The Cold War Presidency

The Cold War Presidency: A Documentary History

THOMAS S. LANGSTON

Tulane University

CQ PRESS

A Division of Congressional Quarterly Inc.

Washington, D.C.

CQ Press
1255 22nd Street, NW, Suite 400
Washington, DC 20037

Phone: 202-729-1900; toll-free, 1-866-4CQ-PRESS (1-866-427-7737)

Web: www.cqpress.com

Composition: Typeset by BMWW, Baltimore, Maryland.

Cover design: Naylor Design Inc.

Cover photo: "The Loneliest Job." President John F. Kennedy in the Oval Office of the White House, February 19, 1961. George Tames/The New York Times/ Redux.

Image and text credits are located on pages 579–581, which are to be considered an extension of the copyright page.

♾ The paper used in this publication exceeds the requirements of the American National Standard for Information Sciences—Permanence of Paper for Printed Library Materials, ANSI Z39.48-1992.

Printed and bound in the United States of America

10 09 08 07 06   1 2 3 4 5

Library of Congress Cataloging-in-Publication Data

Langston, Thomas S.
  The Cold War presidency : a documentary history / Thomas S. Langston.
    p. cm.
  Includes bibliographical references and index.
  ISBN-13: 978-1-933116-38-9 (alk. paper)
  ISBN-10: 1-933116-38-2 (alk. paper)
  1. Presidents—United States—History—20th century—Sources. 2. United States—Foreign relations—1945–1989—Sources. 3. United States—Politics and government—1945–1989—Sources. 4. Cold War—Sources. I. Title.

  E176.1.L265 2006
  973.92—dc22   2006034845

For my brother, Herbert Atom Langston,
named by our father for a favorite uncle and the Atomic Age

Contents

Documents

Thomas S. Langston is professor and chair of political science at Tulane University. He is the author of five previous books on the presidency and the U.S. military, including *Uneasy Balance: Civil-Military Relations in Peacetime America since 1783* (2003) and *With Reverence and Contempt: How Americans Think about Their President* (1995), as well as two books in CQ Press's American Presidents Reference Series: *Lyndon Baines Johnson* (2002) and *George Washington* (2003).

Preface

Since 1789, when the Constitution of the United States was adopted, there has never been any doubt that the president is integral to the nation's security. The framers of the Constitution designed the office of the president with war hero George Washington in mind, and although they neither desired nor expected America's presidents to take the nation to war anytime soon, they were realists and knew that peace was difficult to sustain. If the new nation were to prosper, it would have to be secure, and its security would depend in large measure on the person entrusted with the presidency. In times of peace, the president, by appointing and receiving ambassadors and negotiating treaties, would take the lead in determining the United States' relations with foreign powers. In times of war, the president would lead the armed forces as the civilian commander in chief. At all times, the president's duty would be to "preserve, protect and defend the Constitution of the United States."

Just how far the president's war powers extend has been the subject of institutional and partisan conflict since 1789. President George Washington's assertion in 1793 of the prerogative to keep the nation out of war, by declaring American neutrality in the conflict that had engulfed France and Britain, spurred the development of the nation's first political parties. A war scare in the next administration, headed by John Adams, so inflamed criticisms of executive power that Adams's successor, Thomas Jefferson, reduced the armed forces and made the executive branch dependent on good relations with Congress. During the Civil War, however, the president's powers grew remarkably, as Abraham Lincoln undertook many initiatives—such as ordering a blockade of Southern ports, suspending the writ of habeas corpus, and issuing the famous Emancipation Proclamation—that, as Lincoln himself acknowledged, would have been plainly unlawful for a president in peacetime. When the Civil War ended, power flowed from the president back to Congress, the states, and the federal judiciary. In fact, each of the United States' nineteenth-century wars established precedents for the expansion of presidential power, and they all left important legacies. But after each one, the president's powers and responsibilities were scaled back. This pattern extended well into the twentieth century.

During World War I, Congress granted President Woodrow Wilson authority to commandeer factories and mines, set prices, take possession of and operate the nation's railways, distribute food and gasoline, censor the news, monitor the mail, and punish the disloyal. By the time the nation returned to war, following the December 7, 1941, surprise attack on Pearl Harbor, a firm precedent had been established and was seized upon by President Franklin Roosevelt. Power again flowed to the presidency during World

War II, as Roosevelt asserted his right to regulate the economy and society at home to support the war abroad.

In all U.S. wars through World War II, as the Constitution's framers had foreseen, the nation turned to its chief executive for leadership. If the president was willing to take on the extraordinary responsibilities of national defense, the public and its many elected and unelected government leaders were willing to grant him extraordinary powers, with the understanding that those powers were temporary. Once each war was over, the armed forces were slashed and the president's powers restrained. As the United States made a habit of fighting only relatively short wars—the nation's longest war prior to the Cold War was the Revolutionary War—for most of the nation's history, the presidency was a *peacetime* institution.

During the Cold War, the extraordinary became the norm. For almost fifty years, from President Harry Truman's presidency through George H. W. Bush's (hereafter George Bush), "permanent emergency" was not an oxymoron but a state of affairs to which presidents, members of Congress, Supreme Court justices, military commanders, and ordinary citizens had to adapt. The emergency was at the same time military, ideological, and psychological.

The Cold War began with the United States' pledge to send military aid to Greece and Turkey, which were threatened by Communist insurgents, and later involved the United States in two extensive armed conflicts, the wars in Korea and Vietnam. Moreover, to deter aggression, both the United States and its superpower rival, the Soviet Union, built vast arsenals of conventional and nuclear weapons and conscripted into military service millions of young men.

The Cold War was also an ideological conflict. The superpowers represented—to themselves as well as to one another—diametrically opposed models of how to organize a human society. In the heated rhetoric of the early Cold War, which was echoed in the 1980s, U.S. officials denounced the Soviet Union as a collectivist hell, where the human spirit was crushed in service of a morally bankrupt "evil empire." Soviet officials accused the United States of seeking to chain the world's poor to the machinery of capitalist global domination.

These military and ideological dimensions shaped the war's consequences for the United States and its presidents. Militarily, once the Cold War turned hot in Korea, with the June 25, 1950, North Korean surprise assault on South Korea, there was no hope of returning to "normal." U.S. presidents accepted the need for a permanently mobilized military force, something the United States had never before maintained. The war was supported across party lines, and both Republicans and Democrats accepted the need for *ideological security* at home. In the early Cold War, the quest for home front safety meant loyalty oaths and Red scares. The more permanent legacy of the desire to make Americans secure at home (so that they might be successful in war abroad) was a vastly expanded welfare state with a commitment to civil rights and other values that were part of the nation's extensive ideological arsenal.

Of course, a large military and a large government cost a great deal of money, and the Cold War presidents all faced the enormous task of managing the financial burdens of a

permanent emergency. The Cold War also cost U.S. presidents and the nation their innocence about global affairs. For decades before the Cold War, the United States had been
one of the world's richest nations but had not been among the world's leaders. During
the Cold War, it became the U.S. president's job to forge and lead an alliance of anti-
Communist nations, often referred to as the "free world."

Once the Soviet Union broke the United States' nuclear monopoly in 1949, the fear
of nuclear war emerged as the psychological dimension of the permanent emergency. This
fear underpinned a further expansion of the president's responsibilities, as it became
imperative that the president, on behalf of the nation, project an image of determination
and willpower at all times. As a result, every Cold War president was required to measure up to the mythic stature of a war leader. For presidents who had trouble striking
the requisite pose—because they were more interested in domestic affairs than war, as was
the case for Lyndon Johnson and Jimmy Carter, or because they undermined their
authority through questionable (even illegal) acts, as with Richard Nixon—the presidency
was a dispiriting trial. But for those commanders in chief who embodied the presumably
iron will of the American people—including, at times, Dwight Eisenhower, John F.
Kennedy, and Ronald Reagan—the Cold War presidency was a gift that kept giving, one
that made its inhabitant the proverbial "most powerful man in the world."

The pressures of Cold War presidential leadership were constant, but some moments
were naturally more intense than others and some presidents more skillful than others.
Among the numerous Cold War crises that confronted U.S. presidents were the Soviet
blockade of Berlin in 1948 and 1949, to which President Truman responded by organizing a sustained military airlift of food and supplies, thereby demonstrating the resolve
plus the remarkable technological, financial, and military power of the Western alliance;
the Taiwan Straits Crises of Eisenhower's presidency, the first in 1955 and the second in
1958, which were resolved peacefully only through Eisenhower's threat of massive retaliation against the People's Republic of China, at the time an ally of the Soviet Union; and
the Cuban Missile Crisis in October 1962, during which President Kennedy ordered a
blockade against Soviet ships carrying nuclear missiles to Cuba.

Following these crises and others, including the disastrous war in Vietnam, superpower
relations became less openly hostile in the 1970s, the era of détente. President Carter even
tried to move away from a bipolar foreign policy and spoke of the Cold War in the past
tense. When the Soviet Union invaded neighboring Afghanistan in 1979, Carter professed
shock and dismay. The next year, the electorate voiced a similar opinion of Carter's leadership and sent him into early retirement. During Ronald Reagan's presidency, drama and
crisis returned—so much so that in 1983, the head of the KGB, the Soviet counterpart
to the U.S. Central Intelligence Agency, came to the chilling conclusion that war with the
United States was imminent. Given this rich variety of experiences, understanding the
Cold War presidency requires taking a careful, historical look at how each of the Cold War
presidents fared.

The Cold War Presidency is a documentary history of nine successive presidents—their goals,
accomplishments, and failures. Each administration is placed in the context of the long-

term expansion of presidential powers that was a by-product of the war and is described and analyzed in the light of the constantly evolving state of U.S. domestic politics at the time. Not every president had equal tools with which to lead in the Cold War, and it is as important to assess each president's political resources as it is to analyze his ambition and personality. Some resources are obvious and easy to measure, such as partisan control of Congress or public approval of the job an incumbent is doing as president. Others are subtler but just as important, such as a president's reputation for trustworthiness or his charisma with a television audience.

The nine presidential chapters narrate the key events in the Cold War from the perspective of the chief executive. Each explores the strengths as well as weaknesses of presidential leadership as exhibited by Presidents Truman through Bush (1945–1993), against the backdrop of constantly changing circumstances at home and abroad. These nine chapters are bracketed by chapters on the origins and aftermath of the Cold War. In the origins chapter, the focus is on the decisions that Presidents Roosevelt and Truman made in response to the decisions and actions of Communist leaders, especially Joseph Stalin. The Cold War was not fated by the results of World War II, but neither was it eagerly chosen. President Roosevelt died before the comprehensive nature of the emerging U.S.-Soviet conflict became obvious. President Truman slowly, and with real regret, acknowledged the plain irreconcilability of American and Soviet aims in Europe, Asia, and the Middle East. In the aftermath chapter, the legacy of the Cold War presidency is viewed from the vantage point of the first two presidential administrations to follow the end of the Cold War. Even before the United States returned to war in the wake of the al-Qaida attacks of September 11, 2001, it was apparent that the pre–Cold War pattern of rapidly shrinking presidential power with the onset of peace had been broken. During the Cold War, the expanded presidency passed a point of no return.

Each chapter's narrative is followed by a selection of documents, including speeches, diary entries, letters, telegrams, press releases, planning memoranda, editorials, reports, congressional resolutions, and treaties. Each document is excerpted and introduced by an explanatory headnote that provides background information and context. The more than 160 documents are cross-referenced in the narrative and in Key Events in the Cold War (Appendix B). Brief profiles of some of the major players in the Cold War are presented in Notable Figures of the Cold War (Appendix A).

Soviet (as well as Soviet bloc and Communist Chinese) interpretations of events are also included, because the other side always has a say in how a war is conducted. The opening of the archives of the former Soviet Union to scholars of the Cold War has dramatically expanded our knowledge of events; in many instances, it has forced historians and political scientists to consider new interpretations of events that they *thought* they understood thoroughly. This book makes extensive use of this new material available to researchers, especially in the documents that follow each narrative.

It is a pleasure to thank the many people who assisted in the production of this book. This is an exciting time to be involved in Cold War studies, thanks in large part to the extraordinary work on formerly secret Communist sources being undertaken by the Cold War

International History Project (www.cwihp.org) at the Woodrow Wilson International Center for Scholars (www.wilsoncenter.org) and the National Security Archive at George Washington University (www.nsarchive.org). Fortuitously, it is also an opportune time for historical studies of the presidency, thanks in no small part to the extraordinary online collection of documents contained in the American Presidency Project, the product of the collaboration of John T. Woolley and Gerhard Peters at the University of California, Santa Barbara (www.presidency.ucsb.edu).

The book was acquired for CQ Press by Doug Goldenberg-Hart. January Layman-Wood developed the manuscript and kept me on track both thematically and with reference to deadlines. Jennifer Campi served more than ably as copy editor, and Anna Schardt kept the project rolling as production editor. The CQ Press editorial team, including interns Cecilia Golombek, Kate Ostrander, Diana Park, and Ilya Plotkin, prepared the key events appendix and assisted in the preparation of the notable figures appendix.

Brooke Longon, a 2005 graduate of Tulane University, provided valuable research assistance for the entire project. Geoffrey Rodriguez provided research assistance at the project's initial stages, courtesy of a grant from the Tulane University Provost's Fund for Student-Faculty Interaction. Rick Wilson, Herbert S. Autry Professor and chair of the Political Science Department at Rice University, and Robert M. Stein, Lena Gohlman Fox Professor of Political Science and dean of Social Sciences at Rice University, graciously hosted me at Rice in the fall of 2005, the "Katrina Term" as it is known at Tulane, during which time a portion of this work was completed. Keeping this book on track, given the dislocations that Hurricane Katrina wrought, required much time at my office, which I would rather have spent with my family—Mary, Jessica, and Taylor. I thank them for their patience and support.

Thomas S. Langston
Tulane University
New Orleans, Louisiana

Origins of the Cold War

A Different Kind of War

On Christmas Day 1945 four thousand soldiers of the United States Army marched through the streets of Manila, the capital of the Philippines, with a singular purpose. They had done their job; they wanted to go home. The army had a well-thought-out plan to bring them back, slowly and orderly. The soldiers demanded to be shipped home now. Weeks later, several thousand U.S. troops in Germany had to be repulsed at bayonet point when they rushed army headquarters, demanding to see their commander. They, too, wanted to go home now. Back home, servicemen's wives, who had organized more than two hundred "Bring Back Daddy" clubs, deluged the offices of their members of Congress with petitions, telegrams, and baby booties. Repre-

The Big Three (from left: British prime minister Winston Churchill, U.S. president Franklin Roosevelt, and Soviet premier Joseph Stalin) met February 4–11, 1945, at Yalta, on the Crimean Peninsula in the Soviet Union. During the conference, the three leaders made plans for the war against Japan, the occupation of Germany, the structure of the United Nations, and the fate of liberated states in Europe. The Yalta agreement proved to be controversial—many of Roosevelt's critics claimed he had "given" Eastern Europe to the Soviets. Source: Library of Congress.

sentatives joined in the fun, demanding that the armed forces speed the return of their soldiers, aviators, sailors, and marines, 12 million of whom were in uniform at the end of World War II.

The generals and officials in Washington were disappointed by the conduct of American service members and their families but not surprised. After every previous American war, there had been a headlong rush away from all things military. This had been particularly true after the Great War, or as it was now known, World War I. Well before World War II ended, Chief of Staff Gen. George Marshall, Secretary of War Henry Stimson, and President Franklin Roosevelt had developed plans to prevent a repeat of what had become an American tradition.

Roosevelt had high hopes for what the United States could achieve after the war. He had been talking about fundamental changes in the relations among nations, he reminded the press in 1944, "on and off the stump since 1919" (**Document 1.1**). At the core of Roosevelt's plan for U.S. postwar policy was his concept of the "Four Policemen." The United States, the Soviet Union, and the United Kingdom—the nations that together had won the war—would keep the peace in Europe, with China's help in Asia. They would collectively occupy defeated Germany for years to come and would pool their resources, including their military might, to quash any movement toward a resumption of war. Through a great power cartel, the United States and its wartime allies would decide among themselves the weighty issues of international affairs. Near their own borders, the major powers might be expected to exercise a high degree of influence but not outright control. In this way, the United States could live up to the promises that Roosevelt had made to the world in the Atlantic Charter, a joint statement of war aims issued by the United States and Britain in 1941, eschewing territorial aggrandizement and affirming the principle of national self-determination.

If the United States was to be one of the world's "policemen," however, it would have to maintain an adequate military force to do the job. The army mutinies of 1945 and 1946 called into question Americans' willingness to perform their assigned role. To accommodate the demands of its personnel, and the Congress that broadly supported these demands, the military repeatedly lowered the number of service points required before a member of the armed forces qualified for discharge. To fill the gaps that this created in the nation's overseas forces—needed for peacekeeping duties in Europe and Asia—the army reduced basic training from seventeen weeks to thirteen, and then to eight, in order to rush recruits overseas as quickly as possible. Through 1945 the military was reducing its net numbers by 1 million per month. Roosevelt—and his successor, Harry Truman—wanted at least to prepare the nation better than before for the possible need to rearm for war. For this purpose, the presidents pressed for Universal Military Training for the nation's young men. Congress rejected the proposal repeatedly, even though the program was backed by its own Select Committee on Postwar Military Policy. Similarly, Congress extended the draft with only the greatest reluctance and shortened the tour of duty to eighteen months.

At the conclusion of World War II, the United States had more power and greater responsibilities than ever before, but did it have the will to use that power and accept those responsibilities? The answer came slowly, over the next several years. What history reveals is that it took one thing more—the realization of a threat—for a consensus to emerge in the United States in support of new American global activism. The result for the United States was a permanent change in both government and society: presidential power expanded, and the public for the first time took war preparedness seriously and did so for decades. The result for the world was the Cold War.

YALTA

Franklin Roosevelt was sometimes idealistic, but he was not delusional. He knew that the United States' great Eastern ally in the war, the Soviet Union, was an ally of convenience. "My children," the president liked to say, paraphrasing a Balkan proverb, "it is permitted

SOVIET EXPANSION IN EUROPE, 1939–1948

Source: Steven W. Hook and John Spanier, *American Foreign Policy Since World War II,* 17th ed. (Washington, D.C.: CQ Press, 2007), 32.

you in time of grave danger to walk with the devil until you have crossed the bridge."[1] The president knew, moreover, that this particular devil was understandably bitter about its losses in the war. American military plans had relied heavily upon Soviet manpower, with the intent of greatly limiting U.S. casualties. As John Lewis Gaddis, a leading historian of the Cold War, notes, "for every American who died in the war, 15 Germans and 53 Russians died."[2] Despite their losses, the Soviets still possessed a massive army at the end of the war, and it was their soldiers who occupied Eastern Europe and the Balkans, from which they had driven the invading German army. Roosevelt thought he could make this cooperative situation work. America was, after all, a fantastically wealthy state now; its economy, its population, and—incredibly—its population's life expectancy had all *grown* during the war. It now accounted for half of the world's manufacturing output. The Soviets, Roosevelt thought, could be enticed by the promise of Western financial aid to continue to cooperate with their Western allies. Besides, Roosevelt had good reason to be supremely confident of his personal negotiating skills. During his lengthy presidency, he had seldom met a person he could not charm.

But Roosevelt met his match in Joseph Stalin, the supreme ruler of the Union of Soviet Socialist Republics (USSR). In February 1945 Stalin and Roosevelt, along with British prime minister Winston Churchill, met for the final time at Yalta (in the Crimea, USSR) to address the future. At this conference, the United States was forced to confront the possibility that its goals and those of the Soviet Union might simply be irreconcilable. The tensions between East and West were evident at Yalta with respect to each of the major issues that the heads of state addressed: the future of Germany, the future of Eastern Europe, the establishment of the United Nations (UN), and the entry of the Soviet Union into the war against Japan.

Roosevelt went to Yalta without a settled American policy on the future of Germany. In the fall of 1944, at a conference at Dumbarton Oaks in Washington, D.C., the president had actually signed onto a plan that would force Germany back in time by dismembering its states, removing its industrial plant, and returning its urban residents to farming life. It is doubtful, however, that Roosevelt ever truly believed in this quixotic vision, and he had come to agree with those, like Churchill, who argued that a permanently weak Germany would weaken Western Europe as a whole. The Soviets, for their part, were keen for reparations to be taken from not only the portion of Germany that their troops might occupy at the close of war, but from the rest of Germany as well. They had suffered the most in defeating Germany and were determined to make the Germans pay.

The Soviets were equally adamant that they emerge from the war with "friendly" states along their borders. Roosevelt acknowledged the Soviet Union's imperative not to be surrounded by hostile nations but hoped it could be accomplished within the framework of national self-determination and democratic governance for Eastern Europe. The different perspectives of the two nations became most apparent in discussions about Poland, the invasion of which had triggered British entry into the war. The Soviets indicated that Poland was for them a matter of "honor and security" and even "life and death"[3]—invaders from Napoleon Bonaparte to Adolf Hitler had attacked Russia through Poland. For the past year, the Soviets had been in physical possession of Poland and supported there a Communist-dominated government seated in Lublin. Meanwhile, the Western powers supported a rival group of Polish exiles in London. If the United States and Britain were to live up to the promise of the Atlantic Charter, the Soviets would have to be persuaded to agree that free elections, in which both "Lublin Poles" and "London Poles" could participate, be the basis for the formation of a new Polish government. At Yalta, Stalin agreed to this demand.

It was, however, a hollow victory for the supporters of the continuation of the wartime alliance. Stalin was contemptuous during the conference about the London Poles, dismissing them as dangerous reactionaries who incited the murder of Soviet troops. Moreover, Roosevelt seems to have understood that Stalin was no more serious about his commitment to free elections and democracy in Eastern Europe than Roosevelt had been in the flowery tributes he paid to the Soviet dictator during the war. Roosevelt had told Stalin during their conversations at Yalta that he needed not a firm commitment, but rather "some gesture" to appease Polish American voters at home. It was, he assured his counterpart, "only a matter of words and details."[4] Considering Roosevelt's habits as a statesman and politician, it would be imprudent to conclude that he intentionally sold out the people of Poland in this way. It is more likely that he still believed that he could overcome Stalin's suspicions of the West, and that over time he could make the Soviets dependent—cheerily dependent, in fact—on American financial support. Once Stalin calmed down, he would presumably come around. In the meantime, Roosevelt would do all he could diplomatically to add substance to the "words and details" of Yalta.

During the war, the Allies spoke often of the work of "the united nations" of the world and began to plan a formal postwar organization that would bring these nations together to harmonize international affairs. The idea of an international body to prevent further war was especially important to Roosevelt. At the fall 1944 Dumbarton Oaks conference, the Allies had drafted the outline of an agreement on such a body. It would have two principal components, each serving a different but vital purpose. To permit all nations a platform from which to voice their concerns and grievances, each state would be a member of and have a single vote in the General Assembly. To settle grave issues that threatened war between states, the great powers would gather in a separate, much smaller assembly, the Security Council. At Yalta, the Soviets demanded and were granted additional votes in the General Assembly for the Ukraine and White Russia. They also held out for a single-power veto in the Security Council, suggesting that Stalin foresaw clearly that the day might come when the Western powers would combine against the Soviets. As the Communists had not yet won the civil war in China, also to be made a charter member of the Security Council, the Soviets could not count on China's support.

The actual text of the Yalta agreement was kept secret. The single American copy was soon locked in a White House safe. The public declarations that were released at the time contained the gist of the agreements on Europe and the UN (**Document 1.2**) but said nothing about one final matter: the entry of the Soviet Union into the war in the Pacific. In February 1945 the atom bomb had yet to be completed and tested, and the U.S. military calculated that Soviet participation in the war against Japan might save the lives of hundreds of thousands of American soldiers. The U.S. ambassador to Moscow, Averell

Harriman, had for months been discussing with Stalin the terms under which Stalin would order the Red Army into combat in the Far East. Shortly before the Yalta conference, Stalin revealed that his price would include American arms and ammunition as well as "political considerations."[5]

Stalin had hoped for a role in the occupation of Japan, but he settled for unimpeded access to the Pacific. To make this dream a reality, the Soviet ruler needed the return of land lost in war against Japan at the turn of the century, plus control of the Chinese Eastern and South Manchurian rail lines. Roosevelt was so concerned about this land-for-war deal that he did not consult Churchill or even his secretary of state before agreeing to Stalin's terms. Nor did he seek the consent of the Chinese; Roosevelt assured Stalin that at the appropriate time, he would inform China of the fact that the United States had given away control of rail lines in Manchuria.

In retrospect, it is clear that power was the motivating force of the Yalta conference and that only two nations had that power. At the time, however, it was far from obvious what Yalta signified. In part, this was because President Roosevelt continued to speak publicly as if nothing had changed in the relationship among the "Big Three." In his final appearance before Congress, upon his return from Yalta, Roosevelt built up the prospects for free elections in Poland and spoke with pride on the Declaration on Liberated Europe that he, Stalin, and Churchill had signed. Roosevelt had a captive audience for such rhetoric in the United States, as for several years the U.S. government had played down the ideological gulf between the capitalist West and the Communist East. This was reflected in a February 1945 public opinion poll that showed that most Americans expected greater trouble for the United States with Britain than with Russia after the war.[6]

If Roosevelt was willing to say, as he did, that "on every point, unanimous agreement was reached" at Yalta, who was Stalin to disagree with him?[7] Besides, Stalin could not publicly declare Soviet motives because doing so would have destroyed all prospect of Allied solidarity, and Stalin needed the alliance to continue, at least for the time being. For Stalin, continuing his alliance with the British and Americans was instrumental; it helped him in his steadfast aim to achieve control of Eastern Europe. Roosevelt had led Stalin to believe at a previous wartime conference (in Tehran, Iran, in early winter 1943) that the Americans would withdraw quickly from Europe after the war. It would be foolish to make the Americans reconsider. Moreover, only by working within the alliance could Stalin hope to secure reparations from the most industrialized area of Germany, which was occupied by the Western states after the war. Finally, Stalin believed that he could play his two Western allies against one another if he continued to work within the alliance.

Stalin, like all true Communists, believed that World War II was a manifestation of the crisis of capitalism. The British and the Americans were bombing their competition. Once they had finished with Germany and Japan, Stalin believed the contradictions between American and British aims would logically lead them to compete with one another. "The crisis of capitalism led to the division of the capitalists into two factions—the one fascist, the other democratic," Stalin lectured one of his subordinates shortly before Yalta. "We are today with one faction against the other, but in the future we shall also be against that faction of capitalists."[8] Stalin was sincerely surprised when the British and Americans worked together after victory in Europe to oppose Soviet ambitions for a postwar mandate in Africa. Until he recognized his error, Stalin was as reluctant as Roosevelt to reveal to the world the tensions that were emerging between the East and the West and, in particular, the Soviet Union and the United States.

FROM SAN FRANCISCO TO POTSDAM

American journalists and politicians began to speculate about what had *really* transpired at Yalta when word leaked of the special provision made for two Soviet satellite states in the UN. Even if this secret had been kept, it would have been revealed on April 25, 1945, at the convening of the UN in San Francisco, California. The conferees, representing forty-six nations, signed the founding Charter of the United Nations (**Document 1.3**) and quarreled over a number of issues that increasingly pitted the Soviets against the West.

The new organization was embraced quickly in the United States. In the Senate, only two members voted against ratification of U.S. membership. It is telling that the public enthusiasm for the organization coexisted with an *overestimation* of its power. As a report from 1947 recounts, "Perhaps because the conception of an organization with power to enforce peace had been so frequently used in official statements and in discussions since 1943, many seemed to have an exaggerated idea of the police power of the United Nations."[9] Roosevelt had certainly done his part to contribute to Americans' high expectations of the UN, an innovation to which he had been wholly committed.

Roosevelt died on April 12, 1945, before he could see the UN born or the war come to an end. He had been president for so long, since March 1933, that a great many Americans were unsure just who was now president. The answer, of course, was Harry Truman, who had been on the job as vice president for eighty-three days, during which Roosevelt had simply ignored him. "I knew the President had a great many meetings with Churchill and Stalin," Truman recorded in his diary. "I was not familiar with any of these things and it was really something to think about."[10] Not surprisingly, Truman had some difficulty settling upon a consistent foreign policy. At first, he seemed intent to bring plain midwestern straightforwardness to America's relations with the Soviet Union, even at the price of unsettling the alliance.

On his way to San Francisco, Soviet foreign minister Vyacheslav Molotov paid a call on the new president. At this famous encounter, Truman bluntly told Molotov that the Soviets had failed to keep their word on Poland. When the minister attempted to change the subject, Truman curtly dismissed him. Shortly after this exchange, however, Truman began to second-guess what he called his "get tough" policy.[11] In early May, after the Germans surrendered, over-zealous bureaucrats in Washington stopped the Lend-Lease program for Russia and Britain in mid-ocean. Under the Lend-Lease Act, passed nine months prior to U.S. entry into the war, the president was authorized to "sell, transfer title to, exchange, lease, lend, or otherwise dispose of " war materiel to the Allies.[12] The pipeline of support was always supposed to end with the war, but by turning around ships already in route, the United States had provoked a fierce protest from the Soviets. Even the hard-liners in the administration, those who were least trustful of Soviet intentions, at this point worried that they might be missing opportunities for constructive dialogue and bargaining. As Truman recounted their argument, Stalin might be more "reasonable" if he were made to know that the United States and Britain were not "ganging up" on him.[13]

Truman had his chance to reassure Stalin of American goodwill when they met at Potsdam, Germany, in the summer of 1945. At Potsdam, the conferees reviewed and in general reaffirmed the commitments made at Yalta. Truman's secretary of state, James F. Byrnes, worked out the details of a package of policies with his Soviet counterpart. By the end of the conference, the Americans, the Soviets, and the British were ready to endorse a consensus deal. Like a good deal in the U.S. Congress, where Byrnes had learned the craft of diplomacy, it had something for everyone (**Document 1.4**).

Stalin received confirmation of a change in the borders of Poland. The Allies agreed that Poland's borders would be shifted more than one hundred miles to the west, requiring a massive resettlement of ethnic Germans who found themselves suddenly residing in a new nation whose language and laws were not their own. Stalin also got private confirmation of the land-for-war deal that would bring the Soviet Union, briefly, into the conflict with Japan.

The Americans obtained Stalin's reaffirmation of the Soviet Union's commitment to join the war in the Pacific. When he recounted in his diary that Stalin had confirmed the Soviet intention to enter the war, Truman added editorially that "I've gotten what I came for."[14] Though Truman had learned during the conference of the successful test of the American atomic bomb, he was perceptive enough to realize that dropping "The Bomb" would not necessarily guarantee Japanese surrender.

The British and Americans both received a pledge from Stalin that free elections would occur in Poland no later than mid-1946. The promise was backed up at the conference by the Communist leader of the provisional government, who was invited to answer questions and provide assurances.

Soviet entry into the war in the Pacific and free elections in Poland were important matters to have settled, but they were not in truth as consequential as they seemed at the time. The atomic bomb did more than the Russian army to end the war in Japan, and Stalin's Potsdam pledge on Poland proved to be no more meaningful than his pledge at Yalta. The most consequential decision taken at Potsdam was on a final issue, that of German occupation and reparations.

Stalin wanted a set figure—10 billion U.S. dollars—in reparations, exclusive of the value of the physical property within the confines of that portion of Germany to be ceded to Poland. The Americans and British proposed that the Soviets take their reparations from the zone of defeated Germany that had been set aside for Soviet forces during the period of immediate postwar occupation. After considerable haggling, the Soviets accepted Byrnes's compromise, which denied them the promise of a set figure. The Western powers that had each been accorded a zone of occupation—Britain, the United States, and France—would give to the Soviets a percentage of the value of whatever industrial plant they decided to remove from their zones. The Western nations believed the zonal agreement they had adopted for the military occupation of Germany was merely a matter of keeping the respective armies from bumping into one another. The arrangement made at Potsdam for reparations broadened and deepened this expedient, and "marked the first step toward the division of that country."[15]

1946: A YEAR OF LEARNING

Over the remainder of 1945, tensions accumulated, making the Western allies and the Soviet Union increasingly wary of one another and weary of negotiation. For the United States, the events in Poland, more than anything else, compelled the United States and the Soviet Union into mutual opposition. A pattern had emerged that became impossible to ignore. Stalin would, when forced, make promises to bring non-Communist Poles into the provisional government and to prepare for open elections, but he would then find it inconvenient to act upon those pledges. Perhaps Roosevelt would have sympathized with Stalin more than Truman did, and thus might have taken less offense on behalf of the United States and the Western allies. Roosevelt, after all, had been at Yalta, and Stalin could be forgiven if he left that conference believing that the American president had accepted Soviet promises on Poland with a nudge and a wink. But even if Roosevelt had finished out his fourth term, he would probably have found that his own public statements had created a momentum, and established a record, that he could not ignore. Any president would have been compelled to try to make the Soviets live up to the plain meaning of the words agreed to at Yalta. As that had never been the Soviets' intention, it was only a matter of time before Soviet imposition of control over Poland drove the Allies apart.

Stalin was not ready, however, for an open break. Back in January 1944, Soviet deputy foreign minister Ivan Maisky had sent Stalin a memorandum regarding Soviet postwar prospects in Europe. They were, Maisky argued, excellent: he expected that the Soviets would quickly be in position to manipulate "popular front" governments across the continent, so that "no power or combination of powers . . . could even think of aggression" against the Soviet Union.[16] The popular front approach, whereby Communists made common cause with bourgeois liberals in forming a government, was working. Resorting instead to harsh measures, as were used in 1939–1941 in the Baltic states, would invite a sharp response from the West.[17] The popular front strategy in the East also helped to provide political cover for the Soviet-dominated Communist parties of Western Europe. Still, as 1945 drew to a close, Stalin must have begun to wonder about the continued benefits to be gained by keeping up appearances with the West.

Particularly troubling to Stalin was his failure to win American support for a share in governing the former imperial possessions of the defeated nations. Stalin wanted African colonial mandates from Italy, which had lost its colonies there when it was defeated along with Nazi Germany. In San Francisco, at the founding of the UN in April 1945, Edward Stettinius, then the American secretary of state, had encouraged the Soviets to think that the United States might support a trusteeship in Africa. But—with the war in Japan behind them—the Americans rebuffed the Soviets at a conference of ministers in London in September. Stalin, sending instructions as he vacationed on the shores of the Black Sea, urged Soviet foreign minister Molotov to threaten not to join in a peace treaty with Italy if the

Western powers would not grant the Soviets' demand. "At worst," Stalin cabled, "the Allies could sign a peace treaty with Italy without us. So what? Then we have a precedent."[18] When Secretary of State Byrnes angrily denounced Molotov's demand, "jumping up" and shouting that it was "Shocking! Shocking! Shocking!" and reminding the diplomat that his country had "never been there," Molotov asked, "So you do not want to give us even a corner of the Mediterranean?"[19]

After another disagreement surfaced at the London conference, over the future of Germany, Stalin exploded in an angry lecture to Molotov, laying bare his attitude toward his recent comrades-in-arms. The Americans intend, he wrote,

> to divert our attention from the Far East, where America assumes a role of tomorrow's friend of Japan . . . ; second, to receive from the USSR a formal sanction for the US playing the same role in European affairs as the USSR, so that the US may hereafter, in league with England, take the future of Europe into their hands; third, to devalue the treaties of alliance that the USSR has already reached with European states; fourth, to pull the rug from under any future treaties of alliance between the USSR and Rumania, Finland, etc.[20]

Like his counterparts in the United States, Stalin was already thinking in Cold War terms of a global struggle between two hostile camps.

The gulf between the two sides became strikingly evident in the following year. Over the course of 1946, the Soviets and the Americans maneuvered for advantage in increasingly blunt rhetoric and in provocative actions that threatened the resumption of actual war. For both sides, 1946 was truly, as the then undersecretary of state Dean Acheson recalled in his memoirs, "a year of learning."[21]

Rhetoric

Stalin took the first rhetorical step toward an open breach, in a "campaign" speech he delivered in Moscow in February 1946 (**Document 1.5**). In Stalin's speech, he returned in public to the language of classical Marxism-Leninism. The late war, he asserted, had not occurred by chance or because of diplomatic bungling or even conflicting national ambitions. Rather, it was the logical outcome of the continuing crisis of capitalism. So long as capitalism reigned supreme in much of the world, capitalist countries would compete with one another, through force, to expand their "spheres of influence." The war, Stalin asserted, had been more than a curse; it was a "great school" that had tested the Soviet system and its people, and it had revealed to the capitalist countries that there was a viable alternative. The results were in: The Soviet system was superior. This was true of its social system, its government, its economy, and even its army.

Hard-liners in the U.S. government read this speech as a "delayed declaration of war."[22] Wanting to put the speech in the context of broader trends in Soviet foreign policy, state department officials in Washington asked for an analysis from the deputy chief of mission in Moscow, George Kennan. Kennan's February 1946 reply became a classic statement of Cold War axioms and the intellectual foundation of the American foreign policy of containment—although the author came quickly to believe that policymakers had misunderstood him (**Document 1.6**).

Kennan's "Long Telegram," as it came to be known, sought to expose the folly of attempting to negotiate to achieve better relations with Moscow. The Soviets did not want a better deal from the West; they wanted victory. They were engaged, he reminded his audience, in a sincere effort to foment worldwide revolution. They would use whatever level of force was necessary to secure control over states adjacent to their territory, and would then seek to undermine neighboring countries though subversion. In considering the appropriate Western response, Kennan pleaded with his superiors to recognize that the Soviet leadership was impervious not only to blandishment but to reason itself. Sensitive only to force, the Soviets must be confronted with strong resistance if the West was not to be overrun.

The telegram received an enthusiastic response in Washington. The secretary of state proclaimed it "splendid," and the influential secretary of the navy, James Forrestal, "virtually adopted the Kennan analysis as his own" and distributed hundreds of copies to policymakers and opinion leaders.[23] A copy was sent, by whom it is not clear, to *Time* magazine, which paraphrased and published it with a map labeled "Communist Contagion." The following year, Kennan publicized his ideas in another classic Cold War statement, an article written under the pseudonym "X," published in the July edition of *Foreign Affairs*.

Kennan's February 1946 telegram had helped to stem the tide of unrealistic thinking among policy elites, but what of the American public? Former British prime minister Winston Churchill attempted to impress upon an American audience the urgency of confronting the Soviet Union, in a speech the next month (**Document 1.7**). Churchill's March 5 speech at Westminster College, in Fulton, Missouri, publicized the term *iron curtain*. An "iron curtain," he warned his distinguished audience, which included President Truman, was descending over Europe. Behind the curtain, small but ruthless Communist parties "have been raised to preeminence and power far beyond their numbers and are seeking everywhere to obtain totalitarian control." This, he remonstrated, was far from being the "liberated Europe" for which the Allies had fought and which the Allies, *including the Soviet Union,* had promised they would support.

If Churchill had left it at that, his speech might have received a better reception. But he saved his most eloquent rhetoric and his most emotional appeals for a description of his preferred cure for the disease of Soviet expansionism. He argued that the United States and Britain must stand together in a great political and military alliance against the Soviet Union. Churchill mused that perhaps one day the two great nations might even join again in a new confederation. Churchill's plea for Anglo-American unity embarrassed Truman, for it went against the grain of America's commitment to the new UN and the nation's emerging color-blind ethos. Stalin picked up on this latter theme in a March interview published in *Pravda,* in which he denounced Churchill as a "warmonger" intent, like Hitler, on unleashing war from "a racist theory" (**Document 1.8**). The former prime minister, he added, had a lot of friends in Washington, D.C., these days.

Stalin was right on this last point. Although the immediate response to Churchill's speech was not what he had hoped, that had perhaps more to do with its overheated tone than with its cold analysis of Soviet behavior. Truman was not yet ready to embrace publicly the reality that Kennan and Churchill described, but he was coming ever closer. Early in the year, Truman had ignored his outspoken secretary of commerce, Henry Wallace, when Wallace seemed to take Stalin's side in a public speech at a dinner for Russian relief. The Soviets, Wallace had said on that occasion, were simply "out to make every boundary secure," in fear "that time is short to prepare for a possible capitalist-provoked war."[24]

On September 12, Wallace gave a similar address to an audience at Madison Square Garden. The "get tough with Russia" policy, he proclaimed, was wrong, for it would only provoke the Russians to get tough in response. A closer alliance with Britain would be pure "folly." Returning to the theme of the Soviets' ambitions along their borders, Wallace blithely compared the influence that the United States exercised in Latin America with Soviet influence in Eastern Europe and said that the United States had no more right to interfere with the Soviets in those nations than the Soviets would have to interfere in the internal affairs of the Western Hemisphere. This was moral obtuseness of a high order, and in the environment of late 1946, it was too much. Though Truman did not like the trouble it caused him among Wallace's numerous friends on the left in the Democratic Party, Truman accepted Wallace's resignation on September 19.

In a telegram to the Kremlin, Soviet ambassador to the United States Nikolai Novikov analyzed Wallace's forced resignation in terms that paralleled those of Kennan's famous telegram to Washington (**Document 1.9**). According to Novikov, the United States was bent on world domination. The growing influence of the Soviets had alarmed American imperialists. For the past year, the "reactionary" forces within the United States had been engaged in political battle with the Rooseveltians and had forged a bipartisan consensus within Congress. In the executive branch, they had taken advantage of the assumption of the presidency by Harry Truman, whom Novikov described as "a politically unstable person but with certain conservative tendencies." The ouster of Wallace, Novikov concluded, "means the victory of the reactionary course that [Secretary of State] Byrnes is conducting in cooperation with [Republican Senators] Vandenberg and Taft."

Novikov's analysis is surprising only in that he seems not to have realized that Byrnes himself had become suspect among the true hard-liners in the Truman administration. The president found Byrnes difficult to deal with on a merely personal level, but officials like Dean Acheson found the secretary suspect on ideological grounds. Even as his doubts about Soviet intentions had flourished, Byrnes continued to believe that it was imperative not to upset the Soviets diplomatically. In the latter half of 1946, Byrnes's influence declined, until he was at last replaced by George Marshall in January 1947, and the influence of men like Acheson, Clark Clifford, James Forrestal, and others with more dependably "conservative tendencies" grew.

Action

Diplomatic relations in 1946 worsened between the Soviets and the Western powers, to the point where some officials actually feared the outbreak of war. The source of trouble was territory at the far periphery of the Soviet Union, beginning in Iran. Iran's importance as a supply route for the Soviets had been demonstrated in the war. The Americans had sent tens of thousands of troops to Iran during the war, where they joined British, Soviet, and Iranian soldiers in finding solutions to the difficult logistical challenges inherent in shipping American Lend-Lease goods to the Soviets and Iranian oil to Britain. All parties had agreed that after the war, the foreign troops would be withdrawn according to the timetable set at the September 1945 London Minister's conference. All troops were to be out of the country by March 2, 1946.

Soon, intelligence reports revealed that the Soviets were increasing, rather than decreasing, their presence. In December 1945 they announced that they had wonderful news to relay to the world. A revolutionary Communist government had been established in Iranian Azerbaijan, the northern province of Iran, bordering Soviet Azerbaijan. The March deadline passed, with Soviet troops still stationed in Iranian Azerbaijan. When Iran, at U.S. and British urging, attempted a tentative troop deployment to the breakaway region, the Soviets threatened to respond with force. The United States and Britain promised their public support to Iran and criticized the Soviets at the UN. When the Security Council voted to take up the issue, the Soviet ambassador to the UN, Andrei Gromyko, walked out in protest. Tensions continued to mount, and in October 1946 the United States and Iran signed an agreement for an American military mission to Iran. The Soviets withdrew in December, however, and Iran reacquired the Azerbaijan province peacefully. The withdrawal, in the opinion of American ambassador George Allen, was credited in Iran to the conviction "that the United States was not bluffing."[25] The Iranians knew what a former Soviet foreign ministry official revealed in a post–Cold War interview: "When the occupation was due to end, Stalin didn't want to leave. He wanted to stay on."[26]

At the same time as the United States and Britain were acting together against the Soviets in Iran, they were beginning to act in concert against their wartime partner with regard to Turkey, another nation along the Soviet periphery. Turkey was of historic importance to Russia, because the Turkish Straits link the Black Sea to the Mediterranean. For hundreds of years, Russia had negotiated and renegotiated the terms of Russian access to the straits. The 1936 Montreaux Convention governed the terms of access during the war. At Yalta, Stalin had begun to demand Western help in revising the terms of that treaty. The Western powers had agreed, proposing in November 1945 that Black Sea powers have unlimited access to the straits. The Americans and the British drew the line, however, at the Soviets' request that they be permitted to establish military bases on Turkish territory to "defend" the straits. Over the course of 1946, the British and the Americans gradually retreated from their commitment to a revision of the Montreaux Convention, while the Soviets continued to insist on a thorough revision, which would include Soviet basing rights. In August the Soviet Union formally petitioned that it be permitted to share in the organization of the means of defense of the straits, a position that was rejected out of hand by Britain and the United States.

But in one final area of great importance to the emerging world order, the United States grew apart from Britain as well as the Soviet Union in 1946. The British had been full partners with the Americans in the Manhattan Project to develop the atomic bomb. After the war, however, Congress reasserted its prerogatives of oversight and passed the Atomic Energy Act, or the McMahon Bill, named for Connecticut senator Brien McMahon, the chairman of the Senate Special Committee on Atomic Energy. The bill, which was signed into law August 1, 1946, took authority for atomic weaponry research away from the U.S. military and placed it in the hands of a civilian agency, the Atomic Energy Commission. In a compromise, the War Department maintained responsibility for stockpiling uranium and other nuclear materials. The act also contravened the late president Roosevelt's private assurances to his British counterpart that the United States would continue to share atomic secrets with the British after the war.

The Truman administration also made it clear in 1946 that the United States would not make a grand gesture of trust to the Soviets by sharing with *them* U.S. atomic secrets. U.S. analysis of the atomic bomb blasts against Japan and forecasts on future developments in atomic weaponry increasingly made it seem that the United States' monopoly in atomic warfare was an advantage to be jealously guarded (**Document 1.10**). Therefore, at the same time as the McMahon Bill was being debated in Congress, the United States developed a plan for the international control of atomic energy that would leave the nation in sole possession of the secret of atomic weapons production.

The American plan—presented on June 14, 1946, to the UN Atomic Energy Commission by highly regarded financier and presidential advisor Bernard Baruch, in his capacity as Truman's representative—called for the creation of an international agency to control and regulate atomic activities. Worldwide, all atomic materials would come under the dominion of the new agency. While the agency would freely disseminate information about the peaceful use of the atom, only its scientists would be permitted to conduct research into the explosive use of atomic energy. To ensure proper regulation, the agency's officials would have the right to inspect atomic facilities around the world. The United States was sensitive to the charge that it merely wished in this way to freeze into place its peculiar advantage in the nuclear field. For this reason, Baruch promised:

> When an adequate system for control of atomic energy, including the renunciation of the bomb as a weapon, has been agreed upon and put into effective operation and condign punishments set up for violations of the rules of control which are to be stigmatized as international crimes, we propose that:
> 1. Manufacture of atomic bombs shall stop;
> 2. Existing bombs shall be disposed of pursuant to the terms of the treaty; and
> 3. The Authority shall be in possession of full information as to the know-how for the production of atomic energy.[27]

The lack of trust that had developed by the summer of 1946 was plain in Baruch's call for special voting provisions in the Security Council to take action when a nation was believed to have violated the conditions of the proposed agreement. Baruch bluntly stated:

> It would be a deception to which I am unwilling to lend myself, were I not to say to you and to our peoples that the matter of punishment lies at the very heart of our present security system. It might as well be admitted, here and now, that the subject goes straight to the veto power contained in the Charter of the United Nations so far as it relates to the field of atomic energy. The Charter permits penalization only by concurrence of each of the five great powers—the Union of Soviet Socialist Republics, the United Kingdom, China, France, and the United States.
>
> There must be no veto to protect those who violate their solemn agreements not to develop or use atomic energy for destructive purposes.[28]

After a Soviet counterproposal was debated and rejected, Baruch's proposal was endorsed, in principle, at the UN on December 31, 1946, but without the concurrence of the Soviet Union, which abstained in the vote. Without Soviet participation, the plan could not move forward, and its practical consequence was to motivate the Americans to improve and enlarge their nuclear armaments and the Soviets to break the American nuclear monopoly as quickly as possible.

ALL OVER BUT THE SHOUTIN'

By the end of 1946, it was no longer possible to pretend that the wartime alliance was still operating. As time passed and all parties sought to advance their particular interests, the benefits to be had from conciliating the other parties diminished, while the costs escalated. The costs of "making nice" came quickly to include the sovereignty of entire nations. While the United States sought to negotiate with the Soviet Union, the latter subjugated Poland, Romania, Bulgaria, Hungary, and other states along its border, while attempting to subvert "capitalist democracy" in favor of "Communist democracy" in nations like France and Italy.

The Cold War did not begin in error. The leaders of the major powers did not simply misunderstand or misperceive one another. They had irreconcilable motives in foreign affairs and the power to act upon them. Almost all of the Cold War's basic features were evident in its origins.

There was a strong ideological component to the Cold War. Ideology was not simply a matter of rhetoric, but of motivation and legitimacy as well. When Stalin sought to explain, publicly and privately, the growing conflict with the West, he did so in the same terms that a Moscow professor of Marxism might have employed. His ideology provided him with readymade explanations of events and a blueprint for action. The ideological challenge was picked up by the United States, which had long seen itself as a nation destined by God to promote human freedom. During the Cold War, the United States would promote freedom actively, not merely by example.

Another important feature was the contest for territory. Once the wartime vision of a collective British/American/Soviet concert of power was discarded as unrealistic, the three nations began in earnest to consolidate their influence within their respective spheres of influence and zones of occupation. The Soviets at first acted cautiously beyond Eastern Europe. Soon, however, conflict over the Straits of Turkey and Iranian Azerbaijan seemed to provide evidence of Communism's expansionist aims.

Finally, there was the centrality of executive power in the conduct of the Cold War. Just as World War II had been the occasion for an expansion of presidential power, the transition back to a state of quasi-war brought with it a return to the centrality of the president in formulating and implementing U.S. policy. In the immediate aftermath of the war, Congress had begun to reassert itself. As an uneasy peace gave way to the Cold War, Congress started once more to defer to the executive, beginning with the formation of a bipartisan, postwar foreign-policy majority on Capitol Hill. It would be up to the president to decide when and where to proclaim to the public that its leadership had returned to war.

Because of the nature of the Cold War, presidential discretion was magnified beyond even that of hot wars such as World Wars I and II and the Civil War. In hot wars, American presidents have been allowed a great deal of latitude to prepare the nation for combat, but ultimately there has come a point at which taking action becomes necessary: the other side lays siege to a fort, sinks a ship, launches a surprise attack, or in some other way makes it plain that a president "has no choice" but to lead the nation into war. The Cold War was different, from its origin to its end. The difference this made in presidential power was plain throughout 1945 and 1946, as first Roosevelt and then Truman struggled to keep the war from starting and, at the same time, to prepare for victory should the war come.

Roosevelt seems to have hoped that he could use his powers of personal persuasion, and America's economic leverage, to close the gap between the rhetoric of Soviet-American friendship and the reality of Soviet-American postwar differences. Truman was, at first, more blunt about that reality, but he too was reluctant to acknowledge the growing rift between the powers. Finally, after Soviet provocations in Iran and Turkey, Truman was ready to act. Still, he waited until yet another crisis arose, this time in Greece, to announce to the world what he had concluded privately months before.

The United States had the resources of a superpower and had assumed the responsibilities of global leadership in World War II. With the emergence of a global threat, the only thing that remained for the Cold War to be revealed was the president's bold assertion of the will to employ American power to meet that threat and fulfill those responsibilities. When Britain announced to the United States early in 1947 that it could no longer police the northern tier of the Mediterranean for the West and that keeping the region free was up to the Americans, President Truman answered the call. With the addition of the puzzle's final piece—the recognition that power in the world was no longer truly multipolar, but bipolar—Britain withdrew, the United States advanced, and the Cold War was on.

NOTES

1. John Lewis Gaddis, *Strategies of Containment* (New York: Oxford University Press, 1982), 3.
2. Ibid., 8.
3. David M. Kennedy, *Freedom from Fear* (New York: Oxford University Press, 1999), 801.
4. From Charles Bohlen's Minutes of the Sixth Plenary Meeting, February 9, 1945, 4:00 p.m., Livadia Palace, in U.S. Department of State, *Foreign Relations of the United States, Conferences at Malta and Yalta, 1945* (Washington, D.C.: U.S. Government Printing Office, 1945), 846.
5. Rudy Abramson, *Spanning the Century: The Life of W. Averell Harriman, 1891–1986* (New York: William Morrow and Company, 1992), 373.
6. Walter Isaacson and Evan Thomas, *The Wise Men: Six Friends and the World They Made* (New York: Touchstone, 1986), 270.
7. Richard Crokcatt, *The Fifty Years War: The United States and the Soviet Union in World Politics, 1941–1991* (New York: Routledge, 1994), 70.
8. Eduard Mark, "Revolution by Degrees: Stalin's National Front Strategy for Europe," Cold War International History Project Working Paper Number 31 (Woodrow Wilson International Center for Scholars, Washington, D.C., February 2001), 44.
9. John C. Cambell, *The United States in World Affairs, 1945–1947*, with the assistance of the research staff of the Council on Foreign Relations and an introduction by John Foster Dulles (New York: Harper and Brothers, 1947), 32.
10. Isaacson and Thomas, *Wise Men*, 256.

11. Ibid., 279.
12. *Public Laws.* Part 1 of *United States Statutes at Large Containing the Laws and Concurrent Resolutions Enacted During the First Session of the Seventy-Seventh Congress of the United States of America, 1941–1942, and Treaties, International Agreements Other than Treaties, and Proclamations,* vol. 55 (Washington, D.C.: U.S. Government Printing Office, 1942), 31–33.
13. Ibid., 281.
14. As quoted by Kennedy, *Freedom from Fear,* 843.
15. Isaacson and Thomas, *Wise Men,* 307.
16. Michael Lind, *The American Way of Strategy: U.S. Foreign Policy and the American Way of Life* (New York: Oxford University Press, 2006).
17. Mark, "Revolution by Degrees," 14–15.
18. Vladimir O. Pechnatov, trans. Vladimir Zubok, " 'The Allies Are Pressing on You to Break Your Will . . .' Foreign Policy Correspondence between Stalin and Molotov and Other Politburo Members, September 1945–December 1946" (Cold War International History Project Working Paper Number 26, Woodrow Wilson International Center for Scholars, Washington, D.C., September 1999), 2.
19. Ibid., 3.
20. Ibid., 5.
21. Dean Acheson, *Present at the Creation: My Years at the State Department* (New York: W. W. Norton, 1969), 196–198.
22. Paul Nitze, interviewed in CNN, *Cold War,* Script for Episode 2: "Iron Curtain," www.cnn.com/SPECIALS/cold.war/episodes/02/script.html.
23. Daniel Yergin, *The Shattered Peace: The Origins of the Cold War and the National Security State* (Boston: Houghton Mifflin, 1977), 170–171.
24. Thomas S. Arms, *Encyclopedia of the Cold War* (New York: Facts on File, 1994), 573.
25. Acheson, *Present at the Creation,* 198.
26. Vladimir Yerofeyev, interviewed in CNN, *Cold War,* Script for Episode 2: "Iron Curtain," www.cnn.com/SPECIALS/cold.war/episodes/02/script.html.
27. "The Baruch Plan," as presented June 14, 1946, to the United Nations Atomic Energy Commission, from the Atomic Archive, www.atomicarchive.com/Docs/Deterrence/BaruchPlan.shtml.
28. Ibid.

Document 1.1
President Franklin Roosevelt's Press Conference on the Development of the United Nations, August 29, 1944

Roosevelt spoke to the press about his plans for the United Nations organization and told a disarming story about the dangers of focusing prematurely on the details of such a body, rather than on the hope that it represented for a world free from war.

. . .

Q.: Mr. President, there was one document on which the three chief delegates had agreed on the general outline for a world security organization which resembled very much your draft of June 15. Would you care to comment on the differences between the two?

The President: My draft of June 15? My goodness, was it that far ahead? What was my draft?

Q.: Mr. Stettinius this morning said it was June 15.

Q.: Your summary of the international security plan.

The President: Oh. To tell you the honest truth, I had forgotten I had done it. Don't say I am claiming authorship, because I haven't compared them. I have had an idea, not since June but way back for a year and a half, on certain general principles. It would be different from the League of Nations, I thought a great deal more workable than the League of Nations, calling for two bodies. On one, membership would be for every Nation—large and small—a little Nation to have just as good a vote as a big Nation. Second, there would be a much smaller working body, talking about terms—I called it council, and that would be aimed primarily at averting a future war. That would be the main function. Then third, there would be some system of a court, or courts, for the judicial determination of disputes between Nations.

Well, I think we all want to put the future peace of the world and the settlement of disputes, working out all kinds of things, like food problems and financial problems and everything else, onto a non-partisan basis. Well, you all got that. I don't remember doing it, but anyway, back in June I had the same idea I had for a year and a half before, and a lot of other people have done it.

It's like back in 1933, when I sent a message to Congress about the Civilian Conservation Corps camps, and they authorized them. And we started the C.C.C. camps. Well, it was something I had been thinking about a great deal, and I had, as a result—after they got going, after everybody liked them—I didn't claim authorship of them, but I did send a message to Congress—I had, I suppose, seven or eight letters from people who said, "I wrote you in nineteen hundred and twenty-nine that we ought to have some kind of camps," or "I wrote you in 1930 and outlined the whole plan. Will you please give me credit for the idea."

Well, I suppose there were five hundred people that have brought the idea of C.C.C. camps to my mind. I merely happened to be in a position where I could properly recommend it to Congress.

Now, on this idea of the relationships between Nations after the war, credit should not go to any one person. People have been talking about it, and I have been talking about it on and off the stump since 1919. I was for the League of Nations. I did all I could to get it. I wasn't the author of it.

Now, on this plan that they are talking about at Dumbarton Oaks, nobody is the author of it. It's a general idea, and they are putting it down on paper in such form that all the Nations of the world can talk it over before they all express their views in a meeting. Nothing is hard and fast. This is the very first step.

And it is obvious they have got to have some kind of an organization—might be called judicial, that is the first step. When they get to that stage, they will take it before a judicial body. If that doesn't work, the next step is to have some kind of meeting place where they will talk it over. Call it the assembly, for want of a better term. I will take a better term if anybody will suggest it.

And if anybody starts to kick over the traces and violates the frontiers of a neighbor country, you have got to have quick action, got to have quick action by some small body, because the time in that case, when you start bombing somebody or invading them, you can't have a man—call him whatever you will—send out notices that there will be a meeting next month on this subject. Next month might be too late. You have got to have a small body that can act quickly for all the other Nations. There are various ways of talking about that. That is why this preliminary conference is being held at Dumbarton Oaks. They are not making final decisions, they are going to make recommendations to all the United Nations of the world.

Well, that's the common sense point of view of what the differences are about, including the political aspects. . . .

Q.: Another point in which there has been a great deal of interest in Washington is what mechanisms you might favor to translate decisions of the council into forceful sanctions on the part of the United States. Would there be reference to the American Congress, sir?

The President: I don't think we have got nearly as far as that yet. I think, again, we are emphasizing the details, not the great object. We are very apt to forget the great object.

And a very good illustration is this. In 1920 I was addressing a very big meeting out of doors up in Michigan—an out of doors meeting, there must have been fifteen or twenty thousand people—and I got to talking about the League.

And some woman got up and said, "I can't be for the League of Nations, it legalizes white slavery." (Laughter)

I said, "Where?"

So she trotted out article something, which authorized the League to set up machinery—the objective was perfectly clear—to put down white slavery by international agreement. And she construed it, because it did not say "put down"—it used the word which meant to work together, to eliminate—I have forgotten what the word was, you can dig it out—but she assumed that it meant to regulate white slavery, and therefore to approve white slavery.

Well, I had a violent discussion with her, and we both left the meeting thoroughly angry.

Now that's what comes of bringing politics or partisanship, or—well, the old word I had used before: picayune—by the way, I found George Washington used that word (laughter)—of bringing carping discussions into the details of a thing like white slavery, or any other current thing.

Now, I don't know how they are going to word anything in regard to the elimination of war, but stepping on it before it grows up. We all know what we mean. I can't give you the details of it, but we are at one—almost—in this country, in wanting to end future wars by stepping on their necks before they grow up.

Now that's plain English. For details, go to a political rally. . . .

Source: "Excerpts from the Press Conference," August 29, 1944, in *Public Papers of the Presidents of the United States: Franklin D. Roosevelt, 1933–1945,* from the American Presidency Project, University of California, Santa Barbara, www.presidency.ucsb.edu.

Document 1.2

Agreement at Yalta on Post–World War II Plans, February 11, 1945

At Yalta, in the Crimea, USSR, the "Big Three"—Stalin, Churchill and Roosevelt—met to make plans for the aftermath of the war. They reached agreement on a number of points, including the division of Germany into zones of occupation and the veto power of permanent members of the planned United Nations Security Council. With regard to Eastern Europe, the leaders agreed—on paper, at least—to move toward free elections and democratic governance. In Poland, Stalin promised to permit "free and unfettered elections." In a secret side agreement with the United States, the Soviets agreed to enter the war against Japan in exchange for territorial concessions. The leaders published a series of statements summarizing the results of their conference.

THE OCCUPATION AND CONTROL OF GERMANY

We have agreed on common policies and plans for enforcing the unconditional surrender terms which we shall impose together on Nazi Germany after German armed resistance has been finally crushed. These terms will not be made known until the final defeat of Germany has been accomplished. Under the agreed plan, the forces of the three powers will each occupy a separate zone of Germany. Coordinated administration and control has been provided for under the plan through a central control commission consisting of the Supreme Commanders of the three powers with headquarters in Berlin. It has been agreed that France should be invited by the three powers, if she should so desire, to take over a zone of occupation, and to participate as a fourth member of the control commission. . . .

DECLARATION ON LIBERATED EUROPE

The Premier of the Union of Soviet Socialist Republics, the Prime Minister of the United Kingdom, and the President of the United States of America have consulted with each other in the common interests of the peoples of their countries and those of liberated Europe. They jointly declare their mutual agreement to concert during the temporary period of instability in liberated Europe the policies of their three Governments in assisting the peoples liberated from the domination of Nazi Germany and the peoples of the former Axis satellite states of Europe to solve by democratic means their pressing political and economic problems.

The establishment of order in Europe and the rebuilding of national economic life must be achieved by processes which will enable the liberated peoples to destroy the last vestiges of Nazism and Fascism and to create democratic institutions of their own choice. This is a principle of the Atlantic Charter—the right of all peoples to choose the form of government under which they will live—the restoration of sovereign rights and self-government to those peoples who have been forcibly deprived of them by the aggressor Nations. . . .

POLAND

A new situation has been created in Poland as a result of her complete liberation by the Red Army. This calls for the establishment of a Polish provisional government which can be more broadly based than was possible before the recent liberation of western Poland. The provisional government which is now functioning in Poland should therefore be reorganized on a broader democratic basis with the inclusion of democratic leaders from Poland itself and from Poles abroad. This new government should then be called the Polish Provisional Government of National Unity.

M. Molotov, Mr. Harriman, and Sir A. Clark Kerr are authorized as a commission to consult in the first instance in Moscow with members of the present provisional government and with other Polish democratic leaders from within Poland and from abroad, with a view to the reorganization of the present government along the above lines. This Polish Provisional Government of National Unity shall be pledged to the holding of free and unfettered elections as soon as possible on the basis of universal suffrage and secret ballot. In these elections all democratic and anti-Nazi parties shall have the right to take part and to put forward candidates.

UNITY FOR PEACE AS FOR WAR

Our meeting here in the Crimea has reaffirmed our common determination to maintain and strengthen in the peace to come that unity of purpose and of action which has made victory possible and certain for the United Nations in this war. We believe that this is a sacred obligation which our Governments owe to our peoples and to all the peoples of the world.

Only with the continuing and growing cooperation and understanding among our three countries and among all the peace-loving Nations can the highest aspiration of humanity be realized—a secure and lasting peace which will, in the words of the Atlantic Charter, "afford assurance that all the men in all the lands may live out their lives in freedom from fear and want."

Victory in this war and establishment of the proposed international organization will provide the greatest opportunity in all history to create in the years to come the essential conditions of such a peace.

Signed:
WINSTON S. CHURCHILL
FRANKLIN D. ROOSEVELT
J. STALIN

Source: Franklin D. Roosevelt, "Joint Statement with Churchill and Stalin on the Yalta Conference," February 11, 1945, in *Public Papers of the Presidents of the United States: Franklin D. Roosevelt, 1933–1945,* from the American Presidency Project, University of California, Santa Barbara, www.presidency. ucsb.edu.

Document 1.3
United Nations Charter, June 26, 1945

As per the agreement reached at Yalta, the Allies organized a postwar conference of forty-six of the world's nations. At this conference, held in San Francisco, California, the United Nations was created. The idealism of the moment is in full evidence in the organization's founding document, particularly in the preamble and first and second articles. The practical limitation to what the body might accomplish in the way of world peace is also apparent in the requirement for unanimity on nonprocedural votes among the permanent members of the Security Council.

WE THE PEOPLES OF THE UNITED NATIONS DETERMINED
- to save succeeding generations from the scourge of war, which twice in our lifetime has brought untold sorrow to mankind, and
- to reaffirm faith in fundamental human rights, in the dignity and worth of the human person, in the equal rights of men and women and of nations large and small, and
- to establish conditions under which justice and respect for the obligations arising from treaties and other sources of international law can be maintained, and
- to promote social progress and better standards of life in larger freedom,

AND FOR THESE ENDS
- to practice tolerance and live together in peace with one another as good neighbors, and
- to unite our strength to maintain international peace and security, and
- to ensure by the acceptance of principles and the institution of methods, that armed force shall not be used, save in the common interest, and
- to employ international machinery for the promotion of the economic and social advancement of all peoples,

HAVE RESOLVED TO COMBINE OUR EFFORTS TO ACCOMPLISH THESE AIMS

Accordingly, our respective Governments, through representatives assembled in the city of San Francisco, who have exhibited their full powers found to be in good and due form, have agreed to the present Charter of the United Nations and do hereby establish an international organization to be known as the United Nations.

CHAPTER I: PURPOSES AND PRINCIPLES

Article 1

The Purposes of the United Nations are:
1. To maintain international peace and security, and to that end: to take effective collective measures for the prevention and removal of threats to the peace, and for the suppression of acts of aggression or other breaches of the peace, and to bring about by peaceful means, and in conformity with the principles of justice and international law,

adjustment or settlement of international disputes or situations which might lead to a breach of the peace. . . .

Article 2

The Organization and its Members, in pursuit of the Purposes stated in Article 1, shall act in accordance with the following Principles.

1. The Organization is based on the principle of the sovereign equality of all its Members. . . .

3. All Members shall settle their international disputes by peaceful means in such a manner that international peace and security, and justice, are not endangered. . . .

CHAPTER III: ORGANS

Article 7

1. There are established as the principal organs of the United Nations:
- a General Assembly
- a Security Council
- an Economic and Social Council
- a Trusteeship Council
- an International Court of Justice
- and a Secretariat. . . .

CHAPTER IV: THE GENERAL ASSEMBLY

Article 12

1. While the Security Council is exercising in respect of any dispute or situation the functions assigned to it in the present Charter, the General Assembly shall not make any recommendation with regard to that dispute or situation unless the Security Council so requests. . . .

CHAPTER V: THE SECURITY COUNCIL

Article 23

1. The Security Council shall consist of fifteen Members of the United Nations. The Republic of China, France, the Union of Soviet Socialist Republics, the United Kingdom of Great Britain and Northern Ireland, and the United States of America shall be permanent members of the Security Council. The General Assembly shall elect ten other Members of the United Nations to be non-permanent members of the Security Council. . . .

2. The non-permanent members of the Security Council shall be elected for a term of two years. In the first election of the non-permanent members after the increase of the membership of the Security Council from eleven to fifteen, two of the four additional members shall be chosen for a term of one year. A retiring member shall not be eligible for immediate re-election. . . .

Article 24

1. In order to ensure prompt and effective action by the United Nations, its Members confer on the Security Council primary responsibility for the maintenance of international peace and security, and agree that in carrying out its duties under this responsibility the Security Council acts on their behalf. . . .

Article 27

1. Each member of the Security Council shall have one vote.
2. Decisions of the Security Council on procedural matters shall be made by an affirmative vote of nine members.
3. Decisions of the Security Council on all other matters shall be made by an affirmative vote of nine members including the concurring votes of the permanent members; provided that . . . a party to a dispute shall abstain from voting. . . .

CHAPTER VII: ACTION WITH RESPECT TO THREATS TO THE PEACE, BREACH OF THE PEACE, AND ACTS OF AGGRESSION

Article 39

The Security Council shall determine the existence of any threat to the peace, breach of the peace, or act of aggression and shall make recommendations, or decide what measures shall be taken in accordance with Articles 41 and 42, to maintain or restore international peace and security. . . .

Article 41

The Security Council may decide what measures not involving the use of armed force are to be employed to give effect to its decisions, and it may call upon the Members of the United Nations to apply such measures. These may include complete or partial interruption of economic relations and of rail, sea, air, postal, telegraphic, radio, and other means of communication, and the severance of diplomatic relations.

Article 42

Should the Security Council consider that measures provided for in Article 41 would be inadequate or have proved to be inadequate, it may take such action by air, sea, or land forces as may be necessary to maintain or restore international peace and security. Such action may include demonstrations, blockade, and other operations by air, sea, or land forces of Members of the United Nations. . . .

Source: United Nations, "Charter of the United Nations," June 26, 1945, www.un.org/aboutun/ charter/.

Document 1.4
Agreement at Potsdam on Postwar Germany, August 1, 1945

At Potsdam, Germany, Truman, Stalin, Churchill, and newly elected British prime minister Clement Atlee met to consider the terms of German occupation and control. The wartime allies agreed on denazification of Germany (and Austria as well); a formula for the distribution of reparations; and the shifting of Poland's borders, at the expense of Germany and to the benefit of the Soviet Union. They also confirmed their earlier commitment to free elections in Eastern Europe.

. . .

II. THE PRINCIPLES TO GOVERN THE TREATMENT OF GERMANY IN THE INITIAL CONTROL PERIOD

A. Political Principles.

1. In accordance with the Agreement on Control Machinery in Germany, supreme authority in Germany is exercised, on instructions from their respective Governments, by the Commanders-in-Chief of the armed forces of the United States of America, the United Kingdom, the Union of Soviet Socialist Republics, and the French Republic, each in his own zone of occupation, and also jointly, in matters affecting Germany as a whole, in their capacity as members of the Control Council.

2. So far as is practicable, there shall be uniformity of treatment of the German population throughout Germany.

3. The purposes of the occupation of Germany by which the Control Council shall be guided are:

   (i) The complete disarmament and demilitarization of Germany and the elimination or control of all German industry that could be used for military production. To these ends:—

      (a) All German land, naval and air forces, the SS., SA., SD., and Gestapo, with all their organizations, staffs and institutions, including the General Staff, the Officers' Corps, Reserve Corps, military schools, war veterans' organizations and all other military and semi-military organizations, together with all clubs and associations which serve to keep alive the military tradition in Germany, shall be completely and finally abolished in such manner as permanently to prevent the revival or reorganization of German militarism and Nazism; . . .

6. All members of the Nazi Party who have been more than nominal participants in its activities and all other persons hostile to Allied purposes shall be removed from public and semi-public office, and from positions of responsibility in important private undertakings. . . .

7. German education shall be so controlled as completely to eliminate Nazi and militarist doctrines and to make possible the successful development of democratic ideas. . . .

11. In order to eliminate Germany's war potential, the production of arms, ammunition and implements of war as well as all types of aircraft and sea-going ships shall be prohibited and prevented. Production of metals, chemicals, machinery and other items that are

directly necessary to a war economy shall be rigidly controlled and restricted to Germany's approved post-war peacetime needs. . . . Productive capacity not needed for permitted production shall be removed in accordance with the reparations plan. . . .

12. At the earliest practicable date, the German economy shall be decentralized for the purpose of eliminating the present excessive concentration of economic power as exemplified in particular by cartels, syndicates, trusts and other monopolistic arrangements.

13. In organizing the German Economy, primary emphasis shall be given to the development of agriculture and peaceful domestic industries. . . .

III. REPARATIONS FROM GERMANY.

1. Reparation claims of the U. S. S. R. shall be met by removals from the zone of Germany occupied by the U. S. S. R., and from appropriate German external assets. . . .

3. The reparation claims of the United States, the United Kingdom and other countries entitled to reparations shall be met from the Western Zones and from appropriate German external assets.

4. In addition to the reparations to be taken by the U. S. S. R. from its own zone of occupation, the U. S. S. R. shall receive additionally from the Western Zones:

   (a) 15 per cent of such usable and complete industrial capital equipment . . . as is unnecessary for the German peace economy . . . from the Western Zones of Germany. . . .

   (b) 10 per cent of such industrial capital equipment as is unnecessary for the German peace economy and should be removed from the Western Zones. . . .

VIII. POLAND.

A. Declaration.

. . .The Three Powers note that the Polish Provisional Government of National Unity, in accordance with the decisions of the Crimea Conference, has agreed to the holding of free and unfettered elections as soon as possible on the basis of universal suffrage and secret ballot in which all democratic and anti-Nazi parties shall have the right to take part and to put forward candidates. . . .

B. Western Frontier of Poland.

. . .The three Heads of Government agree that, pending the final determination of Poland's western frontier, the former German territories east of a line running from the Baltic Sea immediately west of Swinamunde, and thence along the Oder River to the confluence of the western Neisse River and along the Western Neisse to the Czechoslovak frontier, including that portion of East Prussia not placed under the administration of the Union of Soviet Socialist Republics in accordance with the understanding reached at this conference and including the area of the former free city of Danzig, shall be under the administration of the Polish State and for such purposes should not be considered as part of the Soviet zone of occupation in Germany. . . .

XII. ORDERLY TRANSFER OF GERMAN POPULATIONS.

The Three Governments, having considered the question in all its aspects, recognize that the transfer to Germany of German populations, or elements thereof, remaining in Poland, Czechoslovakia and Hungary, will have to be undertaken. They agree that any transfers that take place should be effected in an orderly and humane manner. . . .

Source: "Potsdam Conference," August 1, 1945, from the Avalon Project at Yale Law School, www .yale.edu/lawweb/avalon/decade/decade17.htm.

Document 1.5
Soviet Premier Joseph Stalin's "Campaign" Speech in Moscow, February 9, 1946

In Joseph Stalin's speech to "voters" in the Stalin Electoral District of Moscow, the Soviet leader provided a classic Marxist account of the origins of the late war and attributed Soviet success in the war to the Communist Party's prewar economic and social policies. The speech shows the tremendous concern that Stalin and other Soviet leaders exhibited toward how the Soviet Union was perceived in the West. The speech alarmed some Washington observers of the Kremlin, who had become accustomed to the more diplomatic way in which the Allies spoke of one another during the war.

The Chairman: Joseph Vissarionovich *Stalin* has the floor.

   (Comrade Stalin's appearance in the rostrum was greeted by the voters with loud cheers lasting several minutes. The entire audience in the Bolshoi Theatre rose to its feet to greet Comrade Stalin. There were continuous cries of "Cheers for great Stalin!" "Long live great Stalin, Hurrah!" "Cheers for our beloved Stalin!")

Comrade *Stalin:* Comrades!

Eight years have passed since the last elections to the Supreme Soviet. This has been a period replete with events of a decisive nature. The first four years were years of intense labour on the part of Soviet people in carrying out the Third Five-Year Plan. The second four years covered the events of the war against the German and Japanese aggressors—the events of the Second World War. Undoubtedly, the war was the main event during the past period.

   It would be wrong to think that the Second World War broke out accidentally, or as a result of blunders committed by certain statesmen, although blunders were certainly committed. As a matter of fact, the war broke out as the inevitable result of the development of world economic and political forces on the basis of present-day monopolistic capitalism. Marxists have more than once stated that the capitalist system of world economy contains the elements of a general crisis and military conflicts, that, in view of that, the development of world capitalism in our times does not proceed smoothly and evenly, but through crises and catastrophic wars. The point is that the uneven development of capitalist countries usually leads, in the course of time, to a sharp disturbance of the equilibrium within the world system of capitalism, and that group of capitalist countries which regards itself as being less secure . . . usually attempts to change the situation and to redistribute "spheres of influence" in its own favour—by employing armed force. As a result of this, the capitalist world is split into two hostile camps, and war breaks out between them. . . .

Thus, as a result of the first crisis of the capitalist system of world economy, the First World War broke out; and as a result of the second crisis, the Second World War broke out. . . .

This does not mean, of course, that the Second World War was a copy of the first. On the contrary, the Second [World War] differed substantially in character from the first. It must be borne in mind that before attacking the Allied countries the major fascist states—Germany, Japan and Italy—destroyed the last remnants of bourgeois-democratic liberties at home and established there a cruel terroristic regime. . . . In [view] of this, the Second World War against the Axis Powers, unlike the First World War, assumed from the very outset the character of an anti-fascist war, a war of liberation, one of the tasks of which was to restore democratic liberties. The entry of the Soviet Union into the war against the Axis Powers could only augment—and really did augment—the anti-fascist and liberating character of the Second World War. . . .

As far as our country is concerned, for her this war was the fiercest and most arduous [war] ever fought in the history of our Motherland.

But the war was not only a curse. It was also a great school which examined and tested all the forces of the people. The war laid bare all facts and events in the rear and at the front, it ruthlessly tore down all the veils and coverings that concealed the actual features of states, governments and parties, and brought them onto the stage without masks and without make-up, with all their defects and merits. The war was something in the nature of an examination of our Soviet system, of our State, of our Government and of our Communist Party, and it summed up their work and said, as it were: Here they are, your people and organizations, their life and work scrutinize them carefully and treat them according to their deserts.

This is one of the positive sides of the war.

For us, for the voters, this is of immense importance, for it helps us quickly and impartially to appraise the activities of the Party and its men, and to draw correct conclusions. . . .

And so, what is the summation of the war?

There is one principal summation upon which all the others rest. This summation is, that towards the end of the war the enemies sustained defeat and we and our Allies proved to be the victors. . . .

Our victory signifies, first of all, that our Soviet *social* system was victorious, that the Soviet social system successfully passed the test of fire in the war and proved that it is fully viable.

As we know, the foreign press on more than one occasion asserted that the Soviet social system was a "dangerous experiment" that was doomed to failure, that the Soviet system was a "house of cards" having no foundations in life and imposed upon the people by the Cheka [the Soviet Secret Police], and that a slight shock from without was sufficient to cause this "house of cards" to collapse.

Now we can say that the war has refuted all these assertions of the foreign press and has proved them to have been groundless. The war proved that the Soviet social system is a genuinely people's system. . . .

More than that. The issue now is not whether the Soviet social system is viable or not, because after the object lessons of the war, no skeptic now dares to express doubt concerning the viability of the Soviet social system. Now the issue is that the Soviet social system has proved to be more viable and stable than the non-Soviet social system, that the Soviet social system is a better form of organization of society than any non-Soviet social system.

Secondly, our victory signifies that our Soviet *state* system was victorious, that our multinational Soviet state passed all the tests of the war and proved its viability. . . .

Thirdly, our victory signifies that the Soviet Armed Forces, our Red Army, was victorious, that the Red Army heroically withstood all the hardships of the war, utterly routed the armies of our enemies, and emerged from the war the victor. *(A voice: "Under Comrade Stalin's leadership!" All rise. Loud and prolonged applause, rising to an ovation.)*

. . . It must not be forgotten that the Red Army is the army which utterly routed the German army, the army which only yesterday struck terror in the hearts of the armies of the European states.

It must be noted that the "critics" of the Red Army are becoming fewer and fewer. More than that. Comments are more and more frequently appearing in the foreign press noting the high qualities of the Red Army, the skill of its men and commanders, and the flawlessness of its strategy and tactics. . . .

Can it be said that before entering the Second World War our country already possessed the necessary minimum of the material potentialities needed to satisfy these main requirements? I think it can. To prepare for this immense task we had to carry out three five-year plans of national-economic development. It was these three five-year plans that enabled us to create these material potentialities. . . .

It is this that explains the storm of debate that was roused in the foreign press at one time by the publication of these figures. Our friends decided that a "miracle" had happened; those who were ill-disposed towards us proclaimed that the five-year plans were "Bolshevik propaganda" and "tricks of the Cheka." But as miracles do not happen and the Cheka is not so powerful as to be able to annul the laws of social development, "public opinion" abroad was obliged to resign itself to the facts.

By what policy was the Communist Party able to create these material potentialities in so short a time?

First of all by the Soviet policy of industrializing the country. . . .

Secondly, by the policy of collectivizing agriculture. . . .

Now a few words about the Communist Party's plans of work for the immediate future. As you know, these plans are formulated in the new five-year plan, which is to be adopted in the very near future. The main tasks of the new five-year plan are to rehabilitate the devastated regions of our country, to restore industry and agriculture to the prewar level, and then to exceed that level to a more or less considerable extent. Apart from the fact that the rationing system is to be abolished in the very near future (*loud and prolonged applause*), special attention will be devoted to the expansion of the production of consumers' goods. . . .

This, then, is my brief report on the activities of the Communist Party during the recent past and on its plans of work for the future. (*Loud and prolonged applause.*)

It is for you to judge to what extent the Party has been and is working on the proper lines (*applause*), and whether it could not have worked better. (*Laughter and applause.*)

It is said that victors are not judged (*laughter and applause*), that they must not be criticized, that they must not be enquired into. This is not true. Victors may and should be judged (*laughter and applause*), they may and should be criticized and enquired into. This is beneficial not only for the cause, but also for the victors (*cries of approval and applause*); there will be less swelled-headedness, and there will be more modesty. (*Laughter and applause.*) I regard the election campaign as the voters' judgment [on] the Communist Party of our country as the ruling party. The result of the election will be the voters' verdict. (*Loud cries of approval and applause.*) The Communist Party of our country would not be worth much if it feared criticism and investigation. The Communist Party is ready to receive the verdict of the voters. (*Loud applause.*) . . .

In conclusion, permit me to express my thanks for the confidence which you have shown me (*loud and prolonged applause. A voice: "Cheers for the great leader of all our victories, Comrade Stalin!"*) by nominating me as a candidate for the Supreme Soviet. You need have no doubt that I will do my best to justify your confidence. (*All rise. Loud and prolonged applause rising to an ovation. Voices in different parts of the hall: "Long live great Stalin, Hurrah!" "Cheers for the great leader of the peoples!" "Glory to great Stalin!" "Long live Comrade Stalin, the candidate of the entire people!" "Glory to the creator of all our victories, Comrade Stalin!"*)

Source: Joseph Stalin, "Speech Delivered by J. V. Stalin at a Meeting of the Voters of the Stalin Electoral District," February 9, 1946, in *Speeches Delivered at Meetings of Voters of the Stalin Electoral District* (Moscow: Foreign Languages Publishing House, 1950), From Marx to Mao, marx2mao.php-webhosting.com/ Stalin/SS46.html.

Document 1.6
The "Long Telegram," George Kennan's Message on the Soviet Outlook, February 22, 1946

In this telegram to the U.S. State Department, George Kennan, a Foreign Service officer expert on Russia, sought to analyze for Washington policymakers recent events in the Soviet Union. Presidential efforts to bargain with the Soviets, Kennan suggested, were bound to fail. The Soviets were motivated by insecurities, both real and imagined, and were fanatically sincere in their ideological pronouncements. Kennan argued that the United States must mobilize all its resources—including, vitally, its spirit and willpower—to confront the challenge of Soviet-led Communism. Although Kennan frequently complained that his thoughts had been misconstrued by those who wielded power in the Truman administration, his ideas provided an intellectual foundation upon which the Cold War strategy of "containment" was constructed.

861.00/2 - 2246: Telegram
The Chargé in the Soviet Union (Kennan) to the Secretary of State
SECRET
Moscow, February 22, 1946—9 p.m. [Received February 22—3:52 p.m.]

. . .

I apologize in advance for this burdening of telegraphic channel; but questions involved are of such urgent importance, particularly in view of recent events, that our answers to them, if they deserve attention at all, seem to me to deserve it at once. There follows

Part 1: Basic Features of Post War Soviet Outlook, as Put Forward by Official Propaganda Machine

Are as Follows:

(a) USSR still lives in antagonistic "capitalist encirclement" with which in the long run there can be no permanent peaceful coexistence. As stated by Stalin in 1927 to a delegation of American workers:

"In course of further development of international revolution there will emerge two centers of world significance: a socialist center, drawing to itself the countries which tend toward socialism, and a capitalist center, drawing to itself the countries that incline toward capitalism. Battle between these two centers for command of world economy will decide fate of capitalism and of communism in entire world."

(b) Capitalist world is beset with internal conflicts, inherent in nature of capitalist society. These conflicts are insoluble by means of peaceful compromise. Greatest of them is that between England and US. . . .

(e) Conflicts between capitalist states, though likewise fraught with danger for USSR, nevertheless hold out great possibilities for advancement of socialist cause, particularly if USSR remains militarily powerful, ideologically monolithic and faithful to its present brilliant leadership. . . .

So much for premises. To what deductions do they lead from standpoint of Soviet policy? To following:

(a) Everything must be done to advance relative strength of USSR as factor in international society. Conversely, no opportunity must be missed to reduce strength and influence, collectively as well as individually, of capitalist powers.

(b) Soviet efforts, and those of Russia's friends abroad, must be directed toward deepening and exploiting of differences and conflicts between capitalist powers. If these eventually deepen into an "imperialist" war, this war must be turned into revolutionary upheavals within the various capitalist countries.

(c) "Democratic-progressive" elements abroad are to be utilized to maximum to bring pressure to bear on capitalist governments along lines agreeable to Soviet interests. . . .

Part 2: Background of Outlook

Before examining ramifications of this party line in practice there are certain aspects of it to which I wish to draw attention.

First, it does not represent natural outlook of Russian people. Latter are, by and large, friendly to outside world, eager for experience of it, eager to measure against it talents they are conscious of possessing, eager above all to live in peace and enjoy fruits of their own labor. . . .

Second, please note that premises on which this party line is based are for most part simply not true. . . .

. . . What does this indicate? It indicates that Soviet party line is not based on any objective analysis of situation beyond Russia's borders; that it has, indeed, little to do with conditions outside of Russia; that it arises mainly from basic inner-Russian necessities which existed before recent war and exist today.

At bottom of Kremlin's neurotic view of world affairs is traditional and instinctive Russian sense of insecurity. Originally, this was insecurity of a peaceful agricultural people trying to live on vast exposed plain in neighborhood of fierce nomadic peoples. To this was added, as Russia came into contact with economically advanced West, fear of more competent, more powerful, more highly organized societies in that area. But this latter type of insecurity was one which afflicted rather Russian rulers than Russian people; for Russian rulers have invariably sensed that their rule was relatively archaic in form fragile and artificial in its psychological foundation, unable to stand comparison or contact with political systems of Western countries. . . .

. . . After establishment of Bolshevist regime, Marxist dogma, rendered even more truculent and intolerant by Lenin's interpretation, became a perfect vehicle for sense of insecurity with which Bolsheviks, even more than previous Russian rulers, were afflicted. In this dogma, with its basic altruism of purpose, they found justification for their instinctive fear of outside world, for the dictatorship without which they did not know how to rule, for cruelties they did not dare not to inflict, for sacrifice they felt bound to demand. . . .

It should not be thought from above that Soviet party line is necessarily disingenuous and insincere on part of all those who put it forward. Many of them are too ignorant of outside world and mentally too dependent to question [apparent omission] self-hypnotism, and who have no difficulty making themselves believe what they find it comforting and convenient to believe. . . .

Part 3: Projection of Soviet Outlook in Practical Policy on Official Level

We have now seen nature and background of Soviet program. What may we expect by way of its practical implementation? . . .

On official plane we must look for following:

(a) Internal policy devoted to increasing in every way strength and prestige of Soviet state: intensive military-industrialization; maximum development of armed forces; great displays to impress outsiders; continued secretiveness about internal matters, designed to conceal weaknesses and to keep opponents in dark.

(b) Wherever it is considered timely and promising, efforts will be made to advance official limits of Soviet power. For the moment, these efforts are restricted to certain neighboring points. . . .

(c) Russians will participate officially in international organizations where they see opportunity of extending Soviet power or of inhibiting or diluting power of others. Moscow sees in UNO [United Nations Organization] not the mechanism for a permanent and stable world society founded on mutual interest and aims of all nations, but an arena in which aims just mentioned can be favorably pursued. . . .

(d) Toward colonial areas and backward or dependent peoples, Soviet policy, even on official plane, will be directed toward weakening of power and influence and contacts of advanced Western nations, on theory that in so far as this policy is successful, there will be created a vacuum which will favor Communist-Soviet penetration. . . .

Part 4: Following May Be Said as to What We May Expect by Way of Implementation of Basic Soviet Policies on Unofficial, or Subterranean Plane, i.e. on Plane for Which Soviet Government Accepts No Responsibility

Agencies utilized for promulgation of policies on this plane are following:

1. Inner central core of Communist Parties in other countries. While many of persons who compose this category may also appear and act in unrelated public capacities, they are in reality working closely together as an underground operating directorate of world communism. . . .

2. Rank and file of Communist Parties. . . . As a rule they are used to penetrate, and to influence or dominate, as case may be, other organizations less likely to be suspected of being tools of Soviet Government. . . .

3. A wide variety of national associations or bodies which can be dominated or influenced by such penetration. These include: labor unions, youth leagues, women's organizations, racial societies, religious societies, social organizations, cultural groups, liberal magazines, publishing houses, etc.

4. International organizations which can be similarly penetrated through influence over various national components. Labor, youth and women's organizations are prominent among them. . . .

7. Governments or governing groups willing to lend themselves to Soviet purposes in one degree or another, such as present Bulgarian and Yugoslav Governments, North Persian regime, Chinese Communists, etc. Not only propaganda machines but actual policies of these regimes can be placed extensively at disposal of USSR

It may be expected that component parts of this far-flung apparatus will be utilized in accordance with their individual suitability, as follows: . . .

(e) Everything possible will be done to set major Western Powers against each other. . . .

(f) In general, all Soviet efforts on unofficial international plane will be negative and destructive in character, designed to tear down sources of strength beyond reach of Soviet control. . . .

Part 5: [Practical Deductions from Standpoint of US Policy]

In summary, we have here a political force committed fanatically to the belief that with US there can be no permanent *modus vivendi* that it is desirable and necessary that the internal harmony of our society be disrupted, our traditional way of life be destroyed, the international authority of our state be broken, if Soviet power is to be secure. . . . Problem of how to cope with this force in [is] undoubtedly greatest task our diplomacy has ever faced and probably greatest it will ever have to face.

(1) Soviet power, unlike that of Hitlerite Germany, is neither schematic nor adventunstic. It does not work by fixed plans. It does not take unnecessary risks. Impervious to logic of

reason, and it is highly sensitive to logic of force. For this reason it can easily withdraw—and usually does when strong resistance is encountered at any point. . . .

(2) Gauged against Western World as a whole, Soviets are still by far the weaker force. Thus, their success will really depend on degree of cohesion, firmness and vigor which Western World can muster. And this is factor which it is within our power to influence.

(3) Success of Soviet system, as form of internal power, is not yet finally proven. It has yet to be demonstrated that it can survive supreme test of successive transfer of power from one individual or group to another. . . .

(4) All Soviet propaganda beyond Soviet security sphere is basically negative and destructive. It should therefore be relatively easy to combat it. . . .

For those reasons I think we may approach calmly and with good heart problem of how to deal with Russia. As to how this approach should be made, I only wish to advance, by way of conclusion, following comments:

(1) Our first step must be to apprehend, and recognize for what it is, the nature of the movement with which we are dealing. We must study it with same courage, detachment, objectivity, and same determination not to be emotionally provoked or unseated by it, with which doctor studies unruly and unreasonable individual.

(2) We must see that our public is educated to realities of Russian situation. . . .

(3) Much depends on health and vigor of our own society. World communism is like malignant parasite which feeds only on diseased tissue. This is point at which domestic and foreign policies meets. . . .

(4) . . . It is not enough to urge people to develop political processes similar to our own. Many foreign peoples, in Europe at least, are tired and frightened by experiences of past, and are less interested in abstract freedom than in security. They are seeking guidance rather than responsibilities. We should be better able than Russians to give them this. And unless we do, Russians certainly will.

(5) Finally we must have courage and self-confidence to cling to our own methods and conceptions of human society. After All, the greatest danger that can befall us in coping with this problem of Soviet communism, is that we shall allow ourselves to become like those with whom we are coping.

KENNAN
800.00B International Red Day/2 - 2546: Airgram

Source: George Kennan, " 'Long Telegram' (Moscow-to-London)," February 22, 1946, from the National Security Archive, George Washington University, www2.gwu.edu/~nsarchiv/coldwar/documents/episode-1/kennan.htm.

Document 1.7
"The Sinews of Peace," Former Prime Minister Winston Churchill's Speech in Fulton, Missouri, March 5, 1946

At Westminster College in Fulton, Missouri, former British prime minister Winston Churchill, accompanied by President Truman, spoke bluntly of Soviet domination over Eastern Europe. An "iron curtain," he said, had descended there. To defend liberty from the threat posed by an expansionist Soviet Union, Churchill proposed an Anglo-American diplomatic, cultural, and military alliance.

. . .When American military men approach some serious situation they are wont to write at the head of their directive the words "over-all strategic concept." There is wisdom in this, as it leads to clarity of thought. What then is the over-all strategic concept which we should inscribe today? It is nothing less than the safety and welfare, the freedom and progress, of all the homes and families of all the men and women in all the lands. . . .

Our American military colleagues, after having proclaimed their "over-all strategic concept" and computed available resources, always proceed to the next step—namely, the method. Here again there is widespread agreement. A world organisation has already been erected for the prime purpose of preventing war, UNO [United Nations Organisation], the successor of the League of Nations, with the decisive addition of the United States and all that that means, is already at work. We must make sure that its work is fruitful, that it is a reality and not a sham, that it is a force for action, and not merely a frothing of words, that it is a true temple of peace in which the shields of many nations can some day be hung up, and not merely a cockpit in a Tower of Babel. Before we cast away the solid assurances of national armaments for self-preservation we must be certain that our temple is built, not upon shifting sands or quagmires, but upon the rock. Anyone can see with his eyes open that our path will be difficult and also long, but if we persevere together as we did in the two world wars—though not, alas, in the interval between them—I cannot doubt that we shall achieve our common purpose in the end.

I have, however, a definite and practical proposal to make for action. Courts and magistrates may be set up but they cannot function without sheriffs and constables. The United Nations Organisation must immediately begin to be equipped with an international armed force. In such a matter we can only go step by step, but we must begin now. I propose that each of the Powers and States should be invited to delegate a certain number of air squadrons to the service of the world organisation. . . .

It would nevertheless be wrong and imprudent to entrust the secret knowledge or experience of the atomic bomb, which the United States, Great Britain, and Canada now share, to the world organisation, while it is still in its infancy. It would be criminal madness to cast it adrift in this still agitated and un-united world. No one in any country has slept less well in their beds because this knowledge and the method and the raw materials to apply it, are at present largely retained in American hands. I do not believe we should all have slept so soundly had the positions been reversed and if some Communist or neo-Fascist State monopolised for the time being these dread agencies. The fear of them alone might easily have been used to enforce totalitarian systems upon the free democratic world, with consequences appalling to human imagination. God has willed that this shall not be and we have at least a breathing space to set our house in order before this peril has to be encountered. . . .

Now I come to the second danger of these two marauders which threatens the cottage, the home, and the ordinary people—namely, tyranny. We cannot be blind to the fact that the liberties enjoyed by individual citizens throughout the British Empire are not valid in a considerable number of countries, some of which are very powerful. In these States control is enforced upon the common people by various kinds of all-embracing police governments. The power of the State is exercised without restraint, either by dictators or by compact oligarchies operating through a privileged party and a political police. It is not our duty at this time when difficulties are so numerous to interfere forcibly in the internal affairs of countries which we have not conquered in war. But we must never cease to proclaim in fearless tones the great principles of freedom and the rights of man which are the joint inheritance of the English-speaking world and which through Magna Carta, the Bill of Rights, the Habeas Corpus, trial by jury, and the English common law find their most famous expression in the American Declaration of Independence.

All this means that the people of any country have the right, and should have the power by constitutional action, by free unfettered elections, with secret ballot, to choose or change the character or form of government under which they dwell; that freedom of speech and thought should reign; that courts of justice, independent of the executive, unbiased by any party, should administer laws which have received the broad assent of large majorities or are consecrated by time and custom. Here are the title deeds of freedom which should lie in every cottage home. Here is the message of the British and American peoples to mankind. . . .

I have now stated the two great dangers which menace the homes of the people: War and Tyranny. I have not yet spoken of poverty and privation which are in many cases the prevailing anxiety. But if the dangers of war and tyranny are removed, there is no doubt that science and co-operation can bring in the next few years to the world, certainly in the next few decades newly taught in the sharpening school of war, an expansion of material well-being beyond anything that has yet occurred in human experience. . . .

Now, while still pursuing the method of realising our overall strategic concept, I come to the crux of what I have travelled here to Say. Neither the sure prevention of war, nor the continuous rise of world organisation will be gained without what I have called the fraternal association of the English-speaking peoples. This means a special relationship between the British Commonwealth and Empire and the United States. This is no time for generalities, and I will venture to be precise. Fraternal association requires not only the growing friendship and mutual understanding between our two vast but kindred Systems of society, but the continuance of the intimate relationship between our military advisers, leading to common study of potential dangers, the similarity of weapons and manuals of instructions, and to the interchange of officers and cadets at technical colleges. It should carry with it the continuance of the present facilities for mutual security by the joint use of all Naval and Air Force bases in the possession of either country all over the world. This would perhaps double the mobility of the American Navy and Air Force. It would greatly expand that of the British Empire Forces and it might well lead, if and as the world calms down, to important financial savings. Already we use together a large number of islands; more may well be entrusted to our joint care in the near future.

The United States has already a Permanent Defence Agreement with the Dominion of Canada. . . . This principle should be extended to all British Commonwealths with full reciprocity. . . . Eventually there may come—I feel eventually there will come—the principle of common citizenship. . . .

A shadow has fallen upon the scenes so lately lighted by the Allied victory. Nobody knows what Soviet Russia and its Communist international organisation intends to do in the immediate future, or what are the limits, if any, to their expansive and proselytising tendencies. I have a strong admiration and regard for the valiant Russian people and for my wartime comrade, Marshal Stalin. There is deep sympathy and goodwill in Britain—and I doubt not here also—towards the peoples of all the Russias and a resolve to persevere through many differences and rebuffs in establishing lasting friendships. We understand the Russian need to be secure on her western frontiers by the removal of all possibility of German aggression. We welcome Russia to her rightful place among the leading nations of the world. We welcome her flag upon the seas. Above all, we welcome constant, frequent and growing contacts between the Russian people and our own people on both sides of the Atlantic. It is my duty however, for I am sure you would wish me to state the facts as I see them to you, to place before you certain facts about the present position in Europe.

From Stettin in the Baltic to Trieste in the Adriatic, an iron curtain has descended across the Continent. Behind that line lie all the capitals of the ancient states of Central and Eastern Europe. Warsaw, Berlin, Prague, Vienna, Budapest, Belgrade, Bucharest and Sofia, all these famous cities and the populations around them lie in what I must call the Soviet sphere, and all are subject in one form or another, not only to Soviet influence but to a very high and, in many cases, increasing measure of control from Moscow. Athens alone—Greece with its immortal glories—is free to decide its future at an election under British, American and French observation. . . . Police governments are prevailing in nearly every case, and so far, except in Czechoslovakia, there is no true democracy.

Turkey and Persia are both profoundly alarmed and disturbed at the claims which are being made upon them and at the pressure being exerted by the Moscow Government. An attempt is being made by the Russians in Berlin to build up a quasi-Communist party in their zone of Occupied Germany. . . .

If now the Soviet Government tries, by separate action, to build up a pro-Communist Germany in their areas, this will cause new serious difficulties in the British and American zones, and will give the defeated Germans the power of putting themselves up to auction between the Soviets and the Western Democracies. Whatever conclusions may be drawn from these facts—and facts they are—this is certainly not the Liberated Europe we fought to build up. . . .

. . . Except in the British Commonwealth and in the United States where Communism is in its infancy, the Communist parties or fifth columns constitute a growing challenge and peril to Christian civilisation. . . .

Last time I saw it all coming and cried aloud to my own fellow-countrymen and to the world, but no one paid any attention. . . . We surely must not let that happen again. This can only be achieved by reaching now, in 1946, a good understanding on all points with Russia under the general authority of the United Nations Organisation and by the maintenance of that good understanding through many peaceful years, by the world instrument, supported by the whole strength of the English-speaking world and all its connections. There is the solution which I respectfully offer to you in this Address to which I have given the title "The Sinews of Peace."

. . . If the population of the English-speaking Commonwealths be added to that of the United States with all that such co-operation implies in the air, on the sea, all over the globe and in science and in industry, and in moral force, there will be no quivering, precarious balance of power to offer its temptation to ambition or adventure. . . .

Source: Winston Churchill, "Sinews of Peace (Iron Curtain)," March 5, 1946, from the Churchill Centre, www.winstonchurchill.org/i4a/pages/index.cfm?pageid= 429.

Document 1.8
Soviet Premier Joseph Stalin's Remarks to the Soviet Press about Churchill's Speech, March 14, 1946

In the Soviet press outlet, Pravda, *Stalin took strong exception to Churchill's "iron curtain" speech. The wartime comity among the great powers was coming to an end.*

Question [Pravda]: How do you assess the recent speech of Mr. Churchill, which he gave in the United States of America?

Answer [Stalin]: My assessment is, it is a dangerous act, calculated to breed strife between allied countries and make their cooperation more difficult.

Question: Could Mr. Churchill's speech be considered as a harm to the progress of peace and security?

Answer: Absolutely, yes. As a matter of fact Mr. Churchill is standing now in the position of a warmonger. And here Mr. Churchill is not alone—he has many friends not only in England but also in the United States. It ought to be mentioned that in this matter Mr. Churchill and his friends strikingly resemble Hitler and his friends. Hitler started the process of unleashing war from the proclamation of a racist theory, according to which only the German-speaking people are a worthy nation. Mr. Churchill is starting his process of unleashing war also from a racist theory, stating that only the English-speaking countries are worthy nations, destined to manage the fate of the world. . . .

. . . Mr. Churchill and his friends in England and in the United States are presenting the non-English-speaking nations with something like an ultimatum: either voluntarily agree to our rule, and everything will be all right, or a war is unavoidable.

But during five years of difficult war nations shed blood for the sake of freedom and independence of their respective countries, and not for the sake of replacing the tyranny of people like Hitler for the tyranny of those like Churchill. Therefore, by all probability, nations which do not speak English, and yet comprise the majority of the world's population, will not conform to the new slavery. . . .

Question: How do you assess the part of Mr. Churchill's speech where he attacks the democratic governments of our neighboring European countries and where he criticizes good neighborly interrelations established between those countries and the Soviet Union?

Answer: This part of Mr. Churchill's speech represents a blend of elements of defamation and elements of rudeness and tactlessness.

Mr. Churchill states that "Warsaw, Berlin, Prague, Vienna, Budapest, Belgrade, Bucharest, Sophia, all those renowned cities and inhabitants of respective regions are in a Soviet zone and all submit in one way or another not only to the Soviet influence, but also in large degree to the growing control of Moscow." Mr. Churchill is qualifying all that as the boundless "expansionist tendencies" of the Soviet Union.

There is no need for any special effort to show that Mr. Churchill is rudely slandering Moscow and the above-mentioned countries neighboring the U.S.S.R.

First, it is particularly absurd to talk about the exclusive control of the Soviet Union in Vienna and Berlin, where the Allied Control Councils exist and whose members represent four powers, and where the Soviet Union has only ¼ of the votes. Occasionally people cannot resist slander, but one must know where to stop.

Secondly, the following matters shall not be forgotten. The Germans carried out the invasion into U.S.S.R. through Finland, Poland, Romania, Bulgaria and Hungary. Germans were able to carry out the invasion through those countries because at the time, there existed regimes hostile to the Soviet Union. As a result of the German invasion, the Soviet Union irrevocably lost about 7 million people during the conduct of war, German occupation, and due to driving away people for servitude labor. In other words, the Soviet Union lost several times more people than England and United States combined. It is possible that in some places, some are inclined to forget the colossal sacrifices of the Soviet Nation, which ensured the liberation of Europe from Hitler's regime.

But the Soviet Union can not forget the sacrifice. Let the question be asked: Is it odd that the Soviet Union, wishing to ensure its safety, in the future works toward having in those countries governments loyal to the Soviet Union? . . .

Mr. Churchill is close to the truth when he speaks about the growing influence of communist parties in Eastern Europe. But it shall be mentioned that he is not exactly correct. Influence of communist parties grew not only in Eastern Europe but almost in all European countries, where fascism once ruled (Italy, Germany, Hungary, Bulgaria, Romania, Ukraine), or where the German, Italian or Hungarian occupation took place (France, Belgium, Holland, Norway, Denmark, Poland, Czechoslovakia, Yugoslavia, Greece, Soviet Union, etc.)

The growing influence of communists shall not be taken as a coincidence. It represents a fully normal phenomenon. . . .

Source: "Stalin Compares Churchill to Hitler," from CNN, *Cold War,* www.cnn.com/SPECIALS/ cold.war/episodes/02/1st.draft/pravda.html.

Document 1.9
Soviet Ambassador Nikolai Novikov's Telegram about Soviet-U.S. Relations, September 27, 1946

*The Soviets had their own interpretation of the growing hostility among the former allies. The Soviet ambassador to the United States, Nikolai Novikov, analyzed events in terms ironically similar to those employed in George Kennan's famous "Long Telegram" (**Document 1.6**).*

The foreign policy of the United States, which reflects the imperialist tendencies of American monopolistic capital, is characterized in the postwar period by a striving for world supremacy. This is the real meaning of the many statements by President Truman and other representatives of American ruling circles; that the United States has the right to lead the world. All the forces of American diplomacy—the army, the air force, the navy, industry, and science—are enlisted in the service of this foreign policy. For this purpose broad plans for expansion have been developed and are being implemented through diplomacy and the establishment of a system of naval and air bases stretching far beyond the boundaries of the United States, through the arms race, and through the creation of ever newer types of weapons. . . .

[1b] Europe has come out of the war with a completely dislocated economy, and the economic devastation that occurred in the course of the war cannot be overcome in a short time. All of the countries of Europe and Asia are experiencing a colossal need for consumer goods, industrial and transportation equipment, etc. Such a situation provides American monopolistic capital with prospects for enormous shipments of goods and the importation of capital into these countries—a circumstance that would permit it to infiltrate their national economies.

Such a development would mean a serious strengthening of the economic position of the United States in the whole world and would be a stage on the road to world domination by the United States.

c) On the other hand, we have seen a failure of calculations on the part of U.S. circles which assumed that the Soviet Union would be destroyed in the war or would come out of it so weakened that it would be forced to go begging to the United States for economic assistance. Had that happened, they would have been able to dictate conditions permitting the United States to carry out its expansion in Europe and Asia without hindrance from the USSR. . . .

. . . Thanks to the historical victories of Soviet weapons, the Soviet armed forces are located on the territory of Germany and other formerly hostile countries, thus guaranteeing that these countries will not be used again for an attack on the USSR. In formerly hostile countries, such as Bulgaria, Finland, Hungary, and Romania, democratic reconstruction has established regimes that have undertaken to strengthen and maintain friendly relations with the Soviet Union. In the Slavic countries that were liberated by the Red Army or with its assistance—Poland, Czechoslovakia, and Yugoslavia—democratic regimes have also been established that maintain relations with the Soviet Union on the basis of agreements on friendship and mutual assistance.

The enormous relative weight of the USSR in international affairs in general and in the European countries in particular, the independence of its foreign policy, and the economic and political assistance that it provides to neighboring countries, both allies and former enemies, has led to the growth of the political influence of the Soviet Union in these countries and to the further strengthening of democratic tendencies in them.

Such a situation in Eastern and Southeastern Europe cannot help but be regarded by the American imperialists as an obstacle in the path of the expansionist policy of the United States.

2a) The foreign policy of the United States is not determined at present by the circles in the Democratic Party that (as was the case during Roosevelt's lifetime) strive to strengthen the cooperation of the three great powers that constituted the basis of the anti-Hitler coalition during the war. The ascendance to power of President Truman, a politically unstable person but with certain conservative tendencies, and the subsequent appointment of (James) Byrnes as Secretary of State meant a strengthening of the influence of U.S. foreign policy of the most reactionary circles of the Democratic party. The constantly increasing reactionary nature of the foreign policy course of the United States, which consequently approached the policy advocated by the Republican Party, laid the groundwork for close cooperation in this field between the far right wing of the Democratic Party and the Republican Party. This cooperation of the two parties, which took shape in both houses of Congress in the form of an unofficial bloc of reactionary Southern Democrats and the old guard of the Republicans headed by (Senator Arthur) Vandenberg and (Senator Robert) Taft, was especially clearly manifested in the essentially identical foreign policy statements issued by figures of both parties. In Congress and at international conferences, where as a rule leading Republicans are represented in the delegations of the United States, the Republicans actively support the foreign policy of the government. This is the source of what is called, even in official statements, "bipartisan" foreign policy.

b) At the same time, there has been a decline in the influence on foreign policy of those who follow Roosevelt's course for cooperation among peace-loving countries. Such persons in the government, in Congress, and in the leadership of the Democratic party are being pushed farther and farther into the background. The contradictions in the field of foreign policy and existing between the followers of (Henry) Wallace and (Claude) Pepper, on the one hand, and the adherents of the reactionary "bipartisan" policy, on the other, were manifested with great clarity recently in the speech by Wallace that led to his resignation from the post as Secretary of Commerce. Wallace's resignation means the victory of the reactionary course that Byrnes is conducting in cooperation with Vandenberg and Taft. . . .

3. . . . The establishment of American bases on islands that are often 10,000 to 12,000 kilometers from the territory of the United States and are on the other side of the Atlantic and Pacific oceans clearly indicates the offensive nature of the strategic concepts of the commands of the U.S. army and navy. . . .

4a) One of the stages in the achievement of dominance over the world by the United States is its understanding with England concerning the partial division of the world on the basis of mutual concessions. . . .

b) . . . In Japan, despite the presence there of only a small contingent of American troops, control is in the hands of the Americans. . . .

6a) Relations between the United States and England are determined by two basic circumstances. On the one hand, the United States regards England as its greatest potential competitor; on the other hand, England constitutes a possible ally for the United States. Division of certain regions of the globe into spheres of influence of the United States and England would create the opportunity, if not for preventing competition between them, which is impossible, then at least of reducing it. At the same time, such a division facilitates the achievement of economic and political cooperation between them. . . .

d) The ruling circles of the United States obviously have a sympathetic attitude toward the idea of a military alliance with England, but at the present time the matter has not yet culminated in an official alliance. Churchill's speech in Fulton calling for the conclusion of an Anglo-American military alliance for the purpose of establishing joint domination over the world was therefore not supported officially by Truman or Byrnes, although Truman by his presence (during the "Iron Curtain" speech) did indirectly sanction Churchill's appeal. . . .

[7]b) The present policy of the American government with regard to the USSR is also directed at limiting or dislodging the influence of the Soviet Union from neighboring countries. In implementing this policy in former enemy or Allied countries adjacent to the USSR, the United States attempts, at various international conferences or directly in these countries themselves, to support reactionary forces with the purpose of creating obstacles to the process of democratization of these countries. In so doing, it also attempts to secure positions for the penetration of American capital into their economies. . . .

Source: "Nikolai Novikov, Soviet Ambassador in Washington, Telegram," September 27, 1946, from Documents Relating to American Foreign Policy: The Cold War, Mount Holyoke College, www .mtholyoke.edu/acad/intrel/novikov.htm.

Document 1.10
United States Strategic Bombing Survey on the Effects of the Atomic Bombs on Hiroshima and Nagasaki, Japan, July 1, 1946

After World War II, President Truman tasked the United States Strategic Bombing Survey, a group of civilian consultants to the secretary of war, with assessing the effectiveness of the atomic bombs used against Japan. The summary report, excerpted here, demonstrates with scientific detachment the ferocity of the new means of destruction that would provide a focus to presidential politics during the Cold War. The president would forever more be "the man with his finger on the button" that could launch a nuclear holocaust.

. . . On 6 August and 9 August 1945, the first two atomic bombs to be used for military purposes were dropped on Hiroshima and Nagasaki respectively. One hundred thousand people were killed, 6 square miles or over 50 percent of the built-up areas of the two cities were destroyed. The first and crucial question about the atomic bomb thus was answered practically and conclusively; atomic energy had been mastered for military purposes and the overwhelming scale of its possibilities had been demonstrated. A detailed examination of the physical, economic, and morale effects of the atomic bombs occupied the attention of a major portion of the Survey's staff in Japan in order to arrive at a more precise definition of the present capabilities and limitations of this radically new weapon of destruction.

Eyewitness accounts of the explosion all describe similar pictures. The bombs exploded with a tremendous flash of blue-white light, like a giant magnesium flare. The flash was of short duration and accompanied by intense glare and heat. It was followed by a tremendous pressure wave and the rumbling sound of the explosion. This sound is not clearly recollected by those who survived near the center of the explosion, although it was clearly heard by others as much as fifteen miles sway. A huge snow-white cloud shot rapidly into the sky and the scene on the ground was obscured first by a bluish haze and then by a purple-brown cloud of dust and smoke.

Such eyewitness accounts reveal the sequence of events. At the time of the explosion, energy was given off in the forms of light, heat, radiation, and pressure. The complete band of radiations, from X- and gamma-rays, through ultraviolet and light rays to the radiant heat of infra-red rays, traveled with the speed of light. The shock wave created by the enormous pressures built up almost instantaneously at the point of explosion but moved out more slowly, that is at about the speed of sound. The superheated gases constituting the original fire ball expanded outward and upward at a slower rate.

The light and radiant heat rays accompanying the flash traveled in a straight line and any opaque object, even a single leaf of a vine, shielded objects lying behind it. The duration of the flash was only a fraction of a second, but it was sufficiently intense to cause third degree burns to exposed human skin up to a distance of a mile. Clothing ignited, though it could be quickly beaten out, telephone poles charred, thatch-roofed houses caught fire. Black or other dark-colored surfaces of combustible material absorbed the heat and immediately charred or burst into flames; white or light-colored surfaces reflected a substantial portion of the rays and were not consumed. Heavy black clay tiles which are an almost universal feature of the roofs of Japanese houses bubbled at distances up to a mile. Test of samples of this tile by the National Bureau of Standards in Washington indicates that temperatures in excess of 1,800° C. must have been generated in the surface of the tile to produce such an effect. . . .

Penetrating rays such as gamma-rays exposed X-ray films stored in the basement of a concrete hospital almost a mile from ground zero. Symptoms of their effect on human beings close to the center of the explosion, who survived other effects thereof, were generally delayed for two or three days. The bone marrow and as a result the process of blood formation were affected. The white corpuscle count went down and the human processes of resisting infection were destroyed. Death generally followed shortly thereafter.

The majority of radiation cases who were at greater distances did not show severe symptoms until 1 to 4 weeks after the explosion. The first symptoms were loss of appetite, lassitude and general discomfort. Within 12 to 48 hours, fever became evident in many cases, going as high as 104° to 105° F., which in fatal cases continued until death. If the fever subsided, the patient usually showed a rapid disappearance of other symptoms and soon regained his feeling of good health. Other symptoms were loss of white blood corpuscles, loss of hair, and decrease in sperm count.

Even though rays of this nature have great powers of penetration, intervening substances filter out portions of them. As the weight of the intervening material increases the percentage of the rays penetrating goes down. It appears that a few feet of concrete, or a somewhat greater thickness of earth, furnished sufficient protection to humans, even those close to ground zero, to prevent serious after effects from radiation.

. . . The blast wave . . . was of far greater extent and duration than that of a high-explosive bomb and most reinforced-concrete structures suffered structural damage or collapse up to 700 feet at Hiroshima and 2,000 feet at Nagasaki. Brick buildings were flattened up to 7,300 feet at Hiroshima and 8,500 feet at Nagasaki. Typical Japanese houses of wood construction suffered total collapse up to approximately 7,300 feet at Hiroshima and 8,200 feet at Nagasaki. Beyond these distances structures received less serious damage to roofs, wall partitions, and the like. Glass windows were blown out at distances up to 5 miles. The blast wave, being of longer duration than that caused by high-explosive detonations, was accompanied by more flying debris. Window frames, doors, and partitions which would have been shaken down by a near-miss of a high-explosive bomb were hurled at high velocity through those buildings which did not collapse. . . .

The above description mentions all the categories of the destructive action by the atomic-bomb explosions at Hiroshima and Nagasaki. There were no other types of action. Nothing was vaporized or disintegrated; vegetation is growing again immediately under the center of the explosions; there are no indications that radio-activity continued after the explosion to a sufficient degree to harm human beings.

Let us consider, however, the effect of these various types of destructive action on the cities of Hiroshima, and Nagasaki and their inhabitants.

Hiroshima is built on a broad river delta; it is flat and little above sea level. The total city area is 26 square miles but only 7 square miles at the center were densely built up. The principal industries, which had been greatly expanded during the war, were located on the periphery of the city. The population of the city had been reduced from approximately 340,000 to 245,000 as a result of a civilian defense evacuation program. The explosion caught the city by surprise. An alert had been sounded but in view of the small number of planes the all-clear had been given. Consequently, the population had not taken shelter. The bomb exploded a little northwest of the center of the built-up area. Everyone who was out in the open and was exposed to the initial flash suffered serious burns where not protected by clothing. Over 4 square miles in the center of the city were flattened to the ground with the exception of some 50 reinforced concrete buildings, most of which were internally gutted and many of which suffered structural damage. Most of the people in the flattened area were crushed or pinned down by the collapsing buildings or flying debris. Shortly thereafter, numerous fires started, a few from the direct heat of the dash, but most from overturned charcoal cooking stoves or other secondary causes. These fires grew in size, merging into a general conflagration fanned by a wind sucked into the center of the city by the rising heat. The civilian-defense organization was overwhelmed by the completeness of the destruction, and the spread of fire was halted more by the air rushing toward the center of the conflagration than by efforts of the fire-fighting organization.

Approximately 60,000 to 70,000 people were killed, and 50,000 were injured. Of approximately 90,000 buildings in the city, 65,000 were rendered unusable and almost all the remainder received at least light superficial damage. The underground utilities of the city were undamaged except where they crossed bridges over the rivers cutting through the city. All of the small factories in the center of the city were destroyed. However, the big plants on the periphery of the city were almost completely undamaged and 94 percent of their workers unhurt. These factories accounted for 74 percent of the industrial production of the city. It is estimated that they could have resumed substantially normal production within 30 days of the bombing, had the war continued. The railroads running through the city were repaired for the resumption of through traffic on 8 August, 2 days after the attack.

Nagasaki was a highly congested city built around the harbor and up into the ravines and river valleys of the surrounding hills. . . . The peak wartime population of 285,000 had been reduced to around 230,00 by August 1945, largely by pre-raid evacuations. . . .

The alarm was improperly given and therefore few persons were in shelters. The bomb exploded over the northwest portion of the city; the intervening hills protected a major portion of the city lying in the adjoining valley. The heat radiation and blast actions of the Nagasaki bomb were more intense than those of the bomb dropped over Hiroshima. Reinforced-concrete structures were structurally damaged at greater distances; the heavy steel-frame industrial buildings of the Mitsubishi steel works and the arms plant were pushed at crazy angles away from the center of the explosion. Contrary to the situation at Hiroshima, the majority of the fires that started immediately after the explosion resulted from direct ignition by the flash.

Approximately 40,000 persons were killed or missing and a like number injured. Of the 52,000 residential buildings in Nagasaki 14,000 were totally destroyed and a further 5,400 badly damaged. Ninety-six percent of the industrial output of Nagasaki was concentrated in the large plants of the Mitsubishi Co. which completely dominated the town. The arms plant and the steel works were located within the area of primary damage. It is estimated that 58 percent of the yen value of the arms plant and 78 percent of the value of the steel works were destroyed. . . .

The Survey has estimated that the damage and casualties caused at Hiroshima by the one atomic bomb dropped from a single plane would have required 220 B-29s carrying 1,200 tons of incendiary bombs, 400 tons of high-explosive bombs, and 500 tons of anti-personnel fragmentation bombs, if conventional weapons, rather than an atomic bomb, had been used. One hundred and twenty-five B-29s carrying 1,200 tons of bombs would have been required to approximate the damage and casualties at Nagasaki. . . .

As might be expected, the primary reaction of the populace to the bomb was fear, uncontrolled terror, strengthened by the sheer horror of the destruction and suffering witnessed and experienced by the survivors. Prior to the dropping of the atomic bombs, the people of the two cities had fewer misgivings about the war than people in other cities and their morale held up after it better than might have been expected. Twenty-nine percent of the survivors interrogated indicated that after the atomic bomb was dropped they were convinced that victory for Japan was impossible. Twenty-four percent stated that because of the bomb they felt personally unable to carry on with the war. Some 40 percent testified to various degrees of defeatism. A greater number (24 percent) expressed themselves as being impressed with the power and scientific skill which underlay the discovery and production of the atomic bomb than expressed anger at its use (20 percent). In many instances, the reaction was one of resignation. . . .

Source: United States Strategic Bombing Survey, *United States Strategic Bombing Survey: Summary Report (Pacific War) 1 July 1946* (Washington, D.C.: U.S. Government Printing Office, 1946), from Digital Micronesia—An Electronic Library and Archive, Charles Sturt University, http://marshall .csu.edu.au/Marshalls/html/WWII/USSBS_Summary.html#teotab.

CHAPTER TWO

Harry Truman

The President Decides on War

Harry Truman was overwhelmed by the magnitude of difficulties that became his responsibility upon the death of Franklin Roosevelt on April 12, 1945. When he learned of the late president's—and his—misfortune on that day, he said he "felt like the moon, the stars, and all the planets had fallen on [him]." [1] As difficult as were the decisions he had to make in the next few months, by the end of the summer he had put the transition behind him, and Allied victory in World War II was complete. In the euphoria of victory, hundreds of thousands of American communities eagerly made plans to celebrate the return of peace, while an even greater number of American

President Harry Truman exits a plane at Gatow Airport in Berlin, Germany, on his way to the Potsdam Conference on July 15, 1945. Like Franklin Roosevelt before him at Yalta, Truman met with his counterparts from the Soviet Union and the United Kingdom, this time to hammer out postwar issues, including the division of Germany. Source: U.S. Army, courtesy of the Harry S. Truman Presidential Museum and Library.

families demanded the immediate return of "the boys" from overseas. As the previous chapter revealed, however, the postwar holiday from war would be short-lived. By late 1946, the reality of the new Cold War with the Soviet Union had become clear to the Truman White House. President Truman's speech to Congress articulating the "Truman Doctrine" brought the new conflict to the public's attention for the first time.

On February 21, 1947, the British ambassador to the United States, Lord Inverchapel, delivered an urgent message to the Department of State: in six weeks' time, Britain would cease to provide aid to Greece and Turkey. The economic wreckage and social dislocations of the war had left a number of European democracies in precarious positions. In the Soviet state of Georgia, troops of the Red Army had massed, prompting military preparations in neighboring Turkey. In nearby Greece, guerilla forces aided by the Communist nations of Yugoslavia, Albania, and Bulgaria were fighting against the restoration of the British-supported monarchy. Within a week of receiving Inverchapel's message, Truman, Secretary of State George Marshall, and Undersecretary of State Dean Acheson met in the White House with legislative leaders to discuss the American response. At this meeting, Acheson spoke passionately about the global implications of what once might have been considered merely local events, and Sen. Arthur Vandenberg, chairman of the Senate Foreign Relations Committee, promised his support to Truman. Vandenberg cautioned the president, however, that if he expected broad bipartisan support, he was going to have to "scare hell out of the country."[2]

THE TRUMAN DOCTRINE

On March 12, 1947, President Truman proceeded to follow Senator Vandenberg's advice in an address before a joint session of Congress. "The peoples of a number of countries of the world have recently had totalitarian regimes forced upon them against their will," the president reminded his audience. "[I]f Greece is to survive as a free nation," it must have assistance, and the United States "must supply this assistance." Inaction would lead to the collapse of democracy in Greece and Turkey, and Communist victory in those countries would lead to "discouragement and possibly failure" throughout Europe. Congress and the president together could prevent such a catastrophe by appropriating roughly $250 million for Greece and $150 million for Turkey—a modest sum, the president stated, when one considered that the United States "contributed $341,000,000,000 toward winning World War II" (**Document 2.1**).

The debate over aid to Greece and Turkey became a debate over the United States' relationship with the Soviet Union and the United States' responsibility for leadership in the postwar world. The influential columnist Walter Lippmann warned that the president's justification for the bill "sounds like the tocsin of an ideological crusade. . . . It cannot be controlled. Its effects cannot be predicted."[3] Conservative Democrats objected to the cost, while liberal Democrats, such as Florida senator Claude Pepper, worried that the legislation would antagonize the Soviets, with whom they still dreamed of reconciliation. In senate hearings, the president's supporters downplayed the precedent being set. Aid to Greece and Turkey, declared Dean Acheson, was not intended to establish a pattern for the future; the United States would respond to requests from other countries "according to the circumstances of each specific case."[4]

In truth, Acheson knew better, as he recalled years later in his memoirs. "The spirit which inspired us all at the time," he wrote, was captured by Joseph M. Jones, an officer in the State Department's public affairs bureau. " 'All . . . were aware,' " Acheson quoted Jones, " 'that a major turning point in American history was taking place. The convergence of massive historical trends upon that moment was so real as to be almost tangible.' "[5] On April 22, the Senate approved the request for funds by a 67-23 vote; two weeks later, the House approved the measure by a similar margin, 287-107. The money plus several hundred U.S. civilian and military trainers and advisers were soon on their way to the Aegean Sea. In the bipartisan implementation of aid to Greece and Turkey, the battle was joined; the Cold War was on.

In the same month as he rallied Congress and the public to fight Communism abroad, President Truman joined the crusade against "Reds" at home. Executive Order 9835 was announced on March 21, 1947 (**Document 2.2**). By this order, the president commanded that loyalty investigations be conducted on all persons applying for positions in the federal government, and that the heads of all government agencies and departments establish procedures to ensure that disloyal persons not be retained in government service. The standard of proof was low. To bar someone from employment, or justify his or her dismissal, it was only necessary to demonstrate that "on all the evidence, reasonable grounds exist for belief that the person involved is disloyal to the Government of the United States." According to the order, "[m]embership in, affiliation with or sympathetic association with" a Communist organization, as identified by the attorney general, was sufficient evidence of disloyalty. Throughout the Cold War, the quest for security from enemies abroad would coincide with an attempt to secure the homeland from subversion. Executive Order 9835, like the Truman Doctrine speech, was only the beginning.

THE MARSHALL PLAN

Greece and Turkey were particularly vulnerable to Communist pressure because they shared borders with Communist states—in the case of Turkey, with the Soviet Union itself. Elsewhere in Europe, the danger was thought to be less urgent but just as deadly. Communists had battled Nazi invaders in France and elsewhere, and many Europeans were loath to consider these resistance fighters, or the Communist superpower that had helped free them from Hitler, in a negative light. Center-left coalitions, which included Communists, governed France, Italy, and Belgium. At the same time, millions of European workers were without jobs, and their would-be employers lacked the capital to put them to work. Europeans on the left thought that, just as the war had discredited fascism and Nazism, the Great Depression of the prewar decade had discredited capitalism, especially the "red tooth and claw" style of unfettered individual competition that had long been celebrated in the United States.[6] Even a skeptical, left-leaning Europe could be expected to accept U.S. aid, but could Europe be persuaded to accept that aid if offered on terms that would promote American interests in forging a united, and non-Communist, Europe?

For that matter, could the U.S. president persuade the American people that it was worthwhile to extend such an offer in the first place? After World War I, isolationist sentiment had forced a hasty American retreat from Europe. With bipartisan passage of the bill to aid Greece and Turkey, it seemed that perhaps this postwar episode would be different, but who could be sure? After all, helping Greece and Turkey required "only" hundreds of millions of dollars. Such an investment did not definitively lock the United States into the troubles of Europe. The European Recovery Program, which came to be known as the "Marshall Plan," by contrast, would cost billions. And with the Marshall Plan, there would be no turning back for the United States.

On June 5, 1947, Secretary of State George Marshall gave a commencement address at Harvard University, in which he called for the United States to provide temporary but massive economic aid to Europe (**Document 2.3**). In the brief address, Marshall spoke bluntly of the "dislocation of the entire fabric of [the] European economy." Europe's requirements, Marshall stated, were simply greater than its resources, and would be for the next three or four years. Either Europe must receive "substantial additional help or face economic, social, and political deterioration of a very grave character." In closing, Marshall encouraged all the nations of Europe, including the Soviet Union, to cooperate on a formal request for the aid that the United States was announcing its willingness to provide.

Within weeks, the Soviets had rejected the Marshall Plan as an attempt to manipulate European political affairs by using food and dollars as tools of politics (**Document 2.4**). Under pressure from the Soviet Union, the Eastern bloc countries likewise renounced their interest in U.S. aid. Communist-state delegates met in Poland in late September to establish Cominform, by which the Soviet Union accelerated its domination of Eastern Europe, isolating the East European economies from the West (**Document 2.5**). The rest of Europe responded to the Marshall Plan more enthusiastically and worked with planners at the State Department, as well as congressional leaders, to draft a request that focused on the provision of grants and credits to rebuild Europe's industrial infrastructure. Some leaders in the West, including British foreign secretary Ernest Bevin, had hoped that the Marshall Plan would break free the nations behind the "iron curtain." Instead, Soviet reaction to the plan solidified Europe's division.

The polarization of East and West Europe into Soviet and Western blocs raised the stakes for the Marshall Plan on Capitol Hill. At hearings on the plan, opposition was minimal. The president demonstrated a deft touch during congressional debate by encouraging the popular association of the plan not with himself but with his enormously popular secretary of state. Former under secretary of state Dean Acheson, who had recently returned to his law practice, embarked on a nationwide speaking tour to promote the plan, while the administration secured endorsements from such disparate groups as the American Bar Association and the United Auto Workers. After a Soviet-backed Communist coup in Czechoslovakia in February 1948, influential senator Robert Taft, R-Ohio, dropped his opposition. Taft, the chairman of the Senate Republican Conference, was nicknamed "Mr. Conservative" for his opposition to what many members of his party saw as the runaway growth of government power under Democratic presidents. Taft's support of the Marshall Plan was a milestone in the development of a bipartisan foreign policy to prosecute the Cold War. On March 31, 1948, the Marshall Plan was adopted by votes even more lopsided than those for aid to Greece and Turkey (67-17 in the Senate, 329-74 in the House).

Over the next four years, the duration of the Marshall Plan, the U.S. government would provide grants to Europe in excess of $11.8 billion and loans totaling $1.5 billion.[7] In retrospect, Truman asserted in his *Memoirs,* the Marshall Plan would surely "go down in history as one of America's greatest contributions to the peace of the world." Without the aid provided by the plan, "it would have been difficult for western Europe to remain free from the tyranny of Communism." [8] Further, by financing recovery using U.S. tax dollars, the United States generated demand for its own manufacturers while aiding Europe. The United States was the world's number one producer and exporter after the war; as other nations began to grow and prosper, they turned naturally to the United States for goods and services. Perhaps most important of all, the plan raised the incomes of European voters. Buttressed by hope for their individual futures, the citizens of Europe proved willing to grant centrist, capitalist governments their support. According to *The Econo-*

mist, the Marshall Plan was "probably the most successful programme of international aid and nation building in history." [9]

ELECTION YEAR CRISES

Before the election year of 1948 was over, the Truman administration would be forced to respond to two additional crises, one foreign, the other domestic. After World War II, the Allies had agreed to a partition of Berlin, giving the United States an outpost in the midst of the Soviet-occupation zone of what would become the nation of East Germany. Tensions within Berlin grew along with the Cold War, and on June 24, 1948, the Soviets imposed a complete land and water blockade of West Berlin. Initially, the Soviets described the blockade as a matter of "technical difficulties," but they soon dropped all pretense. They resented a Western presence so deep into Soviet-occupied territory and did not believe the United States would risk war to preserve it. The American military commander in Germany, Gen. Lucius Clay, immediately began airlifting supplies into Berlin as a temporary expedient while awaiting a decision from the president on the official U.S. response.

General Clay urged the president to send an armed convoy into Berlin. Instead, President Truman ordered that the temporary airlift be expanded and kept in place as long as necessary to secure a peaceful settlement in Berlin. The United States, with assistance from the United Kingdom and France, would supply all the external needs of Berlin by air (**Document 2.6**). The airlift was an organizational and military marvel, but it was also a politically risky move. Ambassador Robert Murphy, the political adviser to Clay, spoke for many hawkish critics of the president when he called Truman's decision "a surrender of our hard-won rights in Berlin." [10] But Truman was determined to stay in Berlin without provoking a shooting war, a prospect which he considered entirely possible.[11] Although every "authority" quoted in the press seemed to "know" that aircraft could not possibly provision Berlin through the winter, they did, and on May 9, 1949, almost a year after the imposition of the blockade, the Soviet commander in Berlin quietly announced its end.

With the hindsight of decades, it is tempting to see the events of the Cold War, and the decisions of the Truman administration about how to fight it, entirely through the prism of *statesmanship*. Harry Truman, like the seasoned veterans of the Foreign Service and the luminaries of the cabinet who guided him, *was* a statesman. But he was also a politician, and 1948 was an election year. The Berlin Crisis was a matter strictly of diplomacy, strategy, logistics, and the avoidance of war. The other crisis that the president had to address in this election year, by contrast, was a matter requiring both a military *and* a political response.

Truman's other crisis was the abysmal showing of Democrats in the midterm elections of 1946, and what that presaged for his upcoming campaign for election to the presidency in his own right. To win in November, Truman would have to do more than rally the nation behind the Cold War; the war was too new and its ultimate costs and benefits too uncertain at the time to provide a sure platform for election. Besides, the president had won his biggest Cold War victories by rising *above* party politics, so he could not now use those bipartisan policies to distinguish himself from the opposition. Nor could Truman count on achieving victory merely by rallying the New Deal faithful. It had been

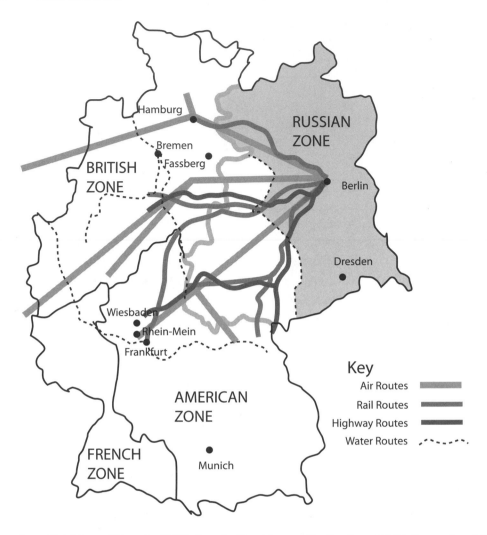

American, British, and French Airlift Supply Corridors to Berlin, June 1948–September 1949.
Source: Courtesy of the Department of History, United States Military Academy, West Point, New York.

almost two decades since Franklin Roosevelt's first presidential election; in that time, the Democratic coalition had enjoyed numerous victories, but factions had emerged that weakened the party. The midterm elections of 1946 had actually brought the Republicans to majority status in the House and Senate for the first time since Herbert Hoover was president. The same Republican-controlled Eightieth Congress that supported the Truman Doctrine and the Marshall Plan rejected so many Truman administration domestic initiatives that the president began to rail against the "Do Nothing Eightieth Congress." Preparing for the 1948 election, Truman decided to sacrifice a portion of his probable support among Southern whites in favor of greater support from urban blacks. He would reach out to black voters by breaking down barriers to their service in the armed forces. In the process, he would aid himself to victory in November and aid the United States in its conduct of the Cold War.

Truman's trusted political confidante, Clark Clifford, analyzed the significance of the black vote in the upcoming election. Black voters, Clifford noted, happened to be concentrated in some key battleground states. Their votes could not be taken for granted. The 1946 results, according to Clifford, had provided disturbing indications that "black voters, having switched to the Democratic party under the New Deal, were starting to drift back to their historic Republican moorings."[12] Truman did not need Clifford to tell him, moreover, that there had been several widely publicized incidents of racial violence against blacks in uniform since the close of the war. Truman had noted these assaults and was deeply angered by them. Finally, civil rights leaders, in particular A. Philip Randolph, head of the Committee against Jim Crow in Military Service and Training, helped the president to see the connection between American civil rights and the Cold War. Given the sacrifices in the late war made by soldiers of all races, blacks were becoming ever more insistent on equality of treatment in the armed forces. If the armed forces were not desegregated soon, warned Randolph early in 1948, while Congress debated a return to the draft, blacks would resist the call to enlist. The president got the message, and made it his own. "Democracy's answer to the challenge of totalitarianism," Truman stated at a campaign appearance in Harlem, "is its promise of equal rights and equal opportunity for all mankind."[13] On July 26, 1948, President Truman issued Executive Order 9981, commanding the desegregation of military service (**Document 2.7**).

Executive orders carry the force of law. That does not, however, make them self-enforcing. The branches of the U.S. armed forces were not of one mind on the president's order, and the army, which had the greatest number of troops, both black and not, was reluctant to change. "The army is not an instrument for social evolution," commented Army Chief of Staff Omar Bradley in a statement following Truman's pronouncement.[14] Secretary of the Army Kenneth Royall, more in sympathy with General Bradley than President Truman, suggested that the army implement the desegregation order by establishing an experimental integrated unit to test the idea in practice. Only after Secretary of Defense Louis Johnson intervened did the army fall into line with the other service branches and put an immediate, official, end to segregation in military life.

If Truman had been a less capable leader, he might have misjudged the strategic as well as political situation in 1947–1948 and have attempted to forge ahead in the Cold War on his own. But Truman realized the limits to his power. (The Republican-controlled Congress was eager, naturally, to remind him.) Truman's success in the early Cold War may, in fact, have been enhanced by the precariousness of his political situation. If Truman wished to recruit majority support for his ideas, he had to broaden the base of support behind his policies abroad as well as at home. As in the case of desegregating the armed forces, he did so by linking domestic initiatives with foreign policy, a practice that became routine in the Cold War.

COLLECTIVE SECURITY

While President Truman met emergency situations with emergency solutions, his administration promoted *collective security* as a long-term strategy for the Cold War. Collective security was, of course, the objective of the United Nations, and Truman would make effective use of the UN. But the keystone of the UN was its Security Council, and the Security Council, because it gave a veto to each of its permanent members, was not adaptable to the distinct interests of either the United States or the Soviet Union. To contain the Soviet Union, a permanent member of the Security Council, a new institutional mechanism to unite the United States and Western Europe was needed. British foreign secretary Ernest Bevin, who became a leader in the search for such a means, recognized that the American public was likely skeptical about entering into any such new alliance. To overcome American reluctance, Europe would have to take the initiative.

In 1947 Bevin joined with French foreign minister Georges Bidault in signing an Anglo-French Treaty of Alliance and Mutual Assistance. The ostensible military threat against which the two nations pledged to cooperate for the next fifty years was Germany, but this was a polite fiction that was dropped as the Cold War's division of Europe hardened. The Treaty of Brussels in the following year brought Belgium, Luxembourg, and the Netherlands into the alliance and built momentum for further expansion.

In light of the commitment of European governments to their own mutual defense, members of the U.S. Congress authorized the Truman administration to join negotiations for membership in the emerging alliance. The symbolic turning point in Washington, D.C., signifying an emerging consensus behind U.S. support for collective security, was Senate passage of a resolution put forward by Senator Vandenberg, a former isolationist (**Document 2.8**). The Vandenberg Resolution stated that it was the "sense of the Senate" that the United States should do what it could to help the UN achieve its potential. This, however, was diplomatic window-dressing. The point of the resolution was to "reaffirm" U.S. policy "to pursue . . . association with regional and other collective arrangements for individual and collective self-defense." "Any armed attack affecting its national security," the resolution stipulated, was cause enough for the United States "to exercise its right of individual or collective self-defense." The State Department was thereby cleared to link the fate of the United States with that of Western Europe, which it did in the April 4, 1949, treaty by which the North Atlantic Treaty Organization (NATO) was formed (**Document 2.9**). The initial signatories, in addition to the United States, were Belgium, Britain, Denmark, France, Iceland, Italy, Luxembourg, the Netherlands, Norway, and Portugal. Greece and Turkey joined before the end of the Truman administration.

Because of the size of its economy, its territory, and its armed forces, and because of its hard-earned prestige in world affairs, the United States entered NATO as its keystone. The military head of NATO has, from the appointment of the first Supreme Allied Commander, Europe (SACEUR), been a four-star general of the United States armed forces. In the approving words of a report issued by the internationalist-minded International Studies Group of the Brookings Institution, "The United States has now accepted an idea that it had consistently rejected throughout its history—the desirability of peacetime alliances with like-minded nations when faced with danger to its own and world security." The report attributed the "conscious basis of this profound change in attitude" not to U.S. experiences in World War II but to the nation's determination to stop the spread of Communism.[15] Fighting the Cold War required a radical break with the American foreign policy tradition.

When President Truman delivered his inaugural address on January 20, 1949, he put the movement toward collective security in context (**Document 2.10**). In response to Soviet designs, the United States must think and act with new resolve, the president stated. In his remarks, the president outlined "four major courses of action." The first was to continue working through the UN. The second was to continue the work of the Marshall Plan and otherwise promote economic recovery. Pursuing collective security, as embodied most significantly in NATO, was the third. The fourth was to embark on "a bold new program for making the benefits of our scientific advances and industrial progress available for the improvement and growth of underdeveloped areas."

This last program, which became known simply as "Point Four," was described by the *Washington Post* as a "Fair Deal Plan for the World," referring to the president's stalled initiatives for the expansion of the New Deal at home.[16] Point Four's emphasis on technology transfer was criticized by those who thought that poor countries—as much as the recovering industrial nations of Europe—needed capital first, not "know how," and the program lasted only two years as a distinct administrative entity. Nevertheless, it was important as both a precedent for the future and a program with immediate public relations benefit. As Truman recounted in his *Memoirs,* "even in countries which were anti-American the relations between the United States technicians and their local counterparts were excellent. The program had the effect of disarming hostile propagandists."[17]

THE TWO EVILS: MCCARTHYISM AND COMMUNIST SUBVERSION

Truman's pursuit of collective security would have been easier had he needed to worry about "hostile propagandists" in foreign countries only. At home, although he could take comfort in his come-from-behind victory at the polls, his leadership was assailed in sometimes vicious tones. Behind the invective was a common anxiety that the threat of Communist domination was more real, more imminent, and more sinister than the president would admit. Given events around the world, it is not hard to see why some Americans came to have this opinion.

In the first year of Truman's full term, the Soviets detonated an atomic bomb and Mao Zedong's Communist Party declared the formation of the People's Republic of China. Relating to the first setback, Gen. Leslie Groves, who had directed the famed Manhattan Project that had developed the American atomic bomb, had thought the Soviets twenty years from their own success. The president made the government's detection of the Soviet bomb test public in a terse and defensive public statement (**Document 2.11**). Communist victory in China similarly stunned the nation. The United States had supported China in its defense against Japan during World War II and had attempted, through nonmilitary means, to promote stalemate if not victory for the anti-Communists in China after the war. Chairman Mao's announcement to the world that "a basic victory has been won in the people's liberation war, and the majority of the people in the nation have gained liberation" (**Document 2.12**) was followed four months later, on February 14, 1950, by the signing of a Soviet-Chinese Treaty of Friendship, Alliance and Mutual Aid.

How had the Soviets so rapidly begun to catch up with the United States in nuclear weaponry? How had Truman "lost" China to Communism?

Wisconsin senator Joseph McCarthy believed he had the answer to both questions: the Truman administration was riddled with Communists. In a speech to a women's club in West Virginia in February 1950, McCarthy warned that "[t]oday we are engaged in a final, all-out battle between communistic atheism and Christianity." McCarthy cited the numbers of persons living under Communist rule, a recitation intended to show the "swiftness of the tempo of Communist victories and American defeats in the cold war." These defeats were attributed to traitors in the U.S. government, particularly in the State Department, such as Alger Hiss (**Document 2.13**).

On January 25, 1950, Alger Hiss had been sentenced to five years in prison for perjury. Hiss was a former New Dealer and a high-ranking State Department employee under Franklin Roosevelt and Harry Truman. The Federal Bureau of Investigation and the House Un-American Activities Committee had investigated him for Communist sympathies. When he appeared before a grand jury in 1948, Hiss gave testimony about his relationship to a confessed member of the American Communist Party, Whittaker Chambers. Chambers had claimed that he and Hiss had been partners in espionage, but Hiss categorically denied knowing Chambers. Hiss's friends were reluctant to believe that the widely admired public servant, who left government service to assume the presidency of the Carnegie Endowment in 1947, was truly a Communist conspirator. Even decades after his conviction for lying about his relationship to Chambers, the Hiss case polarized liberals and conservatives in American politics.

Documents released in the aftermath of the Cold War have demonstrated to most analysts that Hiss was indeed a Soviet agent, and that he was hardly alone in being so. Scores of men and women in high government positions were in fact members of the American Communist Party, which was "controlled, financed, and run entirely by the leadership of the Communist Party of the Soviet Union."[18] At the time, though, McCarthy's vicious personal attacks on the innocent as well as the guilty made it seem as if the prosecution of Hiss and the wider pattern of "Red baiting" were merely partisan efforts to detract attention from the failures of the Republican Party in Congress, which was precisely what the president alleged.

Referring directly to the Hiss trial and Dean Acheson's appearance as a character witness on Hiss's defense, McCarthy drew the following connection in his speech. "[V]ery recently," he said, "the Secretary of State proclaimed his loyalty to a man guilty of what has always been considered as the most abominable of all crimes—being a traitor to the people who gave him a position of great trust—high treason." Men like Hiss, McCarthy asserted, were still in the State Department. In fact, McCarthy said, he possessed a list of more than 200 persons—the number changed from speech to speech—of questionable integrity who were at that time employed at the State Department. The State Department, he stated, was fully aware of these employees' treasonous associations. Clearly, by McCarthy's reasoning, there was sympathy, if not collusion, with Communists at the highest reaches of government. The senator repeated these charges, and added new ones, in a rambling six-hour speech on the floor of the senate on February 20.

President Truman shot back rhetorically, accusing McCarthy of deceit. At a March 30 news conference at Key West, Florida, the president offered his opinion that the senator's attacks were the result of a desperate effort on the part of the Republicans to find an issue on which they might win back control of Congress. "They tried 'statism.' They tried 'welfare state.' They tried 'socialism.' And," the president went on, "there are a certain number of members of the Republican Party who are trying to dig up that old malodorous dead horse called 'isolationism.' And in order to do that, they are perfectly willing to sabotage the bipartisan foreign policy of the United States." It was, said Truman, just another attempt to make news and win votes with a "false and fatuous" issue.[19]

Although many Republicans were as appalled with the senator's tactics as were most Democrats, the president could not merely wish away McCarthy's attacks, any more than he could ignore the Soviet atomic bomb or the victory of Chairman Mao. But what was the best response to these threats? Truman favored sensible preparation, certainly, and reform in the organization and strategy of the armed forces, but he was absolutely opposed to putting the nation back on a wartime foundation.

COLD WAR STICKER SHOCK

President Truman was deeply committed to the Cold War, but even he was reluctant to embrace what some of his own leading strategists argued were the imperatives of fighting it. The United States needed, most simply, to rearm and repopulate its armed forces. After the end of World War II, Congress had acted in traditional American fashion by slashing defense spending, troop levels, and armaments. In a debate over personnel policy, the administration favored Universal Military Training (UMT), short-term education and indoctrination of young American men along military lines, to provide a large pool of recruits or conscripts in the event of a return to war. In Truman's plan, as the president explained it in a special message delivered to a joint session of Congress in October 1945, upon reaching eighteen years of age or graduating from high school, young men who were not very disabled would undergo one year of basic military training. Afterward, these men would be required to serve in the organized reserves for six years.[20] Truman routinely downplayed the rigors of UMT. Not all men called to service would even have to train for the military, the president insisted on other occasions; some might be trained in other vital fields.[21] Congress, however, balked at UMT; "[i]ts opponents succeeded by emphasizing the philosophical conflict between American values of individualism and liberty on one side and compulsion on the other." [22] To meet the immediate need for troops, Congress approved a "temporary" draft reinstatement in 1948, after a brief hiatus during which no draft law was in effect (March 1947–July 1948).

Draft reinstatement was a success, in that it enabled the services to meet their troop requirements. Still, retrenchment, not expansion, seemed to be the goal of the Truman administration, guided as it was by conventional concerns about excessive government spending in "peacetime." Despite having the means to raise troop levels and the apparent need to do so in the face of Communist gains in China and the Soviet Union, Secretary of Defense Louis Johnson—with Truman's support—cut the organized reserves and worked with like-minded members of Congress to reduce regular army troop levels from 677,000 in 1949 to less than 600,000 the following year.[23] Admirals, generals, soldiers, and sailors grew to hate Secretary Johnson—they "damned him day and night" in the words of one artillery officer aboard a ship headed for Korea in 1950—but he was greatly admired on Capitol Hill.[24] "Enervating overpreparation" was the real enemy, in the words of a Senate Appropriations Committee report of the time, which envisioned the United States pitted against a "cunning and patient enemy who fully realizes the debilitating influences of a war-geared economy over a long period of time."[25] President Truman could not have said it better himself.

In the summer of 1949, the president summoned his top military and economic advisers and read to them from a prepared statement. The budget deficit was unacceptably large, he observed. Congress was unwilling to raise taxes, and a stagnant economy was reducing growth in government revenues. Therefore, said the president, getting to the point, "adjustments downward must be made" in national security.[26] Accordingly, the president set a $13 billion annual ceiling for what he would ask Congress to appropriate for defense spending. Further, he would approve a request of only $4 billion for complementary foreign assistance.

In line with his demand for greater economy in 1949, the president cancelled a proposed supercarrier for the navy. Secretary of the Navy James Forrestal resigned in protest. The navy's top admirals chose not to resign but rather to lobby vigorously against the president's alleged favoritism for the air force. This "Revolt of the Admirals" highlighted the difficulties of forging consensus behind an American response to Communist gains in the early Cold War and the priority the president placed on limiting the costs of the war. Truman favored an air-based strategy of nuclear deterrence as it was less expensive, and less intrusive, than rebuilding American ground and naval forces. Internationalists in 1949 and 1950 came to worry that the United States was undermining its collective security endeavors in Europe, because Truman seemed so reluctant to provide the troops and the nonnuclear armaments necessary to that defense. But the president was deaf to such complaints, even when they originated from within the Executive Office of the President.

On April 7, 1950, the National Security Council (NSC) added its voice to the debate over the apparent gap between American objectives in the Cold War and the government's willingness to ask its citizens to sacrifice in pursuit of those goals. Its report, NSC 68, called for massive and sustained rearmament to fight the Cold War (**Document 2.14**). The need was urgent, as war with the Soviets, in the opinion of the NSC, was possible by 1954, at which time the Soviets would be capable of a nuclear attack on the United States. Recent Communist gains, moreover, raised the specter that "any substantial further extension of the area under the domination of the Kremlin would raise the possibility that no coalition adequate to confront the Kremlin with greater strength could be assembled."

Truman had called for the report himself, but the budget-minded president "would have burned NSC-68 gladly," in the words of a noted military historian.[27] The NSC's recommendations were just too expensive. Although the report spoke eloquently of the necessity to guard against military overspending as well as underspending, the report's authors had a different idea than Truman did about how much was too much. At the same time as the president had mandated a ceiling of $13 billion for defense and $4 billion for foreign aid, the NSC was envisioning annual budgets of $40 billion and $10 billion, respectively. Paul Nitze, the principal author of the report, warned in the document that the "destruction not only of this Republic but of civilization itself" was at stake and "will not await our deliberations." Truman, unmoved, ordered follow-up studies.

THE KOREAN WAR

The events of June 25, 1950, did what the NSC could not—they dramatically shifted the debate over war preparations and military spending. For a time, at least, budgetary stringency would not take primacy over the apparent need for a stronger U.S. military. On that day (which was June 24 in Washington), North Korean troops invaded South Korea. The president learned of the attack in a phone call with Dean Acheson. Acheson proposed that the United States ask for an emergency meeting of the UN Security Council. This was a momentous recommendation; it would be the first time in American history that a U.S. president would respond to an enemy attack against U.S. national interests by securing international approval in New York rather than by rallying congressional support in Washington, D.C. Following Acheson's initiative, the United States proposed, and the Security Council passed, a resolution condemning the invasion (**Document 2.15**). On June 27 President Truman issued a statement to the nation, in which he narrated events (**Document 2.16**): "In Korea," government forces were attacked by invaders from the north. In response, "the Security Council of the United Nations called upon the invading troops to cease hostilities and to withdraw. . . . In these circumstances I have ordered United States air and sea forces" into battle.

Ironically, only the chance absence of the Soviet representative to the Security Council, who was boycotting meetings to protest the UN's refusal to recognize the People's Republic of China, had made it possible for the United States to thus work through the new international organization. But even if the Soviets had been attending Security Council meetings, Truman may have at least taken the issue to the Council before taking action, for he was reluctant to rely on the U.S. Congress for authorization to respond aggressively to the Korean crisis. The legislature, he believed, was poorly suited to handle the sort of decisions that should more properly be left to the commander in chief. After all, as Truman once told his staff, "the president has the power to keep the country from going to hell," and he was determined to use that power to send help to Korea as soon as possible.[28]

Previous presidents who had bypassed Congress in times of crisis, such as Abraham Lincoln, had sought constitutional refuge in after-the-fact congressional resolutions or, like Franklin Roosevelt, had directly challenged Congress to lead, follow, or get out of the way. Simply to ignore Congress, as if it had no constitutional responsibility in such a situation, was something new and one of the most important and controversial Cold War precedents set by Harry Truman.

At the time, however, congressional representatives from both parties joined in rancorous applause when Truman's statement of June 27 was read before the House and

Senate, informing them that the president had ordered air and naval forces into action. Republican senator William Knowland of California expressed the sentiment of virtually all representatives who cared to speak for the record when he called for "overwhelming support" for the president from all Americans, regardless of party.[29] The *Washington Post* expressed similar opinions in an editorial of June 28, 1950. In a cascade of clichés, the editors lionized Truman: "These are days calling for steady nerves, for a strict eye on the ball, and for a renewed resolve to keep our purposes pure in the grapple we have undertaken with men who would plunge the world into darkness. The occasion has found the man in Harry Truman."

A month into the war, on July 19, the president addressed the nation and explained in stark terms the consequences should the United States lose the war (**Document 2.17**). "What is at stake here," Truman stated, "is nothing less than our own national security and the peace of the world." Although his talk focused on events in Asia, the president drew the public's attention to the wider implications of the fighting there. The assault in Korea demonstrated, he said, that the "international Communist movement is willing to use armed invasion to conquer independent nations." The attack, the president explained, had originated from the northern part of the nation, to which the Soviet Union had withdrawn its forces to after the end of World War II. The implication was clear: Stalin had something to do with this conflict, which was in reality a proxy war in the wider Cold War. Many years later, after files from the former Soviet archives were opened to scholars for the first time, Truman's claim would be subjected to rigorous analysis and found to have been correct (**Document 2.18**).

Because the invasion of Korea put into a new perspective the urgency of events in Europe and throughout the world, Truman told the nation in that July address that he would call upon Congress to approve a supplemental emergency appropriation of $10 billion for national defense. "It will be necessary," said the president, in the spirit of sacrifice familiar to a generation that had overcome both depression and world war, "to make substantial increases in taxes." At least some of NSC 68's recommendations would be acted upon, after all.

TRUMAN FIRES MACARTHUR

Unfortunately for the president, the commitment to common sacrifice for a common cause did not last. After a daring amphibious landing at Inchon that marked the beginning of a successful U.S.-led counteroffensive, Chinese "volunteers" donned North Korean uniforms and entered the war. Gen. Douglas MacArthur, the U.S. commander of the allied forces, urged President Truman to respond with an all-out attack on Communist China. Reasoning that the United States would have to confront China militarily at one time or another, MacArthur argued that 1950 was the time. The president, backed by the Joint Chiefs of Staff (JCS), demurred. They wanted no wider war, not with the Chinese and most definitely not with the Soviets, who might attack in Asia or Europe, or both. The president and his military advisers, in fact, came soon to accept a return to the status quo on the Korean peninsula as a satisfactory conclusion to the war.

MacArthur, though concerned at first that he would not be able to achieve the return to a divided Korea, fought hard to broaden the administration's goal in the war. Unable to persuade the president to give him control of either the means to be employed or the ends to be sought in the war, MacArthur turned to the press to broadcast his views. On August 17, he sent a message to the Veterans of Foreign Wars declaring that if only the president would permit him to accept military assistance from the Nationalist Chinese on Formosa (Taiwan), the United States could dominate "every Asiatic port from Vladivostok [in the Soviet Union] to Singapore."[30] More was to come. On December 1, in an interview with *U.S. News and World Report,* MacArthur accused the administration of imposing upon him "an enormous handicap, without precedent in military history" by denying him the authority to attack China. The president and the Joint Chiefs of Staff both issued directives, clearly intended for MacArthur, that henceforth no military commander would speak publicly on military or foreign policy. MacArthur stubbornly continued to defy orders and to speak out against the pursuit of limited objectives through limited means in a limited war.

In his *Memoirs,* Truman remarked that he should have fired MacArthur after his December 1 outburst but did not out of his high regard for the general. Of course Truman was also no fool, and he well understood MacArthur's immense popularity at home. MacArthur had been the hero of the Pacific in World War II, and the risky landing at Inchon, which he had designed and led, had eclipsed even his victories in the prior war. But MacArthur was attempting to dictate military strategy to the commander in chief, something that no self-respecting chief executive could let go unchallenged.

On April 5, 1951, MacArthur at last went too far. On that day, with the general's permission, House minority leader Joseph W. Martin Jr., R-Mass., entered into the *Congressional Record* a recent letter from MacArthur (**Document 2.19**). "It seems strangely difficult for some to realize," MacArthur wrote, "that here in Asia is where the Communist conspirators have elected to make their play of global conquest." If America were to lose "the war to Communism in Asia the fall of Europe is inevitable." In a famous closing statement, the general intoned that "there is no substitute for victory."

The next day, Dean Acheson and George Marshall both urged the president to be cautious in his response. "If you relieve MacArthur," said Acheson, "you will have the biggest fight of your administration."[31] The president, however, was determined. By issuing statements at variance with administration policy, MacArthur had confused world perception of U.S. policy, defied his commander in chief, and undermined the doctrine of civilian command of the military.

Truman was sensibly reluctant to ask the Joint Chiefs personally whether they would support the removal of MacArthur. If they said no, then he would have only magnified his troubles. Instead, he sent Marshall, the secretary of state and a retired five-star general, to solicit their views. In their session with Marshall, the chiefs looked over the documentary record of the president's orders regarding public statements by officers and the general's repeated defiance of orders. They expressed dismay at MacArthur's challenge to civilian supremacy over the military. They were also disturbed by what they saw as the commander's demoralizing loss of self-confidence, which caused him to doubt whether he could achieve even the limited aims that the administration sought in Korea without broadening the war. They unanimously agreed that MacArthur had to go.

On April 11, the president issued a press release and made a radio address justifying the removal of the general from his command (**Documents 2.20 and 2.21**). He also made public the order in which he relieved the general of command. The president's order had been sent through military channels, but its receipt had not been acknowledged. Afraid that the general would quit before Truman could fire him, the president had decided to use the media to broadcast his assertion of civilian supremacy.

Just eight days later, the enraged commander appeared in Washington, D.C., having been awarded the privilege of addressing a joint session of Congress. "Old soldiers never die," MacArthur said in his one of his finer rhetorical flourishes, "they just fade away."[32] MacArthur's words proved prophetic, but they hardly seemed so at the time.

The public responded by burning the president in effigy on both coasts. The Los Angeles City Council adjourned for a day of "sorrowful contemplation of the political assassination" of the sainted general.[33] Editorial opinion was similarly heated, especially in the newspapers of the Hearst syndicate. Congressional Republicans, eager to embarrass the president and energized by a deepening public frustration with a war in which "victory" was being redefined as not losing, initiated public hearings into the general's dismissal and, by extension, the president's conduct of the war.

These investigatory hearings were actually a compromise measure, because numerous Republicans had expressed a desire to move immediately to impeachment. Representative Martin wanted "impeachments," in the plural, while Sen. William Jenner of Indiana proclaimed that only through impeachment could the nation learn the identity of the *true* decision makers in the White House, for events had made plain to Jenner that the administration was "in the hands of a secret inner coterie which is directed by the agents of the Soviet Union."[34] Within forty-eight hours of the news breaking, congressional Republicans received almost 45,000 telegrams, almost all angrily demanding the removal of the president.

The day after MacArthur's address to Congress, the general was the honored subject of a ticker tape parade in New York City where a reported crowd of 7.5 million greeted the general—more people than had been on hand in 1945 to hail Dwight Eisenhower after victory in the World War II. After the parade, MacArthur returned to Washington to testify for three days before a joint session of the Senate Foreign Relations and Armed Services committees. Truman's policy in Korea, MacArthur stated, had no purpose but "to go on indefinitely . . . indecisively, fighting with no mission."[35]

The testimony of the Joint Chiefs of Staff greatly defused the situation. Gen. Omar Bradley, the chairman of the JCS and an immensely popular man in his own right, criticized MacArthur's testimony in *military* terms. Widening the war by accepting the help of the Nationalist Chinese and attacking Communist China, Bradley stated, would "involve us in a wrong war at the wrong place and against a wrong enemy."[36] The chiefs of staff of the army and air force, and the chief naval officer, all agreed. President Truman, in a June 25 speech at Tullahoma, Tennessee, described MacArthur and his backers as saying "Take a chance"—take a chance that the Soviets won't jump into a fight in Asia if we attack China; take a chance that our allies in Europe won't disown us for committing all our resources to Asia; take a chance that "we won't have a third world war. . . . This is not a policy," proclaimed Harry Truman, it is "Russian roulette." [37]

COMPROMISE IN A WAR OF ABSOLUTES

Truman survived the backlash for firing MacArthur but not the backlash for the war. Truman's handling of the war was widely disparaged, and the president left office with his standing in the polls severely battered. It did not help that in the closing months of his presidency, the Supreme Court agreed to hear a case challenging a presidential assertion of prerogative power and overruled the commander in chief. The nation's steel mill owners were in conflict with the unions representing the majority of their workers. The administration's Wage Stabilization Board, a wartime agency created for the Korean conflict that was based on similar institutions utilized in the world wars, had recommended a wage increase. The owners refused to comply unless they were permitted a significant increase in the price they could charge for their product. (Wartime price controls made the government the arbiter of such decisions.) Rebuffed, the mill owners insisted that wages would not rise; the union replied that it would carry through with its threat to strike. Declaring in a nationwide address that it was his "plain duty" to prevent a stoppage in steel production and blaming the crisis on the reckless actions of the owners, Truman issued an executive order on April 8, 1952, instructing his commerce secretary to seize the mills and operate them with the assistance of the U.S. Army. If the president has the authority to do that, an incredulous journalist asked at a news conference, could he seize the newspapers and broadcast stations too? "Under similar circumstances," Truman replied.[38]

The American people and the Court were not so sure. Victory in Korea, however that was defined, would not be put at risk by a stoppage of steel production. The United States and the other parties to the conflict had entered truce talks shortly after MacArthur's dismissal. Although the president warned that "other 'Koreas' " might result from "evidence of a slowdown in our rearmament," this chain of reasoning led further and further from any immediate threat to the nation or its soldiers.[39] Moreover, the president and Congress were at the time engaged in a dispute over labor law. In 1947, over the president's veto, Congress had passed the Taft-Hartley Law, which contained provisions for a "cooling-off" period to prevent a strike; Truman had simply ignored the law in ordering the immediate turnover of the mills. In addition, when Congress had debated Taft-Hartley, it had expressly rejected an amendment to the law which would have granted the president emergency seizure powers.

In *Youngstown Sheet and Tube Co. v. Sawyer* (1952), the Supreme Court overturned the president's action. Though the Court's verdict was clear, its reasoning was not. All six justices in the majority issued their own opinions seeking to explain the outcome. The president was peeved, but he was powerless to respond except through tight-lipped complaint at a news conference (**Document 2.22**). To Truman's critics, who were many at the time, the showdown seemed merely another illustration of the president's "talent for trouble." [40]

In truth, the episode was more than that. It was a reflection of the paradox for presidential power posed by the Cold War.

There was nothing particularly new in the presidency about suffering a backlash after overreaching.[41] What was new was the way in which the pressures of the Cold War seemed to compel presidents to overreach. Perhaps Truman had not truly had to grasp at the steel mills, but as president in a time of crisis—and after building his entire presidency since 1947 on the foundation of the necessity of strong leadership in the face of Communist aggression—it was only natural for the president to consider such a bold move his "plain duty."

This was the logic of Cold War. Like all wars, the Cold War provided incentives for the centralization of authority within the national government and enhanced the leverage of the presidency within an expanded governmental domain. With the articulation of the Truman Doctrine, the president became the center of "action" in Washington, D.C. It was his policy that members of Congress debated, his decisions that ultimately sent hundreds of thousands American service members to new postings and billions of dollars to new beneficiaries of American aid. And when the conflict turned hot in Korea, it was his staff that prepared and then implemented massive new budgets for defense. Most telling, when Communists invaded South Korea, the president simply took from Congress the power to decide that the nation was going to war. At first, Congress cheered. But when Communist Chinese armies crossed the border with North Korea, the president scaled back U.S. war aims and means. Then Congress, reflecting as always the mood of the nation, expressed frustration.

In the Korean War, the old goal of unconditional surrender was obsolete. The risks of all-out war were simply too great; unconditional "victory" might mean unparalleled devastation to the victor as well as the vanquished. With this thought in mind, Truman accepted a tactical retreat to the 38th parallel in Korea, so as to husband strength for the long term. This was surely prudent, but it was not rousing.

What Truman did not know at the time, and his critics did not seem to realize either, is that all the presidents of the Cold War would find themselves in similar binds. To wage the Cold War required presidents, on occasion, to "scare hell" out of the American people. This was, incidentally, a boon to presidential power. But rallying the public, not to mention the world, is not just exhausting, it is enervating. Expectations, once raised, must be satisfied in politics. If not, there can be hell to pay. Thus Harry Truman became the first in a succession of Cold War presidents to find themselves forced to pursue compromise in a war of absolutes.

NOTES

1. William DeGregorio, *The Complete Book of U.S. Presidents* (New York: Wings Books, 1993), 523.
2. Joseph Marion Jones, *The Fifteen Weeks, February 21–June 5, 1947* (New York: Viking, 1955), 139–145.
3. Ronald Steel, *Walter Lippmann and the American Century* (New York: Vintage, 1981), 438–39.
4. David McCullough, *Truman* (New York: Simon and Schuster, 1992), 549.

5. Dean Acheson, *Present at the Creation: My Years in the State Department* (New York: Norton, 1969), 220.

6. David Reynolds, "Marshall Plan Commemorative Section: The European Response: Primacy of Politics," in *Foreign Affairs* (May/June 1997), www.foreignaffairs.org.

7. The George C. Marshall Foundation, "Marshall Plan Information," www.marshallfoundation .org/marshall_plan_information.html.

8. Harry S. Truman, *Memoirs,* vol. 2, *Years of Trial and Hope* (Garden City, New York: Doubleday, 1956), 119.

9. *The Economist,* "Marshall Plan" entry in "Economics A–Z," www.economist.com/research/ economics.

10. Acheson, *Present at the Creation,* 263.

11. Truman, *Memoirs,* 123.

12. Robert J. Donovan *Conflict and Crisis: The Presidency of Harry S. Truman, 1945–1948.* (New York: Norton, 1997), 245.

13. Thomas S. Langston. *With Reverence and Contempt: How Americans Think about Their President.* Baltimore: Johns Hopkins University Press, 1997), 41.

14. Richard M. Dalfiume, *Desegregation of the U.S. Armed Forces; Fighting on Two Fronts, 1939–1953* (Columbia: University of Missouri Press, 1969), 172.

15. Brookings Institution, *Major Problems of United States Foreign Policy* (Menasha, Wis.: George Banta Publishing Company, 1949), 46.

16. McCullough, *Truman,* 731.

17. Truman, *Memoirs,* 237.

18. Ronald Radosh, "The Two Evils: Communism, McCarthyism, and the Truth," *The New Republic* (May 11, 1998): 38.

19. "The President's News Conference at Key West," March 30, 1950, in *Public Papers of the Presidents of the United States: Harry S Truman, 1945–1953,* from the American Presidency Project, University of California, Santa Barbara, www.presidency.ucsb.edu.

20. Harry S. Truman, "Address before a Joint Session of Congress on Universal Military Training," October 23, 1945, in *Public Papers of the Presidents of the United States: Harry S. Truman, 1945–1953,* from the American Presidency Project, University of California, Santa Barbara, www.presidency.ucsb.edu.

21. Harry S. Truman, "Remarks at the Armed Forces Dinner," May 19, 1950, in *Public Papers of the Presidents of the United States: Harry S. Truman, 1945–1953,* from the American Presidency Project, University of California, Santa Barbara, www.presidency.ucsb.edu.

22. Thomas S. Langston, *Uneasy Balance: Civil-Military Relations in Peacetime America since 1783* (Baltimore: Johns Hopkins University Press, 2003), 64.

23. George Q. Flynn, *The Draft, 1940–1973* (Lawrence: University Press of Kansas, 1993), 109.

24. Dale R. Herspring, *The Pentagon and the Presidency: Civil-Military Relations from FDR to George W. Bush* (Lawrence: University Press of Kansas, 2005), 73.

25. Dennis S. Ippolito, *Uncertain Legacies: Federal Budget Policy from Roosevelt through Reagan* (Charlottesville: University Press of Virginia, 1990), 100.

26. Aaron Friedberg, *In the Shadow of the Garrison State: America's Anti-Statism and Its Cold War Grand Strategy* (Princeton: Princeton University Press, 2000), 105.

27. Geoffrey Perret, *A Country Made by War: From the Revolution to Vietnam—the Story of America's Rise to Power* (New York: Vintage, 1989), 448.

28. McCullough, *Truman,* 897.

29. Ibid., 781.

30. Herspring, *Pentagon and the Presidency,* 79.

31. McCullough, *Truman,* 839.

32. Douglas MacArthur, "Old Soldiers Never Die," typescript speech for General MacArthur's Farewell Address to the United States Congress, April 19, 1951, from American Treasures of the

Library of Congress, Memory Gallery C: The Postwar Era, www.loc.gov/exhibits/treasures/trm048.html, p. 12.

33. McCullough, *Truman*, 845.
34. John W. Spanier, *The Truman-MacArthur Controversy and the Korean War* (New York: Norton, 1965), 212.
35. McCullough, *Truman*, 853.
36. Military Situation in the Far East, *Hearings Before the Committee on Armed Services and the Committee on Foreign Relations, United States Senate, Eighty-Second Congress, First Session, to Conduct an Inquiry into the Military Situation in the Far East and the Facts Surrounding the Relief of General of the Army Douglas MacArthur from His Assignments in that Area,* part 2. (Washington, D.C.: United States Government Printing Office, 1951), 753.
37. McCullough, *Truman*, 856.
38. Langston, *With Reverence and Contempt,* 95.
39. Ibid., 96.
40. McCullough, *Truman*, 899.
41. Richard M. Pious, *The American Presidency* (New York: Basic Books, 1979).

Document 2.1
The Truman Doctrine, President Harry Truman's Speech to Congress, March 12, 1947

At the end of February 1947, the British ambassador to the United States delivered an urgent message to the State Department. The British government had decided that it had no choice but to end its aid to Greece and Turkey. Greece was under assault from Communist insurgents, and Turkey was trying desperately to arm itself against a growing Soviet threat, but the United Kingdom was all but bankrupt following World War II. Would the United States accept the responsibility of protecting these nations from Communist aggression? In Truman's words, "I wanted no hedging in this speech. This was America's answer to the surge of expansion of Communist tyranny. It had to be clear and free of hesitation or double talk" (Harry S. Truman, Memoirs, vol. 2, Years of Trial and Hope [Garden City, N.Y.: Doubleday, 1956], 105). The president spoke before a joint session of Congress.

. . . Greece is today without funds to finance the importation of those goods which are essential to bare subsistence. Under these circumstances the people of Greece cannot make progress in solving their problems of reconstruction. Greece is in desperate need of financial and economic assistance to enable it to resume purchases of food, clothing, fuel and seeds. These are indispensable for the subsistence of its people and are obtainable only from abroad. Greece must have help to import the goods necessary to restore internal order and security so essential for economic and political recovery.

The Greek Government has also asked for the assistance of experienced American administrators, economists and technicians to insure that the financial and other aid given to Greece shall be used effectively in creating a stable and self-sustaining economy and in improving its public administration.

The very existence of the Greek state is today threatened by the terrorist activities of several thousand armed men, led by Communists, who defy the government's authority at a number of points, particularly along the northern boundaries. A Commission appointed by the United Nations Security Council is at present investigating disturbed conditions in northern Greece and alleged border violations along the frontier between Greece on the one hand and Albania, Bulgaria, and Yugoslavia on the other.

Meanwhile, the Greek Government is unable to cope with the situation. The Greek army is small and poorly equipped. It needs supplies and equipment if it is to restore authority to the government throughout Greek territory.

Greece must have assistance if it is to become a self-supporting and self-respecting democracy.

The United States must supply this assistance. We have already extended to Greece certain types of relief and economic aid but these are inadequate.

There is no other country to which democratic Greece can turn.

No other nation is willing and able to provide the necessary support for a democratic Greek government. . . .

As in the case of Greece, if Turkey is to have the assistance it needs, the United States must supply it. We are the only country able to provide that help.

I am fully aware of the broad implications involved if the United States extends assistance to Greece and Turkey, and I shall discuss these implications with you at this time.

One of the primary objectives of the foreign policy of the United States is the creation of conditions in which we and other nations will be able to work out a way of life free from coercion. This was a fundamental issue in the war with Germany and Japan. Our victory was won over countries which sought to impose their will, and their way of life, upon other nations.

To ensure the peaceful development of nations, free from coercion, the United States has taken a leading part in establishing the United Nations. The United Nations is designed to make possible lasting freedom and independence for all its members. We shall not realize our objectives, however, unless we are willing to help free peoples to maintain their free institutions and their national integrity against aggressive movements that seek to impose upon them totalitarian regimes. This is no more than a frank recognition that totalitarian regimes imposed upon free peoples, by direct or indirect aggression, undermine the foundations of international peace and hence the security of the United States.

The peoples of a number of countries of the world have recently had totalitarian regimes forced upon them against their will. The Government of the United States has made frequent protests against coercion and intimidation, in violation of the Yalta agreement, in Poland, Rumania, and Bulgaria. I must also state that in a number of other countries there have been similar developments.

At the present moment in world history nearly every nation must choose between alternative ways of life. The choice is too often not a free one.

One way of life is based upon the will of the majority, and is distinguished by free institutions, representative government, free elections, guarantees of individual liberty, freedom of speech and religion, and freedom from political oppression.

The second way of life is based upon the will of a minority forcibly imposed upon the majority. It relies upon terror and oppression, a controlled press and radio, fixed elections, and the suppression of personal freedoms.

I believe that it must be the policy of the United States to support free peoples who are resisting attempted subjugation by armed minorities or by outside pressures.

I believe that we must assist free peoples to work out their own destinies in their own way. . . .

It would be an unspeakable tragedy if these countries, which have struggled so long against overwhelming odds, should lose that victory for which they sacrificed so much. Collapse of free institutions and loss of independence would be disastrous not only for them but for the world. Discouragement and possibly failure would quickly be the lot of neighboring peoples striving to maintain their freedom and independence. . . .

I therefore ask the Congress to provide authority for assistance to Greece and Turkey in the amount of $400,000,000 for the period ending June 30, 1948. In requesting these funds, I have taken into consideration the maximum amount of relief assistance which would be furnished to Greece out of the $350,000,000 which I recently requested that the Congress authorize for the prevention of starvation and suffering in countries devastated by the war.

In addition to funds, I ask the Congress to authorize the detail of American civilian and military personnel to Greece and Turkey, at the request of those countries, to assist in the tasks of reconstruction, and for the purpose of supervising the use of such financial and material assistance as may be furnished. I recommend that authority also be provided for the instruction and training of selected Greek and Turkish personnel. . . .

The United States contributed $341,000,000,000 toward winning World War II. This is an investment in world freedom and world peace.

The assistance that I am recommending for Greece and Turkey amounts to little more than ⅒ of 1 percent of this investment. It is only common sense that we should safeguard this investment and make sure that it was not in vain.

Source: Harry S. Truman, "Special Message to the Congress on Greece and Turkey: The Truman Doctrine," March 12, 1947, in *Public Papers of the Presidents of the United States: Harry S. Truman, 1945–1953,* from the American Presidency Project, University of California, Santa Barbara, www.presidency. ucsb.edu.

Document 2.2
Truman Loyalty Oath, Executive Order 9835, March 21, 1947

The Cold War was fought both at home and abroad. Though fears of Communist influence were greatly exaggerated in the "Red Scare," there were Communists in the U.S. government as the Cold War got under way, and the president intended to reveal them and drive them out of the government.

Whereas each employee of the Government of the United States is endowed with a measure of trusteeship over the democratic processes which are the heart and sinew of the United States; and

Whereas it is of vital importance that persons employed in the Federal service be of complete and unswerving loyalty to the United States; and

Whereas, although the loyalty of by far the overwhelming majority of all Government employees is beyond question, the presence within the Government service of any disloyal or subversive person constitutes a threat to our democratic processes; and

Whereas maximum protection must be afforded the United States against infiltration of disloyal persons into the ranks of its employees, and equal protection from unfounded accusations of disloyalty must be afforded the loyal employees of the Government:

Now, Therefore, by virtue of the authority vested in me by the Constitution and statutes of the United States, including the Civil Service Act of 1883 (22 Stat. 403), as amended, and section 9A of the act approved August 2, 1939 (18 U.S.C. 61i), and as President and Chief Executive of the United States, it is hereby, in the interest of the internal management of the Government, ordered as follows:

PART I—INVESTIGATION OF APPLICANTS

1. There shall be a loyalty investigation of every person entering the civilian employment of any department or agency of the executive branch of the Federal Government. . . .
6. An investigation shall be made of all applicants at all available pertinent sources of information and shall include reference to:

   1. Federal Bureau of Investigation files.
   2. Civil Service Commission files.
   3. Military and naval intelligence files.
   4. The files of any other appropriate government investigative or intelligence agency.
   5. House Committee on un-American Activities files.
   6. Local law-enforcement files at the place of residence and employment of the applicant, including municipal, county, and State law-enforcement files.
   7. Schools and colleges attended by applicant.
   8. Former employers of applicant.
   9. References given by applicant.
   10. Any other appropriate source. . . .

PART II—INVESTIGATION OF EMPLOYEES

1. The head of each department and agency in the executive branch of the Government shall be personally responsible for an effective program to assure that disloyal civilian officers or employees are not retained in employment in his department or agency. . . .

PART V—STANDARDS

1. The standard for the refusal of employment or the removal from employment in an executive department or agency on grounds relating to loyalty shall be that, on all the evidence, reasonable grounds exist for belief that the person involved is disloyal to the Government of the United States.
2. Activities and associations of an applicant or employee which may be considered in connection with the determination of disloyalty may include one or more of the following:

1. Sabotage, espionage, or attempts or preparations therefor, or knowingly associating with spies or saboteurs;
2. Treason or sedition or advocacy thereof;
3. Advocacy of revolution or force or violence to alter the constitutional form of government of the United States;
4. Intentional, unauthorized disclosure to any person, under circumstances which may indicate disloyalty to the United States, of documents or information of a confidential or non-public character obtained by the person making the disclosure as a result of his employment by the Government of the United States;
5. Performing or attempting to perform his duties, or otherwise acting, so as to serve the interests of another government in preference to the interests of the United States.
6. Membership in, affiliation with or sympathetic association with any foreign or domestic organization, association, movement, group or combination of persons, designated by the Attorney General as totalitarian, fascist, communist, or subversive, or as having adopted a policy of advocating or approving the commission of acts of force or violence to deny other persons their rights under the Constitution of the United States, or as seeking to alter the form of government of the United States by unconstitutional means. . . .

Source: Executive Order no. 9835, *Code of Federal Regulations,* title 3, sec. 627 (1943–48).

Document 2.3
The Marshall Plan, Secretary of State George Marshall's Commencement Address at Harvard University, June 5, 1947

Undersecretary of State Dean Acheson first proposed to President Truman a massive economic aid program for Europe, as a complement to the Truman Doctrine. An ad hoc committee within the executive branch worked out the details of the proposal. Still reeling from the Republican victory in the midterm elections of 1946, Truman astutely delegated responsibility for unveiling the plan, which would require bipartisan support from Congress, to George Marshall, his immensely popular secretary of state. Although the aid offer was intended to crack apart the "iron curtain," the division of Europe was instead hardened after the Soviets rejected participation in the recovery effort on behalf of themselves and the Eastern Europe countries which they dominated. Over the four years of its existence, the Marshall Plan disbursed almost $13 billion in aid and credits, and it was pivotal in the economic recovery, and concomitant political moderation, of Western Europe.

. . .The truth of the matter is that Europe's requirements for the next three or four years of foreign food and other essential products—principally from America—are so much greater than her present ability to pay that she must have substantial additional help or face economic, social, and political deterioration of a very grave character.

The remedy lies in breaking the vicious circle and restoring the confidence of the European people in the economic future of their own countries and of Europe as a whole. . . .

It is logical that the United States should do whatever it is able to do to assist in the return of normal economic health in the world, without which there can be no political stability and no assured peace. Our policy is directed not against any country or doctrine but against hunger, poverty, desperation, and chaos. Its purpose should be the revival of a working economy in the world so as to permit the emergence of political and social conditions in which free institutions can exist. Such assistance, I am convinced, must not be on a piecemeal basis as various crises develop. Any assistance that this Government may render in the future should provide a cure rather than a mere palliative. Any government that is willing to assist in the task of recovery will find full cooperation, I am sure, on the part of the United States Government. Any government which maneuvers to block the recovery of other countries cannot expect help from us. Furthermore, governments, political parties, or groups which seek to perpetuate human misery in order to profit therefrom politically or otherwise will encounter the opposition of the United States.

It is already evident that, before the United States Government can proceed much further in its efforts to alleviate the situation and help start the European world on its way to recovery, there must be some agreement among the countries of Europe as to the requirements of the situation and the part those countries themselves will take in order to give proper effect to whatever action might be undertaken by this Government. . . . The initiative, I think, must come from Europe. . . .

Source: Department of State Bulletin 16, no. 415 (June 15, 1947): 1159–1160, from the Internet Modern History Sourcebook, www.fordham.edu/halsall/mod/1947marshallplan1.html.

Document 2.4
Soviet Deputy Foreign Minister Andrei Vyshinsky's Speech to the United Nations on the Marshall Plan, September 25, 1947

Andrei Vyshinsky explained the Soviet point of view on the Marshall Plan at a speech before the United Nations. It was, said the Soviet diplomat, nothing more than economic imperialism, and nothing less than a violation of the fundamental principles that the United States had agreed to uphold by joining the United Nations.

The so-called Truman Doctrine and the Marshall Plan are particularly glaring examples of the manner in which the principles of the United Nations are violated, of the way in which the organization is ignored.

As the experience of the past few months has shown, the proclamation of this doctrine meant that the United States government has moved towards a direct renunciation of the principles of international collaboration and concerted action by the great powers and towards attempts to impose its will on other independent states, while at the same time obviously using the economic resources distributed as relief to individual needy nations as an instrument of political pressure. This is clearly proved by the measures taken by the United States government with regard to Greece and Turkey which ignore and bypass the United Nations as well as by the measures proposed under the so-called Marshall Plan in Europe. This policy conflicts sharply with the principle expressed by the General Assembly in its resolution of 11 December 1946, which declares that relief supplies to other countries "should . . . at no time be used as a political weapon."

As is now clear, the Marshall Plan constitutes in essence merely a variant of the Truman Doctrine adapted to the conditions of postwar Europe. . . .

Source: Andrei Vyshinsky, "Vyshinsky speech to the UN," September 25, 1947, from CNN, *Cold War,* www.cnn.com/SPECIALS/cold.war/episodes/03/documents/vyshinsky.

Document 2.5
Communist Information Bureau (Cominform) Manifesto on Communist Solidarity, October 5, 1947

The purpose of the Communist Information Bureau (Cominform) was to disseminate propaganda and encourage Communist solidarity. The French and Italian Communist parties, members of Cominform, worked to undermine support in Western Europe for the Marshall Plan. Their failure, and the obvious Soviet domination of the pact, served to isolate rather than promote Communism within the West.

Manifesto Proclaiming the Cominform

In the international situation brought about by the Second World War and in the period that followed fundamental changes took place. The characteristic aspect of these changes is a new balance of political forces interplaying in the world arena, a shift in the relationship between states which were the victors in the Second World War, and their reevaluation.

As long as the war lasted the Allied states fighting against Germany and Japan marched in step and were one. Nevertheless, in the Allies' camp already during the war there existed differences regarding the aims of the war as well as the objectives of the post-war and world organization. The Soviet Union . . . believed that the main objective of the war was the rebuilding and strengthening of democracy in Europe, the liquidation of fascism and the prevention of a possible aggression on behalf of Germany. . . .

The United States of America and with them England placed as their war aim a different goal—the elimination of competition on the world market. . . .

Two opposite political lines have crystallized. On one extreme the USSR and the democratic countries aim at whittling down imperialism and the strengthening of democracy. On the other hand the United States of America and England aim at the strengthening of imperialism and choking democracy. . . .

In these conditions the anti-imperialist democratic camp has to close its ranks and draw up and agree on a common platform to work out its tactics against the chief forces of the imperialist camp, against American imperialism, against its English and French allies, against the Right-Wing Socialists above all in England and France. To frustrate those imperialistic plans of aggression we need the efforts of all democratic and anti-imperialist forces in Europe. . . .

Resolution of Conference of Communist Parties on Establishing the Cominform

. . . Experience has shown that . . . division between Communist parties is incorrect and harmful. . . .

Because of this, members of the conference agreed upon the following:

First, to set up an Information Bureau of representatives of the Communist Party of Yugoslavia, the Bulgarian Workers Party (of Communists), the Communist Party of Rumania, the Hungarian Communist Party, the Polish Workers Party, the Communist Party of the Soviet Union (Bolshevik), the Communist Party of France, the Communist Party of Czechoslovakia, and the Communist Party of Italy. . . .

Source: Edward H. Judge and John W. Langdon, *The Cold War: A History through Documents* (Upper Saddle River, N.J.: Prentice Hall, 1999), 38.

Document 2.6
Berlin Airlift Statistics, June 24, 1948–May 12, 1949

In response to a Soviet blockade of the Allied-occupied western sector of Berlin, the United States, with British (and French) assistance, conducted a fifteen-month airlift to supply food, fuel, and other essential items to the people of West Berlin. "Operation Vittles" was a remarkable demonstration of logistical skill and air power. By comparison, the multinational effort to supply Sarajevo (during the Bill Clinton presidency) delivered just short of 180,000 tons of cargo over three and a half years. In Berlin, more supplies than that were airlifted each month during the peak period, March 1949 through July 1949.

Berlin Airlift Statistics

		Cargo (short tons)				Passengers	
	Flights	Total	Food	Coal	Other	In	Out
USA	189,963	1,783,572.7	296,319.3	1,421,118.8	66,134.6	25,263	37,486
UK	87,606	541,936.9	240,386	164,910.5	136,640.4	34,815	130,091
Total	277,569	2,325,509.6	536,705.3	1,586,029.3	202,775	60,078	167,577

Source: Table adapted from "Berlin Airlift Summary" in Roger G. Miller, *To Save a City: The Berlin Airlift, 1948–1949* (College Station: Texas A&M University Press, 2000), Appendix 1.

Document 2.7
Desegregation of the Armed Forces, Executive Order 9981, July 26, 1948

African American troops had served in all American wars since the Revolution, but as late as World War II they were still kept apart from white troops in barracks as well as in battle. Civil rights leaders lobbied the president to bypass Congress and desegregate the armed forces through executive order. Out of anger at publicized instances of mistreatment of African American veterans, and because it would help him win election in 1948 and the United States win the ideological struggle of the Cold War, President Truman issued Executive Order 9981 in the summer of 1948.

Whereas it is essential that there be maintained in the armed services of the United States the highest standards of democracy, with equality of treatment and opportunity for all those who serve in our country's defense:

Now therefore, by virtue of the authority vested in me as President of the United States, by the Constitution and the statutes of the United States, and as Commander in Chief of the armed services, it is hereby ordered as follows:

1. It is hereby declared to be the policy of the President that there shall be equality of treatment and opportunity for all persons in the armed services without regard to race, color, religion or national origin. This policy shall be put into effect as rapidly as possible, having due regard to the time required to effectuate any necessary changes without impairing efficiency or morale.

2. There shall be created in the National Military Establishment an advisory committee to be known as the President's Committee on Equality of Treatment and Opportunity in the Armed Services, which shall be composed of seven members to be designated by the President.

3. The Committee is authorized on behalf of the President to examine into the rules, procedures and practices of the armed services in order to determine in what respect such rules, procedures and practices may be altered or improved with a view to carrying out the policy of this order. The Committee shall confer and advise with the Secretary of the Air Force, and shall make such recommendations to the President and to said Secretaries as in the judgment of the Committee will effectuate the policy hereof.

4. All executive departments and agencies of the Federal Government are authorized and directed to cooperate with the Committee in its work, and to furnish the Committee such information or the services of such persons as the Committee may require in the performance of its duties.

5. When requested by the Committee to do so, persons in the armed services or in any of the executive departments and agencies of the Federal Government shall testify before the Committee and shall make available for the use of the Committee such documents and other information as the Committee may require.

6. The Committee shall continue to exist until such time as the President shall terminate its existence by Executive Order.

Source: Executive Order no. 9981, *Federal Register* 13 (1948): 4313, from U.S. Department of State, Bureau of International Information Programs, *Basic Readings in U.S. Democracy,* usinfo.state.gov/usa/infousa/facts/democrac/35.htm.

Document 2.8
The Vandenberg Resolution on the North Atlantic Treaty Organization, June 11, 1948

Sen. Arthur Vandenberg of Michigan had been an isolationist before World War II. In the early Cold War, he provided critical support from the Republican side of the aisle to President Harry Truman. His resolution of support for U.S. participation in a new collective security organization to protect Western Europe enabled the United States to play a leading role in the formation of the North Atlantic Treaty Organization (NATO).

Whereas peace with justice and the defense of human rights and fundamental freedoms require international cooperation through more effective use of the United Nations: Therefore be it

Resolved, That the Senate reaffirm the policy of the United States to achieve international peace and security through the United Nations so that armed force shall not be used except in the common interest, and that the President be advised of the sense of the Senate that this Government, by constitutional process, should particularly pursue the following objectives within the United Nations Charter:

1. Voluntary agreement to remove the veto from all questions involving pacific settlements of international disputes and situations, and from the admission of new members.
2. Progressive development of regional and other collective arrangements for individual and collective self-defense in accordance with the purposes, principles, and provisions of the Charter.
3. Association of the United States, by constitutional process, with such regional and other collective arrangements as are based on continuous and effective self-help and mutual aid, and as affect its national security.
4. Contributing to the maintenance of peace by making clear its determination to exercise the right of individual or collective self-defense under article 51 should any armed attack occur affecting its national security.
5. Maximum efforts to obtain agreements to provide the United Nations with armed forces as provided by the Charter, and to obtain agreement among member nations upon universal regulation and reduction of armaments under adequate and dependable guaranty against violation.
6. If necessary, after adequate effort toward strengthening the United Nations, review of the Charter at an appropriate time by a General Conference called under article 109 or by the General Assembly.

Source: "Vandenberg Resolution," U.S. Senate Resolution 239, 80th Congress, 2d session, June 11, 1948, from the Avalon Project at Yale Law School, www.yale.edu/lawweb/avalon/decade/decad040 .htm.

Document 2.9
The North Atlantic Treaty, April 4, 1949

Collective security alliances became a central feature of the Cold War. The North Atlantic Treaty Organization (NATO) promoted the political and military interdependence of Western Europe and the United States.

The Parties to this Treaty reaffirm their faith in the purposes and principles of the Charter of the United Nations and their desire to live in peace with all peoples and all governments.

They are determined to safeguard the freedom, common heritage and civilisation of their peoples, founded on the principles of democracy, individual liberty and the rule of law.

They seek to promote stability and well-being in the North Atlantic area.

They are resolved to unite their efforts for collective defence and for the preservation of peace and security.

They therefore agree to this North Atlantic Treaty:

Article 1

The Parties undertake, as set forth in the Charter of the United Nations, to settle any international dispute in which they may be involved by peaceful means in such a manner that international peace and security and justice are not endangered, and to refrain in their international relations from the threat or use of force in any manner inconsistent with the purposes of the United Nations.

Article 2

The Parties will contribute toward the further development of peaceful and friendly international relations by strengthening their free institutions, by bringing about a better understanding of the principles upon which these institutions are founded, and by promoting conditions of stability and well-being. They will seek to eliminate conflict in their international economic policies and will encourage economic collaboration between any or all of them.

Article 3

In order more effectively to achieve the objectives of this Treaty, the Parties, separately and jointly, by means of continuous and effective self-help and mutual aid, will maintain and develop their individual and collective capacity to resist armed attack.

Article 4

The Parties will consult together whenever, in the opinion of any of them, the territorial integrity, political independence or security of any of the Parties is threatened.

Article 5

The Parties agree that an armed attack against one or more of them in Europe or North America shall be considered an attack against them all, and consequently they agree that, if such an armed attack occurs, each of them, in exercise of the right of individual or collective self-defence recognised by Article 51 of the Charter of the United Nations, will assist the Party or Parties so attacked by taking forthwith, individually, and in concert with the other Parties, such action as it deems necessary, including the use of armed force, to restore and maintain the security of the North Atlantic area.

Any such armed attack and all measures taken as a result thereof shall immediately be reported to the Security Council. Such measures shall be terminated when the Security Council has taken the measures necessary to restore and maintain international peace and security. . . .

Article 9

The Parties hereby establish a Council, on which each of them shall be represented to consider matters concerning the implementation of this Treaty. The Council shall be so organised as to be able to meet promptly at any time. The Council shall set up such subsidiary bodies as may be necessary; in particular it shall establish immediately a defence committee which shall recommend measures for the implementation of Articles 3 and 5. . . .

Source: NATO, "The North Atlantic Treaty," April 4, 1949, www.nato.int/docu/basictxt/treaty.htm.

Document 2.10
President Harry Truman's Inaugural Address, January 20, 1949

President Truman stunned Republicans and pollsters with his victory in the 1948 presidential election. In his subsequent inaugural address, he outlined a four-point program to win the Cold War. "Point Four" indicated that the administration would not neglect peaceful means to win friends and combat Communism in the Third World.

[Delivered in person at the Capitol]
Mr. Vice President, Mr. Chief Justice, fellow citizens:

I accept with humility the honor which the American people have conferred upon me. I accept it with a resolve to do all that I can for the welfare of this Nation and for the peace of the world.

In performing the duties of my office, I need the help and the prayers of every one of you. I ask for your encouragement and for your support. The tasks we face are difficult. We can accomplish them only if we work together.

Each period of our national history has had its special challenges. Those that confront us now are as momentous as any in the past. Today marks the beginning not only of a new administration, but of a period that will be eventful, perhaps decisive, for us and for the world.

It may be our lot to experience, and in a large measure bring about, a major turning point in the long history of the human race. The first half of this century has been marked by unprecedented and brutal attacks on the rights of man, and by the two most frightful wars in history. The supreme need of our time is for men to learn to live together in peace and harmony.

The peoples of the earth face the future with grave uncertainty, composed almost equally of great hopes and great fears. In this time of doubt, they look to the United States as never before for good will, strength, and wise leadership.

It is fitting, therefore, that we take this occasion to proclaim to the world the essential principles of the faith by which we live, and to declare our aims to all peoples.

The American people stand firm in the faith which has inspired this Nation from the beginning. We believe that all men have a right to equal justice under law and equal opportunity to share in the common good. We believe that all men have a right to freedom of thought and expression. We believe that all men are created equal because they are created in the image of God.

From this faith we will not be moved.

The American people desire, and are determined to work for, a world in which all nations and all peoples are free to govern themselves as they see fit, and to achieve a decent and satisfying life. Above all else, our people desire, and are determined to work for, peace on earth—a just and lasting peace—based on genuine agreement freely arrived at by equals.

In the pursuit of these aims, the United States and other like-minded nations find themselves directly opposed by a regime with contrary aims and a totally different concept of life.

That regime adheres to a false philosophy which purports to offer freedom, security, and greater opportunity to mankind. Misled by that philosophy, many peoples have sacrificed their liberties only to learn to their sorrow that deceit and mockery, poverty and tyranny, are their reward.

That false philosophy is communism.

Communism is based on the belief that man is so weak and inadequate that he is unable to govern himself, and therefore requires the rule of strong masters.

Democracy is based on the conviction that man has the moral and intellectual capacity, as well as the inalienable right, to govern himself with reason and justice.

Communism subjects the individual to arrest without lawful cause, punishment without trial, and forced labor as the chattel of the state. It decrees what information he shall receive, what art he shall produce, what leaders he shall follow, and what thoughts he shall think.

Democracy maintains that government is established for the benefit of the individual, and is charged with the responsibility of protecting the rights of the individual and his freedom in the exercise of those abilities of his.

Communism maintains that social wrongs can be corrected only by violence.

Democracy has proved that social justice can be achieved through peaceful change.

Communism holds that the world is so widely divided into opposing classes that war is inevitable.

Democracy holds that free nations can settle differences justly and maintain a lasting peace.

These differences between communism and democracy do not concern the United States alone. People everywhere are coming to realize that what is involved is material well-being, human dignity, and the right to believe in and worship God.

I state these differences, not to draw issues of belief as such, but because the actions resulting from the Communist philosophy are a threat to the efforts of free nations to bring about world recovery and lasting peace.

Since the end of hostilities, the United States has invested its substance and its energy in a great constructive effort to restore peace, stability, and freedom to the world.

We have sought no territory. We have imposed our will on none. We have asked for no privileges we would not extend to others.

We have constantly and vigorously supported the United Nations and related agencies as a means of applying democratic principles to international relations. We have consistently advocated and relied upon peaceful settlement of disputes among nations.

We have made every effort to secure agreement on effective international control of our most powerful weapon, and we have worked steadily for the limitation and control of all armaments.

We have encouraged, by precept and example, the expansion of world trade on a sound and fair basis.

Almost a year ago, in company with 16 free nations of Europe, we launched the greatest cooperative economic program in history. The purpose of that unprecedented effort is to invigorate and strengthen democracy in Europe, so that the free people of that continent can resume their rightful place in the forefront of civilization and can contribute once more to the security and welfare of the world.

Our efforts have brought new hope to all mankind. We have beaten back despair and defeatism. We have saved a number of countries from losing their liberty. Hundreds of millions of people all over the world now agree with us, that we need not have war—that we can have peace.

The initiative is ours.

We are moving on with other nations to build an even stronger structure of international order and justice. We shall have as our partners countries which, no longer solely concerned with the problem of national survival, are now working to improve the standards of living of all their people. We are ready to undertake new projects to strengthen a free world.

In the coming years, our program for peace and freedom will emphasize four major courses of action.

First, we will continue to give unfaltering support to the United Nations and related agencies, and we will continue to search for ways to strengthen their authority and increase their effectiveness. We believe that the United Nations will be strengthened by the new nations which are being formed in lands now advancing toward self-government under democratic principles.

Second, we will continue our programs for world economic recovery.

This means, first of all, that we must keep our full weight behind the European recovery program. We are confident of the success of this major venture in world recovery. We believe that our partners in this effort will achieve the status of self-supporting nations once again.

In addition, we must carry out our plans for reducing the barriers to world trade and increasing its volume. Economic recovery and peace itself depend on increased world trade.

Third, we will strengthen freedom-loving nations against the dangers of aggression.

We are now working out with a number of countries a joint agreement designed to strengthen the security of the North Atlantic area. Such an agreement would take the form of a collective defense arrangement within the terms of the United Nations Charter.

We have already established such a defense pact for the Western Hemisphere by the treaty of Rio de Janeiro [1947].

The primary purpose of these agreements is to provide unmistakable proof of the joint determination of the free countries to resist armed attack from any quarter. Every country participating in these arrangements must contribute all it can to the common defense.

If we can make it sufficiently clear, in advance, that any armed attack affecting our national security would be met with overwhelming force, the armed attack might never occur.

I hope soon to send to the Senate a treaty respecting the North Atlantic security plan.

In addition, we will provide military advice and equipment to free nations which will cooperate with us in the maintenance of peace and security.

Fourth, we must embark on a bold new program for making the benefits of our scientific advances and industrial progress available for the improvement and growth of underdeveloped areas.

More than half the people of the world are living in conditions approaching misery. Their food is inadequate. They are victims of disease. Their economic life is primitive and stagnant. Their poverty is a handicap and a threat both to them and to more prosperous areas.

For the first time in history, humanity possesses the knowledge and skill to relieve suffering of these people.

The United States is pre-eminent among nations in the development of industrial and scientific techniques. The material resources which we can afford to use for assistance of other peoples are limited. But our imponderable resources in technical knowledge are constantly growing and are inexhaustible.

I believe that we should make available to peace-loving peoples the benefits of our store of technical knowledge in order to help them realize their aspirations for a better life. And, in cooperation with other nations, we should foster capital investment in areas needing development.

Our aim should be to help the free peoples of the world, through their own efforts, to produce more food, more clothing, more materials for housing, and more mechanical power to lighten their burdens. . . .

Such new economic developments must be devised and controlled to the benefit of the peoples of the areas in which they are established. Guarantees to the investor must be balanced by guarantees in the interest of the people whose resources and whose labor go into these developments.

The old imperialism—exploitation for foreign profit—has no place in our plans. What we envisage is a program of development based on the concepts of democratic fair-dealing.

All countries, including our own, will greatly benefit from a constructive program for the better use of the world's human and natural resources. Experience shows that our commerce with other countries expands as they progress industrially and economically.

Greater production is the key to prosperity and peace. And the key to greater production is a wider and more vigorous application of modern scientific and technical knowledge.

Only by helping the least fortunate of its members to help themselves can the human family achieve the decent, satisfying life that is the right of all people.

Democracy alone can supply the vitalizing force to stir the peoples of the world into triumphant action, not only against their human oppressors, but also against their ancient enemies—hunger, misery, and despair.

On the basis of these four major courses of action we hope to help create the conditions that will lead eventually to personal freedom and happiness for all mankind. . . .

Events have brought our American democracy to new influence and new responsibilities. They will test our courage, our devotion to duty, and our concept of liberty.

But I say to all men, what we have achieved in liberty, we will surpass in greater liberty.

Steadfast in our faith in the Almighty, we will advance toward a world where man's freedom is secure.

To that end we will devote our strength, our resources, and our firmness of resolve. With God's help, the future of mankind will be assured in a world of justice, harmony, and peace.

Source: Harry S. Truman, "Inaugural Address," January 20, 1949, in *Public Papers of the Presidents of the United States: Harry S. Truman, 1945–1953,* from the American Presidency Project, University of California, Santa Barbara, www.presidency.ucsb.edu.

Document 2.11
President Harry Truman Informs the Public that the Soviet Union Has Detonated an Atomic Bomb, September 23, 1949

U.S. military and scientific experts were confident in 1949 that the Soviets were years, perhaps decades, from overcoming the technological hurdles involved in producing a nuclear weapon. The president's terse and defensive statement announcing the Soviet achievement hints at the nation's shock.

I believe the American people, to the fullest extent consistent with national security, are entitled to be informed of all developments in the field of atomic energy. That is my reason for making public the following information.

We have evidence that within recent weeks an atomic explosion occurred in the U.S.S.R.

Ever since atomic energy was first released by man, the eventual development of this new force by other nations was to be expected. This probability has always been taken into account by us.

Nearly 4 years ago I pointed out that "scientific opinion appears to be practically unanimous that the essential theoretical knowledge upon which the discovery is based is already widely known. There is also substantial agreement that foreign research can come abreast of our present theoretical knowledge in time." And, in the Three-Nation Declaration of the President of the United States and the Prime Ministers of the United Kingdom and of Canada, dated November 15, 1945, it was emphasized that no single nation could in fact have a monopoly of atomic weapons.

This recent development emphasizes once again, if indeed such emphasis were needed, the necessity for that truly effective enforceable international control of atomic energy which this Government and the large majority of the members of the United Nations support.

Source: Harry S. Truman, "Statement by the President on Announcing the First Atomic Explosion in the U.S.S.R.," September 23, 1949, in *Public Papers of the Presidents of the United States: Harry S. Truman, 1945–1953,* from the American Presidency Project, University of California, Santa Barbara, www.presidency.ucsb.edu.

Document 2.12
Mao Zedong Announces the Founding of the People's Republic of China, October 1, 1949

At the end of the World War II, the United States supported the Kuomintang Party's claim to be the legitimate ruler of all China. U.S. diplomatic efforts were not sufficient, however, to prevent a return to civil war and the eventual triumph of Mao Zedong's Communist Party. Mao waited until his forces had secured complete success on the battlefield and driven their opponents to the island of Taiwan before declaring victory and pronouncing the creation of a new regional power.

The people throughout China have been plunged into bitter suffering and tribulations since the Chiang Kai-shek Kuomintang reactionary government betrayed the fatherland, colluded with imperialists, and launched the counter-revolutionary war. Fortunately, our People's Liberation Army, backed by the whole nation, has been fighting heroically and selflessly to defend the territorial sovereignty of our homeland, to protect the people's lives and property, to relieve the people of their sufferings, and to struggle for their rights, and it eventually wiped out the reactionary troops and overthrew the reactionary rule of the Nationalist Government. Now the People's War of Liberation has been basically won, and the majority of the people have been liberated. On this foundation, the first session of the Chinese People's Political Consultative Conference, composed of delegates of all the democratic parties and people's organizations of China, the People's Liberation Army, the various regions and nationalities of the country, and the overseas Chinese and other patriotic elements, has been convened. Representing the will of the whole nation, [this session of the conference] has enacted the organic law of the Central People's Government of the People's Republic of China, elected Mao Zedong as chairman of the Central people's Government; . . . proclaimed the founding of the People's Republic of China and decided upon Beijing as the capital of the People's Republic of China. . . . At the same time, the Central People's Government Council decided to declare to the governments of all other countries that this government is the sole legal government representing all the people of the People's Republic of China. This government is willing to establish diplomatic relations with any foreign government that is willing to observe the principles of equality, mutual benefit, and mutual respect of territorial integrity and sovereignty.

MAO ZEDONG
Chairman
The Central People's Government
The People's Republic of China

Source: Michael Y. M. Kau and John K. Leung, eds., *The Writings of Mao Zedong, 1949–1976,* vol. 1, *September 1949–December 1955* (Armonk, N.Y.: M. E. Sharpe, 1986), 10–11.

Document 2.13
"Enemies from Within," Senator Joseph McCarthy's Speech to the Republican Women's Club of Wheeling, West Virginia, February 9, 1950

By the start of 1950, many Americans were anxiously asking how to account for the recent U.S. setbacks in the Cold War. Senator McCarthy provided an easy answer: the Truman adminis-tration was under the control of Communists! In a speech in West Virginia, McCarthy blasted away at the Truman administration. Truman's White House was not only soft on Communists, but absolutely fond of them. How else, the senator implied, could one explain the employment within the State Department alone of some 205 Communists and Communist sympathizers? After reporters challenged the senator's numbers, he changed the claim to a mere 57, the figure that appears below in the text of the speech entered by the senator in the Congressional Record *on February 20.*

. . . Today we are engaged in a final, all-out battle between communistic atheism and Chris-tianity. The modern champions of communism have selected this as the time. And, ladies and gentlemen, the chips are down—they are truly down. . . .

Ladies and gentlemen, can there be anyone here tonight who is so blind as to say that the war is not on? Can there by anyone who fails to realize that the Communist world has said, "The time is now" that this is the time for the show-down between the democratic Chris-tian world and the Communistic atheist world? Unless we face this fact, we shall pay the price that must be paid by those who wait too long.

Six years ago . . . there was within the Soviet orbit, 180,000,000 people. Lined up on the antitotalitarian side there were in the world at the time roughly 1,625,000,000 people. Today, only six years later, there are 800,000,000 people under the absolute domination of Soviet Russia—an increase of over 400 percent. On our side, the figure has shrunk to around 500,000,000. In other words, in less than six years, the odds have changed from 9 to 1 in our favor to 8 to 5 against us. This indicates the swiftness of the tempo of Communist vic-tories and American defeats in the cold war. As one of our outstanding historical figures once said, "When a great democracy is destroyed, it will not be from enemies from without, but rather because of enemies from within." . . .

The reason why we find ourselves in a position of impotency is not because our only pow-erful potential enemy has sent men to invade our shores, but rather because of the traitor-ous actions of those who have been treated so well by this Nation. It has not been the less fortunate, or members of minority groups who have been selling this Nation out, but rather those who have had all the benefits that the wealthiest Nation on earth has had to offer—the finest homes, the finest college education and the finest jobs in government we can give.

This is glaringly true in the State Department. . . .

I have here in my hand a list of 57 cases of individuals who would appear be either card carrying members or certainly loyal to the Communist Party, but who nevertheless are still helping to shape our foreign policy. . . .

As you know, very recently the Secretary of State proclaimed his loyalty to a man guilty of what has always been considered as the most abominable of all crimes—being a traitor to the people who gave him a position of great trust. The Secretary of State in attempting to justify his continued devotion to the man who sold out the Christian world to the athe-istic world, referred to Christ's Sermon on the Mount. . . .

When this pompous diplomat in striped pants, with a phony British accent, proclaimed to the American people that Christ on the Mount endorsed communism, high treason, and betrayal of a sacred trust, the blasphemy was so great that it awakened the dormant indig-nation of the American people. . . .

He has lighted the spark which is resulting in a moral uprising and will end only when the whole sorry mess of twisted, warped thinkers are swept from the national scene so that we may have a new birth of honesty and decency in government.

Source: Joseph McCarthy, "Speech at Wheeling, West Virginia," February 9, 1950, reprinted in Michael P. Johnson, ed., *Reading the American Past,* vol. 2 (Boston: Bedford Books, 1998), 191–195.

Document 2.14
National Security Council Report #68 (NSC 68) on National Security Objectives and Programs, April 7, 1950

The staff of the National Security Council (NSC) urged the president to effect a rapid and dra-matic increase in defense spending. The nation was at war, the NSC warned in its most famous report, but had yet to accept the consequences. The president, ever mindful of budget deficits and his weak hold over Congress, was not persuaded. The report's recommendations were ignored until the return to hot war in Korea.

VII. PRESENT RISKS

A. General

. . . Even if there were no Soviet Union we would face the great problem of the free soci-ety, accentuated many fold in this industrial age, of reconciling order, security, the need for participation, with the requirement of freedom. We would face the fact that in a shrinking world the absence of order among nations is becoming less and less tolerable. The Kremlin design seeks to impose order among nations by means which would destroy our free and democratic system. The Kremlin's possession of atomic weapons puts new power be-hind its design, and increases the jeopardy to our system. It adds new strains to the uneasy equilibrium-without-order which exists in the world and raises new doubts in men's minds whether the world will long tolerate this tension without moving toward some kind of order, on somebody's terms.

The risks we face are of a new order of magnitude, commensurate with the total struggle in which we are engaged. For a free society there is never total victory, since freedom and democracy are never wholly attained, are always in the process of being attained. But defeat at the hands of the totalitarian is total defeat. These risks crowd in on us, in a shrinking world of polarized power, so as to give us no choice, ultimately, between meeting them effectively or being overcome by them.

B. Specific

It is quite clear from Soviet theory and practice that the Kremlin seeks to bring the free world under its dominion by the methods of the cold war. The preferred technique is to subvert by infiltration and intimidation. Every institution of our society is an instrument which it is sought to stultify and turn against our purposes. Those that touch most closely our material and moral strength are obviously the prime targets, labor unions, civic enterprises, schools, churches, and all media for influencing opinion. The effort is not so much to make them serve obvious Soviet ends as to prevent them from serving our ends, and thus to make them sources of confusion in our economy, our culture, and our body politic. The doubts and diversities that in terms of our values are part of the merit of a free system, the weaknesses and the problems that are peculiar to it, the rights and privileges that free men enjoy, and the disorganization and destruction left in the wake of the last attack on our freedoms, all are but opportunities for the Kremlin to do its evil work. . . .

At the same time the Soviet Union is seeking to create overwhelming military force, in order to back up infiltration with intimidation. In the only terms in which it understands strength, it is seeking to demonstrate to the free world that force and the will to use it are on the side of the Kremlin, that those who lack it are decadent and doomed. In local incidents it threatens and encroaches both for the sake of local gains and to increase anxiety and defeatism in all the free world.

The possession of atomic weapons at each of the opposite poles of power, and the inability (for different reasons) of either side to place any trust in the other, puts a premium on a surprise attack against us. It equally puts a premium on a more violent and ruthless prosecution of its design by cold war, especially if the Kremlin is sufficiently objective to realize the improbability of our prosecuting a preventive war. It also puts a premium on piecemeal aggression against others, counting on our unwillingness to engage in atomic war unless we are directly attacked. We run all these risks and the added risk of being confused and immobilized by our inability to weigh and choose, and pursue a firm course based on a rational assessment of each.

The risk that we may thereby be prevented or too long delayed in taking all needful measures to maintain the integrity and vitality of our system is great. The risk that our allies will lose their determination is greater. And the risk that in this manner a descending spiral of too little and too late, of doubt and recrimination, may present us with ever narrower and more desperate alternatives, is the greatest risk of all. . . .

But there are risks in making ourselves strong. A large measure of sacrifice and discipline will be demanded of the American people. They will be asked to give up some of the benefits which they have come to associate with their freedoms. Nothing could be more important than that they fully understand the reasons for this. The risks of a superficial understanding or of an inadequate appreciation of the issues are obvious and might lead to the adoption of measures which in themselves would jeopardize the integrity of our system. At any point in the process of demonstrating our will to make good our fundamental purpose, the Kremlin may decide to precipitate a general war, or in testing us, may go too far. These are risks we will invite by making ourselves strong, but they are lesser risks than those we seek to avoid. Our fundamental purpose is more likely to be defeated from lack of the will to maintain it, than from any mistakes we may make or assault we may undergo because of asserting that will. No people in history have preserved their freedom who thought that by not being strong enough to protect themselves they might prove inoffensive to their enemies.

IX. POSSIBLE COURSES OF ACTION

Introduction. Four possible courses of action by the United States in the present situation can be distinguished. They are:

  a. Continuation of current policies, with current and currently projected programs for carrying out these policies;
  b. Isolation;
  c. War; and
  d. A more rapid building up of the political, economic, and military strength of the free world than provided under (a), with the purpose of reaching, if possible, a tolerable state of order among nations without war and of preparing to defend ourselves in the event that the free world is attacked. . . .

The Third Course—War

Some Americans favor a deliberate decision to go to war against the Soviet Union in the near future. It goes without saying that the idea of "preventive" war—in the sense of a military attack not provoked by a military attack upon us or our allies—is generally unacceptable to Americans. Its supporters argue that since the Soviet Union is in fact at war with the free world now and that since the failure of the Soviet Union to use all-out military force is explainable on grounds of expediency, we are at war and should conduct ourselves accordingly. Some further argue that the free world is probably unable, except under the crisis of war, to mobilize and direct its resources to the checking and rolling back of the Kremlin's drive for world dominion. This is a powerful argument in the light of history, but the considerations against war are so compelling that the free world must demonstrate that this argument is wrong. The case for war is premised on the assumption that the United States could launch and sustain an attack of sufficient impact to gain a decisive advantage for the free world in a long war and perhaps to win an early decision.

The ability of the United States to launch effective offensive operations is now limited to attack with atomic weapons. A powerful blow could be delivered upon the Soviet Union, but it is estimated that these operations alone would not force or induce the Kremlin to capitulate and that the Kremlin would still be able to use the forces under its control to dominate most or all of Eurasia. This would probably mean a long and difficult struggle during which the free institutions of Western Europe and many freedom-loving people would be destroyed and the regenerative capacity of Western Europe dealt a crippling blow.

Apart from this, however, a surprise attack upon the Soviet Union, despite the provocativeness of recent Soviet behavior, would be repugnant to many Americans. Although the American people would probably rally in support of the war effort, the shock of responsibility for a surprise attack would be morally corrosive. Many would doubt that it was a "just war" and that all reasonable possibilities for a peaceful settlement had been explored in good faith. Many more, proportionately, would hold such views in other countries, particularly in Western Europe and particularly after Soviet occupation, if only because the Soviet Union would liquidate articulate opponents. It would, therefore, be difficult after such a war to create a satisfactory international order among nations. Victory in such a war would have brought us little if at all closer to victory in the fundamental ideological conflict. . . .

D. The Remaining Course of Action—A Rapid Build-up of Political, Economic, and Military Strength in the Free World

A more rapid build-up of political, economic, and military strength and thereby of confidence in the free world than is now contemplated is the only course which is consistent with progress toward achieving our fundamental purpose. The frustration of the Kremlin design requires the free world to develop a successfully functioning political and economic system and a vigorous political offensive against the Soviet Union. These, in turn, require an adequate military shield under which they can develop. It is necessary to have the military power to deter, if possible, Soviet expansion, and to defeat, if necessary, aggressive Soviet or Soviet-directed actions of a limited or total character. The potential strength of the free world is great; its ability to develop these military capabilities and its will to resist Soviet expansion will be determined by the wisdom and will with which it undertakes to meet its political and economic problems.

Source: U.S. National Security Council, "NSC 68: United States Objectives and Programs for National Security," April 7, 1950, from the Federation of American Scientists, www.fas.org/irp/offdocs/nsc-hst/nsc-68.htm.

Document 2.15
UN Security Council Resolution 82 Condemning the Attack on South Korea, June 25, 1950

In response to the surprise attack of Allied-occupied South Korea by Communist troops from the north, Truman turned not to Congress but to the newly established United Nations for support. The Soviet Union, a permanent member of the Security Council, was boycotting meetings at the time to protest the UN's refusal to acknowledge the People's Republic of China, making it possible for the United States to secure the unanimity of permanent members present and voting required for passage of a Security Council resolution condemning the attack in Korea.

The Security Council,

Recalling the finding of the General Assembly in its resolution 293 (IV) of 21 October 1949 that the Government of the Republic of Korea is a lawfully established government having effective control and jurisdiction over that part of Korea where the United Nations Temporary Commission on Korea was able to observe and consult . . . ; that this Government is based on elections which are a valid expression of the free will of the electorate of that part of Korea and which were observed by the Temporary Commission; and that this is the only such Government in Korea,

Mindful of the concern expressed by the General Assembly . . . about the consequences which might follow unless Member States refrained from acts derogatory to the results sought to be achieved by the United Nations in bringing about the complete independence and unity of Korea. . . .

Noting with grave concern the armed attack on the Republic of Korea by forces from North Korea,

Determines that this action constitutes a breach of the peace; and

Calls for the immediate cessation of hostilities;

Calls upon the authorities in North Korea to withdraw forthwith their armed forces to the 38th parallel; . . .

Calls upon all Member States to render every assistance to the United Nations in the execution of this resolution and to refrain from giving assistance to the North Korean authorities.

Source: United Nations Security Council, "Resolution 82: Complaint of Aggression upon the Republic of Korea," June 25, 1950, www.un.org/documents/sc/res/1950/scres50.htm.

Document 2.16
President Harry Truman's Decision to Send Troops to Aid South Korea, White House Press Release, June 27, 1950

Two days after the start of the Korean War, President Truman issued a press release announcing his decision to send air and naval forces to aid in the defense of South Korea. Near the end of his statement, he announced a decision that was of little moment at the time: that the United States would tie itself to the French effort in Vietnam, Laos, and Cambodia, "Indochina."

In Korea the Government forces, which were armed to prevent border raids and to preserve internal security, were attacked by invading forces from North Korea. The Security Council of the United Nations called upon the invading troops to cease hostilities and to withdraw to the 38th parallel. This they have not done, but on the contrary have pressed the attack. The Security Council called upon all members of the United Nations to render every assistance to the United Nations in the execution of this resolution. In these circumstances I have ordered United States air and sea forces to give the Korean Government troops cover and support.

The attack upon Korea makes it plain beyond all doubt that communism has passed beyond the use of subversion to conquer independent nations and will now use armed invasion and war. It has defied the orders of the Security Council of the United Nations issued to preserve international peace and security. In these circumstances the occupation of Formosa [Taiwan] by Communist forces would be a direct threat to the security of the Pacific area and to United States forces performing their lawful and necessary functions in that area.

Accordingly I have ordered the 7th Fleet to prevent any attack on Formosa. . . .

I have also directed that United States Forces in the Philippines be strengthened and that military assistance to the Philippine Government be accelerated.

I have similarly directed acceleration in the furnishing of military assistance to the forces of France and the Associated States in Indochina and the dispatch of a military mission to provide [close] working relations with those forces. . . .

Source: Harry S. Truman, "Statement by the President on the Situation in Korea," June 27, 1950, in *Public Papers of the Presidents of the United States: Harry S. Truman, 1945–1953,* from the American Presidency Project, University of California, Santa Barbara, www.presidency.ucsb.edu.

Document 2.17
President Harry Truman Addresses the Public about Korea, July 19, 1950

In a radio and television address, Truman takes his case for war to the people. After reviewing the basic facts of the war's origins—emphasizing that it began with an unprovoked attack from North Korea, organized after World War II by the Soviets—Truman puts the war in the context of the global struggle against Communism. In the section of the speech reprinted here, the president concludes the speech by speaking of the United States' need to put itself back on a war footing.

. . . [T]he fact that Communist forces have invaded Korea is a warning that there may be similar acts of aggression in other parts of the world. The free nations must be on their guard, more than ever before, against this kind of sneak attack.

It is obvious that we must increase our military strength and preparedness immediately. There are three things we need to do.

First, we need to send more men, equipment, and supplies to General MacArthur.

Second, in view of the world situation, we need to build up our own Army, Navy, and Air Force over and above what is needed in Korea.

Third, we need to speed up our work with other countries in strengthening our common defenses.

To help meet these needs, I have already authorized increases in the size of our Armed Forces. These increases will come in part from volunteers, in part from Selective Service, and in part from the National Guard and the Reserves.

I have also ordered that military supplies and equipment be obtained at a faster rate.

The necessary increases in the size of our Armed Forces, and the additional equipment they must have, will cost about $10 billion, and I am asking the Congress to appropriate the amount required.

These funds will be used to train men and equip them with tanks, planes, guns, and ships, in order to build the strength we need to help assure peace in the world.

When we have worked out with other free countries an increased program for our common defense, I shall recommend to the Congress that additional funds be provided for this purpose. This is of great importance. The free nations face a worldwide threat. It must be met with a worldwide defense. The United States and other free nations can multiply their strength by joining with one another in a common effort to provide this defense. This is our best hope for peace.

The things we need to do to build up our military defense will require considerable adjustment in our domestic economy. We have a tremendously rich and productive economy, and it is expanding every year.

Our job now is to divert to defense purposes more of that tremendous productive capacity—more steel, more aluminum, more of a good many things.

Some of the additional production for military purposes can come from making fuller use of plants which are not operating at capacity. But many of our industries are already going full tilt, and until we can add new capacity, some of the resources we need for the national defense will have to be taken from civilian uses.

This requires us to take certain steps to make sure that we obtain the things we need for national defense, and at the same time guard against inflationary price rises.

The steps that are needed now must be taken promptly.

In the message which I sent to the Congress today, I described the economic measures which are required at this time.

First, we need laws which will insure prompt and adequate supplies for military and essential civilian use. I have therefore recommended that the Congress give the Government power to guide the flow of materials into essential uses, to restrict their use for nonessential purposes, and to prevent the accumulation of unnecessary inventories.

Second, we must adopt measures to prevent inflation and to keep our Government in a sound financial condition. One of the major causes of inflation is the excessive use of credit. I have recommended that the Congress authorize the Government to set limits on installment buying and to curb speculation in agricultural commodities. In the housing field, where Government credit is an important factor, I have already directed that credit restraints be applied, and I have recommended that the Congress authorize further controls.

As an additional safeguard against inflation, and to help finance our defense needs, it will be necessary to make substantial increases in taxes. This is a contribution to our national security that every one of us should stand ready to make. As soon as a balanced and fair tax program can be worked out, I shall lay it before the Congress. This tax program will have as a major aim the elimination of profiteering.

Third, we should increase the production of goods needed for national defense. We must plan to enlarge our defense production, not just for the immediate future, but for the next several years. This will be primarily a task for our businessmen and workers. However, to help obtain the necessary increases, the Government should be authorized to provide certain types of financial assistance to private industry to increase defense production.

Our military needs are large, and to meet them will require hard work and steady effort. I know that we can produce what we need if each of us does his part—each man, each woman, each soldier, each civilian. This is a time for all of us to pitch in and work together. . . .

If prices should rise unduly because of excessive buying or speculation, I know our people will want the Government to take action, and I will not hesitate to recommend rationing and price control.

We have the resources to meet our needs. Far more important, the American people are unified in their belief in democratic freedom. We are united in detesting Communist slavery.

We know that the cost of freedom is high. But we are determined to preserve our freedom—no matter what the cost.

I know that our people are willing to do their part to support our soldiers and sailors and airmen who are fighting in Korea. I know that our fighting men can count on each and every one of you.

Our country stands before the world as an example of how free men, under God, can build a community of neighbors, working together for the good of all.

That is the goal we seek not only for ourselves, but for all people. We believe that freedom and peace are essential if men are to live as our Creator intended us to live. It is this faith that has guided us in the past, and it is this faith that will fortify us in the stern days ahead.

Source: Harry S. Truman, "Radio and Television Address to the American People on the Situation in Korea," July 19, 1950, in *Public Papers of the Presidents of the United States: Harry S. Truman, 1945–1953,* from the American Presidency Project, University of California, Santa Barbara, www.presidency.ucsb.edu.

Document 2.18
Soviet and Chinese Involvement in the Korean War, According to the Soviet Foreign Ministry, August 9, 1966

The DPRK (Democratic People's Republic of Korea or, more simply, North Korea) did not move forward with its plans for attack until its leader, Kim Il Sung, had gained Joseph Stalin's approval. According to this document, part of a formerly secret internal history of the Korean War written by members of the Soviet Foreign Ministry, Stalin gave his consent only after Kim persuaded him that the United States would not intervene. Kim similarly persuaded Chairman Mao to stand ready to assist the Koreans in case of Japanese intervention. Once the war was on, and Truman made the decision to support the South, the conflict became a proxy test of wills as well as military capabilities.

. . . After separate elections in 1948 in South Korea and the formation of the puppet government of Rhee Syngman, on the one hand, and the formation of the DPRK, on the other, relations between the North and the South of the country were sharply aggravated. The Seoul regime, as well as the DPRK, declared its claim to be the authority in all of Korea. The situation at the 38th parallel became even more tense in 1948 after the withdrawal of Soviet and American troops from Korea.

During this period, Kim Il Sung and other Korean leaders were firmly determined to unify the country by military means, without devoting the necessary attention to studying the possibility that existed at that time for peaceful reunification through the broad development of the democratic movement in South Korea.

In the DPRK, a people's army was created which in manpower and equipment significantly surpassed the armed forces of South Korea. By January 1, 1950, the total number of DPRK troops was 110,000; new divisions were hastily being formed.

Calculating that the USA would not enter a war over South Korea, Kim Il Sung persistently pressed for agreement from Stalin and Mao Zedong to reunify the country by military means.

Stalin at first treated the persistent appeals of Kim Il Sung with reserve, noting that "such a large affair in relation to South Korea . . . needs much preparation," but he did not object in principle. The final agreement to support the plans of the Koreans was given by Stalin at the time of Kim Il Sung's visit to Moscow in March–April 1950. Following this, in May, Kim Il Sung visited Beijing and secured the support of Mao. . . .

At Stalin's order, all requests of the North Koreans for delivery of arms and equipment for the formation of additional units of the KPA [Korean People's Army] were quickly met. The Chinese leadership sent to Korea a division formed from Koreans who had been serving in the Chinese army, and promised to send food aid and to transfer one army closer to Korea "in case the Japanese enter on the side of South Korea." . . .

During Kim Il Sung's visit to Beijing in May 1950, Mao Zedong, in conversation with him, underscored his conviction that the Americans would not become engaged in a war "for such a small territory as Korea" and stated that the Chinese government would transfer one of their armies to the region of Mukden in order to render the necessary assistance in case the South Koreans drew Japanese soldiers into military action. The Chinese leadership based their calculation on the fact that the American troops would not take part in the war, and they did not intend to aid the DPRK by means of the entrance of a large number of their troops.

In August 1950 American planes began bombing Chinese territory near the Yalu. In October 1950, soon after the American landing at Inchon, the front line moved close to the Korean-Chinese border and the enemy's artillery began to fire on Chinese territory. Ships of the American Seventh Fleet entered the Taiwan Straits.

By that time the Korean People's Army had virtually disintegrated as a fighting force. Remnants of military units that escaped encirclement were making their way toward China to regroup.

The Chinese government, under pressure from Stalin, adopted the decision to send volunteers to Korea only after a real threat to the security of China had arisen and the very existence of the DPRK had been called into question. . . .

The entry of the Chinese volunteers into the war and the active participation of Soviet military advisers, who participated in the planning of all major offensive operations, brought about a vital breakthrough in the course of military events. . . .

Source: Kathryn Weathersby, ed. and trans., "New Findings on the Korean War," *Cold War International History Project Bulletin,* no. 3 (Fall 1993): 1, 14–18, www.cwihp.org.

Document 2.19
"No Substitute for Victory," General Douglas MacArthur's Letter Denouncing President Harry Truman's Conduct of the War, April 5, 1951

After the Chinese Army entered the war, total victory over North Korea seemed to the U.S. military a lost cause without taking the fight directly to the Chinese mainland. If the United States attacked China, however, the consequences might include a global nuclear war. Unwilling to take such risks, Truman limited his war aims and the means available to his commanders. Theater commander Gen. Douglas MacArthur assailed the president's strategy as appeasement.

Dear Congressman Martin:

I am most grateful for your note of the eighth forwarding me a copy of your address of February 12. The latter I have read with much interest, and find that with the passage of years you have certainly lost none of your old time punch.

My views and recommendations with respect to the situation created by Red China's entry into war against us in Korea have been submitted to Washington in the most complete detail. Generally these views are well known and clearly understood, as they follow the conventional pattern of meeting force with maximum counter force as we have never failed to do in the past. . . .

It seems strangely difficult for some to realize that here in Asia is where the Communist conspirators have elected to make their play for global conquest, and that we have joined the issue thus raised on the battlefield; that here we fight Europe's war with arms while the diplomats there still fight it with words; that if we lose the war to communism in Asia the fall of Europe is inevitable, win it and Europe most probably would avoid war and yet preserve freedom. As you point out, we must win. There is no substitute for victory.

With renewed thanks, and expressions of most cordial regard, I am,

Faithfully yours,

DOUGLAS MacARTHUR

Source: Congressional Record, 82d Cong., 1st sess., 1951, 97, pt. 3:3380.

Document 2.20
President Harry Truman Fires General Douglas MacArthur, April 11, 1951

Gen. Douglas MacArthur's outburst of April 5, 1951, had been merely the most recent in a long line of provocations. On April 11, the president finally relieved the general of his command, releasing to the public a statement justifying the order; the order itself; and five supporting documents, including copies of orders from the Joint Chiefs of Staff to the general commanding that he issue no statement on war policy without prior authorization.

[1.] Statement by the President:

With deep regret I have concluded that General of the Army Douglas MacArthur is unable to give his wholehearted support to the policies of the United States Government and of the United Nations in matters pertaining to his official duties. In view of the specific responsibilities imposed upon me by the Constitution of the United States and the added responsibility which has been entrusted to me by the United Nations, I have decided that I must make a change of command in the Far East. I have, therefore, relieved General MacArthur of his commands and have designated Lt. Gen. Matthew B. Ridgway as his successor.

Full and vigorous debate on matters of national policy is a vital element in the constitutional system of our free democracy. It is fundamental, however, that military commanders must be governed by the policies and directives issued to them in the manner provided by our laws and Constitution. In time of crisis, this consideration is particularly compelling.

General MacArthur's place in history as one of our greatest commanders is fully established. The Nation owes him a debt of gratitude for the distinguished and exceptional service which he has rendered his country in posts of great responsibility. For that reason I repeat my regret at the necessity for the action I feel compelled to take in his case.

[2.] Order by the President to General MacArthur:

I deeply regret that it becomes my duty as President and Commander in Chief of the United States military forces to replace you as Supreme Commander, Allied Powers; Commander in Chief, United Nations Command; Commander in Chief, Far East; and Commanding General, U.S. Army, Far East.

You will turn over your commands, effective at once, to Lt. Gen. Matthew B. Ridgway. You are authorized to have issued such orders as are necessary to complete desired travel to such place as you select.

My reasons for your replacement will be made public concurrently with the delivery to you of the foregoing order, and are contained in the next following message. (See attached Statement by the President.) . . .

Source: Harry S. Truman, "Statement and Order by the President on Relieving General MacArthur of His Commands," April 11, 1951, in *Public Papers of the Presidents of the United States: Harry S. Truman, 1945–1953,* from the American Presidency Project, University of California, Santa Barbara, www.presidency.ucsb.edu.

Document 2.21
President Harry Truman Defends His Conduct of the War and the Dismissal of a War Hero, Radio Address, April 11, 1951

President Truman knew he would be damned by General MacArthur's many supporters. In a public radio address, he made the case for the dismissal, going so far as to present documentary evidence of the commander's refusal to comply with orders that he cease and desist from issuing strategic statements at variance with those of his commander in chief. The president's speech was not popular. The people did not so much care whether MacArthur had the legal right to say what he did; they cared whether he was right in what he said. Most Americans thought he was.

My fellow Americans:

I want to talk to you plainly tonight about what we are doing in Korea and about our policy in the Far East.

In the simplest terms, what we are doing in Korea is this: We are trying to prevent a third world war. . . .

If history has taught us anything, it is that aggression anywhere in the world is a threat to the peace everywhere in the world. When that aggression is supported by the cruel and selfish rulers of a powerful nation who are bent on conquest, it becomes a dear and present danger to the security and independence of every free nation.

This is a lesson that most people in this country have learned thoroughly. This is the basic reason why we joined in creating the United Nations. And, since the end of World War II, we have been putting that lesson into practice—we have been working with other free nations to check the aggressive designs of the Soviet Union before they can result in a third world war.

That is what we did in Greece, when that nation was threatened by the aggression of international communism.

The attack against Greece could have led to general war. But this country came to the aid of Greece. The United Nations supported Greek resistance. With our help, the determination and efforts of the Greek people defeated the attack on the spot.

Another big Communist threat to peace was the Berlin blockade. That too could have led to war. But again it was settled because free men would not back down in an emergency.

The aggression against Korea is the boldest and most dangerous move the Communists have yet made.

The attack on Korea was part of a greater plan for conquering all of Asia.

I would like to read to you from a secret intelligence report which came to us after the attack on Korea. It is a report of a speech a Communist army officer in North Korea gave to a group of spies and saboteurs last May, 1 month before South Korea was invaded. The report shows in great detail how this invasion was part of a carefully prepared plot. Here, in part, is what the Communist officer, who had been trained in Moscow, told his men: "Our forces," he said, "are scheduled to attack South Korean forces about the middle of June. . . . The coming attack on South Korea marks the first step toward the liberation of Asia."

Notice that he used the word "liberation." This is Communist double-talk meaning "conquest." . . .

That is what the Communist leaders are telling their people, and that is what they have been trying to do.

They want to control all Asia from the Kremlin. . . .

The whole Communist imperialism is back of the attack on peace in the Far East. It was the Soviet Union that trained and equipped the North Koreans for aggression. The Chinese Communists massed 44 well-trained and well-equipped divisions on the Korean frontier. These were the troops they threw into battle when the North Korean Communists were beaten.

The question we have had to face is whether the Communist plan of conquest can be stopped without a general war. Our Government and other countries associated with us in the United Nations believe that the best chance of stopping it without a general war is to meet the attack in Korea and defeat it there.

That is what we have been doing. It is a difficult and bitter task.

But so far it has been successful.

So far, we have prevented world war III.

So far, by fighting a limited war in Korea, we have prevented aggression from succeeding, and bringing on a general war. And the ability of the whole free world to resist Communist aggression has been greatly improved.

We have taught the enemy a lesson. He has found that aggression is not cheap or easy, Moreover, men all over the world who want to remain free have been given new courage and new hope. They know now that the champions of freedom can stand up and fight, and that they will stand up and fight. . . .

But you may ask why can't we take other steps to punish the aggressor. Why don't we bomb Manchuria and China itself? Why don't we assist the Chinese Nationalist troops to land on the mainland of China?

If we were to do these things we would be running a very grave risk of starting a general war. If that were to happen, we would have brought about the exact situation we are trying to prevent. . . .

A number of events have made it evident that General MacArthur did not agree with that policy. I have therefore considered it essential to relieve General MacArthur so that there would be no doubt or confusion as to the real purpose and aim of our policy.

It was with the deepest personal regret that I found myself compelled to take this action. General MacArthur is one of our greatest military commanders. But the cause of world peace is much more important than any individual.

The change in commands in the Far East means no change whatever in the policy of the United States. We will carry on the fight in Korea with vigor and determination in an effort to bring the war to a speedy and successful conclusion. The new commander, Lt. Gen. Matthew Ridgway, has already demonstrated that he has the great qualities of military leadership needed for this task.

Source: Harry S. Truman, "Radio Report to the American People on Korea and on U.S. Policy in the Far East," April 11, 1951, in *Public Papers of the Presidents of the United States: Harry S. Truman, 1945–1953,* from the American Presidency Project, University of California, Santa Barbara, www .presidency.ucsb.edu.

Document 2.22
President Harry Truman on the Supreme Court's War Powers Ruling, News Conference, June 5, 1952

Near the close of the Truman administration, the Supreme Court overruled the president's assertion of prerogative powers to resolve a labor-management dispute in the nation's steel mills. The president's war powers, the Court decided, had limits, and Truman had breached them. Truman's pique was evident at his news conference three days later.

. . .

[4.] Q.: Can you tell us anything about the steel situation?

The President: No. I have no comment on it.

Q.: Do you plan to use the Taft-Hartley law at all?

The President: No comment.

Q.: When could you comment on the Supreme Court decision?

The President: Never. [Laughter]

Q.: Mr. President, was that question when will you comment, sir?

The President: Yes.

Q.: Mr. President, you have said that the Supreme Court—that nobody could take away your powers that were inherent in the Constitution. I wonder if you could elucidate that now?

The President: I will at a later date. Not today. The best thing for you to do is to read the Constitution of the United States. It can be amended only by one method.

[5.] Q.: Are you intending to—do you have in mind a message to Congress on new legislation to handle labor disputes?

The President: No.

Q.: None?

The President: None in contemplation at the present time.

Q.: Do you think we need it?

The President: I don't know.

Source: "The President's News Conference of June 5, 1952," in *Public Papers of the Presidents of the United States: Harry S. Truman, 1945–1953,* from the American Presidency Project, University of California, Santa Barbara, www.presidency.ucsb.edu.

CHAPTER THREE

Dwight Eisenhower
Defense within Limits

In July 1953, the summer after he assumed the presidency, Dwight Eisenhower sat down one evening with his diary to contemplate the contradictions of capitalism. The famous Marxist revolutionary Vladimir Lenin had been at least half right, the president concluded (**Document 3.1**). In capitalist countries such as the United States, there was indeed a "contradiction" between what was good for the individual and the system in the short term and what was necessary for the long-term survival of both. Too many persons focused exclusively on the short term. The solution: only effective leadership could bridge the gap between what people

President Dwight Eisenhower delivers his "Atoms for Peace" speech to the United Nations on December 8, 1953. In his address Eisenhower called on the Soviet Union to join the United States in diverting nuclear material and called for the creation of an International Atomic Energy Agency. Source: United Nations/Department of Public Information.

naturally desired and what they must be taught to value. The president was confident that he could provide that leadership. It was urgent that he do so, moreover, for "Ike" was much more than the golfer-without-a-care that he was so often depicted as being. President Eisenhower was, in fact, in a hurry to save his country, and the world, from ruin.

A graduate of West Point and a career soldier, General Eisenhower had been selected by President Franklin Roosevelt to command Operation Overlord, the decisive cross-channel invasion of the continent of Europe launched on June 6, 1944. Eisenhower's D-Day campaign eventually led to another—his sweeping victory at the head of the Republican ticket in the presidential election of 1952. His victory came as no surprise to political observers, even though Democrats had reigned in the White House since 1933. The outgoing president, Harry Truman, had led the nation into the anxiety-filled Cold War and its first hot conflict, the unpopular war in Korea. Moreover, the Truman administration was hampered by an inflationary economy and charges of corruption.

Eisenhower, free from the taint of prior political associations, seemed the ideal man for the times. His promise during the campaign merely to "go to Korea" inspired millions of voters who believed that the general's mere presence would surely bring that conflict to an end. He won in a popular- and electoral-vote landslide, even defeating his Democratic opponent, Adlai Stevenson, in three states of the former Confederacy—a part of the nation whose voters were at that time still hostile to most Republican candidates. The election proved that the people of America truly did "like Ike," but what, if anything, did Ike stand for? What would be the Eisenhower presidency's purpose?

Eisenhower believed his first priority as president was to calm Americans' fears. Excessive fear, he said repeatedly in public appearances, threatened the long-term survival of the nation and the world. As a candidate for office, in a highly publicized speech before the American Legion National Convention at Madison Square Garden in New York City, he had spoken of the dangerous effect of fear in a climate of military competition:

> Now fear is a climate that nourishes bankruptcy in dollars and morals alike. Those afraid seek security in a heedless extravagance that breeds waste of substance and corruption of men. Fear is a climate that, if long endured, is as costly in its toll on material resources, on lives, on the spirit of men as defeat in war. In an era of chronic fear can be heard the death rattle of a nation.[1]

After election, the president returned to this theme repeatedly, as in his first State of the Union address on February 2, 1953. "We anticipated a world of peace and cooperation" after World War II, Eisenhower observed. Unfortunately, "aggressive Communism" had brought about a "world of turmoil."[2] Defeating the enemy would take strength over a long period of time. Too many people, motivated by fear, wanted to win the Cold War tomorrow. Others, motivated by the same fear, thought only of their selfish desires. According to Eisenhower, these people seemed to think that they best enjoy today because they might not be here tomorrow. If Americans did not control their fears, the enemy might defeat them without having to fire a single shot.

As a corrective to hysteria, President Eisenhower espoused what he proudly called a "middle-of-the-road" philosophy.[3] To steer this course, Eisenhower had to avoid doing both too much to win the war *today* and too little. President Truman, Eisenhower believed, had wanted to do too much, which had threatened the durability of the nation's economy, battered as it was by high levels of wartime taxation. Although twenty-first century liberals tend to be internationalist doves—those who support American involvement abroad, but not necessarily the expansion of American military power—mainstream liberals during Eisenhower's presidency were eager to expand America's military and willing to resort to the use of force. They were "hawks," and "big-spending" ones at that, from the perspective of their opponents. It was the socially and economically conservative isolationists in the Republican Party who threatened to do too little. They, too, were hawks of a sort, but only favored the use of force to defend the physical territory of the United States. Following the lead of Republican senator Robert Taft of Ohio, the isolationists longed to return to the days of modest defense budgets and modest American involvement in world affairs. It would take a great deal of political skill to pursue a middle course between these two dominant political positions. Eisenhower was not always successful in the effort, but he never changed his destination.

KOREA, THE COLD WAR, AND THE GARRISON STATE

Eisenhower did indeed go to Korea in November 1952, even before he assumed office. The situation on the ground remained grim. Peace negotiations, opened in July 1951, were stalled over the issue of the repatriation of Chinese and North Korean prisoners of war (POWs). The two Communist governments insisted upon the return of all their POWs, while the United States and its allies insisted upon the right of individual prisoners to choose whether to return to their home countries. In the intensely ideological climate of the time, replete with charges of "brainwashing" by both sides, this was a deadly serious issue. Meanwhile, combat continued sporadically. Eisenhower had an idea of how to move forward, but he wanted to do so without a return to full-scale battles. For this reason, while in Korea, the president-elect never gave the UN supreme commander, U.S. Gen. Mark Clark, an opportunity to present him with his views in private. Eisenhower knew that Clark, like many in the military establishment, wanted to resume the offensive with a frontal assault on the North Koreans and their Chinese allies. Eisenhower thought such ideas "border[ed] on madness."[4] He saw an easier way out: He would communicate to the North Koreans and the Chinese his willingness to use nuclear weapons. So as not publicly to back the enemy into a corner, he conveyed his intent indirectly.

The parading of the army's new 280 mm field gun, "The Atomic Cannon," at the incoming president's inaugural parade was certainly dramatic, if not entirely subtle. Then there was the inaugural address itself, which Eisenhower devoted exclusively to foreign and military affairs. At the midway point of a "century of trial," the president said, "[s]cience seems ready to confer upon us, as its final gift, the power to erase human life from this planet." The United States would face this peril with confidence, however, because of the stakes involved in a contest where "freedom is pitted against slavery; lightness against the dark." As for the enemy, such as the men who ruled North Korea and Communist China, they "know no god but force."[5] If it was force they wanted, the president implied, it would be force they received.

Once in office, the president first consulted with an invigorated National Security Council (NSC) on the situation in Korea. Though he rejected the advice of hard-liners in the NSC, including Secretary of State John Foster Dulles, to let General Clark pursue the military unification of the Korean peninsula, the president used diplomatic back channels to let the enemy know that in the spring, he would "move decisively," as he recalled in his memoirs, "without inhibition in our use of weapons."[6] This was followed by the actual transfer of atomic warheads to forward bases in Okinawa, Japan, a move that the enemy was bound to pick up on. Shortly thereafter, the Chinese and North Koreans accepted the principle of truly voluntary repatriation of POWs. Peace negotiations resumed. The outcome, a return to a divided Korea, was "acceptable," according to Stephen Ambrose, a leading historian of the Eisenhower presidency, "only because [Eisenhower] had put his own immense prestige behind it."[7] One might go further and observe that it was *possible* only because Eisenhower used his immense prestige as a military commander to make a credible threat of the use of unrestrained nuclear force.

While pursuing a peaceful, if not precisely a diplomatic, resolution to the war in Korea, the president responded to a "peace offensive" in the wider Cold War from an unlikely source. Joseph Stalin, the beguiling, belligerent, and ruthless Soviet dictator, died March 4, 1953. His immediate successor, Georgi Malenkov, lost little time publicly proclaiming the Soviet Union's allegedly long-standing but frequently misunderstood desire for peace. Many Western officials quickly discounted the new Soviet rhetoric as empty talk. Eisenhower was not certain and, in any event, saw an opportunity to score a propaganda victory of his own with a positive response. The result was a speech, delivered April 16, 1953, entitled "The Chance for Peace" (**Document 3.2**).

In this speech, the president spoke of his desire for the international control of atomic energy and a verifiable arms limitation agreement. The speech made headlines for its remarks on the true costs of war and war preparedness. Speaking as a tired warrior, the president pictured "humanity hanging from a cross of iron." He said, "Every gun that is made, every warship launched, every rocket fired signifies, in the final sense, a theft from those who hunger and are not fed, those who are cold and are not clothed."

In the light of the president's concern to steer a middle course in the quest for security, "The Chance for Peace" was more than just great rhetoric; it was a piece of grand strategy. The Cold War, Eisenhower was quite certain, could be won only through cool restraint. If too many resources were diverted to war preparedness, the nation would be bankrupted. If people's fears were not settled, they would demand just such a diversion of resources. The United States would then suffer—before the whole experiment ended in bankruptcy—under a government with inflated powers, a so-called garrison state.[8]

About a year later, on March 17, 1954, at one of his weekly press conferences, the president elaborated on the same theme, asking and answering his own question during an exchange on military strategy:

> What are we talking about? It is, I think, there is too much hysteria. . . . We fear the men in the Kremlin, we fear what they will do to our friends around them; we are fearing what unwise investigators will do to us here at home as they try to combat subversion or bribery or deceit within. We fear depression, we fear the loss of jobs. All of these, with their impact on the human mind makes us act almost hysterically, and you find hysterical reactions.

"[T]he answer" to America's problems and fears, according to Eisenhower, was "a faith in the destiny of America."[9]

The public responded favorably to Eisenhower's initial calls for a cooling of the Cold War. It was fortunate for the president that his message had such approval from the broad public at the start of his presidency, because he faced serious problems right away with the nation's political and military elite. Perhaps foremost among Eisenhower's difficulties was disagreement over the budget for national security.

The president desired to impose substantial cuts on the fiscal year 1954 budget that his administration had inherited from President Truman, who was already too conservative a spender to please many hawkish liberals. Eisenhower, backed by his budget director and secretary of the Treasury, wanted to cut almost $10 billion, and he wanted the majority of the dollars to come from the military. The military establishment, naturally, objected

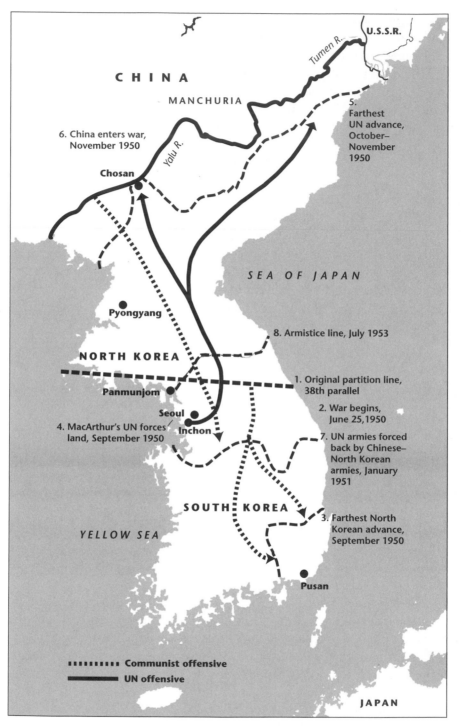

THE KOREAN WAR, 1950–1953

Source: Steven W. Hook and John Spanier, *American Foreign Policy Since World War II*, 17th ed. (Washington, D.C.: CQ Press, 2007), 70.

and aired its grievances publicly. The president, however, managed to overcome the "spenders" in his first year and to keep his administration on track by rallying conservative anti-spenders ("deficit hawks") within Congress.

Early in his presidency, then, Eisenhower established a pattern. In pursuit of moderation in the Cold War, he would threaten vastly immoderate (nuclear) action against external foes while downsizing conventional military forces despite the vocal opposition of high-ranking members of the military establishment. This pattern would continue throughout his presidency.

THE NEW LOOK

To develop his ideas regarding national security into a doctrine that would guide his administration, Eisenhower relied heavily upon the National Security Council, with assistance from ad hoc groups of experts outside the government. The first major product of the thorough planning process that characterized Eisenhower's drafting of foreign policy was NSC 162/2 (**Document 3.3**). The drafters of this document took as their point of departure NSC 68, which had been composed under President Truman (**Document 2.14**). Truman's administration, as Eisenhower saw it, had failed to see that "the purpose of America is to defend a way of life rather than merely to defend property, houses, or lives."[10] Whereas NSC 68 had seen the Cold War building rapidly to a "year of maximum danger"—and therefore called for an urgent and massive buildup in U.S. military power while contradictorily warning of the dangers of overspending—NSC 162/2 envisioned a lengthy, indefinite struggle and advised fiscal restraint.

Eisenhower's security experts disagreed, though, on how much restraint was too much. As a consequence, the drafters of NSC 162/2 battled over such seeming minutia as whether U.S. policy would "place emphasis on" or merely "include" "the capability of inflicting massive retaliatory damage by offensive striking power." Eisenhower, motivated by his desire to draw down the expensive conventional military forces that had been built up for the Korean War, insisted upon the former. The United States would contain Soviet aspirations by threatening massive retaliatory strikes in the event of an aggressive act. This, the president hoped, would keep the peace *and* keep the nation from becoming both bankrupt and militarized.

Eisenhower's policy had its limitations. It was not clear whether the threat of nuclear attack would in fact deter every or even most conceivable acts of Communist aggression. Would the threat be credible in, say, a localized war in a remote third-world nation, where the Soviets might attempt to disguise their involvement? In addition, the American policy would become obsolete were the Soviets ever to achieve nuclear parity. The president's concern on this point led him to contemplate the conditions under which a preemptive nuclear strike might be justified (**Document 3.4**). Despite his private doubts, the president employed his sometimes bellicose secretary of state, John Foster Dulles, to publicize what became known as the "New Look" defense policy and its doctrine of "Massive Retaliation" (**Document 3.5**).

THE NEW LOOK IN ACTION: FIRST-TERM CRISES

In Eisenhower's first term, the United States and its allies faced a number of Cold War crises. As a consequence, the New Look was tested in Europe, the Middle East, Latin America, and Asia.

Indochina/Vietnam

American opposition to the reimposition of French imperialism in Laos, Cambodia, and the territory that became Vietnam was an early casualty of the Cold War. With tensions rising between Moscow and Washington, D.C., in the immediate aftermath of World War II, during which time the Japanese had driven the French out of Southeast Asia, it became more important to placate the French than to promote the principle of national self-determination. After almost ten years of battle, however, the French government in the early 1950s began to look toward a negotiated withdrawal. The Vietminh, led by the veteran Communist stalwart Ho Chi Minh, received substantial economic and military assistance from the People's Republic of China and had proven a formidable foe. By winter 1953 the French were eager to reach a diplomatic settlement with the Vietminh at a forthcoming international conference in Geneva. The Vietminh, although aspiring to total victory even at this early stage of what would be their decades' long war, had been pressured by the Chinese into accepting the inevitability of peace talks. But both sides wished to arrive at the bargaining table having recently won major concessions in combat.

When the French seized and fortified Dien Bien Phu, a remote district capital near the Laotion border, on November 20, 1953, the Vietminh decided to concentrate and attack. The French, isolating themselves almost 200 miles west of Hanoi in the hope of thus defending nearby Laos, had anticipated an assault but not the severity of that assault. The French command had discounted the ability of the Vietminh to take advantage of the hills surrounding the encampment. In this, they fatally underestimated their opponents, who managed to bring, among other items, 100 rocket launchers across mountain trails in pieces, which they then reassembled upon the high ground overlooking the French troops. The Vietminh assault began March 13, 1954. Human-wave tactics urged upon the fighters by their Chinese advisers gave way to patient tunneling, and the greatly outnumbered French grew desperate.

As the situation deteriorated, the French began to lobby the United States for help. The United States had been heavily subsidizing the cost of the French war in Indochina since the Truman years. Now the French wanted not just dollars but American bombs, if not American troops. Adm. Arthur Radford, chairman of the Joint Chiefs of Staff, supported the notion of U.S. bombing raids in Vietnam, even suggesting the use of tactical nuclear weapons. Privately, Eisenhower made clear what he thought of this idea: "You boys must be crazy," he told his most gung-ho advisors at a meeting of the NSC.[11]

Not wanting to reject the French entreaty outright, the president deferred first to the bipartisan leadership of Congress. Congressional leaders passed the buck back to the president, joining strong rhetorical support for the French with a list of implausible conditions to be met before the United States would intervene directly. Eisenhower was thus able to avoid the risks of another war in Asia while not seeming to deviate from his new policy. The cause of freedom in Vietnam, he insisted at a press conference of April 7, 1954, was critical (**Document 3.6**). If Vietnam should fall, it could lead to the collapse of other regimes in the region. They might fall like "dominoes," he said, employing but not coining a metaphor that would become a familiar part of American Cold War rhetoric. The president rattled the proverbial saber but made sure that it would not be drawn. The final defeat at Dien Bien Phu came on May 6, when the Vietminh launched an offensive from all sides, captured the compound, and took prisoner the entire French headquarters staff.

In the aftermath, the French negotiated their withdrawal from Vietnam, leaving the nation divided between a Western-allied South Vietnam and a Communist-allied North Vietnam. In September the United States, along with France, the United Kingdom, and several regional powers (Australia, New Zealand, Thailand, and Pakistan), entered into a mutual defense pact, the Southeast Asia Treaty Organization (SEATO; **Document 3.7**). They agreed in this treaty not only to come to one another's aid in the case of attack but also to join one another in resisting with force an attack "against any State or territory which the Parties by unanimous agreement may hereafter designate." In an addendum to the treaty, the parties designated South Vietnam one such state.

The First Taiwan Straits Crisis

The island nation of the Republic of China (ROC, known as Taiwan or Formosa) lies 100 miles off the mainland of China. The Quemoy and Matsu islands, also occupied by the ROC, are just a few miles offshore. ROC possession and fortification of these islands had been a source of constant tension between the two Chinas. The United States' allies in the region, including Britain and Australia, urged President Eisenhower to pressure ROC president Chiang Kai-shek to withdraw from them his government's forces. Rather than withdraw, Chiang in August 1954 sent more troops and called for a "holy war" against the mainland. In remarks intended for the U.S. public as well as its Congress, Chiang urged American military support for a war of national unification. The mainland government of the People's Republic of China (PRC) replied with incendiary language of its own, issuing a declaration calling for the "liberation" of Taiwan from the clutches of the ROC. The PRC followed up with a guerrilla raid upon and, starting on September 3, the sustained artillery shelling of the islands.

Over the ensuing months, the PRC, the ROC, and the United States engaged in moves and countermoves designed to test one another's commitments and secure an outcome favorable to their own interests. The danger of all-out war was grave, because the Soviet Union had pledged to defend the PRC if American forces attacked. But would the United States intervene militarily if the PRC invaded just the contested islands, not Taiwan itself?

Admiral Radford, joined by the chiefs of the navy and air force, recommended placing American soldiers on the ground on the islands, as well as carrying out bombing raids upon the mainland. President Eisenhower, however, had no intention of possibly starting a world war over Quemoy and Matsu. At the same time, he felt that he could not simply abandon a historic American ally. Although he appreciated the precariousness of Taiwan's hold on these islands, he agreed with Chiang that their possession was important to sustaining the morale of the Taiwanese people. How, then, could the PRC be forced to back off, without going to war?

Eisenhower's answer was to employ the New Look's doctrine of massive retaliation. First, the American secretary of state and his ROC counterpart signed a mutual defense pact that included "other territories under the jurisdiction of the parties." After that failed to wind down the conflict, the president engineered passage of a congressional resolution granting him seemingly unlimited discretion to use necessary force to defend American interests at risk in the continuing conflict (**Document 3.8**). To clarify for his adversary the stakes involved, the president at a press conference on March 16, 1955, stated his willingness to use nuclear weapons "against strictly military targets" in a general war in the Far East. In the event of such a war, he stated, he saw "no reason why they shouldn't be used just exactly as you would use a bullet or anything else."[12] After this, the PRC indirectly but unmistakably signaled its desire to relax tension in the area and remain at peace with the United States. A tacit cease-fire was achieved by the end of May.

The threat of massive retaliation had, it seemed, worked. The ROC kept possession of its island garrisons, the PRC shelling ceased, and there was no wider war. There was, however, reason for concern. If the PRC had not backed down, the United States might well have been backed into a truly major war—with the Soviet Union as well as China. Today, it seems that that threat was actually not as great as it seemed at the time. Mao Zedong, the founder of Communist China and the PRC Communist Party chairman, it appears, was also bluffing. His intent seems to have been to convince the Soviet Union that its vital Asian ally was under an imminent threat from the United States, so that the Soviets would increase their assistance for China's nuclear weapons program.[13] Even if this surmise is correct, Eisenhower had no choice but to take the PRC's actions seriously. Fortunately, Mao decided—for whatever reason—not to test Eisenhower's resolve, and this game of nuclear "chicken" ended without a headlong crash.

Covert Ops

Another way to keep costs down while still actively pursuing success in the Cold War was through covert action. Covert action was especially inviting where the outcome that the United States desired was more complicated than the mere cessation of hostilities. Covert operations (or ops) had the additional advantage of allowing the United States to encroach on the Communist world—that is, to take at least small steps beyond mere containment. These were important benefits, but were covert ops *American*? Spies, after all, did more than just uncover the enemy's secrets. Covert operatives in modern as well as ancient times engaged in such unsavory acts as sabotage, subversion, bribery, and worse. This bothered many American policymakers, but not so much that they were willing to renounce "black ops." Air force general Jimmy Doolittle spoke for many persons in and out of government when, in a report to Eisenhower on the role of the American intelligence community, he wrote, "It is now clear we are facing an implacable enemy whose avowed objective is world domination. . . . There are no rules in such a game. Hitherto acceptable norms of human conduct do not apply."[14]

The Eisenhower administration first employed covert means in Iran. At the close of World War II, the Soviets had threatened to join Iranian Azerbaijan with an Azeri Soviet province across the border. Under American pressure, and with the incentive of American and British promises of oil concessions, the Soviets withdrew. The Americans and the British thereafter supported Iranian autonomy under Western tutelage.

In 1951 the Western-allied monarch of Iran, Shah Mohammed Reza Pahlavi, was forced by the Iranian parliament (the Majlis) to name as prime minister Mohammed Mosaddegh, a rival figure. Upon assuming office, the prime minister sought to enforce the nationalization of the country's oil industry, a step approved by the parliament in March. The British responded by withdrawing all technical support for the industry and imposing a blockade against Iranian efforts to ship oil out of the country. The British, with American help, also orchestrated a complicated covert op.

Although the new Iranian prime minister was lionized in much of the Western press, his politics were questioned in London and Washington. Director of Central Intelligence Allen Dulles considered him a Communist sympathizer and feared that the Soviets would intervene in Iran to support him. The Central Intelligence Agency (CIA) therefore worked with British intelligence to bring down the prime minister. By employing a variety of tactics, including the manipulation of public demonstrations and more coercive measures, they brought about a pro-Shah military coup against the prime minister.

The following year, the CIA acted against another putative Communist, this time in Guatemala. Jacobo Arbenz had been elected president of Guatemala in 1950; after taking office, he initiated a program of land reform. The U.S.-owned United Fruit Company, the largest employer and landowner in Guatemala, protested vehemently about the compensation set for its expropriated land. In part because Arbenz had allied with the Communist Party in securing passage of the Agrarian Reform Law, unsympathetic observers in the West concluded—in the words of the American ambassador at the time—that if Arbenz "is not a communist, he will certainly do until one comes along." [15]

After a shipment of arms from Communist Czechoslovakia was discovered on its way to Guatemala, President Eisenhower ordered the U.S. Navy to patrol the coasts and ordered the transfer of arms to neighboring countries. In Honduras, one of those contiguous states, the CIA was already helping pro-American Guatemalan colonel Carlos Castillo Armas train an "army" of about 200 troops. On June 18, 1954, they were cut loose to launch their "invasion." The CIA used false radio broadcasts to exaggerate the size of the invading force and to incite Guatemalans to rally against Arbenz. After the Guatemalan Army turned against the president, Arbenz resigned and fled first to Mexico and from there to Czechoslovakia. Armas assumed power, while President Eisenhower and Secretary of State Dulles, lauded the patriotic restoration of conservative rule carried out by "loyal citizens of Guatemala." [16]

The apparent short-term success of these CIA operations gave the agency confidence and seemed to set a precedent for the use of covert means in the Cold War. That this was at best a complicated legacy would become apparent in the first months of the succeeding presidency.

Suez and Hungary

Heading toward reelection, President Eisenhower faced two more Cold War crises. In one case, naturally enough, the Soviets were the instigators. In the other, two of the United States' closest allies were to blame. In both cases, Eisenhower responded characteristically by deciding *not* to act.

Suez. After Egypt's charismatic pan-Arabist leader Gamal Abdel Nasser came to power in a coup in 1952, the U.S. government attempted to forge a relationship with Egypt's new government. The centerpiece of America's commitment to Egypt was to be the Aswan High Dam, a massive development project for which the Americans, with the British, would provide financing upwards of a quarter billion dollars. When, however, Nasser recognized the People's Republic of China and entered into an agreement to purchase military goods from Czechoslovakia, a Soviet client state, the Western powers renounced their agreement.

Nasser announced that he would raise the money himself by nationalizing the Suez Canal and claiming its profits for Egypt. Nasser knew that this would provoke the West. Two-thirds of the oil used in Western Europe traveled through the canal, and the corporation that owned and operated the canal was owned by French private investors and the British government. The French government, moreover, already had reason to view Nasser as an enemy, as he supported the rebels fighting against the French colonial government in neighboring Algeria.

The French, therefore, concocted a plan. They would first transfer military equipment to Israel, which had been engaged for months in border warfare against Egypt. Israel would use that equipment to make a surprise attack in Egypt's Sinai Peninsula. The Israeli Defense Forces would drive the Egyptians back to the canal, whereupon France, in concert with Britain, would enter the game. France and Britain, citing their historic and practical interest in the canal, would insist upon the immediate disengagement and withdrawal of combat forces. Israel, continuing to play its part in this charade, would graciously accede to the European demand. Egypt, it was predicted, would not. (To ensure Egyptian non-cooperation, Egypt would be given only hours to consider the demand.) At that point, the British and French would send their own military forces to "protect" the canal. The United States, it was assumed, would approve of the outcome if not the methods used to achieve it. Incredibly, the plan worked, from the Israeli attack on October 29, 1956, up to the last assumption.

President Eisenhower was angry. Not only did he consider the British and French occupation of the Canal Zone an anachronistic "Victorian" stunt that would play into the hands of Soviet propaganda about the West, but he also felt personally slighted at having been misled by allied governments.[17] The Soviet Union was also aggrieved, and threatened Britain and France with "dangerous consequences" for their transgressions, including attacks on their capitals by "all types of modern weapons of destruction."[18] Early on Election Day in the United States, the CIA reported that the Soviet Union had secretly promised Egypt that it would "do something" in the Middle East soon.[19] The president was sufficiently alarmed to inquire about the availability of nuclear submarines in the Mediterranean.

Eisenhower defused the crisis by taking the matter to the United Nations General Assembly. Predictably, the General Assembly, after ten days' debate, condemned the attack and demanded a withdrawal of European forces. In addition, the United States employed its economic leverage directly upon its allies. During the fighting, Nasser had ordered the sinking of all the ships presently in the canal, which resulted in gas rationing and economic distress in Europe. The United States alone had the economic power to relieve the resultant tension in Western Europe. It declined to do so until the British and French reversed their actions. A cease-fire was reached on November 6, and invading forces withdrew in early 1957, to be replaced by the UN's first contingent of "peacekeepers" (the armed constabulary of the first United Nations Emergency Force [UNEF I]).

One reason why Eisenhower was so tough on his allies during the Suez Crisis was that he was contending simultaneously with another crisis, an anti-Soviet revolt in Hungary that was put down by Soviet troops. He would have opened himself up to the charge of hypocrisy had he condemned Soviet intervention in Eastern Europe but supported European intervention in the Sinai Peninsula. The president may also have been tempted to act decisively in the Suez Crisis because his power to influence the outcome of that conflict was so much greater than his ability to control events behind the iron curtain.

Hungary. Ever since President Roosevelt's alleged capitulation to Soviet intentions at Yalta, the Republican Party had returned time and again, as in the 1952 party platform, to the imperative to undo the "tragic blunder" made at Yalta.[20] It was never clear, however, what the Republicans were prepared to do about the situation in Eastern Europe. After all, so long as the Republicans were the opposition party, it was a largely theoretical issue.

As it happened, when he set about to give form to the first Republican postwar policy for Europe, President Eisenhower continued for the most part the policies of the Truman administration. In both administrations, U.S. priorities were to enhance the capability of the North Atlantic Treaty Organization (NATO), to integrate West Germany into the alliance (which occurred in May 1955), and to concentrate on the forward defense of the West against invasion by the Soviet Union and its Warsaw Pact "allies." For the dissidents and rebels actually fighting to reverse Soviet control of Eastern Europe, Eisenhower intended, like Truman before him, to provide only moral and covert support. The Voice of America and Radio Free Europe broadcast news from the West into the East, and the CIA on occasion helped individual dissidents and those seeking escape. Stalin's death in March 1953, however, put pressure on this stable and cautious set of policies.

Within a number of Eastern European nations, Stalin's death led to conflict over the direction of government policy. Anti-Stalinist protests occurred in East Germany, Poland, and Hungary. After deadly confrontations between demonstrators and Hungarian security forces on the night of October 23, 1956, the Soviets ordered their own troops into battle. During the first two weeks of intense fighting, and for months afterward while the Soviets defeated the rebellion and reasserted their control, the Hungarian resistance sent urgent appeals to the West for help.

In response, the United States sought to allay the fears not of the Hungarian resistance but of the Soviet attackers, so that they would not "be tempted to resort to very extreme measures and even to precipitate global war."[21] The United States further attempted to assuage Soviet anxieties by indicating that if the Soviets should lose a satellite, NATO did not intend to bring the lost nation into its orbit. As the president said in his second inaugural address (January 21, 1957), when other nations, "in time of want or peril," ask for the United States' help, they can receive it honorably, knowing that Americans "no more seek to buy their sovereignty than we would sell our own." Against this backdrop, the president's homage to the "heroes" of the recent uprising in the same speech rang somewhat hollow. "Budapest," said the president, "is no longer merely the name of a city," but a "new and shining symbol of man's yearning to be free."[22] As a practical matter, the United States helped the International Red Cross clothe, feed, and shelter some 200,000 Hungarians who made it over the border to Austria, and accepted large numbers of émigrés to the United States from among the refugees.

As a logical consequence of Eisenhower's decision to pursue a middle-of-the-road policy in a war of absolutes, there was often, as in this case, a gap between the rhetoric and the reality of the American position in the Cold War. This affected President Eisenhower's relations with both the military and Congress.

THE MIDDLE WAY IS TESTED AT HOME AND ABROAD

President Eisenhower's relations with the Joint Chiefs of Staff were not always cordial. The military establishment wanted to continue to build up; the president was determined to draw down. The end result was a compromise on policy—and a number of dramatic, public confrontations between the commander in chief and his principal military advisers. The president's relationship with Congress was similarly tense. Unexpectedly, it was often members of his own party who gave the president the most trouble, especially during the first two years of his first term, when Republicans enjoyed a short-lived majority status in both houses.

The Joint Chiefs of Staff

The Joint Chiefs of Staff (JCS) are the nation's highest-ranking admirals and generals. As organized when Eisenhower began his presidency, the JCS gave each of the independent armed forces a place at the table in discussions of military affairs and advised the president and the secretary of defense. Dwight Eisenhower knew well the institution of the JCS and its personnel. He had, in fact, served for more than two years as army chief of staff following World War II. Later, taking time away from his "day job" as president of Columbia University, he had struggled on behalf of President Truman to forge consensus among the chiefs as they fought one another over postwar roles and missions. The wartime JCS was made a permanent institution in the 1947 National Security Act. Eisenhower's personal relationship with all of the chiefs might have made for a great working relationship, but it was not to be. The difficulty was Eisenhower's New Look military policy.

The New Look directly challenged the services, with the exception of the air force, to reduce personnel and armaments. At a deeper level, the New Look might even be said to have challenged the relevance of the profession of arms itself. If international peace were truly to be maintained through deterrence alone and wars fought by the pushing of buttons, of what use were traditional military forces and their traditional codes of honor? It was no surprise, then, that the military establishment fought back against the New Look. What was surprising was military leaders' willingness to take public their displeasure with the strategy's principal designer.

Through their testimony on Capitol Hill and leaks to the press, the chiefs attempted to undermine the New Look. Eisenhower's response was multifaceted. He exercised the prerogatives of executive command, especially in changing personnel; appealed to the public; and led Congress to reform the JCS itself.

The chiefs and the president fought first over the fiscal year 1954 budget. The chiefs were invited as a body to attend a meeting of the NSC on March 25, 1953. Army Chief of Staff Gen. J. Lawton Collins, "spoke first . . . concluding that the proposed cut would have not only grave military implications for the national security, but would give rise to equally serious political and diplomatic difficulties."[23] The other chiefs followed, all with equally dire descriptions of the harm to be done by the president's proposed savings. It was too much for Eisenhower, causing him to "observe that perhaps the Council should have a report as to whether national bankruptcy or national destruction would get us first."[24]

Failing to persuade the president of the error of his ways in private, the chiefs voiced their objections before Congress. Air Force Chief of Staff Gen. Hoyt Vandbenberg testified that the civilian defense secretary, Charles Wilson, had forced the chiefs to accept unwise cuts in their budgets. In response, Eisenhower cleaned house in the JCS, accepting the resignation of his mutinous air commander and declining to keep in office the other members. Vandenberg had served since 1948. His last, single-year appointment was granted to provide continuity during the Korean War. Army Chief of Staff Gen. J. Lawton Collins and the chairman of the JCS, Gen. Omar Bradley, had served since 1949. Only Adm. William Fechteler, the chief naval officer since 1951, could truly be said to have been "sacked" in this move, by being denied a customary second, two-year term. Nevertheless, the military (and the press) interpreted the move as an assault upon the military establishment.

Underscoring the president's eagerness for a new start, he put the incoming chiefs to work right away, before they were formally installed in office. Incoming chairman Adm. Arthur William Radford, an air power enthusiast, even got the new body to sign off collectively on such basic elements of the Eisenhower viewpoint on defense as the primacy of massive retaliation and the importance of a durable economy.

In 1955 the president once again had difficulty with the JCS. This time, the principal antagonist was the Army Chief of Staff Gen. Matthew Ridgway. Before he was named to his post in the clean sweep of 1953, Ridgway had been carefully vetted by the administration on his willingness to abide by civilian direction. He was, however, still a military professional and felt it his duty, first and foremost, to promote the security of the nation. As chief of staff for the nation's principal ground arm, the pressure upon Ridgway was intense. The army had the most to lose of all the services in the implementation of the New Look, and the general was concerned, alarmed even, at the depths of the cuts that Eisenhower desired.

The president's fiscal year 1956 budget was especially disturbing to believers in large U.S. ground forces, as it proposed to reduce the army to just over 1 million troops by the summer of 1956. This represented a substantial decrease from the levels of only two years before, when the army had 1.17 million personnel in uniform. Asked at a congressional hearing on January 31, 1955, whether the proposed cut affected the "safety of the country," Ridgway replied, "I think it does, sir" (**Document 3.9**). Ridgway went on to testify that the proposed reduction in force levels had not been cleared by the JCS.

President Eisenhower replied to Ridgway at a press conference a few days later (**Document 3.10**). Eisenhower suggested that while the general was entitled to his opinion, as the chief of a military service he necessarily suffered the limitation of a "parochial" vantage point from which to comment on such matters. Moreover, with regard to the charge that he had ignored the advice of his chiefs, the president remarked that he had not failed to hear them—he simply did not agree with them. He stated, "I know exactly who agrees with me and who doesn't and now they are entitled to their opinions, but I have to make the decisions."

The consequence was another reshuffling of the JCS. The president ousted Ridgway at the close of his first two-year tour and replaced him with Gen. Maxwell Taylor. In a parting shot at his commander in chief, Ridgway wrote a farewell, ostensibly addressed to the secretary of defense, which was published in the *New York Times*. In that letter, Ridgway deplored the controversial reductions in force and challenged the assertion that he had only a parochial view of defense matters. "Present United States military forces cannot support fully American diplomacy," the general asserted. To fulfill its many promises to come to the aid of nations when threatened by Communist encroachment, the United States was in need of military power "real and apparent to all concerned, and . . . capable of being applied promptly, selectively and with the degree of violence appropriate to the occasion." What the United States had instead was a nuclear arsenal soon to be matched by the Soviet Union and "military detachments which are not mutually supporting, which have little or no strategic mobility or their own, and which are difficult to reinforce because of the lack of truly mobile and adequate military reserves."[25]

Congressional Relations

The Republican Party majorities in the House and Senate that greeted Eisenhower upon first coming to office were short-lived, expiring after the midterm elections of 1954. He could not, in any event, have governed even for those first two years merely by rallying "his" party. The Republicans, like the Democrats, were not ideologically uniform in the 1950s, making bipartisanship a necessity. Republicans, in addition, were by habit as well as inclination skeptical of executive power. They had no intention of relinquishing their skepticism just because Dwight Eisenhower was president. President Eisenhower after all, had come to the party late, after a highly political but nonpartisan career in the armed services. Merely keeping the Republicans on Capitol Hill from breaking openly with his administration was a challenge for the president.

One of the first instances of this difficulty revolved around Sen. John W. Bricker, a Republican from Ohio first elected in the immediate postwar elections of 1946. From 1951 until he lost his seat after the elections of 1958, Bricker crusaded against the expansion of executive power and U.S. entanglement in world affairs. In what became a ritual, the senator proposed each year a constitutional amendment to prohibit the negotiation of treaties that abridged constitutional rights or freedoms of Americans (**Document 3.11**). Like many members of his party, Bricker believed that this was precisely what President Franklin Roosevelt had done in his negotiations at Yalta and in the establishment of the United Nations. Senator Bricker's particular fear (shared by the United States Chamber of Commerce and the American Medical Association) was that the UN might proclaim rights of humanity that would force the United States, and all other member nations, to implement socialist governments.

The president deplored Bricker's amendment privately and thought the senator "almost psychopathic" on the subject. Bricker's amendment, Eisenhower believed, would tie the president's hands in foreign policy and force the nation back toward isolationism. Nevertheless, he and members of his Cabinet sang the senator's praises as a well-meaning patriot.[26] Finally, the president was forced by the momentum that the amendment had acquired within a Republican-controlled Congress to state his opposition publicly, though not plainly. Bricker's amendment, "as analyzed for me by the secretary of state," Eisenhower said in 1953, would have negative implications for the conduct of diplomacy.[27] In part because the president had still not made plain his personal opposition, the amendment resurfaced the next year and gained such support that the president at last expressed himself without subterfuge. He was, he stated, "unalterably opposed" to the amendment's passage. With the president's prestige on the line, the administration held onto just enough votes to block the amendment's progress.

Sen. Joseph McCarthy, R-Wis., gave the White House even more grief. McCarthy was extremely popular, especially though hardly exclusively among Republicans. Reelected to the senate in the same year as Eisenhower first won the White House, he was rewarded by his colleagues with chairmanship of the Permanent Investigations Subcommittee of the Senate Government Operations Committee.

McCarthy, who had bedeviled President Truman, quickly signaled that he had no intention of toning down his rhetoric for Eisenhower's sake. His first target within the Eisenhower circle was Charles Bohlen, who had advised President Roosevelt on the Soviet Union and whom Eisenhower wished to appoint ambassador to the Soviet Union. Though Bohlen had tried to warn Roosevelt not to place too much faith in Stalin, he had been at Yalta when, as the Republicans saw it, Roosevelt had given away Eastern Europe to the Russian dictator. That was enough for Senator McCarthy. Eisenhower's secretary of state, John Foster Dulles, was forced in Senate testimony to promise virtually to exclude Bohlen from policymaking in exchange for his confirmation.

Ironically, Eisenhower, like Truman before him, agreed with the Wisconsin senator on the urgent need to ferret subversives out of the government. Eisenhower continued

Truman's executive loyalty program, although he decentralized its administration. But McCarthy, Eisenhower knew, was hunting not so much Communists as publicity. "Senator McCarthy is, of course, so anxious for the headlines," the president recorded in his diary on April 1, 1953, "that he is prepared to go to any extremes in order to secure some mention of his name in the public press." To confront him directly, Eisenhower concluded, would only reward him. "I really believe that nothing will be so effective in combating his particular kind of troublemaking as to ignore him. This he cannot stand."[28] Eisenhower refused to be drawn into debate with the senator, even at the expense of seeming to be intimidated.

Privately, the president worked through his press secretary, James Hagerty, to use the media to discredit McCarthy. Hagerty and members of the congressional leadership, including Democratic Minority Leader Lyndon Johnson, stage managed the congressional hearings that brought McCarthy down. Eisenhower and Johnson both realized that the public might well have second thoughts about McCarthy if they ever got a close look at him in action. The result was the Army-McCarthy hearings, the McCarthy subcommittee's investigation into alleged subversion within the highly regarded U.S. Army, carried live on the ABC and Dumont networks from April 22 to June 17, 1954. McCarthy's bullying behavior, relayed live to millions of viewers in 188 hours of broadcast time, laid the foundation for a bipartisan censure vote in the Senate, which passed 67-22, on December 2.[29] The senator had outlived his usefulness, even to his own party. McCarthy guessed who was ultimately behind his downfall, but nobody paid much attention when he lashed out at President Eisenhower. The president's "hidden hand" strategy had worked, once again.

The Arms Race

When Eisenhower entered the White House, the United States possessed clear superiority in nuclear arms. The Americans had detonated the world's first hydrogen bomb (H-bomb), or fusion-powered nuclear weapon, just before the presidential election of 1952. Although the Soviets followed with their own tests within a year, the United States had a clear edge in the technology required not only to develop but to deliver such weapons. This was important because the H-bomb was exponentially more powerful than the atomic bombs that the United States had used against Japan in 1945. Another feature of the new weapon that demanded attention was that there was no theoretical limit to its size or power. The finite weight that could be either carried or projected into space was the only limit on the size or power of the H-bomb.

With H-bombs in the arsenals of the superpowers, President Eisenhower decided that the public should be informed about the new weapons and what an arms race for thermonuclear advantage would entail. This went against the general grain of Eisenhower's approach to public relations in the Cold War, as the news was meant to incite rather than to calm fears. If it was fear-mongering, though, it was fear-mongering in the service of disarmament. Keeping the peace through the threat of massive retaliation with nuclear bombs was, after all, a pretty frightening prospect, even if it was meant to be a corrective to the more fearful policy of arming to the teeth for a year of maximum of danger. How much better, the president reasoned, it would be simply to make peace and to employ atomic power for civilian purposes.

Consequently, in a speech before the UN on December 8, 1953, the president spoke in unusually open terms about the magnitude and capabilities of the American nuclear arsenal (**Document 3.12**). Since the day that the United States first detonated an atomic weapon, the president stated, atomic weaponry "has moved forward at such a pace that every citizen of the world should have some comprehension . . . of the extent of its development." Mere atomic bombs, the president noted, are twenty-five times as powerful as they once were, while "hydrogen weapons are in the ranges of millions of tons of TNT equivalent." He explained, "A single air group whether afloat or land-based, can now deliver to any reachable target a destructive cargo exceeding in power all the bombs that fell on Britain in all of World War II." Within the U.S. armed forces, every branch "is capable of putting this weapon to military use." The only sane response to the continuing growth of the arms race, Eisenhower intimated, is to demand that it stop. As a first step, the president proposed an "Atoms for Peace" diversion program. The Soviets should join with the United States in diverting some portion of its nuclear material to civilian purposes. The proposed International Atomic Energy Agency (IAEA) would create a "uranium bank" for the collection and distribution of fissile material.

At the UN, Communist and Western delegates all joined in the applause, while the Gallup Poll showed a ten-point boost in the president's approval rating among American adults. But was Eisenhower serious? The Soviets thought not, and they rejected his proposal promptly. Eisenhower himself confessed in his diary that even if the Soviets surprised Cold War skeptics and accepted the offer, the diversion of nuclear material to civilian purposes would come at a greater price to their weaponry program than to that of the Americans (**Document 3.13**). As it happened, the race continued and the number of nuclear weapons in the U.S. arsenal alone increased from 1,000 to 23,000 over the course of Eisenhower's presidency.

Although the arms race accelerated, there continued through the Eisenhower years to be efforts at entering into a sustained dialogue on arms limitation. At Geneva in 1955, the heads of state of the United States, the Soviet Union, the United Kingdom, and France met for the first time since the World War II. Their agenda included, among other topics, the arms race. The Soviets had done their part to make the meeting possible when they relented in their prior demand that disarmament begin with the abolition of all nuclear weapons; the Soviets, with their smaller nuclear arsenals and their advantage in conventional forces in Europe, had relatively little to lose and much to gain from such a process.

Eisenhower ignored Secretary of State Dulles's advice not to smile when meeting with the Soviets and focused his efforts on the establishment of personal trust. He also sought a breakthrough (and headlines) by proposing "Open Skies." The two sides would, under this plan, actually help each other spy on their military capabilities. They would begin by exchanging maps of their countries, indicating the location of military installations and assets. Nikita Khrushchev, head of the Soviet Communist Party but not yet the undisputed executive of the Soviet state, rejected the idea out of hand as a "transparent espionage device."[30] Nevertheless, all sides agreed to continue discussions aimed at the limitation or at least control of nuclear weapons and even such goals as the reunification of Germany.

As a result, the "Spirit of Geneva" was hailed worldwide and led to the first American-Soviet summit of the Cold War, when Khrushchev visited the United States in September 1959.

SECOND TERM DÉJÀ VU

In the era of the New Look, vigilance truly was the price of liberty. Deterrence by the threat of massive retaliation invited the United States' adversaries to test American resolve again and again. The first such test of Eisenhower's second term came, once more, in the Taiwan Straits.

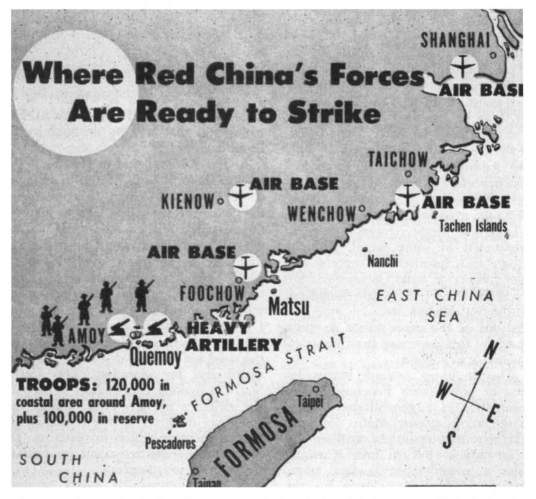

This image from an April 15, 1955, story in *U.S. News* depicts China's troop positions during the first Taiwan Straits Crisis, in which the United States supported Taiwan (Formosa) and its fortification of the islands of Quemoy and Matsu, while the Soviet Union supported mainland China. Both superpowers had to decide to what lengths they would go to defend their allies. *Source: U.S. News,* April 15, 1955, 23.

The Second Taiwan Straits Crisis

In the summer of 1958, the Communist PRC resumed shelling Taiwanese troops on the islands of Quemoy and Matsu. This time, Communist China also established a naval blockade to interdict supply service to the islands. Since the truce of four years before, the Western-allied ROC now had almost 100,000 soldiers on the islands, an increase of roughly 100 percent, enhancing the threat of invasion to the mainland.

President Eisenhower met this crisis in much the same way as he had resolved the earlier one. First, he perceived these events as a premeditated test of Western will. Second, the administration analyzed the threat to Taiwan in terms of the domino theory. If Quemoy and Matsu were to fall, the failure of American resolve to protect them would encourage the Communist enemy, who would seek progressively more territory.

On the basis of this analysis, the president gave a repeat performance of the brinkmanship that had ended the first crisis over the same groups of islands. U.S. naval destroyers were ordered to escort Taiwanese merchant vessels past the blockade. If the Chinese had fired on one of the American vessels, the United States and Communist China, which was closely allied at the time with the Soviet Union, would have been at war. Fortunately, the Chinese did not put Eisenhower's threat to the test and offered to stop shelling the islands in return for the cessation of American naval escorts. After the president made a vague and complex threat at a press conference on October 1, 1958, all sides backed off from provocative acts; however, to preserve its honor the PRC at first insisted on the right to fire artillery shells at the islands every other day, causing the president to wonder aloud whether he was caught in a "Gilbert and Sullivan war."[31]

The Middle East

In Eisenhower's second term, the superpowers moved into the power vacuum created in the Middle East by the humiliation of the French and British at the Suez Canal. Concerned by the gains that the other side seemed to be making, the president requested congressional passage of a resolution granting him authority to use force in the region to protect American interests. The former general wanted, cried Sen. Hubert Humphrey, D-Minn., a "predated declaration of war."[32] The critics, however, were greatly outnumbered, as most members agreed with Georgia Democratic senator Richard Russell's observation that there existed a "shadowland between the President's authority to use Armed Forces and the necessity for a declaration of war."[33] Even Senator Bricker supported what came to be known as the Eisenhower Doctrine (**Document 3.14**).

The first test of the doctrine came in the kingdom of Jordan in the spring of 1957. The regime of the pro-Western monarch of Jordan, King Hussein, was threatened by domestic unrest following his dismissal of a Nasserite prime minister and the declaration of martial law. President Eisenhower threatened the use of force against Hussein's enemies within the state (who were spurred on daily by Radio Cairo to commit regicide), ordered units of the Sixth Fleet into the eastern Mediterranean, and granted Hussein emergency economic aid in order to stabilize his rule.

The fullest use of the Eisenhower Doctrine came in Lebanon the next year. Lebanon's Maronite Christian president, Camille Chamoun, was openly supportive of the Eisenhower

Doctrine. With the United States seemingly standing behind him, Chamoun overreached in 1958 when he sought to run for an unprecedented second term as chief executive. The Lebanese constitution carefully divided power among the state's religious groups and prescribed rotation in office as a safeguard against any one faction gaining a preponderance of power. Chamoun's unbridled display of ambition provoked an uprising among Lebanese Muslims. Chamoun blamed not himself but Egypt and Syria for inciting the unrest, and he called for American help in May.

The U.S. response was at first cautious, as Chamoun's allegation of outside interference was supported by scant evidence. On July 14, however, the pro-Western king of Iraq and his premier were overthrown by a coup which brought a socialist government to power. President Eisenhower immediately responded to what he now saw as a "crisis of formidable proportions." On July 15, a force of 10,000 U.S. Marines came ashore in Lebanon and established a temporary garrison until a new president could be elected and installed in office. As for the Soviets, they opted to stay out of this fight, even though Egyptian leader Gamal Abdel Nasser personally lobbied Khrushchev in Moscow for help.

Conflict over Budgets and Strategy

President Eisenhower, looking ahead to his second term, entered the following resolution in his diary: "During my [second] term of office, unless there is some technical or political development that I do not foresee—or a marked inflationary trend in the economy (which I will battle to the death)—I will not approve any obligational or expenditure authorities for the Defense Department that exceed something on the order of $38.5 billion mark." [34] The president would have difficulty keeping his resolution.

The 1950s, on the whole, were a time of remarkable economic growth for the United States, but not all years were equally good. In 1957 the economy wavered. As it did so, the president became engaged in an embarrassing conflict over his fiscal year 1958 budget requests. This time, ironically, the majority sentiment in Congress seemed to be that the president had asked for too much. His budget, though balanced, would set a record for "peacetime" spending. It was not so much the budget itself, however, as the politics of its presentation that harmed the president.

On January 16, 1957, the very day that the president's first post-reelection budget was delivered to Congress, Treasury Secretary George Humphrey warned of a "depression that will curl your hair" if the budget's alleged big-spending ways were not curbed. [35] The budget reflected the priorities of what the president and others termed "modern republicanism." There were moderate planned increases for defense spending and foreign aid, as well as aid for school construction and social welfare programs. Further tax cuts, a priority of the Old Guard, would have to wait.

In an attempt to downplay his cabinet member's insubordination, the president made it seem as if he too were opposed to the Eisenhower budget. At a press conference just two days after his second inauguration, Eisenhower explained, "As the process of appropriating this money goes on everybody that is examining the many details—and any of you that have looked at a budget know how many details are in it, there are literally thousands and thousands—anybody that is examining that seriously ought to find some place where he might save another dollar." He continued, "So with the thought behind the Secretary's statements I am in complete agreement."[36]

If the secretary of the Treasury *and* the president did not favor the administration's spending program, just who was in control at the White House? During the early months of 1957, the executive departments were required to forward lists of further cuts in their programs. Democrats at first suspected the president of a clever conspiracy of some kind, while departmental staffs at the Pentagon and elsewhere "felt themselves the victims of a backstairs *coup*."[37] The president, shifting rhetorically "back and forth between defense of his budget and good words for the economizers" lost control of the budget process altogether.[38] The only good news for the president was that this fiasco had transpired in a climate of budget-busting. The end result, a smaller budget, was in line with the president's primary directive: to keep the country going down a middle path of a sensible defense, supported by sustainable spending.

Just two years later, the mood of Congress and significant elements of the public had changed. Eisenhower still felt he had to guard the Treasury as he had during his first year in office. But by 1959 there was a $10 billion difference between what the president wished to propose for defense ($40 billion) and what the military and civilian leaders of the Department of Defense, as well as their supporters on Capitol Hill, desired. These advocates for an expanded defense program were joined by the Atomic Energy Commission, panels of civilian experts on defense, and major commentators on national security, both civilians and recently retired officers, all of whom wanted more weapons, more personnel, and more spending. There was even considerable enthusiasm building among national security experts for space exploration, which the president thought on the whole an enormous waste. President Eisenhower still believed, as he told his cabinet, that "the Communist objective is to make us spend ourselves into bankruptcy."[39] With a presidential election nearing, Democrats adopted the theme that the president's mania for savings, not the hypothetical bankruptcy that the president feared, was endangering the nation.

The president's second-term critics also pressed him on strategy. The New Look deemphasized conventional forces, creating doubt as to the purpose of American troops deployed abroad. Were they mere "tripwires," or were they expected to provide a credible force for defense in their own right? The issue became urgent as the American nuclear advantage declined during the course of Eisenhower's second term. As the Cold War rivalry moved toward parity in nuclear weapons—some presumed experts even said that the Soviets had overtaken the United States. Could the United States still rely on the threat of massive retaliation? If massive retaliation was obsolete, what should replace it as a doctrine of U.S. nuclear strategy?

Critics of the New Look, including retired general Matthew Ridgway, who wrote and made speeches on the topic, called for a more flexible U.S. defense policy. What Ridgway envisioned was a strategy that would give a president a full range of options to fight a full range of possible wars, from a guerrilla insurgency to a full-scale nuclear exchange. Eisenhower remained reluctant to entertain even the possibility of putting U.S. forces back into a limited war, such as Korea had been; as for the possibility of the exchange of nuclear weapons, he termed that idea "race suicide." Ridgway, however, was part of a whole new group of defense professionals, many of them civilians, who challenged such assumptions. They wanted the United States to reconfigure a portion of its forces to take on the challenge of small wars and spoke of nuclear exchange in the novel terms of nuclear *warfighting*.

Some of these ideas were acted upon in Eisenhower's second term, even though the president himself was skeptical of their merit. In the army, the "pentomic division" was introduced. Its objective was to enhance maneuverability, dispersion, and survivability on a nuclear battlefield. All army divisions, in addition, were equipped with tactical nuclear weapons during the Eisenhower presidency. Still, for those who watched the bottom line, it seemed like little more than a shell game. The overall quantities by which army forces are typically measured were still in decline. The U.S. Army, composed of more than 1.5 million personnel in 1953, had fewer than 1 million personnel in 1958 and had decreased from twenty combat divisions to fifteen. In 1953 the defense budget was $34 billion. In 1958 it had climbed only to $41 billion, not far off the mark that Eisenhower had resolved to observe. But of that $41 billion, the army's share was just $9 billion, considerably less than when Eisenhower took office.

THE SHOCK OF THE NEW

The 1950s were years of rapid technological change. One area of technology that was integral to the Cold War was that for the delivery of nuclear warheads. The United States started the Cold War with a significant advantage in heavy bombers capable of carrying nuclear payloads over intercontinental distances. But the future belonged to missiles, including intermediate range ballistic missiles (IRBMs) and intercontinental ballistic missiles (ICBMs). The Eisenhower administration gave priority to the development of IRBMs, permitting each of the armed services to develop its own such missile. The army and air force deployed, respectively, the Thor and Jupiter missiles in late 1957, while the navy continued work on its submarine-launched ballistic missile (SLBM), the Polaris. Thor and Jupiter missiles could reach targets at distances as great as 1,500 miles.

In the ICBM field, the United States similarly had a multiplicity of efforts underway during Eisenhower's presidency, none of them yet successful when on August 26, 1957, the Soviets launched their first ICBM. Shortly after that milestone, on October 4, 1957, the Soviets employed an ICBM to launch into orbit the first manmade satellite, Sputnik. Sputnik was not only first, it was heavy. Its 184-pound weight led the CIA to conclude that the Soviet Union was now capable of launching a two-megaton warhead at a target as far as 5,000 miles away. American experts further believed that the Soviets could have approximately a dozen ICBMs with these capabilities operational by the end of 1958.

The president tried at first to downplay the event. Golfing when the news broke, the president saw no reason to cut short his game. At the White House, the press secretary even told reporters, "We never thought of our program as one which was in a race with the Soviets."[40] Few Americans were so sanguine. The editors of the *New Republic* compared the Russian success to that of the voyage of Columbus. Sen. Stuart Symington, a

Democrat from Truman's home state of Missouri, demanded that Eisenhower call Congress into special session to address the event, while Sen. Richard Russell, D-Ga., observed darkly that "We now know beyond a doubt that the Russians have the ultimate weapon." In the popular press, the launch of the Russian satellite was compared frequently to the surprise attack by the Japanese at Pearl Harbor. Many Americans blamed not just the president and the government, but the entire "age" in American life. Sen. Henry Styles Bridges, R-N.H., lamented that "[t]he time has clearly come to be less concerned with . . . the height of the fin on the car and to be more prepared to shed blood, sweat and tears if this country and the Free World are to survive." [41]

The president at first faltered in response. In his first public appearance after the Soviet launch, he seemed, in the words of a historian of the American response to Sputnik, "unsure and unclear of what the Russian satellite signified." [42] Shortly afterward, he sought, typically, a compromise authorizing the secretary of defense to seek funds above and beyond the previously set $38 billion dollar ceiling for defense spending—but not nearly so far above and beyond as his critics desired. The president also hastened as much as possible the launch of a comparable American product. An effort to rush the launch of a small American satellite via the navy's experimental Vanguard rocket failed dramatically in December, but on the last day of January 1958, the U.S. Army's rocketry program, under the direction of the legendary rocket scientist Werner von Braun, launched a Jupiter C rocket carrying a thirty-one pound satellite dubbed "Explorer."

At the same time, however, the president rejected recommendations from a committee that he had formed to examine defense issues before the Sputnik surprise. The Gaither Committee (named for its chairman, H. Rowan Gaither, who was the head of the Ford Foundation) had been granted considerable autonomy by the president. The committee repaid the president by going well beyond its charge to raise concerns about fundamental principles of Eisenhower's defense policy. The committee warned that the United States was not adequately prepared for a possible Soviet attack and recommended a significant increase in U.S. military spending, an expansion of civil defense, and an increase in the U.S. missile arsenal. The president coolly received the report at a meeting of the NSC on November 7. The committee chairman was disappointed that even the public reaction to Sputnik could not move Eisenhower to embrace a plan for a $40 billion defense budget. The president did, however, embrace the committee's recommendations for a reform of the Defense Department and the JCS.

The obvious duplication in the military's missile development programs had almost certainly helped the Soviets gain the edge in launching the first satellite. While the Americans had been wasting time and effort among redundant programs, the Soviets had been focused on a single missile design. This realization spurred congressional and public interest in defense reform. Changes in the defense establishment that eventually made it into law in the Defense Reorganization Act of 1958 included a transfer of authority from interagency commissions such as the Office of Defense Mobilization to the president, who in turn vested more power in the Office of the Secretary of Defense (OSD). As a consequence of this change in law, OSD at long last gained the ability to coordinate and rationalize weapons acquisition plans, formerly jealously guarded by the individual branches of the armed forces.

Two other significant innovations in the defense field in 1958 were the creation of the (Defense) Advanced Research Projects Agency (ARPA, also commonly known as DARPA), and the National Aeronautics and Space Administration (NASA). ARPA's creation was announced by Neil McElroy, Eisenhower's second secretary of defense, in testimony before the House Armed Services Committee on January 13, 1958. "Such long range programs as the antimissile missile and the military satellite programs," he stated, "are in the research and exploratory development stages. . . . To handle them, I am establishing within the Department of Defense an Advanced Research Projects Agency."[43] The president included $350 million for ARPA in his budget for fiscal year 1959. The agency proved to be greatly useful, as it catalyzed the development of dual-use technologies, including the Internet.

The legal authority for NASA was established when the president signed into law on July 29, 1958, the National Aeronautics and Space Act of 1958. The nucleus for the new agency was the existent National Advisory Committee for Aeronautics (NACA). Significantly, NASA, like NACA, was a civilian agency. The president intended for space exploration to be conducted outside the framework of the military competition of the Cold War.

When the president was challenged by his military chiefs on these reforms, he pulled rank. "I don't care who is against this thing," he said at one point in the debate. "It just happens I have got a little bit more experience in military organization and the directing of unified forces than anyone else on the active list."[44] To overcome congressional reluctance to tinker with the defense establishment, the administration even took the highly unusual step of orchestrating a letter-writing campaign among the nation's leading business executives, including some who had benefited greatly under the old system. Sputnik had brought the nation together, allowing the president to achieve more than he otherwise would likely have been able to in a long-sought reorganization of the Pentagon.

THE ARMS RACE AND THE SINO-SOVIET SPLIT

Shortly after the launch of Sputnik, Democrats in Congress, led by a young senator from Massachusetts named John F. Kennedy, began to decry a "missile gap" with the Soviets. Many others worried also about an apparent "bomber gap." This, it seemed, would be a good time for the United States to rethink its approach to the arms race, either by attempting to slow the pace of work on both sides or by speeding up the American response to recent Soviet gains.

President Eisenhower, naturally, favored the former course of action, beginning with a ban on further testing of nuclear weapons, which had been discussed in defense and diplomatic circles for years. To advance the cause of a test ban, Eisenhower proposed in January 1958 to meet with his Soviet counterpart after meetings of foreign ministers had been completed. After a series of diplomatic moves, the two sides reached agreement in principle on a ban against new atmospheric testing and agreed to an exchange of visits by their heads of state. Khrushchev, as long anticipated, would come first to the United

States. Afterward, the American president would travel to the Soviet Union. In preparation, American vice president Richard Nixon in July 1959 met with the Soviet leader in Europe, where the two engaged in the famous "kitchen debate" (**Document 3.15**).

The Soviet premier made his historic visit to the United States in September 1959. The media coverage—incessant and on the whole positive—encouraged the president. Eisenhower believed that such exchanges built trust, and he began to look forward to returning Khrushchev's visit. In May 1960, according to the plans agreed to by both parties, Eisenhower and Khrushchev would go first to Paris, where they would hold a joint summit with the United States' major Western allies. Afterward, the president would travel to Moscow. In anticipation, President Eisenhower proposed early in 1960 to extend the scope of the proposed nuclear test ban to include not only atmospheric testing but oceanic and space testing as well. The Soviets countered by proposing also to include underground testing in the treaty, which was a highly controversial move because of scientific uncertainty about detecting underground blasts.

In the weeks before Paris, then, the administration worked in an atmosphere that mixed optimism with caution. To ensure that the American side could take into its meetings the best available information on the Soviet arsenal, the president agreed two weeks before the joint summit to just one more fly-over of the Soviet Union by the United States' secret spy plane, the U-2. Eisenhower personally gave his okay for a flight on May 1. Later that day, Eisenhower's military liaison, Gen. Andrew Goodpaster, telephoned the president to say that the plane had been reported missing. Two days later, a NASA spokesperson issued a preestablished cover story, indicating that a weather plane operated by NASA had been lost on a routine flight over Turkey (**Document 3.16**). The White House issued a release at about the same time, stating that the president had ordered an inquiry into the event.

The cover story held until May 7, when Premier Khrushchev made a surprise speech in which he revealed that the Soviets had recovered fragments of a spy plane on Soviet soil and the pilot as well, whom he reported to be "alive and kicking."[45] This was quite a revelation, because the president had been told that the pilot could not have survived a U-2 crash. Pilot Gary Powers had, however, survived. He had also chosen to live rather than take his own life before capture, a choice for which some Americans criticized him. As a result, the U.S. State Department was forced to acknowledge that it was indeed a spy plane flying over the Soviet Union that had gone down on May 1, although the State Department denied that the plane's flight had been approved in Washington, much less by the president himself (**Document 3.17**).

It might have been possible for President Eisenhower to maintain plausible deniability of his involvement in the U-2 mission, but on May 11 he came clean nonetheless in a terse statement accepting responsibility and affirming his belief that the spy flight had been a necessary endeavor (**Document 3.18**). At the Paris summit, the president refused to discuss the matter further, and the Soviet premier brought the meeting to an abrupt close, just three hours after its start, with a tirade against American duplicity and an unmet demand for an apology.

In retrospect, it appears that Khrushchev may have been motivated in this diplomatic maneuver not so much by his concern over the ostensible issue but out of concern, once again, for the Soviet Union's troubled relationship with China. In April 1960 Chairman Mao had launched "Maoism," the doctrine of achieving Communist revolution through the imitation of the example of Chairman Mao, in a bid for Chinese leadership of the Communist world. At the same time, Mao began to speak loosely of the acceptability—even desirability—of general war with the West, and publicly condemned as "revisionism" Khrushchev's notion of the peaceful spread of socialism.[46]

Khrushchev's goal at Paris may have been to upstage his Chinese rival by a show of belligerence against their common adversary. Afterward, when Mao continued his attack upon Khrushchev, the two exchanged bitter denunciations. In reply to Mao's bellicosity, Khrushchev stated that "only madmen and maniacs can now call for another world war," and ordered the withdrawal from the PRC of the Soviet Union's military and scientific advisers and halted its assistance to Chinese industrial projects, particularly the development of a Chinese nuclear arsenal.[47]

CONCLUSION

When he left office, Americans still "liked Ike." A majority of them, in fact, approved of the way he was handling his presidency every year he was in office. (That is, the results from polls taken throughout every year averaged over 50 percent support.) His popular support as president was both broad and deep, but contemporary academic and intellectual commentators were not so sure about him. They tended to downgrade Eisenhower's accomplishments and to support the orthodox liberal critique of his administration and the entire decade as a time of conformity and lassitude. Since the 1980s, however, experts have come to a greater appreciation of Eisenhower's achievements—so much so that there has now been a revision to the revision in the literature, leaving us not back where we started, but at a point where it is possible to acknowledge both the positive and negative attributes of Eisenhower as president.

"Long faces don't win wars," Eisenhower repeatedly told his cabinet.[48] To prevail in the Cold War, Eisenhower felt he needed to project just the right image: not scared, but concerned; not hostile, but resolute. By holding the line against fear and hostility, the president felt he could hold the line against the twin dangers of Communist encroachment abroad and a garrison state at home. To contain Communists abroad, the president relied heavily upon repeated threats, or bluffs. In this way he kept peace with the Soviets and Chinese.

More negatively, one can say that Eisenhower succeeded merely in pushing the United States into future major conflicts, especially in Asia. The president's public legacy in Vietnam was replete with tough-talking statements about the necessity of avoiding Communist victory. It would not help his successors at all that he had prevented the introduction of American troops or planes into combat there, because he had achieved this by sleight of hand. Lastly, by leaving his successor with an ill-conceived plan for the invasion of Cuba, complete with a paramilitary force of Cuban exiles, Eisenhower virtually guaranteed that whoever followed him would confront a Cold War crisis in his first months in office.

What troubled Eisenhower when he left office, however, was whether the nation could continue to maintain its resolve, without giving way to panic. Too many Americans, the president believed, were doubting themselves and their country, openly asking and secretly wondering whether in some way "they" were in fact better than "us." Such anxiety is precisely what Eisenhower had struggled to overcome. He returned to the theme in his famous Farewell Address (**Document 3.19**), in which he spoke darkly of the threat to the nation from the growing "military-industrial complex," which lived off the fear of the people. It would be up to the next president to deal with this new threat, as well as all the other problems unresolved in the eight years of Eisenhower's presidency.

NOTES

1. "Text of General Eisenhower's Address to the American Legion Convention," *New York Times,* August 26, 1952.
2. Dwight D. Eisenhower, "Annual Message to Congress on the State of the Union," February 2, 1953, in *Public Papers of the Presidents of the United States: Dwight D. Eisenhower, 1953–1961,* from the American Presidency Project, University of California, Santa Barbara, www.presidency.ucsb.edu.
3. Dwight D. Eisenhower, *The Eisenhower Diaries,* ed. Robert H. Ferrell (New York: W. W. Norton, 1981), 234, 243–45.
4. Dale R. Herspring, *The Pentagon and the Presidency: Civil-Military Relations from FDR to George W. Bush* (Lawrence: University Press of Kansas, 2005), 90.
5. Dwight D. Eisenhower, "Inaugural Address," January 20, 1953, in *Public Papers of the Presidents of the United States: Dwight D. Eisenhower, 1953–1961,* from the American Presidency Project, University of California, Santa Barbara, www.presidency.ucsb.edu.
6. Dwight D. Eisenhower, *Mandate for Change, 1953–1956: The White House Years* (Garden City, N.Y.: Doubleday, 1963), 181.
7. Stephen E. Ambrose, *Eisenhower* (New York: Simon and Schuster, 1983), 331.
8. Political scientist Harold Lasswell popularized the term. See his *National Security and Individual Freedom* (New York: McGraw-Hill, 1950).
9. "The President's News Conference," March 17, 1954, in *Public Papers of the Presidents of the United States: Dwight D. Eisenhower, 1953–1961,* from the American Presidency Project, University of California Santa Barbara, www.presidency.ucsb.edu.
10. Robert R. Bowie and Richard H. Immerman, *Waging Peace: How Eisenhower Shaped an Enduring Cold War Strategy* (New York: Oxford University Press, 1998), 42–45.
11. Ambrose, *Eisenhower,* 362–363.
12. "The President's News Conference," March 16, 1955, in *Public Papers of the Presidents of the United States: Dwight D. Eisenhower, 1953–1961,* from the American Presidency Project, University of California, Santa Barbara, www.presidency.ucsb.edu.
13. Jun Chang and Jon Halliday, *Mao: The Unknown Story* (New York: Knopf, 2005), 396, 397.
14. Ambrose, *Eisenhower,* 377.
15. Christopher J. Pach and Elmo Richardson, *The Presidency of Dwight D. Eisenhower,* rev. ed. (Lawrence: University Press of Kansas, 1991), 88.
16. Ibid., 90.
17. Ibid., 133.
18. Daniel J. Yergin, *The Prize: The Epic Quest for Oil, Money and Power* (New York: Free Press, 1993), ch. 24.
19. Ambrose, *Eisenhower,* 431.
20. "Republican Party Platform of 1952," from the American Presidency Project, University of California, Santa Barbara, available online at www.presidency.ucsb.edu.

21. Saki Dockrill, *Eisenhower's New Look National Security Policy, 1953–61* (New York: St. Martin's Press, 1996), 161.

22. Dwight D. Eisenhower, "Second Inaugural Address," January 21, 1957, in *Public Papers of the Presidents of the United States: Dwight D. Eisenhower, 1953–1961,* from the American Presidency Project, University of California, Santa Barbara, www.presidency.ucsb.edu.

23. "Memorandum of Discussion at the 138th Meeting of the National Security Council, Wednesday, March 25, 1953," in United States Department of State, *Foreign Relations of the United States, 1952–1954,* William Z. Slany, ed., vol. 2, *National Security Affairs* (in two parts), part 1 (Washington, D.C.: U.S. Government Printing Office, 1984), 259.

24. Ibid., 260.

25. Anthony Ceriero, "Ridgway Assails U.S. Policy Stress on Air and Atom; Sees Soviet Peril" *New York Times,* July 15, 1955.

26. Eisenhower, *Eisenhower Diaries,* 233.

27. Pach and Richardson, *Presidency of Dwight D. Eisenhower,* 61.

28. Eisenhower, *Eisenhower Diaries,* 233–234.

29. Thomas Doherty, "The Army-McCarthy Hearings," in *The Encyclopedia of Television,* ed. Horace Newcomb (New York: Taylor and Francis, 1997), from the Museum of Broadcast Communications, www.museum.tv/archives/etv/A/htmlA/army-mccarthy/army-mccarthy.htm.

30. Robert A. Divine, *Eisenhower and the Cold War* (New York: Oxford University Press, 1981), 121.

31. Stephen Ambrose, *Eisenhower,* vol. 2, *The President* (New York: Simon and Schuster, 1984), 485.

32. Pach and Richardson, *Presidency of Dwight D. Eisenhower,* 161.

33. Ibid.

34. Eisenhower, *Eisenhower Diaries,* 337. Undated entry, probably late December 1956.

35. "Secretary Warns Outlays and Taxes Must Decrease; Defends Budget but Believes It Can Be Trimmed—Says He Opposes Several Programs—Fears Incurring Deficits," *New York Times,* January 17, 1957.

36. "The President's News Conference," January 23, 1957, in *Public Papers of the Presidents of the United States: Dwight D. Eisenhower, 1953–1961,* from the American Presidency Project, University of California, Santa Barbara, www.presidency.ucsb.edu.

37. Richard P. Neustadt, *Presidential Power: The Politics of Leadership* (New York: John Wiley and Sons, 1960), 69.

38. Ibid., 70.

39. Ambrose, *Eisenhower,* 484.

40. Robert A. Divine, *The Sputnik Challenge* (New York: Oxford University Press, 1993), xiv.

41. Ibid., xvi.

42. Ibid., 8.

43. Eugene M. Emme, comp., *Aeronautics and Astronautics: An American Chronology of Science and Technology in the Exploration of Space, 1915–1960* (Washington, D.C.: NASA, 1961), 94–105, in National Aeronautics and Space Administration, "Aeronautics and Astronautics Chronology, 1958," www.hq.nasa.gov/office/pao/History/Timeline/1958.html.

44. Divine, *Sputnik Challenge,* 132.

45. *Current Digest of the Soviet Press,* June 8, 1960, 3–7.

46. Chang and Halliday, *Mao,* 463.

47. Ibid., 464.

48. Ambrose, *Eisenhower,* 372.

Document 3.1
President Dwight Eisenhower's Diary Entry on the Contradictions of Capitalism, July 2, 1953

Shortly after taking office, the president reflected in his diary on the challenges facing the United States. In an ironic reflection of the extent to which the Cold War permeated American thought in the 1950s, President Eisenhower contrasted his views with those of the early Marxist revolutionary Vladimir Lenin. In a brief diary entry a few weeks later the president gave a name to his beliefs, referring to "the middle-of-the-road philosophy (my philosophy)."

Daily I am impressed by the short-sightedness bordering upon tragic stupidity of many who fancy themselves to be the greatest believers in and supporters of capitalism (or a free competitive economy), but who blindly support measures and conditions that cannot fail in the long run to destroy any free economic system.

Lenin held, of course, that capitalism contains within itself what he calls "contradictions" which not only make certain of its inadequacy as a basis of government, but which he claimed are certain to bring about revolution of the proletariat.

The first of these contradictions he called the capital-labor contradiction. He claimed that there were no restraints upon the power of the capitalists—the great corporations and the syndicates—to confront the masses with the choice between the extremes of abject acceptance of a condition of slavery on one hand or bloody revolution on the other.

The second contradiction in the capitalistic system he described as the inevitable conflict between separate groups of capitalists each struggling for the sources of raw materials and other means of production. In essence, of course, this meant capitalistic wars. . . .

His third contradiction was the inherent conflict, as he argued, between the advanced, industrialized nations of the world and the dependent masses of backward peoples. . . .

Any material contemplation of the points raised by Lenin could easily show that his intentions had plausibility only when considered in terms of extremism. All human experience tends to show that human progress, where advanced numbers of people and intricate relationships are concerned, is possible only as extremes are avoided and solutions to problems are found in a great middle way that has regard for the requirements, desires, and aspirations of the vast majority. . . .

Of course there have been happenings in history that would seemingly give a certain validity to some of these communistic arguments. . . . [T]he principal contradiction in the whole system comes about because of the inability of men to forego immediate gain for a long time good. I believe that the educational process has convinced the vast majority of Americans, for example, that the true interests of labor and capital within our society follow courses that are far more nearly parallel than conflicting. I believe that capitalistic—that is to say, self-governing—nations have long ago foreseen that any kind of war is too high a price to pay for the hope of additional territory. I believe, also, that, in the high average of cases, industrialized countries approach the problem of relationships with backward areas on the basis of mutual benefit and advancement.

But when it comes to the making of decisions as between the immediate and selfish interest of a nation, a group, or an individual on the one hand, and on the other the long-term good of the world, the nation, or the individual, we do not yet have a sufficient number of people who are ready to make the immediate sacrifice in favor of a long-term investment. . . .

The general conclusion of these meandering thoughts is that leadership must find a way to bring men and nations to a point where they will give to the long-term promise the same value that they give to immediate and individual gains. . . .

Source: Dwight D. Eisenhower, Diary Series, entry dated July 2, 1953, Diary–Copies of DDE Personal 1953–1954 (2), Box 9, Dwight D. Eisenhower Library.

Document 3.2
"The Chance for Peace," President Dwight Eisenhower's Speech before the American Society of Newspaper Editors, April 16, 1953

In the aftermath of the death of Soviet premier Joseph Stalin, President Eisenhower appealed to the new Soviet leadership in a speech laced with powerful statements on the human costs of the Cold War. The president spoke at the Statler Hotel in Washington, D.C.

. . . What can the world, or any nation in it, hope for if no turning is found on this dread road [of the arms race]?

The worst to be feared and the best to be expected can be simply stated.

The worst is atomic war.

The best would be this: a life of perpetual fear and tension; a burden of arms draining the wealth and the labor of all peoples; a wasting of strength that defies the American system or the Soviet system or any system to achieve true abundance and happiness for the peoples of this earth.

Every gun that is made, every warship launched, every rocket fired signifies, in the final sense, a theft from those who hunger and are not fed, those who are cold and are not clothed. This world in arms is not spending money alone.

It is spending the sweat of its laborers, the genius of its scientists, the hopes of its children.

The cost of one modern heavy bomber is this: a modern brick school in more than 30 cities.

It is two electric power plants, each serving a town of 60,000 population.

It is two fine, fully equipped hospitals. It is some 50 miles of concrete highway.

We pay for a single fighter plane with a half million bushels of wheat.

We pay for a single destroyer with new homes that could have housed more than 8,000 people.

This, I repeat, is the best way of life to be found on the road the world has been taking.

This is not a way of life at all, in any true sense. Under the cloud of threatening war, it is humanity hanging from a cross of iron. . . .

. . . [T]he new Soviet leadership now has a precious opportunity to awaken, with the rest of the world, to the point of peril reached and to help turn the tide of history. . . .

Source: Dwight D. Eisenhower, "Address 'The Chance for Peace' Delivered Before the American Society of Newspaper Editors," April 16, 1953, in *Public Papers of the Presidents of the United States: Dwight D. Eisenhower, 1953–1961,* from the American Presidency Project, University of California Santa Barbara, www.presidency.ucsb.edu.

Document 3.3
National Security Council Report #162/2 (NSC 162/2) on National Security Policy, October 30, 1953

Upon taking office, President Eisenhower initiated a review of American security policy. After considerable debate within the National Security Council, the president authorized the following statement of American doctrine. It was the touchstone of Eisenhower's "New Look" security policy, and the official underpinning of "massive retaliation."

Top Secret

BASIC NATIONAL SECURITY POLICY

General Considerations

Basic Problems of National Security Policy:
1. a. To meet the Soviet threat to U.S. security,
    b. In doing so, to avoid seriously weakening the U.S. economy or undermining our fundamental values and institutions.

The Soviet Threat to the United States:
2. The primary threat to the security, free institutions, and fundamental values of the United States is posed by the combination of:
    a. Basic Soviet hostility to the non-communist world, particularly to the United States.
    b. Great Soviet military power.
    c. Soviet control of the international communist apparatus and other means of subversion or division of the free world. . . .
6. b. When both the USSR and the United States reach a stage of atomic plenty and ample means of delivery, each will have the probable capacity to inflict critical damage on the other, but is not likely to be able to prevent major atomic retaliations. This could create a stalemate, with both sides reluctant to initiate general warfare; although if the Soviets believed that initial surprise held the prospect of destroying the capacity for retaliation, they might be tempted into attacking.
    c. Although Soviet fear of atomic reaction should still inhibit local aggression, increasing Soviet atomic capability may tend to diminish the deterrent effect of U.S. atomic power against peripheral Soviet aggression. It may also sharpen the reaction of the

USSR to what it considers provocative acts of the United States. If either side should miscalculate the strength of the other's reaction, such local conflicts could grow into general war, even though neither seeks nor desires it. To avoid this, it will in general be desirable for the United States to make it clear to the USSR the kind of actions which will be almost certain to lead to this result, recognizing, however, that as general war becomes more devastating for both sides the threat to resort to it becomes less available as a sanction against local aggression.

7. The USSR will continue to rely heavily on tactics of division and subversion to weaken the free world alliances and will to resist Soviet power. Using both the fear of atomic warfare and the hope of peace, such political warfare will seek to exploit differences among members of the free world, neutralist attitudes, and anti-colonial and nationalist sentiments in underdeveloped areas. . . .

Defense Against the Soviet Threat:

9. In the face of the Soviet threat, the security of the United States requires:
   a. Development and maintenance of:
      (1) A strong military posture, with emphasis on the capability of inflicting massive retaliatory damage by offensive striking power;
      (2) U.S. and allied forces in readiness to move rapidly initially to counter aggression by Soviet bloc forces and to hold vital areas and lines of communication; and
      (3) A mobilization base, and its protection against crippling damage, adequate to insure victory in the event of general war.
   b. Maintenance of a sound, strong and growing economy, capable of providing through the operation of free institutions, the strength described in a above over the long pull and of rapidly and effectively changing to full mobilization.
   c. Maintenance of morale and free institutions and the willingness of the U.S. people to support the measures necessary for national security. . . .
      [15. b.] The major deterrent to aggression against Western Europe is the manifest determination of the United States to use its atomic capability and massive retaliatory striking power if the area is attacked. . . .

40. a. A strong, healthy and expanding U.S. economy is essential to the security and stability of the free world. In the interest of both the United States and its allies, it is vital that the support of defense expenditures should not seriously impair the basic soundness of the U.S. economy by undermining incentives or by inflation. . . .

41. To support the necessarily heavy burdens for national security, the morale of the citizens of the United States must be based both on responsibility and freedom for the individual. The dangers from Soviet subversion and espionage require strong and effective security measures. Eternal vigilance, however, is needed in their exercise to prevent the intimidation of free criticism. It is essential that necessary measures of protection should not be so used as to destroy the national unity based on freedom, not fear.

Source: William Z. Slany, ed., *Foreign Relations of the United States, 1952–1954,* vol. 2, *National Security Affairs,* part 1 (Washington, D.C.: Government Printing Office, 1984), 578–596.

Document 3.4
President Dwight Eisenhower's Memorandum to Secretary of State John Foster Dulles about a First Strike, September 8, 1953

In a memorandum to his secretary of state, President Eisenhower advanced in writing an ongoing conversation on national security and the Cold War. The sophistication of Eisenhower's memorandum belies the common misperception that in his relationship with the secretary of state, the president was the pupil and the cabinet member the master. A remarkable feature of this memorandum is the president's musings regarding a nuclear first strike.

I.

With respect to your outlined argument for reconsideration of security policies, I am in general agreement with the points you make. The following are specific comments:

A. I am doubtful whether we can, as a practical matter, greatly increase the emphasis we are now placing upon assuring our lead in non-conventional weapons. . . .

C. I note that you say the United States has put thirty billion dollars of economic aid into Europe during the six years—1946–51. I assume you have looked up these figures, but I have often heard Paul Hoffman [the administrator of the Economic Cooperation Administration, i.e., the Marshall Plan] say that the total was something on the order of fourteen billion under ECA. [The president was right; the figure was roughly twelve billion.]. . .

A general comment is that programs for informing the American public, as well as other populations, are indispensable if we are to do anything except to drift aimlessly, probably to our own eventual destruction.

There is currently much misunderstanding among us. Our own people want tax relief; but they are not well informed as to what drastic tax reduction would mean to the security of the country. They have hoped, and possibly believed, that the Armistice achieved on the Korean battlefield is a prelude to an era of better relations between ourselves and Russia. The individual feels helpless to do anything about the foreign threat that hangs over his head and so he turns his attention to matters of immediate interest—farm supports, Taft-Hartley Act, taxes, drought relief, and partisan politics. Abroad we and our intentions are suspect because we are known to be big and wealthy, and believed to be impulsive and truculent.

If we are to attempt real revision in policies—some of which may temporarily, or even for a very extended time, involve us in vastly increased expenditures, we must begin now to educate our people in the fundamentals of these problems.

Among other things, we should describe the capabilities now and in the near future of the H-bomb, supplemented by the A-bomb. We should patiently point out that any group of people, such as the men in the Kremlin, who are aware of the great destructiveness of these weapons—and who still decline to make any honest effort toward international control by collective action—must be fairly assumed to be contemplating their aggressive use. It would follow that our own preparation could no longer be geared to a policy that attempts only to avert disaster during the early "surprise" stages of a war, and so gain time for full mobilization. Rather, we would have to be constantly ready, on an instantaneous basis, to inflict greater loss upon the enemy than he could reasonably hope to inflict upon us. This would be a deterrent—but if the contest to maintain this relative position should have to continue indefinitely, the cost would either drive us to war—or into some form of dictatorial government. In such circumstances, we would be forced to consider whether or not our duty to future generations did not require us to initiate war at the most propitious moment that we could designate.

I realize that none of this is new to you—in fact, we talked it all over the other day. I put it down here merely to emphasize the fact that a re-study of our position, and even the adoption on a unanimous basis of radically revised policies by the President, the Cabinet, and the bi-partisan leaders of the Congress, would not, in themselves, be sufficient to assure the accomplishment of the resulting objectives. *We must have the enlightened support of Americans* and the informed understanding of our friends in the world. Moreover, all of these people would have to understand that increased military preparation had been forced upon us because every honest peaceful gesture or offer of our own had been summarily rejected by the Communists. . . .

II.

With respect to the draft of your speech to the United Nations, I started out on page one to suggest certain editorial corrections. However, I then remembered that you had said that you had done no editing whatsoever, and so I abandoned that effort.

I think, of course, that the speech will be timely and informative. My chief comment is one of a rather general character. As I read it, I had the impression, particularly in the first part, that the speech is intended as a new indictment of the Bolshevik Party, the USSR, and the Communist Governments in the world. Now I have no quarrel with indicting and condemning them, but I wonder whether or not in front of the United Nations Assembly, this would be the proper approach. . . . The recital, therefore, of past misdeeds, including broken faith, calumny, or anything else, would be made—let us say—regretfully, and only to establish the basis for proceeding more constructively in the future.

I shall not belabor this point further. You can decide whether or not it has any validity. But I think that the speech can be made positive and clear without giving the impression to our opponents or to our friends that we are merely concerned with showing that we have been very nice people, while the others have been very wicked indeed. . . .

Source: Dwight D. Eisenhower, "Top Secret to John Foster Dulles," September 8, 1953, document 404 in *The Papers of Dwight David Eisenhower,* ed. Louis Galambos and Daun van Ee (Baltimore, Md.: The Johns Hopkins University Press, 1996) 14:504–507. Available online from the Dwight D. Eisenhower Memorial Commission, www.eisenhowermemorial.org/presidential-papers/first-term/documents/404.cfm.

Document 3.5
"Massive Retaliation," Secretary of State John Foster Dulles's Speech to the Council on Foreign Relations, January 12, 1954

In a celebrated speech to the Council on Foreign Relations in New York City, Secretary of State John Foster Dulles contrasted the Eisenhower administration's foreign policy, which emphasized "massive retaliatory power," with the crisis-driven policies that prevailed under President Truman and turned a famous threat by Vladimir Lenin against its author.

It is now nearly a year since the Eisenhower Administration took office. . . . Tonight I should like to present an overall view of those policies which relate to our security.

First of all, let us recognize that many of the preceding foreign policies were good. . . . But we need to recall that what we did was in the main emergency action, imposed on us by our enemies. . . . We did not send our army into Korea because we judged in advance that it was sound military strategy to commit our Army to fight land battles in Asia. Our decision had been to pull out of Korea. It was Soviet-inspired action that pulled us back.

We did not decide in advance that it was wise to grant billions annually as foreign economic aid. We adopted that policy in response to the Communist efforts to sabotage the free economies of Western Europe.

We did not build up our military establishment at a rate which involved huge budget deficits, a depreciating currency, and a feverish economy because this seemed, in advance, a good policy. Indeed, we decided otherwise until the Soviet military threat was clearly revealed. . . .

Emergency measures are costly; they are superficial; and they imply that the enemy has the initiative. They cannot be depended on to serve our long-time interests.

This "long time" factor is of critical importance. The Soviet Communists are planning for what they call "an entire historical era," and we should do the same. They seek, through many types of maneuvers, gradually to divide and weaken the free nations by overextending them in efforts which, as Lenin put it, are "beyond their strength so that they come to practical bankruptcy." . .

In the face of this strategy, measures cannot be judged adequate merely because they ward off immediate danger. It is essential to do this, but it is also essential to do so without exhausting ourselves.

When the Eisenhower administration applied this test, we felt that some transformations were needed. . . .

We need allies and collective security. This can be done by placing more reliance on deterrent power and less dependence on local defensive power.

This is accepted practice so far as local communities are concerned. We keep locks on our doors, but we do not have an armed guard in every home. We rely principally on a community security system so well equipped to punish any who break in and steal that, in fact, would-be aggressors are generally deterred. That is the modern way of getting maximum protection at bearable cost. What the Eisenhower administration seeks is a similar international security system. We want, for ourselves and the other free nations, a maximum deterrent at a bearable cost. . . .

Local defenses must be reinforced by the further deterrent of massive retaliatory power. A potential aggressor must know that he cannot always prescribe battle conditions that suit him. . . .

Let us now see how this concept has been applied to foreign policy, taking first the Far East.

In Korea this administration effected a major transformation . . . because the aggressor . . . was faced with the possibility that fighting might, to his own great peril, soon spread beyond the limits and methods which he had selected.

I have said in relation to Indochina that, if there were open Red Chinese army aggression there, that would have "grave consequences which might not be confined to Indochina." . . .

If we turn to Europe, we see readjustments in the NATO collective security effort. . . . At the April meeting of the NATO Council, the United States put forward a new concept, now known as that of the "long haul." . . . The West German Republic needs to be freed from the armistice; and new political arrangements should be made to assure that rearmed Germans will serve the common cause and never serve German militarism. . . .

In the ways I outlined we gather strength for the long-term defense of freedom. We do not, of course, claim to have found some magic formula that insures against all forms of Communist success. It is normal that at some times and at some places there may be setbacks to the cause of freedom. What we do expect to insure is that any setbacks will have only temporary and local significance, because they will leave unimpaired those free world assets which in the long run will prevail. . . .

If we persist in the courses I outline we shall confront dictatorship with a task that is, in the long run, beyond its strength. For unless it changes, it must suppress the human desires that freedom satisfies—as we shall be demonstrating. If the dictators persist in their present course, then it is they who will be limited to superficial successes, while their foundation crumbles under the tread of iron boots.

Source: John Foster Dulles, "Outlines of Strategy: Address by the Secretary of State (Dulles) before the Council on Foreign Relations, New York, January 12, 1954," in *Documents on American Foreign Relations 1954,* ed. Peter V. Curl (New York: Harper and Brothers for the Council on Foreign Relations, 1955), 7–15.

Document 3.6
President Dwight Eisenhower's Press Conference on the H-Bomb, Subversion, and "Falling Dominoes," April 7, 1954

In one of his weekly press conferences, Eisenhower employed a metaphor of "falling dominoes" to describe the stakes involved in the Cold War contest for Indochina. What happened in Vietnam, the president stated, was of "incalculable" importance to the West. The highly elastic "domino theory" continued to guide American policy in Vietnam through the next two decades.

Q. Robert Richards, Copley Press: Mr. President, would you mind commenting on the strategic importance of Indochina to the free world? I think there has been, across the country, some lack of understanding on just what it means to us.

The President: You have, of course, both the specific and the general when you talk about such things.

First of all, you have the specific value of a locality in its production of materials that the world needs.

Then you have the possibility that many human beings pass under a dictatorship that is inimical to the free world.

Finally, you have broader considerations that might follow what you would call the "falling domino" principle. You have a row of dominoes set up, you knock over the first one, and what will happen to the last one is the certainty that it will go over very quickly. So you could have a beginning of a disintegration that would have the most profound influences.

Now, with respect to the first one, two of the items from this particular area that the world uses are tin and tungsten. They are very important. There are others, of course, the rubber plantations and so on.

Then with respect to more people passing under this domination, Asia, after all, has already lost some 450 million of its peoples to the Communist dictatorship, and we simply can't afford greater losses.

But when we come to the possible sequence of events, the loss of Indochina, of Burma, of Thailand, of the Peninsula, and Indonesia following, now you begin to talk about areas that not only multiply the disadvantages that you would suffer through loss of materials, sources of materials, but now you are talking really about millions and millions and millions of people.

Finally, the geographical position achieved thereby does many things. It turns the so-called island defensive chain of Japan, Formosa, of the Philippines and to the southward; it moves in to threaten Australia and New Zealand.

It takes away, in its economic aspects, that region that Japan must have as a trading area or Japan, in turn, will have only one place in the world to go—that is, toward the Communist areas in order to live.

So, the possible consequences of the loss are just incalculable to the free world.

Source: "The President's News Conference," April 7, 1954, in *Public Papers of the Presidents of the United States: Dwight D. Eisenhower, 1953–1961,* from the American Presidency Project, University of California, Santa Barbara, www.presidency.ucsb.edu.

Document 3.7
Southeast Asia Collective Defense Treaty, September 8, 1954

In the following treaty, the United States, Australia, France, the United Kingdom, New Zealand, Pakistan, the Philippines, and Thailand pledged to come to the aid of one another in the event of armed attack against a signatory party in the treaty area, or in the event of such an attack "against any State or territory which the Parties by unanimous agreement may hereafter designate." In a protocol agreed to simultaneously with the treaty, the signatories agreed to extend the treaty to Cambodia, Laos, "and the free territory under the jurisdiction of the State of Vietnam." The principal function of the treaty organization was to legitimize the U.S. presence in Vietnam following French withdrawal.

The Parties to this Treaty,

Recognizing the sovereign equality of all the Parties,

Reiterating their faith in the purposes and principles set forth in the Charter of the United Nations and their desire to live in peace with all peoples and all governments,

Reaffirming that, in accordance with the Charter of the United Nations, they uphold the principle of equal rights and self-determination of peoples, and declaring that they will earnestly strive by every peaceful means to promote self-government and to secure the independence of all countries whose peoples desire it and are able to undertake its responsibilities,

Desiring to strengthen the fabric of peace and freedom and to uphold the principles of democracy, individual liberty and the rule of law, and to promote the economic well-being and development of all peoples in the treaty area,

Intending to declare publicly and formally their sense of unity, so that any potential aggressor will appreciate that the Parties stand together in the area, and

Desiring further to coordinate their efforts for collective defense for the preservation of peace and security,

Therefore agree as follows:

ARTICLE I

The Parties undertake, as set forth in the Charter of the United Nations, to settle any international disputes in which they may be involved by peaceful means in such a manner that international peace and security and justice are not endangered, and to refrain in their international relations from the threat or use of force in any manner inconsistent with the purposes of the United Nations.

ARTICLE II

In order more effectively to achieve the objectives of this Treaty, the Parties, separately and jointly, by means of continuous and effective self-help and mutual aid will maintain and develop their individual and collective capacity to resist armed attack and to prevent and counter subversive activities directed from without against their territorial integrity and political stability.

ARTICLE III

The Parties undertake to strengthen their free institutions and to cooperate with one another in the further development of economic measures, including technical assistance, designed both to promote economic progress and social well-being and to further the individual and collective efforts of governments toward these ends.

ARTICLE IV

1. Each Party recognizes that aggression by means of armed attack in the treaty area against any of the Parties or against any State or territory which the Parties by unanimous agreement may hereafter designate, would endanger its own peace and safety, and agrees that it will in that event act to meet the common danger in accordance with its constitutional processes. Measures taken under this paragraph shall be immediately reported to the Security Council of the United Nations.

2. If, in the opinion of any of the Parties, the inviolability or the integrity of the territory or the sovereignty or political independence of any Party in the treaty area or of any other State or territory to which the provisions of paragraph 1 of this Article from time to time apply is threatened in any way other than by armed attack or is affected or threatened by any fact or situation which might endanger the peace of the area, the Parties shall consult immediately in order to agree on the measures which should be taken for the common defense.

3. It is understood that no action on the territory of any State designated by unanimous agreement under paragraph 1 of this Article or on any territory so designated shall be taken except at the invitation or with the consent of the government concerned. . . .

UNDERSTANDING OF THE UNITED STATES OF AMERICA

The United States of America in executing the present Treaty does so with the understanding that its recognition of the effect of aggression and armed attack and its agreement with reference thereto in Article IV, paragraph 1, apply only to communist aggression but affirms that in the event of other aggression or armed attack it will consult under the provisions of Article IV, paragraph 2.

In witness whereof, the undersigned Plenipotentiaries have signed this Treaty.

Done at Manila, this eighth day of September, 1954.

Source: "Southeast Asia Collective Defense Treaty (Manila Pact)," September 8, 1954, from the Avalon Project at Yale Law School, www.yale.edu/lawweb/avalon/intdip/usmulti/usmu003.htm.

Document 3.8
Formosa Resolution, Joint Resolution by the U.S. Congress, January 29, 1955

Congress reacted quickly and affirmatively to President Eisenhower's request for a resolution proclaiming American determination to defend Formosa in the first Taiwan Strait Crisis. Buoyed by this expression of government solidarity, the president went to the brink of war, threatening at a press conference on March 16 to order the use of tactical nuclear weapons "against a strictly military target" in defense of Taiwan.

Joint Resolution by the Congress, January 29, 1955

Whereas the primary purpose of the United States, in its relations with all other nations, is to develop and sustain a just and enduring peace for all; and

Whereas certain territories in the West Pacific under the jurisdiction of the Republic of China are now under armed attack, and threats and declarations have been and are being made by the Chinese Communists that such armed attack is in aid of and in preparation for armed attack on Formosa and the Pescadores;

Whereas such armed attack if continued would gravely endanger the peace and security of the West Pacific area and particularly of Formosa and the Pescadores; and

Whereas the secure possession by friendly governments of the Western Pacific island chain, of which Formosa is a part, is essential to the vital interests of the United States and all friendly nations in or bordering upon the Pacific Ocean; and

Whereas the President of the United States on January 6, 1955, submitted to the Senate for its advice and consent to ratification Mutual Defense Treaty between the United States of America and the Republic of China, which recognizes that an armed attack in the West Pacific area directed against territories, therein described, in the region of Formosa and the Pescadores, would be dangerous to the peace and safety of the parties to the treaty: Therefore be it

Resolved by the Senate and House of Representatives of the United States in Congress assembled, That the President of the United States be and hereby is authorized to employ the Armed Forces of the United States as he deems necessary for the specific purpose of securing and protecting Formosa and the Pescadores against armed attack, this authority to include the securing and protecting of such related positions and territories of that area now in friendly hands and the taking of such other measures as he judges to be required or appropriate in assuring the Defense of Formosa and the Pescadores. . . .

Source: Formosa Resolution, Joint Resolution 159, 84th Cong., 1st sess., January 29, 1955, reproduced in U.S. Department of State, *Foreign Relations of the United States, 1955–1957,* vol. 2, *China,* ed. John P. Glennon (Washington, D.C.: U.S. Government Printing Office, 1986), 162–163.

Document 3.9
Army Chief of Staff General Matthew Ridgway Criticizes Proposed Army Cuts in Congressional Testimony, January 31, 1955

In an unusual public display of military dissent with the commander in chief, Army Chief of Staff Gen. Matthew Ridgway accepted the invitation of members of Congress to criticize the president's proposal to reduce the size of the nation's ground and amphibious forces.

[Army] Secretary [Robert T.] Stevens: . . . My own view, up to the moment, is that . . . scientific advances and improved weapons do possibly justify some smaller total personnel in the standing army. . . .

Mr. [Paul Joseph] Kilday (D–TX): . . . May I propound the same question to the Chief of Staff . . . ?

General Ridgway: . . . The overall strength of the Army in a hypothetical future global war would, in my opinion, be considerably less than the overall strength of the Army in the last such conflict, namely, World War II. However, it is my reasoned judgment that . . . the depth of the battle zone, the necessity for rapid concentration, dispersion and rapid reconcentration, the requirement for increased maintenance personnel for all these complicated weapons and their controlling system—all point clearly to me to the probability that for a structural field force of given composition the need will be for more rather than for fewer men. . . .

Mr. [Overton] Brooks (D–LA): General, you see our situation there [in the Far East] and how deeply concerned the committee is in reference to cutting down the Army in a crisis when we have those in charge of the destinies of Red China threatening war on the United States and then we come out and reduce our force by 140,000 men.

Does that affect the safety of the country?

General Ridgway: I think it does, sir. . . .

Mr. Brooks: . . . Should we reduce the size of our Army by 140,000 men at this particular critical time in our international affairs and will we jeopardize our position in the Far East or will we jeopardize the safety of this country?

General Ridgway: I think we should not reduce it. I think we do jeopardize the security to a degree.

Mr. Brooks: And, of course, you are opposing the reduction of the Army by 140,000 men. I agree with you, I will say that.

General Ridgway: May I say this, sir: It isn't up to me or to any other officer in uniform to oppose a decision by the constituted authorities of our Government. I stand on but one position, sir. Whatever be the decisions, the Army will execute them to the utmost of its capability, with unswerving loyalty, with the means assigned to it.

Source: House of Representatives, Committee on Armed Services, *Briefing on National Defense, No. 3, 84th Congress, 1st Session* (Washington, D.C.: U.S. Government Printing Office, 1955): 318–319, 343–344.

Document 3.10

The President Replies to General Ridgway in His Press Conference of February 2, 1955

President Eisenhower diplomatically but firmly replied to the challenge of the army chief of staff (see **Document 3.9***) and the other members of the Joint Chiefs of Staff.*

Q. Marvin Arrowsmith, Associated Press: Mr. President, General Ridgway told the House Armed Services Committee 2 days ago that he is against the projected cut in Army strength, and he said he believes that the proposed cut jeopardized national security to a degree. How do you feel about that, and is there any possibility of the reduction order being rescinded?

The President: Well, I assume that you are asking me the question so far as it affects the executive department. My decision in this matter was not reached lightly; it was reached after long study of every opinion I could get, in consultation with every single individual in this Government that I know of that bears any responsibility whatsoever about it.

General Ridgway was questioned in the Congress as to his personal convictions; naturally, he had to express them.

His responsibility for national defense is, you might say, a special one, or, in a sense, parochial. He does not have the overall responsibility that is borne by the Commander in Chief, and by him alone, when it comes down to making the recommendations to the Congress.

My recommendations, I repeat, were made from my best judgment of what is the adequate defense structure for these United States, particularly on the long-term basis. That decision has not been altered, and at this moment I don't see any chance of its being altered.

Q. Sarah McClendon, El Paso Times: Mr. President, in that same connection, your letter of January 5th to Mr. Wilson, I believe, mentioned that recent scientific and technological developments made it necessary for us not to use as many men as we might otherwise use.

Well, the Joint Chiefs of Staff, in their testimony before the House Armed Services Committee, don't agree with this. They say, no.

Will you have any further conferences with them on this?

The President: I confer with the Joint Chiefs of Staff through their chairman several times a week, every week. I am never out of touch with them. I know their opinions, and I know exactly who agrees with me and who doesn't.

Now, they are entitled to their opinions, but I have to make the decisions.

Source: "The President's News Conference," February 2, 1955, in *Public Papers of the Presidents of the United States: Dwight D. Eisenhower, 1953–1961,* from the American Presidency Project, University of California, Santa Barbara, www.presidency.ucsb.edu.

Document 3.11
Senator John Bricker's Proposed Amendment to the U.S. Constitution, 1953

Sen. John Bricker, R-Ohio, proposed to amend the Constitution to prohibit the president from reaching understandings with foreign governments without consulting with Congress. The proposal was endorsed in the Republican Party platform in 1952.

SECTION 1.

A provision of a treaty which conflicts with this Constitution shall not be of any force or effect.

SECTION 2.

A treaty shall become effective as internal law in the United States only through legislation which would be valid in the absence of treaty.

SECTION 3.

Congress shall have power to regulate all executive and other agreements with any foreign power or international organization. All such agreements shall be subject to the limitations imposed on treaties by this article.

SECTION 4.

The congress shall have power to enforce this article by appropriate legislation.

Source: "The Bricker Amendment," in *Ohio History Central: An Online Encyclopedia of Ohio History* (Columbus: Ohio Historical Society, 2005), www.ohiohistorycentral.org/entry.php?rec=1398.

Document 3.12
"Atoms for Peace," President Dwight Eisenhower's Address to the United Nations, December 8, 1953

*In his second such initiative of his first year in office (see **Document 3.2**) President Eisenhower addressed the UN General Assembly on the nuclear arms race. The speech began with a candid review of where the United States stood in the development of its highly secret nuclear arsenal, and ended with a plea to the Soviet Union to join the United States in diverting nuclear weapons material to peaceful purposes.*

. . . On July 16, 1945, the United States set off the world's first atomic explosion. Since that date in 1945, the United States of America has conducted 42 test explosions.

Atomic bombs today are more than 25 times as powerful as the weapons with which the atomic age dawned, while hydrogen weapons are in the ranges of millions of tons of TNT equivalent.

Today, the United States' stockpile of atomic weapons, which, of course, increases daily, exceeds by many times the explosive equivalent of the total of all bombs and all shells that came from every plane and every gun in every theatre of war in all of the years of World War II.

A single air group, whether afloat or land-based, can now deliver to any reachable target a destructive cargo exceeding in power all the bombs that fell on Britain in all of World War II.

In size and variety, the development of atomic weapons has been no less remarkable. The development has been such that atomic weapons have virtually achieved conventional status within our armed services. In the United States, the Army, the Navy, the Air Force, and the Marine Corps are all capable of putting this weapon to military use.

But the dread secret, and the fearful engines of atomic might, are not ours alone.

In the first place, the secret is possessed by our friends and allies, Great Britain and Canada, whose scientific genius made a tremendous contribution to our original discoveries, and the designs of atomic bombs.

The secret is also known by the Soviet Union. . . .

Even against the most powerful defense, an aggressor in possession of the effective minimum number of atomic bombs for a surprise attack could probably place a sufficient number of his bombs on the chosen targets to cause hideous damage.

Should such an atomic attack be launched against the United States, our reactions would be swift and resolute. But for me to say that the defense capabilities of the United States are such that they could inflict terrible losses upon an aggressor—for me to say that the retaliation capabilities of the United States are so great that such an aggressor's land would be laid waste—all this, while fact, is not the true expression of the purpose and the hope of the United States. . . .

To hasten the day when fear of the atom will begin to disappear from the minds of people, and the governments of the East and West, there are certain steps that can be taken now.

I therefore make the following proposals:

The Governments principally involved, to the extent permitted by elementary prudence, to begin now and continue to make joint contributions from their stockpiles of normal uranium and fissionable materials to an International Atomic Energy Agency. We would expect that such an agency would be set up under the aegis of the United Nations.

The ratios of contributions, the procedures and other details would properly be within the scope of the "private conversations" I have referred to earlier.

The United States is prepared to undertake these explorations in good faith. Any partner of the United States acting in the same good faith will find the United States a not unreasonable or ungenerous associate.

Undoubtedly initial and early contributions to this plan would be small in quantity. However, the proposal has the great virtue that it can be undertaken without the irritations and mutual suspicions incident to any attempt to set up a completely acceptable system of worldwide inspection and control.

The Atomic Energy Agency could be made responsible for the impounding, storage, and protection of the contributed fissionable and other materials. The ingenuity of our scientists will provide special safe conditions under which such a bank of fissionable material can be made essentially immune to surprise seizure.

The more important responsibility of this Atomic Energy Agency would be to devise methods whereby this fissionable material would be allocated to serve the peaceful pursuits of mankind. Experts would be mobilized to apply atomic energy to the needs of agriculture, medicine, and other peaceful activities. A special purpose would be to provide abundant electrical energy in the power-starved areas of the world. Thus the contributing powers would be dedicating some of their strength to serve the needs rather than the fears of mankind. . . .

Source: Dwight D. Eisenhower, "Address Before the General Assembly of the United Nations on Peaceful Uses of Atomic Energy" December 8, 1953, in *Public Papers of the Presidents of the United States: Dwight D. Eisenhower 1953–1961,* from the American Presidency Project, University of California, Santa Barbara, www.presidency.ucsb.edu.

Document 3.13
President Dwight Eisenhower's Diary Entry on His "Atoms for Peace" Speech, December 10, 1953

*In his diary, President Eisenhower described the multiple purposes served by his dramatic speech before the United Nations (**Document 3.12**).*

. . . There has been much speculation on what I was trying to do in a talk that dealt principally with the field of atomic energy and atomic warfare and made definite proposals for international action in promoting the peaceful use of atomic science and materials.

The reasons were several. Of these, the first and principal one was exactly as stated—to make a clear effort to get the Soviet Union working with us in some phase of this whole atomic field that would have only peace and the good of mankind as a goal.

(b). If we were successful in getting even the tiniest of starts, it was believed that gradually this kind of talk and negotiation might expand into something broader—that at least a faint possibility existed that Russia's concern, bordering upon fright, of the certain results of atomic warfare might lead her, in her own self-interests, to participate in this kind of joint humanitarian effort. . . .

(d). Another reason was that even in the event that the USSR would cooperate in such a plan for "propaganda purposes" that the United States could unquestionably afford to reduce its atomic stockpile by two or three times the amounts that the Russians might contribute to the United Nations agency, and still improve our relative position in the cold war and even in the event of the outbreak of war.

(e). Another important reason was to give the population of our country the feeling—the certain knowledge—that they had not poured their substance into this whole development with the sole purpose and possibility of its being used for destruction. This effort also gave the opportunity to tell America and the world a very considerable story about the size and strength of our atomic capabilities, but to do it in such a way as to make this presentation an argument for peaceful negotiation rather than to present it in an atmosphere of truculence, defiance, and threat.

Underlying all of this, of course, is the clear conviction that as of now the world is racing toward catastrophe—that something must be done to put a brake on this movement. Certainly there is none so foolish as to think that the brake can be composed only of words and protestations, however eloquent or sincere. But ideas expressed in words must certainly have a function in getting people here and elsewhere thinking along these lines and helping to devise ways and means by which the possible disaster of the future can be avoided.

Source: Dwight D. Eisenhower, Diary Series, entry dated December 10, 1953, DDE Diary Oct.–Dec. 1953, Box 4, Dwight D. Eisenhower Library.

Document 3.14
The Eisenhower Doctrine, President Dwight Eisenhower's Speech to Congress, January 5, 1957

To curb the "evil influence" of Egyptian leader Gamal Abdel Nasser's pan-Arab aspirations, and to prevent the Soviet Union from filling the "vacuum" created by Britain and France's humiliation at Suez the year before, President Eisenhower asked Congress in this speech to grant him discretionary authority to use both the carrot of special economic and military aid and the stick of armed force to repel Communist encroachment in the Middle East.

International Communism, of course, seeks to mask its purposes of domination by expressions of good will and by superficially attractive offers of political, economic and military aid. But any free nation, which is the subject of Soviet enticement, ought, in elementary wisdom, to look behind the mask.

Remember Estonia, Latvia and Lithuania! In 1939 the Soviet Union entered into mutual assistance pacts with these then dependent countries; and the Soviet Foreign Minister, addressing the Extraordinary Fifth Session of the Supreme Soviet in October 1939, solemnly and publicly declared that "we stand for the scrupulous and punctilious observance of the pacts on the basis of complete reciprocity, and we declare that all the nonsensical talk about the Sovietization of the Baltic countries is only to the interest of our common enemies and of all anti-Soviet provocateurs." Yet in 1940, Estonia, Latvia and Lithuania were forcibly incorporated into the Soviet Union.

Soviet control of the satellite nations of Eastern Europe has been forcibly maintained in spite of solemn promises of a contrary intent, made during World War II.

Stalin's death brought hope that this pattern would change. And we read the pledge of the Warsaw Treaty of 1955 that the Soviet Union would follow in satellite countries "the principles of mutual respect for their independence and sovereignty and noninterference in domestic affairs." But we have just seen the subjugation of Hungary by naked armed force. In the aftermath of this Hungarian tragedy, world respect for and belief in Soviet promises have sunk to a new low. International Communism needs and seeks a recognizable success. . . .

Under these circumstances I deem it necessary to seek the cooperation of the Congress. Only with that cooperation can we give the reassurance needed to deter aggression, to give courage and confidence to those who are dedicated to freedom and thus prevent a chain of events which would gravely endanger all of the free world. . . .

. . . [T]he United States through the joint action of the President and the Congress, or, in the case of treaties, the Senate, has manifested in many endangered areas its purpose to support free and independent governments—and peace—against external menace, notably the menace of International Communism. Thereby we have helped to maintain peace and security during a period of great danger. It is now essential that the United States should manifest through joint action of the President and the Congress our determination to assist those nations of the Mid East area, which desire that assistance.

The action which I propose would have the following features.

It would, first of all, authorize the United States to cooperate with and assist any nation or group of nations in the general area of the Middle East in the development of economic strength dedicated to the maintenance of national independence.

It would, in the second place, authorize the Executive to undertake in the same region programs of military assistance and cooperation with any nation or group of nations which desires such aid.

It would, in the third place, authorize such assistance and cooperation to include the employment of the armed forces of the United States to secure and protect the territorial integrity and political independence of such nations, requesting such aid, against overt armed aggression from any nation controlled by International Communism. . . .

Source: Dwight D. Eisenhower, "Special Message to Congress on the Situation in the Middle East," January 5, 1957, in *Public Papers of the Presidents of the United States: Dwight D. Eisenhower 1953–1961,* from the American Presidency Project, University of California, Santa Barbara, www .presidency.ucsb.edu.

Document 3.15
"The Kitchen Debate" between Vice President Richard Nixon and Premier Nikita Khrushchev, July 24, 1959

In the summer of 1959, preparatory to President Dwight Eisenhower's visit to Moscow follow-ing Soviet premier Khrushchev's historic visit to the United States, the American vice president met with the Soviet leader in Moscow. Their unrehearsed debate at an "American National Exhibit" demonstrated the tenacity of both participants and the wide-ranging differences between the superpowers. The New York Times *provided its readers with the following edited transcript of their remarks.*

Khrushchev: . . . "How long has America existed? Three hundred years?"

Nixon: "One hundred and fifty years."

Khrushchev: "One hundred and fifty years? Well then we will say America has been in exis-tence for 150 years and this is the level she has reached. We have existed not quite 42 years and in another seven years we will be on the same level as America. When we catch you up, in passing you by, we will wave to you. Then if you wish we can stop and say: Please follow up. Plainly speaking, if you want capitalism you can live that way. That is your own affair and doesn't concern us. We can still feel sorry for you but since you don't understand us—live as you do understand. . . ."

Nixon: "There are some instances where you may be ahead of us, for example in the development of the thrust of your rockets for the investigation of outer space; there may be some instances in which we are ahead of you—in color television, for instance."

Khrushchev: "No, we are up with you on this, too. We have bested you in one technique and also in the other."

Nixon: "You see, you never concede anything."

Khrushchev: "I do not give up."

Nixon: "Wait till you see the picture. . . ."

Nixon [*Halting Khrushchev at model kitchen in model house*]: "You had a very nice house in your exhibition in New York. My wife and I saw and enjoyed it very much. I want to show you this kitchen. It is like those of our houses in California."

Khrushchev [*after Nixon called attention to a built-in panel-controlled washing machine*]: "We have such things."

Nixon: "This is the newest model. This is the kind which is built in thousands of units for direct installation in the houses." He added that Americans were interested in making life easier for their women.

Mr. Khrushchev remarked that in the Soviet Union, they did not have "the capitalist attitude toward women."

Nixon: "I think that this attitude toward women is universal. What we want to do is make easier the life of our housewives."

He explained that the house could be built for $14,000 and that most veterans had bought houses for between $10,000 and $15,000.

Nixon: "Let me give you an example you can appreciate. Our steelworkers, as you know, are on strike. But any steelworker could buy this house. They earn $3 an hour. This house costs about $100 a month to buy on a contract running 25 to 30 years."

Khrushchev: "We have steelworkers and we have peasants who also can afford to spend $14,000 for a house."

He said American houses were built to last only 20 years, so builders could sell new houses at the end of that period.

"We build firmly. We build for our children and grandchildren."

Mr. Nixon said he thought American houses would last more than 20 years, but even so, after 20 years many Americans want a new home or a new kitchen, which would be obsolete then. The American system is designed to take advantage of new inventions and new techniques, he said.

Khrushchev: "This theory does not hold water."

He said some things never got out of date—furniture and furnishings, perhaps, but not houses. He said he did not think houses. He said he did not think that what Americans had written about their houses was all strictly accurate.

Nixon [pointing to television screen]: "We can see here what is happening in other parts of the home." . . .

Khrushchev: "Don't you have a machine that puts food into the mouth and pushes it down? Many things you've shown us are interesting but they are not needed in life. They have no useful purpose. They are merely gadgets. . . ."

Source: "Moscow 'Kitchen Debate': Nixon-Khrushchev Discussion, July 24, 1959," transcript in *New York Times,* July 25, 1959, from CNN, *Cold War,* www.cnn.com/SPECIALS/cold.war/episodes/14/documents/debate/.

Document 3.16
The Eisenhower Administration Launches a Cover Story for the U-2 Crisis, NASA Statement to the Press, May 3, 1960

After an American U-2 spy plane was lost over the Soviet Union, the Eisenhower administration presented the press with a prearranged cover story in a press briefing by an official of the National Aeronautics and Space Administration.

A NASA U-2 research airplane, being flown in Turkey on a joint NASA-USAF Air Weather Service mission, apparently went down in the Lake van, Turkey, area at about 9:00 a.m. (3:00 a.m., e.d.t.) Sunday, May 1.

During the flight in southeast Turkey, the pilot reported over the emergency frequency that he was experiencing oxygen difficulties. The flight originated in Adana with a mission to obtain data on clear air turbulence.

A search is now underway in the Lake Van area.

The pilot is an employee of Lockheed Aircraft under contract to NASA.

The U-2 program was initiated by NASA in 1956 as a method of making high-altitude weather studies.

Source: "Statement of May 3," *Department of State Bulletin* 42, no. 1091 (May 23, 1960; Pub. no. 6999): 817.

Document 3.17
The Eisenhower Administration Refines the U-2 Cover Story, Statement to the Press, May 7, 1960

After Chairman Khrushchev revealed on May 7 that the Soviets had recovered the wreckage of a spy plane and captured its pilot, the administration had to change its story. The authorities in Washington still hoped to maintain the innocence, however, of "the authorities in Washington."

The Department of State has received the text of Mr. Khrushchev's further remarks about the unarmed plane which is reported to have been shot down in the Soviet Union. As previously announced, it was known that a U-2 spy plane was missing. As a result of the inquiry ordered by the President it has been established that insofar as the authorities in Washington are concerned there was no authorization for any such flight as described by Mr. Khrushchev.

Nevertheless it appears that in endeavoring to obtain information now concealed behind the Iron Curtain a flight over Soviet territory was probably undertaken by unarmed civilian U-2 plane.

It is certainly no secret that, given the state of the world today, intelligence collection activities are practiced by all countries, and postwar history certainly reveals that the Soviet Union has not been lagging behind in this field. . . .

It is in relation to the danger of a surprise attack that planes of the type of unarmed civilian U-2 aircraft have made flights along the frontiers of the free world for the past 4 years.

Source: "Department of State, May 7," *Department of State Bulletin* 42, no. 1091 (May 23, 1960; Pub. no. 6999): 818–819.

Document 3.18
President Dwight Eisenhower Takes Responsibility for the U-2 Flight, News Conference, May 11, 1960

President Eisenhower, downcast at the public response to the administration's transparent attempt to maintain plausible deniability, told his son, John, "We're going to take a beating on this. And I'm the one, rightly, who is going to have to take the brunt" (Chester J. Pach Jr. and Elmo Richardson, The Presidency of Dwight D. Eisenhower, *rev. ed. [Lawrence: University of Kansas Press, 1991], 217.) Eisenhower acknowledged responsibility in the prepared remarks with which he began one of his regular press conferences.*

The President [reading]: I have made some notes from which I want to talk to you about this U-2 incident.

A full statement about this matter has been made by the State Department, and there have been several statesmanlike remarks by leaders of both parties.

For my part, I supplement what the Secretary of State has had to say, with the following four main points. After that I shall have nothing further to say—for the simple reason I can think of nothing to add that might be useful at this time.

The first point is this: the need for intelligence-gathering activities.

No one wants another Pearl Harbor. This means that we must have knowledge of military forces and preparations around the world, especially those capable of massive surprise attacks.

Secrecy in the Soviet Union makes this essential. In most of the world no large-scale attack could be prepared in secret, but in the Soviet Union there is a fetish of secrecy and concealment. This is a major cause of international tension and uneasiness today. Our deterrent must never be placed in jeopardy. The safety of the whole free world demands this. . . .

My second point: the nature of intelligence-gathering activities.

These have a special and secret character. They are, so to speak, "below the surface" activities. . . .

These activities have their own rules and methods of concealment which seek to mislead and obscure—just as in the Soviet allegations there are many discrepancies. For example, there is some reason to believe that the plane in question was not shot down at high altitude. The normal agencies of our Government are unaware of these specific activities or of the special efforts to conceal them.

Third point: how should we view all of this activity?

It is a distasteful but vital necessity.

We prefer and work for a different kind of world—and a different way of obtaining the information essential to confidence and effective deterrents. Open societies, in the day of present weapons, are the only answer.

This was the reason for my "open skies" proposal in 1955, which I was ready instantly to put into effect—to permit aerial observation over the United States and the Soviet Union which would assure that no surprise attack was being prepared against anyone. I shall bring up the "open skies" proposal again at Paris—since it is a means of ending concealment and suspicion.

My final point is that we must not be distracted from the real issues of the day by what is an incident or a symptom of the world situation today.

This incident has been given great propaganda exploitation. The emphasis given to a flight of an unarmed nonmilitary plane can only reflect a fetish of secrecy.

The real issues are the ones we will be working on at the summit-disarmament, search for solutions affecting Germany and Berlin, and the whole range of East-West relations, including the reduction of secrecy and suspicion.

Frankly, I am hopeful that we may make progress on these great issues. This is what we mean when we speak of "working for peace."

And as I remind you, I will have nothing further to say about this matter. [Ends reading]. . . .

Q. Edward T. Foillard, Washington Post: Mr. President, do you think the outlook for the summit conference has changed, or has been changed, in the last week or so?

The President: Not decisively at all, no.

Source: "The President's News Conference," May 11, 1960, in *Public Papers of the Presidents of the United States: Dwight D. Eisenhower, 1953–1961,* from the American Presidency Project, University of California, Santa Barbara, www.presidency.ucsb.edu.

Document 3.19

President Dwight Eisenhower's Farewell Address, Radio and Television Speech, January 17, 1961

*In his valedictory remarks, the president elaborated on the centerpiece of his philosophy (see **Document 3.1**): the need to strike a balance between immediate desires and future needs. If the United States departed from the middle way of pursuing peace through moderated expenditures and the avoidance of war, Eisenhower warned, it risked falling into the embrace of the "military-industrial complex."*

My fellow Americans:

Three days from now, after half a century in the service of our country, I shall lay down the responsibilities of office as, in traditional and solemn ceremony, the authority of the Presidency is vested in my successor.

This evening I come to you with a message of leave-taking and farewell, and to share a few final thoughts with you, my countrymen. . .

III.

Throughout America's adventure in free government, our basic purposes have been to keep the peace; to foster progress in human achievement, and to enhance liberty, dignity and integrity among people and among nations. To strive for less would be unworthy of a free and religious people. Any failure traceable to arrogance, or our lack of comprehension or readiness to sacrifice would inflict upon us grievous hurt both at home and abroad.

Progress toward these noble goals is persistently threatened by the conflict now engulfing the world. It commands our whole attention, absorbs our very beings. We face a hostile ideology—global in scope, atheistic in character, ruthless in purpose, and insidious in method. Unhappily the danger it poses promises to be of indefinite duration. To meet it successfully, there is called for, not so much the emotional and transitory sacrifices of crisis, but rather those which enable us to carry forward steadily, surely, and without complaint the burdens of a prolonged and complex struggle—with liberty the stake. Only thus shall we remain, despite every provocation, on our charted course toward permanent peace and human betterment.

Crises there will continue to be. In meeting them, whether foreign or domestic, great or small, there is a recurring temptation to feel that some spectacular and costly action could become the miraculous solution to all current difficulties. A huge increase in newer elements of our defense; development of unrealistic programs to cure every ill in agriculture; a dramatic expansion in basic and applied research—these and many other possibilities, each possibly promising in itself, may be suggested as the only way to the road we wish to travel.

But each proposal must be weighed in the light of a broader consideration: the need to maintain balance in and among national programs—balance between the private and the public economy, balance between cost and hoped for advantage—balance between the clearly necessary and the comfortably desirable; balance between our essential requirements as a nation and the duties imposed by the nation upon the individual; balance between actions of the moment and the national welfare of the future. Good judgment seeks balance and progress; lack of it eventually finds imbalance and frustration.

The record of many decades stands as proof that our people and their government have, in the main, understood these truths and have responded to them well, in the face of stress and threat. But threats, new in kind or degree, constantly arise. I mention two only.

IV.

A vital element in keeping the peace is our military establishment. Our arms must be mighty, ready for instant action, so that no potential aggressor may be tempted to risk his own destruction.

Our military organization today bears little relation to that known by any of my predecessors in peacetime, or indeed by the fighting men of World War II or Korea.

Until the latest of our world conflicts, the United States had no armaments industry. American makers of plowshares could, with time and as required, make swords as well. But now we can no longer risk emergency improvisation of national defense; we have been compelled to create a permanent armaments industry of vast proportions. Added to this, three and a half million men and women are directly engaged in the defense establishment. We annually spend on military security more than the net income of all United States corporations.

This conjunction of an immense military establishment and a large arms industry is new in the American experience. The total influence-economic, political, even spiritual—is felt in every city, every State house, every office of the Federal government. We recognize the imperative need for this development. Yet we must not fail to comprehend its grave implications. Our toil, resources and livelihood are all involved; so is the very structure of our society.

In the councils of government, we must guard against the acquisition of unwarranted influence, whether sought or unsought, by the military-industrial complex. The potential for the disastrous rise of misplaced power exists and will persist.

We must never let the weight of this combination endanger our liberties or democratic processes. We should take nothing for granted. Only an alert and knowledgeable citizenry can compel the proper meshing of the huge industrial and military machinery of defense with our peaceful methods and goals, so that security and liberty may prosper together.

Akin to, and largely responsible for the sweeping changes in our industrial-military posture, has been the technological revolution during recent decades.

In this revolution, research has become central; it also becomes more formalized, complex, and costly. A steadily increasing share is conducted for, by, or at the direction of, the Federal government.

Today, the solitary inventor, tinkering in his shop, has been overshadowed by task forces of scientists in laboratories and testing fields. In the same fashion, the free university, historically the fountainhead of free ideas and scientific discovery, has experienced a revolution in the conduct of research. Partly because of the huge costs involved, a government contract becomes virtually a substitute for intellectual curiosity. For every old blackboard there are now hundreds of new electronic computers.

The prospect of domination of the nation's scholars by Federal employment, project allocations, and the power of money is ever present—and is gravely to be regarded.

Yet, in holding scientific research and discovery in respect, as we should, we must also be alert to the equal and opposite danger that public policy could itself become the captive of a scientific-technological elite.

It is the task of statesmanship to mold, to balance, and to integrate these and other forces, new and old, within the principles of our democratic system—ever aiming toward the supreme goals of our free society.

V.

Another factor in maintaining balance involves the element of time. As we peer into society's future, we—you and I, and our government—must avoid the impulse to live only for today, plundering, for our own ease and convenience, the precious resources of tomorrow. We cannot mortgage the material assets of our grandchildren without risking the loss also of their political and spiritual heritage. We want democracy to survive for all generations to come, not to become the insolvent phantom of tomorrow. . . .

So—in this my last good night to you as your President—I thank you for the many opportunities you have given me for public service in war and peace. I trust that in that service you find some things worthy; as for the rest of it, I know you will find ways to improve performance in the future.

You and I—my fellow citizens—need to be strong in our faith that all nations, under God, will reach the goal of peace with justice. May we be ever unswerving in devotion to principle, confident but humble with power, diligent in pursuit of the Nation's great goals.

To all the peoples of the world, I once more give expression to America's prayerful and continuing aspiration:

We pray that peoples of all faiths, all races, all nations, may have their great human needs satisfied; that those now denied opportunity shall come to enjoy it to the full; that all who yearn for freedom may experience its spiritual blessings; that those who have freedom will understand, also, its heavy responsibilities; that all who are insensitive to the needs of others will learn charity; that the scourges of poverty, disease and ignorance will be made to disappear from the earth, and that, in the goodness of time, all peoples will come to live together in a peace guaranteed by the binding force of mutual respect and love.

Source: Dwight D. Eisenhower, "Farewell Radio and Television Address to the American People," January 17, 1961, in *Public Papers of the Presidents of the United States, Dwight D. Eisenhower, 1953–1961,* from the American Presidency Project, University of California, Santa Barbara, www.presidency .ucsb.edu.

CHAPTER FOUR

John F. Kennedy

Taking the Fight to the Enemy

I n his inaugural address (**Document 4.1**), President John F. Kennedy presented himself to the world as the leader of a new generation of Americans. It was the duty and privilege of this new generation, he said, to defend freedom itself at a moment of great peril. This speech, one of the most famous of all presidential communications, won such widespread acclaim that it obscured for a time the fact that Kennedy and his running mate, Lyndon Johnson, had won in November 1960 by the narrowest of margins.

The speech, a "call to action which Americans have needed to hear for many a year," in the words of the *Denver Post*,[1] can be read as a veritable Cold War catechism:

President John F. Kennedy signs the Proclamation for Interdiction of the Delivery of Offensive Weapons to Cuba on October 23, 1962. Source: John F. Kennedy Presidential Library and Museum/Cecil Stoughton.

Q. What is the greatest threat to freedom?

A. *Soviet-led communism.*

Q. Where is the battleground upon which the fight for freedom is to be waged?

A. *Everywhere. The Cold War is not a war of static fronts, but a dynamic global struggle.*

Q. By what means will America and the West defend themselves against communism?

A. *In two ways:*

　I. With a flexible military strategy backed by a full array of weapons and forces. No longer will the United States rely on the crude threat of nuclear annihilation.

　II. With cadres of compassion. Communists exploit poverty and hopelessness; Americans must lift the people of the third world out of poverty and place them on the path of modernization.

Q. What is the role of ordinary Americans?

A. *To sacrifice for victory without limit.*

Dwight Eisenhower had come into office determined to combat fearfulness. The public's role was to calm down. Eight years later, John F. Kennedy charged that under Eisenhower, confidence had turned to complacency. As a result, America had lost both prestige and power. What the public needed to do now was to *get going*. Through action, Kennedy believed, the nation's confidence would be restored.

THREAT AND RESPONSE

Kennedy's inaugural address was itself a response to a perceived threat issued to the incoming administration by Soviet premier Nikita Khrushchev in a speech of January 6, 1961. On that occasion, Khrushchev had spoken of the inevitability of Communist triumph, not through world war but "national liberation wars." These, the Soviet leader had asserted, promised the "only way of bringing imperialism to heel." The ongoing war in Vietnam and the Castro regime in Cuba were cited as examples.[2] The American president-elect interpreted the speech, published by the Soviets just two days before the American inaugural, as a "calculated personal test."[3]

Kennedy's reaction reflected more than a personal competitiveness. The Cold War, like hot wars before it, magnified the importance of the president. Starting in the late 1950s, the Cold War brought forth a veritable cult of presidential power. Kennedy, as a candidate for the office, gave voice to the wisdom of his time when he remarked:

> [I]f this nation is to reassert the initiative in foreign affairs, it must be presidential initiative. If we are to rebuild our prestige in the eyes of the world, it must be presidential prestige. . . . If the President does not move, if his party is opposed to progress then the nation does not move—and there is no progress.[4]

Louis XIV could not have said it any better.[5]

Khrushchev, ironically, may have intended his remarks as a challenge not to Kennedy, but to Mao. Chairman Mao Zedong, the revolutionary hero of Communist China, had recently challenged his Soviet counterpart for leadership of the international Communist movement in the third world. Khrushchev's speech was designed to demonstrate the continuing relevance of the Soviet Union to the global Communist cause. Nevertheless, the Soviet threat was not merely a figment of the new president's imagination. In fact, the Soviets had recently scored a considerable victory in the Cold War. By forging an alliance with Cuba's revolutionary government, they had brought the specter of international communism within ninety miles of America's shores.

Threat: The Bay of Pigs

On March 17, 1960, President Dwight Eisenhower had approved a covert action program against the new Cuban government of Fidel Castro. The most ambitious part of the plan was for the Central Intelligence Agency (CIA) to train more than 1,000 Cuban exiles intent on overturning Castro's 1959 revolution against General Fulgencio Batista. At a military base in Guatemala, these volunteers received instruction in military tactics preparatory to an invasion of their homeland. Just three months into his presidency, Kennedy gave the CIA the green light to proceed.

On April 15, 1961, eight American B-26 bombers, flying from Nicaragua, destroyed almost half of Cuba's air force. Two days later, the refugee army made an amphibious assault at the Bay of Pigs. Unfortunately for them, roughly 25,000 soldiers of the Cuban armed forces, with armored vehicles and tanks, greeted the "surprise" attack. Within two days, 149 CIA-trained, anti-Communist counterrevolutionaries had been killed; almost all the rest had been taken prisoner. What had gone wrong?

To this day, many Cuban-Americans and some writers hold President Kennedy responsible for the failure: "if only" the president had sent bombers to finish the mission of destroying the Cuban air force before the invasion; "if only" he had deployed the U.S. Air Force itself on the day of the landing; "if only" any number of tactical decisions had been made differently, then things would have turned out better. Most historians and political scientists, however, blame the plan itself and the process that allowed it to be carried out.

The Bay of Pigs was, in the title of an authoritative book on the topic, a "perfect failure" of decision making.[6] There were four significant mistakes in decision making; any one of them alone probably would have been sufficient to doom the operation.

First, the plan assumed that the United States' hand in the invasion could be hidden from the world despite the operation's size and rampant press speculation regarding an imminent American attack against Castro. Press inquiries about an invasion forced the president to pledge at a press conference on April 12 that there would not be "under any conditions an intervention in Cuba by the US Armed Forces."[7] Three days later, one of the Cuban pilots who took part in the April 15 raids landed his bomber in Florida to announce that he was a defector from Castro's air force. The press quickly uncovered the distinguishing marks of a plane straight out of the American arsenal. Once the American cover story was blown, the president decided that it would be up to the Cuban counterrevolutionaries to finish the job without additional American military cover.

Second, the CIA plan had internal contradictions. In the event that the initial landing and invasion did not fare well, the Cuban volunteers were to melt into the mountains where they would carry on as a guerilla force. This had made sense in conjunction with the landing site in the original CIA plan. But in what proved to be a futile effort to maintain the element of surprise, that site had been abandoned for another—eighty miles from the mountains.

Third, the plan relied for success upon the actions of others. The CIA never intended the small volunteer force to overthrow the government of Castro. It was to be the spark, rather, for a general uprising. This element of the plan not only underestimated Castro's popularity, but his ruthless efficiency as well. On the day of the invasion, Cuban security forces began a massive operation in which 200,000 potential enemies of the state were detained under guard.

Finally, those who recognized the plan's flaws decided to keep their reservations to themselves. This included the members of the Joint Chiefs of Staff (JCS) and their chairman, Gen. Lyman Lemnitzer.

How could so many things have gone wrong, so quickly, in the development of this plan?

Scholars have studied the decision-making process that led to this botched operation for answers. Their basic insight is that the new president, in reacting against the formality of the outgoing administration's National Security Council (NSC) planning process, went too far. The informality that characterized the Kennedy presidency had some benefits. It meant that anyone within the president's orbit with a good idea could have it heard. But it also made it easier for Kennedy's formal advisers, such as the chairman of the JCS, to remain silent, letting those eager to talk and to take responsibility do so.

"Group Think" may also have warped the outcome of the small, principals-only discussion sessions that Kennedy liked to rely upon. Participants in intense, small group settings—such as those that met to review the Cuban operation with the new president—tend to become keenly reluctant to speak against an emerging consensus. The esprit of the group becomes more important than the opinions of its members. Kennedy's informality magnified the danger of Group Think, because those present in the critical ad hoc meetings that the president relied upon to make decisions knew that their presence depended not on the formal office that they held but on the pleasure of the president.

Another reason for the failure at the Bay of Pigs is that it may have been in some sense *intended*. President Kennedy certainly hoped for the best from the invasion but seems to have chosen to proceed with the plan in part because he could not think of a better solution to what those in the White House called the "disposal problem."[8] Once 1,400 Cuban exiles had been armed, trained, and motivated to defeat Cuban communism, could the United States simply cancel their mission? What would the disappointed freedom fighters have had to say? Probably, they would have entertained the American and world press with bitter denunciations against the Democratic president who had lacked the guts to follow through with an operation begun by his Republican predecessor.

Some historians even argue that the lead planners of the CIA mission themselves realized that their plan would almost surely fail. In which case, they may have concluded, the inexperienced president in the Oval Office could be persuaded to save the day by authorizing what they and other hawks had wanted all along: an overt American invasion to overthrow Fidel Castro.[9]

Response

The president did not crack, but he took the defeat hard. He put on a brave, some said bellicose, front in a highly publicized speech on April 20, 1961, to the American Society of Newspaper Editors (**Document 4.2**). In that speech, Kennedy spoke with remorse about the recent defeat of the "small band of freedom fighters" in Cuba but disclaimed responsibility for their fate. "[T]his was a struggle," he said, "of Cuban patriots against a Cuban dictator." The president was adamant that the fight would continue, and he warned that the United States would not always be so reluctant to join in.

At a press conference the following day, the president went further in acknowledging responsibility without actually revealing the extent of U.S. participation (**Document 4.3**). "Defeat," the president famously remarked on this occasion, "is an orphan," but the president had no choice but to accept paternity. The president's response was not limited, however, to words or even to the predictable removal of the director of the CIA, Allen Dulles, and the CIA's director for plans, Richard Bissell.

On November 30, the president launched a wide-ranging covert operation in Cuba as bold as the invasion at the Bay of Pigs. Operation Mongoose, with a budget of approximately $50 million per year, engaged in sabotage, the incitement of rebellion, political and physical harassment, and (attempted) assassination. The JCS even recommended consideration at one point of a "Remember the Maine" incident.[10] A pretext for invasion, they stated in a planning document "could be arranged in several forms."[11]

By the end of its first year, 400 U.S. personnel and more than 1,000 Cubans living on the island had been placed on the Mongoose payroll, and the president had turned over operational command of the top-secret, multiagency initiative to his most trusted lieutenant—Attorney General Robert Kennedy, his brother. In January 1962 the administration used a military training exercise in the Caribbean, code-named ORTSAC, to signal the steadiness of its determination to act against Castro.[12]

The president also demonstrated a determination to score victories against communism beyond Cuba. The battle that had been lost in Cuba, the president repeatedly affirmed in the days after the invasion, was just a single battle in a wider war. Specifically, the president drew a connection between events in the Caribbean and those in Southeast Asia. In Vietnam, Kennedy suggested, the United States was about to draw the line (**Document 4.4**).

First, however, the U.S. armed forces would have to be enhanced and the nation's commitment to its overall security expanded. This had been one of Kennedy's themes in his recent campaign, and events in Cuba had given it new urgency. On May 25, the president delivered a special message "on urgent national needs" to Congress (**Document 4.5**). In the address, the president requested a range of actions, including a multibillion dollar expansion of the nation's civil-defense program and a new goal for NASA: "landing a man on the moon and returning him safely to the earth" by the end of the decade. The next month, the president spoke to the graduating class at the United States Military Academy at West Point, New York, describing the challenges and opportunities that lay before the new officers in an era of the global Cold War (**Document 4.6**).

Threat: Summitry and a New Berlin Crisis

Over two days of talks in Vienna on June 3–4, 1961, Kennedy and Khrushchev exchanged views on a range of issues, including the Eisenhower administration's nuclear test ban proposals and even events at the Bay of Pigs. Khrushchev hectored the president, who in the opinion of participants appeared "absolutely shook [shaken]," and even "shattered."[13]

Following lunch on the second day, the president suggested that the two leaders meet privately, with only their interpreters and note takers present. The topic would be Berlin, for Khrushchev had at the conference renewed a threat he had first made to President Eisenhower: He would negotiate a peace treaty with the German Democratic Republic (GDR, or East Germany), formalizing the division of Europe and asserting to the world the Soviet Union's commitment to the territorial integrity and sovereignty of the GDR. Either he would do this in December, or the Western powers and the Soviets could enter into an interim agreement providing for a withdrawal of Western forces from Berlin within six months. Either way, the premier asserted, the Western powers in Berlin would soon be reduced to the status of interlopers—illegitimate guests in the Communist capital of a Communist country. In their private meeting, the president pressed the premier on the meaning of this ultimatum.

Kennedy "reiterated his hope that relations between the two countries would develop in a way that would avoid direct contact or confrontation between them." To this, Khrushchev replied that "if the President insisted on US rights after the signing of a peace treaty and that if the borders of the GDR—land, air, or sea borders—were violated, they would be defended." Krushchev stated bluntly that "force would be met by force."[14]

Kennedy pursued the threat, stating that "either Mr. Khrushchev did not believe the US was serious or the situation in that area was so unsatisfactory that it had to take this drastic action." Kennedy was referring, with diplomatic ambiguity and grammatical awkwardness, to an unfolding crisis in East Berlin. The Communist authorities could not prevent their population, especially skilled workers, from fleeing to the West. The problem had grown to the point that the GDR and the Soviets were indeed desperate. In the month following the summit, 30,000 East Germans entered West Berlin to stay. Khrushchev ignored the president's reference to the internal problems of the GDR. Instead, he affirmed his threat: "[I]f the US wanted war," he said, "that was its problem."[15]

Response

Upon their return to their respective capitals, the showdown between the president and the premier gathered momentum. President Kennedy gave a nationally televised speech in which he elaborated on his call in May for a new civil defense program. The need, the president suggested, was now urgent and he pressed Congress to provide new funds for

> immediate objectives: to identify and mark space in existing structures—public and private—that could be used for fall-out shelters in case of attack; to stock those shelters with food, water, first-aid kits and other minimum essentials for survival . . . to improve our air-raid warning and fall-out detection systems, including a new household warning system which is now under development.

The effort, he assured his audience, was well worth it, for "[I]n the event of an attack, the lives of those families which are not hit in a nuclear blast and fire can still be saved."[16] As if to underscore the seriousness of the situation, the president went on to note that the appropriation of these extra funds would result in a $5 billion budget deficit.

Premier Khrushchev interpreted the president's speech as a virtual declaration of war. Having apparently decided that this was a president he might push around, he added to the threats offered in Vienna. The Soviets, he warned, had the capacity to deliver a 100-megaton bomb—and their scientists were eager to use it. Ultimately, however, Khrushchev backed away from a direct confrontation by acting upon the underlying problem within East Berlin.

Work on the infamous Berlin Wall began in the middle of the night of August 12–13, 1961. The wall, at first a fence of barbed wire, was completed and reinforced over the next several months. Although the situation along the 100-mile border during construction of the barricade was sometimes tense—there was a sixteen-hour standoff by Soviet and American tanks in late October—the wall effectively sealed the once embarrassingly porous border. Over time, it would come to be seen as both a symbol of Communist oppression and a provocation to the West. At the time, it was understood by Kennedy for what it was—"a hell of a lot better than a war."[17]

Kennedy prudently tested Khrushchev's meaning with the construction of the wall by sending an armed convoy overland to West Berlin. It was neither stopped nor harassed. The Soviets did not formally renounce their ultimatum, but let it pass without notice or action. The Berlin crisis, for the moment, was over.

Threat: The Cuban Missile Crisis

By late in his first year in office, President Kennedy and the members of his Cabinet had themselves abandoned one of their previous claims: that of a missile gap between the United States and the Soviet Union. There had always been more than a bit of campaign hyperbole behind the claim of a missile gap. On September 21, 1961, a new National Intelligence Estimate—a secret CIA report—confirmed that the Soviet intercontinental ballistic missile (ICBM) program was far behind worst-case speculations of the previous year. Although the Soviets had certainly made progress, they had not achieved parity with, much less an advantage over, the United States in the deployment of strategic forces. Nonetheless, the president intended to proceed with those aspects of his military buildup that had been justified by reference to the alleged American deficiency. And he would do so after publicly revealing the true status of the arms race.

The president intended, it seems, to humiliate his Soviet counterpart. The United States, the administration informed the public, had several times the nuclear power of the Soviet Union. Kennedy's administration disseminated this news with a major speech personally approved by the president and delivered by Deputy Secretary of Defense Roswell Gilpatric on October 21, 1961. The American advantage was so great, Gilpatric said, that the United States could survive a first strike and then retaliate with devastating counterforce in the event of a nuclear war. In ICBMs alone, the United States had between a four-to-one and an eight-to-one advantage in numbers, as well as a further advantage in reliability and accuracy. With regard to all nuclear warheads, the Americans had seventeen times the Soviets' number of weapons.

The president wanted still more weapons for two reasons. First, in the supercharged atmosphere of the 1960s, the failure to push an advantage was perceived as a loss. In the "game" of nuclear deterrence, the personal factor could not be discounted. It would make no difference how great the U.S. advantage was if the other side doubted the American will to use nuclear weapons. The slightest deviation from the path of "toughness" might crack the American reputation for resolve.

Second, the president was inspired by proponents of the "New Economics," who thought that large defense budgets helped, not hurt, the economy. Their message was that President Eisenhower and Secretary of the Treasury George Humphrey had held old-fashioned views of the economy, and that their obsessive fear of inflation and budget deficits had "kept policy thinking in too restrictive a mold."[18] Enhanced public spending on defense, moreover, was far less controversial among members of Congress and the public than expanded spending on social programs.

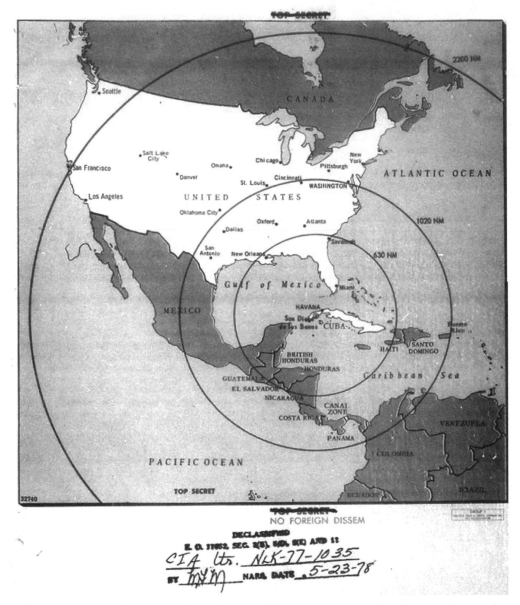

A declassified map of the western hemisphere used during secret Kennedy administration meetings in October 1962 shows the full range of the nuclear missiles under construction in Cuba. *Source:* John F. Kennedy Presidential Library and Museum.

Khrushchev, tempted already by what he perceived as Kennedy's weakness in the Bay of Pigs and at Vienna, was now provoked by Kennedy's candor. Against the opposition of some members of the Politburo, the executive committee of the Soviet Communist Party and therefore the leading organization of state control in the Soviet Union, the Soviet premier resolved to take a shortcut toward nuclear parity. He would do so by following the example of the Americans themselves, who in April 1962 had completed the installation of fifteen nuclear-tipped missiles in Turkey, a NATO ally and Soviet neighbor. The Soviets would reply in kind and raise the stakes. They would ship to Cuba forty medium and intermediate range ballistic missile launchers, with respective ranges of 1,100 and 2,200 miles, along with two missiles and one nuclear warhead for each. To complement this force, the Soviets would send attack submarines, fighter jets, bombers, surface-to-air missiles, tanks, and 40,000 troops. The operation was begun in July 1862. By October, the eighty-five ships that the Soviets dedicated to this mission had made more than 105 trips.

Naturally, Khrushchev presented this decision to his Cuban friend as a step toward that nation's defense. The United States, he asserted, might try again to overthrow Fidel Castro, and the next time, the Americans might not rely on subterfuge and refugees. Castro knew better. As he remarked years later:

> I don't know what Khrushchev was striving for, but it seems to me that his assurances about the defense of Cuba being his main goal notwithstanding, Khrushchev was setting strategic goals for himself. . . . Personally, I believe that along with his love for Cuba Khrushchev wanted to fix the strategic parity in the cheapest way.[19]

Khrushchev's son revealed after the Cold War that his father's goal was to surprise the West with a fait accompli. Once the operation was complete, the premier planned to travel to Cuba himself and reveal the missiles. This was to happen shortly after the American midterm elections. (The Soviets were savvy enough about electoral politics to realize that doing so during the election season would greatly increase the pressure upon the president to react.) Khrushchev, according to his son, believed that in the lull after their elections, the Americans would "make a fuss, make more of a fuss, and then accept."[20]

Perhaps because of his confidence in American acquiescence, Khrushchev and his generals were as reckless of discovery as Kennedy and his generals had been the year before in the buildup to the Bay of Pigs. Should the Americans take photographs of the missiles from their spy planes, Soviet defense officials asserted to the Politburo, they would find nothing, because the missiles would blend in with the palm trees.

In late summer and early fall 1962, rumors began to circulate of strange happenings in Cuba. Cubans spying for the CIA reported, among other things, unusual boasts from Cuba's military chief, Raul Castro, as well as his brother, Fidel; enormous trucks ferrying secret cargoes through the streets at night—trucks so large that they toppled street signs; and Soviet military personnel who would not allow even Cuban officers to go near their new equipment. In the United States, word leaked of these discoveries, and several Republicans in Congress began to air their own suspicions about what they meant. Senators Kenneth Keating of New York and Homer Capehart of Indiana began to urge the president in September to prepare for a U.S. invasion, just in case.

In early September, the president issued a statement on Cuba meant to calm anxieties, while simultaneously requesting standby authority from Congress to call up 150,000 reservists. Even without evidence of what, exactly, the Soviets were up to in Cuba, the situation there was becoming news—and a major issue in the elections of 1962.

The White House was uncertain what to do because the administration was at first reluctant to believe that the Soviets would take such a brazen step. Kennedy's new director of central intelligence, John McCone, speculated that the administration's critics were right and that the Soviets had transported nuclear weapons to Cuba, but he could not produce hard evidence. The CIA's own analysts disagreed with their chief. When the administration confirmed the presence in Cuba of surface-to-air missiles, Soviet ambassador Anatoly Dobrynin met with Robert Kennedy to pass along the Soviet premier's guarantee that the Soviets would place no surface-to-*surface* missiles or other offensive weapons in Cuba. The president replied in a White House statement of September 4 that "[w]ere it otherwise the gravest issues would arise."[21]

In early October, the president authorized the resumption of U-2 spy flights, which he had temporarily halted to lessen tensions in the area. Finally, on October 15, analysts at the National Photographic Interpretation Center discovered unmistakable evidence of nuclear-missile launching sites under construction in Cuba.

"He can't do that to me!" the president proclaimed. This, Kennedy soon decided, was the test of all tests. If he failed to take decisive action, he told his close aide, Ken O'Donnell, he would forever be remembered as "looking away" while Khrushchev gained the upper hand in the Cold War. Senator Keating was looking good for president of the United States in 1965, the president somberly observed when first studying the photographs with National Security Adviser McGeorge Bundy.[22]

Response

Once again, Kennedy relied upon an informal decision-making process, meeting continuously with an ad hoc group he dubbed the Executive Committee of the NSC, or EXCOMM. In addition to meeting with EXCOMM in multiple, almost continuous sessions during the crisis, the president met privately with small subsets of its members, mostly those with whom he had a personal relationship. Kennedy magnified the informality of the process by using his brother, unbeknownst to EXCOMM's other members, to relay private messages to Khrushchev via the Soviet ambassador.

The decision-making process was, on paper at any rate, as personal and informal—and therefore dangerous—as it had been in the Bay of Pigs. This time, however, Kennedy made the process work. In part, this was because he had learned to be skeptical of "expert" advice, particularly from the military. In addition, there was virtually no limit to the "downside" should the situation get out of hand. In the Bay of Pigs, failure in fact came with *benefits,* namely it provided a solution to the "disposal problem." In the Cuban Missile Crisis, the costs associated with failure were potentially huge. With this extra motivation, the president proved able to resist the pressure to foreclose options with a hasty and irrevocable decision.

The crisis unfolded at first in private, as Kennedy and the fourteen members of EXCOMM considered a range of options before going public on October 22, 1962. In EXCOMM meetings, Kennedy at first played the role of facilitator, encouraging everyone to speak their mind and then pressing them to defend their recommendations, which ranged initially from capitulation to a nuclear assault on the Soviet Union. The group also spent many hours debating the course of action that the military almost immediately recommended: the invasion of Cuba.

The Joint Chiefs suggested a week's intensive aerial bombardment followed by an invasion with a force of 25,000 men. Within three weeks of dropping the first bomb, 90,000 U.S. military personnel could be on the ground in Cuba. A number of more limited assault options were also considered, such as a bombing campaign aimed exclusively at the missile sites. There was considerable disagreement within the room over the highly important issue of the likely Soviet response to any of these plans.

The president consistently expressed concern at EXCOMM discussions over first-order Soviet reprisals, which he expected to include an invasion of West Berlin. The collective and foreboding nature of the conversations in the first few days of the crisis is nicely illustrated in the following exchange, which took place at 11:00 a.m. on October 18, among the president, Attorney General Robert Kennedy, National Security Adviser McGeorge Bundy, Secretary of Defense Robert McNamara, and Chairman of the JCS Gen. Maxwell Taylor.

R. Kennedy: "What do we do when really . . . I think he moves into Berlin?"
M. Bundy: "If we could trade off Berlin, and not have it our fault. . ."
(Bundy alone laughs)
R. McNamara: "Well, when we're talking about taking Berlin, what do we *mean* exactly? Do they take it with Soviet troops?"
President: "That's what I would see, anyway."
R. McNamara: "I think there's a real possibility of that. We have U.S. troops there. What do they do?"
M. Taylor: "They fight."
R. McNamara: "They fight. I think that's perfectly clear."
President: "And they get overrun."
R. McNamara: "Yes, they get overrun, exactly."
R. Kennedy: "Then what do we do?"
M. Taylor: "Go to general war, assuming we have time for it."
President: "You mean nuclear exchange?"
M. Taylor: "Guess you have to."[23]

It was around the time of this exchange that the president began to move away from invasion, toward a blockade. "The question, *really*," the president announced moments after the above remarks, was "what action we take which *lessens* the chance" of such an outcome.[24]

On October 18, the president also met in the Oval Office with Soviet foreign minister Andrei Gromyko. It was a strained conversation, made more so by the fact that the president did not yet wish to reveal that the Soviets' secret had been uncovered (**Document 4.7**). The president recited to Gromyko previous Soviet assurances regarding the transfer of offensive weapons to Cuba, to which Gromyko added new promises of good behavior. The president indicated his satisfaction, repeatedly stating that the United States had no intention of invading the island and would even make such a guarantee if it would be helpful. He warned, however, that "grave" consequences would follow from any deviation from the Soviet position on introducing offensive weapons to Cuba. The president's threatening remarks made no impression on the minister, who reported blithely to his superiors in the Kremlin the next day that the situation in Washington was "completely satisfactory" (**Document 4.8**).

Early the next day, in a tense meeting with the full JCS, the president reviewed where matters stood. He was leaning, he indicated, toward a blockade in order merely to force the removal of the missiles. That would be a good enough outcome, he stated, because we "don't really have to invade Cuba." The Communist outpost in the Caribbean, he said, might simply be "one of the difficulties that we live with in life."[25]

The Joint Chiefs were not inclined to be so philosophical. They argued, variously, that a blockade would lead to a wider war; that a bombing campaign against the missile sites would be less provocative; that the longer the United States waited to replace the objectionable Cuban regime, the more difficult it would be to do so; and that a weak U.S. response in Cuba would bring about precisely what the president wished to prevent—a Soviet assault on West Berlin. The chiefs were, among themselves, positively contemptuous of the president's preferred course of action. "Almost as bad as the appeasement at Munich," offered Air Force Chief of Staff General Curtis LeMay. "Weak," contributed Gen. Earl Wheeler of the army.[26]

Despite the Joint Chiefs' objections, the president had made his decision. Before leaving for a campaign function on October 19, he instructed two of his most loyal subordinates, his brother and his secretary of defense, to lead the EXCOMM toward a consensus behind a blockade. The following day, the president ordered the JCS to begin preparations for a blockade. On October 22, the Strategic Air Command initiated an alert of its B-52 nuclear bombers, guaranteeing that one-eighth of the force was always airborne.

The same day, after revealing the news first to seventeen congressional leaders from both parties, the United States' major allies, and the Soviet Union, the president at last went public in a televised speech to the nation (**Document 4.9**). Remarkably, the president had managed to keep secret the very thing that so many in the press had speculated about for months. The *New York Times,* the *Washington Post,* and the *New York Herald Tribune* had all pieced together the essence of the story. All three papers had agreed to hold their stories after requested to do so by the president or the secretary of defense. It was imperative, the publishers and journalists were told, that Khrushchev not be allowed to make the first "move" in what was bound to be a delicate "game" of diplomatic—and possibly military—maneuver.

The president's brief remarks to the public were grim. He quoted first from the false promises made to him only recently by the Soviet foreign minister, before bringing up the lesson of the 1930s: not to appease aggressors. After announcing that as one of his "initial steps," he had ordered a blockade or "quarantine" to be put in place in a few days' time, the president warned that should a nuclear missile be launched against the United States from Cuba, the United States would respond with a "full retaliatory response upon the Soviet Union." Only the Soviets, he said, could now pull the world back from the "abyss."[27] After the speech, three of five Americans surveyed expected armed conflict to result; fully 20 percent expected "world war."[28]

Ambassador Dobrynin analyzed Kennedy's speech for Moscow (**Document 4.10**). American hard-liners, the Soviet minister reported, on the basis of allegedly inside information, were now in control of the administration. They were urging the president to regard the situation in Cuba as an opportunity to "demonstrate his character" by taking up the challenge of the Soviet Union. Dobrynin wrote of the Soviet delivery of missiles to Cuba as having itself already damaged the United States' reputation as the "leader of the capitalist world," thereby provoking the president's allegedly warlike response. This time, the president seemed willing to "go pretty far" with the Soviets in reply. But reading somewhat between the lines, Dobrynin's overall advice seems to have been to proclaim victory and go home. After a short period of reflection, Khrushchev too came to the realization that the president meant what he said; the Soviets had "missed our chance."[29]

Before coming to this realization, however, Khrushchev at first ordered the captains of Soviet ships approaching the blockade zone to hold course, an order quietly countermanded at the prompting of his more cool-headed Politburo ally, Anastas Mikoyan. Publicly, the Soviets warned that their ships did not intend to observe the quarantine line and that U.S. ships would be sunk if they attempted to molest Soviet vessels. In anticipation of a confrontation, Secretary of Defense McNamara, upon the advice of the JCS, on October 24 took the Strategic Air Command to DEFCON 2 (Defense Condition 2, a heightened state of alert). On a five point scale, this was just one step from DEFCON 1, or maximum force readiness, which was itself one step from actual war.

October 24 was the day that the blockade would formally go into effect. On that date, the first Soviet ships came to within sight of awaiting American naval vessels. Over the course of the day, several Soviet ships stopped in the water and then changed course. Navy officers, White House officials, and high-level appointees from the State Department debated, however, what to do about those Soviet ships that appeared to be continuing on course to Cuba. After considerable discussion at the highest levels, a decision was made to interdict a Soviet-chartered but non–Soviet bloc ship, the Lebanese freighter *Marucla*. On October 26, American sailors boarded the vessel. After a search revealed no indication of contraband, it was permitted to continue for Havana.

The slow pace at which the quarantine unfolded permitted time for both sides to continue internal debates and to seek public advantage. On the American side, the U.S. ambassador to the United Nations, Adlai Stevenson, made a memorable presentation to the UN Security Council in which he provided visual evidence of the Soviet missile sites and dramatically confronted the Soviet representative. Before placing his evidence on easels, Stevenson confronted Soviet ambassador Valerian Zorin:

And while we are asking questions, let me ask you why your Government—your Foreign Minister—deliberately, cynically deceived us about the nuclear build up in Cuba.

And finally, the other day, Mr. Zorin, I remind you that you did not deny the existence of these weapons. Instead, we heard that they had suddenly become defensive weapons. But today again if I heard you correctly, you now say that they do not exist, or that we haven't proved they exist, with another fine flood of rhetorical scorn.

All right, sir, let me ask you one simple question: Do you, Ambassador Zorin, deny that the U.S.S.R. has placed and is placing medium- and intermediate-range missiles and sites in Cuba? Yes or no—don't wait for the translation—yes or no?

[Silence from the Soviet delegate]

You can answer yes or no. You have denied they exist. I want to know if I understood you correctly. I am prepared to wait for my answer until hell freezes over, if that's your decision.[30]

Ambassador Zorin replied with bluster of his own, dismissing Stevenson's photographic evidence as a forgery and accusing the American president of acting like a "highway robber."[31] Internal debates continued in the United States. When the chief of naval operations, Admiral George Anderson Jr., bristled at the secretary of defense's micromanagement of the navy's blockade, claiming that his service had been conducting such operations (presumably without civilian interference) "since the days of John Paul Jones,"

McNamara replied with the memorable line that it was "not a blockade" that the navy was conducting "but a means of communication between Kennedy and Khrushchev." [32]

During this period of communication by blockade, Soviet troops on the island continued to assemble missiles and uncrate bombers, leading the president, by October 26, once again to consider direct military action, including possibly an invasion. Before the end of the day, and before Kennedy could come to a firm conclusion to employ greater force, Khrushchev sent to the president a message that seemed to offer a way out: the Soviets would remove the missiles and the Americans would pledge not to invade Cuba (**Document 4.11**).

As this was essentially the same deal that Kennedy had hinted at in his meeting with the Soviet foreign minister, the prospects for a peaceful resolution to the crisis appeared to be quite good. But the administration had not yet had a chance to respond when another letter arrived (**Document 4.12**). This time, the Soviet premier demanded that the United States pledge not only not to invade Cuba but also to remove NATO missiles from Turkey. The president was quick to concede, among his advisers, the logic of the proposal. We "can't very well invade," he remarked, "when we could have gotten them out by making a deal on the same missiles in Turkey." [33] The United States' major European allies had, in fact, through the entire crisis been troubled by the apparent double standard implied by the U.S. position on the two sets of weapons. Still, to give up the NATO missiles under pressure would be to acknowledge weakness, the perception of which was anathema under the unwritten rules of nuclear deterrence and personally abhorrent to the president.

The president's solution was to work out a secret, explicit trade on the missiles along the lines suggested by Khrushchev in his second letter. Only the president, the Soviet premier, and their most loyal associates were ever to know that a quid pro quo had been arranged. In the West, what began as a presidential cover story took on, over decades of repetition and embellishment, the character of myth. According to this myth, the president ingeniously decided to ignore the second letter and accept the first. The president's brother, the story continued, met privately with the Soviet ambassador to explain that the president could not possibly trade away NATO missiles but would graciously agree to consider the issue of their utility at a later date. The Soviet emissary was given no choice, the legend continues, but to be content with this vague commitment. The opening of some of the archives of the former Soviet Union after the end of the Cold War made available documents revealing that, in reality, the president sent his brother on this private errand to accept the terms contained in the famous second letter (**Document 4.13**).

Khrushchev apparently had no difficulty granting Kennedy's wish that their agreement be kept secret. Intriguingly, the premier may have been motivated not to demand the embarrassment of his adversary because he believed the president was on the verge of losing control of his presidency. What Khrushchev took away from reading Dobrynin's telegram reporting on his meeting with Robert Kennedy was that "[e]ven though the President himself is very much against starting a war over Cuba, an irreversible chain of events could occur against his will. . . . The American army could get out of control." [34] The Soviet top command was so anxious about an American invasion, whether ordered by the constitutional executive or a military junta, that when they learned via the press that Kennedy was to speak to the American people on the very evening of the meeting between Robert Kennedy and Dobrynin, they anticipated an announcement of invasion. A formal exchange of letters between the two countries was soon arranged, specifying the public component of the settlement (**Document 4.14**).

There was tremendous relief in both capitals, but not everyone joined in the celebratory mood. Ironically, the two groups that were perhaps most upset were the leaders of the American military and the Communist government of Cuba. "We have been had," was the collective feeling among the JCS and the Castro regime. The U.S. military had to content itself with the knowledge that although the president had—for the first time—renounced the notion of invading Cuba, the administration always hedged its promise with qualifications and continued with its covert operations against the regime. For their part, the Cubans and the Soviets patched up their relationship. While Cuba could not serve the Soviets as a strategic counterweight in the direct superpower rivalry, the Cuban military proved highly useful to the Soviets in the 1970s, sending ground troops to Africa on behalf of the Communist cause.

Unfortunately, the greatest legacy of the peaceful resolution of the Cuban Missile Crisis was the spur that it gave to the arms race. With the failure of the Cuban gambit, the Soviets had no choice but to build up their nuclear ICBM force if they were to forge a more favorable correlation of forces with the United States. The way in which the crisis was resolved—with the American president seemingly forcing his will upon the Soviet premier—added another, more personal motivation to the Soviet desire to catch up. It was not good for Soviet prestige among its allies and associates to be shown up so by the Americans.

BEYOND CRISIS

Not everything that happened in the 1960s happened in the midst of a nerve-wracking crisis. There was a continuous press on a number of policy fronts related to the Cold War, including the arms race and the struggle for the "hearts and minds" of the world's poor.[35]

The Arms Race and the Sino-Soviet Rift

There was complexity—some said ambivalence—in the Kennedy administration's pursuit of arms reductions. On the one hand, the president continued the Eisenhower administration's pursuit of a test ban treaty. In a June 10, 1963, speech at American University in Washington, D.C., the president spoke memorably of his and the nation's desire for peace and of the importance of the proposed treaty (**Document 4.15**). Even the Soviets, the president said, want peace. A relaxation of Cold War tensions was imperative so that all sides could come closer to their common objective. Just two weeks later, in brief remarks upon being welcomed to Berlin, the president returned to more familiar Cold War rhetoric, expressing his solidarity with the people of West Berlin in the famous sentence, "Ich bin ein Berliner" (**Document 4.16**). To be a citizen of Berlin, the president explained, was the proudest boast of a free person because Berlin was the front line in the struggle of absolutes that was the Cold War.

The duality in the president's rhetoric reflected the complexity of the Cold War in the 1960s, in particular the weakening of the Communist bloc. Although U.S. policymakers of the Cold War are routinely condemned for having been blind to the reality of Communist diversity, the Sino-Soviet split was headline news, so to speak, within the executive branch from the time of the late Eisenhower administration forward. China had been chafing for years at playing "younger brother" to the Soviet Union's self-assigned role of "older brother." As far back as the Chinese civil war (1927–1950), Stalin had worried about Chairman Mao Zedong's ambitions to challenge Soviet leadership. Stalin had been right to worry, his successors discovered. In the final year of the Eisenhower presidency, the Chinese government criticized "peaceful coexistence" as revisionist heresy and attempted to break Soviet client states away from their patrons in Moscow.

President Kennedy was quite aware of the Sino-Soviet split. In the summer of 1963 he tried to persuade the Soviets at the Nuclear Test Ban talks in Moscow to join him in taking military action against the Chinese. Specifically, the president instructed his test ban treaty negotiator, Averell Harriman, "to elicit K[hrushchev]'s view of means of limiting or preventing China's nuclear development and his willingness either to take Soviet action or to accept U.S. action aimed in this direction."[36] The premier rebuffed the proposed joint preemptive strike against their common antagonist.

Significantly, the proposed Nuclear Test Ban Treaty would bar signatories from helping other states gain nuclear weapons. The treaty, formally the "Treaty Banning Nuclear Weapons Tests in the Atmosphere, in Outer Space, and Under Water," was signed in Moscow by the United States, the United Kingdom, and the Soviet Union on August 5, 1963, and went into effect October 10 (**Document 4.17**). It was a significant first step toward nonproliferation, but it did not limit underground tests of nuclear weapons. China and France, which were both nuclear powers, declined to sign. After Khrushchev signed the treaty, Mao allowed, for the first time, direct criticism of the Soviet premier by name. The chair of the Atomic Energy Commission, Glenn Seaborg, thought that, in retrospect, the president was probably more motivated to conclude negotiations for this agreement by his concern for China than by his worries about the Soviet Union.

Still, there were limits to how far the United States might want to go in any relationship of convenience with the Soviet Union. The Soviets and the Chinese, after all, continued to cooperate on a number of fronts and were both still highly motivated by Communist ideology. In addition, their rivalry spurred them at times to compete with one another in their antagonism to the West and in their support of Communist revolutions around the world.

Hearts and Minds

Europe's old empires were in the final stages of collapse when Kennedy took office. In 1960 alone, seventeen nations became independent in Africa. These countries and their peers had a choice to make: were they to align with the East, the West, or one another? To help them to make the "right" choice, the Kennedy administration promised both military assistance, when needed, and nonmilitary assistance.

There was at times tension within the administration between those who were oriented toward seeing the fight for the third world primarily as a military encounter and those who prioritized the fight against poverty. The latter group favored reliance on the Agency for International Development (AID), the "Food for Peace" program, and the Peace Corps, which was created in response to an administration proposal. The president sought to utilize the advice and talents of both hawks and doves on the third world, but he sometimes could not keep out of the bureaucratic warfare between the two. When G. Mennen Williams, assistant secretary of state for African affairs, was criticized within the administration for saying that Africa "was for Africans," the president at a press conference quipped that he "didn't know who else Africa should be for." [37]

The quip came easily, but in practice it was difficult for the president to steer a steady course in his administration's policy toward Africa and the rest of the third world. A secessionist movement in the mineral-rich province of Katanga created a rift within Congo as well as within the world political community that also threatened to divide the administration, especially once the Congolese government turned to the Soviets for help. President Kennedy rejected pressure to draw a parallel between Katanga and Hungary, where the Soviets had used force to crush a pro-democracy rebellion, but used the CIA to provide limited assistance to the secessionist province in any event.

For America's Western allies, the relinquishing of African colonies was often a bitter experience, but the United States had never been a traditional imperialist power and had long condemned European colonialism. It could not always side with the former imperial powers. In response to events in Ghana, the administration chose to err on the other side of the divide. Ghana had become a republic in July 1960. Shortly after winning the nation's first election for president, Kwame Nkrumah proclaimed himself president for life and began to employ harsh tactics, in particular the preventive detentions of political opponents. Nkrumah was a socialist-inspired pan-Africanist, but he was wary of both the United States and the Soviet Union. The United States chose in this instance not to take action against the mildly Marxist third-world dictator but rather to provide aid to his officially nonaligned state. In October 1962, during the Cuban Missile Crisis, the United States was repaid when the government of Ghana refused to grant landing rights to Soviet planes for refueling.

The Peace Corps was another component of the Kennedy Cold War arsenal. Kennedy had proposed the corps in the final week of his presidential campaign. Once in office, the president made two critical decisions that enhanced the new agency's prospects for success. He put it in the hands of Sargent Shriver, his brother-in-law and a passionate advocate for programs to alleviate poverty, and he followed the advice of Shriver and Vice President Lyndon Johnson when deciding to propose the agency as a stand-alone organization rather than placing it under the direction of a traditional component of the bureaucracy, such as the Agency for International Development. The Peace Corps was quickly approved and funded by Congress and became one of the most widely praised legacies of the Kennedy presidency.

In Latin America Peace Corps volunteers were integrated into a broad program known as the Alliance for Progress. The president announced the Alliance initiative at the White House on March 13, 1961, calling it a "vast cooperative effort, unparalleled in magnitude and nobility of purpose." [38] The program, which was intended to unite North and South American nations, combined three principal elements: monetary aid ($20 billion over ten years, from a mix of public and private sources), land and tax reform, and democratization. Because the Alliance did not address the problem of preexisting debt, net capital outlays to Latin America were only marginally affected by this seemingly generous program. At the end of the day, debt-ridden Latin American nations ended up with minimal new money to distribute, and the redistributive efforts of the Alliance stood little chance of implementation.

Rather than a decade of reform and stabilization, Latin America entered a decade of coups and countercoups. Often, the American president was found on the side of the coup makers. In this "most dangerous area in the world," as Kennedy once described it, it was important to be alert to the slightest indication of anti-Western intent.[39] The CIA therefore became one of the administration's most important tools in the region.

The CIA was also important to the Kennedy administration in its efforts in Southeast Asia. Kennedy was determined, especially after the shock of the Bay of Pigs, that the United States demonstrate its resolve in Laos and Vietnam. In Laos the president in his first year in office accepted an uneasy truce and a formal declaration of Laotion neutrality. In Vietnam the president wanted a clear win. As Kennedy said after the Bay of Pigs disaster and the Laotian settlement to John Kenneth Galbraith, an academic adviser whom the president would appoint U.S. ambassador to India, there were "just so many concessions that one [could] make to the communists in one year and survive politically."[40]

During the Kennedy presidency, the U.S. military commitment to South Vietnam increased substantially, as suggested by the number of U.S. military advisers in the country: their number stood at 1,000 when Kennedy came into office and at about 16,000 in November 1963. The president's most important decision with respect to South Vietnam, however, was to withdraw his support from South Vietnamese president Ngo Dinh Diem and his brother and co-ruler, Ngo Dinh Nhu. On August 24, 1963, Assistant Secretary of State for Far Eastern Affairs Roger Hilsman sent a cable to the U.S. ambassador in Vietnam, Henry Cabot Lodge, instructing him that if Diem remained "obdurate" about the urgent need to remove his notorious brother from the government, and otherwise reform his administration, "then we are prepared to accept the obvious implication that we can no longer support Diem. You may also tell appropriate military commanders we will give them direct support in any interim period of breakdown of central government mechanism."[41] The president authorized this "green light" signal to Diem's rivals, and he and his top aides closely monitored the situation in Saigon. The United States, Kennedy decided at an August 29 White House meeting, would not actively engage in coup plotting with officers in Diem's army, but would support a coup "that has a good chance of succeeding."[42] On November 1, 1963, the coup took place, during the course of which Diem and his brother were killed.

Weeks later, Kennedy himself was assassinated as he rode in a motorcade in Dallas, Texas.

CONCLUSION

President Kennedy came into office having made a promise to "get the nation moving again." His administration was indeed one of constant movement, but the moves that Kennedy made proved to be largely reactions to the moves of others. It was difficult to plan in an atmosphere of constant change, and it was especially difficult to focus on the long term when near-term crises followed one another with a discouraging regularity.

President Kennedy's biggest reactive move was his management of the Cuban Missile Crisis. In this, he won the respect of the West and of commentators and historians for keeping the crisis from turning into a catastrophe. The president's most lasting proactive move was the decision to respond aggressively to the Soviet and Chinese challenge in the third world. The United States, too, wanted the allegiance of the world's poor, and it was prepared to do new things to win that support.

The approach that the Kennedy administration followed in the Cold War had two sides, a peaceful one and a military one. Kennedy's hopes for a peaceable solution were epitomized in the Peace Corps. His passion for military action was epitomized by the army's Special Forces, the "Green Berets" in which the president took a deep, personal interest. In the succeeding administration, it was the military half of the Kennedy legacy that flourished.

NOTES

1. "Editorial Comment Across the Nation on President Kennedy's Inaugural," "Moscow Radio Gives News," and Hart Phillips, "Castro Suggests Amity with the U.S.," *New York Times,* January 21, 1961.
2. Michael Beschloss, *The Crisis Years: Kennedy and Khrushchev, 1960–1963* (New York: Harper Collins, 1991), 60.
3. Arthur M. Schlesinger Jr., *Robert Kennedy and His Times* (Boston: Houghton Mifflin, 1978), 422–433.
4. John F. Kennedy, *Freedom of Communication, Part I: The Speeches, Remarks, Press Conferences and Statements of Senator John F. Kennedy, August 1 through November 7, 1960, 87th Congress, 1st Session,* ed. U.S. Senate Committee on Commerce (Washington, D.C.: United States Government Printing Office, 1961), 992–993.
5. The French Sun King (1638–1715) was famously said to have boasted "L'état, c'est moi" ("I am the State").
6. Trumbull Higgins, *The Perfect Failure: Kennedy, Eisenhower, and the CIA at the Bay of Pigs* (New York: W. W. Norton and Company, 1989).
7. "The President's News Conference," April 12, 1961 in *Public Papers of the Presidents of the United States: John F. Kennedy, 1961–1963,* from the American Presidency Project, University of California, Santa Barbara, www.presidency.ucsb.edu.
8. The quotation is from Arthur M. Schlesinger, *A Thousand Days: John F. Kennedy in the White House* (Boston: Houghton Mifflin, 1965). See Joan Didion, "Miami, 'La Lucha,' " *New York Review of Books,* June 11, 1987, www.nybooks.com/articles/4740.
9. Lucien S. Vanenbrouke, "The 'Confessions' of Allen Dulles: New Evidence on the Bay of Pigs," *Diplomatic History* 8 (February 1984): 365–375.
10. On February 15, 1898, the USS *Maine* exploded and sank in Havana harbor, taking the lives of 266 of its crew members. Americans suspected sabotage by the Spanish authorities who ruled Cuba, and "Remember the Maine" became a battle cry during the Spanish-American War that began in April.
11. L. L. Lemnitzer, Chairman of the Joint Chiefs of Staff, "Justification for U.S. Military Intervention in Cuba," Memorandum for the Secretary of Defense, March 13, 1962, from the National Security Archive, George Washington University, www.gwu.edu/~nsarchiv/news/20010430/doc1.pdf.
12. ORTSAC is, of course, Castro spelled backwards.
13. So said Lem Billings and Averell Harriman, respectively. Vice President Johnson, rather unkindly, said "Khrushchev scared the poor little fellow dead." The president himself said it was "like dealing with [his own] Dad. All give and no take." All quotations from Beschloss, *Crisis Years,* 234.
14. James N. Giglio and Stephen G. Rabe, *Debating the Kennedy Presidency* (Lanham, Md.: Rowman and Littlefield Publishers, 2003), 76–78.

15. Ibid., 78.

16. Giglio and Rabe, *Debating the Kennedy Presidency,* 79.

17. Ibid., 27.

18. Christopher A. Preble, *John F. Kennedy and the Missile Gap* (DeKalb: Illinois University Press, 2004), 38.

19. Georgy K. Shakhnazavolv, " 'I Know Something About the Cuban Missile Crisis,' Notes from a Conversation with Fidel Castro, 5 November 1987," *Cold War International History Bulletin,* no. 5 (Spring 1995): 87–89.

20. The younger Khrushchev, as quoted in Max Frankel, *High Noon in the Cold War: Kennedy, Khrushchev, and the Cuban Missile Crisis* (New York: Ballantine Books, 2004), 11.

21. Ibid., 33.

22. Ibid., 75.

23. Sheldon M. Stern, *Averting "The Final Failure": John F. Kennedy and the Secret Cuban Missile Crisis Meetings* (Palo Alto, Calif.: Stanford University Press, 2003), 105.

24. Ibid.

25. Ibid., 127.

26. Ibid., 123–129.

27. John F. Kennedy, "Radio and Television Report to the American People on the Soviet Arms Buildup in Cuba," October 22, 1962, in *Public Papers of the Presidents of the United States: John F. Kennedy 1961–1963,* from the American Presidency Project, University of California, Santa Barbara, www.presidency.ucsb.edu.

28. Frankel, *High Noon,* 121.

29. Ibid.

30. Statement by Ambassador Stevenson to United Nations Security Council, October 25, 1962, *Department of State Bulletin* 47, no. 1220 (November 12, 1962): 737–740.

31. William Fulton, "Adlai, Red Battle in U.N., Defies Russian to Deny Giving Rockets to Cuba," *Chicago Daily Tribune,* October 26, 1962.

32. Stern, *Averting "The Final Failure,"* 233.

33. Frankel, *High Noon,* 150.

34. Nikita Sergeevich Khrushchev, *Khrushchev Remembers,* trans. and ed. Strobe Talbott (New York: Bantam Books, 1971), 551–552.

35. The phrase "winning the hearts and minds of the people" was used widely throughout the Cold War. It echoes a Biblical passage, Philippians 4:7.

36. Jung Chang and Jon Halliday, *Mao: The Unknown Story* (New York: Knopf, 2005), 480–481, drawing from the archived notes of Ambassador Harriman.

37. James N. Giglio, *Presidency of John F. Kennedy* (Lawrence: University Press of Kansas, 2006), 223.

38. John F. Kennedy, "Address at a White House Reception for Members of Congress and for the Diplomatic Corps of the Latin American Republics," March 13, 1961, in *Public Papers of the Presidents of the United States: John F. Kennedy 1961–1963,* from the American Presidency Project, University of California, Santa Barbara, www.presidency.ucsb.edu.

39. Stephen G. Rabe, *The Most Dangerous Area in the World: John F. Kennedy Confronts Communist Revolution in Latin America* (Chapel Hill: University of North Carolina Press, 1999), 267.

40. Giglio, *Presidency of John F. Kennedy,* 240.

41. State-Saigon Cable 243, "Eyes Only—Ambassador Lodge," August 24, 1963, in John Prados, "JFK and the Diem Coup," National Security Archive, George Washington University, www.gwu.edu/~nsarchiv/NSAEBB/NSAEBB101/vn02.pdf.

42. State-Saigon Cable 272, "Top Secret Eyes Only for Ambassador Lodge and General Harkins," August 29, 1963, in John Prados, "JFK and the Diem Coup," National Security Archive, George Washington University, www.gwu.edu/~nsarchiv/NSAEBB/NSAEBB101/vn12.pdf.

Document 4.1
"Pay Any Price, Bear Any Burden," President John F. Kennedy's Inaugural Address, January 20, 1961

President Kennedy's inaugural address is one of the best-known presidential speeches. In it, the president summoned a new generation to the task of "defending freedom in its hour of maximum danger" and evoked a spirit of common sacrifice for the common good. He also issued a warning to America's adversaries: the nation would "pay any price, bear any burden . . . to assure the survival and the success of liberty."

Vice President Johnson, Mr. Speaker, Mr. Chief Justice, President Eisenhower, Vice president Nixon, President Truman, Reverend Clergy, fellow citizens:

We observe today not a victory of party but a celebration of freedom—symbolizing an end as well as a beginning—signifying renewal as well as change. For I have sworn before you and Almighty God the same solemn oath our forebears prescribed nearly a century and three quarters ago.

The world is very different now. For man holds in his mortal hands the power to abolish all forms of human poverty and all forms of human life. And yet the same revolutionary beliefs for which our forebears fought are still at issue around the globe—the belief that the rights of man come not from the generosity of the state but from the hand of God.

We dare not forget today that we are the heirs of that first revolution. Let the word go forth from this time and place, to friend and foe alike, that the torch has been passed to a new generation of Americans—born in this century, tempered by war, disciplined by a hard and bitter peace, proud of our ancient heritage—and unwilling to witness or permit the slow undoing of those human rights to which this nation has always been committed, and to which we are committed today at home and around the world.

Let every nation know, whether it wishes us well or ill, that we shall pay any price, bear any burden, meet any hardship, support any friend, oppose any foe to assure the survival and the success of liberty.

This much we pledge—and more.

To those old allies whose cultural and spiritual origins we share, we pledge the loyalty of faithful friends. United, there is little we cannot do in a host of cooperative ventures. Divided, there is little we can do—for we dare not meet a powerful challenge at odds and split asunder. . . .

To those peoples in the huts and villages of half the globe struggling to break the bonds of mass misery, we pledge our best efforts to help them help themselves, for whatever period is required—not because the communists may be doing it, not because we seek their votes, but because it is right. If a free society cannot help the many who are poor, it cannot save the few who are rich.

To our sister republics south of our border, we offer a special pledge—to convert our good words into good deeds—in a new alliance for progress—to assist free men and free governments in casting off the chains of poverty. But this peaceful revolution of hope cannot become the prey of hostile powers. Let all our neighbors know that we shall join with them to oppose aggression or subversion anywhere in the Americas. And let every other power know that this Hemisphere intends to remain the master of its own house.

To that world assembly of sovereign states, the United Nations, our last best hope in an age where the instruments of war have far outpaced the instruments of peace, we renew our pledge of support—to prevent it from becoming merely a forum for invective—to strengthen its shield of the new and the weak—and to enlarge the area in which its writ may run.

Finally, to those nations who would make themselves our adversary, we offer not a pledge but a request: that both sides begin anew the quest for peace, before the dark powers of destruction unleashed by science engulf all humanity in planned or accidental self-destruction.

We dare not tempt them with weakness. For only when our arms are sufficient beyond doubt can we be certain beyond doubt that they will never be employed. . . .

Let both sides unite to heed in all corners of the earth the command of Isaiah—to "undo the heavy burdens . . . (and) let the oppressed go free." . . .

All this will not be finished in the first one hundred days. Nor will it be finished in the first one thousand days, nor in the life of this Administration, nor even perhaps in our lifetime on this planet. But let us begin.

In your hands, my fellow citizens, more than mine, will rest the final success or failure of our course. Since this country was founded, each generation of Americans has been summoned to give testimony to its national loyalty. The graves of young Americans who answered the call to service surround the globe.

Now the trumpet summons us again—not as a call to bear arms, though arms we need—not as a call to battle, though embattled we are—but a call to bear the burden of a long twilight struggle, year in and year out, "rejoicing in hope, patient in tribulation"—a struggle against the common enemies of man: tyranny, poverty, disease and war itself. . . .

In the long history of the world, only a few generations have been granted the role of defending freedom in its hour of maximum danger. I do not shrink from this responsibility—I welcome it. I do not believe that any of us would exchange places with any other people or any other generation. The energy, the faith, the devotion which we bring to this endeavor will light our country and all who serve it—and the glow from that fire can truly light the world.

And so, my fellow Americans: ask not what your country can do for you—ask what you can do for your country.

My fellow citizens of the world: ask not what America will do for you, but what together we can do for the freedom of man.

Finally, whether you are citizens of America or citizens of the world, ask of us here the same high standards of strength and sacrifice which we ask of you. With a good conscience our only sure reward, with history the final judge of our deeds, let us go forth to lead the land we love, asking His blessing and His help, but knowing that here on earth God's work must truly be our own.

Source: John F. Kennedy, "Inaugural Address," January 20, 1961, in *Public Papers of the Presidents of the United States: John F. Kennedy, 1961–1963,* from the American Presidency Project, University of California, Santa Barbara, www.presidency.ucsb.edu.

Document 4.2
"More Difficult Than War," President John F. Kennedy's Speech before the American Society of Newspaper Editors in Washington, D.C., April 20, 1961
In this speech before the American Society of Newspaper Editors, President Kennedy outlined the lessons of failure at the Bay of Pigs: "Soft" societies were no match for the iron discipline of Communist states. The free world would have to demonstrate its mettle some other time, in some other place.

. . . The President of a great democracy such as ours, and the editors of great newspapers such as yours, owe a common obligation to the people: an obligation to present the facts, to present them with candor, and to present them in perspective. It is with that obligation in mind that I have decided in the last 24 hours to discuss briefly at this time the recent events in Cuba.

On that unhappy island, as in so many other arenas of the contest for freedom, the news has grown worse instead of better. I have emphasized before that this was a struggle of Cuban patriots against a Cuban dictator. While we could not be expected to hide our sympathies, we made it repeatedly clear that the armed forces of this country would not intervene in any way.

Any unilateral American intervention, in the absence of an external attack upon ourselves or an ally, would have been contrary to our traditions and to our international obligations. But let the record show that our restraint is not inexhaustible. Should it ever appear that the inter-American doctrine of non-interference merely conceals or excuses a policy of nonaction—if the nations of this Hemisphere should fail to meet their commitments against outside Communist penetration—then I want it clearly understood that this Government will not hesitate in meeting its primary obligations which are to the security of our Nation!

Should that time ever come, we do not intend to be lectured on "intervention" by those whose character was stamped for all time on the bloody streets of Budapest! Nor would we expect or accept the same outcome which this small band of gallant Cuban refugees must have known that they were chancing, determined as they were against heavy odds to pursue their courageous attempts to regain their Island's freedom.

But Cuba is not an island unto itself; and our concern is not ended by mere expressions of nonintervention or regret. This is not the first time in either ancient or recent history that a small band of freedom fighters has engaged the armor of totalitarianism.

It is not the first time that Communist tanks have rolled over gallant men and women fighting to redeem the independence of their homeland. Nor is it by any means the final episode in the eternal struggle of liberty against tyranny, anywhere on the face of the globe, including Cuba itself.

Mr. Castro has said that these were mercenaries. According to press reports, the final message to be relayed from the refugee forces on the beach came from the rebel commander when asked if he wished to be evacuated. His answer was: "I will never leave this country." That is not the reply of a mercenary. He has gone now to join in the mountains countless other guerrilla fighters, who are equally determined that the dedication of those who gave their lives shall not be forgotten, and that Cuba must not be abandoned to the Communists. And we do not intend to abandon it either! . . .

. . . But there are from this sobering episode useful lessons for us all to learn. Some may be still obscure, and await further information. Some are clear today.

First, it is clear that the forces of communism are not to be underestimated, in Cuba or anywhere else in the world. The advantages of a police state—its use of mass terror and arrests to prevent the spread of free dissent—cannot be overlooked by those who expect the fall of every fanatic tyrant. If the self-discipline of the free cannot match the iron discipline of the mailed fist—in economic, political, scientific and all the other kinds of struggles as well as the military—then the peril to freedom will continue to rise. . . .

Third, and finally, it is clearer than ever that we face a relentless struggle in every corner of the globe that goes far beyond the clash of armies or even nuclear armaments. The armies are there, and in large number. The nuclear armaments are there. But they serve primarily as the shield behind which subversion, infiltration, and a host of other tactics steadily advance, picking off vulnerable areas one by one in situations which do not permit our own armed intervention. . . .

We dare not fail to see the insidious nature of this new and deeper struggle. We dare not fail to grasp the new concepts, the new tools, the new sense of urgency we will need to combat it—whether in Cuba or South Viet-Nam. And we dare not fail to realize that this struggle is taking place every day, without fanfare, in thousands of villages and markets—day and night—and in classrooms all over the globe.

The message of Cuba, of Laos, of the rising din of Communist voices in Asia and Latin America—these messages are all the same. The complacent, the self-indulgent, the soft societies are about to be swept away with the debris of history. Only the strong, only the industrious, only the determined, only the courageous, only the visionary who determine the real nature of our struggle can possibly survive.

No greater task faces this country or this administration. No other challenge is more deserving of our every effort and energy. Too long we have fixed our eyes on traditional military needs, on armies prepared to cross borders, on missiles poised for flight. Now it should be clear that this is no longer enough—that our security may be lost piece by piece, country by country, without the firing of a single missile or the crossing of a single border.

We intend to profit from this lesson. We intend to reexamine and reorient our forces of all kinds—our tactics and our institutions here in this community. We intend to intensify our efforts for a struggle in many ways more difficult than war, where disappointment will often accompany us.

For I am convinced that we in this country and in the free world possess the necessary resource, and the skill, and the added strength that comes from a belief in the freedom of man. And I am equally convinced that history will record the fact that this bitter struggle reached its climax in the late 1950's and the early 1960's. Let me then make clear as the President of the United States that I am determined upon our system's survival and success, regardless of the cost and regardless of the peril!

Source: John F. Kennedy, "Address before the American Society of Newspaper Editors," April 20, 1961, in *Public Papers of the Presidents of the United States: John F. Kennedy, 1961–1963,* from the American Presidency Project, University of California, Santa Barbara, www.presidency.ucsb.edu.

Document 4.3
"Defeat Is an Orphan," President John F. Kennedy's Press Conference about the Bay of Pigs, April 21, 1961

At a press conference at the White House, President Kennedy acknowledged responsibility for the botched operation in Cuba without actually revealing the extent of American involvement.

The President: Gentlemen, I have several announcements to make.

I know that many of you have further questions about Cuba. I made a statement on that subject yesterday afternoon. We are continuing consultations with other American Republics. Active efforts are being made by ourselves and others on behalf of various individuals, including any Americans who may be in danger. I do not think that any useful national purpose would be served by my going further into the Cuban question this morning. I prefer to let my statement of yesterday suffice for the present. . . .

Q.: Sir, since last Saturday a certain foreign policy situation has given rise to many conflicting stories. During that time reporters in Washington have noticed that there's been a clamming up of information from formerly useful sources. To my knowledge the State Department and the White House have not attempted to take a representative group of reporters and say, "These are the facts as we know them," and this morning we are not permitted to ask any further questions about this foreign policy situation. In view of the fact we are taking a propaganda lambasting around the world, why is it not useful, sir, for us to explore with you the real facts behind this, or our motivations?

The President: Well, I think, in answer to your question, that we have to make a judgment as to how much we can usefully say that would aid the interest of the United States. One of the problems of a free society, a problem not met by a dictatorship, is this problem of information. A good deal has been printed in the paper and I wouldn't be surprised if those of you who are members of the press will be receiving a lot of background briefings in the next day or two by interested people or interested agencies.

There's an old saying that victory has 100 fathers and defeat is an orphan. And I wouldn't be surprised if information is poured into you in regard to all of the recent activities. . . .

But I will say to you . . . that I have said as much as I feel can be usefully said by me in regard to the events of the past few days. Further statements, detailed discussions, are not to conceal responsibility because I'm the responsible officer of the Government—and that is quite obvious—but merely because I do not believe that such a discussion would benefit us during the present difficult situation.

Source: "The President's News Conference," April 21, 1961, in *Public Papers of the Presidents of the United States: John F. Kennedy 1961–1963,* from the American Presidency Project, University of California, Santa Barbara, www.presidency.ucsb.edu.

Document 4.4
President John F. Kennedy Speaks off the Record to Members of the Press in Washington, D.C., on the Bay of Pigs, April 25, 1961

At the State Department, the president spoke off the record to members of the press about the Bay of Pigs. In this setting, Kennedy frankly acknowledged that the invasion was planned in Washington and suggested to his audience that it had enjoyed the enthusiastic endorsement of the nation's military and spy chiefs. The president also linked the struggle in Cuba to that taking place elsewhere, in particular, in Vietnam.

. . .

Q.: Mr. President, how badly damaged do you think United States prestige abroad has been, as a result of our involvement in the abortive Cuban invasion attempt, and what can we do to restore it to its previous state?

The President: Well, I think the prestige of the United States has been hurt because a failure hurts. As to what we can do to restore it, that's a matter which we are considering. But I think that we are going to have to recognize that in these next years there are going to be many setbacks, and I hope many successes.

But in this struggle, which, after all, we are seeing a similar kind of struggle being carried on by the communists in Viet Nam—but that kind of support of guerillas is not regarded—which is far more brutal, and directed as I have said to eliminating important groups within the society—that does not seem to be regarded very critically in the United Nations and elsewhere. But we will have to—I think our prestige, our survival are all at stake, and will be for the next ten years.

I know of no sure formula for success. All we can attempt to do is try to secure the best judgments of the people who have the most experience, and try, and if we fail, then we are going to try again.

Q.: Mr. President—

The President: Perhaps in a different way, however, next time. . . .

Q.: Mr. President, if you had the Cuban decision to make over again, what would you have done differently? [Laughter]

The President: Well, we hope that by the time General Taylor can conclude his analysis—I will say that, speaking here privately, many meetings were held on this matter.

Many people—whose experience had carried them through many years—judgments were reached, in both military and other branches of the Government. And this was not—when the decision was made, those who were most involved thought that this effort would be worthwhile, on the assumption that if it did not succeed there, that they could carry on as guerillas.

But it failed. So quite obviously, with the advantage of hindsight, a good many different decisions would have been made. But I must say that a good many people, with long military experience and all the rest, looked at this, and were wrong. . . .

Q.: Mr. President, now that you have been in office for three months, how do you like it?

The President: Well, I liked it better up to about nine days ago. [Laughter; applause]

Source: "JFK, Backgrounder at State," in Thomas W. Benson, *Writing JFK: Presidential Rhetoric and the Press in the Bay of Pigs Crisis* (College Station: Texas A&M University Press, 2004), 86–99.

Document 4.5
President John F. Kennedy Pledges to Land a Man on the Moon, Special Message to the U.S. Congress, May 25, 1961

In a special message to Congress on "urgent national needs," President Kennedy called for Congress and the states to embrace the need for civil defense (that is, fallout shelters) and pledged to land a man on the moon before the end of the decade.

. . . One major element of the national security program which this nation has never squarely faced up to is civil defense. This problem arises not from present trends but from national inaction in which most of us have participated. In the past decade we have intermittently considered a variety of programs, but we have never adopted a consistent policy. Public considerations have been largely characterized by apathy, indifference and skepticism; while, at the same time, many of the civil defense plans have been so far-reaching and unrealistic that they have not gained essential support.

This Administration has been looking hard at exactly what civil defense can and cannot do. It cannot be obtained cheaply. It cannot give an assurance of blast protection that will be proof against surprise attack or guaranteed against obsolescence or destruction. And it cannot deter a nuclear attack.

We will deter an enemy from making a nuclear attack only if our retaliatory power is so strong and so invulnerable that he knows he would be destroyed by our response. If we have that strength, civil defense is not needed to deter an attack. If we should ever lack it, civil defense would not be an adequate substitute.

But this deterrent concept assumes rational calculations by rational men. And the history of this planet, and particularly the history of the 20th century, is sufficient to remind us of the possibilities of an irrational attack, a miscalculation, an accidental war, for a war of escalation in which the stakes by each side gradually increase to the point of maximum danger which cannot be either foreseen or deterred. It is on this basis that civil defense can be readily justifiable—as insurance for the civilian population in case of an enemy miscalculation. It is insurance we trust will never be needed—but insurance which we could never forgive ourselves for foregoing in the event of catastrophe. . . .

Federal appropriations for civil defense in fiscal 1962 under this program will in all likelihood be more than triple the pending budget requests; and they will increase sharply in subsequent years. . . .

Finally, if we are to win the battle that is now going on around the world between freedom and tyranny, the dramatic achievements in space which occurred in recent weeks should have made clear to us all, as did the Sputnik in 1957, the impact of this adventure on the minds of men everywhere, who are attempting to make a determination of which road they should take. Since early in my term, our efforts in space have been under review. With the advice of the Vice President, who is Chairman of the National Space Council, we have examined where we are strong and where we are not, where we may succeed and where we may not. Now it is time to take longer strides—time for a great new American enterprise—time for this nation to take a clearly leading role in space achievement, which in many ways may hold the key to our future on earth.

I believe we possess all the resources and talents necessary. But the facts of the matter are that we have never made the national decisions or marshaled the national resources required for such leadership. We have never specified long-range goals on an urgent time schedule, or managed our resources and our time so as to insure theft fulfillment.

Recognizing the head start obtained by the Soviets with their large rocket engines, which gives them many months of lead-time, and recognizing the likelihood that they will exploit this lead for some time to come in still more impressive successes, we nevertheless are required to make new efforts on our own. For while we cannot guarantee that we shall one day be first, we can guarantee that any failure to make this effort will make us last. We take an additional risk by making it in full view of the world, but as shown by the feat of astronaut [Alan] Sheppard, this very risk enhances our stature when we are successful. But this is not merely a race. Space is open to us now; and our eagerness to share its meaning is not governed by the efforts of others. We go into space because whatever mankind must undertake, free men must fully share.

I therefore ask the Congress, above and beyond the increases I have earlier requested for space activities, to provide the funds which are needed to meet the following national goals:

First, I believe that this nation should commit itself to achieving the goal, before this decade is out, of landing a man on the moon and returning him safely to the earth. No single space project in this period will be more impressive to mankind, or more important for the long-range exploration of space; and none will be so difficult or expensive to accomplish. . . .

This decision demands a major national commitment of scientific and technical manpower, materiel and facilities, and the possibility of their diversion from other important activities where they are already thinly spread. It means a degree of dedication, organization and discipline which have not always characterized our research and development efforts. It means we cannot afford undue work stoppages, inflated costs of material or talent, wasteful interagency rivalries, or a high turnover of key personnel.

New objectives and new money cannot solve these problems. They could in fact, aggravate them further—unless every scientist, every engineer, every serviceman, every technician, contractor, and civil servant gives his personal pledge that this nation will move forward, with the full speed of freedom, in the exciting adventure of space. . . .

I have not asked for a single program which did not cause one or all Americans some inconvenience, or some hardship, or some sacrifice. But they have responded—and you in the Congress have responded to your duty—and I feel confident in asking today for a similar response to these new and larger demands. It is heartening to know, as I journey abroad, that our country is united in its commitment to freedom—and is ready to do its duty.

Source: John F. Kennedy, "Special Message to the U.S. Congress on Urgent National Needs," May 25, 1961, in *Public Papers of the Presidents of the United States: John F. Kennedy, 1961–1963,* from the American Presidency Project, University of California, Santa Barbara, www.presidency.ucsb.edu.

Document 4.6
President John F. Kennedy's Commencement Speech at the United States Military Academy at West Point, New York, June 6, 1962

In this commencement address at the United States Military Academy at West Point, New York, President Kennedy spoke with conviction about the sort of military force he believed the nation required to prevail in the Cold War.

. . . [T]he period just ahead in the next decade will offer more opportunities for service to the graduates of this Academy than ever before in the history of the United States, because all around the world, in countries which are heavily engaged in the maintenance of their freedom, graduates of this Academy are heavily involved. Whether it is in Viet-Nam or in Laos or in Thailand, whether it is a military advisory group in Iran, whether it is a military attaché in some Latin American country during a difficult and challenging period, whether it is the commander of our troops in South Korea—the burdens that will be placed upon you when you fill those positions as you must inevitably, will require more from you than ever before in our history. The graduates of West Point, the Naval Academy, and the Air Academy in the next 10 years will have the greatest opportunity for the defense of freedom that this Academy's graduates have ever had. . . .

. . . Your strictly military responsibilities, therefore, will require a versatility and an adaptability never before required in either war or in peace. They may involve the command and control of modern nuclear weapons and modern delivery systems, so complex that only a few scientists can understand their operation, so devastating that their inadvertent use would be of worldwide concern, but so new that their employment and their effects have never been tested in combat conditions.

On the other hand, your responsibilities may involve the command of more traditional forces, but in less traditional roles. Men risking their lives, not as combatants, but as instructors or advisers, or as symbols of our Nation's commitments. The fact that the United States is not directly at war in these areas in no way diminishes the skill and the courage that will be required, the service to our country which is rendered, or the pain of the casualties which are suffered.

To cite one final example of the range of responsibilities that will fall upon you: you may hold a position of command with our special forces, forces which are too unconventional to be called conventional, forces which are growing in number and importance and significance, for we now know that it is wholly misleading to call this "the nuclear age," or to say that our security rests only on the doctrine of massive retaliation.

Korea has not been the only battleground since the end of the Second World War. Men have fought and died in Malaya, in Greece, in the Philippines, in Algeria and Cuba and Cyprus, and almost continuously on the Indo-Chinese Peninsula. No nuclear weapons have been fired. No massive nuclear retaliation has been considered appropriate. This is another type of war, new in its intensity, ancient in its origin—war by guerrillas, subversives, insurgents, assassins, war by ambush instead of by combat; by infiltration, instead of aggression, seeking victory by eroding and exhausting the enemy instead of engaging him. . . . [T]hese are the kinds of challenges that will be before us in the next decade if freedom is to be saved, a whole new kind of strategy, a wholly different kind of force, and therefore a new and wholly different kind of military training.

. . . In the years ahead, some of you will serve as advisers to foreign aid missions or even to foreign governments. Some will negotiate terms of a cease-fire with broad political as well as military ramifications. Some of you will go to the far corners of the earth, and to the far reaches of space. Some of you will sit in the highest councils of the Pentagon. Others will hold delicate command posts which are international in character. Still others will advise on plans to abolish arms instead of using them to abolish others. Whatever your position, the scope of your decisions will not be confined to the traditional tenets of military competence and training. You will need to know and understand not only the foreign policy of the United States but the foreign policy of all countries scattered around the world who 20 years ago were the most distant names to us. You will need to give orders in different tongues and read maps by different systems. You will be involved in economic judgments which most economists would hesitate to make. . . .

Our forces, therefore, must fulfill a broader role as a complement to our diplomacy, as an arm of our diplomacy, as a deterrent to our adversaries, and as a symbol to our allies of our determination to support them. . . .

Source: John F. Kennedy, "Remarks at West Point to the Graduating Class of the U.S. Military Academy," June 6, 1962, in *Public Papers of the Presidents of the United States: John F. Kennedy, 1961–1963,* from the American Presidency Project, University of California, Santa Barbara, www.presidency .ucsb.edu.

Document 4.7
Soviet Foreign Minister Andrei Gromyko's Record of his Meeting with President John F. Kennedy, October 20, 1962

In a historic meeting on October 18, 1962, President Kennedy concealed his knowledge that the Soviets had violated their pledge regarding the shipment of nuclear weapons to Cuba, while hinting repeatedly at an exchange: remove the missiles and the president would renounce any attempt to repeat the invasion of Cuba. Both sides threatened "grave" consequences should their conflict over Cuba escalate. This account was written by Soviet foreign minister Andrei Gromyko for the benefit of the Soviet Foreign Ministry.

During the meeting with President Kennedy at the White House on 18 October I transmitted to him, his spouse and other members of his family regards from the head of the Soviet government N. S. Khrushchev and from Nina Petrovna.

Kennedy expressed his gratitude to N. S. Khrushchev for the regards.

Further I said that I would like to give an account of the Soviet government policy on a number of important issues. . . .

It is well known to you, Mr. President, the attitude of the Soviet government and personally of N. S. Khrushchev toward the dangerous developments connected with the USA administration position on the issue of Cuba. An unrestrained anti-Cuban campaign has been going on in the USA for a long time and apparently there is a definite USA administration policy behind it. Right now the USA are making an attempt to blockade Cuban trade with other states. [Gromyko speaks here of a trade embargo, not the military blockade, or "quarantine," that was to come.] There is talk about a possibility of actions of organized policy in this region under the USA aegis.

But all of this amounts to a path that can lead to grave consequences, to a misfortune for all mankind, and we are confident that such an outcome is not desired by any people, including the people of the USA.

The USA administration for some reason considers that the Cubans must solve their domestic affairs not at their discretion, but at the discretion of the USA. But on what grounds? Cuba belongs to the Cuban people, not to the USA or any other state. And since it is so, then why are the statements made in the USA calling for an invasion of Cuba? What do the USA need Cuba for?

Who can in earnest believe that Cuba represents a threat to the USA? If we speak about dimensions and resources of the two countries—the USA and Cuba—then it is clear that they are a giant and a baby. The flagrant groundlessness of such charges against Cuba is obvious. . . .

Is it possible, Mr. President, for the Soviet Union, taking into account all of this, to sit cross-handed and to be a detached onlooker? You say that you like frankness. Giving an account of the Soviet government position frankly as well, I would like to stress that nowadays is not the middle of the XIX century, is not the time of colonial partition and not the times when a victim of aggression could raise its voice only weeks and months after an assault. American statesmen frequently declare that the USA is a great power. This is correct, the USA is a great power, a rich and strong power. And what kind of power is the Soviet Union?

You know that N. S. Khrushchev was positively impressed by your realistic statement during the Vienna meeting about the equality of forces of the two powers—the USSR and USA. But insofar as it is so, inasmuch as the USSR is also a great and strong power it cannot be a mere spectator while there is appearing a threat of unleashing a large war either in connection with the Cuban issue or [with a] situation in whatever other region of the world.

You are very well aware of the Soviet government attitude toward such an action of the USA, as the decision about the draft of 150 thousand reservists. The Soviet government is convinced that if both of our countries favor a lessening of international tension and a solution of unsettled international problems, then such steps should be avoided because they are intended for sharpening the international situation.

If it came to the worst, if a war began, certainly, a mobilization of an additional 150 thousand reservists to the USA armed forces would not have significance. And undoubtedly you are very well aware of this. For the present is not the year 1812 when Napoleon was setting all his hopes upon the number of soldiers, of sabres and cannons. Neither is it 1941, when Hitler was relying upon his mass armies, automatic rifles, and tanks. Today life and and military equipment have made a large step forward. Nowadays the situation is quite different and it would be better not to rely on armaments while solving disputed problems.

So far as the aid of the Soviet Union to Cuba is concerned, the Soviet government has declared and I have been instructed to reaffirm it once more, our aid pursues exclusively the object of rendering Cuba assistance to its defensive capacity and development of its peaceful economy. . . .

Having listened to our statement, Kennedy said . . . that the USA administration had no intentions to launch an aggression against Cuba. Suddenly, Mr. Khrushchev, without notifying me, began to increase at a brisk pace supplies of armaments to Cuba, although there was no threat on our side that could cause such a necessity. If Mr. Khrushchev addressed me on this issue, we could give him corresponding assurances on that score. The build-up of the Cuban military might has badly impressed the American people and the USA congress. As President I was trying to calm public opinion and I have declared that, taking into account the kind of aid rendered by the Soviet Union to Cuba, we must keep cool and self-controlled. But I was not able to find a satisfactory explanation for those actions of the Soviet Union.

Kennedy said later, that . . . [t]he actions of the Soviet Union create a very complicated situation and I don't know where the whole thing can bring us. The present situation is, perhaps, the most dangerous since the end of the Second World War. We, certainly, take on trust statements of the Soviet Union about the sort of armaments supplied by you to Cuba. As President I am trying to restrain those people in the USA who are favoring an invasion of Cuba. . . .

I answered Kennedy that once there was an attempt to organize an invasion of Cuba and it is known what was the end of the affair. From different official statements and your own statements, Mr. President, everybody know what were the circumstances and how that invasion was arranged. Everybody knows also that the USA administration needs only to move a finger and no Cuban exiles, nor those who support them in the USA and some countries of the Caribbean, would dare launch any adventure against Cuba.

At this moment Kennedy put in a remark that he had already had an exchange of opinions with N. S. Khrushchev on the issue of the invasion of Cuba in 1961 and had said that it was a mistake.

I should be glad, Kennedy stressed, to give assurances that an invasion would not be repeated neither on the part of Cuban refugees, nor on the part of the USA armed forces.

But the issue is, Kennedy said, that as a result of the USSR government's action in July of the current year the situation suddenly has changed for the worse. . . .

Kennedy said that, to make things completely clear on this issue, he would like to announce once more that the USA do not have any intentions to invade Cuba. Nevertheless, intensified armaments supplies to Cuba on the part of the Soviet Union, which began in July of the current year, have complicated the situation greatly and made it more dangerous. . . .

[Kennedy, reading from a recent speech] "There is no evidence of any organized combat force in Cuba from any Soviet bloc country; of military base provided to Russia; of a violation of the 1934 treaty relating to Guantanamo; of the presence of offensive ground-to-ground missiles; or of other significant offensive capability either in Cuban hands or under Soviet direction and guidance.

Were it to be otherwise, the gravest issues would arise."

The conversation lasted 2 hours and 20 minutes. There were present: on the American side—Rusk, Thompson, Hillenbrandt and Akalovsky, on the Soviet side—Semenov, Dobrynin, and Sukhodrev.

A. GROMYKO

Source: Andrei Gromyko, "Cable from the Soviet Foreign Minister Gromyko on 18 October 1962 Meeting with President Kennedy (excerpts)," October 20, 1962, from the Cold War International History Project, Woodrow Wilson International Center for Scholars, www.cwihp.org.

Document 4.8
Soviet Foreign Minister Andrei Gromyko Assures the Kremlin that the "Situation Is Completely Satisfactory," Telegram to the Central Committee of the Communist Party, October 19, 1962

Soviet foreign minister Andrei Gromyko came away from his October 18 meeting at the White House without realizing that President Kennedy had discovered the Soviet Union's recent activities in Cuba. He was completely unmoved by the president's implicit threat regarding "the gravest issues" that would arise were the Soviets to place nuclear weapons in Cuba. In this telegram, Gromyko reports directly to the top leadership at the Kremlin, the Central Committee of the Communist Party, Soviet Union (CC CPSU).

TOP SECRET
Making Copies Prohibited
Copy No. 1
CIPHERED TELEGRAM
    To the CC CPSU
Everything which we know about the position of the USA government on the Cuban question allows us to conclude that the overall situation is completely satisfactory. This is confirmed by official announcements of American officials, including Kennedy, in his discussion with us on October 18, and all information which reaches us via unofficial channels and from representatives of other countries.

There is reason to believe that the USA is not preparing an intervention in Cuba and has put its money on obstructing Cuba's economic relations with the USSR and other countries, so as to destroy its economy and to cause hunger in the country, and in this way creating dissatisfaction among the population and prompting an uprising against the regime. This is based on a belief that the Soviet Union will not over a long period be able to provide Cuba with everything it needs.

The main reason for this American position is that the Administration and the overall American ruling circles are amazed by the Soviet Union's courage in assisting Cuba. Their reasoning is thus: The Soviet government recognizes the great importance which the Americans place on Cuba and its situation, and how painful that issue is to the USA. But the fact that the USSR, even knowing all that, still provides such aid to Cuba, means that it is fully committed to repulsing any American intervention in Cuba. There is no single opinion as to how and where that rebuff will be given, but that it will be given—they do not doubt.

In these last days the sharpness of the anti-Cuban campaign in the USA has subsided somewhat, while the sharpness of the West Berlin question has stood out all the more. Newspapers bleat about the approaching crisis vis-à-vis West Berlin, the impending in the very near future signing of the agreement with the GDR, and so on. The goal of such a change in the work of the propaganda machine is to divert somewhat public attention from the Cuba issue. All this is not without the participation of the White House.

Even the rumor to the effect that the Soviet Union has made it known that it can soften its position on the Cuban issue if the West will soften its own position in West Berlin was basically intended to mollify the public vis-à-vis Cuba.

The wide publication of the results of an election survey conducted here by the Gallup (sic) Institute showing that the vast majority of Americans are against an American intervention in Cuba serves this same goal. In this regard, we have to note that the leadership of the institute in the past traditionally were more sympathetic to Republicans. Therefore, its publication in this case deserves special attention. This was not done without the encouragement of the White House either; in this way a nudge was given to the extremist groups in Congress which support extreme measures.

Also deserving of attention is the fact that Congress has now "gone on recess." This suggests that the pressure on Kennedy from the extreme groups in Congress will be less during the recess.

The position of the USA allies, particularly the British, also played a role. They did not support calls for the unleashing of aggression against Cuba, although they equally approved of other anti-Cuban steps of the USA.

It is not possible, of course, to be completely insured against USA surprises and adventures, even in the Cuba issue; all the same, taking into account the undeniable objective facts and the corresponding official public statements, and also the assurances given to us that the USA has no plans for intervention in Cuba (which undeniably commits them in many respects), it is possible to say that in these conditions a USA military adventure against Cuba is almost impossible to imagine.

19/X-62 A. GROMYKO

Source: Andrei Gromyko, "Telegram from Soviet Foreign Minister A. A. Gromyko to the CC CPSU," October 19, 1962, from the Cold War International History Project, Woodrow Wilson International Center for Scholars, www.cwihp.org.

Document 4.9
President John F. Kennedy Informs the Public of Offensive Weapons in Cuba, Radio and Television Address, October 22, 1962

President Kennedy, via an address carried on radio and television, informed the public about the threat from Cuba. The United States will not "shrink," the president said, from the risk of "worldwide nuclear war" to secure the removal of Soviet weapons.

Good evening, my fellow citizens:

This Government, as promised, has maintained the closest surveillance of the Soviet military buildup on the island of Cuba. Within the past week, unmistakable evidence has established the fact that a series of offensive missile sites is now in preparation on that imprisoned island. The purpose of these bases can be none other than to provide a nuclear strike capability against the Western Hemisphere. . . .

This urgent transformation of Cuba into an important strategic base—by the presence of these large, long-range, and clearly offensive weapons of sudden mass destruction—constitutes an explicit threat to the peace and security of all the Americas, in flagrant and deliberate defiance of the Rio Pact of 1947, the traditions of this Nation and hemisphere, the joint resolution of the 87th Congress, the Charter of the United Nations, and my own public warnings to the Soviets on September 4 and 13. This action also contradicts the repeated assurances of Soviet spokesmen, both publicly and privately delivered, that the arms buildup in Cuba would retain its original defensive character, and that the Soviet Union had no need or desire to station strategic missiles on the territory of any other nation. . . .

Only last Thursday, as evidence of this rapid offensive buildup was already in my hand, Soviet Foreign Minister Gromyko told me in my office that he was instructed to make it clear once again, as he said his government had already done, that Soviet assistance to Cuba, and I quote, "pursued solely the purpose of contributing to the defense capabilities of Cuba," that, and I quote him, "training by Soviet specialists of Cuban nationals in handling defensive armaments was by no means offensive, and if it were otherwise," Mr. Gromyko went on, "the Soviet Government would never become involved in rendering such assistance." That statement also was false.

Neither the United States of America nor the world community of nations can tolerate deliberate deception and offensive threats on the part of any nation, large or small. . . .

. . . [T]his secret, swift, and extraordinary buildup of Communist missiles—in an area well known to have a special and historical relationship to the United States and the nations of the Western Hemisphere, in violation of Soviet assurances, and in defiance of American and hemispheric policy—this sudden, clandestine decision to station strategic weapons for the first time outside of Soviet soil—is a deliberately provocative and unjustified change in the status quo which cannot be accepted by this country, if our courage and our commitments are ever to be trusted again by either friend or foe.

The 1930's taught us a clear lesson: aggressive conduct, if allowed to go unchecked and unchallenged, ultimately leads to war. This nation is opposed to war. We are also true to our word. Our unswerving objective, therefore, must be to prevent the use of these missiles against this or any other country, and to secure their withdrawal or elimination from the Western Hemisphere.

Our policy has been one of patience and restraint, as befits a peaceful and powerful nation, which leads a worldwide alliance. We have been determined not to be diverted from our central concerns by mere irritants and fanatics. But now further action is required—and it is under way; and these actions may only be the beginning. We will not prematurely or unnecessarily risk the costs of worldwide nuclear war in which even the fruits of victory would be ashes in our mouth—but neither will we shrink from that risk at any time it must be faced.

Acting, therefore, in the defense of our own security and of the entire Western Hemisphere, and under the authority entrusted to me by the Constitution as endorsed by the resolution of the Congress, I have directed that the following initial steps be taken immediately:

First: To halt this offensive buildup, a strict quarantine on all offensive military equipment under shipment to Cuba is being initiated. All ships of any kind bound for Cuba from whatever nation or port will, if found to contain cargoes of offensive weapons, be turned back. This quarantine will be extended, if needed, to other types of cargo and carriers. We are not at this time, however, denying the necessities of life as the Soviets attempted to do in their Berlin blockade of 1948.

Second: I have directed the continued and increased close surveillance of Cuba and its military buildup. . . .

Third: It shall be the policy of this Nation to regard any nuclear missile launched from Cuba against any nation in the Western Hemisphere as an attack by the Soviet Union on the United States, requiring a full retaliatory response upon the Soviet Union. . . .

. . . [F]inally: I call upon Chairman Khrushchev to halt and eliminate this clandestine, reckless, and provocative threat to world peace and to stable relations between our two nations. I call upon him further to abandon this course of world domination, and to join in an historic effort to end the perilous arms race and to transform the history of man. He has an opportunity now to move the world back from the abyss of destruction—by returning to his government's own words that it had no need to station missiles outside its own territory, and withdrawing these weapons from Cuba by refraining from any action which will widen or deepen the present crisis—and then by participating in a search for peaceful and permanent solutions. . . .

But it is difficult to settle or even discuss these problems in an atmosphere of intimidation. That is why this latest Soviet threat—or any other threat which is made either independently or in response to our actions this week—must and will be met with determination. Any hostile move anywhere in the world against the safety and freedom of peoples to whom we are committed—including in particular the brave people of West Berlin—will be met by whatever action is needed. . . .

Source: John F. Kennedy, "Radio and Television Report to the American People on the Soviet Arms Buildup in Cuba," October 22, 1962, in *Public Papers of the Presidents of the United States: John F. Kennedy, 1961–1963,* from the American Presidency Project, University of California, Santa Barbara, www.presidency.ucsb.edu.

Document 4.10
Soviet Ambassador to the United States Anatoly Dobrynin's Telegram Analyzing President John F. Kennedy's Actions, October 23, 1962

In this telegram, Anatoly Dobrynin, Soviet ambassador to the United States, informs Moscow of the mood in Washington following President Kennedy's October 22 speech, relays information about secret White House internal debates on foreign policy, and recommends measures to give an "appropriate rebuff" to the United States.

TOP SECRET
Making Copies Prohibited
Copy No. 1
CIPHERED TELEGRAM

. . . An analysis of the public statements which Kennedy has made, his message to N. S. Khrushchev, and also the statements of officials who are close to the White House and the State allow us to make, as it is presented to us, a preliminary conclusion that the measures which have been undertaken by the Kennedy Administration in regard to Cuba are the product of a range of domestic and foreign policy considerations, the most important of which, apparently, are the following.

1. To try to "take up the gauntlet" of that challenge which Kennedy believes has been thrown down by the Soviet Union to the USA in the form of military deliveries to Cuba. Regarding this, insofar as up to now a direct military attack by the USA on Cuba is not on the table (the President, as is known, also persistently stressed this during the meeting with A. A. Gromyko), Kennedy evidently is counting on the Soviet Union in this case not responding with military actions directly against the USA itself or by delivering a blow to their positions in West Berlin. As a result, in Kennedy's thinking, the United States will succeed in establishing at least in part the correlation of forces which existed in the world before July, that is before the announcement of our military deliveries to Cuba, which delivered a serious blow to the USA's positions as the leader of the capitalist world and even more constrained their freedom of action on issues like the one in West Berlin.

Kennedy apparently believes that a further demonstration by the United States of indecisiveness and lack of will to risk a war with the Soviet Union for the sake of its positions would unavoidably lead to an even quicker and more serious undermining of their positions around the globe.

2. That which Kennedy said yesterday in his appeal to the American people and the complex of measures which were announced in this connection by the USA government in fact touch not only upon Cuba alone or our deliveries of weapons to it, or even our missiles for Cuba. More to the point, it is a decision connected with a certain risk and determined by a whiff of adventurism, to try to bring to a stop now the development of events in the whole world, which are generally disadvantageous to the USA.

In this regard, some information which we have just received by confidential means and which we are now reconfirming, may be interesting. According to this information, prior to the President's decision a hot discussion was conducted recently in the government regarding the future foreign policy course of the USA following the appearance of information about the deliveries of Soviet missiles to Cuba. R. Kennedy, McNamara, Rusk, Chief of the CIA McCone, and the Chairman of the Joint Chiefs of Staff asserted that since Vienna the status quo in the world had changed, and had changed not to the benefit of the USA, as a result of the well-known development of the Cuban events, in particular the open deliveries of Soviet weapons to Cuba. The issue is not the weapons themselves, insofar as they do not have much significance from a purely military point of view, rather it is that great political loss which the Kennedy government suffered in the eyes of the whole world and particularly of its American allies and neighbors when it (the USA government) turned out to be not in a position—for the first time in the history of the USA—to prevent "the penetration and establishment of influence" by another great power, the USSR, in the Western Hemisphere itself. What then of the obligations of the USA in other parts of the world? And all this is happening at a moment—as asserted by representatives of the military brass—when America for the time being still has an advantage over the Soviet Union in nuclear missiles, an advantage which is gradually being liquidated by the successes of Soviet weapons, and now also by the creation of a missile base in Cuba in direct proximity with the USA. . . .

. . . Precisely on the Cuban issue it is best for President Kennedy to take a firm position and to "demonstrate his character." This approximately was the basic argument of those government representatives who support a more hard-line course of action (several of them speculated also that the President maintains the opinion that the Soviet government apparently does not particularly believe in the President's steadfastness following the failure of last year's incursion in Cuba). It follows, evidently, to recognize that the supporters of this course for the time being have taken the upper hand in the USA government.

3. Having created the extraordinary situation around Cuba, the Kennedy administration is hoping that in that situation it will be able quickly to get from its NATO allies and from the Latin American countries support for its course towards the full isolation of Cuba from the "free world," and the ultimate overthrow of the current government of Cuba. . . . [T]he Kennedy administration is succeeding in binding the governments of these [Latin American] countries to its will under conditions of the prewar psychosis which has now been created in the USA. . . .

4. On the domestic political plane, Kennedy obviously is counting on his last step to pull the rug out from under the legs of the Republicans, whose leadership in recent days officially announced that they consider the Cuban issue a fundamental issue of the election campaign, having in essence accused the administration of inactivity on that issue. . . .

. . . [T]his time he is ready to go pretty far in a test of strength with the Soviet Union, hoping that in the location of the conflict (Cuba) which was chosen by him, the President, the USA has a greater chance than the USSR, and that in the final analysis the Soviet government will refuse to increase the military power of Cuba, not wishing to let a major war break out. Under these conditions it is seen as expedient, while observing the necessary precautions, to at the same time review certain steps which would demonstrate the resolve of the USSR to give an appropriate rebuff to the USA and which would make the USA vulnerable to the possibility of actions which we may take in response. In particular, as it seems to us, it would be possible to review the question of hinting to Kennedy in no uncertain terms about the possibility of repressions against the Western powers in West Berlin (as a first step, the organization of a blockade of ground routes, leaving out for the time being air routes so as not to give grounds for a quick confrontation). . . .

23.X.62 A. DOBRYNIN

Source: Anatoly Dobrynin, "Telegram from Soviet Ambassador to the USA Dobrynin to the USSR MFA," October 23, 1962, from the Cold War International History Project, Woodrow Wilson International Center for Scholars, www.cwihp.org.

Document 4.11
Soviet Premier Nikita Khrushchev's First Letter to President John F. Kennedy Offering to Resolve the Cuban Missile Crisis, October 26, 1962

In the midst of a rambling letter repeating Soviet complaints about American actions and attitudes and taking the president to task for the Bay of Pigs attack and his alleged misrepresentation of Soviet intentions, Soviet premier Nikita Khrushchev suggested that he would order the removal of the offending armaments in exchange for an American pledge not to invade Cuba.

Dear Mr. President:

. . . Now we have already publicly exchanged our evaluations of the events around Cuba and each of us has set forth his explanation and his understanding of these events. Consequently, I would judge that, apparently, a continuation of an exchange of opinions at such a distance, even in the form of secret letters, will hardly add anything to that which one side has already said to the other.

I think you will understand me correctly if you are really concerned about the welfare of the world. Everyone needs peace: both capitalists, if they have not lost their reason, and, still more, Communists, people who know how to value not only their own lives but, more than anything, the lives of the peoples. We, Communists, are against all wars between states in general and have been defending the cause of peace since we came into the world. We have always regarded war as a calamity, and not as a game nor as a means for the attainment of definite goals, nor, all the more, as a goal in itself. Our goals are clear, and the means to attain them is labor. War is our enemy and a calamity for all the peoples. . . .

I see, Mr. President, that you too are not devoid of a sense of anxiety for the fate of the world understanding, and of what war entails. What would a war give you? You are threatening us with war. But you well know that the very least which you would receive in reply would be that you would experience the same consequences as those which you sent us. And that must be clear to us, people invested with authority, trust, and responsibility. We must not succumb to intoxication and petty passions, regardless of whether elections are impending in this or that country, or not impending. These are all transient things, but if indeed war should break out, then it would not be in our power to stop it, for such is the logic of war. I have participated in two wars and know that war ends when it has rolled through cities and villages, everywhere sowing death and destruction.

In the name of the Soviet Government and the Soviet people, I assure you that your conclusions regarding offensive weapons on Cuba are groundless. It is apparent from what you have written me that our conceptions are different on this score, or rather, we have different estimates of these or those military means. Indeed, in reality, the same forms of weapons can have different interpretations.

You are a military man and, I hope, will understand me. Let us take for example a simple cannon. What sort of means is this: offensive or defensive? A cannon is a defensive means if it is set up to defend boundaries or a fortified area. But if one concentrates artillery, and adds to it the necessary number of troops, then the same cannons do become an offensive means, because they prepare and clear the way for infantry to attack. The same happens with missile-nuclear weapons as well, with any type of this weapon. . . .

But, Mr. President, do you really seriously think that Cuba can attack the United States and that even we together with Cuba can attack you from the territory of Cuba? Can you really think that way? How is it possible? We do not understand this. Has something so new appeared in military strategy that one can think that it is possible to attack thus. I say precisely attack, and not destroy, since barbarians, people who have lost their sense, destroy. . . .

You have now proclaimed piratical measures, which were employed in the Middle Ages, when ships proceeding in international waters were attacked, and you have called this "a quarantine" around Cuba. Our vessels, apparently, will soon enter the zone which your Navy is patrolling. I assure you that these vessels, now bound for Cuba, are carrying the most innocent peaceful cargoes. Do you really think that we only occupy ourselves with the carriage of so-called offensive weapons, atomic and hydrogen bombs? Although perhaps your military people imagine that these (cargoes) are some sort of special type of weapon, I assure you that they are the most ordinary peaceful products.

Consequently, Mr. President, let us show good sense. I assure you that on those ships, which are bound for Cuba, there are no weapons at all. The weapons which were necessary for the defense of Cuba are already there. I do not want to say that there were not any shipments of weapons at all. No, there were such shipments. But now Cuba has already received the necessary means of defense. . . .

We were very grieved by the fact—I spoke about it in Vienna—that a landing took place, that an attack on Cuba was committed, as a result of which many Cubans perished. You yourself told me then that this had been a mistake. I respected that explanation. You repeated it to me several times, pointing out that not everybody occupying a high position would acknowledge his mistakes as you had done. I value such frankness. For my part, I told you that we too possess no less courage; we also acknowledged those mistakes which had been committed during the history of our state, and not only acknowledged, but sharply condemned them.

If you are really concerned about the peace and welfare of your people, and this is your responsibility as President, then I, as the Chairman of the Council of Ministers, am concerned for my people. Moreover, the preservation of world peace should be our joint concern, since if, under contemporary conditions, war should break out, it would be a war not only between the reciprocal claims, but a world wide cruel and destructive war.

Why have we proceeded to assist Cuba with military and economic aid? The answer is: We have proceeded to do so only for reasons of humanitarianism. At one time, our people itself had a revolution, when Russia was still a backward country. We were attacked then. We were the target of attack by many countries. The USA participated in that adventure. This has been recorded by participants in the aggression against our country. A whole book has been written about this by General Graves, who, at that time, commanded the US Expeditionary Corps. Graves called it "The American Adventure in Siberia."

We know how difficult it is to accomplish a revolution and how difficult it is to reconstruct a country on new foundations. We sincerely sympathize with Cuba and the Cuban people, but we are not interfering in questions of domestic structure, we are not interfering in their affairs. The Soviet Union desires to help the Cubans build their life as they themselves wish and that others should not hinder them.

You once said that the United States was not preparing an invasion. But you also declared that you sympathized with the Cuban counter-revolutionary emigrants, that you support them and would help them to realize their plans against the present Government of Cuba. It is also not a secret to anyone that the threat of armed attack, aggression, has constantly hung, and continues to hang over Cuba. It was only this which impelled us to respond to the request of the Cuban Government to furnish it aid for the strengthening of the defensive capacity of this country.

If assurances were given by the President and the Government of the United States that the USA itself would not participate in an attack on Cuba and would restrain others from actions of this sort, if you would recall your fleet, this would immediately change everything. I am not speaking for Fidel Castro, but I think that he and the Government of Cuba, evidently, would declare demobilization and would appeal to the people to get down to peaceful labor. Then, too, the question of armaments would disappear, since, if there is no threat, then armaments are a burden for every people. . . .

Source: Nikita Khrushchev, "Chairman Khrushchev's Message of October 26, 1962," from "Messages Exchanged by President Kennedy and Chairman Khrushchev During the Cuban Missile Crisis of October 1962," in "Significant Documents Declassified under Executive Order 11652," *Department of State Bulletin* 69, no. 1795 (November 19, 1973), 640–645.

Document 4.12
Soviet Premier Nikita Khrushchev's Second Letter to President John F. Kennedy on the Cuban Missile Crisis, October 27, 1962

Before Kennedy had replied to the Soviet premier's offer of a deal in his first such letter (Document 4.11), another letter arrived, adding a further requirement to achieve the removal of Soviet missiles from Cuba: the removal of US missiles from Turkey.

. . . You are disturbed over Cuba. You say that this disturbs you because it is 90 miles by sea from the coast of the United States of America. But Turkey adjoins us; our sentries patrol back and forth and see each other. Do you consider, then, that you have the right to demand security for your own country and the removal of the weapons you call offensive, but do not accord the same right to us? You have placed destructive missile weapons, which you call offensive, in Turkey, literally next to us. How then can recognition of our equal military capacities be reconciled with such unequal relations between our great states? This is irreconcilable. . . .

I therefore make this proposal: We are willing to remove from Cuba the means which you regard as offensive. We are willing to carry this out and to make this pledge in the United Nations. Your representatives will make a declaration to the effect that the United States, for its part, considering the uneasiness and anxiety of the Soviet State, will remove its analogous means from Turkey. . . .

We, in making this pledge, in order to give satisfaction and hope of the peoples of Cuba and Turkey and to strengthen their confidences in their security, will make a statement within the framework of the Security Council to the effect that the Soviet Government gives a solemn promise to respect the inviolability of the borders and sovereignty of Turkey, not to interfere in its internal affairs, not to invade Turkey, not to make available our territory as a bridgehead for such an invasion, and that it would also restrain those who contemplate committing aggression against Turkey, either from the territory of the Soviet Union or from the territory of Turkey's other neighboring states.

The United States Government will make a similar statement within the framework of the Security Council regarding Cuba. . . .

These are my proposals, Mr. President.

Respectfully yours,

N. KHRUSHCHEV

Source: Nikita Khrushchev, "Chairman Khrushchev's Message of October 27, 1962," from "Messages Exchanged by President Kennedy and Chairman Khrushchev During the Cuban Missile Crisis of October 1962," in "Significant Documents Declassified under Executive Order 11652," *Department of State Bulletin* 69, no. 1795 (November 19, 1973), 649–650.

Document 4.13
Soviet Ambassador to the United States Anatoly Dobrynin Recounts Arrangement with Attorney General Robert Kennedy, Cable to the Soviet Foreign Ministry, October 27, 1962

President Kennedy accepted Premier Khrushchev's offers: the first in public and the second in the strictest of confidences. Only the opening of the former Soviet Union's archives revealed that the United States did indeed accede to the removal of its missiles from Turkey as a part of the deal that resolved the Cuban Missile Crisis. In this cable to the Soviet Foreign Ministry, Soviet ambassador to the United States Anatoly Dobrynin recounts how the arrangement was reached.

TOP SECRET

Making Copies Prohibited

Copy No. 1

CIPHERED TELEGRAM

Late tonight R. Kennedy invited me to come see him. We talked alone.

The Cuban crisis, R. Kennedy began, continues to quickly worsen. . . . "The USA government is determined to get rid of those bases—up to, in the extreme case, of bombing them, since, I [R. Kennedy] repeat, they pose a great threat to the security of the USA. But in response to the bombing of these bases, in the course of which Soviet specialists might suffer, the Soviet government will undoubtedly respond with the same against us, somewhere in Europe. A real war will begin, in which millions of Americans and Russians will die. We want to avoid that any way we can, I'm sure that the government of the USSR has the same wish. However, taking time to find a way out is very risky (here R. Kennedy mentioned as if in passing that there are many unreasonable heads among the generals, and not only among the generals, who are 'itching for a fight'). The situation might get out of control, with irreversible consequences."

"In this regard," R. Kennedy said, "the president considers that a suitable basis for regulating the entire Cuban conflict might be the letter N. S. Khrushchev sent on October 26 and the letter in response from the President, which was sent off today to N. S. Khrushchev through the US Embassy in Moscow. The most important thing for us," R. Kennedy stressed, "is to get as soon as possible the agreement of the Soviet government to halt further work on the construction of the missile bases in Cuba and take measures under international control that would make it impossible to use these weapons. In exchange the government of the USA is ready, in addition to repealing all measures on the "quarantine," to give the assurances that there will not be any invasion of Cuba and that other countries of the Western Hemisphere are ready to give the same assurances—the US government is certain of this."

"And what about Turkey?" I asked R. Kennedy.

"If that is the only obstacle to achieving the regulation I mentioned earlier, then the president doesn't see any unsurmountable difficulties in resolving this issue," replied R. Kennedy. "The greatest difficulty for the president is the public discussion of the issue of Turkey. Formally the deployment of missile bases in Turkey was done by a special decision of the NATO Council. To announce now a unilateral decision by the president of the USA to withdraw missile bases from Turkey—this would damage the entire structure of NATO and the US position as the leader of NATO, where, as the Soviet government knows very well, there are many arguments. In short, if such a decision were announced now it would seriously tear apart NATO."

"However, President Kennedy is ready to come to agree on that question with N. S. Khrushchev, too. I think that in order to withdraw these bases from Turkey," R. Kennedy said, "we need 4–5 months. This is the minimal amount of time necessary for the US government to do this, taking into account the procedures that exist within the NATO framework. On the whole Turkey issue," R. Kennedy added, "if Premier N. S. Khrushchev agrees with what I've said, we can continue to exchange opinions between him and the president, using him, R. Kennedy and the Soviet ambassador. However, the president can't say anything public in this regard about Turkey," R. Kennedy said again. R. Kennedy then warned that his comments about Turkey are extremely confidential; besides him and his brother, only 2–3 people know about it in Washington.

"That's all that he asked me to pass on to N. S. Khrushchev," R. Kennedy said in conclusion. "The president also asked N. S. Khrushchev to give him an answer (through the Soviet ambassador and R. Kennedy) if possible within the next day (Sunday) on these thoughts in order to have a business-like, clear answer in principle. . . . The request for a reply tomorrow," stressed R. Kennedy, "is just that—a request, and not an ultimatum. The president hopes that the head of the Soviet government will understand him correctly."

I noted that it went without saying that the Soviet government would not accept any ultimatums and it was good that the American government realized that. . . .

I should say that during our meeting R. Kennedy was very upset; in any case, I've never seen him like this before. True, about twice he tried to return to the topic of "deception," (that he talked about so persistently during our previous meeting), but he did so in passing and without any edge to it. He didn't even try to get into fights on various subjects, as he usually does, and only persistently returned to one topic: time is of the essence and we shouldn't miss the chance.

After meeting with me he immediately went to see the president, with whom, as R. Kennedy said, he spends almost all his time now.

27/X-62 A. DOBRYNIN

Source: Anatoly Dobrynin, "Dobrynin's Cable to the Soviet Foreign Ministry," October 27, 1962, in Jim Hershberg, "Anatomy of a Controversy: Anatoly F. Dobrynin's Meeting with Robert F. Kennedy, Saturday, 27 October 1962," *Cold War International History Project Bulletin*, no. 5 (Spring 1995): 75, 77–80, www.cwihp.org.

Document 4.14
President John F. Kennedy and Soviet Premier Nikita Khrushchev Exchange Formal Letters Ending the Cuban Missile Crisis, October 27 and 28, 1962

The leaders of the two superpowers exchanged formal letters signifying their understanding of the (public) agreements they had reached to end the crisis in Cuba. The president's letter was released to the press on the evening of October 27 and was sent to the U.S. embassy in Moscow, with instructions that it "be delivered as soon as possible to highest available Soviet official."

Dear Mr. Chairman:

I have read your letter of October 26th with great care and welcomed the statement of your desire to seek a prompt solution to the problem. The first thing that needs to be done, however, is for work to cease on offensive missile bases in Cuba and for all weapons systems in Cuba capable of offensive use to be rendered inoperable, under effective United Nations arrangements.

Assuming this is done promptly, I have given my representatives in New York instructions that will permit them to work out this weekend—in cooperation with the Acting Secretary General and your representative—an arrangement for a permanent solution to the Cuban problem along the lines suggested in your letter of October 26th. As I read your letter, the key elements of your proposals—which seem generally acceptable as I understand them—are as follows:

1) You would agree to remove these weapons systems from Cuba under appropriate United Nations observation and supervision; and undertake, with suitable safeguards, to halt the further introduction of such weapons systems into Cuba.

2) We, on our part, would agree—upon the establishment of adequate arrangements through the United Nations to ensure the carrying out and continuation of these commitments—(a) to remove promptly the quarantine measures now in effect and

(b) to give assurances against an invasion of Cuba. I am confident that other nations of the Western Hemisphere would be prepared to do likewise.

If you will give your representative similar instructions, there is no reason why we should not be able to complete these arrangements and announce them to the world within a couple of days. The effect of such a settlement on easing world tensions would enable us to work toward a more general arrangement regarding 'other armaments,' as proposed in your second letter which you made public. I would like to say again that the United States is very much interested in reducing tensions and halting the arms race; and if your letter signifies that you are prepared to discuss a detente affecting NATO and the Warsaw Pact, we are quite prepared to consider with our allies any useful proposals.

But the first ingredient, let me emphasize, is the cessation of work on missile sites in Cuba and measures to render such weapons inoperable, under effective international guarantees. The continuation of this threat, or a prolonging of this discussion concerning Cuba by linking these problems to the broader questions of European and world security, would surely lead to an intensification of the Cuban crisis and a grave risk to the peace of the world. For this reason I hope we can quickly agree along the lines in this letter and in your letter of October 26th.

JOHN F. KENNEDY

The Soviet leader's reply was broadcast in English from Moscow the following day, to speed receipt in the days before the "hotline."

Dear Mr. President:

I have received your message of October 27. I express my satisfaction and thank you for the sense of proportion you have displayed and for realization of the responsibility which now devolves on you for the preservation of the peace of the world.

I regard with great understanding your concern and the concern of the United States people in connection with the fact that the weapons you describe as offensive are formidable weapons indeed. Both you and we understand what kind of weapons these are.

In order to eliminate as rapidly as possible the conflict which endangers the cause of peace, to give an assurance to all people who crave peace, and to reassure the American people, who, I am certain, also want peace, as do the people of the Soviet Union, the Soviet Government, in addition to earlier instructions on the discontinuation of further work on weapons construction sites, has given a new order to dismantle the arms which you described as offensive, and to crate and return them to the Soviet Union.

Mr. President, I should like to repeat what I had already written to you in my earlier messages—that the Soviet Government has given economic assistance to the Republic of Cuba, as well as arms, because Cuba and the Cuban people were constantly under the continuous threat of an invasion of Cuba. . . .

I regard with respect and trust the statement you made in your message of October 27, 1962, that there would be no attack, no invasion of Cuba, and not only on the part of the United States, but also on the part of other nations of the Western Hemisphere, as you said in your same message. Then the motives which induced us to render assistance of such a kind to Cuba disappear.

It is for this reason that we instructed our officers—these means as I had already informed you earlier are in the hands of the Soviet officers—to take appropriate measures to discontinue construction of the aforementioned facilities, to dismantle them, and to return them to the Soviet Union. . . .

Thus in view of the assurance you have given and our instructions on dismantling, there is every condition for eliminating the present conflict. . . .

Respectfully yours,

N. KHRUSHCHEV

Source: John F. Kennedy, "Telegram from the Department of State to the Embassy in the Soviet Union," October 27, 1962, and Nikita Khrushchev, "Letter from Chairman Khrushchev to President Kennedy," October 28, 1962, documents 67 and 68 in U.S. Department of State, *Foreign Relations of the United States, 1961–1963,* vol. 6, *Kennedy-Khrushchev Exchanges,* ed. Charles S. Sampson, www.state.gov/www/about_state/history/volume_vi/exchanges.html.

Document 4.15
President John F. Kennedy's Commencement Address at American University, Washington, D.C., June 10, 1963

In a commencement address at American University, President Kennedy spoke of world peace and of his hopes for a relaxation of tensions between the United States and the Soviet Union. Peace, he said, was a "process" of mutual engagement, marked by small but tangible agreements. To advance progress toward one such agreement, the president took this opportunity to declare that the United States would conduct no further nuclear tests in the atmosphere "so long as other states do not do so." The president also took the occasion to honor the Soviets for their presumed mutual commitment to peace, and for the great sacrifices they made during World War II.

. . . Some say that it is useless to speak of world peace or world law or world disarmament—and that it will be useless until the leaders of the Soviet Union adopt a more enlightened attitude. I hope they do. I believe we can help them do it. But I also believe that we must reexamine our own attitude—as individuals and as a Nation—for our attitude is as essential as theirs. . . .

First: Let us examine our attitude toward peace itself. Too many of us think it is impossible. Too many think it unreal. But that is a dangerous, defeatist belief. It leads to the conclusion that war is inevitable—that mankind is doomed—that we are gripped by forces we cannot control.

We need not accept that view. Our problems are manmade—therefore, they can be solved by man. And man can be as big as he wants. No problem of human destiny is beyond human beings. Man's reason and spirit have often solved the seemingly unsolvable—and we believe they can do it again.

I am not referring to the absolute, infinite concept of universal peace and good will of which some fantasies and fanatics dream. I do not deny the value of hopes and dreams but we merely invite discouragement and incredulity by making that our only and immediate goal.

Let us focus instead on a more practical, more attainable peace—based not on a sudden revolution in human nature but on a gradual evolution in human institutions—on a series of concrete actions and effective agreements which are in the interest of all concerned. . . .

There is no single, simple key to this peace—no grand or magic formula to be adopted by one or two powers. Genuine peace must be the product of many nations, the sum of many acts. It must be dynamic, not static, changing to meet the challenge of each new generation. For peace is a process—a way of solving problems. . . .

Second: Let us reexamine our attitude toward the Soviet Union. It is discouraging to think that their leaders may actually believe what their propagandists write. . . . [I]t is sad to read these Soviet statements—to realize the extent of the gulf between us. But it is also a warning—a warning to the American people not to fall into the same trap as the Soviets, not to see only a distorted and desperate view of the other side, not to see conflict as inevitable, accommodation as impossible, and communication as nothing more than an exchange of threats.

No government or social system is so evil that its people must be considered as lacking in virtue. As Americans, we find communism profoundly repugnant as a negation of personal freedom and dignity. But we can still hail the Russian people for their many achievements—in science and space, in economic and industrial growth, in culture and in acts of courage.

Among the many traits the peoples of our two countries have in common, none is stronger than our mutual abhorrence of war. Almost unique, among the major world powers, we have never been at war with each other. And no nation in the history of battle ever suffered more than the Soviet Union suffered in the course of the Second World War. . . .

So, let us not be blind to our differences—but let us also direct attention to our common interests and to the means by which those differences can be resolved. And if we cannot end now our differences, at least we can help make the world safe for diversity. For, in the final analysis, our most basic common link is that we all inhabit this small planet. We all breathe the same air. We all cherish our children's future. And we are all mortal.

Third: Let us reexamine our attitude toward the cold war, remembering that we are not engaged in a debate, seeking to pile up debating points. We are not here distributing blame or pointing the finger of judgment. We must deal with the world as it is, and not as it might have been had the history of the last 18 years been different.

We must, therefore, persevere in the search for peace in the hope that constructive changes within the Communist bloc might bring within reach solutions which now seem beyond us. We must conduct our affairs in such a way that it becomes in the Communists' interest to agree on a genuine peace. Above all, while defending our own vital interests, nuclear powers must avert those confrontations which bring an adversary to a choice of either a humiliating retreat or a nuclear war. To adopt that kind of course in the nuclear age would be evidence only of the bankruptcy of our policy—or of a collective death-wish for the world.

To secure these ends, America's weapons are nonprovocative, carefully controlled, designed to deter, and capable of selective use. Our military forces are committed to peace and disciplined in self-restraint. Our diplomats are instructed to avoid unnecessary irritants and purely rhetorical hostility.

For we can seek a relaxation of tensions without relaxing our guard. And, for our part, we do not need to use threats to prove that we are resolute. We do not need to jam foreign broadcasts out of fear our faith will be eroded. We are unwilling to impose our system on any unwilling people—but we are willing and able to engage in peaceful competition with any people on earth. . . .

I am taking this opportunity, therefore, to announce two important decisions in this regard.

First: Chairman Khrushchev, Prime Minister Macmillan, and I have agreed that high level discussions will shortly begin in Moscow looking toward early agreement on a comprehensive test ban treaty. Our hopes must be tempered with the caution of history—but with our hopes go the hopes of all mankind.

Second: To make clear our good faith and solemn convictions on the matter, I now declare that the United States does not propose to conduct nuclear tests in the atmosphere so long as other states do not do so. We will not be the first to resume. Such a declaration is no substitute for a formal binding treaty, but I hope it will help us achieve one. Nor would such a treaty be a substitute for disarmament, but I hope it will help us achieve it. . . .

. . . "When a man's ways please the Lord," the Scriptures tell us, "he maketh even his enemies to be at peace with him." And is not peace, in the last analysis, basically a matter of human rights—the right to live out our lives without fear of devastation-the right to breathe air as nature provided it—the right of future generations to a healthy existence? . . .

Source: John F. Kennedy, "Commencement Address at American University in Washington," June 10, 1963, in *Public Papers of the Presidents of the United States: John F. Kennedy, 1961–1963,* from the American Presidency Project, University of California, Santa Barbara, www.presidency.ucsb.edu.

Document 4.16:
"Ich bin ein Berliner," President John F. Kennedy's Speech at the Rudolf Wild Platz, Berlin, June 26, 1963

In the final summer of his presidency and his life, President Kennedy was greeted by enormous crowds during a trip to Europe. The highlight of the trip, which generated more than twenty special reports on American network television, was the president's visit to West Berlin. On the fifteenth anniversary of the start of the Berlin airlift, Kennedy reaffirmed the West's commitment to the defense of the besieged city. The president condemned the Berlin Wall as proof of the "failures of communism."

I am proud to come to this city as the guest of your distinguished Mayor, who has symbolized throughout the world the fighting spirit of West Berlin. And I am proud to visit the Federal Republic with your distinguished Chancellor who for so many years has committed Germany to democracy and freedom and progress, and to come here in the company of my fellow American, General Clay, who has been in this city during its great moments of crisis and will come again if ever needed.

Two thousand years ago the proudest boast was "civis Romanus sum." Today, in the world of freedom, the proudest boast is "Ich bin ein Berliner."

I appreciate my interpreter translating my German!

There are many people in the world who really don't understand, or say they don't, what is the great issue between the free world and the Communist world. Let them come to Berlin. There are some who say that communism is the wave of the future. Let them come to Berlin. And there are some who say in Europe and elsewhere we can work with the Communists. Let them come to Berlin. And there are even a few who say that it is true that communism is an evil system, but it permits us to make economic progress. Lass' sic nach Berlin kommen. Let them come to Berlin.

Freedom has many difficulties and democracy is not perfect, but we have never had to put a wall up to keep our people in, to prevent them from leaving us. I want to say, on behalf of my countrymen, who live many miles away on the other side of the Atlantic, who are far distant from you, that they take the greatest pride that they have been able to share with you, even from a distance, the story of the last 18 years. I know of no town, no city, that has been besieged for 18 years that still lives with the vitality and the force, and the hope and the determination of the city of West Berlin. While the wall is the most obvious and vivid demonstration of the failures of the Communist system, for all the world to see, we take no satisfaction in it, for it is, as your Mayor has said, an offense not only against history but an offense against humanity, separating families, dividing husbands and wives and brothers and sisters, and dividing a people who wish to be joined together.

What is true of this city is true of Germany—real, lasting peace in Europe can never be assured as long as one German out of four is denied the elementary right of free men, and that is to make a free choice. In 18 years of peace and good faith, this generation of Germans has earned the right to be free, including the right to unite their families and their nation in lasting peace, with good will to all people. You live in a defended island of freedom, but your life is part of the main. So let me ask you, as I close, to lift your eyes beyond the dangers of today, to the hopes of tomorrow, beyond the freedom merely of this city of Berlin, or your country of Germany, to the advance of freedom everywhere, beyond the wall to the day of peace with justice, beyond yourselves and ourselves to all mankind.

Freedom is indivisible, and when one man is enslaved, all are not free. When all are free, then we can look forward to that day when this city will be joined as one and this country and this great Continent of Europe in a peaceful and hopeful globe. When that day finally comes, as it will, the people of West Berlin can take sober satisfaction in the fact that they were in the front lines for almost two decades.

All free men, wherever they may live, are citizens of Berlin, and, therefore, as a free man, I take pride in the words "Ich bin ein Berliner."

In this address, Kennedy refers to Mayor Will Brandt, Chancellor Adenauer, and Gen. Lucius D. Clay. *Source:* John F. Kennedy, "Remarks in the Rudolf Wild Platz, Berlin," June 26, 1963, in *Public Papers of the Presidents of the United States: John F. Kennedy, 1961–1963,* from the American Presidency Project, University of California, Santa Barbara, www.presidency.ucsb.edu.

Document 4.17
The Partial Test Ban Treaty, August 5, 1963

The United States, the Soviet Union, and the United Kingdom agreed in 1963 to the Cold War's first limits on nuclear weapons testing. The treaty was signed in Moscow by the American secretary of state and the foreign ministers of the UK and the Soviet Union. It was ratified quickly by the U.S. Senate and went into effect on October 10, 1963. A comprehensive test ban treaty would not be signed until 1996, after the end of the Cold War.

The Governments of the United States of America, the United Kingdom of Great Britain and Northern Ireland, and the Union of Soviet Socialist Republics, hereinafter referred to as the "Original Parties,"

Proclaiming as their principal aim the speediest possible achievement of an agreement on general and complete disarmament under strict international control in accordance with the objectives of the United Nations which would put an end to the armaments race and eliminate the incentive to the production and testing of all kinds of weapons, including nuclear weapons,

Seeking to achieve the discontinuance of all test explosions of nuclear weapons for all time, determined to continue negotiations to this end, and desiring to put an end to the contamination of mans environment by radioactive substances,

Have agreed as follows:

ARTICLE I

1. Each of the Parties to this Treaty undertakes to prohibit, to prevent, and not to carry out any nuclear weapon test explosion, or any other nuclear explosion, at any place under its jurisdiction or control:
   (a) in the atmosphere; beyond its limits, including outer space; or under water, including territorial waters or high seas; or
   (b) in any other environment if such explosion causes radioactive debris to be present outside the territorial limits of the State under whose jurisdiction or control such explosion is conducted. It is understood in this connection that the provisions of this subparagraph are without prejudice to the conclusion of a Treaty resulting in the permanent banning of all nuclear test explosions, including all such explosions underground, the conclusion of which, as the Parties have stated in the Preamble to this Treaty, they seek to achieve.
2. Each of the Parties to this Treaty undertakes furthermore to refrain from causing, encouraging, or in any way participating in, the carrying out of any nuclear weapon test explosion, or any other nuclear explosion, anywhere which would take place in any of the environments described, or have the effect referred to, in paragraph 1 of this Article. . . .

Source: U.S. Department of State, "Treaty Banning Nuclear Weapon Tests in the Atmosphere, in Outer Space and Under Water," August 5, 1963, www.state.gov/t/ac/trt/4797.htm#treaty.

CHAPTER FIVE

Lyndon Johnson
The Credibility Gap

The Cold War frustrated even as it empowered American presidents. The frustrations became intense in the 1960s and 1970s. The result was a line of presidents who, by exercising powers granted to them by virtue of their status as wartime chief executives, undermined their standing with the American public. Of the four presidents who held office from 1964 through 1980, none was elected twice; one resigned under pressure; two lost bids to remain in office; and one, Lyndon Johnson, withdrew from the presidency under political assault from his own party. It has never been easy to be president; it has seldom been as difficult as it was in the 1960s and 1970s. The Cold War was a major reason why.

Would the Cold War ever be won? Could it even be "fought"? Was it really necessary for Americans to keep sacrificing their own blood and money for the defense of other peoples? And why weren't those other people more grateful? As the nation

President Lyndon Johnson jots notes during a March 27, 1968, meeting in the Cabinet Room. Four days later, in a major speech about the Vietnam War, Johnson announced that he would not seek another term in office. Source: Lyndon Baines Johnson Library and Museum/Yoichi R. Okamoto.

entered into the third decade of cold war in the mid-1960s, these questions took on new urgency. There were four principle reasons why:

- To start with, the Soviets were catching up in the arms race. They had made dramatic breakthroughs in the past, but the Americans had always been able to push back and push ahead. Now things were beginning to look different. The Soviet buildup in intercontinental ballistic missiles (ICBMs) was especially dramatic during the Johnson years.
- Second, the superpowers took sides against one another in an increasing number of conflicts throughout the third world. Both Soviet and American leaders viewed revolutions, coups, border skirmishes, and outright wars in and between developing countries through the prism of the Cold War.

- Third, the Cold War began to undermine the presidency as other persons, institutions, and nations began to react against the decisions made and actions taken by presidents. The president's discretionary authority to set foreign policy in the fight against communism was thus called into question not just by college students and protestors, but also by senators and heads of state. The United States' allies in Europe and Asia were no longer as willing to take direction from across the Atlantic as they had been just after World War II.

- Finally, the beginning of economic distress at home led many Americans to seek a retreat from the global commitments of a superpower, and skepticism about the Cold War began to emerge.

Lyndon Johnson was not unique in facing these difficulties, but he was the first of four successive presidents who failed to overcome them. His failure was particularly tragic, because he wanted so badly to do good and to lift up the American people, especially those who were poor or otherwise out of the mainstream of America's middle-class prosperity. Johnson's vision for the nation, articulated in his wildly successful campaign for election in 1964, was to create a "Great Society," in which all Americans would reap benefits. The Great Society was to be the culmination of all the progressive legislation that had been passed before, especially the New Deal programs of President Franklin Roosevelt.

Johnson had entered politics as a Democrat during the New Deal era by winning a seat in the House of Representatives in a 1937 special election. He became a favorite of President Roosevelt, who helped Representative Johnson direct government aid to his poor district in the Texas hill country. When he won a Senate seat in 1948, it seemed that Johnson had found his niche. The Senate, which has fewer institutionally defined roles than the House, places a premium on personal persuasion. Lyndon Johnson, a masterful persuader in one-on-one sessions, thrived in this environment, rising to become Senate majority leader, a post he held from 1954 to 1960.

As majority leader under President Eisenhower, Johnson had steered a moderate course. As president, he saw an opportunity to act boldly and took it, pushing through Congress a flood of legislation that expanded the government's role in individuals' lives; his initiatives included Medicare and Medicaid, federal aid to secondary schools, desegregation of public accommodations, and the federal enforcement of voting rights in the states—and came close to eclipsing the legislative record of Johnson's model, President Roosevelt.

Foreign policy did not play a major part in Johnson's plans to achieve either national or personal greatness. To gain legislative passage of the new government programs that would usher in a Great Society, the president needed to keep the public and Congress focused intently on domestic issues. Johnson knew from personal experience in the 1940s that once a president turned to war, the public and Congress would demand a stop to "luxuries" such as new progressive domestic programs.

Unfortunately for Johnson, the Cold War could not be put aside indefinitely. After serving out the remainder of President John F. Kennedy's elected term and then a single term in his own right, President Johnson stunned the nation by announcing in March 1968 that he would not run for a second term as president. Coming from a man who had quested for power all his life and believed he had so much to offer the nation as president, this was a shock. The Cold War presidency expanded the president's capacities in all respects, especially in foreign affairs, but for a president interested primarily in the home front, being the leader of the free world could be more of a curse than a blessing. Among other difficulties, being a Cold War president, especially in the first two decades of the conflict, meant jumping from one crisis to another.[1]

CRISIS MANAGEMENT

The first Cold War crisis that Lyndon Johnson faced was his assumption of the presidency following the assassination of President John F. Kennedy. "I thought it was a conspiracy," the president stated plainly, looking back on the events of November 22, 1963 (**Document 5.1**). If the Soviets, or Soviet-directed agents from some other nation, had killed Kennedy, then "who would they shoot next? And what was going on in Washington?" Johnson wondered as he made his way from the hospital in Dallas, where Kennedy had been pronounced dead, to the president's plane

Lyndon Johnson was always a good man in a crisis, in the sense that he maintained his poise and could sustain intense focus and discipline over many days, with minimal sleep. As vice president, he had been miserable and had given himself over to self-pity and reckless behavior, including excessive drinking. Lyndon Johnson had never wanted to be vice anything. He strove all his life for power, and he had risen to become one of the most effective Senate majority leaders ever during Dwight Eisenhower's presidency. The vice presidency was offered to Johnson as a consolation prize for having failed to win the 1960 Democratic Party nomination for president. Massachusetts senator John F. Kennedy, who won the nomination, wanted Johnson, a Texan, on the ticket for geographical balance, not because he wanted Johnson's assistance formulating policy in the White House. Most of Johnson's friends did not even think he would accept the post, because it is well known to be a frustrating position. A vice president is, as the saying goes, a heartbeat from the presidency, but he has no executive authority in his own right. Although President Kennedy tried to keep Johnson busy, he could not make him like being Number Two.

At the moment when the assassin's bullets struck the Kennedy motorcade in Dallas, Lyndon Johnson regained control of himself once more under the life-giving pressure of a crisis. After being sworn in aboard Air Force One while it sat on the tarmac at Love Field, the new president returned to Washington, D.C. He went to work immediately, seeking to win the loyalty and confidence of the assassinated president's top appointees, in order to project to the nation the "leadership and purpose and continuity" that he believed the American people needed at that moment.[2] He met personally with as many of Kennedy's people as he could, urging them all to stay and promising to carry forward Kennedy's agenda in domestic and foreign affairs.

Johnson also quickly arranged for a prominent commission of respected citizens, led by the Supreme Court chief justice Earl Warren, to study the assassination. Johnson had to use all his persuasive powers to get Warren to take the potentially troublesome job of chairing the committee. He also persuaded his friend from the senate, Sen. Richard Russell,

D-Ga., to serve. Johnson pushed the commission not to drag out their investigation. When, after ten months of work, the Warren Commission concluded that a lone gunman had killed the president and wounded the governor of Texas, Johnson praised the commission's fast work.

The president wanted to put the assassination investigation behind him for two reasons. First, as long as the public was fixated on who killed Kennedy, the president would not be able to mobilize support for his legislative goals. Second, the president worried about what might be uncovered in a more thorough investigation. If the Reds had had a hand in Kennedy's death, the president seemed to believe that it would be better for the nation simply not to know. Johnson always doubted the Warren Commission's findings, but he did not say so publicly until he had retired.

Although President Johnson would indeed push forward with his Great Society legislation, he was often interrupted by crises. None was as dramatic as the event that began his presidency, but all required his complete attention—in the climate of the Cold War, virtually any crisis involving almost any foreign nation could escalate out of control.

Latin America

Johnson handled his first several crises in Latin America adeptly. Shortly after coming to office, the president had attempted to ease the antagonism between the U.S. executive branch and Fidel Castro by ordering a halt to U.S. efforts to assassinate the Cuban dictator. Despite this, in February 1964 Castro's troops cut off the water supply to the U.S. military base at Guantanamo Bay. Johnson handled the situation quietly. Learning that contingency plans had been made for just such a provocation, Johnson ordered the military to put them into action. When Castro offered to restore water, the United States told him not to bother.

Later in 1964 the administration faced another problem in Latin America when anti-United States rioting in Panama led to the deaths of four U.S. soldiers. Anti-Communists in the administration believed that if Castro's agents were not in fact controlling events, they would surely take advantage of the situation if it were not brought quickly under control. In his oral history for the Johnson Presidential Library, Thomas Mann, known as "Mr. Latin America" in the Johnson administration, speculated that the Panamanian government had exploited U.S. anxieties about Cuba by secretly supporting the riots while publicly blaming Castro for them.[3] The goal of the Panamanians, according to Mann, was to pressure the United States to renegotiate the historic treaty for control of the Panama Canal. Whether he had been manipulated by an ally or not, President Johnson waited until after the November 1964 election and then instructed the State Department to seek a new treaty with Panama. Eventually, under the next Democratic president, Jimmy Carter, a treaty was signed to transfer the canal to Panamanian control.

The overall policy that the Johnson administration followed in Latin America was in line with the president's handling of these incidents. The president downplayed the Alliance for Progress, created under President Kennedy for the purpose of spreading democracy and prosperity, and emphasized the Cold War stakes in the region. In remarks to U.S. ambassadors in March 1964, Mann articulated what came to be known as the

Mann Doctrine. It might also have been called the Johnson Doctrine, for it encapsulated President Johnson's perspective on foreign affairs in Latin America. Economic growth and anti-communism were to be the United States' top priorities in Latin America. The United States would support governments able to withstand or contain Communists and Communist-leaning leftists, and to maintain order. According to critics of the policy, this gave a green light to military coup plotters.

Two weeks after Mann's remarks, on April 1, 1964, the Brazilian armed forces took power from President Joao Goulart, who had been struggling for radical land reform in the face of harsh opposition from conservatives. Although Goulart was a leader of the Labor Party, not the Communist Party, he was suspected of having ties to foreign Marxist governments. The U.S. ambassador to Brazil welcomed the news of his ouster, calling the coup "the greatest victory of the West against Communism, greater than Cuba's nuclear disarmament, greater than the crisis of the Berlin Wall."[4] Within twelve hours of the coup, the United States formally recognized the new military government. Had the coup turned violent, the U.S. armed forces had in place a contingency plan to come to the assistance of the Brazilian military. As the president had told Undersecretary of State George Ball the day before Goulart's ouster, "I think we ought . . . be prepared to do everything that we need to do. . . . We just can't take this one," referring to the ideologically suspect Goulart.[5]

In 1965 President Johnson did send U.S. armed forces into a Latin American country to fight leftist factions vying for control of the government. Following a coup against Juan Bosch, the democratically elected president of the Dominican Republic, rebels supporting Bosch's reinstallation besieged the pro-U.S. government of Donald Reid Cabral, who had the backing of the nation's armed forces. The U.S. ambassador urged President Johnson to send in the marines to take on the leftists among Bosch's supporters. After receiving the blessing of a bipartisan group of congressional leaders, Johnson ordered some 22,000 troops to the country to evacuate U.S. citizens and defend the Dominican Republic's military government.

The president's penchant for hyperbole got him into trouble in this incident, foreshadowing the "credibility gap" that would beset his handling of the war in Vietnam. At one point, Johnson attempted to justify U.S. involvement by claiming that "some fifteen hundred innocent people were murdered and shot and their heads cut off." When challenged on this assertion, Johnson telephoned the ambassador and ordered him to "go down there"—to the site of the fighting—"and see if you can find some of those people who were beheaded."[6] The ambassador was able to confirm the discovery of just two. A large majority of the public supported the president's policy nonetheless, but Sen. J. William Fulbright, D-Ark., chairman of the Senate Foreign Relations Committee, publicly questioned the president's statements justifying the troop deployment. The editors of *Newsweek* magazine observed that the president seemed to be "touchy, bitter and exasperated" in his handling of foreign affairs.[7] Johnson's crisis management skills were being put to a hard test.

Two years later, Johnson claimed an important, if controversial, symbolic victory against Communist guerillas in Latin America. On October 9, 1967, Bolivian special forces, trained by American Green Berets, captured and killed the revolutionary icon Ernesto Guevara de la Serna, commonly known as Che Guevara. The Argentine-born Guevara had been a founder of revolutionary Cuba and had held top posts in Fidel Castro's government. At the time of his death, he was in Bolivia attempting to spread Marxist revolution.

Africa and the Middle East

In Africa, the Johnson administration more directly continued the policy set by President Kennedy. The United States thus continued to support President Joseph Mobutu in the Congolese civil war. The victory of Mobutu's forces in November 1965 against Cuban-backed revolutionary Patrice Lumumba was regarded as a victory for containment of communism in the third world. Although Mobutu's supporters in the United States were chagrined by his excesses—he publicly executed political rivals to consolidate his power and nationalized foreign firms—the U.S. government valued Mobutu as an ally in the Cold War. He supported anti-Communist guerilla groups in Angola that were also supported by the United States, and he maintained cordial relations with most Western nations. Elsewhere in Africa, President Johnson supported economic development programs, in conjunction with the World Bank and European countries. Johnson tasked the U.S. ambassador to Ethiopia, Edward Korry, with devising a program of aid. Korry, however, found little support within the government to commit serious funds to Africa, and policy toward the continent remained ad hoc and reactive throughout the Johnson years.

In the Middle East, the biggest challenge to the Johnson presidency came in the Six-Day Arab-Israeli War of June 1967. U.S. policy had been cautiously pro-Israel since the creation of that state in 1948. With the rise of Egyptian president Gamal Abdel Nasser and his Soviet-backed version of pan-Arabism, the United States had begun to work even more closely with Israel and anti-Nasser Arab governments, as well as with the anti-Nasser government of Iran. Nasser's authorization of a Viet Cong mission in Cairo and his aid to Congolese rebels gave the United States additional reasons to work against him.

President Johnson and his foreign affairs advisers, in particular Secretary of State Dean Rusk, tried to avert the Six-Day War. The decision, however, was not in their hands, and during the conflict, the United States could only seek to restrain the triumphant Israeli military. With stunning success, Israel occupied the Sinai Peninsula and the Gaza Strip, previously held by Egypt, as well as the West Bank of the Jordan River and East Jerusalem, previously claimed by Jordan. Israeli forces proved equally effective against the army of Syria, a Soviet client state. With Israeli troops fifty miles from the Syrian capital of Damascus, the hot line providing direct Teletype communication between the leaders of the United States and the Soviet Union carried threats that the Soviets would send troops to protect their friends. The Americans responded by ordering the Sixth Fleet to sail toward the eastern Mediterranean. Ultimately, Israel agreed to claim from Syria only the strategically significant Golan Heights, and U.S. and Soviet forces stood down.

After this short but consequential war, U.S. problems in the region grew more severe. Soviet arms shipments flowed to Palestinians in Jordanian refugee camps. (Palestinians had been resettled into such camps in Jordan and Lebanon following the warfare that occasioned the establishment of the state of Israel.) Oil-rich Arab states, including Saudi Arabia, Iraq, and Kuwait, imposed an oil embargo against the United States.

Fortunately for President Johnson, this first Middle Eastern oil embargo failed before summer's end, and the president was able to mollify Arab resentment of U.S. support for Israel by increasing American assistance to moderate Arab states. This was part of a policy described by National Security Adviser McGeorge Bundy as dividing "good Arabs" (especially the Saudis) from "bad Arabs."[8] As anti-Israel radicalism increased after the Six-Day War, moderate Arab states such as Saudi Arabia grew closer to the United States. They too were threatened by the radicals, who thought most Arab governments were not doing enough to avenge an Arab defeat. The Johnson administration offered military arms to such moderate states in return for their assistance in relaxing tensions in the region.

Over the course of Johnson's last two years in office, his administration also increased the U.S. commitment of arms and other types of aid to Israel. It was an open secret that the Israelis were developing, if they had already not succeeded in building, workable nuclear weapons in the mid-1960s. At the same time, they pursued aircraft delivery capability from the United States. In 1966 Israel obtained American A-4E Skyhawks (and, later, F-4E Phantoms) under the condition that the aircraft not be used to deliver nuclear weapons. The U.S. State Department wanted to link the aircraft sales to a right of continuous inspection of Israeli nuclear research and production facilities, but this was overridden by the president. (Although the United States denied it at the time, the aircraft were delivered in September 1969 "with nuclear capable hardware intact.")[9]

The legacy of Johnson's decisions on Middle East policy was a "three pillars" strategy. The Americans would work through Israel, Saudi Arabia, and Iran, while the Soviets continued to exert considerable influence in Egypt, in Syria, and within the Palestinian Liberation Organization (PLO), the dominant institution speaking for the stateless Palestinians. Saudi Arabia and Iran were thus positioned to succeed Britain as the guarantor of regional stability in the Persian Gulf.[10] Under President Johnson, U.S. financial aid and military supplies flowed more freely than ever before to the "pillars."

Korea and Czechoslovakia

The tensest places in world affairs during the lengthy period of 1947–1991 were those whose borders had been frozen artificially at the onset of the Cold War. In the years before Johnson came to office, the United States had intervened in divided Korea, had sent thousands of military advisers to divided Vietnam, and had risked nuclear war over divided Berlin and China. The fate of Eastern Europe had engendered heated rhetoric and partisan divisions, and the Soviets had sent troops to the region to quash rebellion, exacerbating superpower tensions. During Lyndon Johnson's presidency, the United States dealt again with provocative acts in Korea and Eastern Europe.

U.S. relations with non-Communist South Korea remained strong throughout the 1960s. The two nations came to an agreement that helped them both: the new civilian government of the Republic of Korea would send troops to South Vietnam, and in exchange, the United States would keep at least an equal number of U.S. troops on Korean soil in defense against a North Korean assault. North Korea refrained from an outright invasion of the South, but it did send commandos to attempt the assassination of the South Korean president on January 21, 1968. (The failed attempt was one of 600 infiltrations from the North in 1968.) Two days later, North Korean armed forces seized the

Pueblo, a U.S. intelligence ship, and its eighty-two crew members. North Korea claimed the ship had violated its territorial waters; the United States insisted that it had not.

One goal of the assault on the *Pueblo* may have been to drive a wedge between the United States and its Korean ally, which the incident did. South Koreans came to resent the enormous attention the United States gave its eighty-two captured crewmen, when millions of South Koreans lived under daily threat of attack from the North. For eleven difficult months, while the North Koreans held their American captives, President Johnson endured the resentment of his Korean allies, worried about Soviet involvement and intentions, kept the congressional hawks at bay in Washington, and allowed time for a diplomatic solution to be found.

In the end, both sides agreed to a farcical resolution. The United States would issue a formal apology for having spied on the North. The North Koreans would distribute this apology internally, thus claiming a propaganda victory against the leader of the anti-Communist world. The United States would simultaneously be permitted to repudiate its apology internationally (which, of course, would never be made known to the North Korean people), thus saving face among its allies.

Although President Johnson and his advisers suspected Soviet complicity in the *Pueblo* incident, recently released documents from Soviet archives suggest that, this time, the president was wrong; the North Koreans acted on their own.[11] In Czechoslovakia, by contrast, there was no ambiguity about Soviet intent. On April 1, 1968, the first secretary of the Communist Party of Czechoslovakia, Alexander Dubcek, openly criticized the nation's Communist policies of the past and proclaimed the legitimacy of human rights. Symbols of the West, including rock music, jazz, pop culture, and miniskirts, blossomed in Prague, the capital, and other cities. Dubcek called his goal, "socialism with a human face." Soviet leaders did not smile in response. After public criticism from the Soviets failed to chill the "Prague Spring," Warsaw Pact forces invaded the country on the night of August 20–21, beginning a lengthy process of the reestablishment of strict Soviet control.[12]

The Soviet news agency TASS (Telegraphy Agency of the Soviet Union) reported that Warsaw Pact forces had entered Czechoslovakia to render "fraternal assistance" to a socialist nation in need.[13] Shortly thereafter, Soviet leader Leonid Brezhnev declared a doctrine of limited sovereignty for Communist nations, asserting that "Czechoslovakia's detachment from the socialist community would have come into conflict with its own vital interests."[14] For his part, President Johnson, who had by then already announced his impending departure from the presidency and had witnessed the American public's declining willingness for sacrifice in foreign affairs, could do nothing but issue a rhetorical rebuke.

ENDURING CHALLENGES

This succession of crises around the world made it difficult for President Johnson to pursue a coherent policy for U.S.-Soviet relations. He tried, nonetheless, and did achieve some success.

The Johnson years were a time of transition in U.S.-Soviet affairs. There was no more talk in the mid-1960s of a "year of maximum danger," and there was no crisis to equal those over the division of Berlin or offensive nuclear weapons in Cuba. But it was not yet a time of reduction of tension. The unsettled nature of relations reflected changes in the relative power of the superpowers and in the world around them—changes that had yet to come to fruition but which had begun to force new thinking in the White House and Kremlin alike.

When Johnson came to office, his Soviet counterpart, Premier Nikita Khrushchev, greeted him with a lecture on the need to refrain from the use of force to settle territorial disputes. The Johnson administration responded with a somewhat-mixed message. The president replied with a conciliatory letter welcoming dialogue and asserting confidence in the ability of both sides to cooperate. Secretary of State Dean Rusk then gave a speech in which he underlined the irreconcilable differences between the two countries and their respective systems of government. Rusk went on to lecture the Soviets; he praised the Chinese for their comparatively better understanding of the nature of nuclear war and criticized the Soviets for their willingness to resort to force in international affairs. Shortly after this speech, the secretary rejected "détente"—a term for the relaxation of tensions between nations, in use in American English for decades—as an "inaccurate" appellation for superpower relations.[15]

The American president and secretary of state were not simply playing good cop, bad cop. There really were opportunities for cooperation between the superpowers, and Johnson was eager to seize them, especially in the arms race. After all, the Soviets and the Americans could reach arms deals by themselves. Although their respective allies' interests had to be considered, the superpowers did not have to negotiate through others when it came to the arms race. In addition, there was an institutionalized bureaucracy—in Washington, D.C., at the United Nations, and even within the Soviet state—that maintained pressure to pursue arms talks. Finally, there was the sheer cost of nuclear weapons to consider. This was troubling for Johnson, for he worked diligently to demonstrate fiscal prudence to defuse the criticism that his many domestic initiatives were too expensive. At the same time, however, the superpowers were still locked in mortal combat around the globe; nothing had happened to diminish the incompatibility of the American and Soviet worldviews.

Soviet-American relations took a step forward following the October 14, 1964, bloodless coup that forced Khrushchev from power. Khrushchev had become a liability in the eyes of many Communist Party elites in the Soviet Union. Personally excitable, he had embarrassed the Soviet Union by his ill-mannered behavior at the United Nations, where he once pounded his shoe on his desk to drive home a point. More important, although he had promised that the Soviet Union would soon overtake the United States in the arms race, he had been forced by the young and inexperienced American president John F. Kennedy to back down from his rash scheme to arm Cuba with offensive nuclear weapons.

Placed under house arrest, Khrushchev was replaced at first with a triumvirate, or troika, consisting of Leonid Brezhnev, general secretary of the Communist Party; Anastas Mikoyan, chairman of the Presidium of the Supreme Soviet (head of state); and Alexei Kosygin, chairman of the Council of Ministers of the Soviet Union or premier. Mikoyan's power quickly faded, leaving Kosygin and Brezhnev in charge. Such power sharing at the apex of the Soviet single-party state was highly unusual. Typically, the general secretary of the party was the undisputed executive, sometimes serving simultaneously as premier, as did Stalin and Khrushchev. (And, indeed, by the end of the decade, Brezhnev had consolidated his power and Kosygin, who retained his title and membership on the politburo, had retreated from leadership.) Johnson was forced to deal with a tricky situation in which he could never be quite certain about the influence within the Soviet state of the person with whom he dealt as his counterpart.

Regardless of who exactly was in charge in the Kremlin, in his January 1965 State of the Union address President Johnson welcomed "the new Soviet leaders" to visit the United States "so they can learn about our country at first hand."[16] The Soviets replied positively via *Pravda*. There were, however, several issues that made the prospects for a summit appear rather dim at the time.

Not So Peaceful Coexistence

The new Soviet leadership kept alive the legacy of "peaceful coexistence." As under Khrushchev, that doctrine dictated a rational anxiety about the possibility of nuclear war with the United States. It indicated nothing, however, about the Soviet Union's general outlook on the use of force in international relations. In fact, from the Soviet point of view, it made sense simultaneously to pursue peaceful coexistence—in the form of new arms control agreements, cultural exchanges, and confidence-building measures—and victory in the global class struggle. Communist victory in the United States and other major Western powers might be a long time in the making, but success by arms was possible in wars of "national liberation," in which the superpowers took sides and fought through their respective proxies.

The Soviets were especially keen to advance the cause of Communist victory in Vietnam because of their growing rift with the Chinese. If the North Vietnamese Communists defeated their American-backed enemy in South, the victory would redound to the credit of not only North Vietnam, but also their principal benefactor. The Soviets and the Chinese both aspired to that role, by offering advice, arms, and even troops. On February 7, 1965, Premier Kosygin, on a visit to Hanoi, North Vietnam, assured his hosts of all the help they might need. To underscore Soviet support for their Vietnamese comrades, 2,000 students staged demonstrations at and an assault upon the U.S. embassy in Moscow two days later. Later that year, the Soviets established surface to air missile (SAM) sites for the defense of Hanoi and threatened publicly to send Soviet "volunteers" to fight side-by-side with Vietnamese patriots if the United States continued its attacks.[17]

In part because the Soviets continued to link events in Vietnam with the status of superpower relations, those relations remained strained throughout Johnson's presidency. By 1968 the two superpowers were publicly feuding over whether relations were improving. President Johnson wished to portray progress. In his January 1968 State of the Union address, he boasted of improved relations. The Soviet press promptly challenged the American president to withdraw from Vietnam if he truly desired to improve U.S.-Soviet relations. Because neither side would budge, this dialogue was essentially replayed that summer, with competing conceptions of reality emerging from the White House and the Kremlin.

Arms Control

President Johnson was very aware of being the one who would have to, as he liked to say, "mash the button" in the event of a nuclear war.[18] The Johnson administration consequently strove for a workable policy on nuclear arms control. The Joint Chiefs of Staff (JCS) wanted the United States to commit itself to an ambitious antiballistic missile (ABM) program to counter the Soviet ABM effort that was in construction around Moscow. As envisioned, the U.S. program would seek first and foremost to protect the first-strike capacity of the United States—the ABMs would *defend* the country's *offensive* weapons. ABM technology was then, as it remains today, of debatable effectiveness. Nobody imagined that even the best ABM technology could destroy *all* incoming nuclear missiles. The very uncertainty of an ABM defense led Secretary of Defense Robert McNamara to strongly oppose the program. To counter an extensive U.S. effort, the Soviets, McNamara reasoned, would simply be encouraged to deploy more and more offensive missiles, against which the United States would deploy more and more defensive missiles, and so on. As an alternative, McNamara favored adding to the U.S. offensive threat by placing multiple independently targeted reentry vehicles (MIRVs)—that is, multiple warheads programmed to hit different targets—on U.S. strategic missiles.

In January 1967 President Johnson began a diplomatic effort to engage the Soviets in arms talks that would encompass ABMs. In June of that year, Johnson and Premier Kosygin met at Glassboro, New Jersey. The "mini summit" achieved little, however, and an exasperated Johnson ordered the secretary of defense to develop a limited U.S. ABM defense. McNamara reluctantly gave the Pentagon the go-ahead. The United States would build a "light" ABM system, ostensibly aimed at protecting the nation against China, but in reality designed to fortify U.S. missile sites and national command centers against a first strike by the Soviet Union, the United States' only true nuclear rival. At the least, this compromise decision took the issue out of the 1968 presidential race. The Republicans would not be able to decry a "missile gap," as the Democrats had in 1960. Under President Richard Nixon, the "Sentinel" ABM program was renamed "Safeguard," and a single ABM site was established to protect retaliatory missile silos at a U.S. air force base. Due to technical difficulties, it was deactivated in 1976 after a few months' operation.[19]

The most concrete achievement in arms control during the Johnson years was the Nuclear Non-Proliferation Treaty (**Document 5.2**). The NPT was unique among major Cold War treaties in that it was negotiated at the United Nations. After the superpowers submitted rival draft treaties to the UN General Assembly, a committee on nuclear arms control helped to facilitate agreement. Under the terms of the treaty, opened for signature on July 1, 1968, nuclear-weapon states (NWS) pledged not to transfer weapons technology to non-nuclear-weapon states. All parties agreed to work toward nuclear disarmament and to acknowledge the right of non-nuclear-weapon states to make peaceful use of nuclear power. The initial signatories included three of the five NWS: the United States, the Soviet Union, and the United Kingdom. France and the People's Republic of China did not sign the NPT until 1992, after the Cold War had ended.

In a less satisfying development, Johnson was forced to suspend the opening of the planned Strategic Arms Limitation Talks (SALT) when the Soviets invaded

Czechoslovakia in August 1968. Last minute back-channel communications between President-elect Richard Nixon and the Soviets finally closed the door for good on the prospects of a breakthrough in arms control during the Johnson presidency. Nixon warned the Soviets that if they wanted a deal that would last, they had best wait for him to take office.

Europe

During the Johnson administration, the superpowers competed aggressively over Europe. Soviet and American leaders were both provoked by events on the ground that threatened to upset the balance of power within Europe. The Soviets expressed considerable anxiety over the possibility that the North Atlantic Treaty Organization (NATO) would adopt a multilateral nuclear force. The Soviets naturally resisted any change in NATO policy that might heighten the threat, from their point of view, to be feared from Western Europe. For the purpose of attempting to rally public opinion in Europe to their side, they argued against the idea of such a multilateral force by referring to the alleged militarization of West Germany. Militarism and Nazism, the Soviets proclaimed, were on the rise again in the Federal Republic of Germany, and NATO's embrace of Germany was largely to blame. The Soviet's preferred solution was the abolition of NATO.

Because of American and British resistance, more so than Soviet alarm, no NATO multilateral nuclear force was created. Instead, in December 1966 NATO established a Nuclear Planning Group and a Nuclear Defense Affairs Committee. The United States would permit routine European input into discussions revolving around the role of nuclear forces in Europe's defense but would not change the duality of Mutual Assured Destruction (MAD).

The alliance was shaken, however, during Johnson's presidency by France's decision to pursue its own nuclear aims outside NATO. France had first detonated a nuclear weapon in 1960 and rapidly built up its nuclear arsenal during the decade. In March 1966, French president Charles de Gaulle called for the removal of NATO bases from French soil. All non-French NATO forces were expelled from France, and the NATO headquarters relocated from Paris to Brussels, Belgium. After making this bold move, de Gaulle made a highly publicized visit to Moscow, where he signed a treaty with the Soviet Union for cooperation on nuclear research. In June, soon after his return from Moscow, de Gaulle announced that France was resigning from the NATO military command, although it retained formal membership in the body.

Inspired by postwar economic growth and prewar memories of national grandeur, de Gaulle envisioned France's playing a mediating role in the superpower conflict. Under his leadership, France had already formally recognized the People's Republic of China. France now manifested its independence in new ways. In a famous speech delivered in Cambodia on September 1, 1966, de Gaulle denounced the U.S. role in the Vietnam War.

During this same period, West Germany's government also exhibited greater independence from the United States. In 1966 two major German parliamentary parties, the Christian Democratic Union and the Social Democratic Party, formed a "Grand Coalition." Under this coalition, Germany's leaders began to build bridges with the Eastern bloc, offering trade incentives for cooperation.

France's decision to leave the military structure of NATO and Germany's decision to forge a consensus government that could reach out to the East together created an apparent crisis in the U.S.-European Cold War alliance. President Johnson responded coolly to these events, however, and kept his administration speaking with a single voice on European matters. Because even de Gaulle acknowledged the legitimacy of the core complaints that Western nations lodged against the Soviets, and because Johnson decided to play down the differences between the United States and its European allies, NATO retained its viability and strength. As a deliberative body, NATO in fact gained in significance during the 1960s, which promoted the development in the 1970s of a truly multilateral détente. With regard to the military alliance, U.S. lobbying paid off in December 1967 when NATO adopted as its own military strategy the Kennedy administration's favored policy of "flexible response."

NATO's continuing military importance was confirmed in the summer of 1968. Amidst growing Soviet concern over events in Eastern Europe, especially Czechoslovakia, the Soviets warned that they might be compelled to intervene militarily *in Germany,* to halt the alleged resurgence of Nazism and militarism. The U.S. Department of State twice asserted in response that NATO would react aggressively to any attack upon the Federal Republic of Germany.

In U.S. domestic politics, President Johnson's handling of the changes under way in Europe helped to keep the United States engaged in the world and the Cold War. In the light of apparent French ingratitude and German independence, Johnson had to fight off NATO critics in the Senate who wanted to decrease the U.S. share of the financial burden of the alliance. The isolationist impulse in American politics is always present. Isolationists believed that if the Europeans did not appreciate the United States, perhaps they should be left to fend for themselves. Johnson thought the United States had no choice but to maintain its leadership by continuing to pay a heavy financial price for Europe's security. Without presidential guidance in this regard, Johnson wrote in retirement, the American people might retreat into isolationism "out of boredom, or frustration . . . lack of money, or out of simple foolishness."[20]

THE VIETNAM WAR

No other event or combination of events in the Cold War was as consequential for the Johnson presidency as the Vietnam War. The war in Vietnam continues to detract from the accomplishments of the Johnson presidency. Thirty-two years after Johnson left office, according to a Gallup poll released on November 17, 2000, 69 percent of Americans reported that they believed it had been a mistake to send troops to fight in Vietnam. The war is remembered by many, moreover, as "one of the most important events of the century." (In a Gallup poll released December 6, 1999, 37 percent of Americans thought so; another 31 percent said it was "important, but not the *most* important event of the century.") An incredible one in four Americans, Gallup reported in November 2000, has visited the Vietnam War Memorial in Washington, D.C.[21]

Commentary on Johnson's handling of the war typically faults him for a range of alleged failings. Military historian and army officer H. R. McMaster portrays the president as conniving with the civilian secretary of defense, Robert McNamara, to shut the military out of decision making for the war.[22] McMaster's account complements the widespread belief of conservatives that in Vietnam, the military was forced to fight with one hand tied behind their backs. Irving Bernstein, meanwhile, joins with a number of other scholars in seeing the war as a reflection of Johnson's troubled personality.[23] Johnson, the story goes, was an oversized Texan fond of making up ancestors who had died at the Alamo. With such a man in the White House, the unreasoned pursuit of even the most suicidal "victory" was a foregone conclusion. Because Lyndon "Davy Crockett" Johnson could brook no dissent, he froze out of White House discussions his few dovish advisers.

Much of the prevailing commentary on President Johnson and the Vietnam War, then, expresses what might be termed counterfactual angst: "if only Kennedy had lived," "if only Johnson had listened to his hawkish advisers," "if only Johnson had listened to his dovish advisers." But what actually happened in "Lyndon Johnson's" Vietnam War? What decisions did the president make, why did he make them, and to what effect?

"Not Anything to Be Concerned About"

As he assumed the presidency, Lyndon Johnson knew he was inheriting a mess in Vietnam. The new president thought that U.S. complicity in the removal (and assassination) of South Vietnamese president Ngo Dinh Diem three weeks before Kennedy's death had been a tragic mistake. Johnson had foreseen that removing Diem would produce political chaos in South Vietnam, and that without a stable government the rebels in South Vietnam, the Viet Cong (VC), and their supporters—the North Vietnamese enemy— would gain strength. Johnson also knew why the United States was in this mess in the first place. He had watched as successive presidents starting with Harry Truman had supported the fight against the Communists in what was then French Indochina. He, like everyone else (but with a closer vantage point), had heard both Dwight Eisenhower and John F. Kennedy boldly vow that America would never let South Vietnam fall to communism. Moreover, Johnson strongly believed that the United States was obligated by its own creation, the Southeast Asia Treaty Organization (see **Document 3.7**), to come to the aid of South Vietnam. "We are party to a treaty," Johnson reminded his old friend, Sen. Richard Russell, D-Ga., "And if we don't pay attention to this treaty, why, I don't guess they [world opinion] think we pay attention to any of them." [24]

During the remainder of 1963 and until the election of the following year, Lyndon Johnson pursued a minimalist approach in the war. His aim was to do just what was necessary to prevent the collapse of South Vietnam, without doing anything that would inflame domestic sentiment over the war. Although he authorized Operation Plan 34A, a series of covert actions, and sent thousands of additional advisers to Vietnam, Johnson deferred a decision on just how far the United States might go to prevent defeat.

The Vietnam War was a central topic of his first press conference as president on December 7, 1963, but Johnson downplayed events there. Secretary McNamara would be stopping by Saigon soon, the president casually announced:

> He is going to be in Paris anyway, and it won't take him too long. He can go there pretty quickly and we want to have him make a few checks out there, not anything to be concerned about, but just to be sure that we are getting maximum efficiency.[25]

Efficiency was something that Johnson and McNamara shared a passion for, and the president proudly went on to proclaim that the secretary had already found new efficiencies in the Pentagon's budget. Defense spending, Johnson promised, would go down by hundreds of millions of dollars during the first year of his presidency.[26]

Johnson put off making tough choices about Vietnam in part to avoid a political fight. He believed that if he openly escalated the war in the midst of the 1964 presidential campaign, the public would assail him. In a telephone conversation with National Security Adviser McGeorge Bundy during the campaign, Johnson recounted a meeting in which he had "just spent a lot of time with the Joint Chiefs":

> The net of it—they say, get in or get out. And I told them. . . . We haven't got any Congress that will go with us, and we haven't got any mothers that will go with us in a war. And nine months I'm just an inherited—I'm a trustee. I've got to win an election, or Nixon or somebody else has. And then you can make a decision. But in the meantime, let's see if we can't find enough things to do to keep them off base.[27]

To keep the issue of Vietnam out of the election, Johnson engineered a nearly unanimous congressional resolution of support. During a covert mission in August 1964 in the Gulf of Tonkin, U.S. vessels reported that they were under torpedo attack. Within hours, limited U.S. reprisal bombing was under way. Within days, Congress rushed to the president's side in the Tonkin Gulf Resolution (**Document 5.3**), granting support for "all necessary measures to repel any armed attack against the forces of the U.S. and to prevent further aggression."

Even though the assault on the ship was evidenced only by ambiguous radar signals and the resolution did not explicitly authorize the war to come, Johnson read a great deal into this expression of support. "I made it clear from the day I took office," the president recounted in his memoirs, "I was not a 'peace at any price man.' The American people knew what they were voting for in 1964."[28] And when the members of Congress voted for the Tonkin Gulf Resolution, the president similarly insisted, they too knew full well that they were authorizing war. In a televised interview, the retired Johnson said:

> It was a shame somebody didn't think of calling it the Fulbright Resolution, like the Fulbright Scholars thing, with his approval, his consent. He [Sen. J. William Fulbright] passed it. He voted for it, eighty-two to one. Don't tell me a Rhodes Scholar didn't understand everything in that Resolution.[29]

The resolution was the "equivalent of a declaration of war," just like Sen. Wayne Morse, D-Ore., complained at the time. Morse, Johnson observed, "was a teacher too," as Johnson had been in his youth. "[H]e could read that language and understand it."[30]

On the other side of the world, Chairman Mao Zedong of the People's Republic of China also read the language of the resolution but was unimpressed. "Scary statements" from Washington, he sought to assure the North Vietnamese leadership, should not frighten them (**Document 5.4**). The Americans had limits to their military force. As long as the North Vietnamese were patient, they could overcome whatever troops the Americans managed to send to Vietnam.

Americanizing the War in Vietnam

After winning the 1964 election, Johnson called for a consideration of options in the war. The administration faced a "trilemma" according to John McNaughton, assistant secretary of defense for international security affairs (**Document 5.5**). The South Vietnamese could not save themselves, McNaughton observed, but each of the three major U.S. responses had serious drawbacks: "Will-breaking" air bombardments against the North might simply annoy, but not defeat, the Communists. Large American troop deployments would have to overcome the "Korea syndrome" in American politics and might simply lead to a situation such as the French faced at Bien Dien Phu, where a large contingent of French forces were besieged and eventually overwhelmed in March–May 1954. Finally, a negotiated withdrawal would be a "humiliation." It was imperative to avoid humiliation, McNaughton reasoned, because "70%" of the reason the United States sought to win in Vietnam was to avoid losing. A loss would cripple the nation's reputation as a "guarantor" of security in the Cold War.

In a different memo drafted by McNaughton and endorsed by Johnson's national security team, the defense department planner put aside his larger worries and presented a different set of three options. Option A called for more tit-for-tat reprisal bombings such as the one ordered immediately after the incident in the Gulf of Tonkin. Option B, described as a "fast full squeeze" of bombing and perhaps even the use of U.S. combat troops, was the Joint Chiefs' preference. The president chose Option C, labeled "progressive squeeze-and-talk," a gradually escalating air war designed to pressure the North Vietnamese leadership.[31]

All that was needed to implement the president's decision was the necessary provocation from the North. It came in February 1965, when joint North Vietnamese/Viet Cong forces attacked Camp Holloway, three miles from Pleiku, in the central highlands. Eight U.S. soldiers were killed and ten aircraft destroyed. The president ordered the air war to commence. Under the name "Rolling Thunder," it broadened into full-scale bombing by B-52s of large areas surrounding defined targets, or so-called carpet bombing. The operation would continue until Johnson ordered a unilateral halt to bombing in March 1968, in order to find a way out of the conflict.

The next step in the U.S. escalation was the introduction of American troops into ground combat, which followed close on the heels of the decision to launch the air war. Air bases required a level of security that the South Vietnamese were not competent to provide. Two months after the attack on Pleiku, through National Security Action Memorandum (NSAM) 328, dated April 6, 1965, the president approved a request for U.S. Marine land and helicopter battalions to defend the air base at Danang. At the same time, the president approved "a change of mission for all Marine Battalions deployed to Vietnam to permit their more active use under conditions to be established and approved by the Secretary of Defense." The national security adviser informed the government via NSAM 328 that it was the president's wish that "these movements and changes should be understood [i.e., perceived] as being gradual and wholly consistent with existing policy." While the actions should be taken "as rapidly as practicable," steps should be taken to "minimize any appearance of sudden changes in policy."[32]

The president knew what he might be getting himself into by approving ground combat for an (initially) limited number of U.S. troops, but he could see no alternative. Even before the bombs began to fall in Rolling Thunder, Secretary of Defense McNamara told the president that the military brass was unanimous about the need for ground troops to protect aircraft and air crews. President Johnson discussed the situation with his old friend from the senate, Richard Russell of Georgia, on March 6, 1965:

> I guess we've got no choice, but it scares the death out of me. I think everybody's going to think, "We're landing the Marines. We're off to battle." . . . Of course, if they come up there, they're going to get them in a fight. Just sure as hell. They're not going to run. Then you're tied down. If they don't, though, and they ruin those airplanes, everybody is going to give me hell for not securing them.[33]

After launching the operation, the president continued to fret. "I think we ought to try to figure out what we can do," he told McNamara. "Now we're off to bombing these people. We're over that hurdle. I don't think anything is going to be as bad as losing, and I don't see any way of winning."[34]

The North Vietnamese, led by Chairman Ho Chi Minh, meanwhile, were buttressed by Chinese encouragement and guarantees. China's foreign minister, Zhou Enlai, spoke candidly with the heads of state of friendly governments, such as Ahmed Ben Bella of Algeria and Ayub Khan of Pakistan, about the situation in Vietnam (**Document 5.6**). In the event of an actual ground attack upon North Vietnam, Zhou stated, the Chinese had given their word to reprise their role in the Korean War; they would enter the conflict with their own massive army. Otherwise, the war would continue, Zhou said, as it was yielding results; South Vietnam was being wrested from the forces of imperialism. As for negotiations with the Americans, Zhou's response was "no way." The Americans wanted an unconditional cease-fire first, but a cease-fire and negotiations, "if viewed objectively," would be "unfavorable to the liberation of the people in South Vietnam."

President Johnson tried in any event to push forward his plans for a negotiated settlement. He offered incentives: if the North Vietnamese would lay down their arms for talks and agree to a peaceful (non-Communist) outcome, the Americans would shower the peninsula with development projects. In a speech at Johns Hopkins University on April 7, 1965, Johnson envisioned a Mekong River equivalent to the mammoth Tennessee Valley Authority hydroelectric, regional planning, and economic development program of the New Deal (**Document 5.7**). The enemy needed to understand, as did the American public, that the United States was serious about the alternative, which was continued fighting. The stakes in Southeast Asia, the president said numerous times, were immense: "We must say in southeast Asia—as we did in Europe—in the words of the Bible: 'Hitherto shalt thou come, but no further.'"[35]

The president's speech was well received at home, but it met with silence from the government in Hanoi. By the summer of 1965, the situation in South Vietnam was deteriorating, and the U.S. commander there, Gen. William Westmoreland, and the U.S. Ambassador to Vietnam, general-turned-diplomat Maxwell Taylor, sent urgent cables to Washington, D.C., requesting authorization for a rapid escalation of forces, as well as a free hand to send U.S. forces into combat independent of the South Vietnamese forces they were there to "assist" and far from the air bases that they had initially been sent to defend. "Westy" wanted some 41,000 more combat troops right away, and 52,000 soon thereafter, which would raise the number of American military personnel in the theater to 175,000. He wrote of his desire to "take the war to the enemy," for which "even greater forces" would perhaps be required in the future.[36] With Westmoreland's request on the table, "the specter of U.S. involvement in a major ground war was there for all to see."[37]

The president heard some dissenting voices at this point—George Ball, undersecretary of state, urged that the United States should look toward withdrawal of its troops, rather than increasing their number—but Johnson decided to escalate. During a July 27, 1965, meeting of his National Security Council, Johnson approved the deployment of about 100,000 more U.S. troops then—which he understood to be but a beginning—but decided to downplay the decision (**Document 5.8**). The following day, President Johnson, in the words of historian Irving Bernstein, "sort of informed the American people that their nation was at war."[38]

On July 28, Johnson announced to the press that he had "today ordered to Vietnam the Air Mobile Division and certain other forces which will raise our fighting strength from 75,000 to 125,000 men almost immediately. Additional forces will be needed later, and they will be sent as requested." He explained that the monthly draft call of 17,000 young men would more than double; recruitment of volunteers would increase; and reserve forces would be called at a later time if needed. A reporter asked whether this meant a change in the U.S. "policy of relying mainly on the South Vietnamese to carry out offensive operations and using American forces to guard American installations and to act as an emergency backup." The president blandly replied, "It does not imply any change in policy whatever."[39]

Waging Limited War

President Johnson had made a momentous decision. He had greatly deepened U.S. involvement in the war, but he denied any change in policy. The Joint Chiefs wanted the president to mobilize the reserve forces—the nation's part-time soldiers, sailors, airmen, and marines, who train on weekends and during summers in case they are needed to respond to war or a national emergency. Secretary of Defense McNamara recommended that Johnson return to Congress for a tax increase to offset inflationary pressures that were certain to flow from the military buildup. Johnson refused to do either of these things.

One reason for Johnson's refusal was his Great Society programs. As McNamara later recounted in a January 8, 1975, interview for the Johnson Presidential Library, the president thought Congress would vote down a war tax. Johnson told McNamara, "[I]f you know so damn much, you go up there [to Congress] and make your own check." McNamara did, and then he went back to tell the president he had been right. Johnson then elaborated on his difficulties: not only would a proposal to raise taxes fail, "but in the process of failure it would impose severe penalties on the Great Society programs," because many members of Congress were eager for an excuse to jump off Johnson's domestic bandwagon.[40]

As Johnson liked to lecture his aides and cabinet secretaries, he had been in Congress when President Harry Truman and the Democratic Party were castigated for not doing enough to whip communism in Korea. He had even been in Congress when President Franklin Roosevelt had been forced to give up some of his biggest dreams for domestic reform, because he had told Congress that the nation had to put 100 percent effort into war instead. Johnson, who thought of the Great Society as "the woman [he] really loved" and the war in Vietnam as "that bitch," was loath to follow their examples.[41]

At the same time, Johnson persuaded himself that further debate would be superfluous. Congress had passed the Tonkin Gulf Resolution, and moreover, the "new economics" of the decade suggested that the old choice of "guns or butter" was obsolete. A nation as wealthy as post–World War II America surely had the resources to do anything it put its mind to.

Still, why did President Johnson take for granted not just the nation's wealth and Congress's support, but also the willpower of the American people? Did not the president have a responsibility to lead the public to "put their mind to" the problem of Vietnam? Perhaps, but that was where President Johnson ran up against a fundamental difficulty of limited war. To wage such a war required perseverance more than passion. An excess of passion, in fact, could have led the nation into World War III.

Johnson worried endlessly that if he pushed too far, if he bombed the wrong target, if U.S. forces stumbled across some hidden trip wire identified in secret agreements between the North Vietnamese and their patrons, the United States would find itself in direct confrontation with China, the Soviet Union, or both. Johnson had reason to worry. As early as 1962, Chairman Mao Zedong had promised that China would come to the aid of North Vietnam if the United States attacked. As it was, during the course of Johnson's war, the Chinese provided the North Vietnamese with anti-aircraft artillery battalions and tens of thousands of troops in support roles.

Mao himself was incredulous at President Johnson's public restraint on the subject of the proxy war as the conflict in Vietnam continued. "Why have the Americans not made a fuss about the fact that more than 100,000 Chinese troops help you in building railways, roads, and airports although they knew about it?" Mao remarked in a September 23, 1968, conversation with the North Vietnamese premier. As his guest suggested, it was simple: "Of course, they are afraid," said Pham Van Dong.[42]

Johnson would have been devastated to hear his opponent's assessment. If the United States did not act with resolution in Vietnam, he told his aide, Bill Moyers, "'they'll think we're yellow and don't mean what we say.' 'Who?' 'The Chinese. The fellas in the Kremlin. They'll be taking the measure of us.'"[43] But Johnson *was* afraid, lamenting from retirement:

People say there's nothing worse than Vietnam. Well, I think there are lots of things worse than Vietnam. World War III would be much worse. The good Lord got me through it without destroying any Russian ships, or Chinese. . . . China and Russia are like two brothers-in-law who don't like each other. One misstep could have kicked off World War III."[44]

In a conversation with Senator Russell in the summer of 1965, the president conjectured that even if the U.S. Air Force merely hit the wrong anti-aircraft site in North Vietnam—one close to the capital, for instance—Russia and China would be "in the war in fifteen minutes." The North Vietnamese, he speculated, were "trying to trap us into doing that."[45] Another problem was that if the president pushed too hard to rally public support for the war at home, he might create a war fever that he could not control. As White House aide Harry McPherson put it, "The big problem he had was trying to rally support just so far. What he was trying to bring off in the American public was something like a semi-satisfactory sexual experience."[46]

Patience Wears Thin

President Johnson's strategy in the Vietnam War began to wear on the patience of the armed forces and the public within just the few years from the introduction of United States into ground combat to the end of Johnson's presidency. Both wanted more results, faster. The president himself was impatient with the war, blaming his generals for a lack of imagination in its conduct.

The military. The military chafed at the restraints that Johnson placed on its conduct of the war. But Johnson too had his complaints about the military. "Bomb, bomb, bomb," Johnson exploded in a meeting of military strategists in February 1965. "You generals have been educated at the taxpayers' expense, and you're not giving me any ideas and solutions for this damn little piss-ant country. Now, I don't need ten generals to come in here ten times and tell me to bomb."[47]

The air war was not without effect, but it could never be so thorough as to succeed completely; it could not block infiltration of the South from the North, especially given the porous sanctuaries of Laos and Cambodia. The North Vietnamese, throughout the war, ferried equipment and personnel into battle along the Ho Chi Minh and the Sihanouk "trails," which were off limits to American military planners during Johnson's presidency. Nor could bombing destroy the industrial base of the North's war effort, because that base was in China and, increasingly, the Soviet Union. On the ground was where the war would be won or lost—and where President Johnson made his most critical decisions.

In the conduct of the air war, Johnson was a micromanager. When it came to combat on the ground, however, the president deferred to the generals. Their strategy was consistent from the summer of 1965, when U.S. forces first engaged in major ground battles, throughout his presidency. In the largely stationary fight to "pacify" the local population by rooting out the VC from villages and towns, the South Vietnamese would bear primary responsibility, assisted by the U.S. Marine Corps and specially trained army soldiers. U.S. armed forces would protect the larger cities and the air bases, but their primary job would be to take the fight to the enemy in search and destroy operations. Eventually, according to the generals, the Communists would realize they had no prospect of victory over the much better equipped and more lethal U.S. forces. If the Communists came out into the open to make a final stand before capitulating, U.S. forces would destroy them in the sort of large-scale warfare for which the U.S. Army—trained and equipped, after all, primarily to meet the Soviet Army on the field of battle in Europe—was particularly well suited.

The details of this overall plan changed over time, but throughout the Johnson presidency, and well into the Nixon administration, the concept remained the same. The U.S. military would simply kill the enemy until they came to their senses and surrendered.[48] Initially, the plan seemed promising. In 1965 and 1966 the North Vietnamese, against Chinese advice, accepted the American invitation of a test of strength. The result was a series of large-scale battles, all won by the United States. In response, the North Vietnamese changed commanders and began to rely more heavily on the operations of smaller units. Once the North Vietnamese adapted to the American approach, the result was a war of no fixed front, where the job of a typical U.S. soldier was, in effect, to be ambushed.

Walking into an ambush could be a "good" thing because it might allow the United States to bring its superior firepower to bear upon the enemy. The search for combat became so intense that even fortified positions would be attacked by U.S. forces, as at Ap Bia Mountain, the infamous "Hamburger Hill," because such an assault promised an opportunity to "attrit" the enemy. To Westmoreland, the only alternative to attrition was an unthinkable war of annihilation.[49]

By pursuing a war of attrition, in which it aimed to win by not losing, the United States left the initiative to the enemy. What would the Americans have to do to win? That depended on what the VC and the North Vietnamese decided to do. How many enemy troops could the American soldiers kill? That too depended on the enemy's willingness to stand and fight. Johnson's choice of strategy left him little choice but to respond to the enemy, and to continue to pour bombs on North Vietnam and troops into South Vietnam.

From the fall of 1963 on, the situation in Vietnam continually challenged the United States to increase its efforts. North Vietnamese and VC troops gained ground in the countryside, and they seemed able to replace however many men they lost to the U.S. and South Vietnamese forces. The Joint Chiefs urged greater bombing, and they were rewarded in 1967 when the president ordered a "hard knock" strike against formerly off-limit targets in the North. The army urgently requested more ground troops, and the United States sent to Vietnam hundreds of thousands of draftees, until U.S. troop deployment peaked at 671,616 in March 1967.

The public. The majority of the American public continued to support the war in Vietnam through 1967 and into Johnson's final year in office (**Document 5.9**). Ironically, given the popular impression of youth attitudes during the decade, support was consistently highest among American adults under thirty years of age (**Document 5.10**). Despite this broad base of support, a minority of Americans steadfastly opposed the war, and a social movement against the war evolved during the Johnson administration.

The anti-war movement bedeviled President Johnson. Given his personal experiences with war in American politics, beginning with his own service in World War II, it is perhaps not surprising that he questioned the legitimacy of anti-war protests. He repeatedly impressed upon his confidantes his conviction that those who organized anti-war resistance, if not all those who ever lifted a sign or chanted a slogan, were agents of international communism. In response to incessant White House pressure for information about foreign control of the protest movement, the Central Intelligence Agency in 1967 established a program of domestic spying, dubbed "CHAOS." The mission of CHAOS, which operated until 1974, was to assemble and analyze intelligence about anti-war activists and other anti-government or anti-administration figures. The CIA, working in conjunction with the Federal Bureau of Investigation, collected information about thousands of American citizens and scores of protest organizations. Repeated negative findings on the key question of foreign control "met with continued skepticism from the White House," in the words of a Senate report on CHAOS.[50] In his darker moments, Johnson was certain that not only were the protestors working for the Soviet Communist Party, but so were leading liberal journalists. Why was it, he asked a former White House fellow who worked with him on his memoirs, in one of his darker moods, "[t]hat you could always find [Soviet ambassador Anatoly] Dobrynin's car in front of [*New York Times* editorialist James] Reston's house the night before Reston delivered a blast on Vietnam?"[51]

Johnson could not seriously suspect his opponents in the Senate of working for the Soviets, so he came up with other explanations for their behavior. Senator Fulbright, the chairman of the Senate Foreign Relations Committee, began hearings on the war in 1966. The tone of the Fulbright hearings could be rough, as illustrated in the following exchange between Johnson's old friend, Senator Wayne Morse, D-Ore., and Gen. Maxwell Taylor. When the senator informed the general that the public was growing disenchanted with the war, Taylor replied, "That is good news for Hanoi." Morse responded, "That's the smear you militarists give to those of us who have honest differences of opinion with you, but I don't intend to get down in the gutter with you and engage in that kind of debate."[52] Johnson forgave Morse for criticizing the war; Morse was consistent, having voted "no" to the Tonkin Gulf Resolution. For Fulbright, however, Johnson felt only scorn. He "couldn't find a president who would name him secretary of state," Johnson complained in retirement, so he sought attention by criticizing the president.[53]

The anti-war movement became broader and deeper in 1967. In that year, Protestant church leaders, professors and students at elite universities and colleges, and civil rights leaders, including Martin Luther King Jr., joined forces against the war. King delivered his first anti-war speech on February 25. The FBI took notice, foreseeing a grim summer of racial violence mixed with "ominous displays of civil disobedience and near seditious activities on the part of Negroes and whites alike" (**Document 5.11**). The FBI's prophecy was fulfilled in October, when a march on Washington evolved into a riot at the Pentagon.

The rally was organized by an umbrella group of anti-war activists, the Mobilization Committee to End the War in Vietnam. Approximately 50,000 people gathered on Saturday, October 21, at the Lincoln Memorial. The majority of them marched across the Potomac River that evening to demonstrate at the Pentagon in Arlington, Virginia. Prepared for the worst, more than 5,000 U.S. soldiers with rifles and bayonets awaited orders inside the Pentagon. Outside, military police assisted by U.S. deputy marshals (who made all actual arrests) attempted to protect the facility. A confrontation ensued, leading to the injury of 47 persons and the arrest of 682.[54] Just days later, the U.S. Senate passed a resolution calling upon the president to send the issue of the Vietnam War to the United

Nations (**Document 5.12**). It was, said Secretary of State Rusk, "both an illusion and a sophistication": the Security Council did not *want* the issue in its lap; not even the Soviets desired that.[55]

In response to the riot, the president threw aside some of his caution about exciting popular emotions and unleashed a peace offensive aimed at domestic opinion. General Westmoreland and General Taylor, the U.S. ambassador to South Vietnam, were ordered home from Saigon to contribute their voices to the chorus predicting victory. We are entering a new phase in the war, Westmoreland told Congress and the press upon his return to the home front. In this phase, "the end begins to come into view."[56] Though Johnson might have meant to stimulate the will of the people to sustain long-term combat—Johnson lectured the public that they could not expect this war to end quickly and conclusively like a football game—the administration's message was widely read as one of reassurance and optimism: We were winning the war. We just needed to stay the course. The editors of the *Washington Post* reported being "encouraged," but issued a prophetic caution:

> [W]hile it [the administration's promise of a war in the process of being won] points persuasively to a time when the war will wither away, it promises no performance that will be subject to precise verification before election day. But just because it is all these things, it carries with it the deadly danger of false hope dashed. The tortured history of Vietnam cries out for caution against overblown hope.[57]

Tet and the Possible Use of Nuclear Weapons

By the end of 1967, Chairman Ho Chi Minh, the leader of North Vietnam, had become impatient. Ho and his military advisers decided that during the Tet holiday, which comes at the lunar new year, the North Vietnamese and the VC would launch what their war planners termed a "General Offensive/General Uprising" throughout South Vietnam. As a first step, starting in January 1968, the North Vietnamese initiated combat in the Central Highlands, along the border with Laos and Cambodia. As many as 10,000 North Vietnamese soldiers were killed in battles that cost 500 American lives. These losses were acceptable to the North Vietnamese, however, because the purpose of the operation was to draw U.S. forces from the cities, the cities being the real prize in the Tet Offensive, which continued until the end of February.

The Tet Offensive, a coordinated assault upon thirty-six South Vietnamese cities and towns, was hardly a victory for the Communists. The cities were not held by the North for long, as the anticipated uprising of the South Vietnamese population did not occur. The VC were in fact routed so extensively that for the remainder of the war, the Communists would rely on regular North Vietnamese Army units to carry the burden of the fight. In Tet, moreover, North Vietnamese soldiers subjected themselves to horrendous casualties in the cities as they had in the feint with which the operation began. Even the much-maligned Army of the Republic of Vietnam (the South Vietnamese) put in a solid performance. Gen. Earle "Bus" Wheeler, the chairman of the Joint Chiefs of Staff, told the president in numerous White House meetings that the situation in Vietnam following Tet

THE VIETNAM WAR

Source: Steven W. Hook and John Spanier, *American Foreign Policy Since World War II,*
17th ed. (Washington, D.C.: CQ Press, 2007), 116.

was fraught with opportunities not just dangers. He said on March 26, 1968, that he could "see no reason for all the gloom and doom we see in the United States press."[58] In strictly military terms, Tet was a catastrophe for the North Vietnamese.

But it was also costly to the Americans. In their effort to "erode the resolve of the American people," the president noted in his memoirs, the Communists got "exactly the reaction they sought."[59] The nightly footage of combat on television left Americans little doubt that they were involved in a bigger war than their president's optimistic rhetoric had prepared them to accept. In truth, Tet shocked the White House too. The situation on the battlefield became so intense at the besieged city of Khe Sanh that military commanders initiated planning for the potential use of tactical nuclear weapons.

A remarkable series of documents reveals the administration's consideration of the potential use of nuclear weapons. On February 1 General Wheeler suggested to General Westmoreland and Adm. Alexander Sharp that they should look into the matter (**Document 5.13**). The admiral replied the next day, informing the chairman of the JCS that planning was already under way. The potential mission even had its own code name, "Fracture Jaw" (**Document 5.14**). That same day, the president's national security adviser, Walt Rostow, wrote to the president in the morning a memorandum, marked "LITERALLY EYES ONLY FOR THE PRESIDENT," in which he suggested that Johnson speak to Chairman Wheeler about his "duty to minimize the likelihood that the nuclear issue would be raised by the JCS" (**Document 5.15**). In handwritten notes on the document that evening, Rostow indicated that the president had taken his advice, talked to Wheeler, and that Wheeler had gone on to speak with Westmoreland about the situation. Although Westmoreland was "confident" that American forces could withstand the siege without the employment of unconventional weapons, protracted poor weather and heavy artillery fire were limiting the effectiveness of the present air campaign. "Planning was moving forward" for the remote possibility that nuclear weapons might be needed.

The president was not pleased to discover that such planning was under way, and the next day Rostow wrote to the boss a mea culpa, taking responsibility for the "fault" that "formal staff work" had been undertaken in advance of a presidential directive (**Document 5.16**). Rostow began by stating that he had not mentioned the possible use of nuclear weapons in any meeting, and that although he had raised the issue with the new secretary of defense, Clark Clifford, he was certain Clifford had not spoken with anyone about it. Rostow admitted having spoken with Gen. Robert Ginsburgh, a member of the National Security Council who was also a member of the JCS staff. Rostow had authorized Ginsburgh to bring the issue to the attention of General Wheeler, but only if Ginsburgh told Wheeler that this was in no way a presidential initiative. Wheeler, Rostow implies, took it from there.

Actually, as the archival record reviewed above shows, Rostow knew, or revealed, only half the story. Sharp and Westmoreland had not waited for Wheeler's order before initiating their own highly secret planning for the deployment of nuclear weapons. Despite this, during a February 16 news conference, the president ridiculed the "gossip and rumors" about nuclear weapons planning for Khe Sanh's defense. The military chiefs and commanders, the president asserted, "have at no time ever considered or made a recommendation in any respect to the deployment of nuclear weapons" (**Document 5.17**). A reporter, the president added, would have to be pretty gullible to believe such talk.

Within the administration and the military establishment, the president was buffeted by discordant advice on how to respond not only to Khe Sanh, but also to the overall situation that the United States now faced in the war. The situation came to a head when General Westmoreland requested 200,000 additional troops. According to Westmoreland, with the additional soldiers, airmen, and marines, the United States, with the South Vietnamese, would be able to take the fight aggressively to the enemy, now that the North Vietnamese had exposed themselves. But in the White House, no one by this point was willing to go along with his request. At a March 4 meeting, Johnson's senior foreign policy advisers, including General Wheeler, presented the president with their consensus advice: Westy would get 22,000 troops, and that was it. To do more would stretch the forces worldwide too thin. Besides, Secretary of Defense Clifford said, by acceding to the commander's request, "we might continue down the road as we have without accomplishing our purpose" (**Document 5.18**).

Outside the administration, the mood was equally dark; support for the president's policy was failing. One of the strongest supporters of the president through the years had been Drew Pearson, a highly respected, nationally syndicated newspaper columnist. In a letter of March 11, 1968, Pearson put the president on notice that he was "preparing a series of columns in disagreement with your Far Eastern policy."[60] Revered newscaster Walter Cronkite had given the president no such warning before he ended a February 27 special broadcast on the war by recommending the United States negotiate a withdrawal "not as victors," but as a nation that had done its best and come up short.

Stunned by the erosion of support and the emergence of peace candidates such as Edmund Muskie and Robert Kennedy in the race for the Democratic Party nomination for president in 1968, Johnson desperately sought a way out of the agony that Vietnam had become. His anguish was visible in a meeting with Generals Wheeler and Creighton Abrams and Secretary of State Rusk on March 26, ten days after President Kennedy's younger brother had entered the race for president. These three were to brief a group of senior foreign policy veterans from previous administrations brought in by Johnson to advise him. In preparing his designated briefers for their meeting with the "Wise Men," Johnson's frustration and anger boiled over. The country's morale was abysmal, he observed. It was the fault of the *New York Times*, the Kennedys, and General Westmoreland's impolitic request for 200,000 additional troops, a supposedly secret request that was the talk of the town. Moreover, the nation's fiscal situation was sorry. And then there was election year politics. "We need more money in an election year," the president summarized, "more taxes in an election year, more troops in an election year and more cuts in an election year" (**Document 5.19**).

Finally, with protestors' chants of "Hey, Hey, LBJ, How many kids did you kill today?" wafting into the White House, the president made two dramatic announcements from the Oval Office on the last day of March 1968. He would unilaterally halt the bombing of almost all of North Vietnam, and he would not stand for reelection in 1968 (**Document 5.20**). Johnson was heartsick. He had for the first time in his life, he said, felt "truly loved" by the American people when he won his landslide election in 1964.[61] Now, he knew that he had failed to unite the country. If he could not provide the unity that was essential for a nation in the conduct of war, and a nation on the verge of what sometimes seemed to be a civil war at home, perhaps someone else could. In Vietnam, from that point until the end of the Johnson presidency, the war stagnated on the ground, and negotiations at last got under way in Paris.

CONCLUSION

The United States would neither go all out in Vietnam under Johnson, nor would it consider withdrawing. The country would simply persevere. Such a strategy required a great deal of patience, perhaps even stoicism, among the public. But Americans, as Johnson knew, were not stoic by nature, which is why he was so fearful of creating a "war psychosis" if he spoke openly to the public about the war. Johnson therefore waited too long to make his case for support aggressively before the public. When he at last spoke up, his message of caution was drowned out by his message of optimism. In the face of the Tet Offensive, it was too little, too late.

Johnson took his failures in Vietnam personally, but would any other president likely have fared differently? In particular, would President Kennedy have done things differently? On the one hand, Kennedy would certainly have had a freer hand than Johnson in making decisions for the war. Johnson said he was continuing Kennedy's policies: if he had decided to do less in Vietnam, he knew he would be pilloried (by none other than the then-hawkish Robert Kennedy) for departing from John Kennedy's legacy. Kennedy, on the other hand, could at least have changed his mind. Still, one must wonder whether Kennedy would have taken the risks involved in withdrawal or even the risks of responding less aggressively than Johnson did to the pressures of the North Vietnamese and the VC. If he had dared to do so, he would likely have lost all influence with Congress, as well as with his own party, and he would have added to an already long list of Cold War embarrassments for the United States.

There is, however, at least one thing that Kennedy might have done differently. Kennedy was the biggest supporter within the government of the U.S. Army Special Forces, the vaunted Green Berets. By ordering greater use of the Special Forces and marines, military analyst Eliot Cohen has suggested, the president might have pushed the military to devise an alternative to a war of attrition. In other words, if the United States had used not more force, but rather less—over an admittedly long time—it might have had a superior outcome in Vietnam.[62] Could Kennedy have forced a reluctant military establishment to pursue such a strategy, surrendering its advantage in firepower and large-scale operations? There is no way to know. But because of Kennedy's special interest in counterinsurgency warfare, and because he was more skeptical generally of military expertise than was Johnson, it remains at least a tantalizing possibility.

Fittingly, the Vietnam War, and President Johnson's role in it, will in many ways remain an enigma. John Roche, a White House aide in the later years of the Johnson presidency, recounted in an interview with this author in 1987 that the president would repeatedly ask him, "What does Ho want?" At Johns Hopkins, Johnson had offered Ho a better life for his people—billions in aid, even a Mekong River equivalent to the great New Deal project, the Tennessee River Authority. "He wants to win," Roche would reply. "He couldn't understand," Roche continued. "You know, maybe [Ho] wanted three post offices, a dam, a Mekong River TVA. . ."

NOTES

1. Some of the material in this chapter is adapted from Thomas S. Langston, *Lyndon Baines Johnson,* American Presidents Reference Series (Washington, D.C.: CQ Press, 2002).
2. Lyndon Baines Johnson, *The Vantage Point: Perspectives on the Presidency, 1963–1969* (New York: Holt, Rinehart and Winston, 1971), 16.
3. Thomas Mann, Oral History Interview, November 4, 1968, Lyndon Johnson Presidential Library.
4. *Encyclopedia of World Biography,* 2d ed. (Farmington Hills, Mich.: Gale Research, 1998), s.v. "João Goulart." Available online from Biography Resource Center, Thomson Gale, http://galenet.galegroup.com/servlet/BioRC.
5. Jim Lobe, Inter Press Service, "Brazil: Documents Shed New Light on US Support for 1964 Coup," March 31, 2004, from Global Policy Forum, www.globalpolicy.org/empire/history/2004/0331coup1964.htm.
6. Robert Dallek, *Flawed Giant: Lyndon Johnson and His Times, 1961–1973* (New York: Oxford University Press, 1998), 267.
7. Ibid.
8. Douglas Little, "Choosing Sides: Lyndon Johnson and the Middle East," in *The Johnson Years,* ed. Robert Divine (Lawrence: University Press of Kansas, 1994), 3: 180.
9. Warner D. Farr, LTC, U.S. Army, "The Third Temple's Holy of Holies: Israel's Nuclear Weapons," *Counterproliferation Papers,* Future Warfare Series no. 2 (Maxwell Air Force Base, Alabama: USAF Counterproliferation Center, Air War College, September 1999), from the Federation of American Scientists, www.fas.org/nuke/guide/isreal/nuke/farr.htm.
10. Britain had claimed Iraq and Palestine as "mandates" after the defeat and dissolution of the Ottoman Empire in World War I. Britain gave up its claims to both territories shortly after World War II but maintained a strong presence in the region, especially in the Persian Gulf, where seven emirates along the coast had granted Britain authority for their defense in nineteenth-century treaties. The emirates did not gain their independence until 1971.
11. Sergery S. Radchenko, "The Soviet Union and the North Korean Seizure of the USS Pueblo: Evidence from Russian Archives" (working paper 47, Cold War International History Project, Woodrow Wilson International Center for Scholars, Washington, D.C.), www.wilsoncenter.org/topics/pubs/CWIHP_WP_47.pdf.
12. Radio Prague, "The Prague Spring," *History OnLine* Virtual Exhibit, http://archiv.radio.cz/history/history14.html.
13. "Statement of Soviet News Agency (TASS), August 21, 1968," in *The Cold War: A History through Documents,* ed. Edward H. Judge and John W. Langdon (Upper Saddle River, N.J.: Prentice Hall, 1999), 145–147.
14. Source Watch, "Brezhnev Doctrine," Center for Media and Democracy, www.sourcewatch.org/index.php?title=Brezhnev_Doctrine.
15. Kenneth J. Hill, *Cold War Chronology: Soviet-American Relations, 1945–1991* (Washington, D.C.: CQ Press, 1993), 145.
16. Lyndon B. Johnson, "Annual Message to Congress on the State of the Union," January 4, 1965, in *Public Papers of the Presidents of the United States: Lyndon B. Johnson, 1963–1969,* from the American Presidency Project, University of California, Santa Barbara, www.presidency.ucsb.edu.

17. Hill, *Cold War Chronology*, 152.

18. Ronnie Dugger, *The Politician: The Life and Times of Lyndon Johnson* (New York: W.W. Norton, 1982), 24.

19. Lt. Col. Charles Costanza, USAF, "Shades of Sentinel: U.S. Missile Defense, Then and Now," *Aerospace Power Journal* 15, no. 3 (Fall 2001): 60–65, www.airpower.maxwell.af.mil/airchronicles/apj/apj01/fal01/costanzo.html.

20. Johnson, *Vantage Point*, 492.

21. Langston, *Lyndon Baines Johnson*, 167–168.

22. H. R. McMaster, *Dereliction of Duty: Lyndon Johnson, Robert McNamara, the Joint Chiefs of Staff, and the Lies That Led to Vietnam* (New York: Harper Perennial, 1997).

23. Irving Bernstein, *Guns or Butter: The Presidency of Lyndon Johnson* (New York: Oxford University Press, 1990). See also Dugger, *The Politician*. The author heard the acclaimed Harvard presidency expert Richard Neustadt deliver a lecture to his American Presidency class in 1984 in which he leaned heavily on the Johnson-as-a-Texan hypothesis, arguing that had only President Kennedy lived, the tragedy in Vietnam would have been avoided. His students gave the professor an ovation in response.

24. President Johnson spoke with Senator Russell on May 27, 1964, as transcribed in Michael R. Beschloss, ed., *Taking Charge: The Johnson White House Tapes, 1963–1964* (New York: Simon and Schuster, 1997), 364.

25. Lyndon Johnson, "The President's First News Conference," December 7, 1963, in *Public Papers of the Presidents of the United States: Lyndon B. Johnson, 1963–1969*, from the American Presidency Project, University of California, Santa Barbara, www.presidency.ucsb.edu.

26. Ibid.

27. Beschloss, *Taking Charge*, 266.

28. Johnson, *Vantage Point*, 68.

29. CBS News, "LBJ: The Decision to Halt the Bombing," CBS special broadcast, February 6, 1970, from the Lyndon B. Johnson Presidential Library.

30. Ibid.

31. "McNaughton's November Draft on Vietnam Aims and Choices" (document 85), in Neil Sheehan et al., *The Pentagon Papers as Published by the* New York Times, (New York: Quadrangle Books, 1971), 374–376.

32. "April '65, Order Increasing Ground Force and Shifting Mission" (document 98), in ibid., 452–453. This order, NSAM 328, was written by McGeorge Bundy and addressed to the secretaries of state and defense and the director of central intelligence.

33. Michael Beschloss, ed., *Reaching for Glory: Lyndon Johnson's Secret White House Tapes, 1964–1965* (New York: Simon and Schuster, 2001), 211.

34. Ibid., 194.

35. Speaking more privately, the president made the same statement in more authentic language: "If we let them take Asia, they're going to try to take us. . . . If you let a bully come in and chase you out of your front yard, tomorrow he'll be on your porch, and the next day, he'll rape your wife in your own bed." As quoted in Beschloss, *Reaching for Glory*, 445.

36. Beschloss, *Reaching for Glory*, 348–349.

37. In the words of the official Department of Defense history of the early war, as recounted in Sheehan et al., *The Pentagon Papers*, 422.

38. Bernstein, *Guns or Butter*, 348.

39. "The President's Press Conference," July 28, 1965, in *Public Papers of the Presidents of the United States: Lyndon Baines Johnson, 1963–1969*, from the American Presidency Project, University of California, Santa Barbara, www.presidency.ucsb.edu.

40. Robert McNamara, Oral History Interview, Lyndon B. Johnson Presidential Library.

41. Doris Kearns Goodwin, *Lyndon Johnson and the American Dream* (New York: St. Martin's Press, 1991), 251.

42. Odd Arne Westad, Chen Jian, Stein Tonnesson, Nguyen Vu Tung, and James G. Hershberg, "77 Conversations between Chinese and Foreign Leaders on the War in Indochina, 1964–1975"

(working paper 22, Cold War International History Project, Wilson International Center for Scholars, Washington, D.C., 1998), www.wilsoncenter.org/topics/pubs/ACFB39.pdf.

43. Michael Lind, *Vietnam: The Necessary War* (New York: Free Press, 1999), 47.

44. Beschloss, *Reaching for Glory*, 444. The president was speaking in retirement to a couple of aides who were assisting in his memoirs project.

45. Ibid., p. 408.

46. Merle Miller, *Lyndon: An Oral History* (New York: Ballantine, 1980), 562–563.

47. David Halberstam, *The Best and the Brightest* (Greenwich, Conn.: Fawcett Crest, 1972), 683–684.

48. On the inflexibility of the U.S. Army's approach to the war, see Michael Lind, *Vietnam: The Necessary War, a Reinterpretation of America's Most Disastrous Military Conflict* (New York: Free Press, 1999), ch. 3.

49. "I see no practical alternative, short of nuclear war, to continue as we are, preparing for the long haul by building up our forces and facilities with [the] objective of gaining a qualitative and quantitative margin over [the] enemy which will wear him down." So wrote General Westmoreland to Adm. Alexander Sharp Jr. on June 11, 1965. Carter Malkasian, "Toward a Better Understanding of Attrition: The Korean and Vietnam Wars," *Journal of Military History* 68, no. 3 (2004): 933.

50. "CIA Intelligence Collection about Americans: CHAOS and the Office of Security" in U.S. Senate, *Final Report of the Select Committee to Study Governmental Operations with Respect to Intelligence Activities,* book 3, *Supplementary Detailed Staff Reports on Intelligence Activities and the Rights of Americans* (Washington, D.C.: U.S. Government Printing Office, 1976), from the Assassination Archives and Research Center Public Library, www.aarclibrary.org/publib/church/reports/book3/html/ChurchB3_0344a.htm.

51. Kearns Goodwin, *Lyndon Johnson and the American Dream,* 317.

52. Michael Maclear, *The Ten Thousand Day War, Vietnam: 1945–1975* (New York: Avon, 1981), 233.

53. Kearns Goodwin, *Lyndon Johnson and the American Dream,* 313.

54. United States Marshals Service Historical Perspective, "U.S. Marshals and the Pentagon Riot of October 21, 1967," www.usmarshals.gov/history/civilian/1967c.htm.

55. This memo summarized the meeting of the "Wise Men" brought in to advise the president on the war. "Memorandum from the President's Assistant (Jones) to President Johnson" (document 377), November 2, 1967, in U.S. Department of State, *Foreign Relations of the United States, 1964–1968,* vol. 5, *Vietnam 1967* (Washington, D.C.: U.S. Government Printing Office, 2002), 969.

56. Editorial, "The New Vietnam War Plan," *Washington Post,* November 26, 1967.

57. Ibid.

58. General Wheeler is quoted by the president in Johnson, *Vantage Point,* 417.

59. Johnson, *Vantage Point,* 384.

60. Langston, *Lyndon Baines Johnson,* 176, 202–203.

61. Kearns Goodwin, *Lyndon Johnson and the American Dream,* 209.

62. See Lind, *Vietnam,* 96–102. See also Albert Hemingway, *Our War Was Different: Marine Combined Action Platoons in Vietnam* (Annapolis, Md.: Naval Institute Press, 1994).

Document 5.1
"I Thought It Was a Conspiracy," President Lyndon Johnson Recalls November 22, 1963, the Day He Became President

Lyndon Johnson became president upon the assassination of John F. Kennedy in a motorcade in Dallas, Texas, on November 22, 1963. After Kennedy was pronounced dead, Johnson took the oath of office aboard Air Force One as it sat on the tarmac at the Dallas airport. His thoughts that day ran to the Cold War; he feared that bullets might soon be followed by missiles. It was a frightening opening to a presidency fraught with anxieties. The first set of recollections reprinted here is drawn from the president's taped conversations with a cabinet member, two White House staffers, and a personal friend, as transcribed by the historian Michael Beschloss. The second set of recollections comes from oral histories researched and collected by biographer Merle Miller.

[*Lyndon Johnson:*] What raced through my mind was that if they had shot our President, driving down there, who would they shoot next? And what was going on in Washington? And when would the missiles be coming? I thought it was a conspiracy and I raised that question, and nearly everybody that was with me raised it. . . .

The reason I went to the airport and didn't take it [oath of office] in the hospital was, first, I wanted to be able to talk to the Attorney General and get the oath. And the second thing was [Secretary of Defense Robert] McNamara had always told me that . . . if you get a warning [of possible nuclear war] . . . the thing they ought to do is get as high in the air as you can because you was least vulnerable there. Flying, a missile doesn't get you. A plane doesn't get you. You have time to think and you have adequate communications.

I thought the most important thing in the world was to decide who was President of this country at that moment. I was fearful that the Communists were trying to take us over. . . .

That evening, the president returned with family members and a few close aides, including Horace Busby and Bill Moyers, to the vice president's residence.

Luci [Baines Johnson, daughter]: It was very late when he got back. He looked like he'd been run over by a truck. And yet very strong. Like a paradox—he looked like part of him had been gutted and another part of him was just as strong and sturdy as an Olympic champion. My mother was very, very pale and in control.

Horace Busby: When the president finally returned home, he was met in the foyer by Mrs. Johnson. They spoke with each other briefly; she returned to her bedroom upstairs, and he came into the sitting room. At one point he asked that the television be turned on. We flicked through the channels and came to a retrospective on Kennedy. He watched it for a few minutes, and then he said, "I guess I know less than anybody about what's happening in the United States." After looking for a while, he kind of put his hands over his eyes and said, "Turn it off. It's all too fresh. I can't watch it." . . .

Eventually the president went upstairs to his bedroom, accompanied by Dr. Hurst. I remember Dr. Hurst speaking to him about possibly taking mild sedation so that he could sleep. The president was emphatic in rejecting this advice, being still quite concerned about whether there might still be more trauma to unfold in conjunction with the day's events.

I was considering leaving when one of the servants came down from the bedroom and said that Mr. Johnson wanted to see me. I had a long episode with him in the bedroom during which he was resting, but each time I tried to leave he called me back. I finally departed. I was the first to leave. . . .

Bill Moyers: That whole night he seemed to have several chambers of his mind operating simultaneously. It was formidable, very formidable.

About three I went to the upstairs bedroom, and I looked down and could see shadowy figures moving through the grounds. The Secret Service had on a heavy guard.

Sources: Michael R. Beschloss, ed., *Taking Charge: The Johnson White House Tapes, 1963–1964* (New York: Simon and Schuster, 1997), 14–15; Merle Miller, *Lyndon: An Oral Biography* (New York: G. P. Putnam's Sons, 1980), 324–325.

Document 5.2
Nuclear Non-Proliferation Treaty, July 1, 1968

The Nuclear Non-Proliferation Treaty was negotiated at the United Nations. The process began with the simultaneous submission of draft treaties by both superpowers in 1965. Three years later, a consensus position was forged, representing the interests of both nuclear-weapon states and non-nuclear-weapon states. The original signatories to the treaty included the United States, the Soviet Union, the United Kingdom, and fifty non-nuclear weapons nations. The Soviet invasion of Czechoslovakia in August 1968 delayed Senate ratification until November 1969.

The Treaty on the Non-Proliferation of Nuclear Weapons (NPT)
Signed at Washington, London, and Moscow July 1, 1968
Ratification advised by U.S. Senate March 13, 1969
Ratified by U.S. President November 24, 1969
U.S. ratification deposited at Washington, London, and Moscow March 5, 1970
Proclaimed by U.S. President March 5, 1970
Entered into force March 5, 1970

The States concluding this Treaty, hereinafter referred to as the "Parties to the Treaty,"

Considering the devastation that would be visited upon all mankind by a nuclear war and the consequent need to make every effort to avert the danger of such a war and to take measures to safeguard the security of peoples,

Believing that the proliferation of nuclear weapons would seriously enhance the danger of nuclear war,

In conformity with resolutions of the United Nations General Assembly calling for the conclusion of an agreement on the prevention of wider dissemination of nuclear weapons,

Undertaking to cooperate in facilitating the application of International Atomic Energy Agency safeguards on peaceful nuclear activities,

Expressing their support for research, development and other efforts to further the application, within the framework of the International Atomic Energy Agency safeguards system, of the principle of safeguarding effectively the flow of source and special fissionable materials by use of instruments and other techniques at certain strategic points,

Affirming the principle that the benefits of peaceful applications of nuclear technology, including any technological by-products which may be derived by nuclear-weapon States from the development of nuclear explosive devices, should be available for peaceful purposes to all Parties of the Treaty, whether nuclear-weapon or non-nuclear-weapon States,

Convinced that, in furtherance of this principle, all Parties to the Treaty are entitled to participate in the fullest possible exchange of scientific information for, and to contribute alone or in cooperation with other States to, the further development of the applications of atomic energy for peaceful purposes,

Declaring their intention to achieve at the earliest possible date the cessation of the nuclear arms race and to undertake effective measures in the direction of nuclear disarmament,

Urging the cooperation of all States in the attainment of this objective,

Recalling the determination expressed by the Parties to the 1963 Treaty banning nuclear weapon tests in the atmosphere, in outer space and under water in its Preamble to seek to achieve the discontinuance of all test explosions of nuclear weapons for all time and to continue negotiations to this end,

Desiring to further the easing of international tension and the strengthening of trust between States in order to facilitate the cessation of the manufacture of nuclear weapons, the liquidation of all their existing stockpiles, and the elimination from national arsenals of nuclear weapons and the means of their delivery pursuant to a Treaty on general and complete disarmament under strict and effective international control,

Recalling that, in accordance with the Charter of the United Nations, States must refrain in their international relations from the threat or use of force against the territorial integrity or political independence of any State, or in any other manner inconsistent with the Purposes of the United Nations, and that the establishment and maintenance of international peace and security are to be promoted with the least diversion for armaments of the world's human and economic resources,

Have agreed as follows:

ARTICLE I

Each nuclear-weapon State Party to the Treaty undertakes not to transfer to any recipient whatsoever nuclear weapons or other nuclear explosive devices or control over such weapons or explosive devices directly, or indirectly; and not in any way to assist, encourage, or induce any non-nuclear-weapon State to manufacture or otherwise acquire nuclear weapons or other nuclear explosive devices, or control over such weapons or explosive devices.

ARTICLE II

Each non-nuclear-weapon State Party to the Treaty undertakes not to receive the transfer from any transferor whatsoever of nuclear weapons or other nuclear explosive devices or of control over such weapons or explosive devices directly, or indirectly; not to manufacture or otherwise acquire nuclear weapons or other nuclear explosive devices; and not to seek or receive any assistance in the manufacture of nuclear weapons or other nuclear explosive devices.

ARTICLE III

1. Each non-nuclear-weapon State Party to the Treaty undertakes to accept safeguards, as set forth in an agreement to be negotiated and concluded with the International Atomic Energy Agency in accordance with the Statute of the International Atomic Energy Agency and the Agency's safeguards system, for the exclusive purpose of verification of the fulfillment of its obligations assumed under this Treaty with a view to preventing diversion of nuclear energy from peaceful uses to nuclear weapons or other nuclear explosive devices. Procedures for the safeguards required by this article shall be followed with respect to source or special fissionable material whether it is being produced, processed or used in any principal nuclear facility or is outside any such facility. The safeguards required by this article shall be applied to all source or special fissionable material in all peaceful nuclear activities within the territory of such State, under its jurisdiction, or carried out under its control anywhere.
2. Each State Party to the Treaty undertakes not to provide: (a) source or special fissionable material, or (b) equipment or material especially designed or prepared for the processing, use or production of special fissionable material, to any non-nuclear-weapon State for peaceful purposes, unless the source or special fissionable material shall be subject to the safeguards required by this article. . . .

ARTICLE V

Each Party to the Treaty undertakes to take appropriate measures to ensure that, in accordance with this Treaty, under appropriate international observation and through appropriate international procedures, potential benefits from any peaceful applications of nuclear explosions will be made available to non-nuclear-weapon States Party to the Treaty on a nondiscriminatory basis and that the charge to such Parties for the explosive devices used will be as low as possible and exclude any charge for research and development. Non-nuclear-weapon States Party to the Treaty shall be able to obtain such benefits, pursuant to a special international agreement or agreements, through an appropriate international body with adequate representation of non-nuclear-weapon States. Negotiations on this subject shall commence as soon as possible after the Treaty enters into force. Non-nuclear-weapon States Party to the Treaty so desiring may also obtain such benefits pursuant to bilateral agreements.

ARTICLE VI

Each of the Parties to the Treaty undertakes to pursue negotiations in good faith on effective measures relating to cessation of the nuclear arms race at an early date and to nuclear disarmament, and on a Treaty on general and complete disarmament under strict and effective international control.

ARTICLE VII

Nothing in this Treaty affects the right of any group of States to conclude regional treaties in order to assure the total absence of nuclear weapons in their respective territories. . . .

ARTICLE X

1. Each Party shall in exercising its national sovereignty have the right to withdraw from the Treaty if it decides that extraordinary events, related to the subject matter of this Treaty, have jeopardized the supreme interests of its country. It shall give notice of such withdrawal to all other Parties to the Treaty and to the United Nations Security Council three months in advance. Such notice shall include a statement of the extraordinary events it regards as having jeopardized its supreme interests.
2. Twenty-five years after the entry into force of the Treaty, a conference shall be convened to decide whether the Treaty shall continue in force indefinitely, or shall be extended for an additional fixed period or periods. This decision shall be taken by a majority of the Parties to the Treaty. . . .

IN WITNESS WHEREOF the undersigned, duly authorized, have signed this Treaty. DONE in triplicate, at the cities of Washington, London and Moscow, this first day of July one thousand nine hundred sixty-eight.

Source: "The Treaty on the Non-Proliferation of Nuclear Weapons (NPT)," July 1, 1968, from the U.S. State Department, www.state.gov/t/isn/trty/16281.htm.

Document 5.3
Tonkin Gulf Resolution, August 7, 1964

On August 2–3, 1964, North Vietnamese patrol boats were suspected of having fired upon an American destroyer, the USS Maddox, *in the Gulf of Tonkin. (The scholarly consensus today is that the first attack was real, but the second report was a false alarm.) President Johnson, who had been waiting for an opportunity to rally Congress behind the war in Vietnam, took the opportunity to request of Congress a show of determination and unity. Congress more than complied when it passed, by overwhelming majorities, this resolution authorizing the president to take "all necessary steps" to assist South Vietnam.*

. . .

Resolved by the Senate and House of Representatives of the United States of America in Congress assembled,

That the Congress approves and supports the determination of the President, as Commander in Chief, to take all necessary measures to repel any armed attack against the forces of the United States and to prevent further aggression.

Section 2. The United States regards as vital to its national interest and to world peace the maintenance of international peace and security in southeast Asia. Consonant with the Constitution of the United States and the Charter of the United Nations and in accordance with its obligations under the Southeast Asia Collective Defense Treaty, the United States is, therefore, prepared, as the President determines, to take all necessary steps, including the use of armed force, to assist any member or protocol state of the Southeast Asia Collective Defense Treaty requesting assistance in defense of its freedom.

Section 3. This resolution shall expire when the President shall determine that the peace and security of the area is reasonably assured by international conditions created by action of the United Nations or otherwise, except that it may be terminated earlier by concurrent resolution of the Congress.

Source: "Tonkin Gulf Resolution," Joint Resolution of Congress (H.J. Res. 1145), August 7, 1964, from the Avalon Project at Yale Law School, www.yale.edu/lawweb/avalon/tonkin-g.htm.

Document 5.4
Chairman Mao Zedong Offers His View of the War in Vietnam,
Conversation with North Vietnamese Leaders, October 5, 1964

Chairman Mao Zedong of China was unimpressed with the "scary statements" emanating from the U.S. government about Vietnam. The chairman offered sound military advice in the following conversation with Pham Van Dong, the prime minister of the Democratic Republic of Vietnam (North Vietnam), and Hoang Van Hoan, a North Vietnamese politburo member. Mao told his comrades that even if the war moved from purely guerrilla operations ("special war") into a limited war in which U.S. forces fought directly against the Communists, the North Vietnamese could win. After all, Mao explained, U.S. military forces were already stretched thinly around the globe.

Mao Zedong: According to Comrade Le Duan, you had the plan to dispatch a division [to South Vietnam]. Probably you have not dispatched that division yet. When you should dispatch it, the timing is important. Whether or not the United States will attack the North, it has not yet made that decision. Now, it is not even in a position to resolve the problem in South Vietnam. If it attacks the North, [it may be forced to] fight for one hundred years, and its legs will be trapped there. . . . The Americans have made all kinds of scary statements. They claim that they will run after and will chase into your country, and that they will attack our air force. In my opinion, the meaning of these words is that they do not want us to fight a big war and our air force to attack their warships. If [we] do not attack their warships, they will not run after you. Isn't this what they mean? . . .

Pham Van Dong: This is also our thinking. The United States is facing many difficulties, and it is not easy for it to expand the war. Therefore our consideration is that we should try to restrict the war in South Vietnam to the sphere of special war, and should try to defeat the enemy within the sphere of special war. . . .

. . . If the United States dares to start a limited war, we will fight it, and will win it.

MAO: Yes, you can win it. The South Vietnamese [regime] has several hundred thousand troops. You can fight against them . . . you can eliminate all of them. To fulfill these tasks is more than possible. It is impossible for the United States to send many troops to South Vietnam. The Americans altogether have 18 army divisions. They have to keep half of these divisions, i.e. nine of them, at home, and can send abroad the other nine divisions. Among these divisions, half are in Europe, and half are in the Asian-Pacific region. . . . As far as the American navy is concerned, they have put more ships in the Western Pacific than in Europe. . . . They have deployed four aircraft carriers near you, but they have been scared away by you. . . .

If the Americans dare to take the risk to bring the war to the North, how should the invasion be dealt with? . . . You must not engage your main force in a head-to-head confrontation with them, and must well maintain your main force. . . .

Source: "Mao Zedong and Pham Van Dong, Hoang Van Hoan, Beijing, 5 October 1964, 7–7:50 (p.m.?)," Conversation 3, in Odd Arne Westad et al., eds., "77 Conversations between Chinese and Foreign Leaders on the Wars in Indochina, 1964–1977" (working paper 22, Cold War International History Project, Woodrow Wilson International Center for Scholars, Washington, D.C., 1998), www.cwihp.org.

Document 5.5

"Why We Fight," Defense Planner John McNaughton's Analysis of U.S. War Aims, November 29, 1964

What was the United States' purpose in the Vietnam War? Why were U.S. soldiers fighting there? Why should it matter so much to Americans whether South Vietnam (SVN) or North Vietnam won control of their faraway land? It irritated Johnson to no end that he had to address such questions repeatedly, *but as this memo from a top foreign policy aide in the Pentagon suggests, the answers were not simple or straightforward. The United States had to fight in Vietnam tomorrow, by the logic of this document, because it was fighting in Vietnam today.*

1. **U.S. aims:**
   70%—To avoid a humiliating U.S. defeat (to our reputation as a guarantor).
   20%—To keep SVN (and the adjacent) territory from Chinese hands.
   10%—To permit the people of SVN to enjoy a better, freer way of life.
   ALSO—To emerge from a crisis without unacceptable taint from methods used.
   NOT—to "help a friend," although it would be hard to stay in if asked out.
2. **The Situation:** The situation in general is bad and deteriorating. The VC [Viet Cong] have the initiative. Defeatism is gaining among the rural population, somewhat in the cities, and even among the soldiers—especially those with relatives in rural areas. The Hop Tac area around Saigon is making little progress; the Delta stays bad; the country has been severed in the north. GVN [Government of Vietnam] control is shrinking to the enclaves, some burdened with refugees. In Saigon we have a remission: Quat is giving hope on the civilian side, the Buddhists have calmed, and the split generals are in uneasy equilibrium.
3. **The preliminary question:** Can the situation in SVN be bottomed out (a) without extreme measures against the DRV [Democratic Republic of Vietnam, or North Vietnam] and/or (b) without deployment of large numbers of U.S. (and other) combat troops inside SVN? The answer is perhaps, but probably no. . . .
5. **The "trilemma":** US policy appears to be drifting. This is because, while there is consensus that efforts within SVN . . . will probably fail to prevent collapse, all three of the possible remedial courses of action have so far been rejected:
   a. Will-breaking strikes on the North . . . are balked (1) by flash-point limits, (2) by doubts that the DRV will cave and (3) by doubts that the VC will obey a caving DRV. (Leaving strikes only a political and anti-infiltration nuisance.)
   b. Large U.S. troop deployments . . . are blocked by "French-defeat" and "Korea" syndromes, and Quat is queasy. (Troops could be net negatives, and be besieged.)
   c. Exit by negotiations . . . is tainted by the humiliation likely to follow.

Effort inside South Vietnam: Progress inside SVN is our main aim. Great, imaginative efforts on the civilian political as well as military side must be made, bearing in mind that progress depends as much on GVN efforts and luck as on added U.S. efforts. While only a few such efforts can pay off quickly enough to affect the present ominous deterioration, some may, and we are dealing here in small critical margins. . . .

Source: First draft of "Annex—Plan for Action for South Vietnam," appended to memorandum from John T. McNaughton, Assistant Secretary of Defense for International Security Affairs, to the Secretary of Defense, March 24, 1965, reprinted in Neil Sheehan et al., *The Pentagon Papers as Published by the* New York Times (New York: Bantam Books, 1971), 432–440 (document 96).

Document 5.6
Chinese Foreign Minister Zhou Enlai Examines the Stakes Involved in the War in Vietnam, March 30, 1965, and April 2, 1965

Chinese foreign minister Zhou Enlai rallied support for the struggle against American "imperialism" among fellow travelers and revolutionary leaders throughout the third world. China, at the time the major international patron of North Vietnam, had no interest in negotiations, which Zhou dismissed as "unfavorable to the liberation of the people . . . if viewed objectively." Zhou also affirms the Chinese government's commitment to send ground troops into the fight, just as they did in Korea, should the Americans attack North Vietnam.

Zhou [to Algerian president Ahmed Ben Bella]: The Vietnam question resulted completely from the trouble made by the Americans. . . . At present, the United States intends to scare Vietnam by expanding the war, hoping that Vietnam will yield to American bombardment, agreeing to negotiate. The United States also intends to scare China, forcing us to accept peace negotiations. Further, the United States is pursuing peace negotiation through the Soviet Union, Britain, France, and other countries. "Unconditional cease-fire"—this is nothing but requesting that the people in South Vietnam should stop armed struggle, that North Vietnam should stop supporting the struggle in South Vietnam, and that the puppet troops in South Vietnam would be given some breathing space, so that the United States would be able to strengthen its military presence in South Vietnam. An unconditional cease fire in South Vietnam? No way. . . . [A]ll these activities are unfavorable to the liberation of the people in South Vietnam, if viewed objectively.

Zhou [to Pakistan's president, Ayub Khan]: The Americans think that by expanding its aggression in South Vietnam and escalating its bombing in North Vietnam, they can bring Vietnam to its knees. This kind of thinking will fail completely.

During my recent visit, the African and European friends [of China's world mission] were all concerned about this issue. . . . I have analyzed and answered [their] questions.

(1) There exists no possibility that Vietnam will yield. . . . The troops the United States is able to send can only occupy a small portion of cities and sea ports. According to America's planning, they can only dispatch, at most, three divisions to South Vietnam. . . . The puppet regime in South Vietnam has changed about a dozen times,

and the Americans can trust virtually none of them. The Ngo Dinh Diem brothers were assassinated by the Americans. . . .

On the other hand, the United States tries to use the bombardment of North Vietnam to force the North to surrender. In August and September last year, the United States bombed North Vietnam once or twice a week. From late March this year to now, there is bombing almost every day. In the face of this, the NLF [National Liberation Front] in South Vietnam stated that no matter how long the bombing lasts, it will continue the fighting, until winning victory. . . . China published an editorial on March 24 in *Renmin ribao [People's Daily]*, expressing determination to support the people in South Vietnam to win victory, preparing to offer all kinds of support, including weapons, to the people in South Vietnam. When the people in South Vietnam are in need, China will send its personnel to fight together with the people in South Vietnam. Although this is only an editorial, It has caused strong reaction in foreign opinions, especially in the United States. Foreign Minister Chen Yi, in his response to the foreign minister of the DRV [Democratic Republic of Vietnam, or North Vietnam], has also confirmed this stand. . . .

After the publication of the *Renmin ribao* editorial and response from Foreign Minister Chen Yi . . . , the United States said that the Chinese were only paying lip service, which would play no role in the resistance by the people in South Vietnam. Sometimes the United States has said that it was uncertain if China would really enter the war. This means that America's policy is not established on a clearly defined foundation. . . . To withdraw is the best way for it save face, but to continue to act recklessly will cause it to lose more face. . . .

(2) Will the war be expanded into a world war? Your Excellency is a marshal. You know that the rules of war are not based on human will. The United States believes that if it does not expand the war in Vietnam to China, China will not support Vietnam. Our position is that even if the war is not expanded to China, still China will support Vietnam. . . . When the war expands, it is impossible to draw a line. This is like the spread of a fire. The United States wants to play with fire and to take the risk. . . . Although the United States threatens that if the war in Indo-China develops into a Korean-type war, it will not, as it did during the Korean War, limit itself to a regional war, but will expand the war to China, so that China will no longer be the shelter. We know this. China is prepared. . . .

The question is: after the expansion of the war, will it continue to expand? Your Excellency asked a moment ago if the war expands to China will the Soviet Union intervene. We are not going to answer this question, because you will be visiting the Soviet Union tomorrow. You can ask the Soviet friends, and let them answer it. . . .

Sources: "Zhou Enlai and Algerian President Ben Bella, Algiers, 30 March 1965" and "Zhou Enlai and Pakistani President Ayub Khan, Karachi, 2 April 1965," Conversations 5 and 6, in Odd Arne Westad et al., eds., "77 Conversations Between Chinese and Foreign Leaders on the Wars in Indochina, 1964–1977" (working paper 22, Cold War International History Project, Woodrow Wilson International Center for Scholars, Washington, D.C., 1998), www.cwihp.org.

Document 5.7
"Peace without Conquest," President Lyndon Johnson's Address at Johns Hopkins University, April 7, 1965

President Johnson sought to address the enemy as well as his own nation when he spoke at length on America's mission in Vietnam in an address at Johns Hopkins University in Baltimore, Maryland. If the North Vietnamese and the South Vietnamese Communists would relent, he stated, the United States would fund a massive development program for the region. The old New Dealer even offered the Vietnamese their own Mekong River equivalent of the Tennessee Valley Authority if they would lay down their arms.

. . . Tonight Americans and Asians are dying for a world where each people may choose its own path to change.

This is the principle for which our ancestors fought in the valleys of Pennsylvania. It is the principle for which our sons fight tonight in the jungles of Viet-Nam.

Viet-Nam is far away from this quiet campus. We have no territory there, nor do we seek any. The war is dirty and brutal and difficult. And some 400 young men, born into an America that is bursting with opportunity and promise, have ended their lives on Viet-Nam's steaming soil.

Why must we take this painful road? . . .

We fight because we must fight if we are to live in a world where every country can shape its own destiny. And only in such a world will our own freedom be finally secure. . . .

THE NATURE OF THE CONFLICT

The world as it is in Asia is not a serene or peaceful place.

The first reality is that North Viet-Nam has attacked the independent nation of South Viet-Nam. Its object is total conquest. . . .

The confused nature of this conflict cannot mask the fact that it is the new face of an old enemy.

Over this war—and all Asia—is another reality: the deepening shadow of Communist China. The rulers in Hanoi are urged on by Peking. This is a regime which has destroyed freedom in Tibet, which has attacked India, and has been condemned by the United Nations for aggression in Korea. It is a nation which is helping the forces of violence in almost every continent. The contest in Viet-Nam is part of a wider pattern of aggressive purposes.

WHY ARE WE IN VIET-NAM ?

Why are these realities our concern? Why are we in South Viet-Nam ?

We are there because we have a promise to keep. Since 1954 every American President has offered support to the people of South Viet-Nam. We have helped to build, and we have helped to defend. Thus, over many years, we have made a national pledge to help South Viet-Nam defend its independence. . . .

We are also there to strengthen world order. Around the globe, from Berlin to Thailand, are people whose well-being rests, in part, on the belief that they can count on us if they are attacked. . . .

We are also there because there are great stakes in the balance. Let no one think for a moment that retreat from Viet-Nam would bring an end to conflict. The battle would be renewed in one country and then another. The central lesson of our time is that the appetite of aggression is never satisfied. To withdraw from one battlefield means only to prepare for the next. We must say in southeast Asia—as we did in Europe—in the words of the Bible: "Hitherto shalt thou come, but no further." . . .

. . .This war, like most wars, is filled with terrible irony. For what do the people of North Viet-Nam want? They want what their neighbors also desire: food for their hunger; health for their bodies; a chance to learn; progress for their country; and an end to the bondage of material misery. And they would find all these things far more readily in peaceful association with others than in the endless course of battle.

A COOPERATIVE EFFORT FOR DEVELOPMENT

These countries of southeast Asia are homes for millions of impoverished people. Each day these people rise at dawn and struggle through until the night to wrestle existence from the soil. They are often wracked by disease, plagued by hunger, and death comes at the early age of 40.

Stability and peace do not come easily in such a land. Neither independence nor human dignity will ever be won, though, by arms alone. It also requires the work of peace. The American people have helped generously in times past in these works. Now there must be a much more massive effort to improve the life of man in that conflict-torn corner of our world.

The first step is for the countries of southeast Asia to associate themselves in a greatly expanded cooperative effort for development. We would hope that North Viet-Nam would take its place in the common effort just as soon as peaceful cooperation is possible. . . .

For our part I will ask the Congress to join in a billion dollar American investment in this effort as soon as it is underway.

And I would hope that all other industrialized countries, including the Soviet Union, will join in this effort to replace despair with hope, and terror with progress.

The task is nothing less than to enrich the hopes and the existence of more than a hundred million people. And there is much to be done.

The vast Mekong River can provide food and water and power on a scale to dwarf even our own TVA.

The wonders of modern medicine can be spread through villages where thousands die every year from lack of care.

Schools can be established to train people in the skills that are needed to manage the process of development.

And these objectives, and more, are within the reach of a cooperative and determined effort. . . .

Source: Lyndon Johnson, "Address at Johns Hopkins University: 'Peace without Conquest,'" April 7, 1965, in *Public Papers of the Presidents of the United States: Lyndon B. Johnson, 1963–1969,* from the American Presidency Project, University of California, Santa Barbara, www.presidency.ucsb.edu.

Document 5.8
Walking a Tightrope in Vietnam, National Security Council Meeting Notes, July 27, 1965

Wanting neither to "put in our big stack [of betting chips] now" or get out, President Johnson decided to temporize. He would continue the Americanization of the war effort in South Vietnam, while attempting to avoid provoking the Soviets or the Chinese. The president's constant concern for American public opinion was also evident on this occasion.

Summary Notes of 553rd NSC Meeting
July 27, 1965—5:40 P.M.–6:20 P.M.
Subject: Deployment of Additional U.S. Troops to Vietnam

The President: Before formalizing decisions on the deployment of additional U.S. forces to Vietnam, he wished to review the present situation with Council members present. Secretary Rusk will deal with the political situation and Secretary McNamara will describe the military situation.

Secretary Rusk:

a. Chinese Communists are most adamant against any negotiations between the North Vietnamese and the U.S./South Vietnamese. The clash between the Chinese Communists and the Russians continues.

b. We have asked many times what the North Vietnamese would do if we stopped the bombing. We have heard nothing in reply.

c. There appear to be elements of caution on the other side. . . .

d. The U.S. actions we are taking should be presented publicly in a low key but in such a way as to convey accurately that we are determined to prevent South Vietnam from being taken over by Hanoi. At the same time, we seek to avoid a confrontation with either the Chinese Communists or the Soviet Union.

Secretary McNamara: Summarized the military situation in Vietnam:

a. The number of Viet Cong forces has increased and the percentage of these forces committed to battle has increased.

b. The geographic area of South Vietnam controlled by the Viet Cong has increased.

c. The Viet Cong have isolated the cities and disrupted the economy of South Vietnam. The cities are separated by the countryside.

d. Increased desertions from the South Vietnamese Army have prevented an increase in the total number of South Vietnamese troops available for combat.

e. About half of all U.S. Army helicopters are now in South Vietnam in addition to over 500 U.S. planes.

The military requirements are:
a. More combat battalions from the U.S. are necessary. A total of 13 additional battalions need to be sent now. On June 15, we announced a total of 75,000 men, or 15 battalions. . . .

The President: The situation in Vietnam is deteriorating. Even though we now have 80 to 90,000 men there, the situation is not very safe. We have these choices:
a. Use our massive power, including SAC [Strategic Air Command], to bring the enemy to his knees. Less than 10% of our people urge this course of action.
b. We could get out on the grounds that we don't belong there. Not very many people feel this way about Vietnam. Most feel our national honor is at stake and that we must keep our commitments there.
c. We could keep our forces at the present level. . . . We could "hunker down." No one is recommending this course.
d. We could ask for everything we might desire from Congress—money, authority to call up the reserves, acceptance of the deployment of more combat battalions. This dramatic course of action would involve declaring a state of national emergency and a request for several billion dollars. Many favor this course. However, if we do go all out in this fashion, Hanoi would be able to ask the Chinese Communists and the Soviets to increase aid and add to their existing commitments.
e. We have chosen to do what is necessary to meet the present situation, but not to be unnecessarily provocative to either the Russians or the Communist Chinese. We will give the commanders the men they say they need. . . . We will get the necessary money in the new budget and will use our transfer authority until January. We will neither brag about what we are doing nor thunder at the Chinese Communists and the Russians.

This course of action will keep us there during the critical monsoon season and possibly result in some gains. Meanwhile, we will push on the diplomatic side. This means that we will use up our manpower reserves. We will not deplete them, but there will be a substantial reduction. Quietly, we will push up the level of our reserve force. We will let Congress push us but, if necessary, we will call the legislators back.

We will hold until January. The alternatives are to put in our big stack now or hold back. . . .

Secretary Fowler: Do we ask for standby authority now to call the reserves but not actually call them?

The President: Under the approved plan, we would not ask for such authority.

Source: "Summary Notes of 553rd National Security Council Meeting, July 27, 1965," in *Public Papers of the Presidents of the United States: Lyndon B. Johnson, 1965* (Washington, D.C.: U.S. Government Printing Office, 1966), 2:388–389.

Document 5.9
Trends in "Hawks" versus "Doves" Regarding the Vietnam War,
December 1967–November 1969

The Tet offensive initially led to increased support for the war in Vietnam. But by March 1968, "doves" outnumbered "hawks" for the first time. By the end of Lyndon Johnson's presidency, "hawks" were heavily outnumbered, as evidenced by the following results from the Gallup Poll Index.

Trends in Hawks versus Doves

People are called "hawks" if they want to step up our military effort in Vietnam. They are called "doves" if they want to reduce our military effort in Vietnam. How would you describe yourself—as a "hawk" or a "dove"?

	December 1967	Late January 1968	Early February 1968	Late February 1968	March 1968	April 1968	Early October 1968	November 1969
Hawk	52%	56%	61%	58%	41%	41%	44%	31%
Dove	35	28	23	26	42	41	42	55
No opinion	13	16	16	16	17	18	14	14

Source: John E. Mueller, *War, Presidents, and Public Opinion* (New York: Wiley, 1973), 107.

Document 5.10
Trends in Public Opinion Regarding the Vietnam War, May 1965–May 1971

Young adults were typically more supportive of the war than were their elders, but Gallup polls indicated that support among all cohorts gradually declined over time. The Tet offensive in the winter of 1967–1968 was a turning point for many Americans.

Trends in Public Opinion on the Vietnam War

	Age Group								
	Under 30			30–49			Over 49		
	Support	Oppose	No opinion	Support	Oppose	No opinion	Support	Oppose	No opinion
May 1965	61%	21%	18%	59%	23%	18%	43%	30%	27%
August 1965	76	14	10	64	22	14	51	29	20
November 1965	75	17	8	68	17	15	57	25	18
March 1966	71	21	8	63	23	14	48	30	22
May 1966	62	29	9	54	32	14	39	42	19
September 1966	53	37	10	56	28	16	39	40	21
November 1966	66	21	13	55	30	15	41	36	23
May 1967	60	31	9	53	34	13	42	42	16
July 1967	62	32	6	52	37	11	37	50	13
October 1967	50	43	7	50	43	7	35	53	12
Early February 1968	51	40	9	44	46	10	36	48	16
March 1968	50	46	4	46	47	7	35	52	13
April 1968	54	38	8	44	46	10	31	54	15
August 1968	45	48	7	39	48	13	27	61	12
Early October 1968	52	44	4	41	49	10	26	64	10
February 1969	47	49	4	43	49	8	31	57	12
September 1969	36	58	6	37	54	9	25	63	12
January 1970	41	54	5	37	54	9	25	62	13
April 1970	43	50	7	40	45	15	25	57	18
March 1970	48	49	3	41	53	6	26	61	13
January 1971	41	52	7	38	55	7	20	67	13
May 1971	34	59	7	30	61	9	23	63	14

Source: John E. Mueller, *War, Presidents, and Public Opinion* (New York: Wiley, 1973), 139.

Document 5.11
The Federal Bureau of Investigation Sees a "Grim" Outlook for the Summer, May 23, 1967

The Federal Bureau of Investigation (FBI) analyzed for the Johnson administration the prospects for racial turbulence and violence in the summer of 1967. Due to the fusion of the anti-war and civil rights movements, and thanks to the dedicated agitation of the Communist Party of the USA (CPUSA), the FBI reported that the outlook was "grim." Of particular concern was the Reverend Martin Luther King Jr.'s decision to join the rank of "demagogues" whose words and actions served to "promote communist aims."

. . . We are now in the midst of an era of protracted racial conflict that has produced a crisis in law enforcement. Along with the seasonal rise in summertime crime, it is painfully evident that racial turmoil has similarly become a summer phenomenon. The racial violence potential is especially high in hot weather in the Nation's urban areas because large numbers of Negroes, living under crowded, depressed conditions in ghettos, take to the streets to escape the heat and seek relaxation and recreation. . . .

. . . There is the added danger this year that the scenes of racial strife in large cities might spread from Negro communities into white neighborhoods and that increased numbers of white people might resort to violence in an effort to counter Negro demonstrations or rioters. . . .

. . . [I]ncessant agitation and propaganda on the part of communists and other subversives and extremists have definitely contributed to Negro unrest and fomented violence. In particular, demagogues like Martin Luther King, Stokely Carmichael, Floyd McKissick, Cassius Clay, and Dick Gregory have fanned the fires of racial discord and animosity. King has now joined . . . civil rights extremists in embracing the communist tactic of linking the civil rights movement with the anti-Vietnam-war protest movement. . . . King's exhortation to boycott the draft and refuse to fight could lead eventually to dangerous displays of civil disobedience and near-seditious activities by Negroes and whites alike. Thus, the antiwar campaign endorsed by King helps to promote communist aims and programs in the United States and abroad. . . .

The innumerable racial riots and disturbances which have plagued the United States since 1964 have had their genesis primarily in the long-smoldering discontent and resentment of Negroes over unequal job, school, and housing opportunities and their deepseated antipathy toward the police. However, constant agitation and propaganda on the part of communists and other subversive and extremist elements have done much to aggravate tension in the ghettos of the Nation's big cities.

. . . Most Negroes realize that the communists are interested in them primarily to exploit racial issues and to create the chaos upon which communism flourishes. Nevertheless, the cumulative effect of this ceaseless agitation and propaganda and the familiar communist charge of "police brutality" cannot be ignored or minimized. . . .

Now that the civil rights and the antiwar protest movements have been joined, with the distinct possibility of ominous displays of civil disobedience and near seditious activities on the part of Negroes and whites alike, the outlook for this summer is grim indeed. The injection of antiwar activities into civil rights activities is bound to intensify the racial discord and heighten the violence potential throughout the country.

In the long run, this consolidated civil rights-peace movement will be detrimental to the national security and the best interests of the Nation, for it will not only tend to encourage the enemy and prolong the Vietnam war but will also have an adverse effect on the cause of civil rights.

Source: Federal Bureau of Investigation, "Racial Violence Potential in the United States This Summer" (Excerpts), May 23, 1967, from the National Security Archive, George Washington University, www.gwu.edu/~nsarchiv/coldwar/documents/episode-13/index.html.

Document 5.12
The Mansfield Resolution on the War in Vietnam, October 25, 1967

Congressional opposition to the war in Vietnam escalated along with the American involvement there. On October 25, 1967, fifty-four senators, led by Senate Majority Leader Mike Mansfield, D-Mont., introduced the following resolution, urging that the United States seek an international solution to its problems in Vietnam by taking the issue before the UN Security Council. The United States had attempted such a move before, in January 1966, but was rebuffed by the Soviets (and the French), who characterized the effort as a ploy to distract attention from aggressive new American actions in the war and from criticism in the U.S. Senate. In 1967 the Senate and, in particular, Mike Mansfield—ironically, often labeled an isolationist— demanded that the president try again.

Whereas the question of the Vietnamese conflict is a matter of which the Security Council of the United Nations is seized by action previously taken by the Council in connection with a letter of the Permanent Representative of the United States dated January 31, 1966, submitting a resolution seeking a settlement of the hostilities, and

Whereas more than one hundred members of the United Nations through their Chiefs of State or Foreign Ministers or Permanent Representatives have expressed their deep concern with the continued hostilities and their desire for a peaceful and honorable settlement of the Vietnamese conflict, thereby be it

Resolved, That it is the sense of the Senate that the President of the United States consider taking the appropriate initiative through his representative at the United Nations to assure that the United States resolution of January 31, 1966, or any other resolution of equivalent purpose be brought before the Security Council for consideration.

Source: Senate Resolution 180, 90th Cong., 1st sess., October 25, 1967.

Document 5.13
Gen. Earle Wheeler, Chairman of the Joint Chiefs of Staff, Raises the
Nuclear Issue with Combatant Commanders in Vietnam, February 1, 1968
During the Tet Offensive in Vietnam, American and South Vietnamese forces were besieged
at Khe Sanh. Fearing that the forces might be overrun, the United States' top military officers
began to consider the possibility that the situation might become so desperate as to call for the use
of nuclear weapons.

FROM: General Wheeler, CJCS
TO: Admiral Sharp, CINCPAC
        General Westmoreland, COMUSMACV

              TOP SECRET   EYES ONLY —JCS   1 February 68

(DELIVER DURING WAKING HOURS TO ADDRESSEES ONLY)

1. There is a considerable amount of discussion around town about the Khe Sanh situation to include the inevitable comparisons with Dien Bien Phu. One question raised
recently in this connection (and I believe it received some consideration at the time of the
Dien Bien Phu siege) is whether tactical nuclear weapons should be used if the situation
in Khe Sanh should become that desperate. I consider such an eventuality unlikely. Nevertheless, I would appreciate your views as to whether there are targets in the area which
lend themselves to nuclear strikes, whether some contingency nuclear planning would be
in order, and what you consider to be some of the more significant pros and cons of using
tac nukes in such a contingency.

2. I do not need a reply quite so urgently as on many of my other requests to you
lately—early next week should suffice. While I know you will have to put a few of your
bright planners on this, I would caution you to hold this subject very closely. Warm
regards.

Source: Memorandum from General Wheeler to Admiral Sharp and General Westmoreland, February 1, 1968, National Security Files, Files of Walt W. Rostow, Box 7, Nuclear Weapons—Contingency
Planning, Lyndon B. Johnson Presidential Library.

Document 5.14
Adm. Alexander Sharp's Reply to Gen. Earle Wheeler on Nuclear Planning, February 2, 1968

In reply to General Wheeler's request for secretive planning regarding the potential use of nuclear weapons in the ongoing battle in Vietnam during the Tet Offensive, Admiral Sharp, commander of the Central Pacific, informed the chairman of the Joint Chiefs of Staff that planning was already in progress under the code name "Fracture Jaw."

FM ADM SHARP, CINCPAC HAWAII
TO GEN WHEELER, CJSC WASHINGTON DC
INFO GEN WESTMORELAND, COMUSMACV VIETNAM
TOP SECRET EYES ONLY RESTRICTED DATA
FRACTURE JAW
A. JCS 01154/011526Z Feb 68

1. IN LINE WITH YOUR OWN THOUGHTS, WESTY AND I EXCHANGED VIEWS SEVERAL DAYS AGO ON THE NEED FOR SOME VERY CLOSELY HELD PLANNING FOR EMPLOYMENT OF TACTICAL NUCLEAR WEAPONS SHOULD THE SITUATION AROUND KHE SANH WARRANT AND SHOULD THE HIGHEST NATIONAL AUTHORITY DIRECT THEIR USE. WHILE AGREEING THAT IT IS HIGHLY UNLIKELY THAT KHE SANH WOULD BECOME SUFFICIENTLY DESPERATE TO CALL FOR THE USE OF TAC NUCS, WE FELT THAT MILITARY PRUDENCE ALONE REQUIRES THAT WE DO SOME DETAILED PLANNING REGARDING UNITS TO BE EMPLOYED, DELIVERY VEHICLES, WEAPON AVAILABILITY, PREFERRED WEAPONS BY TYPE AND YIELD, CONSTRAINTS, PREFERRED DELIVERY MEANS, TACTICS AND OTHER OPERATIONAL DETAILS.

2. CONSIDERING THE SENSITIVITY OF THIS MATTER, WE ARE ACCOMPLISHING THE PLANNING UNDER THE STRICTEST SECURITY IN OKINAWA WITH A SPECIAL PLANNING TEAM. . . . TO SIMPLIFY REFERENCE TO THE HIGHLY CLASSIFIED PROJECT, THE UNCLASSIFIED NICKNAME OF FRACTURE JAW HAS BEEN ASSIGNED. THE PLANNING IS CURRENTLY WELL UNDERWAY.

3. . . . I FORWARDED TO WESTY ON 29 JANUARY A MESSAGE DESCRIBING STEP BY STEP THE PROCEDURES FOR REQUESTING THE SELECTIVE RELEASE OF NUCLEAR WEAPONS. HE HOLDS THE NECESSARY DOCUMENTS AND AUTHENTICATORS AND THE PURPOSE OF MY MESSAGE WAS TO HIM A SIMPLIFIED REMINDER FOR HIS USE. ADDITIONALLY, MY MESSAGE INFORMS HIM OF THE TYPE AND LOCATION OF TACTICAL NULCEAR WEAPONS AVAILABLE AND BEST SUITED FOR THE PURPOSE. AIR DELIVERED TACTICAL NUCLEAR WEAPONS PROVIDE THE IMMEDIATE CAPABILITY. SUITABLE WEAPONS ARE AVAILABLE [section redacted for security purposes]

4. THE FOREGOING IS TO GIVE YOU A QUICK SKETCH OF OUR TAC NUC PLANNING AND TO LET YOU KNOW THAT I BELIEVE WE ARE PREPARED FOR THIS EVENTUALITY, UNLIKELY AS IT MIGHT BE. UPON COMPLETION OF THE PLANNING NOW UNDERWAY IN OKINAWA, OUR PLANS AND PREPARATIONS WILL BE REFINED.

5. ANSWERS TO YOUR QUESTIONS AS TO WHETHER THERE ARE TARGETS IN THE KHE SANH AREA AND THE PROS AND CONS OF USING TAC NUCS IN SUCH A CONTINGENCY WILL BE PROVIDED SUBSEQUENTLY.

6. THIS ENTIRE SUBJECT HAS BEEN VERY CLOSELY HELD IN MY STAFF AND I HAVE CAUTIONED EACH COMMANDER TO HOLD STAFF OFFICERS ON THE STRICTEST NEED TO KNOW BASIS. WARM REGARDS.

Source: Telegram from Adm. Alexander Sharp to General Earle Wheeler, February 2, 1968, National Security Files, Files of Walt W. Rostow, Box 7, Nuclear Weapons—Contingency Planning, Lyndon B. Johnson Presidential Library.

Document 5.15
National Security Adviser Walt Rostow's Memo Concerning the "Nuclear Issue" and the Tet Offensive, February 2, 1968

In this memo, National Security Adviser Walt Rostow warns President Johnson that the military might raise the "nuclear issue" with him directly and advises him on how to avoid this "circumstance."

Memorandum
Friday, February 2, 1968—8:30 a.m.
SECRET   SENSITIVE
LITERALLY EYES ONLY FOR THE PRESIDENT
Mr. President:

One reason for my particular concern for the battle of Khe Sanh is a desire to avoid a situation of battlefield crisis in which Westy and the JCS would ask you to release tactical nuclear weapons.

I have felt that every action ought to be taken now that could prevent such a circumstance from arising.

That is why it may be worth offering Westy now an extra reserve division; although if the 81st Airborne and/or the two Marine brigades were sent out, you would undoubtedly have to call up the reserves.

I am not making that recommendation. But you may wish to talk privately with Clark Clifford about the advisability of: *[handwritten notation in margin: circled "A"]*

—communicating privately to Bus Wheeler that it is his duty to minimize the likelihood that the nuclear issue would be raised by the JCS;

—asking Westy back-channel if he wants an extra airborne division or other reserve forces on the spot. (He would—almost surely—accept.)

W. W. Rostow

[Handwritten Continuation/Notes]

. . .

The President communicated "A" to Gen Wheeler.

He replied:

—contingency most remote, although planning going forward;

—Westy "confident". . .

—Will accelerate answer to key questions from Westy:

What if bad weather protracted?

What if artillery too continuous for a/c and choppers.

8:35 p.m.

Source: Memorandum from Walt W. Rostow to President Lyndon Johnson, National Security Files, Files of Walt W. Rostow, Box 7, Nuclear Weapons—Contingency Planning, Lyndon B. Johnson Presidential Library.

Document 5.16
National Security Adviser Walt Rostow's Memo Detailing His Conversations on Nuclear Contingency Plans, February 3, 1968

President Johnson apparently learned, possibly in his conversation of the preceding day with General Wheeler, that the military had already *addressed the nuclear issue in their planning (see* **Document 5.14**). *In this memorandum, the president's national security adviser seems to respond to a series of questions from the boss about exactly who he had talked to about nuclear weapons and explains that he had not meant to set in motion formal staff work for a nuclear contingency.*

SECRET/SENSITIVE/EYES ONLY

Saturday, February 3, 1968—12:30 p.m.

Mr. President:

I thought you would not wish me to discuss the nuclear weapons matter in a meeting. I did not discuss this question with Gen. Taylor.

I did discuss it with Clark Clifford, but I am 100% sure he did not raise it with the Pentagon. The discussion was yesterday and he confined his advice to saying I had the duty to share my anxiety with you verbally.

I have discussed various aspects of the matter over the past ten days or so with Bob Ginsburgh. It first arose in my mind from recollection that the issue was raised with us by the French at the time of the crisis at Dienbienphu.

In particular, we chatted informally about three matters:

1. Could such a question arise at Khe Sanh?

2. Would nuclear weapons be relevant?

3. What steps could be taken to minimize the likelihood that the question would arise?

With respect to 2, he asked me one day if he might explore the question informally with General Wheeler.

I told him he could if it was understood:

— this was in no sense a "White House request";

— the matter had never even been raised with the President, let alone by the President.

I did not envisage that any formal staff work would be set in train.

The fault, therefore, is mine.

W. W. ROSTOW

Source: Memorandum from Walt W. Rostow to President Lyndon Johnson, February 3, 1968, National Security Files, Files of Walt W. Rostow, Box 7, Nuclear Weapons—Contingency Planning, Lyndon B. Johnson Presidential Library.

Document 5.17

President Lyndon Johnson's Press Conference on Rumors of Possible Use of Nuclear Weapons in Vietnam, February 16, 1968

The president addressed "the gossip and rumors" about nuclear weapons being considered for use in Vietnam. He denied that any such planning had taken place, now or at any time during his years in the executive branch. In a nice Johnsonian touch, he chided the press for being so gullible and naïve as to believe such outrageous rumors.

. . .

Q.: Mr. President, could you address yourself, please, sir, to the gossip and rumors about nuclear weapons in Vietnam?

The President: I think the Press Secretary covered that very well.

The President must make the decision to deploy nuclear weapons. It is one of the most awesome and grave decisions any President could be called upon to make.

It is reasonably apparent and known to all that it is very much against the national interest to carry on discussions about deployment of nuclear weapons; so much so that the act, itself, tries to guard against that.

I have been in the executive branch of the Government for 7 years. I think I have been aware of the recommendations made by the Joint Chiefs of Staff, by the Secretary of State, and by the Secretary of Defense during that period.

So far as I am aware, they have at no time ever considered or made a recommendation in any respect to the deployment of nuclear weapons. They are on our planes on training missions from time to time.

We do have problems. There are plans with our allies concerning what they do.

There is always a person available to me who has full information in connection with their deployment, as you newspapermen know. I think if any serious consideration were ever given, and God forbid there ever will be, I don't think you would get it by some anonymous caller to some committee of the Congress. I think most of you know that, or ought to know that.

No recommendation has been made to me. Beyond that, I think we ought to put an end to that discussion. . . .

Source: "The President's News Conference of February 16, 1968," in *Public Papers of the Presidents of the United States: Lyndon B. Johnson, 1963–1969,* from the American Presidency Project, University of California, Santa Barbara, www.presidency.ucsb.edu.

Document 5.18
The President's Team Considers Gen. William Westmoreland's Request for 200,000 Additional Troops, Meeting Notes, March 4, 1968

During the winter of 1967–1968, the North Vietnamese and the South Vietnamese Communists launched a large, coordinated assault, known as the Tet Offensive. The American and South Vietnamese forces denied the enemy victory on the battlefield during Tet, but the civilian command was shaken. The U.S. military commander, Gen. William Westmoreland, wanted 200,000 more U.S. troops to shore up defenses and to pursue the enemy; he would get but a tenth of that number. The following "Notes of the President's Meeting with Senior Foreign Policy Advisers (Cabinet Room)" were taken by Deputy Press Secretary Tom Johnson. Attending were the president, Vice President Hubert Humphrey, Secretary of State Dean Rusk, Secretary of Defense Clark Clifford, Chair of the JCS Gen. Earle Wheeler, Deputy Secretary of Defense Paul Nitze, CIA Director Richard Helms, retired chairman of the JCS Gen. Maxwell Taylor, Secretary of the Treasury Henry Fowler, National Security Adviser Walt Rostow, Press Secretary George Christian, and Special Assistant Marvin Watson (joined for conclusion). The meeting began at 5:33 p.m. It ended at 7:20 p.m.

The President: As I told you last week, I wanted you to return today with your recommendations in response to General Westmoreland's request. . . . As I understand it, Clark Clifford, Secretary Rusk, and Rostow and others have been meeting on these questions in conjunction with the Joint Chiefs of Staff.

Walt Rostow: That is correct.

Clark Clifford: Paul Nitze and I started to work on this Friday night. As you could understand, with the time pressure we placed upon ourselves there still may need to be refinements and adjustments to the program I will discuss.

We have tried to make this document clear and understandable. (Undersecretary Nitze passed out prior to the meeting copies of a "Draft Memorandum for the President"). . . .

As you know, from time to time, the military leaders in the field ask for additional forces. We have, in the past, met these requests until we are now at the point where we have agreed to supply up to 525,000 men to General Westmoreland. He has now asked for 205,000 additional troops. . . .

Your senior advisers have conferred on this matter at very great length. There is a deep-seated concern by your advisers. There is a concern that if we say, yes, and step up with the addition of 205,000 more men that we might continue down the road as we have been without accomplishing our purpose—which is for a viable South Vietnam which can live in peace.

We are not convinced that our present policy will bring us to that objective.

As I said before, we spent hours discussing this matter. For a while, we thought and had the feeling that we understood the strength of the Viet Cong and the North Vietnamese. You will remember the rather optimistic reports of General Westmoreland and Ambassador Bunker last year.

Frankly, it came as a shock that the Viet Cong and North Vietnamese had the strength of force and skill to mount the Tet offensive—as they did. They struck 34 cities, made strong inroads in Saigon and in Hue. There have been very definite effects felt in the countryside.

At this stage, it is clear that this new request by General Westmoreland brings the President to a clearly defined watershed:

1. Do you continue to go down the same road of "more troops, more guns, more planes, more ships?"

2. Do you go on killing more Viet Cong and more North Vietnamese and killing more Viet Cong and more North Vietnamese?

There are grave doubts that we have made the type of progress we had hoped to have made by this time. As we build up our forces, they build up theirs. We continue to fight at a higher level of intensity.

Even were we to meet this full request . . . it is likely that by March he [General Westmoreland] may want another 200,000 to 300,000 men with no end in sight. . . .

We recommend an immediate decision to deploy to Vietnam an estimated total of 22,000 additional personnel. We would agree to get them to General Westmoreland right away. It would be valuable for the general to know they are coming so he can make his plans accordingly. This is as far as [we] are willing to go. . . .

The President: Westmoreland is asking for 200,000 men, and you are recommending 20,000 or so?

Clark Clifford: The strategic reserves in the United States are deeply depleted. They must be built up. Senator Russell has said this. We do not know what might happen anywhere around the world, but to face an emergency we will need to strengthen the reserve. . . .

We are not sure the present strategy is the right strategy—that of being spread out all over the country with a seek and destroy policy.

We are not convinced that this is the right way, that it is the right long-term course to take. We are not sure under the circumstances which exist that a conventional military victory, as commonly defined, can be had. . . .

We can no longer rely just on the field commander. He can want troops and want troops and want troops and want troops. We must look at the overall impact on us, including the situation here in the United States. We must look at our economic stability, our other problems in the world, our other problems at home; we must consider whether or not this thing is tying us down so that we cannot do some of the other things we should be doing; and finally, we must consider the effects of our actions on the rest of the world—are we setting an example in Vietnam through which other nations would rather not go if they are faced with a similar threat? . . .

Secretary Rusk: Mr. President, without a doubt, this will be one of the most serious decisions you will have made since becoming President. This has implications for all of our society.

First, on the review of strategic guidance: we want the Vietnamese to do their full share and be able to survive when we leave. This was one of the things that saved us in Korea. The question is whether substantial additional troops would eventually increase or decrease South Vietnamese strength.

. . . Many of us would like to see the ARVN [the Army of the Republic of Vietnam, or the South Vietnamese Army] equipped better and supplied with the M-16 rifles.

We must also consider what would happen to our NATO troop policies. To reduce NATO troops is a serious matter indeed. . . .

Dick Helms: I feel that the study of the last 3–4 days has shown that we must replenish our Strategic Reserve. If you look at the conditions throughout the world, you can easily see that we need it.

Rusk: I would go to Congress for specific actions, not for a statement of policy such as the Tonkin Gulf Resolution. We do not want a general declaration.

The President: In the Senate we face a real problem. Anything that requires any authority may result in a filibuster.

Wheeler: If we could provide Westy with the troops he wants I would recommend they be sent. They cannot be provided. This [the 22,000] is what we can do by 15 June. . . .

General Taylor: We are all for this recommendation tonight—but all for different reasons. I frankly was startled to learn that we can't send more than 22,000 men.

I also want to know if this is a year of despair or a year of opportunity. I think it is the latter. Westy may get into trouble between now and June. He could lose a lot of politically valuable terrain.

We should bear this in mind. . . . Let's not delude ourselves about ARVN. They will try—they will give us the right answers—but don't count on them to do too much in a short period of time.

The President: Have you told Westmoreland you would only send this number and we could give no more by June 1?

Wheeler: No, I will tell him after this meeting.

The President: Tell him to forget the 100,000 [sic]. Tell him 22,000 is all we can give at the moment. If the ARVN are not equipped as well as the Vietcong, isn't that a sad commentary on us?

Source: David M. Barrett, ed., *Lyndon B. Johnson's Vietnam Papers: A Documentary Collection* (College Station: Texas A&M University Press, 1997), 643–651.

Document 5.19
President Lyndon Johnson Prepares His Generals to Brief the "Wise Men," Meeting Notes, March 26, 1968

President Johnson's anger at his domestic foes boils over in these "Notes of the President's Meeting with General Earle Wheeler, CJCS, and General Creighton Abrams, Commander of U.S. Forces in Vietnam [and Sec. Rusk]," taken March 26, 1968. The group gathered in the Family Dining Room of the White House from 10:30 a.m. to 12:15 p.m. It is clear from the discussion that the president has had about all he can take by this time—of both the presidency and the war in Vietnam. The notes were taken by Deputy Press Secretary Tom Johnson.

The President: I want you to meet with that group today. Stress that you have worked with the South Vietnamese closely. Tell them, in candor, we want to talk to you about the South Vietnamese. Give them the factual, cold honest picture as you see it. We don't want an inspirational talk or a gloom talk. Nitze won't even testify. It is the civilians that are cutting our guns out.

We weren't caught asleep during Tet. They lost 50,000. They are trying their damndest to recover.

Give them your plan, hope and belief.

[Sentence sanitized.] I want both of you at lunch. I want General Abrams to give us the whole pictures—pros and cons.

The bitterness has built up here. We hope we aren't attacked while this is going on.

General Ridgway said the strategic reserves are down to nothing. He said he thinks we have more commitments than we can handle.

Secretary Rusk: If we can't see some reasonable date, this country can't support a bottomless pit.

General Wheeler: The ARVN [South Vietnam's army] is doing well. The morale is good.

The President: Stress that.

General Wheeler: Westy said he understands the situation in the U.S. . . .

The President: Our fiscal situation is abominable. We have a deficit running over 20 [billion dollars]. We are not getting the tax bill. The deficit could be over 30. If it does, the interest rate will rise. The British pound may fall. The Canadian pound may fall. The dollar will be in danger. Unless we get a tax bill it will be unthinkable.

They say to get $10 in taxes we must get $10 in reductions of appropriations. We have to take one half from non-Vietnam defense expenditures. That will cause hell with [Georgia Democratic senator Richard] Russell, if we don't do that we have hell. What happens when you cut poverty, housing and education?

This is complicated by the fact that it is an election year. I don't give a damn about the election. I will be happy just to keep doing what is right and lose the election.

There has been a panic in the last three weeks. It is caused by Ted Kennedy's report on corruption and the ARVN and the GVN [Government of (South) Vietnam] being no good. And now a release that Westmoreland wants 206,000 more men, and a call-up of 400,000. That would cost $15 billion. That would hurt the dollar and gold.

The leaks to the *New York Times* hurt us. The country is demoralized. You must know about it. It's tough you can't have communications. A worker writes a paper for Clifford group and it's all over Georgetown. The people are trying to save us from ourselves. You must bear this in mind. Bobby [Democratic senator and presidential candidate Robert Kennedy, brother of President John F. Kennedy, and a bitter rival to President Johnson] advocated: (1) Rusk resigning. (2) Placing the war in the hands of a Commission. I said no.

I will have overwhelming disapproval in the polls and elections. I will go down the drain. I don't want the whole alliance and military pulled in with it. . . .

How can we get this job done? We need more money in an election year, more taxes in an election year, more troops in an election year and more cuts in an election year.

As yet I cannot tell them what they expect to get in return. We have no support for the war. This is caused by the 206,000 troop request, leaks, Ted Kennedy and Bobby Kennedy. . . .

I want you to tell them [the Wise Men] all the things that are true. Be sure it's factual. If you soldiers were as gloomy and doomy as the civilians you would have surrendered.

Source: David M. Barrett, ed., *Lyndon B. Johnson's Vietnam Papers: A Documentary Collection* (College Station: Texas A&M University Press, 1997), 706–710.

Document 5.20
President Lyndon Johnson Announces a Unilateral Bombing Halt and Withdraws from the Presidential Election, March 31, 1968

President Johnson did not often address the American people via television, and he did not often devote a major speech to the Vietnam War. He did both these things at the end of March 1968, in a speech in which he announced a de-escalation of the war. At the end of the speech, he announced that he would not seek reelection.

Good evening, my fellow Americans:

Tonight I want to speak to you of peace in Vietnam and Southeast Asia.

No other question so preoccupies our people. No other dream so absorbs the 250 million human beings who live in that part of the world. No other goal motivates American policy in Southeast Asia.

For years, representatives of our Government and others have traveled the world—seeking to find a basis for peace talks.

Since last September, they have carried the offer that I made public at San Antonio. That offer was this:

That the United States would stop its bombardment of North Vietnam when that would lead promptly to productive discussions—and that we would assume that North Vietnam would not take military advantage of our restraint.

Hanoi denounced this offer, both privately and publicly. Even while the search for peace was going on, North Vietnam rushed their preparations for a savage assault on the people, the government, and the allies of South Vietnam.

Their attack—during the Tet holidays—failed to achieve its principal objectives.

It did not collapse the elected government of South Vietnam or shatter its army—as the Communists had hoped.

It did not produce a "general uprising" among the people of the cities as they had predicted.

The Communists were unable to maintain control of any of the more than 30 cities that they attacked. And they took very heavy casualties.

But they did compel the South Vietnamese and their allies to move certain forces from the countryside into the cities.

They caused widespread disruption and suffering. Their attacks, and the battles that followed, made refugees of half a million human beings.

The Communists may renew their attack any day.

They are, it appears, trying to make 1968 the year of decision in South Vietnam—the year that brings, if not final victory or defeat, at least a turning point in the struggle. This much is clear:

If they do mount another round of heavy attacks, they will not succeed in destroying the fighting power of South Vietnam and its allies.

But tragically, this is also clear: Many men—on both sides of the struggle—will be lost. A nation that has already suffered 20 years of warfare will suffer once again. Armies on both sides will take new casualties. And the war will go on.

There is no need for this to be so.

There is no need to delay the talks that could bring an end to this long and this bloody war.

Tonight, I renew the offer I made last August—to stop the bombardment of North Vietnam. We ask that talks begin promptly, that they be serious talks on the substance of peace. We assume that during those talks Hanoi will not take advantage of our restraint.

We are prepared to move immediately toward peace through negotiations.

So, tonight, in the hope that this action will lead to early talks, I am taking the first step to deescalate the conflict. We are reducing—substantially reducing—the present level of hostilities.

And we are doing so unilaterally, and at once.

Tonight, I have ordered our aircraft and our naval vessels to make no attacks on North Vietnam, except in the area north of the demilitarized zone where the continuing enemy buildup directly threatens allied forward positions and where the movements of their troops and supplies are clearly related to that threat.

The area in which we are stopping our attacks includes almost 90 percent of North Vietnam's population, and most of its territory. Thus there will be no attacks around the principal populated areas, or in the food-producing areas of North Vietnam. . . .

On many occasions I have told the American people that we would send to Vietnam those forces that are required to accomplish our mission there. So, with that as our guide, we have previously authorized a force level of approximately 525,000.

Some weeks ago—to help meet the enemy's new offensive—we sent to Vietnam about 11,000 additional Marine and airborne troops. They were deployed by air in 48 hours, on an emergency basis. But the artillery, tank, aircraft, medical, and other units that were needed to work with and to support these infantry troops in combat could not then accompany them by air on that short notice.

In order that these forces may reach maximum combat effectiveness, the Joint Chiefs of Staff have recommended to me that we should prepare to send—during the next 5 months—support troops totaling approximately 13,500 men.

A portion of these men will be made available from our active forces. The balance will come from reserve component units which will be called up for service.

The actions that we have taken since the beginning of the year
- to reequip the South Vietnamese forces,
- to meet our responsibilities in Korea, as well as our responsibilities in Vietnam,
- to meet price increases and the cost of activating and deploying reserve forces,
- to replace helicopters and provide the other military supplies we need, all of these actions are going to require additional expenditures.

The tentative estimate of those additional expenditures is $2.5 billion in this fiscal year, and $2.6 billion in the next fiscal year.

These projected increases in expenditures for our national security will bring into sharper focus the Nation's need for immediate action: action to protect the prosperity of the American people and to protect the strength and the stability of our American dollar. . . .

Now let me give you my estimate of the chances for peace:
- the peace that will one day stop the bloodshed in South Vietnam,
- that will permit all the Vietnamese people to rebuild and develop their land,
- that will permit us to turn more fully to our own tasks here at home.

I cannot promise that the initiative that I have announced tonight will be completely successful in achieving peace any more than the 30 others that we have undertaken and agreed to in recent years.

But it is our fervent hope that North Vietnam, after years of fighting that have left the issue unresolved, will now cease its efforts to achieve a military victory and will join with us in moving toward the peace table. . . .

I believe that a peaceful Asia is far nearer to reality because of what America has done in Vietnam. I believe that the men who endure the dangers of battle—fighting there for us tonight—are helping the entire world avoid far greater conflicts, far wider wars, far more destruction, than this one.

The peace that will bring them home someday will come. Tonight I have offered the first in what I hope will be a series of mutual moves toward peace.

I pray that it will not be rejected by the leaders of North Vietnam. I pray that they will accept it as a means by which the sacrifices of their own people may be ended. And I ask your help and your support, my fellow citizens, for this effort to reach across the battle-field toward an early peace.

Finally, my fellow Americans, let me say this:

Of those to whom much is given, much is asked. I cannot say and no man could say that no more will be asked of us.

Yet, I believe that now, no less than when the decade began, this generation of Americans is willing to "pay any price, bear any burden, meet any hardship, support any friend, oppose any foe to assure the survival and the success of liberty."

Since those words were spoken by John F. Kennedy, the people of America have kept that compact with mankind's noblest cause.

And we shall continue to keep it.

Yet, I believe that we must always be mindful of this one thing, whatever the trials and the tests ahead. The ultimate strength of our country and our cause will lie not in powerful weapons or infinite resources or boundless wealth, but will lie in the unity of our people.

This I believe very deeply.

Throughout my entire public career I have followed the personal philosophy that I am a free man, an American, a public servant, and a member of my party, in that order always and only.

For 37 years in the service of our Nation, first as a Congressman, as a Senator, and as Vice President, and now as your President, I have put the unity of the people first. I have put it ahead of any divisive partisanship.

And in these times as in times before, it is true that a house divided against itself by the spirit of faction, of party, of region, of religion, of race, is a house that cannot stand.

There is division in the American house now. There is divisiveness among us all tonight. And holding the trust that is mine, as President of all the people, I cannot disregard the peril to the progress of the American people and the hope and the prospect of peace for all peoples.

So, I would ask all Americans, whatever their personal interests or concern, to guard against divisiveness and all its ugly consequences.

Fifty-two months and 10 days ago, in a moment of tragedy and trauma, the duties of this office fell upon me. I asked then for your help and God's, that we might continue America on its course, binding up our wounds, healing our history, moving forward in new unity, to clear the American agenda and to keep the American commitment for all of our people.

United we have kept that commitment. United we have enlarged that commitment.

Through all time to come, I think America will be a stronger nation, a more just society, and a land of greater opportunity and fulfillment because of what we have all done together in these years of unparalleled achievement.

Our reward will come in the life of freedom, peace, and hope that our children will enjoy through ages ahead.

What we won when all of our people united just must not now be lost in suspicion, distrust, selfishness, and politics among any of our people.

Believing this as I do, I have concluded that I should not permit the Presidency to become involved in the partisan divisions that are developing in this political year.

With America's sons in the fields far away, with America's future under challenge right here at home, with our hopes and the world's hopes for peace in the balance every day, I do not believe that I should devote an hour or a day of my time to any personal partisan causes or to any duties other than the awesome duties of this office—the Presidency of your country.

Accordingly, I shall not seek, and I will not accept, the nomination of my party for another term as your President.

But let men everywhere know, however, that a strong, a confident, and a vigilant America stands ready tonight to seek an honorable peace—and stands ready tonight to defend an honored cause—whatever the price, whatever the burden, whatever the sacrifice that duty may require.

Thank you for listening. Good night and God bless all of you.

Source: Lyndon Johnson, "The President's Address to the Nation Announcing Steps to Limit the War in Vietnam and Reporting His Decision Not to Seek Reelection," March 31, 1968, in *Public Papers of the Presidents of the United States: Lyndon B. Johnson, 1963–1969,* from the American Presidency Project, University of California, Santa Barbara, www.presidency.ucsb.edu.

CHAPTER SIX

Richard Nixon

Détente and the China Card

Richard Nixon won the election of 1968; the Vietnam War lost. Hubert Humphrey, the sitting vice president, had secured his party's nomination at the Democrats' riotous convention in Chicago. He struggled throughout the campaign under the weight of the "Johnson-Humphrey administration's" conduct of the war. His attempt, late in the campaign season, to disassociate himself from President Lyndon Johnson's highly unpopular war leadership helped make the contest close, but it was a classic case of too little, too late. Besides, Richard Nixon had already laid claim to what was essentially the same political real estate: While defeat was unthinkable, escalation was out of the question. The war, both candidates agreed, must end.

Nixon's recitation of this message was polished. The former vice president to Dwight Eisenhower knew a thing or two about defeating a Democratic opponent

President Richard Nixon and First Lady Patricia Nixon visit the Great Wall of China on February 24, 1972. Source: Nixon Presidential Materials, National Archives and Records Administration.

tied to an unpopular war. Like Ike in 1952, Nixon in 1968 suggested that, if elected, he would bring a stalemated conflict in Asia to a satisfactory close. Nixon, however, did not have the military credentials to get by with an Eisenhower-like promise merely to "go to Vietnam." Instead, he played to his own strength—his reputation for intellect. He had devised a plan, he said, that would end the war. He would reveal his secret plan upon election.

The only candidate who did not run against the war that year was the independent, George Wallace. Wallace, the segregationist governor of Georgia, and Gen. Curtis LeMay, his running mate and former air force chief of staff, appealed to voters alienated from the bipartisan Cold War consensus on civil rights and the war in Vietnam. Civil rights for African Americans had been backed, at last, by national-minded Democrats as well as Republicans. Starting with Harry Truman, Cold War presidents had consistently backed civil rights as necessary to counter Soviet propaganda in the third world about how the United States treated its own nonwhite population. Courage in civil rights was not a popular message among white Southerners. Nor was another Cold War imperative, caution in Vietnam. President Johnson had constantly worried that if he made a misstep in that war, he would unwittingly bring the Chinese and perhaps the Soviets into the conflict. Critics of Johnson's cautious approach demanded that the United States unleash its full military power to win in Vietnam. By rallying voters, many of them in the Deep South, who opposed these policies, the pro-war team of Wallace and LeMay won roughly 10 million votes. This was a sizable number for a third-party candidate and sufficient to prevent either major party candidate from gaining a majority of the popular vote, but it was hardly enough for victory. Overall, the 1968 presidential election resulted in an overwhelming repudiation of the Vietnam War and an extremely narrow margin of victory for Nixon, who picked up 31.8 million votes to Humphrey's 31.3 million.

Richard Nixon took his slim margin of victory as a challenge and a caution. Frustrated because he could not plausibly claim a mandate, especially with Congress still under the firm control of Democrats in both houses, he felt challenged to do better next time. In the reelection campaign, he would be certain to secure his right flank to ward off a repeat challenge from Wallace or any other potential spoiler. The election's cautionary message was even simpler: be rid of war. "I'm not going to end up like LBJ," Nixon resolved, "holed up in the White House afraid to show my face on the street. I'm going to put a stop to that war. Fast."[1] It was a good thing that the president-elect had that secret plan of his.

A SECRET PLAN

Of course, there was no secret plan to end the war. But Nixon's transition team had a basic concept, which they refined before the inauguration. To reduce American casualties, which Nixon believed were driving public dissatisfaction with the war, the U.S. Army would draw down its numbers in Vietnam. To compensate for the diminished role of the army, the United States would increase its efforts to help South Vietnamese ground forces become more effective and more lethal. In addition, U.S. airpower would put "irresistible pressure" upon the enemy in the North, while the Central Intelligence Agency (CIA), working in conjunction with special operations personnel from the U.S. and South Vietnamese armed forces, would target the already decimated Communist insurgency in the South.[2] Nixon's plan also looked beyond the battlefield. Through "linkage," the United States would induce the Soviet and Chinese patrons of North Vietnam to persuade their client to accept a negotiated settlement.

"Vietnamization," as the plan came to be known, was but an element of a comprehensive effort to redirect American policy in the Cold War. The American people, the president believed, were tiring of the Cold War and turning inward. Vietnamization would permit the president to reverse this growing impulse toward isolation.[3]

During his first six months in office, President Nixon announced the first concrete steps in his plan: troop withdrawals and a commitment to end the highly unpopular draft. The withdrawals began in June 1969, with an announcement that 25,000 troops would soon be brought home. This began a process of periodic withdrawal announcements. Rather than put forth a timetable for a series of withdrawals, the president preferred to declare each withdrawal individually. The military rationale for this approach was plain. Releasing a withdrawal timetable would tell the enemy just how long they had to hang on before they would be left to settle their conflict with the South Vietnamese directly. It was also good politics to hoard the withdrawal announcements until they were most needed at home.

Within a year, the U.S. military commitment to South Vietnam had shrunk from 540,000 to 475,000 troops. Over the same time, there was a considerable drop in American casualties, from 8,400 battle deaths in the first half of 1969 to 3,900 in the second half.[4] It helped that the North Vietnamese were focused on domestic priorities of their own—rebuilding from the bombing campaign of the late Johnson years and reorganizing their South Vietnamese cadres into a Provisional Revolutionary Government, the successor to the National Liberation Front (NLF).

The anticipation that the United States would need fewer service personnel in Vietnam permitted the Nixon administration to push ahead in its first year with a plan to end military conscription. Thanks in part to the post–World War II baby boom, military service had gone from being a rite of passage for a generation to a burden carried by a minority. In 1958, 70 percent of twenty-six-year-old American men had been military veterans. The comparable figure in 1966 was only 46 percent. Further, the Selective Service had responded to the decreased need for personnel by adopting the practice of "channeling," the wide-ranging granting of deferments—millions of which went to students in college or graduate school.

The result was not, as was often supposed, a "conscripted horde of youths" forced to die for their country in the Vietnam War.[5] Draftees accounted for only half of all field forces in Vietnam and just one-third of those killed in combat. Likewise, combat deaths of African Americans, at twelve percent of all American combat deaths, were not disproportionate. Nonetheless, it was difficult to justify sending *anyone* to risk his life for a cause to which so many Americans were no longer committed. Moreover, liberal critics of the draft had been lately joined by conservatives, who saw military service as a form of "taxation" and favored a return to a volunteer military.

In March 1969 Nixon appointed a commission to study the future of the draft. The commission's chair, Thomas Gates, was a leading advocate of an All Volunteer Force. Within a year, the Gates Commission issued a report that came to the predictable conclusion that the draft should end. Even before the commission's work was finished, however, Nixon replaced the system's draft boards with a lottery. With few exceptions, a young man's prospects of being called to service would now depend on chance alone. The following year, on the way toward the abolition of conscription altogether in 1973, the administration limited eligible men's vulnerability to the lottery to a single year. If you weren't drafted in your nineteenth year of life, you were home free forever.

Nixon put these changes in military personnel policy into perspective when he revealed his plan for Vietnamization in a press conference at Guam on July 25, 1969. He elaborated on the plan in his legendary speech to the "silent majority" on November 3 (**Document**

6.1), and he made it the centerpiece of his first annual report to Congress on foreign affairs the following February. On all these occasions, the president articulated a consistent message. The United States could not and would not "conceive all the plans, design all the programs, execute all the decisions, and undertake all the defense of the free nations of the world." The people of the countries being helped would have to carry a greater part of the load from now on. "We shall look," the president said, "to the nation directly threatened to assume the primary responsibility of providing the manpower for its defense." [6] This was the crux of the matter, and it was enshrined as the Nixon Doctrine.

Nixon knew that his doctrine would be controversial. Even within his administration, there were those who feared the announcement would demoralize America's allies and give hope to its enemies. Nixon's statement at Guam had been in fact an end run around his own national security adviser, Henry Kissinger, as well as the State Department. The president was not intended to make news that day. Nixon was sensitive to the issues raised by critics within his administration, but he thought he could prove them wrong by demonstrating that burden sharing did not mean giving up. In Vietnam, he meant to increase the pressure on the enemy by increasing the pressure on the South Vietnamese to take up a greater share of the fight. Perhaps it was wishful thinking to pair the pursuit of victory with the pursuit of disengagement, but this was the path Nixon chose. The *way* in which the president chose to advance his doctrine reveals a great deal about Richard Nixon's strengths and weaknesses as a Cold War president.

A SECRET WAR

War breeds secrets as surely as it enlarges government and expands executive power. Never before Nixon, however, had a Cold War president tried to conduct a major military operation in secret. That is what President Nixon did when he ordered Operation Menu, an open-ended bombing campaign against North Vietnamese positions in Cambodia. Cambodia was ostensibly neutral in the Cold War, but the North Vietnamese used the port of Sihanoukville (Kampong Saom) as their own, moved freely across the border, and—it was believed—had set up within Cambodia a regional headquarters for the war, the Central Office for South Vietnam (COSVN).

Fear of domestic political backlash had prevented President Johnson from ordering significant incursions into Cambodia. In Nixon's calculations, this made action against targets there all the more attractive. By ordering that the war be expanded into Cambodia, Nixon intended to demonstrate to the Communists that he would not be paralyzed by domestic politics: here was an American president to be reckoned with, one who was willing to hide violence behind a veil of peaceful rhetoric. This was the first step in Nixon's "madman" gambit by which he hoped to frighten the enemy into believing that he might stop at nothing to get his way in Vietnam.

To prevent disclosure, the president controlled the operation from the White House and the National Security Council. The secretary of the air force was not informed, and those who did know—all the military personnel in the chain of command, down to the pilots who flew the missions—were ordered to lie.[7] The enemy might have revealed the bombing, but doing so would have given the lie to their claim not to be in Cambodia. As for the government of Cambodia, historians debate whether Prince Sihanouk even knew of the operation beforehand. Nixon coupled his secret expansion of the military's mission with an equally secret signal to the Soviets. Late in 1969, by order of the president, the Joint Chiefs of Staff undertook a Readiness Test in which B-52s from the Strategic Air Command were loaded with nuclear weapons and flown over Alaska. The exercise, undisclosed to the public, was easily detectable to the Soviet Union.[8] The United States, Nixon wanted the Soviets to believe, was ready for anything. If the Soviets knew what was good for them, they would put pressure on North Vietnam to accept a negotiated settlement with the South.

The results of these secret operations were discouraging. North Vietnam continued to insist that the first step in any peace process be full withdrawal of American military forces from Vietnam. This was so clearly unacceptable to the Americans and the South Vietnamese that it was interpreted as merely a pretext for the continuation of war. For their part, the Soviets insisted that although they continued to serve as the North's industrial base, they had no influence over their strong-willed protégés in Hanoi.

On March 18, 1970, almost a year into Operation Menu, Laos' prime minister, Gen. Lon Nol, deposed Sihanouk while the prince was on a diplomatic mission to Moscow and Beijing. Gen. Creighton Abrams, the American commander in Vietnam, saw an opportunity in this change of government: Lon Nol was overtly pro-Western, and a ground attack against North Vietnamese positions inside Cambodia would serve as a show of support to a new friend in the region. (Lon Nol, however, was apparently not consulted and was dismayed at the potentially destabilizing influence of the operation once it commenced.) The ground operation began April 29, with 20,000 troops, 15,000 of them American and the rest South Vietnamese. As a leading text on U.S. military history laconically describes the results, "The logistical damage to the NVA was significant, but the accompanying political results discouraged the administration."[9]

The president knew the political stakes were high in opening a new front in an old war, but he was willing to "go for broke."[10] Although by this time America's major European allies had themselves grown weary of the war, the president continued to view the battle in broad geopolitical terms. It was vital, he believed, for the United States to be seen as having kept its word in Vietnam. "It would be the easiest thing in the world for me simply to order our troops out of there," he said to John Ehrlichman, a close White House aide, "but if I did none of our allies could count on the United States' word again."[11] What was more, the president truly believed he could get the war "wound up" in 1970 with a big push, if the United States did not "crumble at home."[12]

An enormous gamble, its very boldness inspired Nixon. About one month prior to Nixon's late April decision, his chief of staff, H. R. "Bob" Haldeman, had been worried. The president seemed to "have lost a lot of the basic 'feel' of the job that he had."[13] The *Apollo 13* crisis mid-month only made things worse. Equipment failure led to several days of high drama during which the fate of the spacecraft's crew was in doubt. The president paid diligent attention but was reduced to a mere spectator. The crisis of opportunity created by Lon Nol's ascent was much more to Nixon's liking. In contemplating whether to expand the ground war into Cambodia, the president exhibited new energy. Going with minimal sleep for days on end, Nixon spent all his waking hours focused on this single issue. Two days before announcing his decision, Nixon went on a long walk around the White House grounds with Ehrlichman, telling him that he would be taking over the domestic side of the presidency for a while and urging him to think through "what you might have to do in terms of police and national guard and all that sort of thing."[14] On the eve of the announcement, the president compared for the benefit of his aides the decision that he had made with those faced by Presidents Kennedy and Eisenhower in the Cuban Missile Crisis and in Lebanon. Nixon thought that his own decision was the hardest, because it was made voluntarily.[15]

On April 30, 1970—at the end of a full day and after approximately three hours of sleep the night before—the president went before the nation to announce an "incursion" into Cambodia (**Document 6.2**). Even within the White House, reaction was harsh. Kissinger thought the decision rash and the speech regrettable: "Apocalyptic in its claim" and "excessive in its pretensions," it needlessly personalized the conflict.[16] The anti-war movement, naturally, shared Kissinger's criticisms and expressed them with less restraint. Up to this moment, Nixon had lowered the volume of the anti-war protestors with his withdrawals and his movement toward a volunteer military. The Cambodian incursion gave new voice to war protestors and Nixon haters.

THE WAR AT HOME

As Nixon took office in 1969, the movement against the Vietnam War was gaining momentum. Indeed, its most successful moment came in Nixon's first year in office. The "Moratorium," a series of peace demonstrations held in Washington, D.C., and several other cities on October 15, 1969, was promoted as an opportunity to take time off from work or school to demonstrate concern about the war. Hundreds of thousands of people—some said millions—participated, the majority of them middle class and middle aged. The Moratorium challenged the popular image of protestors as radical students and received highly favorable treatment in the media. The president was so concerned that he decided to strike back with his speech rallying support from the "silent majority" on November 3, in advance of a second Moratorium planned for November 15. Nixon and his speechwriters knew that, to the great detriment of the anti-war movement, the general public sometimes conflated responsible dissent with radical, even revolutionary assaults on authority. Unfortunately for the anti-war movement, the radical fringe soon took center stage.

The most influential of the youth movements was the Students for a Democratic Society (SDS). SDS was an offshoot of the League for Industrial Democracy, an American socialist organization tracing its roots back to the early 1900s. The founders of SDS, including Tom Hayden and Paul Booth, were intent on revolutionizing American society, starting with colleges and universities. Its principles—idealistic, even utopian—were anti-materialist and anti-capitalist. The Cold War was the backdrop to its famous statement of principles, the Port Huron Statement, issued in summer 1962. "Our work," said the statement's signatories, "is guided by the sense that we may be the last generation in the experiment with living." [17] SDS's purpose, however, was not to end the war, but to transcend it, through participatory politics and egalitarian economics. Once the political process and the economic system were remade, everything else would fall into place. This highbrow agenda was soon replaced by resistance to the war in Vietnam. From 1965 to 1968, SDS, along with unaffiliated campus radicals across the nation, moved from the pursuit of vague ideals to active resistance against the government. In 1969 SDS began to break apart. In its confrontation with the reality of the war, the organization's leadership had been forced to take a stand on just how far they were prepared to go to stop it. In that year, the protestors were forced out by the bomb-throwers; SDS was hijacked by a faction of its most extreme members, the Weather Underground.

The "Weathermen" were an offshoot of the Maoist Revolutionary Youth Movement, itself a faction within SDS. They were not so much anti-war as anti-American. Having persuaded themselves that global revolution was imminent, they decided to help it along by embracing violence. After minimal success in inciting riots in the cities, the Weather Underground came to specialize in the bombing of government and military installations. They were not alone. In the name of revolution, a number of other radical groups such as the Black Panther Party and the Symbionese Liberation Army committed acts of violence, including armed robbery, kidnapping, and murder.

On elite college campuses, radicals from "the underground" were lionized and their tactics—including even the use of deadly force—imitated. From January 1969 through April 1970, there were more than 1,000 bombings or bombing attempts, which caused forty-one deaths. The majority of the bombings took place on college campuses. Less than 10 percent of the bombings were attributable to simple criminal activity; radicals of one stripe or another were responsible for the rest. In an indication of how anti-war violence overlapped with racial violence, black extremists were credited with 20 percent and white extremists with 14 percent of the explosions. During the same period, there were well over 7,000 arrests for violent acts of all types at colleges and universities. The violence of the "movement" caused some government officials to speak publicly of a violent response. After a fatal confrontation between protestors and police near the University of California at Berkeley, Governor Ronald Reagan garnered both hatred and praise when he said: "If it takes a bloodbath, let's get it over with. No more appeasement." [18]

Violence peaked after Nixon's April 30, 1970, speech on Cambodia. On May 4, in a confused series of events, four students were killed by National Guardsmen at Kent State University in Ohio. The president, in Haldeman's words, was "very disturbed. Afraid his decision set it off." [19] Nixon's private sensitivity to this tragedy was undermined by a callous statement he made in public just two days later. "Bums," he said, were "blowing up the campuses." [20] In one of the more bizarre moments in Cold War presidential history, on May 9, 1970, the president made an impromptu visit to talk to some of the "bums" at the Lincoln Memorial, where thousands of youthful protestors were encamped. Contrary to myth, the president did not just talk football to the unimpressed collegians. He tried to talk policy, to "connect" on matters of substance. It didn't work.

Unable to connect with the protestors, the president went back to his base. After several hundred construction workers in Lower Manhattan attacked anti-war protestors at a rally in May 1970, the president invited leaders of the workers' union to the White House. The White House also enlisted the evangelist Billy Graham as well as the comedian Bob Hope and other mainstream entertainment icons to speak out in support of the president. Later, Elvis Presley volunteered his services in a famous impromptu visit to the White House in December 1970. "The drug culture, the hippie elements, the SDS, Black Panthers, etc.," the King wrote in a hand-written letter requesting a meeting, "do NOT consider me as their enemy or as they call it The Establishment. I call it America and I love it. Sir, I can and will be of any service that I can to help The Country out."[21]

Before the crisis unleashed by Nixon's speech of April 30 was over, the White House had taken on the feel, in the words of White House counsel Chuck Colson, of a Latin American presidential palace awaiting a coup. Elements of the Eighty-second Airborne were secreted in the Old Executive Office Building to provide firepower that the Secret Service did not possess. But within weeks of the Cambodia incursion, the president decided to de-escalate the war at home. Characteristically, however, he sought to do so through secrecy and deception.

On May 31, 1970, at the "Western" White House in California, Nixon ordered his national security team to rally around a new statement of policy. The combat phase of the Cambodia operation was all but over; the United States was at that point merely providing support to South Vietnamese troops when necessary to protect American lives. "That is what we will say publicly," he stated. "But now, let's talk about what we will actually do." The military should "put the air in there and not spare the horses." "Just do it," he instructed. "Don't come back and ask permission each time."[22]

Frustrated by his critics, Nixon increasingly turned to the powers of the presidency to take unilateral action. When news of the secret bombing of Cambodia leaked, the president was furious. To catch the miscreant, Nixon ordered the Federal Bureau of Investigation (FBI) to conduct an investigation of potential leak sources. Four journalists and thirteen presidential appointees were placed under electronic surveillance. Unfortunately for the president, the director of the FBI, the legendary and stubborn J. Edgar Hoover, argued with the White House over the suitability of certain targets. Nixon's solution was to take the task in-house with the creation of a Special Investigations Unit. In June 1971, when the *New York Times* began to publish excerpts of a top-secret Pentagon study of the Vietnam War, he was ready.

Even before the Supreme Court, in a June 30, 1971, 6-3 decision, refused to stop publication of what were called the *Pentagon Papers* (**Document 6.3**), the president had decided this was an ideal occasion to employ his clandestine White House operation. Nixon wanted to punish Daniel Ellsberg, the former Defense Department official who had admitted sending the *New York Times* a copy of the study, which he had stolen from the RAND Corporation, the think tank where he was employed at the time. Even though the history contained in the *Pentagon Papers* ended with the Johnson administration, Nixon felt it was "despicable" to release government secrets in wartime and demanded of his aides that Ellsberg and the whole "Kennedy elite" be made to pay for their actions.[23] Kissinger added fuel to the fire. He later recounted reminding the president of the stakes involved: "If Hanoi concluded that our domestic support was eroding, for whatever reason, it was bound to hold fast to its position. The war would continue; there would be no chance of peace in 1971 except through capitulation."[24]

In the summer of 1971, the Special Investigations Unit was therefore put to work to undermine Ellsberg. Nixon urged on his special operatives. "I want him exposed," he reportedly told Colson, "I don't care how you do it but get it done."[25] In room 16 of the Old Executive Office Building, where the unit labored, David Young hung a sign on the door: "Plumbers." Inside, Young and a team of other Nixon campaign operatives, including G. Gordon Liddy and E. Howard Hunt,[26] pored over the transcripts of wiretaps on Ellsberg and analyzed his cancelled checks—all obtained illegally through White House contacts in the shadowy world of ex-CIA agents and Cuban-American veterans of the Bay of Pigs. Apparently not content with what they found through these sources, the Plumbers conducted a break-in at the office of Ellsberg's psychiatrist, Dr. Lewis Fielding, in September 1971.

Eventually, government prosecutors learned of the break-in. Feeling they had no choice, they revealed what they knew to Judge W. Matthew Byrne Jr., who was presiding over Ellsberg's trial for espionage, theft, and conspiracy in federal district court in Massachusetts. After the administration refused to comment on the prosecutors' report (and after newspaper stories revealed that the judge had recently met with White House officials to discuss the president's alleged interest in hiring Byrne for the top spot at the FBI), the judge dismissed the case. The Plumbers' operation had backfired, and Ellsberg was set free.

Ironically, the president might have had more success against his critics had he trusted his basic foreign policy and simply left his critics alone. Vietnamization was gradually reducing U.S. troop levels and casualties. By the end of 1971, fewer than 157,000 American service personnel remained in South Vietnam. Over the last six months of the year, 276 Americans died from wounds sustained in combat for a total of 2,357 deaths in 1971, compared with 11,616 in 1969 and 6,081 in 1970.

As a result, the anti-war movement lost its ability to mobilize large crowds. The American drawdown also diminished the likelihood of a repeat of such incidents as the My Lai Massacre, which was reported publicly in November 1969. By the 1972 presidential campaign, the anti-war movement had become so anemic that the president had to instigate a "mob attack" against his limousine at a campaign rally in San Jose, California. "Wanting some confrontation," in Haldeman's words, the president delayed his departure to permit time for protestors to organize, and then provoked them by standing on the hood of his car and flashing his trademark "V for Victory" sign.[27]

The president was similarly combative against his critics in Congress, who were much more vocal and prolific. That "politics stops at the water's edge" is a myth, despite what generations of Americans have been taught about the way things *used* to be, back in the Cold War and back in the Good Old Days before that. Foreign affairs have regularly been at the core of party differences. The first American political parties, the Federalists and the Republicans, broke out into open factional fighting because of their vigorous disagreement over

President George Washington's foreign policy. When the United States began for the first time to exert sustained influence abroad at the turn of the twentieth century, the Democratic and Republican parties were sharply divided over the foreign policy of William McKinley and Theodore Roosevelt.

The periods during World Wars I and II were modestly different, though "consensus" was sometimes achieved only by criminalizing party differences. In the Great War, it was a federal offense to say or write anything injurious to the war effort. During World War II, the Democratic administration managed to maintain considerable support for its conduct of the war from the people at large and their representatives in Congress, and it did so by relying more on persuasion than intimidation. When the shooting stopped, however, party differences again reemerged.

In the early Cold War, both parties and their leaders worked strenuously to "return" to what was in fact a mythic era, one of routine harmony in foreign affairs. Bad history proved nevertheless to be good politics to the mid-1960s. Some more liberal politicians and commentators said the return to Eden had gone too far, to the extent that difference was interpreted as deviance, and dissent as disloyalty. Other, more conservative political actors were just grateful for the appearance of solidarity in a conflict where everyone agreed national will was critical to success. The parties would occasionally launch partisan attacks against one another for alleged apostasy, but that only underlined their devotion to a common creed. For almost two decades, virtually all American politicians agreed on the vital importance of battling Communists. Those who did not were shunned and marginalized.

As time passed, however, political fissures widened. Disagreement over the implementation of America's consensual foreign policy goal came to overlap with disagreements over domestic issues, promoting the formation of new factions within the major parties. Finally, late in the Johnson administration, leading members of the Democratic Party dissociated themselves from the Vietnam War. A number of hawkish Democrats abandoned the party in response and helped to elect the Republican Nixon president. It would take many more years, however, before this seismic shift in the party system would at last, after the Cold War had ended, bring about a Republican majority in Congress. The result was that Nixon found himself in an awkward situation. There had been many instances of divided party government in the United States before, but it had been almost 100 years since a president had been elected without having at least one house of Congress under the control of his party. Moreover, the Democratic majority that Nixon faced was more united, *in opposition,* than had been the Democratic majority with which Eisenhower had worked for six of his eight years as president. The Democrats were not shy about letting the president know what they thought about his foreign policy. In Nixon's first term, the Senate took up eighty-six Vietnam War resolutions. The great majority of them, like the Cooper-Church Amendment of June 1970, expressed the sentiment of the body against the president's conduct of the war (**Document 6.4**). Votes on these resolutions and on other measures related to the war, such as military appropriations bills, were highly partisan throughout Nixon's years in office.[28]

Nixon's battles at home led him to redefine success in Vietnam. Although the president never took seriously Vermont Republican senator George Aiken's pithy comment of October 19, 1966, that the United States should "declare victory and go home," he did come to believe that, by staying in Vietnam too long, the administration risked alienating the American public and America's allies from the wider Cold War.[29] As a consequence, the "good enough" definition of success in Vietnam came to be an agreement under which the United States could complete its withdrawal as a matter of choice—without appearing to have been forced out. Once the North and South Vietnamese resumed their fight to the finish, the American contribution would be limited to airpower. A "decent interval" would separate the American pullout from whatever happened then.

The president endorsed the decent interval scenario on numerous occasions from early 1971 on. In talking to Kissinger, his national security adviser, in March of that year, Nixon displayed no illusions about the prospects for the South Vietnamese following an international agreement that would permit a U.S. withdrawal (**Document 6.5**). The point was to get out, as the two men made clear later that month in a conversation in which they put the need for withdrawal into the context of the upcoming campaign for Nixon's reelection (**Document 6.6**). Vietnam, Kissinger and Nixon agreed, could not be allowed to consume two presidents in succession. There were, after all, other foreign policy issues that meant more to Nixon personally. In an April 14 telephone call, Nixon and Kissinger weighed the costs and benefits of one such issue, changing the relationship between the United States and Communist China. Not least among the benefits of pursuing such a change was that it would divert attention from Vietnam (**Document 6.7**). The linkage between Vietnam and China was further reinforced by Kissinger in his historic visit to brief the Chinese foreign minister in confidence on the president's initiative. In editing the briefing book that his aides had assembled for him in preparation, Kissinger inserted in his own handwriting the remark, "We want a decent interval. You have our assurance" (**Document 6.8**).

THE OPENING TO CHINA

President Nixon sent numerous diplomatic signals to the Communist People's Republic of China (PRC) to indicate his government's interest in forging a new relationship. He made use of the unilateral power of a president to ease travel and trade restrictions. He also conveyed diplomatic messages to the Chinese leadership through a trusted intermediary, the Communist (but anti-Soviet) dictator of Romania. The PRC was, as it happens, interested.

The Chinese had become anxious about Soviet intentions. Soviet-Chinese relations had become so strained recently that the two countries had engaged in armed clashes along their border. In 1971, when India and Pakistan went to war, the Soviets supported India, China's historic rival. Chinese domestic politics also played a role in explaining China's openness to a new relationship with the United States. By 1971 Maoism had failed as a world revolutionary model, and Chairman Mao Zedong's latest dramatic domestic initiative, the Great Proletarian Cultural Revolution, had led to economic turmoil at the end of the 1960s and into the 1970s. China was in desperate need of access to the Western technology that might enable the Chinese to restore their country to some measure of economic viability.

Nixon and Mao were ready for a mutual opening. But what of the American public? Attitudes toward mainland China had been particularly bitter during the Cold War within Nixon's own party. Republican leaders routinely railed against the Democrats for having "lost" China to the Communists in the first place. The Republicans had, however, an enduring fascination with the "Orient." Even during the decades of American isolationism, the Grand Old Party was never truly isolated from Asia. Democratic Party liberals, for their part, could be counted on to support any policy that promised to tone down the harsh rhetoric fueled by the fear of monolithic communism. To prepare the American people for a change in orientation toward China, Nixon needed merely a pretext—the diplomatic equivalent of an accidental encounter by the watercooler of two old corporate rivals.

Mao provided just such an excuse for the initiation of a dialogue, by seizing upon the chance encounter of Chinese and American Ping-Pong players at a world tournament in Japan on April 4, 1971 (**Document 6.9**). At Mao's order, the Chinese team invited the American team to tour China. The trip, hastily arranged for April 11–17, was a sensation, and "Ping-Pong diplomacy" won rave reviews in the American press (**Document 6.10**). Nixon followed up this "citizens' diplomacy" by sending Kissinger as his special envoy on a secret trip that July to meet with his Chinese counterpart, Zhou Enlai. Zhou was seemingly not impressed, even when Alexander Haig, Kissinger's deputy, in a follow-up mission that took place in January of 1972, promised to give to the Chinese U.S. intelligence on Soviet troop positions (**Document 6.11**). Zhou boasted to Mao that Kissinger was so eager for a new relationship that he was like a loose woman "tarting herself up and offering herself at the door."[30] His assessment was a bit unfair, but Zhou and Mao knew that Nixon was on a deadline set by the rules of democratic politics. Without any worries about democratic accountability on their part, Zhou and Mao could more easily afford to play the part of reluctant suitor. The next month, during President Nixon's visit to China, Mao toyed with the Americans, turning their anxiety about third world revolution against them and dismissing the Americans' argument about Soviet encirclement (**Documents 6.12 and 6.13**).

Mao may have been more in control of the relationship than Nixon, but it was the American president who claimed the glory for having made the climactic public visit to the capital of his adversary. This was the sort of dramatic, personal event that was ideal for television, and viewers throughout the world were able to follow Nixon's progress at the epochal meeting. The drama was greatly enhanced by the secrecy with which the trip was planned. The White House had managed to avoid leaks about the preparatory moves, so that Nixon's summer 1971 announcement of the January 1972 summit took everyone (including a very displeased Soviet leadership) by surprise.

Domestically, the reaction was not at first what Nixon had hoped for. Supporters of Taiwan were outraged when, in the interim between the announcement and Nixon's trip, the non-Communist Republic of China lost its seat in the United Nations to the PRC. President Nixon had pursued a "Two Chinas" compromise but lost control of the situation.

His ambassador to the UN, George Bush, had been kept in the dark about the White House's diplomatic overtures to the PRC, which weakened the influence that he might have been able to exert within the organization. When the positive vote to expel Taiwan was reported to the General Assembly, third-world delegates literally danced with joy at the apparent humiliation of the United States and its client state. Congress retaliated by withholding funds from the body.

As historian Melvin Small writes, though, "No amount of dancing in the UN aisles could deter Nixon from his dramatic visit to China, which captivated the world from 21 to 27 February 1972."[31] The Nixon trip was covered extensively by the media. Fully 98 percent of Americans were aware of the visit by its end. The president engaged in mostly small talk with the ailing but still dangerous ultimate leader of Communist China. Nixon had actually gone to China without a guarantee of meeting Mao personally. Perhaps for this reason, he took the position of a "supplicant seeking favors" in his audience with Mao. While Nixon gushed with praise for Mao's wisdom, Mao offered little in return, although he did tell Nixon that his book, *Six Crises,* was "not a bad book."[32]

The trip was marked at its end with the issuance of a formal communiqué on February 27, 1972 (**Document 6.13**). In it, the United States and China agreed that neither would "seek hegemony in the Asia Pacific region" and that both were "opposed to efforts by any other country or group of countries," such as the Soviet Union, "to establish such hegemony." With regard to Taiwan, each nation issued its own understanding of the situation. The United States acknowledged that Taiwan was a part of China, which represented no change in American policy, but insisted that Taiwan and the PRC should resolve their differences peacefully. Once those differences were in fact resolved, the Americans stated, the United States would then be able to fulfill its "ultimate objective" of withdrawing its troops and bases from Taiwan. The Americans did not mention the U.S.-Taiwan defense treaty negotiated when Nixon was vice president. Kissinger attempted to redress this omission by making reference to the treaty in his remarks to the press on the last day of the trip.

Despite these bumps in the road, Nixon's strategic move had something in it for virtually everyone, and political leaders from both sides of the aisle soon came around to offer their support. Conservatives appreciated how Nixon had driven a wedge between the two most powerful Communist countries in the world. Conservative commentator, magazine editor, and talk show host William F. Buckley Jr. at first lampooned Nixon's new apparent love for Communists, but he then joined another icon of the right, California governor Ronald Reagan, in endorsing Nixon's initiative. Liberals applauded the retreat from bellicosity that the move indicated and hoped that it might be followed by a similarly bold new approach to the Soviet Union.

DÉTENTE

By the time Richard Nixon became president, the Soviet Union and the United States were both weary of the Cold War. The state of near-perpetual crisis that had prevailed when Nixon served as vice president had only worsened in subsequent years. Nixon agreed with defense experts who argued that normalizing relations with the Soviets was necessary to prevent another flare-up like the Cuban Missile Crisis. Nixon and those who advised him also believed that the arms race with the Soviets had become simply too costly. The "Go-Go" years of the 1960s were fading, and the government was now being forced to confront the painful choice between "guns and butter" that fast economic growth—and a healthy dose of wishful thinking—had permitted the Johnson administration to ignore.[33] Nixon had, finally, a further reason for wanting to ease tensions with the Soviets. When he looked at the Soviet Union from the vantage point of the presidency, he saw a changed country. The Union of Soviet Socialist Republics, he believed, was becoming more normal: less prone to taking ideologically inspired risks and more concerned with (and hence more amenable to persuasion with regard to) the quality of life of its own people.

For their part, the Soviets, led by Communist Party chairman Leonid Brezhnev, also had been forced to confront certain hard truths. The Soviet economy was in trouble and needed access to Western technology and goods. Also, the PRC had grown in stature and power and seemed to some Russians to be emerging as the true adversary of the Soviet Union. Tensions between the Communist powers were sufficiently bad that in early 1969 the Soviet leadership actually debated a preemptive attack on Chinese nuclear missile bases. A relaxation of tensions between the superpowers also appealed to the Soviets because it would presumably signal to the world that the planet's most modern nation, the United States, recognized the Soviet Union as its equal, rather than as an aberration to be erased from history. Under such conditions, ideological struggle would naturally continue, but the vitriolic rhetoric of days past would be confined to lower-level operatives, not heads of state (**Document 6.14**).

A final incentive for détente was to be found in developments in Western Europe. Would the Americans really fight to preserve the freedom of their allies in the event of a Soviet or Warsaw Pact (the Soviet counterpart to the North Atlantic Treaty Organization) invasion, or might the Americans hold back? Could the future of warfare in Europe be a tense peace between the superpowers—guaranteed by mutual assured destruction—and war between Western Europe and the Warsaw Pact? In the event of such a European war, if the United States withheld its nuclear force, the Warsaw Pact, with its marked advantage in conventional forces, was bound to prevail. Questions of this sort had long complicated the United States' relationship with its NATO partners. In the late 1960s, former West German Chancellor Willy Brandt became foreign minister in a coalition government under Chancellor Kurt Kiesinger. In this position, Brandt developed the policy of looking to the East, or "Ostpolitik," which was a key element of German foreign policy when Nixon assumed the presidency. Brandt led West Germany to accept the principle of nonaggression with the Soviet Union and to acknowledge at least implicitly the division of the German nation. If Nixon did not soften U.S. policy regarding Eastern Europe, the United States would be out of touch with realities on the ground in the frontline European state in the Cold War. Ostpolitik provided the foundation for the Quadripartite Agreement, signed by the United States, the Soviet Union, Britain, and France on September 3, 1971. This agreement normalized the partition of Berlin and guaranteed Western access to West Berlin (**Document 6.15**).

In forging détente, Nixon relied heavily on his national security adviser, Henry Kissinger, routinely ignoring the secretary of state and his department of career diplomats. Beginning in 1969, Nixon and the Soviet ambassador to the United States, Anatoly Dobrynin, began a series of private meetings. At first, Kissinger insisted through this back channel upon the concept of linkage, the idea that progress in one area of superpower relations might be made dependent on another. Specifically, the Nixon administration tried to persuade the Soviets that if they wanted to get progress in bilateral relations, they would have to give America some help in Southeast Asia, by pushing the North Vietnamese toward a negotiated settlement. By summer, though, when it became apparent that the Soviets either had little actual influence over the North Vietnamese or little interest in using what influence they had, the administration signaled its willingness to move ahead with the Soviets without first winning their assistance in Vietnam. After all, there was a stalled agenda on arms control awaiting immediate action.

By 1969 the practice of summitry had evolved to the point where there was a permanent bureaucracy within the executive branch (and therefore a permanent interest) dedicated to the pursuit of arms control agreements. Presidents came and went, but once created by statute in 1961, the Arms Control and Disarmament Administration (ACDA) was, seemingly, forever. Outside of government, there had developed a small but influential group of experts in arms control, at think tanks and universities and within the print media, who also constituted a sort of permanent lobby for the continuation of what had truly become a "peace process."

Picking up where the Johnson administration had left off, President Nixon's negotiators were soon able to present to him a completed nonproliferation treaty, which the president signed in November 1969. At that time, the two sides of negotiators began to meet again publicly in the Strategic Arms Limitation Talks (SALT) and on the issue of antiballistic missiles (ABMs). Nixon wanted to use the challenge of American technological breakthroughs in the latter as leverage to induce the Soviets to come to terms on the former. To make this linkage work, the president first had to excite hawks within Congress to fight off an effort by liberals to block spending on the ABM program in order to inflate the credit he would receive from the Soviets in trading it away. On this occasion, Nixon won his high-stakes game of deception, though when the time came to make the swap, some hawkish members of Congress, as well as hawks within the international security policy network, felt betrayed.

Even though the superpowers recognized early on that they were close to an agreement, political maneuvering delayed a settlement and summit. First, it was the Soviets who balked at a heads of state meeting in 1970. They knew full well that Nixon was eager for a summit before the congressional elections of that year and resented being used for American political ends. In July 1971 Nixon repaid the Soviets by announcing that he would travel first to China. Nixon's announcement diminished the drama in Brezhnev's August 10, 1971, invitation to Nixon to come to Moscow the following year.

At the May 1972 summit in Moscow, the superpowers at last signed the first SALT agreement, SALT I, and a treaty limiting ABMs. SALT I (**Document 6.16**) was not as coherent as it might have been had Nixon relied less on Kissinger's back-channel maneuverings and more on the formal negotiations conducted by the ACDA experts. Also, despite several years of foot-dragging in scheduling the summit, the two sides left a number of complex issues to be settled in back rooms while the heads of state made small talk before the cameras. Nevertheless, it was the first agreement of the Cold War actually to limit the production of new nuclear arms.

SALT I was an interim accord that was to expire in five years. During that time, it froze the number of intercontinental ballistic missiles (ICBMs) and permitted an increase up to agreed levels of submarine-launched ballistic missiles (SLBMs). The freeze seemed to favor the Soviets numerically, but the Americans had an advantage in strategic bombers and forward-deployed nuclear delivery systems, neither of which were included in the treaty. Although SALT I was a complex numerical agreement, it was criticized by some for its failure actually to reduce arms. (The treaty set out of bounds the development of certain *new* weapons but did not compel the destruction of any weapons already in existence.) Even its contribution to stability in the arms race was doubtful, as it placed no restrictions on warheads, merely the missiles that launched them. This had become an important distinction, due to the development of multiple independently targeted reentry vehicles (MIRVs). With MIRV technology, a single missile could launch multiple warheads, each aimed at a different target. SALT I was, in the opinion of a leading U.S. expert, "not significant as an arms control measure."[34] It was, nonetheless, as Kissinger put it, "better certainly than nothing." Congress agreed, supporting SALT by joint resolution at the end of September 1972.

SALT I was placed before both houses of Congress because it was not actually a treaty but rather an interim agreement that was supposed to be merely the first in a series of accords. The ABM deal, signed simultaneously at the same summit, was a true treaty and was also of greater consequence (**Document 6.17**). By limiting the ABM defenses that each side might deploy, the ABM treaty foreclosed the possibility of a destabilizing departure from the logic of mutual assured destruction (MAD). MAD had become accepted as a balance of terror, where each side possessed a critical second-strike capability to respond to a nuclear first strike by the other. If ABMs proliferated to the point where retaliatory nuclear missiles might not be able to reach their targets, the nuclear balance would no longer be cause for confidence but an invitation to a preventive strike. The treaty allowed each superpower to have only two ABM sites: one for its capital (so that a second-strike order could be given) and one for an ICBM launch area (so that a second-strike order could be carried out).[35]

Later in the year of Nixon's first summit, Congress gave its assent to a Nixon administration proposal to grant the Soviet Union most-favored-nation (MFN) status as a trading partner. Ironically, the anti-capitalists in the Kremlin used the agreement to corner the grain market by purchasing huge quantities of U.S. wheat in 1972 and 1973. Once the Soviets had thus driven up the price, they resold at a profit on the world market. This was embarrassing enough to the administration, but Senator Henry "Scoop" Jackson of Washington, a Democratic cold warrior who opposed détente, used the issue of trade concessions to focus scrutiny upon the Soviet Union's record of human rights abuse.

Using the language of moral condemnation rather than the Nixonian language of the balance of power, Jackson labored to link U.S. trade concessions to the Soviets with Soviet concessions on the treatment of Soviet Jews seeking to emigrate (**Document 6.18**). Jews in the Soviet Union faced ingrained anti-Semitism, as well as the official atheism of the Soviet state. Many sought to emigrate to Israel; so many were refused that the term "Refusenik," came into common usage, to describe a person refused permission to leave the Soviet state. When Jackson's proposal was introduced on October 4, 1972, as an amendment to a trade reform bill, the Soviets reacted angrily. The most significant repercussions, however, were in the realm of U.S. domestic politics, as Jackson's crusade against Soviet human rights violations became a cause around which a number of hawkish Democrats rallied. These Democrats would eventually join the other hawks who had already abandoned the Democratic Party, and they would join the Republicans as "neoconservatives."

Nixon, after signing the SALT and ABM agreements, had come back to the United States to give a triumphal speech to a joint session of Congress on June 1, 1972. This was, he said, the "beginning of the end of the era which began in 1945."[36] Nixon surely claimed too much in this statement, but the Moscow summit had indeed begun a process whereby the two nations would deal with one another, at least at certain levels, routinely and without hostility. The Americans and the Soviets continued to work toward a SALT II Treaty, while meeting regularly through a Standing Consultative Commission to resolve differences over the implementation of SALT I. The Soviets and Americans also signed numerous smaller agreements and treaties over the next several years. At the Moscow gathering itself, the two sides signed a statement of "Basic Principles of Relations," which the Americans dismissed as merely symbolic but the Soviets understood as a critical step toward normalizing relations. In the Basic Principles, the two sides agreed to abstain from seeking "unilateral advantage at the expense of the other" and agreed to the principle of "peaceful coexistence," though this last phrase meant different things to different people.[37] More than twenty agreements were signed in Nixon's first term in office alone, including agreements to ban nuclear weapons from the oceans, to promote scientific and technical cooperation and exchanges, and to convene a Conference on Security and Cooperation in Europe.

"PEACE WITH HONOR" IN VIETNAM

Early in 1972, the last U.S. maneuver battalion was withdrawn from the ground war in Vietnam. The Americans and the South Vietnamese were now pursuing a passive strategy, focusing on the defense of highly fortified cities, bases, and village enclaves. The initiative was thus left to the North Vietnamese, who determined to launch a spring offensive in 1972 with the goal of driving the South Vietnamese president out of power, regaining territory, and then preparing for the post-American phase of the war. The United States' response was Operation Linebacker, the massive bombing of the North. This time, U.S. bombers struck deep into North Vietnamese territory, hitting a range of targets previously deemed off-limits. To heighten the effect of these retaliatory strikes, Nixon employed the "madman" ruse again, utilizing Kissinger to tell the North Vietnamese that the president was "going crazy."[38]

In addition, the United States mined North Vietnam's major harbor. The military chiefs had long recommended this tactic. This time, they "took the unheard of and insubordinate step" of telling the president that they would "walk out the door" if the president said "no."[39] The chiefs added to this threat an emotional appeal. "Let us make these bastards pay for the American blood they've spilled," they entreated the president. Nixon gave them the answer they wanted, but he also used the opportunity to pass responsibility for success to the chiefs. "This is your chance," he said, "to use military power effectively to win this war."[40]

Unfortunately for the chiefs, it was too late. Bombs and mines could not win the war at this late stage—when the American public had long since lost the will to "pay any price" for victory. As the CIA reported in hindsight, although the mining operation slowed the ability of the North Vietnamese to move supplies to the field, it did not reduce supplies and imports to a level below what was needed to sustain the war. Mines and bombs might destroy and kill, but only ground troops could hold territory. Even the damage caused by the mines and bombs was limited by the fact that this was a proxy war, in which neither side dared strike directly at the other. In response to the new U.S. tactics, the PRC—even in the midst of its opening with the United States and against the backdrop of a widening Sino-Soviet rift—cooperated with the Soviet Union to remove the mines and to build pipelines to send oil overland from the Soviet Union to North Vietnam.

Meanwhile, peace negotiations continued. In October 1972 the North Vietnamese unilaterally announced that they and the United States had reached a general agreement which would lead to U.S. withdrawal. The United States was forced to confirm the agreement, before the South Vietnamese, who wanted the Americans to hold out for tougher terms than the North would accept, undermined it. Under the terms of the deal that had been struck by negotiators in Paris, the Americans agreed that the North Vietnamese would continue to hold territory in the South that they had recently occupied by force, and the North Vietnamese agreed to drop their demand that South Vietnamese president Nguyen Van Thieu be removed from office. All sides agreed to the release of prisoners of war (POWs). Nixon was irritated at the North Vietnamese for grabbing the headlines with the early announcement, but it was a relief for the administration at last to be able to say that "peace is at hand." Kissinger actually uttered this famous line himself at a televised press conference on October 26, 1972, rather than waiting for the president to speak, which added to Nixon's annoyance at how the diplomatic end had been played out in public. Still, the apparent imminence of a peace settlement contributed to Nixon's landslide victory for reelection in November 1972.

South Vietnam's president then complicated the situation, however, by balking at the terms that the Americans had settled upon. Thieu was grateful that the Americans had insisted upon his continuance in office, but he was disappointed that they had permitted North Vietnamese troops to retain possession of territory in South Vietnam. While the South Vietnamese and Americans bickered amongst themselves, the North Vietnamese seemed to be having second thoughts of their own when their representatives walked out of talks in Paris on December 12. The Americans responded, once more, by bombing

North Vietnam. After Kissinger formally broke off talks in Paris, the president unleashed Linebacker II, from December 15 to December 30. The "Christmas Bombing" campaign, as the press christened the operation, was even more intense than the bombing of the North before the American election. The president, with a historic electoral victory behind him, reveled in this show of strength. Critics of the war reacted wildly; the Swedish premier went so far as to compare the United States to Nazi Germany. In the White House, though, Kissinger agreed with the president that the administration still had a "lot of friends in the country" and that "brutal unpredictability" was the "best course" for the president to take to force the North Vietnamese to conclude peace talks.[41]

As for Thieu, President Nixon was prepared at this point to cut him out of a formal deal if necessary. If that happened, there would be no formal cease-fire "but we could argue," Haldeman recounted the president saying, that "South Vietnam is now in a position where they can stand on their own feet."[42] But Nixon provided private assurances sufficient to overcome Thieu's doubts. As Nixon wrote in a private letter dated November 14,

> far more important than what we say in the agreement on this issue is what we do in the event the enemy renews its aggression. You have my absolute assurance that if Hanoi fails to abide by the terms of this agreement, it is my intention to take swift and severe retaliatory action.[43]

In the face of this typically Nixonian argument—with its distinction between "what we say" and "what we do"—Thieu relented, although he declined to sign the peace accords on the same page that carried the signature of the representative of the Communist Provisional Revolutionary Government (PRG) of South Vietnam.

Finally, on January 23, 1973, the Nixon administration was able to announce the end of American involvement in the Vietnam War. This time, the president got to make the announcement himself (**Document 6.19**). The United States, South Vietnam, North Vietnam and the PRG had on that day signed the Paris Peace Agreement, which called for the cessation of hostilities, the return of POWs within sixty days, and the withdrawal of U.S. troops within the same time. "Peace with honor" had been achieved.

Relaxing after his final election and his administration's final negotiation with the North Vietnamese, Nixon read the reviews of his announcement from the nation's newspapers with disappointment. Reaction was positive, but muted and anxious for the future. The president blamed Kissinger and the rest of his top-level aides and cabinet members. Kennedy's men, the president observed, had backed their president even in failure. Here the president had achieved peace with honor in a war that had bedeviled presidents before him, including Kennedy, but the press, following Kissinger, was not giving the president his due. The president remonstrated:

> The basic line here [should be] the character, the lonely man in the White House, with little support from government, active opposition from the Senate and some House members, overwhelming opposition from media and opinion leaders, including religious, education, and business, but strong support from labor. The President alone held on and pulled it out.[44]

That was what the newspapers should record; that was what Kissinger should say.

As a political professional, Nixon should have known better than to anticipate more praise, regardless of whether Kissinger read his lines accurately or not. The deal was transparently weak, and in any event, it was soon violated. The South Vietnamese leadership had never really accepted the idea of leaving North Vietnam in control of territory within the South's borders. The South Vietnamese Army therefore soon initiated skirmishes with the enemy. The North Vietnamese, meanwhile, showed by their actions that they fully expected to resume large-scale warfare against the South. They widened and reinforced the Ho Chi Minh trail, laid oil pipeline through South Vietnamese territory that they controlled to just north of Saigon, and increased their troop presence within the South. By fall 1973 South and North Vietnam were deeply involved in a "post-war war."[45] In April 1974 the North Vietnamese initiated what would be their final offensive. The "decent interval" had passed quickly.

THE IMPERIAL PRESIDENCY

By April 1974, when the North Vietnamese launched the final maneuver that would end the war, President Nixon was in no position politically to respond with force. He was, rather, near the end of a two-year battle with his numerous "enemies" at home, a battle that he himself had launched.

The president had first come to office without a popular majority and without his own party in control of even one branch of Congress. Through his first term, he had restrained himself on numerous occasions when he may have wished to throw down a gauntlet to Congress and to his "enemies." In domestic policy, he compromised so often with the Democratic-controlled Congress that he effectively co-opted their agenda for environmental protection, the expansion of Social Security, and the promotion of civil rights. Nixon's 1972 victory in reelection had left him emboldened. It had been a stunning personal triumph—a landslide of historic proportions. It was, however, just that: a *personal* victory, a "lonely landslide" against a disastrous Democratic nominee, Sen. George McGovern of South Dakota. In the House, the president's party picked up twelve seats, to return to the exact division of seats they had enjoyed when Nixon first came to office: 243 for the Democrats, 192 for the Republicans. In the Senate, the president's party lost two seats, enlarging the Democratic majority to 57 to 43.

The president acted, however, as if he had won a sweeping mandate. This election, to Nixon, was the culminating and resounding response to a lifetime of putdowns and slights. Now he was determined to get tough—and to get even. He proceeded to act against his own branch of government as well as against Congress with the same sort of ruthless abandon and sleight of hand with which he had achieved success in foreign policy during his first term.

The president began by brusquely greeting his cabinet members the day after "their" victory. After perfunctory remarks, he left the room, leaving Haldeman, as chief of staff, to tell them all that the president wanted their letters of resignation. Six of these letters were accepted immediately. This began a sustained effort to reorganize the executive branch by centralizing authority within the White House staff and by coordinating and even merging the management of cabinet departments. The boldest effort at attempted reinvention of government since before the Cold War soon stalled as the upper reaches of the administration became absorbed in the Watergate scandal.

Before losing his momentum, though, the president also challenged Congress. He impounded appropriated funds and withdrew support for Great Society legacy programs, such as Model Cities, which he had been hesitant to attack in his first term. Nixon knew his actions would expand his list of enemies, but he truly believed that, by clever use of executive power and exploitation of his personal popularity with the people, he could destroy the old New Deal coalition and create a "New Majority" in support of a "New American Revolution."[46]

The Democrats who were the majority in Congress had other ideas, and they fought back. Congress passed in Nixon's truncated second term a number of laws designed to restrict the president's freedom of action. The Case-Church Amendment of June 26, 1973, forbade use of appropriated funds to deploy American forces in Cambodia, Laos, or Vietnam without the explicit authorization of Congress. The ban's supporters did not realize just how big a step they had taken, because Nixon had not revealed to Congress his private assurances to President Thieu. It was only the beginning.

In November 1973 Congress overrode Nixon's veto and passed into law the War Powers Resolution (**Document 6.20**). The act requires the president to consult with Congress in order to send American forces into hostilities. Once forces are deployed into combat or even into a situation where hostilities are imminent, the president has sixty days to win congressional approval. Otherwise, the president is to remove the forces. The War Powers Act has never been accepted by an American president, during or after the Cold War, and has been routinely "ignored, evaded, or otherwise minimized" by commanders in chief.[47] Still, it is a historic reflection of the interinstitutional struggle between the executive and legislative branches, and of how that struggle was intensified during the Cold War.

The Supreme Court also responded to Nixon's aggressive use of executive power. Nixon thought of himself as a wartime president and believed that as such, he had to have wide discretion in the use of the government's powers. The Supreme Court took exception to this stark view of unrelenting war and unrelenting institutional deference to the executive. This was apparent in the *Pentagon Papers* decision and even more so in the Court's decision that forced the president to release the secret tapes he had made of conversations within the White House.

In getting to this point, Nixon had gone for broke. He had run his 1972 campaign with no holds barred, even after the Democratic Party lurched to the left and nominated McGovern, whose candidacy caused a substantial split in the party. Rather than sit back and watch his opponents commit electoral suicide, Nixon permitted his campaign organization to get out of hand and then participated in the cover-up of their crimes.

In 1972 the personnel of Nixon's Special Investigations Unit known as the Plumbers took jobs in the president's campaign. It was a Plumbers' offshoot operating out of the Committee to Reelect the President (CRP to Republicans, CREEP to others) that broke into the offices of the Democratic National Committee in the Watergate complex in Washington, D.C., on June 17, 1972. When he learned that his own people had been caught

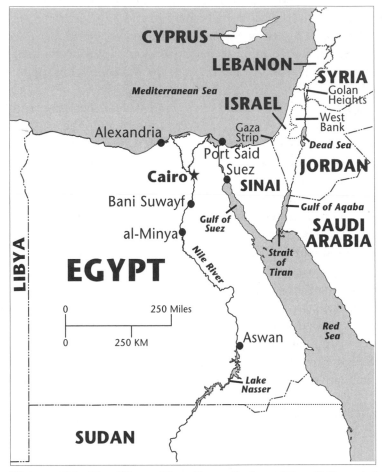

Theater of the Yom Kippur War—Egypt, Syria, and Israeli-Occupied Sinai and Golan Heights. *Source:* CQ Press, *The Middle East,* 10th ed. (Washington, D.C.: CQ Press, 2005), 223.

in the break-in at the Watergate, Nixon immediately decided upon a cover-up. Reflexively, the president played the card of national security. In the famous "smoking gun" tape of June 23, Nixon instructed Haldeman to have the CIA tell the FBI to "stay the hell out of this" because it is "a national security thing."[48] The president was worried that an investigation would turn up evidence about not just the dirty tricks and illegal acts of his campaign workers, but the Fielding break-in during the Ellsberg episode.

From February 1973, when the Senate empanelled a select committee to investigate the Watergate burglary and associated allegations of corruption in the Nixon campaign, until Nixon's resignation on August 9, 1974, Nixon's presidency was reduced to a struggle for existence. No modern president, however, can simply wall himself off from events, and even while fighting for his political life, Nixon was forced to handle one more Cold War crisis: the October 1973 Arab-Israeli War.

The Yom Kippur War began on October 6 and lasted sixteen days. In a coordinated, surprise assault, Syria and Egypt initiated the conflict in the Golan Heights and the Sinai, respectively. Egypt's president Anwar al-Sadat had threatened war with Israel repeatedly, but his threats had become routine and were discounted as mere theater. Israel was thus caught unprepared; the nation lost 1,000 soldiers killed in battle in the first day and one-third of its tanks in the first week. Kissinger and Nixon were also taken by surprise, but they quickly decided to use the conflict as an opportunity to advance their Cold War aims. Reasoning that Israel would be more willing to agree to a compromise peace with the Arab states if the Israelis "finally realized that the allegedly backward Arab nations could use modern weaponry to launch a successful offensive," the Nixon administration reacted slowly to Israel's urgent request for supplies.[49] But the United States soon began to send the necessary equipment in earnest, quickly outpacing a similar effort made on behalf of the Arab states by the Soviet Union.

The crisis, however, was not over. With help from the Americans, the Israelis reversed their losses and were poised to inflict additional damage against the Egyptian Army, which they had pursued into Egypt. Even after Kissinger and Brezhnev worked out a cease-fire agreement on October 21, 1973, in Moscow, which was then ratified in the United Nations, the Israeli Defense Force continued its offensive. In response, Sadat invited both superpowers immediately to deploy peacekeepers in the region. The Soviets had never before had a direct military presence in the region, though, and the Americans were loathe to see them take such a step. The Americans declined the request and expected the Soviets to do likewise. The Soviets, however, issued a statement indicating that they reserved the right to act unilaterally to uphold peace in the Middle East.

In the White House, this was seen as a deliberate provocation: a threat by the Soviets to intervene with force in the Middle East. Fearing that the Politburo meant to take advantage of a distracted president, Kissinger, the chairman of the Joint Chiefs of Staff, the director of the CIA, the secretary of defense, and Nixon's new chief of staff, Gen. Alexander Haig, took charge of the situation, ordering a worldwide U.S. military alert. The Soviets quickly insisted that the Americans had misunderstood their intentions; on the ground in Egypt, the Israelis agreed to adhere to the cease-fire. An Arab oil embargo, imposed against the U.S. during the war, was lifted in March 1974.

Though he was not clearly in command anymore, even in the midst of such a crisis as was caused by the Yom Kippur War, the president continued to insist that he should be accorded the respect and latitude that historically had been granted to wartime chief executives. He had no choice, however, but to continue to face his critics, who were by this time using the "I" word—"impeachment" (**Document 6.21**). Like other wartime presidents, he attempted to assert "executive privilege," in Nixon's case, to withhold from congressional and judicial investigators the secret tapes that would reveal his misdeeds. In a unanimous decision, the Court, in the aptly titled case *U.S. v. Nixon* (418 U.S. 683 [1974]), upheld for the first time the concept of executive privilege but denied that it shielded Nixon in this instance. Nixon's attorney, James St. Clair, had hinted in oral argument before the Court that his client might simply refuse to obey a Court order to release the tapes, forcing a constitutional showdown. The Court called the president's bluff. Once the tapes were in the public domain, Nixon's presidency was doomed.

All the sordidness of Watergate went back to Nixon's anger at the collapse during his secret war in Cambodia of a mythic tradition whereby Americans naturally rallied around the president on foreign policy, putting differences of party aside. The Watergate scandal was in fact a manifestation of an institutional conflict that was itself an outgrowth of the decades-long war against communism. Perhaps no other modern president would have allowed the conflict to get so out of hand, but any other modern president unfortunate enough to be in Richard Nixon's shoes in the final years of the Vietnam War would also have been tempted to lash out at the many opponents of executive power. The war abroad had come to seem an extension of a war at home.

CONCLUSION

In times of war, the presidency's powers have historically expanded. The federal courts have, moreover, routinely waited until the return of peace before daring to rule against the unilateral expansion of executive power. This had been the pattern of the Civil War and the two world wars. Every student of history, and every president, knew that in times of true crisis, the executive power of the presidency had been permitted to expand so as to provide energy, dispatch, and secrecy—the qualities that Alexander Hamilton had identified as essential attributes of executive power. Of course, America had never been in a war like the Cold War before, a war with no end in sight. The Vietnam War was itself unusually long for Americans used to a few years of overt fighting and then a rush back to domestic priorities. Under these conditions, a prudent politician would have acted with caution to claim the mantle of executive indulgence that had been worn by previous commanders in chief. That was not Nixon's way.

In a post-presidency, televised interview with David Frost, the president spoke as candidly as he ever did about Watergate and his forced resignation from office. In that interview, Nixon presented a lawyerly defense, one steeped in both the peculiar logic of the courtroom and the aura of the wartime presidency. Of those persons who, while employed for the president, engaged in burglary, wiretaps, and other plainly illegal activities, Nixon famously asserted that they were *not guilty* of a crime, because they had been acting under orders from the president, who was himself acting under necessity. Like Abraham Lincoln before him, Nixon went on to say, he had perhaps stretched the law, but he had done so to save the nation. This was war—at home as well as abroad (**Document 6.22**).

When Nixon came to office, the American public was weary of the Vietnam War. By the time he left—largely on account of how he conducted his presidency—the same public was so weary of presidential power and presidential wars that pollsters found a stunning return to isolationist impulses. Nixon had, quite simply, failed. Above all else, he had wanted to keep his nation engaged in world affairs and committed to its allies, yet when asked whether they would support the use of American force under a broad range of conditions, a majority of the public said "no" to the defense of American allies in Europe and Asia. Besides defending the American homeland itself, a majority of American adults in the mid-1970s were willing to sanction the use of force only to defend one other nation: Canada. Many expert commentators at the time wrote, however, as if the resurgence of isolationism (or defeatism) hardly mattered. The Cold War was routinely written of at this time in the past tense. It had all apparently been a big mistake, or perhaps even a figment of an overheated imagination. Over the next two presidencies, American military forces were used only in attempts to rescue American hostages. Nixon's legacy demoralized even Chairman Mao Zedong of the PRC, who complained, "I have come to be regarded as a right-wing opportunist."[50]

NOTES

1. Melvin Small, *The Presidency of Richard Nixon* (Lawrence: University Press of Kansas, 2003), 132.
2. Jeffrey Kimball, *The Vietnam War File: Uncovering the Secret History of Nixon-Era Strategy* (Lawrence: University Press of Kansas, 2003) 11.
3. Henry Brandon, *The Retreat of American Power* (New York: Dell, 1974), 81.
4. Melvin Small, *At the Water's Edge: American Politics and the Vietnam War* (New York: Ivan R. Dee, 2005), 148.
5. Allan R. Millet and Peter Maslowski, *For the Common Defense*, rev. and exp. ed. (New York: Free Press, 1994), 587.
6. Richard Nixon, "First Annual Report to the Congress on United States Foreign Policy for the 1970s," February 18, 1970, in *Public Papers of the Presidents of the United States: Richard Nixon, 1969–1974*, from the American Presidency Project, University of California, Santa Barbara, www.presidency.ucsb.edu.
7. Dale R. Herspring, *The Pentagon and the Presidency: Civil-Military Relations from FDR to George W. Bush* (Lawrence: University Press of Kansas, 2005), 195.
8. Kimball, *Vietnam War File*, 231.
9. Millett and Maslowski, *For the Common Defense*, 592.
10. Richard Nixon, *Memoirs*, as quoted in Michael Maclear, *Vietnam: The Ten Thousand Day War* (London: Methuen, 1981), 295.
11. Maclear, *Vietnam*, 290.
12. H. R. Haldeman, *The Haldeman Diaries: Inside the Nixon White House* (New York: Putnam, 1994), 184.
13. Ibid., 150.
14. Maclear, *Vietnam*, 296.
15. Haldeman, *Haldeman Diaries*, 157.
16. Alan Shank, *Presidents and Foreign Policy: Countdown to Ten Controversial Decisions* (Albany: State University of New York Press, 1997), 159.
17. Students for a Democratic Society, "Port Huron Statement," from the Sixties Project, University of Virginia at Charlottesville, www3.iath.virginia.edu/sixties/HTML_docs/Resources/Primary/Manifestos/SDS_Port_Huron.html.
18. Small, *Presidency*, 157.
19. Haldeman, *Haldeman Diaries*, 159.
20. The president made the statement about "bums" on a visit to the Pentagon on May 1, 1970, while speaking to a group of Pentagon employees. See in-text note 1 in "The President's News Conference of May 8, 1970," in *Public Papers of the Presidents of the United States: Richard*

Nixon, 1969–1974, from the American Presidency Project, University of California, Santa Barbara, www.presidency.ucsb.edu.

21. "When Nixon Met Elvis," online exhibit produced by the National Archives and Records Administration, www.archives.gov/exhibits/when_nixon_met_elvis/index.html.

22. Cal Woodward, Associated Press, "Documents Show Nixon Deception on Cambodia," *Washington Post,* November 16, 2005.

23. Richard Nixon, *RN: The Memoirs of Richard Nixon,* vol. 1 (New York: Warner Books, 1978), 511.

24. Henry Kissinger, *White House Years* (Boston: Little, Brown, 1979), 737, 1021.

25. Charles W. Colson, *Born Again* (Old Tappan, N.J.: Chosen Books, 1976), 56.

26. Young, a special assistant to the National Security Council, was officially on loan to the Domestic Council, but he was actually working on Nixon's campaign. Liddy, a former FBI special agent and former White House staffer, was at the time the general counsel to the Nixon campaign. Hunt, a former CIA spy, performed "black bag" (that is, illegal) operations for the Nixon campaign.

27. Small, *At the Water's Edge,* 161.

28. Barbara Hinckley, *Less Than Meets the Eye: Foreign Policy Making and the Myth of the Assertive Congress* (Chicago: University of Chicago Press, 1994), 84.

29. Joe Klein, "A Rush to War—Now a Rush Out of One?" *Time* Web exclusive, October 5, 2003, www.time.com/time/columnist/klein (locate by date in list of past articles).

30. Jung Chang and Jon Halliday, *Mao: The Unknown Story* (New York: Knopf, 2005), 583.

31. Small, *Presidency,* 122.

32. Ibid., 123.

33. John Brooks, *The Go-Go Years: The Drama and Crashing Finale of Wall Street's Bullish 60s* (New York: Allworth Press, 1998).

34. Raymond Garthoff, "SALT," in *The Oxford Companion to American Military History,* ed. John Whiteclay Chambers (New York: Oxford University Press, 2000), 632, 633.

35. In a protocol signed two years later, both sides agreed to reduce to one the number of allowed ABM sites.

36. Richard Nixon, "Address to a Joint Session of the Congress on Returning from Austria, the Soviet Union, Iran, and Poland," in *Public Papers of the Presidents of the United States: Richard Nixon, 1969–1974,* from the American Presidency Project, University of California, Santa Barbara, www.presidency.ucsb.edu.

37. "Paper Agreed upon by the United States and the Soviet Union," Document 116 in Office of the Historian, U.S. Department of State, *Foreign Relations of the United States, 1969–1976,* vol. 1, *Foundations of Foreign Policy* (Washington, D.C.: U.S. Government Printing Office, 2003), www.state.gov/r/pa/ho/frus/nixon/i/20706.htm.

38. Kimball, *Vietnam War File,* 20.

39. Herspring, *The Pentagon and the Presidency,* 207.

40. Ibid., p. 208.

41. Haldeman, *Haldeman Diaries,* 679.

42. Ibid., 680.

43. Jerold L. Schecter, "The Final Days: The Political Struggle to End the Vietnam War," in *Gerald Ford and the Politics of Post-War America,* vol. 2, ed. Bernard J. Firestone and Alexi Ugrinsky (Westport, Conn.: Greenwood Press/Hofstra University, 1993), 541.

44. Haldeman, *Haldeman Diaries,* 698–699.

45. Allan E. Goodman, "Paris Peace Agreement," in Chambers, *Oxford Companion to American Military History,* 528.

46. Nixon spoke of a "new American revolution" in his January 22, 1971, State of the Union address. The term "new majority" is used to describe what Nixon called the "silent majority" in his famous November 3, 1969, "Address to the Nation on the War in Vietnam." November 3, 1969, in the same source. See Robert Mason, *Richard Nixon and the Quest for a New*

Majority (Chapel Hill: University of North Carolina Press, 2003); addresses named above in Richard Nixon, *Public Papers of the Presidents of the United States: Richard Nixon, 1969–1974,* from the American Presidency Project, University of California, Santa Barbara, www.presidency .ucsb.edu.

47. Richard M. Pious, "The War Powers Resolution," in Chambers, *Oxford Companion to American Military History,* 787.
48. Small, *Presidency,* 277.
49. Ibid., 133.
50. Chang and Halliday, *Mao,* 596.

Document 6.1
President Richard Nixon Asks for the Support of the "Silent Majority" for "Vietnamization," November 3, 1969

President Nixon attempted in this speech to mobilize the great majority of Americans who neither fought against nor fought in the Vietnam War. He rallied them to support a new Cold War policy, which came to be known as the Nixon Doctrine. Under this doctrine, the United States would help other nations fight for their freedom against Communist forces, but America would no longer make the sort of open-ended promise that previous presidents had made to the government of South Vietnam (and a host of other nations). Through "Vietnamization," the U.S. role in the Vietnam War would be brought into alignment with the president's new doctrine.

. . . Tonight I want to talk to you on a subject of deep concern to all Americans and to many people in all parts of the world—the war in Vietnam.

I believe that one of the reasons for the deep division about Vietnam is that many Americans have lost confidence in what their Government has told them about our policy. The American people cannot and should not be asked to support a policy which involves the overriding issues of war and peace unless they know the truth about that policy.

Tonight, therefore, I would like to answer some of the questions that I know are on the minds of many of you listening to me.

How and why did America get involved in Vietnam in the first place?

How has this administration changed the policy of the previous administration?

What has really happened in the negotiations in Paris and on the battlefront in Vietnam?

What choices do we have if we are to end the war?

What are the prospects for peace? Now, let me begin by describing the situation I found when I was inaugurated on January 20.

—The war had been going on for 4 years.

—31,000 Americans had been killed in action.

—The training program for the South Vietnamese was behind schedule.

—540,000 Americans were in Vietnam with no plans to reduce the number.

—No progress had been made at the negotiations in Paris and the United States had not put forth a comprehensive peace proposal.

—The war was causing deep division at home and criticism from many of our friends as well as our enemies abroad.

In view of these circumstances there were some who urged that I end the war at once by ordering the immediate withdrawal of all American forces.

From a political standpoint this would have been a popular and easy course to follow. After all, we became involved in the war while my predecessor was in office. I could blame the defeat which would be the result of my action on him and come out as the peacemaker. Some put it to me quite bluntly: This was the only way to avoid allowing Johnson's war to become Nixon's war. . . .

Now, many believe that President Johnson's decision to send American combat forces to South Vietnam was wrong. And many others—I among them—have been strongly critical of the way the war has been conducted.

But the question facing us today is: Now that we are in the war, what is the best way to end it?

In January I could only conclude that the precipitate withdrawal of American forces from Vietnam would be a disaster not only for South Vietnam but for the United States and for the cause of peace.

For the South Vietnamese, our precipitate withdrawal would inevitably allow the Communists to repeat the massacres which followed their takeover in the North 15 years before. . . .

For the future of peace, precipitate withdrawal would . . . be a disaster of immense magnitude.

—A nation cannot remain great if it betrays its allies and lets down its friends.

—Our defeat and humiliation in South Vietnam without question would promote recklessness in the councils of those great powers who have not yet abandoned their goals of world conquest.

—This would spark violence wherever our commitments help maintain the peace—in the Middle East, in Berlin, eventually even in the Western Hemisphere.

Ultimately, this would cost more lives. It would not bring peace; it would bring more war.

For these reasons, I rejected the recommendation that I should end the war by immediately withdrawing all of our forces. I chose instead to change American policy on both the negotiating front and battlefront.

In order to end a war fought on many fronts, I initiated a pursuit for peace on many fronts.

In a television speech on May 14, in a speech before the United Nations, and on a number of other occasions I set forth our peace proposals in great detail.

—We have offered the complete withdrawal of all outside forces within 1 year.

—We have proposed a cease-fire under international supervision.

—We have offered free elections under international supervision. . . .

Hanoi has refused even to discuss our proposals. They demand our unconditional acceptance of their terms, which are that we withdraw all American forces immediately and unconditionally and that we overthrow the Government of South Vietnam as we leave. . . .

At the time we launched our search for peace I recognized we might not succeed in bringing an end to the war through negotiation. I, therefore, put into effect another plan to bring peace—a plan which will bring the war to an end regardless of what happens on the negotiating front.

It is in line with a major shift in U.S. foreign policy which I described in my press conference at Guam on July 25. Let me briefly explain what has been described as the Nixon Doctrine—a policy which not only will help end the war in Vietnam, but which is an essential element of our program to prevent future Vietnams.

We Americans are a do-it-yourself people. We are an impatient people. Instead of teaching someone else to do a job, we like to do it ourselves. And this trait has been carried over into our foreign policy.

In Korea and again in Vietnam, the United States furnished most of the money, most of the arms, and most of the men to help the people of those countries defend their freedom against Communist aggression.

Before any American troops were committed to Vietnam, a leader of another Asian country expressed this opinion to me when I was traveling in Asia as a private citizen. He said: "When you are trying to assist another nation defend its freedom, U.S. policy should be to help them fight the war but not to fight the war for them."

Well, in accordance with this wise counsel, I laid down in Guam three principles as guidelines for future American policy toward Asia:

—First, the United States will keep all of its treaty commitments.

—Second, we shall provide a shield if a nuclear power threatens the freedom of a nation allied with us or of a nation whose survival we consider vital to our security.

—Third, in cases involving other types of aggression, we shall furnish military and economic assistance when requested in accordance with our treaty commitments. But we shall look to the nation directly threatened to assume the primary responsibility of providing the manpower for its defense.

After I announced this policy, I found that the leaders of the Philippines, Thailand, Vietnam, South Korea, and other nations which might be threatened by Communist aggression, welcomed this new direction in American foreign policy.

The defense of freedom is everybody's business—not just America's business. And it is particularly the responsibility of the people whose freedom is threatened. In the previous administration, we Americanized the war in Vietnam. In this administration, we are Vietnamizing the search for peace. . . .

I recognize that some of my fellow citizens disagree with the plan for peace I have chosen. Honest and patriotic Americans have reached different conclusions as to how peace should be achieved.

In San Francisco a few weeks ago, I saw demonstrators carrying signs reading: "Lose in Vietnam, bring the boys home."

Well, one of the strengths of our free society is that any American has a right to reach that conclusion and to advocate that point of view. But as President of the United States,

I would be untrue to my oath of office if I allowed the policy of this Nation to be dictated by the minority who hold that point of view and who try to impose it on the Nation by mounting demonstrations in the street.

For almost 200 years, the policy of this Nation has been made under our Constitution by those leaders in the Congress and the White House elected by all of the people. If a vocal minority, however fervent its cause, prevails over reason and the will of the majority, this Nation has no future as a free society.

And now I would like to address a word, if I may, to the young people of this Nation who are particularly concerned, and I understand why they are concerned, about this war.

I respect your idealism.

I share your concern for peace. I want peace as much as you do. There are powerful personal reasons I want to end this war. This week I will have to sign 83 letters to mothers, fathers, wives, and loved ones of men who have given their lives for America in Vietnam. It is very little satisfaction to me that this is only one-third as many letters as I signed the first week in office. There is nothing I want more than to see the day come when I do not have to write any of those letters.

—I want to end the war to save the lives of those brave young men in Vietnam.

—But I want to end it in a way which will increase the chance that their younger brothers and their sons will not have to fight in some future Vietnam someplace in the world.

—And I want to end the war for another reason. I want to end it so that the energy and dedication of you, our young people, now too often directed into bitter hatred against those responsible for the war, can be turned to the great challenges of peace, a better life for all Americans, a better life for all people on this earth.

I have chosen a plan for peace. I believe it will succeed.

If it does succeed, what the critics say now won't matter. If it does not succeed, anything I say then won't matter.

I know it may not be fashionable to speak of patriotism or national destiny these days. But I feel it is appropriate to do so on this occasion.

Two hundred years ago this Nation was weak and poor. But even then, America was the hope of millions in the world. Today we have become the strongest and richest nation in the world. And the Wheel of destiny has turned so that any hope the world has for the survival of peace and freedom will be determined by whether the American people have the moral stamina and the courage to meet the challenge of free world leadership.

Let historians not record that when America was the most powerful nation in the world we passed on the other side of the road and allowed the last hopes for peace and freedom of millions of people to be suffocated by the forces of totalitarianism.

And so tonight—to you, the great silent majority of my fellow Americans—I ask for your support.

I pledged in my campaign for the Presidency to end the war in a way that we could win the peace. I have initiated a plan of action which will enable me to keep that pledge.

The more support I can have from the American people, the sooner that pledge can be redeemed; for the more divided we are at home, the less likely the enemy is to negotiate at Paris.

Let us be united for peace. Let us also be united against defeat. Because let us understand: North Vietnam cannot defeat or humiliate the United States. Only Americans can do that. . . .

Source: Richard Nixon, "Address to the Nation on the War in Vietnam," November 3, 1969, in *Public Papers of the Presidents of the United States: Richard M. Nixon 1969–1974,* from the American Presidency Project, University of California, Santa Barbara, www.presidency.ucsb.edu.

Document 6.2
President Richard Nixon's Address to the Nation on the Cambodian Incursion, April 30, 1970

Vietnamization was put to the test on the battlefield in Southeast Asia in the spring of 1970, when the U.S. Army and the Army of the Republic of Vietnam (ARVN, the South Vietnamese Army) launched an assault against North Vietnamese forces in Cambodia, whose new government had recently aligned itself with the United States. ARVN forces did not perform well, and the much-sought after hidden headquarters of the North Vietnamese Army remained elusive. Although the invasion was limited to fifteen miles beyond the border in an area under the de facto control of the North Vietnamese Army, the anti-war movement in the United States erupted in outrage against what it interpreted as an expansion of the Vietnam War into another country.

. . . Ten days ago, in my report to the Nation on Vietnam, I announced a decision to withdraw an additional 150,000 Americans from Vietnam over the next year. I said then that I was making that decision despite our concern over increased enemy activity in Laos, in Cambodia, and in South Vietnam.

At that time, I warned that if I concluded that increased enemy activity in any of these areas endangered the lives of Americans remaining in Vietnam, I would not hesitate to take strong and effective measures to deal with that situation.

Despite that warning, North Vietnam has increased its military aggression in all these areas, and particularly in Cambodia.

After full consultation with the National Security Council, Ambassador Bunker [Ellsworth Bunker, U.S. ambassador to Vietnam], General Abrams, and my other advisers, I have concluded that the actions of the enemy in the last 10 days clearly endanger the lives of Americans who are in Vietnam now and would constitute an unacceptable risk to those who will be there after withdrawal of another 150,000.

To protect our men who are in Vietnam and to guarantee the continued success of our withdrawal and Vietnamization programs, I have concluded that the time has come for action.

Tonight, I shall describe the actions of the enemy, the actions I have ordered to deal with that situation, and the reasons for my decision.

Cambodia, a small country of 7 million people, has been a neutral nation since the Geneva agreement of 1954—an agreement, incidentally, which was signed by the Government of North Vietnam.

American policy since then has been to scrupulously respect the neutrality of the Cambodian people. We have maintained a skeleton diplomatic mission of fewer than 15 in Cambodia's capital, and that only since last August. For the previous 4 years, from 1965 to 1969, we did not have any diplomatic mission whatever in Cambodia. And for the past 5 years, we have provided no military assistance whatever and no economic assistance to Cambodia.

North Vietnam, however, has not respected that neutrality.

For the past 5 years—as indicated on this map that you see here—North Vietnam has occupied military sanctuaries all along the Cambodian frontier with South Vietnam. Some of these extend up to 20 miles into Cambodia. The sanctuaries are in red and, as you note, they are on both sides of the border. They are used for hit and run attacks on American and South Vietnamese forces in South Vietnam.

These Communist occupied territories contain major base camps, training sites, logistics facilities, weapons and ammunition factories, airstrips, and prisoner-of-war compounds.

For 5 years, neither the United States nor South Vietnam has moved against these enemy sanctuaries because we did not wish to violate the territory of a neutral nation. Even after the Vietnamese Communists began to expand these sanctuaries 4 weeks ago, we counseled patience to our South Vietnamese allies and imposed restraints on our own commanders.

In contrast to our policy, the enemy in the past 2 weeks has stepped up his guerrilla actions and he is concentrating his main forces in these sanctuaries that you see on this map where they are building up to launch massive attacks on our forces and those of South Vietnam.

North Vietnam in the last 2 weeks has stripped away all pretense of respecting the sovereignty or the neutrality of Cambodia. Thousands of their soldiers are invading the country from the sanctuaries; they are encircling the capital of Phnom Penh. Coming from these sanctuaries, as you see here, they have moved into Cambodia and are encircling the capital.

Cambodia, as a result of this, has sent out a call to the United States, to a number of other nations, for assistance. Because if this enemy effort succeeds, Cambodia would become a vast enemy staging area and a springboard for attacks on South Vietnam along 600 miles of frontier—a refuge where enemy troops could return from combat without fear of retaliation.

North Vietnamese men and supplies could then be poured into that country, jeopardizing not only the lives of our own men but the people of South Vietnam as well.

Now confronted with this situation, we have three options.

First, we can do nothing. Well, the ultimate result of that course of action is clear. . . . Our second choice is to provide massive military assistance to Cambodia itself. Now unfortunately, while we deeply sympathize with the plight of 7 million Cambodians whose country is being invaded, massive amounts of military assistance could not be rapidly and effectively utilized by the small Cambodian Army against the immediate threat. . . .

Our third choice is to go to the heart of the trouble. That means cleaning out major North Vietnamese and Vietcong occupied territories—these sanctuaries which serve as bases for attacks on both Cambodia and American and South Vietnamese forces in South Vietnam. Some of these, incidentally, are as close to Saigon as Baltimore is to Washington. This one, for example [indicating], is called the Parrot's Beak. It is only 33 miles from Saigon.

Now faced with these three options, this is the decision I have made.

In cooperation with the armed forces of South Vietnam, attacks are being launched this week to clean out major enemy sanctuaries on the Cambodian-Vietnam border. . . .

Tonight, American and South Vietnamese units will attack the headquarters for the entire Communist military operation in South Vietnam. This key control center has been occupied by the North Vietnamese and Vietcong for 5 years in blatant violation of Cambodia's neutrality.

This is not an invasion of Cambodia. The areas in which these attacks will be launched are completely occupied and controlled by North Vietnamese forces. Our purpose is not to occupy the areas. Once enemy forces are driven out of these sanctuaries and once their military supplies are destroyed, we will withdraw.

These actions are in no way directed to the security interests of any nation. Any government that chooses to use these actions as a pretext for harming relations with the United States will be doing so on its own responsibility, and on its own initiative, and we will draw the appropriate conclusions.

Now let me give you the reasons for my decision.

A majority of the American people, a majority of you listening to me, are for the withdrawal of our forces from Vietnam. The action I have taken tonight is indispensable for the continuing success of that withdrawal program.

A majority of the American people want to end this war rather than to have it drag on interminably. The action I have taken tonight will serve that purpose.

A majority of the American people want to keep the casualties of our brave men in Vietnam at an absolute minimum. The action I take tonight is essential if we are to accomplish that goal.

We take this action not for the purpose of expanding the war into Cambodia but for the purpose of ending the war in Vietnam and winning the just peace we all desire. . . .

My fellow Americans, we live in an age of anarchy, both abroad and at home. We see mindless attacks on all the great institutions which have been created by free civilizations in the last 500 years. Even here in the United States, great universities are being systematically destroyed. Small nations all over the world find themselves under attack from within and from without.

If, when the chips are down, the world's most powerful nation, the United States of America, acts like a pitiful, helpless giant, the forces of totalitarianism and anarchy will threaten free nations and free institutions throughout the world.

It is not our power but our will and character that is being tested tonight. The question all Americans must ask and answer tonight is this: Does the richest and strongest nation in the history of the world have the character to meet a direct challenge by a group which rejects every effort to win a just peace, ignores our warning, tramples on solemn agreements, violates the neutrality of an unarmed people, and uses our prisoners as hostages?

If we fail to meet this challenge, all other nations will be on notice that despite its overwhelming power the United States, when a real crisis comes, will be found wanting. . . .

Source: Richard Nixon, "Address to the Nation on the Situation in Southeast Asia," April 30, 1970, in *Public Papers of the Presidents of the United States: Richard M. Nixon 1969–1974,* from the American Presidency Project, University of California, Santa Barbara, www.presidency.ucsb.edu.

Document 6.3
The Supreme Court's Per Curiam Opinion on the *Pentagon Papers* Case, June 30, 1971

Daniel Ellsberg, a defense analyst with a troubled conscience, leaked to the press the contents of a 7,000-page secret history of the war in Vietnam, which covered events from 1945 to 1968. The Nixon White House attempted to stop the publication of the document, but the Supreme Court held that the First Amendment guarantee of free expression, as applied in this case, prohibited after-the-fact censorship. The Court fundamentally disagreed with the Nixon administration about the significance of this breach of confidence to the interests of the nation.

403 U.S. 713
New York Times Co. v. United States
Certiorari to the United States Court of Appeals for the Second Circuit
No. 1873 Argued: June 26, 1971 — Decided: June 30, 1971 [*]
PER CURIAM

We granted certiorari in these cases in which the United States seeks to enjoin the New York Times and the Washington Post from publishing the contents of a classified study entitled "History of U.S. Decision-Making Process on Viet Nam Policy." *Post,* pp. 942, 943.

"Any system of prior restraints of expression comes to this Court bearing a heavy presumption against its constitutional validity." *Bantam Books, Inc. v. Sullivan,* 372 U.S. 58, 70 (1963); see also *Near v. Minnesota,* 283 U.S. 697 (1931). The Government "thus carries a heavy burden of showing justification for the imposition of such a restraint." *Organization for a Better Austin v. Keefe,* 402 U.S. 415, 419 (1971). The District Court for the Southern District of New York, in the *New York Times* case, and the District Court for the District of Columbia and the Court of Appeals for the District of Columbia Circuit, in the *Washington Post* case, held that the Government had not met that burden. We agree.

---

*Together with No. 1885, *United States v. Washington Post Co. et al.,* on certiorari to the United States Court of Appeals for the District of Columbia Circuit.

The judgment of the Court of Appeals for the District of Columbia Circuit is therefore affirmed. The order of the Court of Appeals for the Second Circuit is reversed, and the case is remanded with directions to enter a judgment affirming the judgment of the District Court for the Southern District of New York. The stays entered June 25, 1971, by the Court are vacated. The judgments shall issue forthwith.

So ordered.

. . .

MR. JUSTICE BRENNAN, concurring.

I.

I write separately in these cases only to emphasize what should be apparent: that our judgments in the present cases may not be taken to indicate the propriety, in the future, of issuing temporary stays and restraining orders to block the publication of material sought to be suppressed by the Government. So far as I can determine, never before has the United States sought to enjoin a newspaper from publishing information in its possession. The relative novelty of the questions presented, the necessary haste with which decisions were reached, the magnitude of the interests asserted, and the fact that all the parties have concentrated their arguments upon the question whether permanent restraints were proper may have justified at least some of the restraints heretofore imposed in these cases. Certainly it is difficult to fault the several courts below for seeking to assure that the issues here involved were preserved for ultimate review by this Court. But even if it be assumed that some of the interim restraints were proper in the two cases before us, that assumption has no bearing upon the propriety of similar judicial action in the future. To begin with, there has now been ample time for reflection and judgment; whatever values there may be in the preservation of novel questions for appellate review may not support any restraints in the future. More important, the First Amendment stands as an absolute bar to the imposition of judicial restraints in circumstances of the kind presented by these cases.

II

The error that has pervaded these cases from the outset was the granting of any injunctive relief whatsoever, interim or otherwise. The entire thrust of the Government's claim throughout these cases has been that publication of the material sought to be enjoined "could," or "might," or "may" prejudice the national interest in various ways. But the First Amendment tolerates absolutely no prior judicial restraints of the press predicated upon surmise or conjecture that untoward consequences may result. Our cases, it is true, have indicated that there is a single, extremely narrow class of cases in which the First Amendment's ban on prior judicial restraint may be overridden. Our cases have thus far indicated that such cases may arise only when the Nation "is at war," *Schenck v. United States*, 249 U.S. 47, 52 (1919), during which times

> [n]o one would question but that a government might prevent actual obstruction to its recruiting service or the publication of the sailing dates of transports or the number and location of troops.

Near v. Minnesota, 283 U.S. 697, 716 (1931). Even if the present world situation were assumed to be tantamount to a time of war, or if the power of presently available armaments would justify even in peacetime the suppression of information that would set in motion a nuclear holocaust, in neither of these actions has the Government presented or even alleged that publication of items from or based upon the material at issue would cause the happening of an event of that nature. . . .

Source: New York Times Co. v. The United States, 430 U.S. 713 (No. 1873), Supreme Court of the United States, Decided June 30, 1971, from the Cornell Law School Legal Information Institute, Supreme Court Collection, http://supct.law.cornell.edu/supct/html/historics/USSC_CR_0403 _0713_ZS.html.

Document 6.4
The Cooper-Church Amendment to the Foreign Military Sales Act, June 29, 1970

Idaho Democratic senator Frank Church and liberal Kentucky Republican senator John Sherman Cooper cosponsored an amendment to an appropriations bill to restrain the president's discretion in the conduct of the Vietnam War. After considerable debate, including a seven-week filibuster, a modified version of the amendment was passed by both houses of Congress in December 1970 and became law in January 1971. By the time of the bill's passage, the president had already withdrawn U.S. ground forces from Cambodia.

AMENDMENT Intended to be proposed by Mr. Cooper (for himself, Mr. Church, Mr. Mansfield, and Mr. Aiken) to H.R. 15628, an Act to amend the Foreign Military Sales Act, viz: At the end of the bill add the following new section:

SEC. 7. The Foreign Military Sales Act is amended by adding at the end thereof the following new section:

"SEC. 47. Prohibition of assistance to Cambodia.

"In order to avoid the involvement of the United States in a wider war in Indochina and expedite the withdrawal of American forces from Vietnam, it is hereby provided that, unless specifically authorized by law hereafter enacted, no funds authorized or appropriated pursuant to this Act or any other law may be expended for the purpose of:

"(1) retaining United States ground forces in Cambodia.

"(2) paying the compensation or allowances of, or otherwise supporting directly or indirectly, any person in Cambodia who (a) furnishes military instruction to Cambodian forces; or (b) engages in any combat activity in support of Cambodian forces.

"(3) entering into or carrying out any contract or agreement to provide military instruction in Cambodia, or persons to engage in any combat activity in support of Cambodian forces.

"(4) supporting any combat activity in the air above Cambodia by United States air forces except for the interdiction of enemy supplies or personnel using the Cambodian territory for attack against or access into South Vietnam."

Source: "Cooper-Church Amendment," U.S. Senate Amendment to the Foreign Military Sales Act, U.S. House Resolution 15628, 91st Cong., 2d Session, version dated June 29, 1970.

Document 6.5
President Richard Nixon Tells National Security Adviser Henry Kissinger to "Get the Hell Out" of Vietnam, Oval Office Conversation, March 11, 1971

In a taped Oval Office conversation with his national security adviser, Henry Kissinger, the president declared his impatience with the war in Vietnam. Nixon and Kissinger shared no apparent illusions about the prospects for peace, with or without a suitable agreement with the North Vietnamese to end the American presence in the war.

President: . . . We know what these people [the South Vietnamese] can or can't do. [unclear] it's going to be close. They're going to take some [racks?]. We've got to get the hell out of there. That's for sure.

Kissinger: No question.

President: . . . I'm not going to allow their weakness and their fear of the North Vietnamese to, to, to delay us. . . . Now we, we've tried everything; we've done everything the military wants. We have, we've done everything to our own satisfaction in order to bring the war to a successful conclusion. I think, I think it's going to work. I think it will, I think, I agree with you that there's a 40 to 50 percent chance, maybe 55, that it will work, that we might even get an agreement. . . . Of course there will still be war out there, back and forth, but the South Vietnamese are not going to be knocked over by the North Vietnamese—not easily, not easily.

Source: Richard Nixon and Henry Kissinger, "Oval Office Conversation no. 466-12, after 4:00 p.m., March 11, 1971, White House Tapes," in Jeffrey Kimball, *The Vietnam War Files: Uncovering the Secret History of Nixon-Era Strategy* (Lawrence: University Press of Kansas, 2004), 144–145.

Document 6.6

President Richard Nixon and National Security Adviser Henry Kissinger Discuss the Fate of Vietnam, Oval Office Conversation, March 19, 1971

In a taped Oval Office conversation, Nixon and Kissinger make some blunt observations about the politics of Vietnamization.

Kissinger: . . . I think that there's a chance of a negotiation [unclear]. Again, it's less than even, but it's still

President: It might be [unclear] boy, [unclear] negotiations. . . . I think we've played the game down to the nut-cutting. It's very much to their advantage to have a negotiation to have us, get us the hell out of there and give us those prisoners.

Kissinger: That's right. That's why—

President: And we've got to do it, and, uh, we know that if they are willing to make that kind of a deal, . . anytime they're ready.

Kissinger: Well, we've got to get enough time to get out; it's got to be because

President: Well, I understand

Kissinger: Because we have to make sure that they don't knock the whole place over.

President: I don't mean [unclear; both talking], but

Kissinger: Our problem is that if we get out, after all the suffering we've gone through

President: We can't have them knocked over brutally.

Kissinger: We can't have them knocked over brutally, to put it brutally, before the election.

President: That's right.

Kissinger: And, uh

President: So that's why, that's why this strategy works pretty well, doesn't it?

Kissinger: That's right. You see, the thing is, as long as we keep our air force there. . . .

Source: Richard Nixon and Henry Kissinger, "Oval Office Conversation no. 471-2, 7:03–7:27 p.m., March 19, 1971, White House Tapes," in Jeffrey Kimball, *The Vietnam War Files: Uncovering the Secret History of Nixon-Era Strategy* (Lawrence: University Press of Kansas, 2004), 148–149.

Document 6.7
President Richard Nixon and National Security Adviser Henry Kissinger
Discuss the Diversionary Benefits of an Opening to China, April 14, 1971

In this telephone conversation, President Nixon and Henry Kissinger discuss the possibility of the mutual opening of China and the United States to one another. The implications for Taiwan and its president, Chiang Kai-shek, are sad, they agree, but news about China-U.S. relations will provide a welcome diversion from the war in Vietnam and provide leverage against the Soviet Union.

Kissinger: Mr. President.

President: Hello, Henry. I was wondering how the—have you checked in to see how they played the Chinese thing today.

Kissinger: Oh, yeah. It was tremendous, it was the lead item on every—I did['nt?] see it myself, I was with Bob Griffin, but I talked to Haig.

President: Yeah.

Kissinger: But he says it has been a tremendous thing on television, it has been the lead item on every television thing and on—

President: You mean rather than Vietnam for a change.

Kissinger: (laughter) Yeah, it's gone on, and on and on. And I found it helpful also with these Michigan Editors. . . .

President: Now on the China thing what we have to realize, Henry, is that in terms of the American public opinion, it is still against Communist China you know.

Kissinger: Right.

President: So we are not making any votes with this.

Kissinger: No, but we are quieting the intellectuals and the newsmen.

President: The intellectuals will worry, they will worry about something, but as we know as we move from the October 7 thing, that doesn't mean that we get much from them, it will just worry them.

Kissinger: That's right.

President: They will think something else is up and the whole thing has got to be played in terms of—how about the Taiwan thing, that's sort of worrisome, not a damn thing we can do about it though is there?

Kissinger: What Taiwan thing?

President: Well, I mean their concern about what we have said.

Kissinger: Right, but they haven't expressed it, yet, have they, I don't think so.

President: Oh, I think there was something in the paper indicating that Taiwan was— [complaining]

Kissinger: Oh, but that's inevitable, they have to say that. . . .

President: Well, Henry, the thing is the story change is going to take place, it has to take place, it better take place when they've got a friend here rather than when they've got an enemy here.

Kissinger: That's right. No, it's a tragedy that it has to happen to Chiang at the end of his life but we have to be cold about it.

President: We have to do what's best for us. . . .

President: Yes, and that he has here an Administration that is not going to just stand by and let Taiwan go down the drain; we're trying to hold their position as best we can.

Kissinger: Exactly. For every reason we have got to have a diversion from Vietnam in this country for a while.

President: That's the point isn't it, yeah.

Kissinger: And we need it for our game with the Soviets.

President: Yeah, yeah. . . .

Source: Richard Nixon and Henry Kissinger, "Record of Kissinger-Nixon Telephone Conversation (Telecon) with Hand-Written Annotation," April 14, 1971, from the National Security Archive, George Washington University, www2.gwu.edu/~nsarchiv/NSAEBB/NSAEBB145/05.pdf.

Document 6.8
National Security Adviser Henry Kissinger Spells out U.S. Aims in Vietnam for the Chinese, July 1971

Henry Kissinger's handwritten notations in his briefing book for his trip to China clearly indicate what the American policy in Vietnam was: withdrawal of American troops, then a continuation of warfare between North and South Vietnamese forces. The "objective realities" of the situation on the ground, meaning the correlation of military forces, would determine the fate of South Vietnam.

On behalf of President Nixon, I want to assure the prime minister solemnly that the United States is prepared to make a settlement that will truly leave the political evolution of South Vietnam to the Vietnamese alone. We are ready to withdraw all of our forces by a fixed date and let objective realities shape the political future. . . .

[In Kissinger's hand:] We want a decent interval. You have our assurance.

Source: Excerpt from the "Indochina" section of the briefing book for Kissinger's July 1971 trip, in Jeffrey Kimball, *The Vietnam War Files: Uncovering the Secret History of Nixon-Era Strategy* (Lawrence: University Press of Kansas, 2004), 187.

Document 6.9
Chairman Mao Zedong Lays the Groundwork for Rapprochement with the United States, April 4, 1971

Mao Zedong's decision to initiate rapprochement with the United States through the device of "Ping-Pong diplomacy" was almost derailed by his own policy that after he had taken his nightly sleeping pills, his words "did not count."

. . . [W]hen the American team expressed a desire to visit China, after other foreign teams had been invited, Mao endorsed a Foreign Ministry recommendation to turn down the request.

But he was clearly uneasy with this decision, and staff noticed that he seemed preoccupied for the rest of the day. That night at 11 o'clock he took a large dose of sleeping pills, and then had dinner with his female nurse-cum-assistant, Wu Xujun. . . . His routine was to take sleeping pills before dinner, so he would fall asleep right after the meal, which he ate sitting at the edge of his bed. . . . This time, Wu recalled,

after he finished eating, he slumped on the table. . . . But suddenly he spoke, mumbling, and it took me a very long time to work out that he wanted me to telephone the Foreign Ministry. . . . "Invite the American team to China." . . .

I was dumbstruck. I thought: this is just the opposite of what he had authorized during the day!

Mao's standing orders were that:

his "words after taking sleeping pills don't count." Did they count now? I was really in a dilemma. . . . I must make him say it again. I pretended nothing was happening and went on eating. . . . After a little while, Mao lifted his head and tried very hard to open his eyes and said to me:

"Little Wu . . . Why don't you go and do what I asked you to do?"

Mao . . . only called me "Little Wu" when he was very serious.

I asked deliberately in a loud voice: "Chairman, what did you say to me? I was eating and didn't hear you clearly. Please say it again."

So Mao repeated, word for word, haltingly, what he had said.

Wu then checked with Mao about the pills rule:

"You've taken sleeping pills. Do your words count?"

Mao waved at me: "Yes, they do! Do it quickly. Otherwise there won't be time."

Mao kept himself awake until Wu returned with the news that she had done what he asked.

Source: Jung Chang and Jon Halliday, *Mao: The Unknown Story* (New York: Alfred A. Knopf, 2005), 580–581.

Document 6.10
Reflections on "Ping-Pong Diplomacy," April 1971

*The hand of Chairman Mao Zedong in the Chinese invitation to American table-tennis play-
ers was evident to the editors of the* New York Times, *who celebrated the emergence of a new
form of dialogue between nations: "Ping-Pong diplomacy."*

. . . The virtues of table tennis as both a form of exercise and spectator sport are well
known. Now Mao Tse-Tung is demonstrating that table tennis can be used as a subtle and
effective instrument of diplomacy. . . . The people of China and the United States, two
of the world's great nations, have been separated from each other much too long; renewed
contacts will advance the cause of understanding between the two countries. . . .

*As one of the first American journalists allowed into the People's Republic of China since the
1949 revolution,* Life *magazine correspondent John Saar wrote firsthand about his journey
behind the Bamboo Curtain.*

. . . The anticipated climax to the visit came with an invitation to meet Premier Chou
En-lai. . . . He made serious response to U.S. team member Glenn Cowan's advocacy of
hippie philosophy, then moved calmly to the historic statement we all were waiting for:
". . . we have opened a new page in the relations of the Chinese and American people.
And I am confident this renewing of friendship . . . will certainly meet with the approval
and support of the great majority of our two peoples."

    [U.S. ping-pong team leader Graham] Steenhoven had no doubts. "I think his hand
of friendship was absolutely sincere." . . .

Life *magazine presidential correspondent Hugh Sidey sought to explain the president's "open
pleasure" at Ping-Pong diplomacy.*

There is a passage in Richard Nixon's writings where he tells about the Chinese word for
"crisis," a favorite term of his in any language. That word, Nixon points out, is made up
of two characters. One of them stands for "danger," the other stands for "opportunity."

    That Oriental footnote, appropriately, is the clue to the President's open pleasure at
the sudden renewal of contact with mainland China. In the power game Nixon plays, men
are drawn to danger not only of necessity but because it provides the greatest stimulus.
And China is a huge mass of unmined opportunity. . . .

Sources: Editorial, "Ping-Pong Diplomacy," *New York Times,* April 10, 1971; John Saar, "A Whole
Country Being Worked Very Hard," *Life,* April 30, 1971, 33; Hugh Sidey, "Thirsting to Get into
China," *Life,* April 30, 1971, 4.

Document 6.11
Deputy National Security Assistant Alexander Haig Lobbies Prime Minister Zhou Enlai to Help Make the President's Visit a Success, January 3, 1972

Henry Kissinger's deputy, Gen. Alexander Haig, sought sympathy in the People's Republic of China for the political risks that President Nixon was prepared to take to improve relations with China. Haig also promised in this conversation with Zhou Enlai (whose name appears here in its alternate form, Chou En-lai) to pass along to the Chinese U.S. intelligence about the Soviet threat to China.

The White House, January 3, 1972
TOP SECRET/SENSITIVE/EXCLUSIVE EYES ONLY
MEMORANDUM OF CONVERSATION
PLACE: The Great Hall of the People
          Peking, China
DATE: Midnight, January 3, 1972

. . .

Haig: I am very honored that the Prime Minister is seeing me personally.

Chou En-lai: Yes, because I heard . . . that you had important matters to convey.

Haig: Yes, Dr. Kissinger and the President asked me to request an audience to give you, in blunt terms, a soldier's assessment of recent events in South Asia and discuss them in context of the President's visit.

Chou En-lai: How is Dr. Kissinger? I heard he had a slight cold.

Haig: He has had a touch of the flu but is much better today.

Chou En-lai: You have to be careful here too because it is snowing. I don't know whether it has snowed in Washington yet. . . .

Haig: . . . [W]e are convinced that the Soviet strategy is first to neutralize the People's Republic and then turn on us. . . . Since the cease fire has gone into effect between India and Pakistan, we have carefully assessed subsequent Soviet actions and we are convinced that they intend to continue their efforts to encircle the People's Republic. We say this based on a number of factors . . . above all, their stepped up expressions of support for Hanoi in its conduct of the war, as well as increased Soviet materiel support for Hanoi. . . . [T]he continuation of the war in Southeast Asia can only give Moscow an opportunity to increase its influence in Hanoi and to further the encirclement of the People's Republic. We feel strongly that Moscow is urging Hanoi in the direction of continued military action and as such, they are forging another link in the chain which is designed to constrain the People's Republic. In all of these circumstances, we also believe that President Nixon's visit takes on a new and immediate significance. . . . In the light of our own strategic interests . . . we are convinced and dedicated to the proposition that the viability of the People's Republic should be maintained. . . .

   . . . One of the steps we are prepared to do unilaterally and without any reciprocity on the part of the People's Republic—is to provide you with our assessments of the

Soviet threat which exists against the People's Republic to the degree that our own technical resources are able to do so . . . perhaps through a third country or through whatever other means you might prefer.

An additional implication of the assessment I have just provided is the fact that we have a major problem developing within the United States. . . . This is a strange merger of forces . . . dedicated to either preventing the President's visit to Peking or to contributing to its failure. The forces which have converged are composed of first the American Left which is essentially pro-Soviet and if it is not truly dominated by Moscow in that sense of the word, it is at least strongly attracted toward Moscow and future U.S. alignment with Moscow. In this instance, the Left has joined in a strange wedding with those conservative elements who are strong supporters of Taiwan. . . .

. . . For this reason, President Nixon and Dr. Kissinger are all the more concerned about making President Nixon's visit a success not only in reality but also in the appearance of the visit itself. . . .

Unfortunately, most American journalists are shallow idiots. . . . For this reason, it is crucial that there be no public embarrassment to the President as a result of his visit to Peking. It is in our mutual interest that the visit reinforce President Nixon's image as a world leader. . . .

Source: Alexander Haig and Chou En-lai, "Haig's Visit and Final Preparations for Nixon's Visit," Memorandum of Conversation at Great Hall of the People, January 3, 1972, from the National Security Archive, George Washington University, www2.gwu.edu/~nsarchiv/NSAEBB/NSAEBB70/doc24.pdf.

Document 6.12
Chairman Mao Zedong Likens U.S. Diplomatic Moves to "a Cat Feeling Sad for a Mouse," Conversation with Chinese Prime Minister Zhou Enlai, January 4, 1972

On the evening of January 4, Premier Zhou Enlai (whose name appears here in its alternate form, Chou En-lai) met with Chairman Mao Zedong to review Gen. Alexander Haig's comments (see Document 6.11) and to consider an appropriate reply.

. . . The Premier then reported that Haig said the Soviet Union was changing its strategy and plotted to surround China using the sub-continent. Chairman said, "Surround China! It would be such a big deal if we asked them to come to our rescue." "Its concerns for us are just like a cat feeling sad for a mouse! . . . This is too serious, worry about us! And then there are Taiwan, the Philippines, South Korea; are *they* not surrounding us? [emphasis added]. . .

When the Premier mentioned that Haig said Nixon was seeking to restore his image as a world leader, the Chairman said: "The Americans are strange. He admits that the so-called pro-Soviet, pro-Taiwan and bureaucratic forces all oppose him domestically. As the President of the United States, Nixon can't even be the leader of the U.S. How can he talk about being a world leader! Surround, surround, we only have two persons here, come surround us!"

Then the Premier showed the draft reply to the oral message to the Chairman. The Chairman said: "Good. I think we can tell him this. After we tell him this, the worst thing that could happen would be that the visit is cancelled. If he hasn't come in twenty-two years, he could wait another 100 years! These Americans, after two nights of good sleep, they have forgotten again. If you don't push him, he's not comfortable. All in all, the worst case would be that the visit is cancelled, in my opinion, in a few years he will come after all."

Finally the Premier asked: "The U.S. side didn't mention anything about the draft joint communiqué except the Taiwan Issue. Shall we leave it as it is?" The Chairman said: "That's fine. If we want to make some change, let's change 'the people want progress' to 'the people want revolution.' Revolution is exactly what they fear. The more they fear it, the more we need to mention it." . . .

Source: "Haig's Preparatory Mission for Nixon's Visit to China in 1972," January 4, 1972, in Diplomatic History Institute of the Chinese Ministry of Foreign Affairs, *Xin zhongguo wenjiao fengyun [New China's Diplomatic Experience]* (Beijing: Shijie zhishi, 1991), 3:71–82, from the National Security Archive, George Washington University, www2.gwu.edu/~nsarchiv/NSAEBB/NSAEBB70/doc26.pdf.

Document 6.13
The Shanghai Communiqué, Joint U.S.-Chinese Statement, February 27, 1972

President Nixon's momentous trip to China was capped with the issuance of a joint communiqué describing a small land of agreement and a vast sea of disagreement. Chairman Mao Zedong's offhand comment (see **Document 6.12***) regarding changing the document's wording to increase American alarm at Chinese revolutionary fervor was clearly acted upon in the negotiations that produced the final wording of this joint statement.*

President Richard Nixon of the United States of America visited the People's Republic of China at the invitation of Premier Chou En-lai of the People's Republic of China from February 21 to February 28, 1972. Accompanying the President were Mrs. Nixon, U.S. Secretary of State William Rogers, Assistant to the President Dr. Henry Kissinger, and other American officials.

President Nixon met with Chairman Mao Tse-tung of the Communist Party of China on February 21. The two leaders had a serious and frank exchange of views on Sino-U.S. relations and world affairs.

During the visit, extensive, earnest, and frank discussions were held between President Nixon and Premier Chou En-lai on the normalization of relations between the United States of America and the People's Republic of China, as well as on other matters of interest to both sides. In addition, Secretary of State William Rogers and Foreign Minister Chi Pengfei held talks in the same spirit.

President Nixon and his party visited Peking and viewed cultural, industrial and agricultural sites, and they also toured Hangchow and Shanghai where, continuing discussions with Chinese leaders, they viewed similar places of interest.

The leaders of the People's Republic of China and the United States of America found it beneficial to have this opportunity, after so many years without contact, to present candidly to one another their views on a variety of issues. They reviewed the international situation in which important changes and great upheavals are taking place and expounded their respective positions and attitudes.

The U.S. side stated: Peace in Asia and peace in the world requires efforts both to reduce immediate tensions and to eliminate the basic causes of conflict. The United States will work for a just and secure peace: just, because it fulfills the aspirations of peoples and nations for freedom and progress; secure, because it removes the danger of foreign aggression. The United States supports individual freedom and social progress for all the peoples of the world, free of outside pressure or intervention. The United States believes that the effort to reduce tensions is served by improving communication between countries that have different ideologies so as to lessen the risks of confrontation through accident, miscalculation or misunderstanding. Countries should treat each other with mutual respect and be willing to compete peacefully, letting performance be the ultimate judge. No country should claim infallibility and each country should be prepared to re-examine its own attitudes for the common good. The United States stressed that the peoples of Indochina should be allowed to determine their destiny without outside intervention; its constant primary objective has been a negotiated solution; the eight-point proposal put forward by the Republic of Vietnam and the United States on January 27, 1972, represents a basis for the attainment of that objective; in the absence of a negotiated settlement the United States envisages the ultimate withdrawal of all U.S. forces from the region consistent with the aim of self-determination for each country of Indochina. . . [T]he United States supports the right of the peoples of South Asia to shape their own future in peace, free of military threat, and without having the area become the subject of great power rivalry.

The Chinese side stated: Wherever there is oppression, there is resistance. Countries want independence, nations want liberation and the people want revolution. This has become the irresistible trend of history. All nations, big or small, should be equal; big nations should not bully the small and strong nations should not bully the weak. China will never be a superpower and it opposes hegemony and power politics of any kind. The Chinese side stated that it firmly supports the struggles of all the oppressed people and nations for freedom and liberation and that the people of all countries have the right to choose their social systems according to their own wishes and the right to safeguard the independence, sovereignty and territorial integrity of their own countries and oppose foreign aggression, interference, control and subversion. All foreign troops should be withdrawn to their own countries.

The Chinese side expressed its firm support to the peoples of Vietnam, Laos, and Cambodia in their efforts for the attainment of their goal and its firm support to the seven-point proposal of the Provisional Revolutionary Government of the Republic of South Vietnam and the elaboration of February this year on the two key problems in the proposal, and to the Joint Declaration of the Summit Conference of the Indo-Chinese Peoples. . . .

There are essential differences between China and the United States in their social systems and foreign policies. However, the two sides agreed that countries, regardless of their social systems, should conduct their relations on the principles of respect for the sovereignty and territorial integrity of all states, nonaggression against other states, noninterference in the internal affairs of other states, equality and mutual benefit, and peaceful coexistence. International disputes should be settled on this basis, without resorting to the use or threat of force. The United States and the People's Republic of China are prepared to apply these principles to their mutual relations.

With these principles of international relations in mind the two sides stated that:

—progress toward the normalization of relations between China and the United States is in the interests of all countries;

—both wish to reduce the danger of international military conflict;

—neither should seek hegemony in the Asia-Pacific region and each is opposed to efforts by any other country or group of countries to establish such hegemony; and

—neither is prepared to negotiate on behalf of any third party or to enter into agreements or understandings with the other directed at other states.

Both sides are of the view that it would be against the interests of the peoples of the world for any major country to collude with another against other countries, or for major countries to divide up the world into spheres of interest.

The two sides reviewed the long-standing serious disputes between China and the United States. The Chinese side reaffirmed its position: The Taiwan question is the crucial question obstructing the normalization of relations between China and the United States; the Government of the People's Republic of China is the sole legal government of China; Taiwan is a province of China which has long been returned to the motherland; the liberation of Taiwan is China's internal affair in which no other country has the right to interfere; and all U.S. forces and military installations must be withdrawn from Taiwan. The Chinese Government firmly opposes any activities which aim at the creation of "one China, one Taiwan, . . . one China, two governments," "two Chinas," and "independent Taiwan" or advocate that "the status of Taiwan remains to be determined."

The U.S. side declared: The United States acknowledges that all Chinese on either side of the Taiwan Strait maintain there is but one China and that Taiwan is a part of China. The United States Government does not challenge that position. It reaffirms its interest in a peaceful settlement of the Taiwan question by the Chinese themselves. With this prospect in mind, it affirms the ultimate objective of the withdrawal of all U.S. forces and military installations from Taiwan. In the meantime, it will progressively reduce its forces and military installations on Taiwan as the tension in the area diminishes.

The two sides agreed that it is desirable to broaden the understanding between the two peoples. To this end, they discussed specific areas in such fields as science, technology, culture, sports and journalism, in which people-to-people contacts and exchanges would be mutually beneficial. Each side undertakes to facilitate the further development of such contacts and exchanges.

Both sides view bilateral trade as another area from which mutual benefit can be derived, and agreed that economic relations based on equality and mutual benefit are in the interest of the people of the two countries. They agree to facilitate the progressive development of trade between their two countries.

The two sides agreed that they will stay in contact through various channels. . . .

Source: "Joint Statement Following Discussions with Leaders of the People's Republic of China," February 27, 1972, in *Public Papers of the Presidents of the United States: Richard Nixon 1969–1974,* from the American Presidency Project, University of California, Santa Barbara, www.presidency.ucsb.edu.

Document 6.14
"Additional Measures to Expose Imperialist Policies," Planning Document by the Central Committee of the Communist Party of the Soviet Union, January 21, 1971

"Peaceful coexistence" did not mean an end to the ideological conflict between the superpowers. This planning document provides insight into the Soviet perspective on landmark Cold War events, such as the establishment of the Peace Corps, as well as the Soviets' preferred view of the United States as a land of violent turmoil.

CENTRAL COMMITTEE. COMMUNIST PARTY
OF THE SOVIET UNION [TsK KPSS]
Additional Measures to Expose Imperialist Policies

We intend to make use of concrete facts to expose capitalist reality, . . . the totalitarian character of a bourgeois state, and the strengthening of reactionary thought in the bourgeois apparatus and in capitalistic society as a whole.

The realization of such measures will permit us to coordinate the Soviet press, radio and television in such a way that the public's attention will be directed to the concrete manifestations of the anti-popular nature of imperialism. . . .

A calendar of this type of events, mainly pertaining to the USA is attached. Similar plans pertaining to other imperialistic states could be developed in the course of work.

We request your review.

Assistant Chief of Propaganda   (A. Iakovlev)
Department, TsK KPSS
January 21, 1971
Attachment 170   Calendar of Certain Events

January 1, 1863—In the USA the Act to free black slaves went into effect. Provides a rationale to point out the severity of the ethnic problem in the United States of America.

January 5, 1957—President Eisenhower in a message to Congress set forth an expansionist U.S. policy for the Near East and Middle East that became known as the "Eisenhower-Dulles Doctrine." . . .

February 9, 1950—Beginning of the "McCarthy Era"

March 1, 1961—Decade of the "Peace Corps USA," an organization engaging in subversive activity in Africa and Asia

March 5, 1946—Churchill's speech at Fulton—the beginning of the "cold war" against socialist countries

March 12, 1947—Acceptance in the USA of Truman's aggressive foreign policy doctrine. . .

March 23, 1947—Truman's order to verify the loyalty of all government employees. . .

April 4, 1969—The leader of the movement for the civil rights of American Negroes, Martin Luther King, is assassinated in the USA.

April 14, 1865—President Abraham Lincoln is assassinated.

April 15–19, 1961—Decade of attempted armed invasion of Cuba by the USA. . .

June 5, 1947—USA adopts expansionist "Marshall Plan"

June 5, 1968—Robert Kennedy assassinated

June 23, 1947—USA adopts anti-labor Taft-Hartley law

June, 1950—Beginning of USA intervention in Korea. . .

Source: Central Committee, Communist Party of the Soviet Union, "Additional Measures to Expose Imperialist Policies," translation available from Library of Congress, "Cold War: Soviet Perspectives," *Revelations from the Russian Archives,* www.loc.gov/exhibits/archives/w2compar.html.

Document 6.15
Quadripartite Agreement on Berlin, September 3, 1971

West German chancellor Willy Brandt pursued his own policy of détente with the East, Ostpolitik. The four-power agreement on the division of Berlin united Brandt's Ostpolitik and Richard Nixon's détente. Under the terms of the agreement, the United States, the Soviet Union, Britain, and France agreed to accept the status of West Berlin. Although Berlin was not a "constituent part" of the Federal Republic, it was tied to West Germany, and no party to the agreement would attempt unilaterally, or by force, to change its status.

By the Governments of the United Kingdom of Great Britain and Northern Ireland, the French Republic, the Union of Soviet Socialist Republics and the United States of America,

Represented by their Ambassadors, who held a series of meetings in the building formerly occupied by the Allied Control Council in the American Sector of Berlin,

Acting on the basis of their quadripartite rights and responsibilities, and of the corresponding wartime and postwar agreements and decisions of the Four Powers, which are not affected,

Taking into account the existing situation in the relevant area,

Guided by the desire to contribute to practical improvements of the situation,

Without prejudice to their legal positions,

Have agreed on the following:

PART I. GENERAL PROVISIONS

1. The four Governments will strive to promote the elimination of tension and the prevention of complications in the relevant area.
2. The four Governments, taking into account their obligations under the Charter of the United Nations, agree that there should be no use or threat of force in the area and that disputes shall be settled solely by peaceful means.
3. The four Governments will mutually respect their individual and joint rights and responsibilities, which remain unchanged.
4. The four Governments agree that, irrespective of the differences in legal views, the situation which has developed in the area, and as it is defined in this Agreement as well as in the other agreements referred to in this Agreement, shall not be changed unilaterally.

PART II: PROVISIONS RELATING TO THE WESTERN SECTORS OF BERLIN

A. The Government of the Union of Soviet Socialist Republics declares that transit traffic by road, rail and waterways through the territory of the German Democratic Republic of civilian persons and goods between the Western Sectors of Berlin and the Federal Republic of Germany will be unimpeded; that such traffic will be facilitated so as to take place in the most simple and expeditious manner; and that it will receive preferential treatment.

   Detailed arrangements concerning this civilian traffic, as set forth in annex I, will be agreed by the competent German authorities. . . .

Source: "Quadripartite Agreement on Berlin," September 3, 1971, available from the German Historical Institute, Washington, D.C., http://germanhistorydocs.ghi-dc.org/document.cfm?document _id=77.

Document 6.16
Strategic Arms Limitation Talks Interim Agreement (SALT I), May 26, 1972

The agreement reached at the conclusion of the first round of Strategic Arms Limitation Talks sought to limit the arms race by imposing numerical as well as qualitative limits on ballistic missile launchers of all types. President Nixon and General Secretary Leonid Brezhnev signed SALT I, an "interim agreement," at a summit meeting in Moscow. It entered into force on October 3, 1972. The treaty was a holding action, whose primary benefit was not its effect on the arms race but its contribution to regularizing U.S.-Soviet relations.

INTERIM AGREEMENT BETWEEN THE UNITED STATES OF AMERICA AND THE UNION OF SOVIET SOCIALIST REPUBLICS ON CERTAIN MEASURES WITH RESPECT TO THE LIMITATION OF STRATEGIC OFFENSIVE ARMS

. . .

ARTICLE I

The Parties undertake not to start construction of additional fixed land-based intercontinental ballistic missile (ICBM) launchers after July 1, 1972.

ARTICLE II

The Parties undertake not to convert land-based launchers for light ICBMs, or for ICBMs of older types deployed prior to 1964, into land-based launchers for heavy ICBMs of types deployed after that time.

ARTICLE III

The Parties undertake to limit submarine-launched ballistic missile (SLBM) launchers and modern ballistic missile submarines to the numbers operational and under construction on the date of signature of this Interim Agreement, and in addition to launchers and submarines constructed under procedures established by the Parties as replacements for an equal number of ICBM launchers of older types deployed prior to 1964 or for launchers on older submarines.

ARTICLE IV

Subject to the provisions of this Interim Agreement, modernization and replacement of strategic offensive ballistic missiles and launchers covered by this Interim Agreement may be undertaken.

ARTICLE V

1. For the purpose of providing assurance of compliance with the provisions of this Interim Agreement, each Party shall use national technical means of verification at its disposal in a manner consistent with generally recognized principles of international law.
2. Each Party undertakes not to interfere with the national technical means of verification of the other Party operating in accordance with paragraph 1 of this Article.
3. Each Party undertakes not to use deliberate concealment measures which impede verification by national technical means of compliance with the provisions of this Interim Agreement. This obligation shall not require changes in current construction, assembly, conversion, or overhaul practices.

ARTICLE VI

To promote the objectives and implementation of the provisions of this Interim Agreement, the Parties shall use the Standing Consultative Commission established under Article XIII of the Treaty on the Limitation of Anti-Ballistic Missile Systems in accordance with the provisions of that Article.

ARTICLE VII

The Parties undertake to continue active negotiations for limitations on strategic offensive arms. The obligations provided for in this Interim Agreement shall not prejudice the scope or terms of the limitations on strategic offensive arms which may be worked out in the course of further negotiations.

ARTICLE VIII

1. This Interim Agreement shall enter into force upon exchange of written notices of acceptance by each Party, which exchange shall take place simultaneously with the exchange of instruments of ratification of the Treaty on the Limitation of Anti-Ballistic Missile Systems.
2. This Interim Agreement shall remain in force for a period of five years unless replaced earlier by an agreement on more complete measures limiting strategic offensive arms. It is the objective of the Parties to conduct active follow-on negotiations with the aim of concluding such an agreement as soon as possible.
3. Each Party shall, in exercising its national sovereignty, have the right to withdraw from this Interim Agreement if it decides that extraordinary events related to the subject matter of this Interim Agreement have jeopardized its supreme interests. It shall give notice of its decision to the other Party six months prior to withdrawal from this Interim Agreement. Such notice shall include a statement of the extraordinary events the notifying Party regards as having jeopardized its supreme interests.

DONE at Moscow on May 26, 1972

Source: "Interim Agreement between the United States of America and the Union of Soviet Socialist Republics on Certain Measures with Respect to the Limitation of Strategic Offensive Arms," May 26, 1972, from the Federation of American Scientists, www.fas.org/nuke/control/salt1/text/salt1.htm.

Document 6.17
Treaty on the Limitation of Anti-Ballistic Missile Systems, May 26, 1972

*In the ABM Treaty, which was concluded simultaneously with SALT I (see **Document 6.16**), the United States and the Soviet Union agreed to leave unchallenged each nation's ability to strike at the other with its nuclear arsenal, thus preserving the "balance of terror" of mutual assured destruction. Under the treaty, each side was permitted only two ABM deployment areas. A protocol to the treaty, agreed to in 1976, reduced the agreed-to deployment areas to one apiece.*

. . .

ARTICLE I

1. Each Party undertakes to limit anti-ballistic missile (ABM) systems and to adopt other measures in accordance with the provisions of this Treaty.

2. Each Party undertakes not to deploy ABM systems for a defense of the territory of its country and not to provide a base for such a defense, and not to deploy ABM systems for defense of an individual region except as provided for in Article III of this Treaty. . . .

ARTICLE III

Each Party undertakes not to deploy ABM systems or their components except that:

(a) within one ABM system deployment area having a radius of one hundred and fifty kilometers and centered on the Party's national capital, a Party may deploy: (1) no more than one hundred ABM launchers and no more than one hundred ABM interceptor missiles at launch sites, and (2) ABM radars within no more than six ABM radar complexes, the area of each complex being circular and having a diameter of no more than three kilometers; and

(b) within one ABM system deployment area having a radius of one hundred and fifty kilometers and containing ICBM silo launchers, a Party may deploy: (1) no more than one hundred ABM launchers and no more than one hundred ABM interceptor missiles at launch sites, (2) two large phased-array ABM radars comparable in potential to corresponding ABM radars operational or under construction on the date of signature of the Treaty in an ABM system deployment area containing ICBM silo launchers, and (3) no more than eighteen ABM radars each having a potential less than the potential of the smaller of the above-mentioned two large phased-array ABM radars.

ARTICLE IV

The limitations provided for in Article III shall not apply to ABM systems or their components used for development or testing, and located within current or additionally agreed test ranges. Each Party may have no more than a total of fifteen ABM launchers at test ranges.

ARTICLE V

1. Each Party undertakes not to develop, test, or deploy ABM systems or components which are sea-based, air-based, space-based, or mobile land-based.

2. Each Party undertakes not to develop, test or deploy ABM launchers for launching more than one ABM interceptor missile at a time from each launcher, not to modify deployed launchers to provide them with such a capacity, not to develop, test, or deploy automatic or semi-automatic or other similar systems for rapid reload of ABM launchers. . . .

ARTICLE XV

1. This Treaty shall be of unlimited duration.

2. Each Party shall, in exercising its national sovereignty, have the right to withdraw from this Treaty if it decides that extraordinary events related to the subject matter of this Treaty have jeopardized its supreme interests. It shall give notice of its decision to the

other Party six months prior to withdrawal from the Treaty. Such notice shall include a statement of the extraordinary events the notifying Party regards as having jeopardized its supreme interests. . . .

Source: "Treaty between the United States of America and the Union of Soviet Socialist Republics on the Limitation of Anti-Ballistic Missile Systems," May 26, 1972, from the Federation of American Scientists, www.fas.org/nuke/control/abmt/text/abm2.htm.

Document 6.18
Senator Henry "Scoop" Jackson Proposes Amendment to the U.S.-Soviet Trade Bill, October 4, 1972

Senator Henry "Scoop" Jackson, D.-Wash., championed the rights of Soviet Jews to emigrate to Israel. He attempted to force President Richard Nixon (and, subsequently, Presidents Gerald Ford and Jimmy Carter) to link Soviet policy on Jewish emigration to the relaxation of trade barriers between the United States and the Soviet Union, a key item on Nixon's agenda for détente. Although his 1972 proposed amendment did not become law, it led the Soviets to ease emigration restrictions and provided a focus for those critics of détente who thought it wrong not to challenge the Soviet Union on moral grounds. When a subsequent Jackson amendment became law in January 1975, the Soviets withdrew from the U.S-Soviet trade agreement.

Mr. JACKSON: Mr. President, I am pleased to submit and send to the desk an amendment in the cause of human rights and individual liberty; and I am proud to be joined in this effort by a bipartisan majority of 72 members of the U.S. Senate. There are times when the depth of our commitment to our own deepest values is put to the test, and this is one of those times.

Last week when I spoke in this Chamber I quoted a great and wise man who, I am certain, would approve of what we are doing here today. The words are those of Alexander Solzhenitzyn, the Russian Nobel laureate, who was prevented by his government from traveling to the West to deliver them:

There are no internal affairs left on our crowded earth.

Despite the effort to silence Solzhenitzyn he has been heard; and because what he says is true, I am confident he will hear us today. . . .

Mr. President, the tyranny the Soviet Government continues to inflict on its minorities of all faiths and persuasions, on its dissidents, its scholars, its scientists, and men of letters is a crime in which all who choose to acquiesce are implicated. To the oppression, which has become commonplace, we have now seen the Soviet authorities add a barbarous ransom on those Russian Jews who seek to emigrate to Israel. It is toward this most recent outrage that we have directed a specific section of our amendment. . . .

Once before, Mr. President, within our memory, the world stood by while an innocent people was all but exterminated. The remnant of that nightmare has established and now defends a brave and proud democracy. In a terrible time, the one bright light in the hopes of the Soviet Jews is the existence of the State of Israel. That Israel should exist is a modern miracle; that the Russian Jews should be denied the right to go there is a cruel and inhuman irony. It must be ended. . . .

Amendment No. 1691

At the end of the bill, add the following new section:

EAST-WEST TRADE AND FUNDAMENTAL HUMAN RIGHTS

Sec. 10. (a) To assure the continued dedication of the United States to fundamental human rights, and notwithstanding any other law, after October 15, 1972, no nonmarket economy country shall be eligible to receive most-favored-nation treatment or to participate in any program of the Government of the United States which extends credits or credit guarantees or investment guarantees, directly or indirectly, during the period beginning with the date on which the President of the United States determines that such country—

(1) denies its citizens the right or opportunity to emigrate; or

(2) imposes more than a nominal tax on emigration or on the visas or other documents required for emigration; for any purpose or cause whatsoever; or

(3) imposes more than a nominal tax, levy, fine, fee, or other charge on any citizen as a consequence of the desire of such citizen to emigrate to the country of his choice, and ending on the date on which the President determines that such country is no longer in violation of paragraph (1), (2) or (3). . . .

Source: Congressional Record, vol. 118, part 25, October 4, 1972 (Washington, D.C.: U.S. Government Printing Office, 1972): 33658-9.

Document 6.19
President Richard Nixon's Address Announcing the End of the (American) War in Vietnam, January 23, 1973

In a radio and television address to the nation, President Nixon announced that "peace with honor" had been achieved in Vietnam.

Good evening:

I have asked for this radio and television time tonight for the purpose of announcing that we today have concluded an agreement to end the war and bring peace with honor in Vietnam and in Southeast Asia.

The following statement is being issued at this moment in Washington and Hanoi:

At 12:30 Paris time today, January 23, 1973, the Agreement on Ending the War and Restoring Peace in Vietnam was initialed by Dr. Henry Kissinger on behalf of the United States, and Special Adviser Le Duc Tho on behalf of the Democratic Republic of Vietnam.

The agreement will be formally signed by the parties participating in the Paris Conference on Vietnam on January 27, 1973, at the International Conference Center in Paris.

The cease-fire will take effect at 2400 Greenwich Mean Time, January 27, 1973. The United States and the Democratic Republic of Vietnam express the hope that this agreement will insure stable peace in Vietnam and contribute to the preservation of lasting peace in Indochina and Southeast Asia.

That concludes the formal statement. Throughout the years of negotiations, we have insisted on peace with honor. In my addresses to the Nation from this room of January 25 and May 8 [1972], I set forth the goals that we considered essential for peace with honor.

In the settlement that has now been agreed to, all the conditions that I laid down then have been met:

A cease-fire, internationally supervised, will begin at 7 p.m., this Saturday, January 27, Washington time.

Within 60 days from this Saturday, all Americans held prisoners of war throughout Indochina will be released. There will be the fullest possible accounting for all of those who are missing in action.

During the same 60-day period, all American forces will be withdrawn from South Vietnam.

The people of South Vietnam have been guaranteed the right to determine their own future, without outside interference. . . .

We shall continue to aid South Vietnam within the terms of the agreement, and we shall support efforts by the people of South Vietnam to settle their problems peacefully among themselves.

We must recognize that ending the war is only the first step toward building the peace. All parties must now see to it that this is a peace that lasts, and also a peace that heals—and a peace that not only ends the war in Southeast Asia but contributes to the prospects of peace in the whole world.

This will mean that the terms of the agreement must be scrupulously adhered to. We shall do everything the agreement requires of us, and we shall expect the other parties to do everything it requires of them. We shall also expect other interested nations to help insure that the agreement is carried out and peace is maintained.

As this long and very difficult war ends, I would like to address a few special words to each of those who have been parties in the conflict.

First, to the people and Government of South Vietnam: By your courage, by your sacrifice, you have won the precious right to determine your own future, and you have developed the strength to defend that right. We look forward to working with you in the future—friends in peace as we have been allies in war.

To the leaders of North Vietnam: As we have ended the war through negotiations, let us now build a peace of reconciliation. For our part, we are prepared to make a major effort to help achieve that goal. But just as reciprocity was needed to end the war, so too will it be needed to build and strengthen the peace.

To the other major powers that have been involved even indirectly: Now is the time for mutual restraint so that the peace we have achieved can last.

And finally, to all of you who are listening, the American people: Your steadfastness in supporting our insistence on peace with honor has made peace with honor possible. . . .

Source: Richard Nixon, "Address to the Nation Announcing Conclusion of an Agreement on Ending the War and Restoring Peace in Vietnam," January 23, 1973, in *Public Papers of the Presidents of the United States: Richard Nixon 1969–1974,* from the American Presidency Project, University of California, Santa Barbara, www.presidency.ucsb.edu.

Document 6.20
The War Powers Resolution, November 7, 1973

The culmination of congressional resistance to the "imperial presidency" was the passage, over President Nixon's veto, of an act intended to prohibit the president from taking the nation to war without adequate consultation with Congress. No president has accepted the constitutionality of the act.

Joint Resolution Concerning the War Powers of Congress and the President.
Resolved by the Senate and the House of Representatives of the United States of America in Congress assembled,

SHORT TITLE
SECTION 1. This joint resolution may be cited as the "War Powers Resolution."

PURPOSE AND POLICY
SEC. 2. (a) It is the purpose of this joint resolution to fulfill the intent of the framers of the Constitution of the United States and insure that the collective judgment of both the Congress and the President will apply to the introduction of United States Armed Forces into hostilities, or into situations where imminent involvement in hostilities is clearly indicated by the circumstances, and to the continued use of such forces in hostilities or in such situations.

(b) Under article I, section 8, of the Constitution, it is specifically provided that the Congress shall have the power to make all laws necessary and proper for carrying into execution, not only its own powers but also all other powers vested by the Constitution in the Government of the United States, or in any department or officer thereof.

(c) The constitutional powers of the President as Commander-in-Chief to introduce United States Armed Forces into hostilities, or into situations where imminent involvement in hostilities is clearly indicated by the circumstances, are exercised only pursuant to (1) a declaration of war, (2) specific statutory authorization, or (3) a national emergency created by attack upon the United States, its territories or possessions, or its armed forces.

CONSULTATION
SEC. 3. The President in every possible instance shall consult with Congress before introducing United States Armed Forces into hostilities or into a situation where imminent

involvement in hostilities is clearly indicated by the circumstances, and after every such introduction shall consult regularly with the Congress until United States Armed Forces are no longer engaged in hostilities or have been removed from such situations.

REPORTING

SEC. 4. (a) In the absence of a declaration of war, in any case in which United States Armed Forces are introduced—

(1) into hostilities or into situations where imminent involvement in hostilities is clearly indicated by the circumstances;

(2) into the territory, airspace or waters of a foreign nation, while equipped for combat, except for deployments which relate solely to supply, replacement, repair, or training of such forces; or

(3) in numbers which substantially enlarge United States Armed Forces equipped for combat already located in a foreign nation; the president shall submit within 48 hours to the Speaker of the House of Representatives and to the President pro tempore of the Senate a report, in writing, setting forth—

   (A) the circumstances necessitating the introduction of United States Armed Forces;

   (B) the constitutional and legislative authority under which such introduction took place; and

   (C) the estimated scope and duration of the hostilities or involvement.

(b) The President shall provide such other information as the Congress may request in the fulfillment of its constitutional responsibilities with respect to committing the Nation to war and to the use of United States Armed Forces abroad.

(c) Whenever United States Armed Forces are introduced into hostilities or into any situation described in subsection (a) of this section, the President shall, so long as such armed forces continue to be engaged in such hostilities or situation, report to the Congress periodically on the status of such hostilities or situation as well as on the scope and duration of such hostilities or situation, but in no event shall he report to the Congress less often than once every six months.

CONGRESSIONAL ACTION

SEC. 5. (a) Each report submitted pursuant to section 4(a)(1) shall be transmitted to the Speaker of the House of Representatives and to the President pro tempore of the Senate on the same calendar day. Each report so transmitted shall be referred to the Committee on Foreign Affairs of the House of Representatives and to the Committee on Foreign Relations of the Senate for appropriate action. If, when the report is transmitted, the Congress has adjourned sine die or has adjourned for any period in excess of three calendar days, the Speaker of the House of Representatives and the President pro tempore of the Senate, if they deem it advisable (or if petitioned by at least 30 percent of the membership of their respective Houses) shall jointly request the President to convene Congress in order that it may consider the report and take appropriate action pursuant to this section.

(b) Within sixty calendar days after a report is submitted or is required to be submitted pursuant to section 4(a)(1), whichever is earlier, the President shall terminate any use of United States Armed Forces with respect to which such report was submitted (or required to be submitted), unless the Congress (1) has declared war or has enacted a specific authorization for such use of United States Armed Forces, (2) has extended by law such sixty-day period, or (3) is physically unable to meet as a result of an armed attack upon the United States. Such sixty-day period shall be extended for not more than an additional thirty days if the President determines and certifies to the Congress in writing that unavoidable military necessity respecting the safety of United States Armed Forces requires the continued use of such armed forces in the course of bringing about a prompt removal of such forces.

(c) Notwithstanding subsection (b), at any time that United States Armed Forces are engaged in hostilities outside the territory of the United States, its possessions and territories without a declaration of war or specific statutory authorization, such forces shall be removed by the President if the Congress so directs by concurrent resolution.

. . . .

INTERPRETATION OF JOINT RESOLUTION
SEC. 8.

. . . .

(d) Nothing in this joint resolution—

(1) is intended to alter the constitutional authority of the Congress or of the President, or the provision of existing treaties; or

(2) shall be construed as granting any authority to the President with respect to the introduction of United States Armed Forces into hostilities or into situations wherein involvement in hostilities is clearly indicated by the circumstances which authority he would not have had in the absence of this joint resolution. . . .

Source: "War Powers Resolution," Public Law 93-148, U.S. House Joint Resolution 542, 93rd Cong., 1st sess., November 7, 1973, from the Avalon Project at Yale Law School, www.yale.edu/lawweb/avalon/warpower.htm.

Document 6.21
President Richard Nixon Discusses the Arab-Israeli War amidst the Impeachment Crisis, News Conference, October 26, 1973

In a press conference in late October 1973, President Nixon spoke about the recently concluded Arab-Israeli War and answered a question regarding his possible impeachment. Calls for Nixon's impeachment had increased following the events of October 20. On that day, in what came to be called the "Saturday Night Massacre," the president had ordered the firing of Watergate Special Prosecutor Archibald Cox and the abolition of the office of the special prosecutor. Attorney General Elliot Richardson and his deputy, William Ruckelshaus, both resigned rather than carry out the order of the president. Finally, the number three person in the Department of Justice, Solicitor General Robert Bork, carried out the president's orders.

The President:

. . . A very significant and potentially explosive crisis developed on Wednesday of this week. We obtained information which led us to believe that the Soviet Union was planning to send a very substantial force into the Mideast, a military force.

When I received that information, I ordered, shortly after midnight on Thursday morning, an alert for all American forces around the world. This was a precautionary alert. The purpose of that was to indicate to the Soviet Union that we could not accept any unilateral move on their part to move military forces into the Mideast. At the same time, in the early morning hours, I also proceeded on the diplomatic front. . . .

What the developments of this week should indicate to all of us is that the United States and the Soviet Union, who admittedly have very different objectives in the Mideast, have now agreed that it is not in their interest to have a confrontation there, a confrontation which might lead to a nuclear confrontation, and neither of the two major powers wants that.

We have agreed, also, that if we are to avoid that, it is necessary for us to use our influence more than we have in the past, to get the negotiating track moving again, but this time, moving to a conclusion—not simply a temporary truce but a permanent peace. . . .

Turning now to the subject of our attempts to get a cease-fire on the home front, that is a bit more difficult. . . .

Q. [Dan Rather, CBS News]: Mr. President, I wonder if you could share with us your thoughts, tell us what goes through your mind when you hear people, people who love this country and people who believe in you, say reluctantly that perhaps you should resign or be impeached.

The President: Well, I am glad we don't take the vote of this room, let me say. And I understand the feelings of people with regard to impeachment and resignation. As a matter of fact, Mr. Rather, you may remember that when I made the rather difficult decision—I thought the most difficult decision of my first term-on December 18, the bombing by B-52's of North Vietnam, that exactly the same words were used on the networks—

I don't mean by you, but they were quoted on the networks—that were used now: tyrant, dictator, he has lost his senses, he should resign, he should be impeached.

But I stuck it out, and as a result of that, we not only got our prisoners of war home, as I have often said, on their feet rather than on their knees, but we brought peace to Vietnam, something we haven't had and didn't for over 12 years.

It was a hard decision, and it was one that many of my friends in the press who had consistently supported me on the war up to that time disagreed with. Now, in this instance I realize there are people who feel that the actions that I have taken with regard to the dismissal of Mr. Cox are grounds for impeachment.

I would respectfully suggest that even Mr. Cox and Mr. Richardson have agreed that the President had the right, constitutional right, to dismiss anybody in the Federal Government. And second, I should also point out that as far as the tapes are concerned, rather than being in defiance of the law, I am in compliance with the law.

As far as what goes through my mind, I would simply say that I intend to continue to carry out, to the best of my ability, the responsibilities I was elected to carry out last November. The events of this past week—I know, for example, in your head office in New York, some thought that it was simply a blown-up exercise; there wasn't a real crisis. I wish it had been that. It was a real crisis. It was the most difficult crisis we have had since the Cuban confrontation of 1962.

But because we had had our initiative with the Soviet Union, because I had a basis of communication with Mr. Brezhnev, we not only avoided a confrontation but we moved a great step forward toward real peace in the Mideast.

Now, as long as I can carry out that kind of responsibility, I am going to continue to do this job. . . .

Source: Richard Nixon, "The President's News Conference of October 26, 1973," in *Public Papers of the Presidents of the United States: Richard Nixon 1969–1974,* from the American Presidency Project, University of California, Santa Barbara, www.presidency.ucsb.edu.

Document 6.22
Former President Richard Nixon Speaks on Presidential Power, Televised Interview, May 9, 1977

Although he longed to be remembered as a peacemaker, President Nixon's thoughts were never far from war. The actions which forced his resignation, he insisted in this televised interview with David Frost, were justified by the "war" at home, over the war abroad.

. . .

Frost: The wave of dissent, occasionally violent, which followed in the wake of the Cambodian incursion, prompted President Nixon to demand better intelligence about the people who were opposing him. To this end, the Deputy White House Counsel, Tom Huston, arranged a series of meetings with representatives of the CIA, the FBI, and other police and intelligence agencies.

These meetings produced a plan, the Huston Plan, which advocated the systematic use of wiretappings, burglaries, or so-called black bag jobs, mail openings and infiltration against antiwar groups and others. Some of these activities, as Huston emphasized to Nixon, were clearly illegal. Nevertheless, the president approved the plan. Five days later, after opposition from J. Edgar Hoover, the plan was withdrawn, but the president's approval was later to be listed in the Articles of Impeachment as an alleged abuse of presidential power.

So what in a sense, you're saying is that there are certain situations, and the Huston Plan or that part of it was one of them, where the president can decide that it's in the best interests of the nation or something, and do something illegal.

Nixon: Well, when the president does it that means that it is not illegal.

Frost: By definition.

Nixon: Exactly. Exactly. If the president, for example, approves something because of the national security, or in this case because of a threat to internal peace and order of significant magnitude, then the president's decision in that instance is one that enables those who carry it out, to carry it out without violating a law. Otherwise they're in an impossible position.

Frost:. . . But, the point is: just the dividing line, is that in fact, the dividing line is the president's judgment?

Nixon: Yes, and the dividing line and, just so that one does not get the impression, that a president can run amok in this country and get away with it, we have to have in mind that a president has to come up before the electorate. We also have to have in mind, that a president has to get appropriations from the Congress. We have to have in mind, for example, that as far as the CIA's covert operations are concerned, as far as the FBI's covert operations are concerned, through the years, they have been disclosed on a very, very limited basis to trusted members of Congress. I don't know whether it can be done today or not.

Frost: Pulling some of our discussions together, as it were; speaking of the Presidency you stated, quote, "It's quite obvious that there are certain inherently government activities, which, if undertaken by the sovereign in protection of the interests of the nation's security are lawful, but which if undertaken by private persons, are not." What, at root, did you have in mind there?

Nixon: Well, what I, at root I had in mind I think was perhaps much better stated by Lincoln during the War between the States. Lincoln said, and I think I can remember the quote almost exactly, he said, "Actions which otherwise would be unconstitutional, could become lawful if undertaken for the purpose of preserving the Constitution and the Nation."

Now that's the kind of action I'm referring to. Of course in Lincoln's case it was the survival of the Union in wartime, it's the defense of the nation and, who knows, perhaps the survival of the nation.

Frost: But there was no comparison was there, between the situation you faced and the situation Lincoln faced, for instance?

Nixon: This nation was torn apart in an ideological way by the war in Vietnam, as much as the Civil War tore apart the nation when Lincoln was president. Now it's true that we didn't have the North and the South—

Frost: But when you said, as you said when we were talking about the Huston Plan, you know, "If the president orders it, that makes it legal," as it were: Is the president in that sense—is there anything in the Constitution or the Bill of Rights that suggests the president is that far of a sovereign, that far above the law?

Nixon: No, there isn't. There's nothing specific that the Constitution contemplates in that respect. I haven't read every word, every jot and every title, but I do know this: That it has been, however, argued that as far as a president is concerned, that in war time, a president does have certain extraordinary powers which would make acts that would otherwise be unlawful, lawful if undertaken for the purpose of preserving the nation and the Constitution, which is essential for the rights we're all talking about.

Source: "Excerpts from Interview with Nixon about Domestic Effects of Indochina War," *New York Times,* May 20, 1977.

CHAPTER SEVEN

Gerald Ford

The Caretaker President

When Gerald Ford became president on August 9, 1974, he inherited a world of troubles. In Vietnam, the United States had withdrawn its combat forces and even brokered a peace treaty, but the war for the hearts and minds of the Vietnamese dragged on. What, if anything, was the United States prepared to do to keep its pledge to protect South Vietnam against a direct North Vietnamese assault? In Western Europe, America's traditional allies were edging closer to the Soviet-controlled East. Would they leave the United States behind, or would the United States find a way to keep its allies in Europe

President Gerald Ford and General Secretary Leonid Brezhnev sign a joint communiqué outlining their progress toward a new Strategic Arms Limitation Treaty (SALT II) in Vladivostok, USSR, on November 24, 1974. Source: Gerald R. Ford Presidential Library and Museum.

united? In Africa, the collapse of colonialism was producing new battlegrounds for conflict between the superpowers. How would the United States respond to Soviet challenges in the third world, now that the public and Congress had turned so decisively against the nation's attempt to hold the line against Communist expansion in Southeast Asia? Unfortunately for President Ford, he was in a uniquely weak position to address such problems.

The Cold War, like all wars, built up executive power, but during Ford's tenure in office, the presidency's preeminence was diminished, even in foreign policy, where presidents are traditionally granted the greatest discretion by Congress and the public. There were a number of reasons why. First, there was the manner of Ford's elevation to his office. Like Harry Truman, the first "accidental" president of the Cold War, Ford had not been elected president. Unlike Truman—or any other chief executive in the nation's history— Ford had never even been elected vice president. In October 1973, while serving as House minority leader, the Michigan Republican had been appointed by President Richard Nixon to fill the vice presidential spot left open by the resignation of Vice President Spiro Agnew. Ford easily gained confirmation by both houses of Congress; he had served in the House since 1949 and had a reputation as a dedicated member who fought fair and worked hard to get along with members on both sides of the aisle. This gave Ford all the constitutional legitimacy he needed when he became president, but it did not give him much political clout. This was a problem because Ford faced large Democratic majorities in Congress. Congressional Democrats, moreover, used their party's dominance in the legislature, and the nation's outrage over the abuses of power associated with the Nixon administration, to challenge Ford for control of the government's agenda in foreign affairs. Finally, Ford faced a Congress, a press, and a public that had learned from recent experience to look with skepticism if not downright disgust at the assertion of presidential power.

THE PRESIDENT STUMBLES

If the president were, somehow, to overcome these many obstacles, and actually lead the nation, he would first have to get the nation's attention. Even this proved to be a problem, as Richard Nixon still claimed the better part of the public's notice. Acting out of a genuine desire to establish the preconditions for leadership, as well as simple sympathy for the former president, who was in poor health from recurring phlebitis and appeared to be dying, Ford pardoned Richard Nixon on Sunday, September 8, 1974. In a statement to the press explaining his pardon decision, Ford spoke of the tragedy of Watergate, of the anguish of the Nixon family, and of the health of the former president. Someone, the president said, must "write the end" to this miserable story. "Only I can do that," Ford said, "and if I can, I must." He then read the pardon proclamation. Richard Nixon had received from the president a "full, free, and absolute" pardon, freeing him from prosecution for any crimes committed while president.[1] Ford had already conditionally pardoned 50,000 draft evaders and deserters, providing them with the opportunity to earn full amnesty and return to the United States. The response had been generally supportive. This time, the response was politically lethal.

Even before Nixon had resigned, the press had speculated about the possibility that Nixon might cut a deal with Ford: the presidency in return for a pardon. Against the backdrop of these stories, Ford's action excited skepticism and fury. The best evidence now available suggests that there was, in fact, no deal.[2] President Ford was forced, though, by insistent questioning to acknowledge that the possibility of a pardon had been a topic of conversation between Ford and Nixon's chief of staff, Gen. Alexander Haig, just days before Nixon's departure from office. Once the firestorm of news coverage of the pardon diminished, Ford reaped a certain benefit from his decision. Nixon was no longer on the front page of the newspapers or at the forefront of peoples' thoughts about the American government. Ford could now attempt to lead. But when he made the attempt, he found that he had done considerable damage to his standing with a number of constituencies, especially Congress. As a result, members of Congress felt even more emboldened than they otherwise might have to challenge the president for leadership in all areas of policy, including the Cold War.

Congress's combative mood was evident in the decision to call President Ford to testify about the pardon before the House Judiciary Committee's Subcommittee on Criminal

Justice. Not since Abraham Lincoln and the Civil War had Congress demanded the appearance of a sitting president. As if being peppered with questions by a congressional committee was not enough, the president was also pilloried by the public. As a result of the pardon, Ford went from being a "superbly average" guy and a "normal, sane, down-to-earth individual"[3] to an "average president" in a month, and then from "average president" to national laughing stock in very little time.[4]

The questioning of Ford's fitness to lead started after an innocent stumble on the ramp of Air Force One as the president disembarked in Austria on June 1, 1975. The president's simple slip was relayed to the nation as highly significant news. On one network, the tape of the incident was replayed eleven times in a single newscast. This embarrassment, it seemed, was the ideal comeuppance for the imperial presidency. When a new late night comedy show, *Saturday Night Live,* went on the air that year, the stumbling president became a standard gag for Chevy Chase, one of the original "Not Ready for Prime Time Players." Chase debuted his kinetic impersonation of the president on November 8, 1975, in episode four of the Emmy Award–winning show.

Confirmation of the president's weak foundation for leadership came in the midterm elections of 1974. In an electoral disaster for Republicans, Democrats picked up forty-three seats in the House, leaving Republicans with just 33 percent of the total seats. In the Senate, the Democrats' gain was three, leaving Republicans with 38 percent of the seats. Republicans had not had such poor representation in Congress since the 1964 Democratic landslide. With these results, Gerald Ford—a Republican in the White House—began to look like a walking anachronism.

The result of all of Ford's troubles—both those he inherited and those he brought on himself—was that, as president, Ford was compelled to rely upon his formal constitutional powers. He relied heavily on vetoes, issuing sixty-six overall, compared with forty-three by Nixon over six years, and fifty-one by Presidents John Kennedy and Lyndon Johnson over their combined eight years. Fifty-five of Ford's vetoes were sustained. Ford's difficulties were perhaps greatest in domestic affairs, but even in foreign and military affairs, Ford was seldom able to take the initiative. Rather, he reacted to events and to the decisions made by a restive Congress.

DÉTENTE

When Gerald Ford came into office, the foreign policy establishment of both parties agreed that détente should be expanded. The normalization of relations between the superpowers that had been achieved since the crisis-filled days of Nikita Khrushchev in the Soviet Union and John F. Kennedy in the United States was remarkable. During the Nixon presidency, the two sides had met cordially in Moscow to sign the Strategic Arms Limitation Talks Interim Agreement (SALT I) in 1972. Perhaps the time was at hand to take the next step: to treat the United States' historic Cold War adversary as a normal nation, with which the United States might disagree on some points, but with which the country might cooperate nonetheless. The first step would be to negotiate a new SALT agreement, as SALT I was set to expire in 1977.

SALT I had been a significant accomplishment, but it was far from complete. It excluded, among other issues, heavy bombers designed to carry nuclear-tipped bombs and missiles. It was also far from entirely satisfactory to many Americans.

Under the treaty, the Soviet Union continued to enjoy an advantage in the total number of intercontinental ballistic missiles (ICBMs). Especially worrying to some in the West was the Soviet SS-9 ICBM, with its very large 20-megaton (later increased to 25-megaton) warhead. SS-9 deployments peaked in 1970 at 313 missiles and remained at that level after SALT I. Such large warheads might threaten U.S. land-based ICBMs, even in heavily protected ("hardened") launch silos. Moreover, while the United States had more multiple independently targeted reentry vehicles (MIRVs)—which allowed a single missile to deliver a number of warheads, each to a discrete target within a large radius—in another technologically advanced field, that of submarine-launched ballistic missiles (SLBMs), the Soviets had the lead in the number of SLBMs and the number of submarines from which to fire them. SALT I froze in place a Soviet numerical superiority. From the vantage point of nuclear arms experts, the American advantage in missile accuracy more than compensated for the greater "throw weight" of the Soviet arsenal, but actual numbers of missiles and submarines made a greater impression on the public than CMP, a mathematical calculation of the counter-military potential of a nuclear force, which took into account missile accuracy.

A final incentive for pushing ahead with SALT II was that, although the presidency had changed hands, the lead negotiator for the United States in the Cold War remained the same. Henry Kissinger stayed to serve Ford in the same dual role of secretary of state and national security adviser that he played at the end of the Nixon administration. Thus, just two months after the start of the Ford presidency, Kissinger traveled to Moscow, where he reached agreement with his Soviet counterpart on the outlines of a SALT II agreement. The agreement would extend the process of negotiations into the indefinite future and would guarantee a rough strategic balance between the superpowers.

With an agreement on basic principles for a new treaty worked out, President Ford and Leonid Brezhnev, the general secretary of the Soviet Union, met in November 1974 in Vladivostok, on the remote Pacific shore of the Soviet Union, to get acquainted and confirm their understanding of the deal they hoped to reach through continued talks. The two leaders made considerable progress, agreeing that in SALT II both sides would place limits on not just ICBMs and SLBMs, but heavy bombers as well. In addition, each side would agree not to exceed an equal number of MIRVs and not to construct new land-based ICBM launchers. In numbers, the deal would limit nuclear delivery "vehicles" or "platforms" to 2,400 and MIRVs to 1,320. The agreement would last for ten years.

President Ford believed that his Vladivostok agreement left only a "few remaining problems" to be "ironed out" by "technicians" before he and Brezhnev could come together once again to sign the actual treaty.[5] This was not, Ford discovered upon returning home, a consensus view. There were, to begin with, some substantial holes in the Vladivostok agreement. New technologies blurred the boundaries of traditional arms negotiation and were not included in discussions at Vladivostok. In particular, the Americans were developing a new generation of cruise missiles. Would their further development and deployment be forbidden under any new treaty based on the agreement that

Ford negotiated? On the Soviet side, their air force had recently unveiled a new heavy bomber, called the "Backfire" by the United States. Was it a strategic bomber, as most American analysts believed, or only a medium bomber unrestricted by the Ford-Brezhnev limits? Again, it was not clear what the answer would be or should be. Finally, the Vladivostok agreement did not reduce the arms stockpiles of the superpowers, which made it suspect to critics who longed for true arms *reductions*.

The president was unable to persuade skeptical members of the U.S. Senate that these were merely technical issues that could safely be left to experts. Although both houses of Congress passed simple resolutions endorsing a SALT II treaty along the lines established at Vladivostok, Ford's congressional liaisons could never find enough votes in the Senate to justify a floor vote on the treaty. Meanwhile, Brezhnev suffered a seizure of undetermined cause shortly after the Vladivostok conference. Anatoly Dobrynin, the Soviet ambassador to the United States, later viewed Brezhnev's illness as a turning point. The Soviet strongman began to lose influence within the Politburo, the Soviet governing body, and interest in SALT II.[6] A planned follow-up summit meeting in Washington, D.C., was postponed repeatedly (first from fall 1974 to spring 1975, then from June to September 1975, and then to 1976) until finally it was abandoned.

President Ford had more success in negotiations that would not require Senate confirmation. His actions, however, were still held up to close scrutiny and criticism. Following months of negotiation in Geneva, the nations participating in the Conference on Security and Cooperation in Europe—the United States, the Soviet Union, and all the countries of Europe (save Chinese-allied Albania)—concluded their work with a three-day Helsinki Final Act. The signatories to the August 1, 1975, Helsinki Final Act, also known as the Helsinki Accords or Declaration, disavowed the use of force to attempt boundary changes in Eastern Europe. This was momentous, for in this way the West accepted at last the post–World War II absorption of the Baltic States into the Soviet empire, the movement of Poland's borders agreed to at Yalta, and the partitioning of Germany. (In 1973 the United States had accepted the admission of both East and West Germany into the United Nations.) The Final Act also put into place confidence-building measures, such as an agreement for prior notice to other signatories before initiating troop movements of more than 25,000 personnel, as in large-scale war games. The most consequential aspect of the agreement, however, was its human rights guarantees.

It might seem odd that the Soviet Union and the countries that it controlled would sign an agreement promising to abide by universal principles of human rights, "including the freedom of thought, conscience, religion or belief," and even "to promote and encourage the effective exercise of civil, political, economic, social, cultural and other rights and freedoms" (**Document 7.1**). The Communist countries did so for two reasons. First, although freedom is typically referred to (as in the Helsinki Accords) as a universal right, it is not universally understood in the same way. Communists reject "bourgeois" freedom as an illusion: the "freedom" to be slaughtered in the charnel house of capitalist wage slavery. True freedom, from the Communist perspective, can only be achieved under Communism. Second, the Helsinki Accords simultaneously proclaimed the signatories' acceptance of the principle of noninterference in the internal affairs of other states. If the

United States were to protest Soviet practices with regard to human rights, the accused could cry foul.

The Helsinki conference was highly controversial in the United States. On the Republican right, California governor Ronald Reagan urged all Americans to oppose the final agreement. Democratic hawk Sen. Henry "Scoop" Jackson of Washington asserted that the president had backed down from the United States' historic commitment to self-determination for the nations of Eastern Europe and the Baltic. It was, he concluded, "a sign of the West's retreat."[7] The president pleaded with his detractors to look to the future, suggesting that the significance of the accords would be determined by the West's effort to hold the Soviets to their agreements.

PROXY WARS, LARGE AND SMALL

Détente changed the venue for the Cold War's most intense conflicts. Overt, nerve-wracking, end-of-the-world showdowns in Europe or the Caribbean were placed out of bounds, but the result was more, rather than fewer, armed confrontations elsewhere. After all, there were continuing differences between the superpowers over goals, and continuing, even growing, opportunities for intervention in third-world states, as nations continued to emerge from colonialism. Moreover, while détente diminished the nuclear arms race, it did not address the "little" arms race in the implements of conventional warfare; that race escalated significantly during the era of détente, as both sides armed their proxies for war.

This outcome was not expected in the United States. President Nixon had hoped that he could use the promise of a relaxation of superpower tensions to induce the Soviets to adopt less assertive policies in the third world. The United States' commitments around the world were supposed to diminish through the application of this policy of linkage. It was not to be. The Soviets had their own ideas about linkage. "Peaceful coexistence," proclaimed the Central Committee of the Soviet Communist Party in 1977, "is a form of class struggle directed at strengthening world socialism, the international Communist, workers' and national liberation movement, the whole anti-imperialist front." Indeed, the movement from Cold War to détente, the Committee asserted, "creates more favorable conditions for strengthening our ideological offensive against imperialism."[8] The timing was held to be ideal during the Ford presidency, because the "general crisis of capitalism" seemed to be deepening. The United States, the world's leading capitalist state, was experiencing rising inflation amid widespread anxiety over oil shortages and recession. To make the situation even more exciting for the Soviets, the United States' long effort to prevent Communist victory in Vietnam was finally coming to an end. The giant was about to suffer a humiliating defeat.

Vietnam
"If they're lucky, they can hold out for a year and a half," Secretary of State Kissinger remarked about the South Vietnamese on January 24, 1973, to his domestic affairs counterpart in the White House, John Erlichman.[9] Perhaps this was all that really could be asked for—a "decent interval" between the signing of an empty peace accord (on January 23,

1973), the withdrawal of American combat forces (completed March 29, 1973), and North Vietnamese victory. Even in private, however, Nixon and Kissinger sometimes expressed a more hopeful view, that American firepower would be sufficient to keep the North Vietnamese from victory. Kissinger later insisted that although he and the president "misjudged the willingness of the American people to defend the agreement," they were not just "writing down surrender terms" at Paris.[10]

Surrender of the South was, however, exactly what the North Vietnamese sought. In the year prior to Ford's assumption of office, the skirmishing of Vietnamese forces, North against South, had intensified, as North Vietnamese commanders probed for weaknesses in South Vietnamese defenses. In December 1974 the North Vietnamese leadership decided to conduct a major offensive that would begin in spring 1975 and culminate, they hoped, in victory in 1976. Once the fighting began on March 1, 1975, U.S. intelligence officers joined *Time* magazine in predicting that, although the Northern offensive was a major operation, "battlefield equilibrium," as *Time* put it, would soon be achieved (**Document 7.2**).

Instead, the South Vietnamese Army of the Republic of Vietnam (ARVN) simply crumbled in the face of the North's assault. Finally, twelve divisions of the North Vietnamese army encircled Saigon, the South Vietnamese capital, which was weakly defended by less than a single ARVN division. On April 21, 1975, South Vietnamese president Nguyen Van Thieu resigned his position in an emotional radio and television address, in which he blamed the United States for the defeat of his nation. The United States had promised to help in the event of a North Vietnamese attack, he said, yet they had done nothing. The new president of South Vietnam, Duong Van Minh, announced unconditional surrender on April 30, 1975. The Vietnam War was over.

Even the Soviets were surprised by the suddenness of South Vietnam's collapse. Yuri Andropov, the chief of the KGB (the Soviet secret police and intelligence bureau), had actually expected the Americans to exploit the situation created on the ground by the sudden North Vietnamese onslaught. "To all intents and purposes the road [to Hanoi] is open," he exclaimed.[11] The North Vietnamese had given the Americans an opportunity to take Hanoi, virtually without opposition. Andropov need not have worried; there was little if any sentiment in the United States to travel up that road. Even had the president wished to do so, Congress would never have permitted such an adventure.

Although Ford well knew Congress' mood, he repeatedly went to the legislature during South Vietnam's collapse to ask for emergency appropriations. On January 28, 1975, Ford asked Congress for $300 million in emergency military assistance and another $6 billion over three years in reconstruction aid. The size of the request was so unrealistic that it would seem that the purpose of asking was in large measure merely to shift blame for the coming failure in Vietnam to Congress (**Document 7.3**). After the final North Vietnamese offensive had begun, Army Chief of Staff Gen. Frederick C. Weyand warned the White House that South Vietnam was on the "brink of total military defeat."[12] Only the immediate resumption of massive U.S. bombing and the infusion of yet more emergency military aid (an additional $700 million) could save the situation, he advised. The president demurred on the bombing but passed the buck on the aid to Congress, which predictably said no. On April 23, at a commencement address at Tulane University, the president announced that Vietnam was "a war that is finished as far as America is concerned" (**Document 7.4**).

In the final chaotic days of the American mission in Vietnam, more than 1,000 Americans and 5,000 Vietnamese "collaborators" were evacuated from the capital. On April 29, 1975, President Ford made a brief statement to the American people following the evacuation, declaring the "close" of the Vietnam "chapter" of American history, and imploring "all Americans to close ranks, to avoid recrimination about the past" and to "look ahead to the many goals we share" (**Document 7.5**).

Four American presidents, from Kennedy to Ford, had led the United States during its lengthy commitment to the defense of South Vietnam. Four presidents had failed to avert defeat. In the process, the presidents had struggled with the issue of proxy war. A proxy war is, by definition, something far less than total war. It is fought when total war between principal adversaries—in this case, the superpowers—is too dangerous to contemplate seriously. To prevent the war in Vietnam from breaching "containment" and becoming total war between nuclear powers, American presidents had declined to fully mobilize the nation behind the proxy war. The Selective Service Administration had permitted numerous exemptions and deferments, to soften the sting of conscription. The National Guard and reserves had been permitted to become safe havens, rather than being integrated into the conflict. Fiscal policy, finally, had been designed to disguise the true economic sacrifice that the war imposed on the economy.

For a long time, Americans had simply pretended that they need not choose between "guns and butter," as a succession of presidents and Congresses ratcheted up military spending while expanding government services at home, all without the harsh levels of taxation familiar from previous hot wars, until war-induced inflation exacted its own "tax" on the American public. Despite the efforts of four American presidents to keep down or diminish the cost and sacrifice of the Vietnam War, the bill grew. Once the war was lost, its costs could no longer be justified by reference to the possibility of victory sometime in the future.

Prime among those costs were the more than 58,000 U.S. military personnel killed, 153,000 wounded, and 2,387 missing in action. Over two million American men and women had served in Vietnam, more than 1.6 million of them in combat roles. But for what had they made these sacrifices? If they had not succeeded in securing freedom for the South Vietnamese, had they at least helped prove the United States' resolve to lead, or take part in, world affairs? The editors of the *New York Times* thought so:

> Only the most simplistic assessment of a major power's international role could portray the end of American involvement in Vietnam and Cambodia as tantamount to a retreat into isolationism. The recognition that its power has limits does not render the United States powerless. A new consciousness that power must be used wisely, without exaggerated faith in its military application alone, is a far cry from isolationism.[13]

Not everyone agreed. Defense Secretary James Schlesinger grimly forecast a slide into isolationism. Henry Kissinger attempted to return the Nobel Prize he had been awarded in 1973 for his part in bringing "peace" to Vietnam. (His co-winner that year, South Vietnam's chief negotiator Le Duc Tho, had refused to accept the prize, because the peace treaty for which he and Dr. Kissinger were being honored had not brought peace.) At a news conference on April 29, 1975, Kissinger forecast that "the outcome will have consequences not only in Asia but in many other parts of the world. To deny these consequences is to miss the possibility of dealing with them."[14] President Ford had no choice but to put the best face possible on the situation. In his speech at Tulane, he insisted that "neither the end of the world nor the end of America's leadership in the world" was presaged in the defeat.

The Rest of the World

Thanks to détente, and to initiatives undertaken by Western Europe's leaders themselves to stabilize relations with the East, the United States' failure in Southeast Asia did not lead to a new crisis in Europe. There was, however, a considerable upsurge in assaults in the third world on Western interests. The late 1970s thus saw a new wave of anti-imperialism, targeting the West.

First off, there were the immediate "dominoes." Cambodia fell, in fact, even before South Vietnam. The U.S. embassy in Cambodia was evacuated on April 12, 1975. The capital city of Phnom Penh fell to the North Vietnamese–supported Khmer Rouge five days later. The Khmer Rouge ("Red Khmer") was a particularly murderous Communist faction, whose reign of terror as the government of Cambodia led to the deaths of almost one-fourth of the nation's entire population, through execution and starvation. In Laos, the North Vietnamese–backed Communist party, the Pathet Lao ("Lao Nation"), claimed victory on August 23, 1975, ending an armed conflict that had begun in 1953. Then there was the continuation of warfare in Africa, pitting American-backed factions against Soviet-backed factions. The most intense fighting was in Angola, a Portuguese colony.

By the time that Portugal recognized Angola's independence on November 11, 1975, three factions that had fought for independence each held power in separate sections of the country. The Soviet Union supported the Marxist Popular Liberation Movement of Angola (MPLA), while the United States' Central Intelligence Agency (CIA), assisted by the People's Republic of China, Zaire, and South Africa, supported the National Liberation Front for Angola (FNLA). Jonas Savimbi headed the third group, the National Union for the Total Independence of Angola (UNITA), which, despite its Maoist ideological origins, secured aid from South Africa in 1975 (and, later, from the United States).

In the United States, President Ford, advised by a special executive branch committee for the oversight of covert operations, authorized large-scale CIA support for FNLA and UNITA. Funds and arms would be funneled to the movements through Zaire and Zambia. American and European mercenaries would be recruited by the CIA to fight with the FNLA. The Soviets, meanwhile, pressured the MPLA, with whom they had a long-term relationship, to forge a unity government in an attempt to undermine popular support for the rival factions. Finally, after American covert aid increased and South African troops began to cross the border in August, Moscow began a massive airlift of supplies, while Cuba sent thousands of combat troops.

After the *New York Times* revealed the United States' involvement in the Angolan war, the House voted to cut off all U.S. covert support in an amendment to a general appropriations bill. After the bill, thus amended, passed the Senate by a 55-22 vote, the president did not bother to use his veto. He signed into law a proscription against his policy to fight Soviet influence in Angola, on February 9, 1976. A senior Soviet diplomat, later a defector, recounted that the Soviets drew the obvious conclusion: "The United States lacked will in Africa."[15] In Communist interpretations of American politics, the "Vietnam Syndrome" was said to have found its echo in an "Angolan Syndrome."[16] Later that year, Angola, under the control of the MPLA, signed a "Treaty of Friendship and Cooperation" with its patron state, giving the Soviet Union free reign to its harbor and air bases. (The MPLA also accepted a gift of East German secret police advisers, who helped the new nation establish its own secret police force, which ferreted out American and Maoist influences alike.)

Over the years 1976 to 1981, the value of Soviet arms transfers to former colonial nations in Africa exceeded that of American transfers by ten to one. The Soviets were activists during this period, while the Americans were forced by domestic political circumstances to be passive in Africa. The results included the establishment of Soviet client states in Mozambique and Ethiopia, as well as Angola. Mozambique's first president, Samora Machel, was attracted to the Soviets for practical as well as ideological reasons. He relied heavily upon the KGB and the East German secret police, the Stasi, to consolidate his power and crush domestic opposition. In Ethiopia, after Emperor Haile Selassie, an American client, was deposed in 1974 and killed in August 1975, Lt. Col. Mengitsu Haile Mariam came to power with a committee of military leaders, the Derg. In order to secure help from Moscow, the Derg purged its pro-Western members and began a counterrevolution. In the ensuing reign of terror, a half million Ethiopians died, according to Amnesty International estimates.[17] In the aftermath, the United States was left with influence only in Somalia, the sworn enemy of its larger, more strategically located neighbor. President Ford wrangled with Congress over the level of aid he might send to American's new, impoverished client state.

CONGRESS RESURGENT

Congress worked to scale back the scope and reach of executive power during the Ford presidency, which led to a decline in the instruments for Cold War leadership available to an American president. The most visible influence that Congress exerted was in its area of traditional, and constitutional, strength: the power of the purse. Congress demonstrated an unusual assertiveness in refusing President Ford funds to resume one overt war, in Vietnam, and one covert operation, in Angola. It was enough to cause the president to chastise Congress for an alleged ambition to be a "virtual co-administrator" of foreign affairs.[18] Ford relied when he could on the veto power. Through the use of the veto, he prevented Congress from putting a ceiling on U.S. arms sales abroad and from proscribing U.S. assistance to countries that violated human rights. But the limits to the veto power as an instrument of foreign policy management were shown in a series of legislative and diplomatic responses to events on the island of Cyprus in late summer 1974.

Ever since Cyprus had secured its independence from the United Kingdom in 1960, there had been tension within the government. The great majority of the population (over

70 percent) was of Greek heritage, but there was a substantial minority (approximately 17 percent) of Turkish Cypriots. In the early 1970s, ultra-nationalist Greek Cypriots, including members of the armed forces, conspired with the Greek military government for union with Greece. After the president of Cyprus, who wished to maintain autonomy from both Turkey and Greece, demanded the withdrawal of potentially disloyal officers from the Cypriot National Guard, Greek loyalists on the island, backed by the Greek government, carried out a coup. While debate over the coup raged in Greece and at the United Nations, Turkish troops landed on Cyprus and took possession of a portion of the island. The coup and the war that followed led to the collapse of the Greek government, the indefinite partition of Cyprus, and a crisis in North Atlantic Treaty Organization (NATO) relations.

Greece and Turkey were both NATO allies and shared responsibility for events in Cyprus. The U.S. Congress, however, imposed an arms embargo on Turkey. The president was unable to engineer the lifting of the embargo, whereupon the Turkish government abrogated its 1969 defense cooperation treaty with the United States and took possession of U.S. military installations in Turkey. In October 1974 Ford and congressional leaders worked out a partial compromise, which permitted the release to Turkey of arms already purchased. The United States military was not invited back into Turkey until 1978, when Congress at last lifted the embargo and resumed U.S. military assistance to Turkey.

Ford similarly failed to lead with regard to the issue of Jewish emigration from the Soviet Union. In 1972 the United States and the Soviet Union had negotiated a three-year trade pact that normalized trade relations by granting to the Soviet Union most-favored-nation (MFN) status as a trade partner. This reduced duties on Soviet goods imported to the United States to levels that were applied to other normal trading partners. (The term "MFN" was changed to the more accurate "NTR," for "normal trade relations," in 1998.) When the agreement was debated in the Senate, Democrat Henry Jackson of Washington led the effort to link trade with the issue of Soviet treatment of Jews seeking to leave for Israel. The issue was kept alive because the Soviets were unwilling to permit migration at the level of demand. In December 1974, under the Ford administration, Henry Kissinger appeared before the Senate to request that the legislators abandon their consideration of Jackson's controversial amendment and permit the administration to use diplomatic means to ease Jewish emigration. "Trust us," was the secretary of state's implied message to a highly skeptical Congress.

President Ford and Kissinger worked out a private arrangement with Soviet ambassador Anatoly Dobrynin, by which up to 45,000 permits for Jewish emigrants would be issued per year. Although Senator Jackson initially approved the deal privately, he later revealed the arrangement and denounced it publicly. Jackson insisted that 45,000 permits were not enough. The president was incensed at what he thought was a crass political maneuver on the part of the senator, who harbored presidential aspirations, but he signed into law a new trade bill on January 3, 1975, which contained an amendment linking Soviet policy on Jewish emigration to improvement in American-Soviet trade relations. In reply, the Soviets abrogated the trade pact, making any further trade reform a lost cause. The Soviets would do without normal trade with the world's largest economy rather than permit embarrassment at the hands of the U.S. Congress. Ambassador Dobrynin believed that this incident, more than any other single event, doomed détente.

Congress also took the lead in the Ford years in forcing changes upon the CIA. The president, as on trade matters, attempted to set the agenda for intelligence reform but failed. The CIA's reputation had been damaged by the Watergate fiasco. One of the burglars arrested at the Democratic National Committee's headquarters in the Watergate complex was E. Howard Hunt, a former CIA agent. Earlier, the same group had broken into the office of a Nixon "enemy's" psychiatrist in Los Angeles, allegedly using CIA equipment and disguises. The Ford White House's attempt at a quiet investigation of its own into CIA misdeeds was derailed by leaks to the press, resulting in a sensational news story about the "family jewels" of the CIA—secrets that included assassination attempts against foreign leaders, the overthrow of governments, and covert operations against American citizens. The CIA, reported investigative journalist Seymour Hersh, had established secret dossiers on at least 10,000 Americans, including "dissident" members of Congress.[19]

In the light of such rumored misdeeds, the president was forced to go public. So, on January 4, 1975, Ford established a committee under the direction of his vice president, Nelson Rockefeller: the United States President's Commission on CIA Activities within the United States. Despite the commission's name, it was charged with a widespread investigation, extending beyond the CIA's alleged domestic misadventures. On the incendiary charge of attempted assassination, the president revealed to reporters off the record in mid-January that such charges might be proved true. The president's remarks were leaked, building expectations regarding what the Rockefeller Commission would later report.

On June 10, 1975, the vice president published his report. It revealed a number of formerly secret and questionable operations, including "Operation Chaos," begun under President Johnson, which collected information about more than 7,000 American citizens. Other revelations included the use of CIA spies to gather information for political purposes and the interception of mail to spy on suspected American radicals. The report considered and rejected allegations of CIA involvement in the Kennedy assassination, and even offered an opinion as to who really shot JFK—Lee Harvey Oswald. The public wanted more. On the issue of CIA assassination of foreign leaders, the commission merely noted that "time did not permit a full investigation before this report was due." Rockefeller only made matters worse when he hinted in a television interview that both President Kennedy and Attorney General Robert Kennedy had been involved in the development and implementation of CIA assassination plots. His intention was presumably to warn Democrats on Capitol Hill and in the press to lay off, lest their zeal to uncover the truth reveal more than they bargained for, but in the climate of the time, Rockefeller's remarks only led to charges of a cover-up.

Idaho senator Frank Church—another Democrat with presidential ambitions—launched an investigation of his own. The senator had high hopes for the Senate Select Committee to Study Governmental Operations with Respect to Intelligence Activities, more commonly known as the Church Committee. He declared that its goal was nothing less than to restore the government "to the genius of the Founding Fathers," and he warned darkly of the prospect "to make tyranny total in America."[20] Director of Central Intelligence William Colby made it difficult for the president to influence the hearings, as he divulged to the committee all the secrets of which he was personally aware.

Over 1975 and 1976, the Church Committee released fourteen reports. The first, "Interim Report: Alleged Assassination Plots Involving Foreign Leaders," provided details on numerous alleged attempts, by the Eisenhower through Nixon administrations, to kill foreign leaders (**Document 7.6**). The committee had investigated rumors of plots to murder heads of state or high government officials in the Congo, the Dominican Republic, South Vietnam, Chile, and Cuba. No evidence was found to support some alleged plots (those that targeted Patrice Lumumba, of the Congo, during Eisenhower's presidency, for instance, or Gen. René Schneider, commander in chief of the Army of Chile, in Nixon's day), and conflicting evidence emerged regarding others (such as Rafael Trujillo of the Dominican Republic). There was in fact no evidence that the CIA had ever actually succeeded in assassinating a foreign leader. With regard to Fidel Castro of Cuba, the record was sensational. Although American intelligence agents, at the behest of Presidents Eisenhower and, especially, Kennedy, had failed to accomplish their goal in Cuba, it was clearly not for lack of trying (**Document 7.7**). Other Church Committee reports revealed extensive domestic spying by the CIA at the behest of American presidents throughout the Cold War, especially under Presidents Johnson and Nixon in reaction to the collapse of support for the war in Vietnam (**Document 7.8**).

President Ford responded to the most damaging revelations—those regarding attempted assassinations—by issuing Executive Order 11905 on February 18, 1976, forbidding the participation of U.S. government employees in political assassination (**Document 7.9**). Presidents Jimmy Carter and Ronald Reagan explicitly reaffirmed Ford's edict in their own executive orders; it has not been publicly revoked since.

A FAREWELL TO ARMS?

With regard to the highly symbolic War Powers Act, passed over President Nixon's veto in November 1973, Ford asserted the presidency's institutional right to commit U.S. troops into combat as the president saw fit. He did not, however, force the issue. President Ford reported to Congress on the use of American troops four times, each time "taking note of" without acknowledging the legality of the War Powers Resolution.[21] In his command of American troops, though, Ford was restrained, introducing forces into combat or imminent hostility only in rescue missions to evacuate Americans from two locations in South Vietnam and on two occasions from Cambodia, as those nations fell to Communist conquerors.

Ordering the U.S. armed forces to conduct rescue operations was not much, but it was something that the president could do unilaterally, without serious challenge by Congress. The single most dramatic such operation ordered by Ford was in response to the Cambodian seizure of a U.S. container ship, the SS *Mayaguez*, on May 12, 1975.

The United States had no diplomatic relations with the Communist government of the Khmer Rouge, headed by the ruthless Pol Pot, so it was difficult to know at first what, if anything, the Cambodian government intended by the seizure of the vessel. Assuming that Cambodia's intentions were as hostile as the act implied, Ford sent 1,000 marines to an American air base in Thailand and ordered a U.S. aircraft carrier and two destroyers to the area. Without waiting for his request for help from United Nations General Secretary Kurt Waldheim to yield results, the president ordered military action the evening of May 14. The U.S. assault began at 7:00 p.m. on May 14 by Washington, D.C., time (6:00 a.m. the next day, Cambodian time)—just ninety minutes after the National Security Council meeting in which the president made his choice for military action. The rationale for acting rapidly with force was articulated bluntly by Secretary Kissinger, who said, "[L]et's look ferocious." [22]

American forces quickly secured the empty vessel and landed on a small island immediately off the shore of Cambodia, where the U.S. government believed the crew of the ship was being held hostage. Though there was no sign of the Americans, the marines were met by a considerably larger force than they had expected, and they engaged the enemy in a difficult daylong fight. In an effort both to overwhelm the enemy and discourage reinforcement, President Ford authorized bomb strikes against targets on the mainland as well as the island.

To negotiate for the release of the hostages, the president relied that day on the press to relay the terms of a deal. The White House press secretary, Ron Nessen, issued a statement via the media: "As soon as you [the Cambodians] issue a statement that you are prepared to release the crew members you hold unconditionally and immediately, we will promptly cease military operations." [23] The Americans had no way of knowing that the crew had actually been set free just minutes after the American assault began. Later in the day, the American crew was picked up from the fishing boat in which they had been released and returned to safety without incident. The bombing, however, continued for several hours to deter attacks on retiring vessels, and perhaps also to "look ferocious." (The final bomb dropped on the island itself was a BLU-82, the largest nonnuclear device in the American arsenal. Due to its size, it had to be launched via parachute from a transport plane.) In the White House, the president micromanaged the crisis, just as President Johnson had when he chose bombing targets in Vietnam from the White House basement. Ford ordered a final air strike on the Cambodian mainland, and he was furious at his cabinet members when he later learned that the order had not been carried out.

The president proclaimed victory in a hurried statement to the press just past midnight, East Coast time, on May 15, 1975. American forces had engaged in combat, the president announced; they had rescued the entire crew of the seized vessel, and they had displayed valor and sacrifice. There was no mention of casualties. The Department of Defense the next day acknowledged a single marine had been killed in action. The American public, eager for good news of just this sort, rallied behind the president, who enjoyed an eleven-point increase in his job approval rating.

Congress stood by. Key members had been informed by White House aides at the time of the action and had expressed satisfaction at this informal consultation. In the *New York Times* on May 23, 1975, constitutional law scholar Raoul Berger took Congress to task for acquiescing in the president's assertion of the sort of presidential discretionary authority that Congress had supposedly rebelled against in the War Powers Act. But even Frank

Church gave his full support to the president, as did columnists and editorial writers around the nation.

The president sought to capitalize on this show of solidarity, saying repeatedly that the *Mayaguez* rescue proved the determination of the United States to lead and to meet challenges to American national interests around the world. The United States was willing to use force, the president asserted repeatedly, and could be trusted by its allies. The president also pointed to his "tough" response to the incident as proof of his strength as president. He was able and willing to make difficult decisions, he said (**Document 7.10**).

There were some troubling aspects of the operation, which became known only after the initial euphoria had begun to wear off. The actual number of American combat deaths was eighteen—fifteen who were killed in the first hour of the operation on the island, and three who were inadvertently left behind and presumed dead. An additional twenty-three troops had died in a helicopter crash in Thailand while preparing for the operation. Forty-one troops had died and another forty-one had been wounded to rescue the thirty-nine civilians on the *Mayaguez*. Further, the Cambodians had relented, it seemed, thanks to the American bombing of the mainland; the deadly assault upon the island had been of little consequence.

The president did not press the point. He did not challenge Congress or the American public to support any other overt use of the armed forces. His later attempt to use military force in a major covert operation in Angola was rebuffed by Congress, as discussed earlier.

THE FINAL SLIP

Typically, an incumbent president faces no serious challenge for his party's nomination for president. The weakness of Ford's political influence, however, was atypical, and the president faced a serious challenge for the Republican nomination. Ford's choice of Nelson Rockefeller, the leading figure of the GOP's northeastern, moderate, "establishment" wing, as his vice president had incensed the conservative wing of the Republican Party. Moreover, the right wing of the party believed that the president had "lost" Vietnam, had surrendered Eastern Europe at Helsinki, and had failed to respond adequately to Soviet challenges to American strength in the arms race and to Western influence in Africa. Finally, the conservatives had a candidate around whom to rally: the former governor of California, Ronald Reagan.

During the primary campaign, Reagan charged that Ford had all but given up in the Cold War. He was joined in this critique by Richard Nixon's former secretary of defense, Melvin Laird. After a major reshuffling of the Ford cabinet on November 2, 1975—dubbed the "Halloween Massacre" by the press—Ford's ousted secretary of defense, James Schlesinger, added his voice to the conservative critique. In early primaries heading toward the Republican convention, Reagan picked up delegates and some surprising victories. A turning point came in North Carolina, where the Californian won an unexpected victory after going on the offensive regarding Ford's alleged weakness in foreign affairs.

Under Ford's stewardship of foreign affairs, said Reagan, the United States had become a "second-rate power." Reagan also criticized Ford for his willingness to consider the renunciation of American control over the Panama Canal. It was a dangerous and weak "give away," said Reagan.[24] Reagan's win in North Carolina kept him in the contest all the way to the convention in Kansas City. Although Ford ultimately secured the nomination in 1976, Reagan's strong showing made him the presumptive candidate four years later and demonstrated Ford's vulnerabilities.

Ford's reaction to Reagan's challenge in the primaries spelled trouble for the policy of détente. At first, the president stuck to his guns. In January 1976, the election year, Ford stated on NBC News, "I think it would be very unwise for a President—me or anyone else—to abandon détente. I think détente is in the best interest of this country."[25] Just three months later, the president announced "we are going to forget the use of the word détente."[26] Reagan stayed on the offensive. "Now, we are told Washington is dropping the word 'détente,' but keeping the policy," he asserted. "But whatever it's called, the policy is what is at fault."[27] In the same month, March 1976, the Committee on the Present Danger (CPD) was reformed. The CPD had been assembled first in 1950, to lobby for a more aggressive foreign and military policy. Its 1976 incarnation was dedicated to the proposition that mainstream elements within both major parties were engaged in an enormous and potentially lethal gamble with the Soviets. SALT II, the CPD proclaimed, was a blunder, and the United States urgently needed to rebuild its military might, from the top down. The CPD added its collective voice to Reagan's in challenging Ford's handling of the Cold War.

Ford held off the challenge from Reagan at the August 1976 Republican National Convention, but in the general election he continued to face challenges from the right. Hardliners from within the administration pushed the president toward an experiment in intelligence: an outside analysis of Soviet capabilities and intentions. Hawks persuaded George Bush—who had taken the position of director of the CIA after the "massacre"—to sign off on a plan for competitive analysis.

In the Intelligence Community Experiment in Competitive Analysis, the CIA would fund its own critics, who would be provided top secret information and briefings, and who would be charged with producing an independent, alternative National Intelligence Estimate on the Soviet threat in 1976. This team (Team "B"), whose members overlapped with the CPD, reviewed the evidence and concluded that the CIA's traditional estimates had grossly understated the Soviet threat because CIA analysts (Team "A") had failed to appreciate just how ruthless, devious, and determined the Soviets truly were (**Document 7.11**). Team B's report was not fully declassified and released until 2004, but during the 1976 campaign, some of its members went public with unclassified popularizations of the report's themes. Major leaks included a story published in *Reader's Digest*, just two months before the general election, by Team B member Lt. Gen. Daniel Graham. Graham had left his position as head of the Defense Intelligence Agency at the end of 1975 and had retired from the army in response to the firing of Defense Secretary Schlesinger.

With "help" like this from within his administration, it was vital that Ford be at his best in the general election campaign against Democratic challenger and former Georgia governor Jimmy Carter. Unfortunately for Ford, he stumbled. He did so famously in a televised debate against his opponent. For his second debate with Carter, the president had prepared for a possible question about Soviet domination in Eastern Europe. His rehearsed answer would have him acknowledge such domination as a fact but deny its legitimacy. Even after Helsinki, the president would assert, the United States took a tough line on Soviet influence in Eastern Europe, refusing officially to recognize the legitimacy of Soviet domination on its periphery. This way, the president could hold aloft a banner of hope, or at least maintain appearances. What Ford came out with, instead, was a clumsy misstatement. "There is no Soviet domination of Eastern Europe," he said, "and there never will be under a Ford administration" (**Document 7.12**). His questioner, stunned by the president's gaffe, immediately gave him the opportunity to clarify his remark. Ford declined to do so, seemingly oblivious to the impression that his statement had created: that here was a man so clueless about Soviet intentions that he did not realize the Soviets had taken control of the nations along their borders. It was a mistake too many for the unfortunate incumbent.

In 1976 Gerald Ford was doubly defeated. He lost the presidential election to Jimmy Carter, and he lost the contest for control of the future of the Republican Party to Ronald Reagan.

NOTES

1. Gerald Ford, "Remarks on Signing a Proclamation Granting Pardon to Richard Nixon," September 8, 1974, in *Public Papers of the Presidents, Gerald Ford, 1974–1977,* from the American Presidency Project, University of California at Santa Barbara, www.presidency.ucsb.edu.
2. Thomas S. Langston, "The Nixon Resignation and the Ford Presidency," in *Watergate and the Resignation of Richard Nixon: Impact of a Constitutional Crisis,* ed. Harry P. Jeffrey and Thomas Maxwell-Long (Washington, D.C.: CQ Press, 2004), 125–138.
3. John Robert Greene, *The Presidency of Gerald Ford* (Lawrence: University Press of Kansas, 1995), 32.
4. Ibid., 53.
5. Gerald Ford, *A Time to Heal: The Autobiography of Gerald R. Ford* (New York: Harper and Row, 1979), 218.
6. Lester H. Brune, *Chronology of the Cold War: 1917–1992* (New York: Routledge, 2005), 329.
7. László Borhi, comp., "The United States and East Central Europe, 1945–1990, Part III, 1968–1984, A Chronology," ed. Csaba Békés, Laura Jordan, and József Litkei, from the Cold War History Research Center, Budapest, www.coldwar.hu/html/en/chronologies/borhi3.html.
8. Quoted in Raymond L. Garthoff, *Détente and Confrontation: American-Soviet Relations from Nixon to Reagan* (Washington, D.C.: Brookings Institution, 1994), 389.
9. John Erlichman, *Witness to Power: The Nixon Years* (New York: Simon and Schuster, 1982), 316.
10. Larry Berman, *No Peace, No Honor: Nixon, Kissinger, and Betrayal in Vietnam* (New York: Free Press, 2001), 263.
11. Christopher M. Andrew and Vasili Mirokhin, *The World Was Going Our Way: The KGB and the Battle for the Third World* (New York: Basic Books, 2005), 13.
12. Greene, *Presidency of Gerald Ford,* 137.
13. Editorial, "After Vietnam," *New York Times,* May 4, 1975.

14. Bernard Gwertzman, "White House Considered the Surrender 'Inevitable,'" *New York Times,* April 30, 1975.

15. Andrew and Mirokhin, *The World Was Going Our Way,* 453.

16. Ibid.

17. Ibid., 457.

18. James L. Sundquist, *Decline and Resurgence of Congress* (Washington, D.C.: Brookings Institution Press, 1982), 291.

19. Seymour Hersh, "Report Massive CIA Spying on Americans; Mail Opened, Wiretaps!" *Chicago Tribune,* December 22, 1974.

20. Stephen F. Knott, "Congressional Oversight and the Crippling of the CIA," November 4, 2001, from History News Network, George Mason University, http://hnn.us/articles/380.html. See also James Bamford's testimony, quoting Church, on pages 33–34 of House Committee of the Judiciary, *Constitution in Crisis: Domestic Surveillance and Executive Power,* Congressional Briefing, January 20, 2006, www.house. gov/judiciary_democrats/nsabriefing/nsabrieftranscript12006.pdf.

21. Duane Tanenbaum, "Gerald Ford and the War Powers Resolution," in *Gerald R. Ford and the Politics of Post-Watergate America,* ed. Bernard Firestone and Alexej Ugrinsky (Westport, Conn.: Greenwood Press, 1992), 2:523–538.

22. Ralph Wetterhahn, *The Last Battle: The Mayaguez Incident and the End of the Vietnam War* (New York: Carroll and Graf Publishers, 2001), 206.

23. Richard G. Head et al., *Crisis Resolution: Presidential Decision Making in the* Mayaguez *and Korean Confrontations* (Boulder, Colo.: Westview Press, 1978), 138.

24. Yanek Mieczkowski, "Gerald Ford," in *The American Presidency,* ed. Alan Brinkley and Davis Dyer (Boston: Houghton Mifflin, 2004), 450.

25. Gerald Ford, "Interview for an NBC News Program on American Foreign Policy," in *Public Papers of the Presidents of the United States: Gerald Ford, 1974–1977,* from the American Presidency Project, University of California, Santa Barbara, www.presidency.ucsb.edu.

26. Anne Hessing Cahn, "Team B: The Trillion Dollar Experiment," *Bulletin of Atomic Scientists* 49, no. 3 (April 1993): 22, 24–27.

27. Davis W. Houck and Amos Kiewe, eds., *Actor, Ideologue, Politician: The Public Speeches of Ronald Reagan* (Westport, Conn.: Greenwood Press, 1993), 155.

Document 7.1

Helsinki Accord, Final Act of the Conference on Security and Co-operation in Europe, August 1, 1975

In Helsinki, Finland, President Gerald Ford and Soviet General Secretary Leonid Brezhnev, along with leaders of 33 other nations, acknowledged the legitimacy of Europe's postwar boundaries and proclaimed their intention to adhere to universal conceptions of human rights in their domestic affairs. The human rights provisions, contained in the third "basket" of Helsinki's Final Act, as the accord is known, spurred dissidence behind the iron curtain.

. . .

The States participating in the Conference on Security and Co-operation in Europe,

Reaffirming their objective of promoting better relations among themselves and ensuring conditions in which their people can live in true and lasting peace free from any threat to or attempt against their security;

Convinced of the need to exert efforts to make détente both a continuing and an increasingly viable and comprehensive process, universal in scope, and that the implementation of the results of the Conference on Security and Cooperation in Europe will be a major contribution to this process;

Considering that solidarity among peoples, as well as the common purpose of the participating States in achieving the aims as set forth by the Conference on Security and Cooperation in Europe, should lead to the development of better and closer relations among them in all fields and thus to overcoming the confrontation stemming from the character of their past relations, and to better mutual understanding;

Mindful of their common history and recognizing that the existence of elements common to their traditions and values can assist them in developing their relations, and desiring to search, fully taking into account the individuality and diversity of their positions and views, for possibilities of joining their efforts with a view to overcoming distrust and increasing confidence, solving the problems that separate them and cooperating in the interest of mankind;

Recognizing the indivisibility of security in Europe as well as their common interest in the development of cooperation throughout Europe and among selves and expressing their intention to pursue efforts accordingly;

Recognizing the close link between peace and security in Europe and in the world as a whole and conscious of the need for each of them to make its contribution to the strengthening of world peace and security and to the promotion of fundamental rights, economic and social progress and well-being for all peoples; . . .

Declare their determination to respect and put into practice, each of them in its relations with all other participating States, irrespective of their political, economic or social systems as well as of their size, geographical location or level of economic development, the following principles, which all are of primary significance, guiding their mutual relations:

I. SOVEREIGN EQUALITY, RESPECT FOR THE RIGHTS INHERENT IN SOVEREIGNTY

The participating States will respect each other's sovereign equality and individuality as well as all the rights inherent in and encompassed by its sovereignty, including in particular the right of every State to juridical equality, to territorial integrity and to freedom and political independence. They will also respect each other's right freely to choose and develop its political, social, economic and cultural systems as well as its right to determine its laws and regulations. . . .

II. REFRAINING FROM THE THREAT OR USE OF FORCE

The participating States will refrain in their mutual relations, as well as in their international relations in general, from the threat or use of force against the territorial integrity or political independence of any State, or in any other manner inconsistent with the purposes of the United Nations and with the present Declaration. No consideration may be invoked to serve to warrant resort to the threat or use of force in contravention of this principle. . . .

III. INVIOLABILITY OF FRONTIERS

The participating States regard as inviolable all one another's frontiers as well as the frontiers of all States in Europe and therefore they will refrain now and in the future from assaulting these frontiers.

Accordingly, they will also refrain from any demand for, or act of, seizure and usurpation of part or all of the territory of any participating State. . . .

VII. RESPECT FOR HUMAN RIGHTS AND FUNDAMENTAL FREEDOMS, INCLUDING THE FREEDOM OF THOUGHT, CONSCIENCE, RELIGION OR BELIEF

The participating States will respect human rights and fundamental freedoms, including the freedom of thought, conscience, religion or belief, for all without distinction as to race, sex, language or religion.

They will promote and encourage the effective exercise of civil, political, economic, social, cultural and other rights and freedoms all of which derive from the inherent dignity of the human person and are essential for his free and full development.

Within this framework the participating States will recognize and respect the freedom of the individual to profess and practice, alone or in community with others, religion or belief acting in accordance with the dictates of his own conscience.

The participating States on whose territory national minorities exist will respect the right of persons belonging to such minorities to equality before the law, will afford them the full opportunity for the actual enjoyment of human rights and fundamental freedoms and will, in this manner, protect their legitimate interests in this sphere.

The participating States recognize the universal significance of human rights and fundamental freedoms, respect for which is an essential factor for the peace, justice and well-being necessary to ensure the development of friendly relations and co-operation among themselves as among all States. . . .

They confirm the right of the individual to know and act upon his rights and duties in this field. . . .

Source: Organization for Security and Co-operation in Europe, "Conference on Security and Co-Operation in Europe Final Act," August 1, 1975, www.osce.org/documents/mcs/1975/08/4044 _en.pdf.

Document 7.2

"Ominous Developments in Vietnam," NSC Staffer William L. Stearman's Memorandum to Secretary of State Henry Kissinger, March 12, 1975

In a memorandum written for Secretary of State and National Security Adviser Henry Kissinger, William Stearman of the National Security Council reported on recent developments in Vietnam. Although Stearman was clearly alarmed at evidence of an "extremely intense" coming offensive from the North Vietnamese, the utter collapse of the South Vietnamese government was not foreseen.

Secret/Sensitive   Urgent Information
MEMORANDUM FOR: SECRETARY KISSINGER
FROM: WILLIAM L. STEARMAN
SUBJECT: Ominous Developments in Vietnam

A number of significant military and political developments in Vietnam provide an ominous indication of North Vietnamese strategy and intentions for the months to come. The high level of military activity since March 10 reinforces this view. These new developments are:

—In December of 1974 the 23rd plenum of the Lao Dong Party Central Committee issues Resolution 23. This may have dealt with a new policy toward the South.

—In late February and early March, high level Soviet and PRC [People's Republic of China] delegations visited Hanoi. Soviet Vice Minister of Foreign Affairs Nikolay Firyubin led the Soviet group. The presence of the PRC delegates and Firyubin may be the result of a major Hanoi policy change relating to the war in South Vietnam.

—Communications intelligence indicates that as of March 10, North Vietnam is apparently deploying to the South an integral unit, the size and identify of which are unknown. This is in addition to the probable movement of elements of the 341st NVA [North Vietnamese Army] Division from Quang Binh in North Vietnam across the DMZ [demilitarized zone] into Quang Tri and the confirmed movement of the 968th Division from Laos into the central highlands.

—The forward element of COSVN [Central Office for South Vietnam, the North Vietnamese supreme military and political headquarters for the war] has expanded its communications and is now in contact with at least three divisions and a number of independent units in the Tay Ninh—Parrots Beak Area. . . .

—Infiltration groups are being dispatched during the current dry season at a rate double that for the same period during the 1973–74 dry season. If the current rate continues, this dry season's infiltration will rival the high level of 1968. . . .

—A large scale military recruitment campaign is being carried out in North Vietnam and the training period for these inductees has been reduced from 4 to 6 months to about 1 month. . . .

—The NVA is continuing to ship large amounts of cargo and additional weapons into the NVN [North Vietnamese] Panhandle, including some tanks and 130 mm guns. Destination of these weapons is unknown, but they are probably enroute to South Vietnam.

—MIGs [Soviet-made fighter aircraft] have been returned to southern North Vietnam. . . .

—Communist troop indoctrination has stressed that fighting in 1975 will be very intensive. Slogans being used to exhort troops on to a high performance are:

- "Repeat 1968"
- "Attack as in 1972"
- "Achieve a Victory like in Bien Dien Phu"

When taken together, these signs indicate that the North Vietnamese spring offensive could be extremely intense and is probably designed to achieve a fundamental change in the balance of power in the South. Many intelligence sources indicate that this fighting is a prelude to a new round of negotiations designed to achieve an implementation of the Paris Accords on North Vietnamese terms.

The probable NVN strategy will be make its gains in the spring and early summer and then offer a cease-fire before the GVN [Government of (South) Vietnam] is able to recoup its losses. Congressional pressure to accept such an offer would no doubt be great—since it would be seen as a chance to end the fighting and to reduce our military aid. As it is unlikely that the GVN will be ready to accept the NVN proposals, the Communists would probably seek to pressure us, through the Congress, into forcing Thieu to acquiesce. We may, therefore, soon be facing a situation in which heavy pressure will be placed on the Executive Branch to accept Hanoi's proposals. These will probably center around establishing the National Council of Reconciliation and Concord with some quasi-governmental powers and providing the Communists complete access to the GVN-controlled population.

Source: Folder "7501509, Ominous Developments in Vietnam," National Security Adviser, from NSC Institutional Files, Gerald R. Ford Library, www.fordlibrarymuseum.gov/library/exhibits/vietnam/750312a.htm.

Document 7.3
President Gerald Ford Answers Questions about Defeat in Vietnam, CBS News Interview, April 21, 1975

In a live, prime-time interview with CBS journalists Walter Cronkite, Eric Sevareid, and Bob Schieffer, President Ford answered questions about the impending South Vietnamese defeat and offered his opinion on how to apportion blame, with the Democratic-controlled Congress receiving the greatest share.

. . .

Mr. Sevareid: Mr. President, one of his [Thieu's] comments was that the United States had led the South Vietnamese people to their deaths. Do you have any specific reply to that one?

The President: Well, there were some public and corresponding private commitments made in 1972–1973 where I think that the President of South Vietnam could have come to the conclusion, as he did, that the United States Government would do two things: one, replace military hardware on a one-for-one basis, keep his military strength sufficiently high so that he could meet any of the challenges of the North; and in addition, there was a commitment that we as a nation would try to enforce the agreements that were signed in Paris in January 1973.

Now, unfortunately, the Congress in August of 1973 removed the latter, took away from the President the power to move in a military way to enforce the agreements that were signed in Paris.

So, we were left then only with the other commitment, and unfortunately, the replacement of military hardware was not lived up to. I, therefore, can understand President Thieu's disappointment in the rather traumatic times that he went through in the last week. I can understand his observations.

Mr. Sevareid: Well, what is the relative weight that you assign to, first, this question of how much aid we sent or didn't send, and his use of it, especially in this pullback? Now, where is the greater mistake, because historically this is terribly important.

The President: Well, it is my judgment—history will be probably more precise—but it is my judgment at the moment that the failure of the Congress to appropriate the military aid requested—the previous administration asked for $1,400 million for this fiscal year; Congress authorized $1 billion; Congress appropriated $700 million; and the failure to make the commitment for this fiscal year of something close to what was asked for certainly raised doubts in the mind of President Thieu and his military that we would be supplying sufficient military hardware for them to adequately defend their various positions in South Vietnam.

Now, the lack of support certainly had an impact on the decision that President Thieu made to withdraw precipitously. I don't think he would have withdrawn if the support had been there. It wasn't there, so he decided to withdraw.

Unfortunately, the withdrawal was hastily done, inadequately prepared, and consequently was a chaotic withdrawal of the forces from Military Regions I, II, and Ill.

Now, how you place the blame, what percentage our failure to supply the arms, what percentage related to a hastily and inadequately prepared withdrawal—the experts, after they study the records, probably can give you a better assessment. But the initial kickoff came for the withdrawal from the failure of our Government to adequately support the military request for help. . . .

Now, unless I am pressed, I don't say the Congress did this or did that. I have to be frank if I am asked the categorical question. . . .

Source: "Interview with Walter Cronkite, Eric Sevareid and Bob Schieffer of CBS News," April 21, 1975, in *Public Papers of the Presidents of the United States: Gerald R. Ford 1974–1977,* from the American Presidency Project, University of California, Santa Barbara, www.presidency.ucsb.edu.

Document 7.4
President Gerald Ford Breaks Free of Vietnam (and Henry Kissinger), Address at Tulane University, April 23, 1975

At Tulane University's commencement, President Ford announced that there would be no attempt at last-minute heroics to save South Vietnam. The content of the president's speech was kept secret from Secretary of State and National Security Adviser Henry Kissinger.

. . . Today, America can regain the sense of pride that existed before Vietnam. But it cannot be achieved by refighting a war that is finished as far as America is concerned. As I see it, the time has come to look forward to an agenda for the future, to unify, to bind up the Nation's wounds, and to restore its health and its optimistic self-confidence.

. . . In New Orleans tonight, we can begin a great national reconciliation. The first engagement must be with the problems of today, but just as importantly, the problems of the future. That is why I think it is so appropriate that I find myself tonight at a university which addresses itself to preparing young people for the challenge of tomorrow.

I ask that we stop refighting the battles and the recriminations of the past. I ask that we look now at what is right with America, at our possibilities and our potentialities for change and growth and achievement and sharing. I ask that we accept the responsibilities of leadership as a good neighbor to all peoples and the enemy of none. I ask that we strive to become, in the finest American tradition, something more tomorrow than we are today.

Instead of my addressing the image of America, I prefer to consider the reality of America. It is true that we have launched our Bicentennial celebration without having achieved human perfection, but we have attained a very remarkable self-governed society that possesses the flexibility and the dynamism to grow and undertake an entirely new agenda, an agenda for America's third century.

So, I ask you to join me in helping to write that agenda. I am as determined as a President can be to seek national rediscovery of the belief in ourselves that characterized the most creative periods in our Nation's history. The greatest challenge of creativity, as I see it, lies ahead.

We, of course, are saddened indeed by the events in Indochina. But these events, tragic as they are, portend neither the end of the world nor of America's leadership in the world.

Let me put it this way, if I might. Some tend to feel that if we do not succeed in everything everywhere, then we have succeeded in nothing anywhere. I reject categorically such polarized thinking. We can and we should help others to help themselves. But the fate of responsible men and women everywhere, in the final decision, rests in their own hands, not in ours.

America's future depends upon Americans—especially your generation, which is now equipping itself to assume the challenges of the future, to help write the agenda for America.

Earlier today, in this great community, I spoke about the need to maintain our defenses. Tonight, I would like to talk about another kind of strength, the true source of American power that transcends all of the deterrent powers for peace of our Armed Forces. I am speaking here of our belief in ourselves and our belief in our Nation.

Abraham Lincoln asked, in his own words, and I quote, "What constitutes the bulwark of our own liberty and independence?" And he answered, "It is not our frowning battlements or bristling seacoasts, our Army or our Navy. Our defense is in the spirit which prized liberty as the heritage of all men, in all lands everywhere."

It is in this spirit that we must now move beyond the discords of the past decade. It is in this spirit that I ask you to join me in writing an agenda for the future. . . .

Source: Gerald R. Ford, "Address at a Tulane University Convocation," April 23, 1975, in *Public Papers of the Presidents of the United States: Gerald R. Ford 1974–1977,* from the American Presidency Project, University of California, Santa Barbara, www.presidency.ucsb.edu.

Document 7.5
President Gerald Ford Announces the End of American Presence in Vietnam, April 29, 1975

On April 29, 1975, Saigon, the capital of the Republic of Vietnam, fell to the invading North Vietnamese Army. In a frantic and humiliating operation, U.S. military personnel and embassy officials evacuated approximately 1,000 U.S. citizens and more than 5,000 South Vietnamese, who were airlifted to safety aboard aircraft carriers and other U.S. Navy vessels. Thousands more South Vietnamese—who had earned certain punishment from the North Vietnamese by working with or for the Americans—were left behind.

During the past week, I had ordered the reduction of American personnel in the United States mission in Saigon to levels that could be quickly evacuated during an emergency, while enabling that mission to continue to fulfill its duties.

During the day on Monday, Washington time, the airport at Saigon came under persistent rocket as well as artillery fire and was effectively closed. The military situation in the area deteriorated rapidly.

I therefore ordered the evacuation of all American personnel remaining in South Vietnam.

The evacuation has been completed. I commend the personnel of the Armed Forces who accomplished it as well as Ambassador Graham Martin and the staff of his mission, who served so well under difficult conditions.

This action closes a chapter in the American experience. I ask all Americans to close ranks, to avoid recrimination about the past, to look ahead to the many goals we share, and to work together on the great tasks that remain to be accomplished.

Source: Gerald R. Ford, "Statement Following Evacuation of United States Personnel from the Republic of Vietnam," April 29, 1975, in *Public Papers of the Presidents of the United States: Gerald Ford 1974–1977,* from the American Presidency Project, University of California, Santa Barbara, www.presidency.ucsb.edu.

Document 7.6
U.S. Congress Reveals CIA Cold War Assassination Plots, Interim Report of the Church Committee, November 11, 1975

Sen. Frank Church, D-Idaho, chaired the Select Committee to Study Government Operations with Respect to Intelligence Activities (the "Church Committee" in the Ninety-Fourth Congress (1975–1976). The Church Committee released fourteen reports, including an interim report on the most dramatic allegation regarding the activities of the CIA: political assassination.

PROLOGUE

The events discussed in this Interim Report must be viewed in the context of United States policy and actions designed to counter the threat of spreading Communism. Following the end of World War II, many nations in Eastern Europe and elsewhere fell under Communist influence or control. The defeat of the Axis powers was accompanied by rapid disintegration of the Western colonial empires. The Second World War had no sooner ended than a new struggle began. The Communist threat, emanating from what came to be called the "Sino-Soviet bloc," led to a policy of containment intended to prevent further encroachment into the "Free World."

United States strategy for conducting the Cold War called for the establishment of interlocking treaty arrangements and military bases throughout the world. Concern over the expansion of an aggressive Communist monolith led the United States to fight two major wars in Asia. In addition, it was considered necessary to wage a relentless cold war against Communist expansion wherever it appeared in the "back alleys of the world." This called for a full range of covert activities in response to the operations of Communist clandestine services.

The fear of Communist expansion was particularly acute in the United States when Fidel Castro emerged as Cuba's leader in the late 1950's. His takeover was seen as the first significant penetration by the Communists into the Western Hemisphere. United States leaders, including most Members of Congress, called for vigorous action to stem the Communist infection in this hemisphere. These policies rested on widespread popular support and encouragement. . . .

The Committee regards the unfortunate events dealt with in this Interim Report as an aberration, explainable at least in part, but not justified, by the pressures of the time. The Committee believes that it is still in the national interest of the United States to help nations achieve self-determination and resist Communist domination. However, it is clear that this interest cannot justify resorting to the kind of abuses covered in this report. Indeed, the Committee has resolved that steps must be taken to prevent those abuses from happening again. . . .

D. SUMMARY OF FINDINGS AND CONCLUSIONS ON THE PLOTS

. . .

The evidence concerning each alleged assassination can be summarized as follows:

Patrice Lumumba (Congo/Zaire).—In the fall of 1960, two CIA officials were asked by superiors to assassinate Lumumba. Poisons were sent to the Congo and some exploratory steps were taken toward gaining access to Lumumba. Subsequently, in early 1961, Lumumba was killed by Congolese rivals. It does not appear from the evidence that the United States was in any way involved in the killing.

Fidel Castro (Cuba).—United States Government personnel plotted to kill Castro from 1960 to 1965. American underworld figures and Cubans hostile to Castro were used in these plots, and were provided encouragement and material support by the United States.

Rafael Trujillo (Dominican Republic).—Trujillo was shot by Dominican dissidents on May 31, 1961. From early in 1960 and continuing to the time of the assassination, the United States Government generally supported these dissidents. Some Government personnel were aware that the dissidents intended to kill Trujillo. Three pistols and three carbines were furnished by American officials, although a request for machine guns was later refused. There is conflicting evidence concerning whether the weapons were knowingly supplied for use in the assassination and whether any of them were present at the scene.

Ngo Dinh Diem (South Vietnam).—Diem and his brother, Nhu, were killed on November 2, 1963, in the course of a South Vietnamese Generals' coup. Although the United States Government supported the coup, there is no evidence that American officials favored the assassination. Indeed, it appears that the assassination of Diem was not part of the Generals' pre-coup planning but was instead a spontaneous act which occurred during the coup and was carried out without United States involvement or support.

General René Schneider (Chile).—On October 25, 1970, General Schneider died of gunshot wounds inflicted three days earlier while resisting a kidnap attempt. Schneider, as Commander-in-Chief of the Army and a constitutionalist opposed to military coups, was considered an obstacle in efforts to prevent Salvador Allende from assuming the office of President of Chile. The United States Government supported, and sought to instigate a military coup to block Allende. . . . Although the CIA continued to support coup plotters up to Schneider's shooting, the record indicates that the CIA had withdrawn active support of the group which carried out the actual kidnap attempt. . . .

Assassination capability (Executive action).—In addition to these five cases, the Committee has received evidence that ranking Government officials discussed, and may have authorized, the establishment within the CIA of a generalized assassination capability. . . .

3. SUMMARY OF FINDINGS AND CONCLUSIONS ON THE ISSUES OF AUTHORITY AND CONTROL

To put the inquiry into assassination allegations in context, two points must be made clear. First, there is no doubt that the United States Government opposed the various leaders in question. . . . Second, the evidence on assassinations has to be viewed in the context of other, more massive activities against the regimes in question. For example, the plots against Fidel

Castro personally cannot be understood without considering the fully authorized, comprehensive assaults upon his regime, such as the Bay of Pigs invasion in 1961 and Operation MONGOOSE in 1962.

Once methods of coercion and violence are chosen, the probability of loss of life is always present. There is, however, a significant difference between a coldblooded, targeted, intentional killing of an individual foreign leader and other forms of intervening in the affairs of foreign nations. Therefore, the Committee has endeavored to explore as fully as possible the questions of how and why the plots happened, whether they were authorized, and if so, at what level.

The picture that emerges from the evidence is not a clear one. This may be due to the system of deniability and the consequent state of the evidence which, even after our long investigation, remains conflicting and inconclusive. Or it may be that there were in fact serious shortcomings in the system of authorization so that an activity such as assassination could have been undertaken by an agency of the United States Government without express authority.

. . . Whether or not the respective Presidents knew of or authorized the plots, as chief executive officer of the United States, each must bear the ultimate responsibility for the activities of his subordinates. . . .

Source: U.S. Senate, *Alleged Assassination Plots Involving Foreign Leaders,* Interim Report of the Select Committee to Study Governmental Operations with Respect to Intelligence Activity, 94th Cong., 1st sess., Report no. 94-465 (Washington, D.C.: U.S. Government Printing Office, 1975), from the Assassination Archives and Research Center Public Library, www.aarclibrary.org/publib/church/reports/ir/contents.htm.

Document 7.7
Summary of CIA Plots against Cuban President Fidel Castro, 1960–1965

Between 1960 and 1965, the Central Intelligence Agency tried numerous times to incapacitate or kill Cuba's Communist leader, Fidel Castro. This program of attempted assassination began under President Dwight Eisenhower and continued into the administration of Lyndon Johnson. Whether either of these presidents or President John F. Kennedy knew of or authorized an attempted "hit" on a foreign leader was not revealed in the separate investigations conducted by Vice President Nelson Rockefeller and Sen. Frank Church. Because every plot failed, and because of the sometimes bizarre details of the means to be employed, what can be pieced together about the CIA's efforts to kill Fidel makes for fascinating, and unintentionally comical, reading.

CIA Plots Targeting Fidel Castro

Year	Purpose	Plot	Outcome
1960	To undermine Fidel Castro's image	Spray broadcast studio with hallucinogen; dust Castro's shoes during trip abroad with thallium, a poison that acts as a depilatory (to make "The Beard" lose his hair)	Never attempted: hallucinogen deemed unreliable; Castro cancelled trip abroad
1960	To "neutralize" the influence of Fidel Castro's brother Raul and others	Provide intelligence and promise cash bounty to anti-Castro Cuban if he could arrange a permanently debilitating "accident" for Raul	Responsible party did not go forward, claimed no opportunity presented itself
1960–1961	To kill Fidel Castro with a poisoned cigar	Slip a poisoned cigar into Fidel's cigar box	Botulinum-laced cigars prepared and delivered to unidentified person; no evidence of disposition
1960–1961	To kill Fidel Castro with a poison pill	The CIA enlisted Mafia boss John Rosselli to arrange a "hit" on Castro	First attempt aborted due to cold feet or loss of access to Castro; second and perhaps third attempts failed when different "asset" either lost access to target, because Castro lost interest in the targeted restaurant, or asset never received "go signal" from CIA handlers

Year	Purpose	Plot	Outcome
1962	To kill Fidel Castro, Raul Castro, and perhaps Che Guevara with poison.	Three-man teams hired by John Rosselli and equipped by the CIA would penetrate the bodyguard of the Cuban leadership	CIA provided supplies and cash; CIA cut off support after first team's apparent failure in Cuba and second team's delay in departure from Florida
1963	To kill Fidel Castro with an exploding sea shell	Booby trap an exotic seashell to attract Castro while skin diving	Plot discarded as impractical
1963	To kill Fidel Castro with a poisoned wet suit	Poison a wet suit to be presented to Castro as "gift" by the American in charge of paying ransom for Bay of Pigs captives	Wetsuit plot either never approved beyond testing or, once approved, would-be-assassin switched wetsuits at own initiative
1961–1965	To kill Fidel Castro by rifle fire or with a poison-pen device	Directly and indirectly provide assassination tools to a highly-placed Cuban, code named AM/LASH	After much talk, a rifle, grenades, and poison-pen were provided to asset in 1963; a specially made rifle-silencer and other equipment provided in 1964. The asset failed to follow through.

Source: Prepared by the author, using information from U.S. Senate, *Alleged Assassination Plots Involving Foreign Leaders,* Interim Report of the Select Committee to Study Governmental Operations with Respect to Intelligence Activity, 94th Cong., 1st sess., Report no. 94-465 (Washington, D.C.: U.S. Government Printing Office, 1975), from the Assassination Archives and Research Center Library, http://www.aarclibrary.org/publib/church/reports/ir/contents.htm.

Document 7.8
Internal Intelligence and the Rights of Americans in the Cold War,
Final Church Committee Report, April 26, 1976

The second book of the Church Committee Reports was devoted to a detailed analysis of the evidence regarding the domestic activities of the CIA and the FBI during the Cold War. The CIA and FBI had clearly overstepped their bounds, engaging in illegal "black bag" operations (break-ins and burglaries) and aggressive counterintelligence operations (COINTELPRO) designed to discredit subversive organizations and individuals. As the report indicates, although the intelligence communities' initial targets may have been would-be American revolutionaries, the agencies' activities expanded to include spying on "rabble rousers" and "key activists," especially those active in the "racial field." In addition to the FBI and CIA, the U.S. Army and the Internal Revenue Service were also employed in this wide-ranging war against domestic enemies, real and imagined.

. . .

II. THE GROWTH OF DOMESTIC INTELLIGENCE: 1936 TO 1976

A. SUMMARY

1. The Lesson: History Repeats Itself

During and after the First World War, intelligence agencies, including the predecessor of the FBI, engaged in repressive activity. A new Attorney General, Harlan Fiske Stone, sought to stop the investigation of "political or other opinions." This restraint was embodied only in an executive pronouncement, however. No statutes were passed to prevent the kind of improper activity which had been exposed. Thereafter, as this narrative will show, the abuses returned in a new form. It is now the responsibility of all three branches of government to ensure that the pattern of abuse of domestic intelligence activity does not recur.

2. The Pattern: Broadening Through Time

Since the re-establishment of federal domestic intelligence programs in 1936, there has been a steady increase in the government's capability and willingness to pry into, and even disrupt, the political activities and personal lives of the people. . . .

3. Three Periods of Growth for Domestic Intelligence

The expansion of domestic intelligence activity can usefully be divided into three broad periods: (a) the pre-war and World War II period; (b) the Cold War era, and (c) the period of domestic dissent beginning in the mid-sixties. . . .

  b. 1946–1963

Cold War fears and dangers nurtured the domestic intelligence programs of the FBI and military, and they became permanent features of government. Congress deferred to the executive branch in the oversight of these programs. The FBI became increasingly isolated from effective outside control, even from the Attorneys General. The scope of investigations of "subversion" widened greatly. Under the cloak of secrecy, the FBI instituted its COINTELPRO operations to "disrupt" and "neutralize" "subversives". The National Security Agency, the FBI, and the CIA re-instituted intrusive wartime surveillance techniques in contravention of law.

c. 1964–1976

Intelligence techniques which previously had been concentrated upon foreign threats and domestic groups said to be under Communist influence were applied with increasing intensity to a wide range of domestic activity by American citizens. These techniques were utilized against peaceful civil rights and antiwar protest activity, and thereafter in reaction to civil unrest, often without regard for the consequences to American liberties. The intelligence agencies of the United States—sometimes abetted by public opinion and often in response to pressure from administration officials or the Congress—frequently disregarded the law in their conduct of massive surveillance and aggressive counterintelligence operations against American citizens. In the past few years, some of these activities were curtailed, partly in response to the moderation of the domestic crisis; but all too often improper programs were terminated only in response to exposure, the threat of exposure, or a change in the climate of public opinion, such as that triggered by the Watergate affair. . . .

C. DOMESTIC INTELLIGENCE IN THE COLD WAR ERA: 1946–1963

1. Main Developments of the 1946–1963 period

. . . The main developments during the Cold War era may be summarized as follows:

a. Domestic Intelligence Authority

During this period there was a national consensus regarding the danger to the United States from Communism; little distinction was made between the threats posed by the Soviet Union and by Communists within this country. Domestic intelligence activity was supported by that consensus, although not specifically authorized by the Congress.

Formal authority for FBI investigations of "subversive activity" and for the agreements between the FBI and military intelligence was explicitly granted in executive directives from Presidents Truman and Eisenhower, the National Security Council, and Attorney General Kennedy. These directives provided no guidance, however, for controlling such investigations.

b. Scope of Domestic Intelligence

The breadth of the FBI's investigation of "subversive infiltration" continued to produce intelligence reports and massive files on lawful groups and law-abiding citizens who happened to associate, even unwittingly, with Communists or with socialists unconnected with the Soviet Union who used revolutionary rhetoric. At the same time, the scope of FBI intelligence expanded to cover civil rights protest activity as well as violent "Klan-type" and "hate" groups, vocal anticommunists, and prominent opponents of racial integration. The vagueness of the FBI's investigative mandate and the overbreadth of its collection programs also placed it in position to supply the White House with numerous items of domestic political intelligence apparently desired by Presidents and their aides.

In response to White House and congressional interest in right-wing organizations, the Internal Revenue Service began comprehensive investigations of right-wing groups in 1961 and later expanded to left-wing organizations. This effort was directed at identifying contributions and ascertaining whether the organizations were entitled to maintain their exempt status.

c. Accountability and Control

Pervasive secrecy enabled the FBI and the Justice Department to disregard as "unworkable" the Emergency Detention Act intended to set standards for aspects of domestic intelligence. The FBI's independent position also allowed it to withhold significant information from a Presidential commission and from every Attorney General, and no Attorney General inquired fully into the Bureau's operations.

During the same period, apprehensions about having a "security police" influenced Congress to prohibit the Central Intelligence Agency from exercising law enforcement powers or performing "internal security functions." Nevertheless, in secret and without effective internal controls, the CIA undertook programs for testing chemical and biological agents on unwitting Americans, sometimes with tragic consequences. The CIA also used American private institutions as "cover" and used intrusive techniques affecting the rights of Americans.

d. Intrusive Techniques

The CIA and the National Security Agency illegally instituted programs for the interception of international communications to and from American citizens, primarily first class mail and cable traffic.

During this period, the FBI also used intrusive intelligence gathering techniques against domestic "subversives" and counterintelligence targets. Sometimes these techniques were covered by a blanket delegation of authority from the Attorney General, as with microphone surveillance; but frequently they were used without outside authorization, as with mail openings and surreptitious entry. Only conventional wiretaps required the Attorney General's approval in each case, but this method was still misused due to the lack of adequate standards and procedural safeguards.

e. Domestic Covert Action

In the mid-fifties, the FBI developed the initial COINTELPRO operations, which used aggressive covert actions to disrupt and discredit Communist Party activities. The FBI subsequently expanded its COINTELPRO activities to discredit peaceful protest groups whom Communists had infiltrated but did not control, as well as groups of socialists who used revolutionary rhetoric but had no connections with a hostile foreign power. . . .

3. Scope of Domestic Intelligence

. . .

c. FBI Political Intelligence for the White House

. . . In 1962 the FBI complied unquestioningly with a request from Attorney General Kennedy to interview a Steel Company executive and several reporters who had written stories about the Steel executive. The interviews were conducted late at night and early in the morning because, according to the responsible FBI official, the Attorney General indicated the information was needed for a White House meeting the next day.

Throughout the period, the Bureau also disseminated reports to high executive officials to discredit its critics. The FBI's inside information on plans of the Lawyers Guild to denounce Bureau surveillance in 1949 gave the Attorney General the opportunity to prepare a rebuttal well in advance of the expected criticism. When the Knoxville Area Human Relations Council charged in 1960 that the FBI was practicing racial discrimination, the FBI did "name checks" on members the Council's board of directors and sent the results to the Attorney General. The name checks dredged up derogatory allegations from as far back as the late thirties and early forties.

d. IRS Investigations of Political Organizations

The IRS program that came to be used against the domestic dissidents of the 1960s was first used against Communists in the 1950s. As part of its COINTELPRO against the Communist Party, the FBI arranged for IRS investigations of Party members, and obtained their tax returns. In its efforts against the Communist Party, the FBI had unlimited access to tax returns: it never told the IRS why it wanted them, and IRS never attempted to find out.

In 1961, responding to White House and congressional interest in right-wing organizations, the IRS began comprehensive investigation of right-wing groups to identify contributors and ascertain whether or not some of them were entitled to their tax exempt status. Left-wing groups were later added, in an effort to avoid charges that such IRS activities were all aimed at one part of the political spectrum. Both right- and left-wing groups were selected for review and investigation because of their political activity and not because of any information that they had violated the tax laws.

While the IRS efforts begun in 1961 to investigate the political activities of tax exempt organizations were not as extensive as later programs in 1969–1973, they were a significant departure by the IRS from normal enforcement criteria for investigating persons or groups on the basis of information indicating noncompliance. By directing tax audits at individuals and groups solely because of their political beliefs, the Ideological Organizations Audit Project (as the 1961 program was known) established a precedent for a far more elaborate program of targeting "dissidents." . . .

4. Accountability and Control

During the Cold War period, there were serious weaknesses in the system of accountability and control of domestic intelligence activity. On occasion the executive chose not to comply with the will of Congress with respect to internal security policy, and the Congressional attempt to exclude U.S. foreign intelligence agencies from domestic activities was evaded. Intelligence agencies also conducted covert programs in violation of laws protecting the rights of Americans. Problems of accountability were compounded by the lack of effective congressional oversight and the vagueness of executive orders, which allowed intelligence agencies to escape outside scrutiny. . . .

b. FBI Covert Techniques

. . .

"Black Bag Jobs."—There is no indication that any Attorney General was informed of FBI "black bag" jobs, and a "Do Not File" procedure was designed to preclude outside discovery of the FBI's use of the technique.

No permanent records were kept for approvals of "black bag jobs," or surreptitious entries conducted for purposes other than installing a "bug." The FBI has described the procedure for authorization of surreptitious entries as requiring the approval of Director Hoover or his Assistant Clyde Tolson. The authorizing memorandum was filed in the Director's office under a "Do Not File" procedure, and thereafter destroyed. In the field office, the Special Agent in Charge maintained a record of approval in his office safe. At the next yearly field office inspection, an Inspector would review these records to ensure that the SAC had secured FBI headquarters approval in conducting surreptitious entries. Upon completion of the review, these records were destroyed.

The only internal FBI memorandum found discussing the policy for surreptitious entries confirms that this was the procedure and states that "we do not obtain authorization from outside the Bureau" because the technique was "clearly illegal." The memorandum indicates that "black bag jobs" were used not only "in the espionage field" but also against "subversive elements" not directly connected to espionage activity. It added that the techniques resulted "on numerous occasions" in obtaining the "highly secret and closely guarded" membership and mailing lists of "subversive" groups. . . .

6. Domestic Covert Action

In its COINTELPRO operation, the FBI went beyond excessive information-gathering and dissemination to the use of secret tactics designed to "disrupt" and "neutralize" domestic intelligence targets. At the outset, the target was the Communist Party, U.S.A. But, consistent with the pattern revealed in other domestic intelligence activities, the program widened to other targets, increasingly concentrating on domestic dissenters. The expansion of COINTELPRO began in the Cold War period and accelerated in the latter part of the 1960s. . . .

D. INTELLIGENCE AND DOMESTIC DISSENT: 1964–1976

1. Main Developments of the 1964–1976 Period

Beginning in the mid-sixties, the United States experienced a period of domestic unrest and protest unparalleled in this century. Violence erupted in the poverty-stricken urban ghettos, and opposition to American intervention in Vietnam produced massive demonstrations.

A small minority deliberately used violence as a method for achieving political goals—ranging from the brutal murder and intimidation of black Americans in parts of the South to the terrorist bombing of office buildings and government-supported university facilities. But three Presidential commissions found that the larger outbreaks of violence in the ghettos and on the campuses were most often spontaneous reactions to events in a climate of social tension and upheaval.

During this period, thousands of young Americans and members of racial minorities came to believe in civil disobedience as a vehicle for protest and dissent.

The government could have set an example for the nation's citizens and prevented spiraling lawlessness by respecting the law as it took steps, to predict or prevent violence. But agencies of the United States, sometimes abetted by public opinion and government officials, all too often disregarded the Constitutional rights of American in their conduct of domestic intelligence operations.

The most significant developments in domestic intelligence activity during this period may be summarized as follows:

a. Scope of Domestic Intelligence

FBI intelligence reports on protest activity and domestic dissent accumulated massive information on lawful activity and law-abiding citizens for vaguely defined "pure intelligence" and "preventive intelligence" purposes related only remotely or not at all to law enforcement or the prevention of violence. The FBI exaggerated the extent of domestic Communist influence, and . . . improperly included groups with no significant connections to Communists. . . .

c. Domestic Covert Action

The FBI developed new covert programs for disrupting and discrediting domestic political groups, using the techniques originally applied to Communists. The most intensive domestic intelligence investigations, and frequently COINTELPRO operations, were targeted against persons identified not as criminals or criminal suspects, but as "rabble rousers," "agitators," "key activists," or "key black extremists" because of their militant rhetoric and group leadership. . . .

2. Scope of Domestic Intelligence

a. Domestic Protest and Dissent: FBI

(1) Racial Intelligence—During the 1960s, the FBI, partly on its own and partly in response to outside requests, developed sweeping programs for collecting domestic intelligence concerning racial matters. These programs had roots in the late 1950s. By the early 1960s, they had grown to the point that the Bureau was gathering intelligence about proposed "civil demonstrations" and the related activities of "officials, committees, legislatures, organizations, etc.," in the "racial field." . . .

Source: U.S. Senate, *Intelligence Activities and the Rights of Americans,* book 2 of the Final Report of the Select Committee to Study Governmental Operations with Respect to Intelligence Activities, 94th Congress, 2nd sess., Report no. 94-755 (Washington, D.C.: U.S. Government Printing Office, 1976), from the Assassination Archives and Research Center Public Library, www.aarclibrary.org/publib/church/reports/book2/contents.htm.

Document 7.9
Prohibition of U.S. Government Employees' Participation in Assassinations, Executive Order 11905, February 18, 1976

In Executive Order 11905, President Ford prohibited the participation of U.S. intelligence agents in the conduct of political assassinations. The order would be updated by the next two presidents (Carter and Reagan). The prohibition's wisdom would be debated after the Cold War ended, as the United States responded to the threat of international terrorism.

By virtue of the authority vested in me by the Constitution and statutes of the United States, including the National Security Act of 1947, as amended, and as President of the United States of America, it is hereby ordered as follows:

SECTION 1. *Purpose.* The purpose of this Order is to establish policies to improve the quality of intelligence needed for national security, to clarify the authority and responsibilities of the intelligence departments and agencies, and to establish effective oversight to assure compliance with law in the management and direction of intelligence agencies and departments of the national government. . . .

SECTION 5. *Restrictions on Intelligence Activities.* Information about the capabilities, intentions and activities of other governments is essential to informed decision-making in the field of national defense and foreign relations. The measures employed to acquire such information should be responsive to the legitimate needs of our Government and must be conducted in a manner which preserves and respects our established concepts of privacy and our civil liberties.

Recent events have clearly indicated the desirability of government-wide direction which will ensure a proper balancing of these interests. This section of this Order does not authorize any activity not previously authorized and does not provide exemption from any restrictions otherwise applicable. Unless otherwise specified, the provisions of this section apply to activities both inside and outside the United States. References to law are to applicable laws of the United States. . . .

(g) Prohibition of Assassination. No employee of the United States Government shall engage in, or conspire to engage in, political assassination. . . .

Source: "President Gerald R. Ford's Executive Order 11905: United States Foreign Intelligence Activities," February 18, 1976, in *Weekly Compilation of Presidential Documents,* February 23, 1976, from the Federation of American Scientists, www.fas.org/irp/offdocs/eo11905.htm.

Document 7.10
President Gerald Ford Answers Questions about the *Mayaguez* Incident, April 1976

On May 12, 1975, shortly after the victory of Communist forces in both Vietnam and Cambodia, a U.S. merchant ship, the Mayaguez, *was seized by Cambodian sailors in international waters. Seeing the situation as an opportunity to buttress American credibility, President Ford ordered a military rescue attempt. In the ensuing battle, the ship's crew was released unharmed, but eighteen U.S. Marines and airmen were killed in an assault on Cambodian forces. During a 1976 presidential election campaign appearance at a public forum in West Bend, Wisconsin, Ford highlighted what he saw as the great symbolic significance of the rescue mission.*

. . .

Q.: Good evening, Mr. President. I would like to know what you think has been your most important decision as President and why?

The President: Well, there were several. It seems some days like that is all it is all day long. I would say that probably the one that took the most forceful action was the decision to make certain that the *Mayaguez,* the merchant ship, was recovered from the Cambodians. That was probably one of the most meaningful decisions because that ship was attacked, it was seized by the Cambodians, and we sent in our forces to get it back, and we got it back. That was a tough decision. . . .

In a question-and-answer session in Evansville, Indiana, on April 23, 1976, President Ford emphasized the "decisiveness" of his administration, as exemplified in his handling of the Mayaguez crisis.

. . .

Q.: Mr. President, first off I would like to congratulate you on your handling of the *Mayaguez* incident. My question is, what is your stand on the Concorde being allowed to land in the United States?

The President: Well, first let me thank you for your comments concerning the *Mayaguez.* That, I think, should be a good warning to any country that thinks they can challenge us. If any country does any act of that kind, I think the *Mayaguez* incident and the action we took ought to be a fair warning to them to the decisiveness of the Ford administration. Now, would you repeat the other question? . . .

At an April 28, 1976, question-and-answer session at Tyler Junior College, in Tyler, Texas, President Ford made a stunning leap in logic when he suggested that because he had stood up to the Cambodians in a single day's combat, the North Koreans had best believe that this *president was so tough, he might use* any *weapon in his arsenal.*

. . .

Q.: Mr. President, I believe that you and former Secretary of Defense Schlesinger have stated that we would engage in limited nuclear warfare in the defense of South Korea. Could you define limited nuclear warfare and the ramifications of such with reference to the Chinese?

The President: I really don't think that I ought to discuss what we would do in any potential—if the potential is there of a war, whether it's limited or nuclear. Certainly we can speculate, but I don't think that I should announce at a forum like this what we would do based on some speculative assumption that we would have a reinvasion by North Korea of South Korea or some other adversary attacking us or attacking an ally.

We have contingency plans to meet all challenges, all challenges. And those plans are available for the Commander in Chief to make a decision on, under any circumstances, and I can assure you that we will meet all challenges. And we have the options as to what we should do. We have the capability to meet those challenges, and this Commander in Chief will meet any challenges in the future as decisively as he did when we took action at the time of the *Mayaguez* affair.

Sources: "Remarks and a Question-and-Answer Session at a Public Forum in West Bend, Wisconsin," April 2, 1976; "Remarks and a Question-and-Answer Session at a Public Forum in Evansville, Indiana," April 23, 1976; and "Remarks and a Question-and-Answer Session at Tyler Junior College, Tyler, Texas," April 28, 1976, in *Public Papers of the Presidents of the United States: Gerald R. Ford 1974–1977,* from the American Presidency Project, University of California, Santa Barbara, www.presidency.ucsb.edu.

Document 7.11

Intelligence Community Experiment in Competitive Analysis, Team "B" Report on Soviet Strategic Objectives, December 1, 1976

Labeled an "experiment" in intelligence analysis, the report of the group of outside experts known as Team "B" was part of a comprehensive assault on détente by conservative critics of Presidents Nixon and Ford and the SALT talks to which they were committed. The top secret report's findings were leaked to the press in October 1976, before it was even printed at the CIA.

SUMMARY

Team "B" found that the NIE [National Intelligence Estimate] . . . series through 1975 has substantially misperceived the motivations behind Soviet strategic programs, and thereby tended consistently to underestimate their intensity, scope, and implicit threat.

This misperception has been due in considerable measure to concentration on the so-called hard data . . . collected by technical means . . . while slighting or misinterpreting the large body of "soft" data concerning Soviet strategic concepts. The failure to take into account or accurately to assess such soft data sources has resulted in the NIEs not addressing themselves systematically to the broader political purposes which underlie and explain Soviet strategic objectives. Since, however, the political context cannot be altogether avoided, the drafters of the NIEs have fallen into the habit of injecting into key judgments of the executive summaries impressionistic assessments based on "mirror-imaging," i.e., the attribution to Soviet decision makers of such forms of behavior as might be expected from their U.S. counterparts under analogous circumstances. This conceptual flaw is perhaps the single gravest cause of the misunderstanding of Soviet strategic objectives found in past and current NIEs. . . .

. . . The drafters of NIE 11-3/8 seem to believe that the Soviet leaders view strategic nuclear weapons much as do their U.S. analogues. Since in the United States nuclear war is generally regarded as an act of mutual suicide that can be rational only as a deterrent threat, it is assumed that the USSR looks at the matter in the same way. The primary concern of Soviet leaders is seen to be the securing of an effective deterrent to protect the Soviet Union from U.S. attack and in accord with the Western concept of deterrence. . . .

Analysis of Soviet past and present behavior, combined with what is known of Soviet political and military doctrines, indicates that these judgments are seriously flawed. The evidence suggests that the Soviet leaders are first and foremost offensively rather than defensively minded. . . . They believe that the probability of a general nuclear war can be reduced by building up one's own strategic forces, but that it cannot be altogether eliminated, and that therefore one has to be prepared for such a war as if it were unavoidable and be ready to strike first if it appears imminent. There is no evidence that the Soviet leadership is ready, let alone eager, to reduce the military budget in order to raise the country's standard of living. Soviet Russia's habitual caution and sensitivity to U.S. reactions are due less to an inherent prudence than to a realistic assessment of the existing global "correlation of forces"; should this correlation (or the Soviet leaders' perception of it) change in their favor, they could be expected to act with greater confidence and less concern for U.S. sensitivities. In fact, there are disturbing signs that the latter development is already taking place, recent evidence of a Soviet willingness to take increased risks (e.g., by threatening unilateral military intervention in the Middle East in October 1973, and supporting the Angola adventure) may well represent harbingers of what lies ahead. . . .

PART ONE: JUDGMENTS OF SOVIET STRATEGIC OBJECTIVES UNDERLYING NIEs AND THE SHORTCOMINGS OF THESE JUDGMENTS

. . . There is no reason to assume that the Soviet leadership, like its U.S. counterpart, regards military expenditures as a waste and wishes to reduce the military budget in order to be able to shift resources to the civilian sector. For one, the priority enjoyed by the Soviet military seems unchallengeable. Secondly, the sharp civilian-military duality, basic to our society, does not exist in the USSR; hence, the Soviet military budget is not clearly differentiated from the civilian one. . . . Having had ample opportunity to observe post-1945 developments in the West, the Soviet leaders seem to have concluded that a population addicted to the pursuit of consumer goods rapidly loses its sense of patriotism, sinking into a mood of self-indulgence that makes it extremely poor material for national mobilization. . . .

It is certainly true that the Russians have been prudent and generally cautious, and that they have avoided rash military adventures of the kind that had characterized nationalist-revolutionary ("fascist") regimes of the 1930's. As the record indicates, whenever they have been confronted with situations that threatened to lead to U.S.-USSR military confrontations, they preferred to withdraw, even at the price of some humiliation. The reason for this cautious behavior, however, lies not in an innate conservatism, but rather in military inferiority, for which reason one cannot count on it recurring as that inferiority disappears. . . .

PART THREE: SOVIET STRATEGIC OBJECTIVES

. . . The ultimate Soviet objective is (as it has been since October 1917) the worldwide triumph of "socialism," by which is meant the establishment of a system which can be best characterized as a regime of state capitalism administered exclusively by a self-perpetuating elite on the model of the Soviet Communist Party. . . .

As seen from Moscow, the United States is something of a paradox in that it is at one and the same time both exceedingly strong and exceedingly weak. Its strength derives primarily from its unique productive capacity and the technological leadership which give it the capacity to sustain a military capability of great sophistication, dangerous to Soviet global ambitions. But the United States is also seen as presently lacking in political will and discipline, unable to mobilize its population and resources for a sustained struggle for world leadership, and devoid of clear national objectives. This assessment has led the Soviet Union to develop a particular strategy vis-à-vis the United States which, under the name first of "peaceful coexistence" and then "détente," has dominated its relations with the United States . . . over the past two decades.

. . . The effect of such a policy of "détente" is expected to be a reduction in the influence of those elements in U.S. society which desire greater military preparedness and military R&D, resulting in a weakening of the United States precisely in that sphere where lies its particular strength. . . .

Soviet motivations for Strategic Arms Limitation Talks should be seen in the same way: They are means to further unilateral advantages instrumental to the continued shift of the strategic balance and to the realization of political gains from the shifting correlation of forces. SALT and the limitations it produces are seen as means of inhibiting U.S. political and military responses to the changing balance of forces. . . .

Source: "Soviet Strategic Objectives: An Alternate View (Report of Team "B")," December 1, 1976, declassified and released March 13, 1996, NARA no. NN3-263-96-002, from the Central Intelligence Agency Electronic Reading Room, www.foia.cia.gov (search by NARA number and publication date).

Document 7.12
President Gerald Ford and Governor Jimmy Carter Debate the Status of Eastern Europe, October 6, 1976

In his second debate with the Democratic nominee for president, Georgia governor Jimmy Carter, President Ford seemed to suggest that he was unaware of Soviet domination of Eastern Europe. The president's misstep came in answer to a question from New York Times *reporter Max Frankel. His slow and defensive response to the ensuing criticism damaged his prospects for reelection, and the entire incident became a part of the folklore of presidential debate history. Pauline Frederick, of National Public Radio, was the debate's moderator.*

. . .

Mr. Frankel: Mr. President, I'd like to explore a little more deeply our relationship with the Russians. They used to brag back in Khrushchev's day that because of their greater patience and because of our greed for—for business deals that they would sooner or later get the better of us. Is it possible that despite some setbacks in the Middle East, they've proved their point? Our allies in France and Italy are now flirting with Communism. We've recognized the permanent Communist regime in East Germany. We've virtually signed, in Helsinki, an agreement that the Russians have dominance in Eastern Europe. We've bailed out Soviet agriculture with our huge grain sales. We've given them large loans, access to our best technology and if the Senate hadn't interfered with the Jackson

Amendment, maybe we—you would've given them even larger loans. Is that what you call a two-way street of traffic in Europe?

Mr. Ford: I believe that we have uh—negotiated with the Soviet Union since I've been president from a position of strength. And let me cite several examples. Shortly after I became president in uh—December of 1974 [sic], I met with uh—General Secretary Brezhnev in Vladivostok and we agreed to a mutual cap on the ballistic missile launchers at a ceiling of twenty-four hundred—which means that the Soviet Union, if that becomes a permanent agreement, will have to make a reduction in their launchers that they now have or plan to have. I've negotiated at Vladivostok with uh—Mr. Brezhnev a limitation on the MIRVing of their ballistic missiles at a figure of thirteen-twenty, which is the first time that any president has achieved a cap either on launchers or on MIRVs. It seems to me that we can go from there to uh—the uh—grain sales. The grain sales have been a benefit to American agriculture. We have achieved a five and three quarter year uh—sale of a minimum six million metric tons, which means that they have already bought about four million metric tons this year and are bound to buy another two million metric tons to take the grain and corn and wheat that the American farmers have produced in order to uh—have full production. And these grain sales to the Soviet Union have helped us tremendously in meeting the costs of the additional oil and—the oil that we have bought from overseas. If we turn to Helsinki—I'm glad you raised it, Mr. uh—Frankel. In the case of Helsinki, thirty-five nations signed an agreement, including the secretary of state for the Vatican— I can't under any circumstances believe that the—His Holiness, the Pope would agree by signing that agreement that the thirty-five nations have turned over to the Warsaw Pact nations the domination of the—Eastern Europe. It just isn't true. And if Mr. Carter alleges that His Holiness by signing that has done it, he is totally inaccurate. Now, what has been accomplished by the Helsinki agreement? Number one, we have an agreement where they notify us and we notify them of any uh—military maneuvers that are to be be undertaken. They have done it. In both cases where they've done so, there is no Soviet domination of Eastern Europe and there never will be under a Ford administration.

Ms. Frederick: Governor Carter?

Mr. Frankel: I'm sorry, I—could I just follow—did I understand you to say, sir, that the Russians are not using Eastern Europe as their own sphere of influence in occupying mo-most of the countries there and in—and making sure with their troops that it's a—that it's a Communist zone, whereas on our side of the line the Italians and the French are still flirting with the possibility of Communism?

Mr. Ford: I don't believe, uh—Mr. Frankel that uh—the Yugoslavians consider themselves dominated by the Soviet Union. I don't believe that the Rumanians consider themselves dominated by the Soviet Union. I don't believe that the Poles consider themselves dominated by the Soviet Union. Each of those countries is independent, autonomous: it has its own territorial integrity and the United States does not concede that those countries are under the domination of the Soviet Union. As a matter of fact, I visited Poland, Yugoslavia and Rumania to make certain that the people of those countries understood that the president of the United States and the people of the United [States] are dedicated to their independence, their autonomy and their freedom.

Ms. Frederick: Governor Carter, may I have your response?

Mr. Carter: (chuckle) Well, in the first place, I'm not criticizing His Holiness the Pope. I was talking about Mr. Ford. The uh—fact is that secrecy has surrounded the decisions made by the Ford administration. In the case of the Helsinki agreement—it may have been a good agreement at the beginning, but we have failed to enforce the so-called basket three part, which insures the right of people to migrate, to join their families, to be free, to speak out. The Soviet Union is still jamming Radio Free Europe—Radio—uh-uh—Radio Free Europe is being jammed. We've also seen a very serious uh—problem with the so-called Sonnenfeldt document, which apparently Mr. Ford has just endorsed, which said that there's an organic linkage between the Eastern European countries and the Soviet Union. And I would like to see Mr. Ford convince the Polish-Americans and the Czech-Americans and the Hungarian-Americans in this country that those countries don't live under the domination and supervision of the Soviet Union behind the Iron—uh—Curtain.

Source: Commission on Presidential Debates, "The Second Carter-Ford Presidential Debate," Debate Transcript, October 6, 1976, www.debates.org/pages/trans76b.html.

CHAPTER EIGHT

Jimmy Carter

Human Rights and a Midcourse Reversal

s a candidate for president, Democrat Jimmy Carter promised Americans a government "as decent, honest, truthful, fair, compassionate, and as filled with love as our people are."[1] A former governor of Georgia with a fiercely developed sense of right and wrong, Carter ran as an outsider in 1976, casting incumbent Gerald Ford in the role of a consummate, if likable, insider—a career politician with a suspiciously long résumé of government service. In November "Jimmy Who?" beat a candidate who to many voters was "the man who pardoned

President Jimmy Carter works at his desk in the Oval Office on February 8, 1977. Source: Jimmy Carter Presidential Library.

Richard Nixon."[2] Democrats, who continued to control the House and Senate as they had since 1954, looked with hope upon the restoration of unified partisan control of the federal government.

Carter was hopeful, too, for he planned to make up for his lack of experience with a surfeit of ideas and plans. As former Carter speechwriter James Fallows once observed, Jimmy Carter came into office with "explicit, thorough positions on every issue under the sun."[3] He was, moreover, considered a quick study and the hardest worker in the White House since Lyndon Johnson. Unlike Johnson, however, Carter did not care much for political give-and-take. Once he mastered a policy issue, he typically wasted little time forming his own opinion about it, and he then acted as if he expected everyone one else to endorse his opinion and embrace his idea, simply "because it was right."[4]

One of President Carter's biggest ideas was that the United States had entered an "Age of Limits": he believed that the nation could not continue on its present course without inviting a disastrous future reckoning. In energy policy, this meant Americans had to learn to conserve; they should turn down the thermostat in winter and wear sweaters indoors, like the president. (In his first nationally televised address, Carter sat by a fire in a cardigan sweater and spoke about energy conservation.) In foreign policy, confronting limits meant moving beyond a Cold War frame of reference. The shape of world politics, the president's foreign policy tutors had taught him on the way to the White House, was no longer bipolar but multipolar. While previous presidents had pursued national advantage in a global contest, President Carter would pursue the common good in an era of global interdependence. The world was just too complex in the mid-1970s, or so the Carter team believed, for a simplistic application of the old Free World versus International Communism perspective.

Leslie Gelb, a Carter administration foreign policy appointee, explained that "the Carter approach" rested upon a belief that "not only is the world far too complex to be reduced to a doctrine, but that there is something inherently wrong with having a doctrine at all."[5] To the extent that the Carter administration pursued a single goal in foreign affairs, it was neither the restoration of détente nor any other Cold War objective, but rather "World Order." The preferred means for its fulfillment was "affirmative" engagement in global affairs, in close association with other nations, especially those of Western Europe and Japan.[6]

Carried to an extreme, as it sometimes was, this point of view suggested not only that the Cold War was less significant than it had once been (or had once been thought to be), but that the Cold War was in fact *over*. Sometimes, early in his presidency, the president spoke of the Cold War in the past tense, as when he reminded a national television audience of the Cuban Missile Crisis, an event "in the era of the Cold War."[7] Carter even dismissed the bedrock Cold War strategy of containment—the idea that Soviet expansion must be contained—as an archaic notion driven by "an inordinate fear of Communism" and proven false by "historical trends."[8] Thus was Carter eager to lay the Vietnam War to rest. One of his first acts as president was to issue a nonconditional presidential pardon to Vietnam War draft evaders. Unlike President Ford's amnesty program, Carter's required neither compensatory community service nor an oath of allegiance. Carter also condemned the war rhetorically as both immoral and unnecessary. The war's failure, the president reasoned, should teach the American people "the danger of our country resorting to military means in a distant place on earth where our security is not being threatened."[9] When the Cold War *was* acknowledged in the Carter White House in the early years, it was subordinated to issues of deeper, more personal interest to the president, namely human rights and nuclear disarmament.

HUMAN RIGHTS

Personal experience and ideals placed human rights at the top of Jimmy Carter's agenda. Carter's involvement in politics grew out of his commitment to civil rights. Heading to the White House, he naturally drew a parallel between civil rights for African Americans in the American south and human rights for all people around the world. Political calculation suggested that Carter's concern be given a place of honor, as Carter's other initiatives in foreign policy were extensions of policies pursued by his Republican predecessors. In arms control, the president had inherited the stalled second Strategic Arms Limitation Talks (SALT II), negotiated by President Ford; on the issue of the Panama Canal, the president intended to carry on the work of Henry Kissinger, national security adviser and secretary of state to Presidents Nixon and Ford. Likewise, with regard to his desire to improve relations with the People's Republic of China, President Carter could make no claim of innovation for his policy, which continued Nixon's. Prioritizing human rights, by contrast, was a novel idea.

Carter's human rights policy, however, was not without its costs. Eventually, it would alienate Cold War hawks because it threatened the country's association with former friends: the leaders of authoritarian but anti-Communist regimes. Initially, though, the president's human rights lens was turned toward the Soviet Union itself, and thus the president attracted support from both post–Cold War liberals, whose prime motivation was the promotion of human rights, and Cold War conservatives, who saw Carter's agenda as an extension of the old battle of ideas against communism. Tellingly, Carter's decision early in his presidency to assert his human rights agenda against the Soviet Union, rather than against a non-Communist nation, happened by accident.

As Jimmy Carter took office in early 1977, an American civil rights attorney named Martin Garbus traveled to Moscow to meet with a high-profile client, Andrei Sakharov. Sakharov was a world-renowned scientist and a dissident who campaigned for human rights in the Soviet Union, under the banner of the Helsinki Accords. In their meeting, Garbus solicited from Sakharov a letter for the U.S. president, which he promised to deliver personally. Denied a meeting at the White House, the attorney released the letter to the State Department and the *New York Times*. In his letter, Sakharov appealed to President Carter to raise his voice in defense of dissidents in the Soviet Union and the Eastern bloc, where they faced a "hard, almost unbearable situation."[10] The Soviet news agency TASS warned President Carter that Sakharov was a "renegade" being used by "some people in Washington" with "a very strong anti-Soviet itch and desire to slander the U.S.S.R. and the Soviet way of life under the cover of the false concern for implementation of the Helsinki decision."[11] Soviet ambassador Anatoly Dobrynin echoed this position.

The president replied on February 5, 1977, in a telegram that was hand delivered to Sakharov at the U.S. embassy in Moscow (**Document 8.1**). Although Carter's message made no explicit criticism of Soviet state behavior and emphasized the global nature of his concern with human rights, the implication was clear: the president of the United States respected Sakharov as a spokesperson for human rights. The Soviet authorities reacted strongly.

They had cause for concern. The August 1975 Helsinki Accords (see Document 7.1), ratified in the United States under President Ford, had encouraged the dissident movement in the Soviet bloc. The results included a number of confrontations between dissidents and Communist governments. Before the incident with Sakharov, a number of prominent dissidents had been arrested, and the Soviets were already bitter at public criticism from the West. In the first weeks of the Carter administration, the State Department had issued a statement condemning Czechoslovakia, a Warsaw Pact nation, for its persecution of Charter 77, a domestic human rights watch group. The Soviets did not care that Secretary of State Cyrus Vance had almost simultaneously stated in an interview that the Carter administration had no desire to link its concern for human rights in Communist countries to issues such as arms control. The Soviets were not about to let the Americans condemn them without consequence.

The Soviets first signaled their displeasure through statements in the Soviet press and protests at the ministerial level. *Pravda* and TASS editorialized in February and March 1977 against "sabotage" from the West.[12] President Carter, *Pravda*'s editors proclaimed, was himself violating the Helsinki agreement by interfering in the internal affairs of a foreign country. The Soviets and their friends in Eastern Europe had every right, the Soviets proclaimed, to act against the likes of Sakharov. The U.S. president apparently did not understand, *Pravda* reasoned, that anti-Soviet dissidents were opponents of détente. These hints to President Carter to tone down his administration's criticisms proved insufficient, as the president on March 1, 1977, met in the White House with Vladimir Bukovsky, a dissident who had been expelled from the Soviet Union. On March 21, the leader of the Soviet government, General Secretary Leonid Brezhnev, joined the conversation in a speech to a Moscow Congress of Trade Union Deputies, in which he accused Carter of interfering in Soviet internal affairs. Carter's words, Brezhnev charged, were inciting false accusations that the Soviet Union in some way threatened the United States.

Carter was not to be deterred. "Surely the Soviets are sophisticated enough," reasoned Carter's press secretary, Jody Powell, in a February 1977 letter to his boss, "to understand that the domestic flexibility we need to make progress in other areas is enhanced by your position on human rights."[13] The president was surprised with the fierceness of Brezhnev's response. Even had the president more accurately estimated the Soviets' likely response, it is doubtful that he would have acted with more caution or spoken with greater tact. He was determined to advance a human rights agenda as president, whatever the cost. "Even if our human rights policy had been a much *more serious* point of contention in Soviet-American relations," Carter later observed in his memoirs, "I would not have been inclined to accommodate Soviet objectives."[14]

As Carter confessed to his diary in the first week of his presidency, "it's almost impossible for me to delay something that I see needs to be done"—no matter if "everybody" was telling him he should instead establish priorities.[15] He saw lobbying on behalf of the human rights of Soviet dissidents as something that "needs to be done." The president also thought that his response to events in the Soviet bloc had ignited a "spark" among the press and the public. He was not about to "douse the growing flames."[16]

To advance his human rights agenda, the president nominated civil rights leader Andrew Young to be ambassador to the United Nations and civil rights expert Patricia Derian to a new post, coordinator for human rights and humanitarian affairs at the State Department. Ambassador Young complicated superpower relations by asserting that the United States held hundreds or even thousands of political prisoners in *its* jails.[17] But the president stuck to the script, devoting his first major foreign policy speech, a commencement address at Notre Dame University on May 22, 1977, to the topic of human rights. "We can no longer separate the traditional issues of war and peace," the president said, "from the new global questions of justice, equity, and human rights." The old East-West conflict needed to be understood from a new North-South (rich world–poor world) point of view. To meet the challenges of a "new world," Carter promised a "new American foreign policy—a policy based on constant decency in its values and on optimism in our historical vision." Détente should be expanded, the president went on to say, so that the Soviets and Americans might join together to address the problems of the developing world (**Document 8.2**).

ARMS CONTROL AND DETERRENCE

The president's pursuit of human rights in the Soviet Union made more difficult his quest for arms control. Brezhnev's expression of frustration with Carter's rhetoric was not simply for effect. Soviet officials, and probably a great many ordinary Soviet citizens as well, were sincere in believing that the dissident movement was part of a vast Western conspiracy, headed perhaps by the Central Intelligence Agency (CIA). Carter's human rights campaign, from the Soviet point of view, represented a significant ratcheting up of the decades-old psychological warfare component of the Cold War.[18] It was all part of a Western plot, as Yuri Andropov, the chief of the KGB, had explained during the Ford years in a memorandum to the Central Committee of the Communist Party. "It should be emphasized," he wrote, "that the anti-socialist activities of hostile elements [dissidents] are linked to the influence of bourgeois propaganda, with the organized subversive activities of imperialist intelligence services and anti-Soviet centers."[19] As if this view were not enough to guarantee a hostile reception for Carter's criticisms, Brezhnev as party secretary had his own contradictory agenda. He had been pursuing "ideological rectification" since 1968, with only a brief respite in 1973, coincident with his visit that year to the United States.[20] It is easy enough to imagine Brezhnev and *his* aides in 1977 assuring themselves that surely the new American president would be sophisticated enough to understand the Soviets' sensitivity to the issue of human rights.

Unfortunately for Carter, he had big ambitions for arms control as well as human rights. He wanted to do more than just finish SALT II, which he thought, like Ford before him, would be a far easier task than it proved to be. Carter wanted, rather, big cuts in nuclear arms, not simply constraints on the pace of the arms race. As president-elect, he had shocked the Joint Chiefs of Staff in his first meeting with them by asking, at the end of a lengthy briefing, "how long would it take" to reduce the American nuclear arsenal to "a few hundred" missiles?[21] The chiefs were surprised not only by the idea, but also by the fact that the commander in chief was not interested in their opinion on the substance of the policy, only on the pace of its implementation. Although the military chiefs did nothing to encourage the president in his pursuit of this agenda, Carter nonetheless continued to pursue the idea of a radical breakthrough in arms talks, from arms *control* to arms *reductions*. In his efforts he was supported by such experts as Paul Warnke, his controversial selection to head the Arms Control and Disarmament Administration. The two superpowers, Warnke famously asserted, were like "apes on a treadmill."[22] The arms race, Warnke and Carter believed, was both barbaric and archaic; it was time to put it in the past.

The president therefore attempted to build pressure for deep cuts in February 1977, his first full month in office. Ignoring a letter he received from Brezhnev criticizing his ideas as "deliberately unacceptable," Carter continued to plow straight ahead.[23] He instructed Secretary of State Vance to propose two deep cut options to the Soviet leader in Moscow at the end of March. In a news conference, Foreign Minister Andrei Gromyko explained that the discussions had failed because the United States had presented proposals that deviated widely from agreements reached at Vladivostok with President Ford. He also complained about President Carter's human rights statements and "interference." It was not until the end of April that both sides agreed to resume talks, in Geneva, using the Vladivostok deal as the basis for further negotiations.[24] This several months' delay in resuming SALT II talks did not seem terribly important at the time, but then a series of events occurred that further deferred action. Although the two sides ultimately reached agreement on a new treaty, the president was forced to pull it from consideration before the Senate could vote on it.

A Multipolar or Bipolar Response to Events in Africa?

The next delay in the SALT II talks occurred when the Soviets and Americans clashed over Soviet intentions in Africa. This conflict exposed a serious disagreement within the administration, between Secretary of State Cyrus Vance and National Security Adviser Zbigniew Brzezinski. The most intense conflict between the superpowers was over events in Ethiopia and Somalia.

Ethiopia had been an American client state since 1953; neighboring Somalia had been dependent on the Soviet Union for military aid since 1963. The Americans had built radar and communication facilities in the Ethiopian province of Eritrea; the Soviets used the Somali's main port as their own. A coup in Ethiopia in 1974, in which Emperor Haile Selassie was deposed, set off a chain of events that led to the two nations switching superpower partners. In February 1977, after a Marxist state was declared in Ethiopia, President Carter cut off aid. Having expelled U.S. advisers, the new Ethiopian government established treaty relations with the Soviets. Somalia's leaders saw this turn of events as an opportunity to seek aid from the Americans as well as Saudi Arabia, Egypt, and Iran— regional powers nervous about Soviet encroachment in the Middle East. On his own initiative, but with high hopes that the United States would ultimately support his bold move, President Siad Barre of Somalia invaded Ethiopia. To protect their new ally, the Soviets arranged for 20,000 Cuban troops to be rushed to the defense of Ethiopia, where Soviet generals directed them in a counterattack.

Jimmy Carter never really settled on a response to the events in Africa. His secretary of state and his UN ambassador, Andrew Young, argued that African nationalism would eventually overcome Soviet imperialism. In a multipolar world, the United States need not rush to respond to every Soviet provocation. Carter was sufficiently persuaded by such arguments to reject all proposals for U.S. military commitment, including the use of covert forces. At the same time, the president was loathe to see the Soviets actually expand their influence over more third-world nations. He was concerned about simultaneous Soviet activity in South Yemen, where a coup brought to power a pro-Soviet government, and Angola, where Cuban troops were battling to establish a Communist government subservient to Moscow. Carter also knew that even if Soviet gains in the present might be erased by Soviet losses in the indefinite future, the political repercussions to Soviet gains were *immediate*. Americans who had been thinking in Cold War terms for more than a generation could not be expected suddenly to think otherwise.

But should Soviet behavior in Africa be linked to other issues, in particular, arms control? Certainly Carter's national security adviser thought so. Throughout 1978 Brzezinski and his staff on the National Security Council (NSC) sought linkage, while Vance and his State Department assistants fought to prevent it. The president's own position was less obvious, which kept the conflict alive. Carter attempted several times in 1978 to clarify his stance. At a press conference on March 2, he rejected "any government policy that has a linkage between the Soviet's involvement . . . and SALT." At the same time, however, he stated, "The two are linked because of actions of the Soviets."[25] Later that month, at Wake Forest University, the president gave a speech in which he stressed the determination of the United States to defend its national interests and spoke in what seemed a newly hawkish tone about superpower relations. While Brzezinski expressed satisfaction with the speech, Vance's chief Soviet affairs deputy, Marshall Shulman, informed the Soviet embassy in Washington, D.C., to pay no attention to the president's rhetoric; Carter had given the speech, he suggested, merely to satisfy domestic political needs.[26]

In June 1978 the president further confused matters in a speech at his alma mater, the United States Naval Academy. In his Annapolis speech, Carter struggled to articulate his administration's beliefs and aims relative to the Soviet Union (**Document 8.3**). While stressing his desire for "cooperation," he acknowledged his willingness to engage in "confrontation." "The United States is adequately prepared," Carter announced, "to meet either choice." He urged the Soviets to work with the Americans to advance human development, yet he was exceptionally explicit in his criticisms of the Soviets, not only for human rights abuses, but also for attempting to "export a totalitarian and repressive form of government" and for using "proxy forces" in Korea, Angola, and Ethiopia. The *Washington Post* commented that the president had given "two speeches."[27] The president's speech writer, James Fallows, later said that the president had stapled together a memorandum from Vance and one from Brzezinski. Although Fallow's account has undeniable appeal, a careful review of the documentary evidence by a political scientist suggests that the president himself actually labored over various drafts to create what he, at least, thought of as a coherent whole.[28]

The president had much greater success in policymaking for the northern African state of Egypt. Egypt's president, Anwar al-Sadat, had expelled most Soviet troops from his country in 1972, and he had demonstrated similar initiative in seeking to forge a new relationship between his nation and its modern nemesis, Israel. In November 1977, to demonstrate Egypt's willingness to break free of old thinking in the stalled peace process, Sadat became the first Arab head of state to visit Israel and to speak before the Israeli Knesset (parliament) in Jerusalem.

Sadat's bold move actually undermined Carter's goal of reviving multilateral peace talks, the so-called Geneva Conference, which had begun after the 1973 Arab-Israeli war. The president, however, moved quickly to capitalize on the possibility for bilateral progress between Israel and Egypt by bringing both Sadat and his Israeli counterpart, Menachem

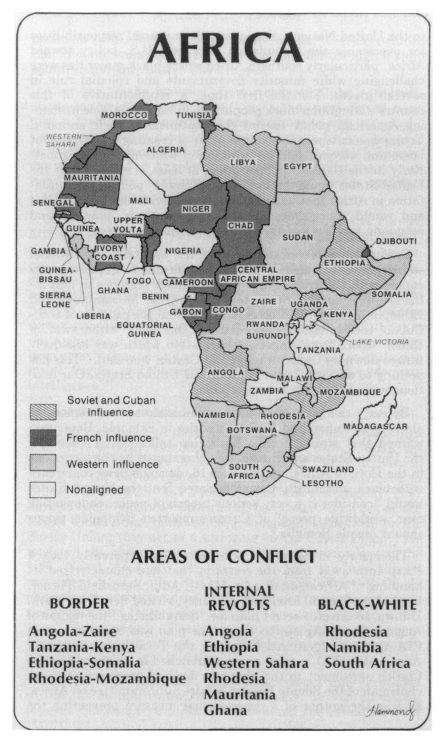

Source: R. C. Schroeder, *Editorial Research Reports 1978*, vol. 2 (Washington, D.C.: CQ Press, 1978). Available online from CQ Electronic Library, CQ Researcher Online, http://library.cqpress.com/cqresearcher/cqresrre1978071400.

Begin, to the presidential retreat in Camp David, Maryland, for intensive talks during September 5–17, 1978. The result was the Camp David Accords, under which Egypt recognized Israel's right to exist and received in exchange the return of territories Israel had captured during the Six-Day War in 1967. Other provisions were aimed, less effectively, at promoting regional peace and a resolution to the problem of Palestinian statehood.

The president might have claimed the accords as a Cold War victory. Egypt had once accepted the patronage of the Soviets, and the Soviets harshly denounced Sadat for making peace with Israel. But Jimmy Carter wanted very much not to be just another Cold War president. By the time he had accepted that the Cold War could not be forgotten or renounced, it was far too late to reinterpret what was, in any event, the diplomatic highlight of his presidency.

Full Diplomatic Relations with China

President Richard Nixon had initiated a process with his famous "opening" to China; the logical culmination would be the establishment of diplomatic relations. There were, however, complications to be worked through on both ends. Thus, although the Chinese welcomed Secretary of State Vance to China in August 1977, they were unreceptive at that time to establishing such relations. Secretary Vance, for his part, downplayed the strategic significance of his government's aims with respect to China, stating that the United States' relations with China were not based on opposition to any other country, meaning, of course, the Soviet Union. The following year, the president tried again, this time dispatching National Security Adviser Brzezinski.

Brzezinski was a proponent of global interdependence and world order, like Vance. He was, however, considerably more hawkish toward the Soviet Union. By this point in the administration, moreover, personal animosity had built up between the two men, which had been magnified in the media. The president realized that he might alarm the Soviets by sending Brzezinski to China, but he rationalized the choice in the same way that he rationalized keeping the two antagonists within his government: his subordinates had limited roles; what truly mattered was what the president thought and said.[29] Although this rationalization was fine in theory, it understated the ability of the president's deputies to influence policy on their own initiative—especially when the president's own preferences were ambiguous or contradictory, or when the president was thousands of miles away and one of his deputies claimed the spotlight. Both circumstances prevailed in this case.

President Carter wanted full diplomatic relations with China, but it was never clear whether he intended to link the pursuit of this goal to American-Soviet relations. As was often the case, he saw merit on both sides of the issue. To be on the safe side, before leaving the United States Brzezinski sought to allay the president's fears about possibly alienating the Soviets and setting back arms talks. Once in China in May 1978, however, Brzezinski accentuated what Vance had been at pains to deny, at one point even referring publicly to American and Chinese joint efforts against the "polar bear to the north."[30] Because Brzezinski's approach suited their own purposes, the Chinese leadership broke the stalemate in discussions; full normalization of relations was at last possible. The Soviets were not pleased, and they warned Carter not to allow himself to be unduly influenced by Brzezinski, whom they viewed as an infamous opponent of détente.

Despite what was, in hindsight, a clear threat of linkage on the part of the Soviets, President Carter made a surprise announcement on December 15, 1978, that all remaining obstacles had been overcome, and the United States of America and the People's Republic of China had agreed to establish full diplomatic relations, effective New Year's Day 1979 (**Document 8.4**). The Soviets were so incensed that they stalled the SALT negotiations. The two sides had been so close to agreement in the SALT talks that the Carter White House had already alerted the major television networks that the president would be needing time for an announcement.[31] Carter, in his memoirs, professes surprise at the Soviet response and shifts the blame to his national security adviser: "I was sure that the announcement, in December . . . would cool the Soviets' willingness to conclude the SALT agreement, but I received a message from Brzezinski" not to worry. Unfortunately, the president continued, "the Soviet leaders were more concerned . . . than we had supposed and than Brzezinski had first indicated."[32]

Trouble in the Senate

Finally, against a backdrop of dismal economic news and a recent shakeup of White House and Cabinet personnel, Carter signed SALT II in a ceremony with General Secretary Brezhnev, in Vienna on June 18, 1979 (**Document 8.5**). "Here today," Carter said at the signing, "we draw boundaries around our fears of one another. As we begin to control our fears, we can better insure our future."[33] The agreement limited growth in the arms race and promoted a degree of stability useful to both nations. Unlike SALT I, SALT II covered all strategic launch platforms for nuclear weapons, including bombers. It set aggregate equal ceilings, so that each side could have no more than 2,400 intercontinental ballistic missiles (ICBMs), submarine-launched ballistic missiles (SLBMs), and strategic bombers. A sublimit of 1,320 was set on MIRVed missiles (those with multiple independently targeted warheads, also known as reentry vehicles). The Soviet Backfire bomber was excluded from the aggregate limits, because the Soviets insisted that it lacked the range to pose a threat to the United States. Still, the Soviet premier promised during the SALT II process to limit production to thirty such bombers per year and not to upgrade their refueling capacity.[34]

But by the time it was signed, SALT II had become even more important in American politics for its symbolic value than for its substantive results. Once debate shifted to the U.S. Senate, where the treaty faced a two-thirds vote hurdle for ratification, the fight over the direction of U.S. foreign policy only became more focused. Those legislators who faulted the president for the mishaps that had occurred on the way to signing SALT II now became determined to send a strong, decisive signal to the Soviets, and to Jimmy Carter, by defeating the treaty.

By the midway point in his presidency, the president was an easy target for such critics. Although the public approved of most of Carter's specific foreign policies, the weakness of his leadership—the way he pursued his policies—had led an overwhelming majority of Americans (62 percent by summer 1979) to believe that America was "becoming weaker" in the world under his presidency.[35] In this environment of anxious public opinion and sharp criticism, some of the president's earlier foreign policy decisions came back to trouble him.

In his campaign for the presidency, Carter had promised to complete the negotiated return of the Panama Canal to Panama, which he did in 1977. Although the senate ratified the Panama Canal Treaties in April 1978, the struggle over U.S. withdrawal, amplified in the press, helped establish a negative image of the president as potentially naïve about the United States' enemies and the need for continued American strength. The president's decision to emphasize "good will and fairness"[36] as reasons for the treaties played into his opponents' hands, leading the *New York Times* to protest that "recent newspaper and television coverage notwithstanding," the Panama Canal Treaties debate "is not about Jimmy Carter's manhood."[37] Moreover, many senators felt the president had taken their votes for granted on the treaties. The Carter White House did not seem to understand, or care, how difficult it had been for many of them to back the president. Every senator had to worry about how his or her next opponent might portray the vote. Elite opinion in the nation was widely supportive of the treaty, but a great many regular Americans were skeptical about giving back something that a previous generation of Americans had won, fair and square. Through his apparent indifference to the practical political problems faced by members of the Senate, the president had alienated the very institution that he would now rely on to ratify SALT II.

The president had similarly alienated each of the major branches of the U.S. armed forces. In 1977 he carried out a campaign promise by ordering the withdrawal of U.S. Army combat forces from South Korea, despite heavy protest by both military and civilian defense leaders. After the third-ranking officer in South Korea, Maj. Gen. John Singlaub, spoke out against the president's intentions, he was recalled to Washington, D.C., and relieved of duty. The Joint Chiefs of Staff (JCS) protested privately when they were asked to advise the president on the *pace* of the withdrawal but not on the policy itself. Although they declined to give their advice under such constraints at first, they were essentially ordered to do so by Secretary of Defense Harold Brown. After all this controversy, the president suspended his own order, ostensibly in response to new intelligence of a North Korean military buildup.

Carter had further angered the defense establishment in his first year by canceling development of the B-1 bomber. The B-1 was intended as an eventual replacement for the U.S. Air Force's aging fleet of B-52s. In his campaign for the presidency, though he refused explicitly to say he would cancel the new bomber, he suggested that it was "pork," a "gross waste of money."[38] Once in office, he initiated a review of the bomber, before announcing on June 30, 1977, that he would zero out funds for its development. The chairman of the JCS, Gen. David Jones, backed the commander in chief on this decision, and Congress went along with it, but the air force took the loss of the B-1 as a bitter defeat.

As for the U.S. Navy, it wanted a phased expansion of its fleet. The centerpiece of the effort in 1977 was to be funding for a new nuclear-powered aircraft carrier. Adm. James L. Holloway III, the chief naval officer (CNO, the representative of the navy in the JCS) helped persuade Congress to appropriate more than $2 billion for the carrier in that year's defense budget. The president thereupon vetoed the defense bill. When Admiral Holloway retired from the service in the summer of 1978, the president snubbed him by declining to meet with him personally, a sign of respect traditionally paid to all outgoing JCS members. The navy, which had great respect for Holloway as a highly decorated naval aviator as well as CNO, was incensed.

The president also faced a Senate in ideological transition. In Carter's election year, only two members of the Watergate Class of 1974 lost their seats in the House. While the Senate barely changed in its partisan composition (from sixty-one Democrats, thirty-seven Republicans, and two independents, to sixty-one, thirty-eight, and one, respectively), fourteen seats changed hands. Among those departing were a number of powerful liberal Democrats, including Stuart Symington of Missouri and John Tunney of California. These two were replaced by Republicans John Danforth and S. I. Hayakawa, respectively. Also among the newcomers were three Republican hardliners, Malcolm Wallop of Wyoming, Orrin Hatch of Utah, and Harrison Schmitt of New Mexico. Then, in the 1978 elections, Republicans picked up three seats in the Senate (and fifteen in the House). Afterward, liberal senators conceded that the sentiment in the Senate had changed. The debate on the defense budget was no longer over how much to cut, but rather over how much to add, and how to spend the new money.[39]

Liberals began to run scared. Missouri senator Thomas Eagleton, best known as the man who was briefly presidential candidate George McGovern's running mate in 1972 before being ousted after he disclosed past mental health problems, was a dedicated liberal in foreign affairs. But when Sen. Paul Tsongas of Massachusetts circulated a letter deploring the use of the SALT II treaty as a vehicle for increased defense spending, Eagleton uncharacteristically declined to sign. He wanted to keep a "low profile" on the treaty, he explained, looking toward his reelection campaign in 1980. (In that campaign, he would boast of having voted for *more than a trillion dollars* in defense spending.)[40]

Likewise, when the Hughes-Ryan Act came up for revision, only fifty members of Congress voted to preserve it in its original form. This "vital reform of the new internationalists" in Congress required that eight separate congressional committees receive reports on covert operations.[41] Congress altered the act to require the president to report only to intelligence committees in both chambers. The most remarkable, and unintentionally comic, example of the new mood in Congress was the fright over a (missing) Soviet brigade in Cuba. In this August 1979 incident, the Senate's progress on SALT II was temporarily halted by the desperate effort of a couple of Senate doves to save their jobs.

During the October 1962 Cuban Missile Crisis, the CIA had discovered the presence of Soviet ground troops in Cuba. As the crisis had been resolved without addressing the issue of the troops, there was no reason to believe that they had ever left. Years later, the CIA was tasked with collecting and reviewing available evidence on Cuban activities, at home and abroad. Following up on an eavesdropping intercept from the National Security Agency (NSA), the CIA quickly "discovered" the presence of perhaps 2,000–3,000 Soviet troops on the island. Unfortunately, the CIA had forgotten that it already knew about these troops, and speculated that they had been introduced in only the past couple of years.

When administration leaders briefed congressional leaders, they asked that the members of the legislative branch keep the information in confidence while the White House sought more information and took the matter up with the Soviets. Sen. Frank Church, a Democrat from Idaho who was facing a tough fight for reelection against an opponent who charged him with habitual softness in the fight against Communists, went public with the "news," and he announced that his vote on SALT II was now uncertain. Church had inherited the chairmanship of the Senate Foreign Relations Committee after the 1978 midterm elections, but he had been unable to gain much leverage over foreign affairs. The Republicans, most of whom now espoused hawkish views on foreign policy, banded together. Although they were still in the minority on the committee, they demanded the right to hire their own staff. Moreover, the Senate Armed Services Committee, which contained a greater proportion of leading members than did Foreign Relations, began to usurp the jurisdiction of the latter committee, even claiming for itself a leading role in the consideration of SALT II. In revealing the new intelligence on Soviet troops, Church had found a way to put himself back in the fight, both for his Senate seat and for the nation's attention.

At first, the Carter administration also seemed to take a hard line against this "new" Soviet threat. The secretary of state declared on September 5, 1979, that he "would not be satisfied with the status quo."[42] Two days later, the president repeated the remark in a brief address to the nation. The Soviets, for their part, rejected out of hand the administration's demand for a change in the status quo. Ironically, their stubbornness was based at least in part on their inflated sense of the competence of the American presidency. "[T]hey could not believe that the United States, with its sophisticated intelligence, had forgotten about the brigade."[43] After several weeks of intense behind-the-scenes conflict within the administration over how to proceed, during which time the CIA realized its mistake, on the first of October the president gave a televised address to the nation on the situation.

In that speech, President Carter tried hard to strike a balance between alarm, no longer justified given that the offending troops had been tolerated by the United States for a long time already, and complacency, which would undermine his effort to win support from Cold War hawks for SALT II ratification. Carter explained that the Soviet troops in Cuba had in fact been on the island since the Cuban Missile Crisis, but he asserted that "[j]ust recently, American intelligence obtained persuasive evidence that some of these Soviet forces had been organized into a combat unit." Because senior administration officials still could not agree on what, if anything, they had (re)discovered in Cuba, the president went on to say that the unit "appears to be" a brigade of "two or three thousand men." Although it was not a "large" force, the president insisted that its presence in Cuba was "a serious matter." Carter then went on to announce several unilateral moves to signal American resolve, including increased surveillance of Cuba, increased military training maneuvers in the region, and the establishment of a new Caribbean joint task force with headquarters at Key West, Florida, to "improve our capability to monitor and to respond rapidly to any attempted military encroachment in this region."[44] The hard-liners within Carter's administration, not to mention his many external critics, viewed these steps as characteristically weak and the speech as "whiny."[45] It was another weak performance by the Carter White House, this time helped along by the dynamics of ideological transformation in Congress.

Partial Victories: SALT II Is Sent to the Floor, and NATO Adopts the "Dual Track"

Clearly, if Carter were to have his treaty, the price would include taking a harder line against the Soviets in some other respect. Thus, on September 7, 1978, the president approved a basing plan for the controversial MX missile. The MX was a new, heavy ICBM with multiple warheads. It was designed as a "counterforce" weapon, one intended to counter, or destroy, the most dangerous of enemy forces, namely Soviet missiles in hardened silos. Unfortunately, the MX was itself an important target for the Soviets' counterforce weapons. Could it survive a first strike? Soviet missiles were not renowned for their accuracy, but the Soviets' newest missile, the SS-20 (which they deployed in March 1976), compensated for inaccuracy with sheer size and weight. Even an indirect hit on American missile silos would destroy the land-based American nuclear deterrent force.

The basing project was therefore held up for several years, while the Pentagon and congressional committees examined multiple options. At last, on June 12, 1979, the president made a decision, in which Congress—for the time being—concurred. The MX missiles would be based along a system of rails, on a "racetrack." By moving the missiles randomly among a large number of possible launch points along the rail system, they could not be targeted successfully. With the president's decision, development of the weapon could proceed. At the same time, the president took the unusual step of previewing his five-year military budget plan months ahead of schedule, to underline his commitment to annual increases above inflation.

Having thus burnished his hard-line credentials, the president was rewarded on November 9, 1979, when the Senate Foreign Relations Committee voted 9 to 6 to recommend approval of SALT II to the full Senate.[46]

Were events finally moving in Carter's favor? The president might be forgiven if he had believed they were. Shortly after the positive vote for SALT II in committee, the president enjoyed a considerable diplomatic victory in U.S. relations with its North Atlantic Treaty Organization (NATO) partners. President Carter had come into office dedicated to strengthening the alliance. He sought a gradual, sustainable increase in NATO defense spending, and he launched a "dual-track" approach to the strengthening of its deterrent force. Under this approach, the United States would *ready for deployment* to Europe ground-launched cruise missiles and Pershing II intermediate-range ballistic missiles. At the same time, the United States would pursue a reduction in Soviet nuclear missiles deployed against Europe, to obviate the need for the *actual deployment* of new American weapons. On December 12, 1979, NATO agreed to the plan (**Document 8.6**).

President Carter achieved this success despite having earlier antagonized the European allies over the matter of the "neutron bomb." The bomb—actually a type of warhead intended to be launched by missile—was a controversial device that was engineered to emit a greater portion of its energy in the form of radiation, relative to blast and heat.

There was a great deal of debate over the deterrent capabilities of such a device. Some theorists argued that the neutron bomb made the West's deterrence more credible, by increasing the lethality of a limited nuclear counterattack against invading Warsaw Pact infantry and artillery. These supporters of the weapon saw it as a highly specialized anti-tank device. But it was a public relations nightmare.

The "ultimate capitalist weapon" would kill people, while sparing buildings.[47] Carter undercut Secretary of State Vance's efforts to achieve consensus within Europe to support the potential deployment of such a weapon, by deciding at the last moment that the Europeans had not met the unofficial condition that he had set for the device's transfer to the continent. The president believed that NATO's European leaders should share in the political liability of the deployment; he now demanded that they specifically request that he make the transfer. The Europeans, believing that the secretary of state surely spoke for the president, had worked out an arrangement that did not call for such an explicit maneuver. They refused to reconsider what they thought was a settled agreement, and the weapon was never deployed. Nor was SALT II ever ratified as action on the floor of the Senate was delayed yet again by ominous developments.

A "Killer Rabbit" and a "Peacock Throne"

President Carter might have known his luck was not going to change when a trivial news item became a front-page joke told at the president's expense. "Bunny Goes Bugs, Rabbit Attacks President" trumpeted the front page of the *Washington Post* on August 30, 1979.[48] The *New York Times* more decorously placed the story on page 16, but the paper gave the president's adversary its lasting moniker: the "killer rabbit."[49] All three television networks led with the tale of a rabbit that attempted to board the commander in chief's small fishing boat on a lake, illustrated by photographs of the president's successful effort to fight it off with a paddle. Some commentators believed that the killer rabbit story emboldened enemies of the United States in Iran.

The Iranian shah (king), Mohammed Reza Pahlavi, was the sort of anti-Communist despot that President Carter's human rights policy was intended to challenge and engage. Carter took a comparatively easy line toward the shah, however, because the Iranian regime was under intense pressure at home, and the alternatives to his continuation in office were unclear. National Security Adviser Brzezinski, predictably, saw the situation in Cold War terms. If the shah fell, the United States would lose listening posts along an important stretch of the Soviet border, and the Soviets might well attempt to influence the new Iranian government.

Street demonstrations against the shah's rule attracted millions of Iranians in November and December 1978, eventually leading to the ruler's abdication of the "Peacock Throne" and departure from the country on January 16, 1979. After warning the Soviet Union not to take advantage of the chaotic situation in Iran, the president returned his attention to other pressing matters.

Carter's first significant decision on Iran was forced by the exiled king's illness. Since fleeing, the shah had been treated, unsuccessfully, for cancer. In October 1979 the shah's condition appeared to worsen. After being informed that the shah required an emergency operation in the United States, the administration was, according to Secretary of State Vance, "faced squarely with a decision in which common decency and humanity had to be weighed against possible harm to our embassy personnel in Tehran."[50] The president made the decision to allow the shah to enter the country for medical treatment. Iranian radicals, vying for power within the not-yet-stable environment of post-revolution Iran, seized the opportunity that the president had provided. On November 4, a group of protestors seized sixty-three Americans at the U.S. embassy in Tehran.

The president at first thought that the embassy takeover had given *him* an opportunity. He canceled plans to debate Sen. Ted Kennedy of Massachusetts for the Democratic Party nomination for president and adopted a stay-at-home strategy in the campaign, focusing his, and therefore the electorate's, attention on his handling of the crisis. In this way, the president made the hostage crisis the "one big test of his leadership."[51] In early 1980, Carter was attempting to "sweep away three years of frustration" by declaring that the hostage crisis was one of only "two major questions that our Nation must resolve."[52] The spokesperson for the State Department, Hodding Carter, actually called ABC News to *thank* them for their innovative late night news program, *America Held Hostage* (the progenitor of Ted Koppel's *Nightline* program), which famously counted off the number of days of the hostage crisis.[53] (The hostages were released after 444 days in captivity, following President Ronald Reagan's inaugural address on January 20, 1981.)

It is difficult to determine the source of Carter's optimism about the hostage crisis. Perhaps he was impressed with the rally-around-the-flag phenomenon. Carter's rally was, after all, even more impressive than that experienced by John F. Kennedy in the Cuban Missile Crisis. The hostage crisis touched off an increase of more than 15 points in Carter's job approval rating. Perhaps he was captivated by the store of presidential resources that had been built up over the course of the postwar years and were available, as he well knew, to a president in a crisis.

Whatever the source of his confidence, Carter proved he was prepared to act. On his own authority, after being blocked by the Soviet Union in the UN Security Council, the president imposed unilateral U.S. sanctions. Before the end of 1979, President Carter banned the import of Iranian oil to the United States and froze all assets of the Iranian government and Iranian Central Bank held in United States financial institutions. (The United States' European and Asian allies did not impose sanctions until April 1980.) The president further ordered immigration restrictions and an embargo on U.S. exports to Iran. Congressional leaders were "invited up [to the White House] to pledge their support and bear witness to Carter's toughness."[54] For a while it seemed that Carter had found his voice and his strength.

The president's actions resonated well with the public, but they did not seem similarly to impress the Iranians. Therefore, the president began planning for a military rescue operation. It launched, and failed, on April 25, 1980.

The mission, Operation Eagle Claw, failed before it even truly began. When not enough troop helicopters made it to Desert One, a refueling position in Iran, the operation was aborted. After the decision was made, a helicopter crashed, killing eight American military personnel. The president studied a copy of Kennedy's famous remarks following the Bay of Pigs disaster, then delivered his own mea culpa, taking responsibility for the mission's failure. Shortly thereafter, the president accepted the resignation of his secretary of state, who had strongly opposed the president's choice to use force.

Carter, especially following the events at Desert One, became a hostage to his own empathy. "The holding of the American hostages," he wrote in his memoirs, "had cast a pall over my own life. . . . Although I was acting in an official capacity as President, I also had deep private feelings that were almost overwhelming. The hostages sometimes seemed like part of my own family." [55] Because the president had invited the public to evaluate his performance as president on the basis of how he handled this crisis, his emotional state could not escape the public's attention. As the bad news from Iran accumulated, the president became visibly distraught, increasing the electorate's anxiety about their president's, and their nation's, plummeting power in the world.

The only foreign policy issue that seriously competed with the hostage crisis for the president's attention in his last year in office was the Soviet invasion of Afghanistan. The Soviet takeover of a neighboring country had a profound effect on Jimmy Carter. It forced the president to abandon SALT II ratification and challenged him to rethink his entire approach to foreign policy.

AFGHANISTAN

At the time Jimmy Carter became president, the State Department had classified Afghanistan as "neutral" but "dependent on the Soviet Union." [56] On April 27, 1978, a military coup brought to power in Afghanistan Nur Mohammed Taraki, the leader of the Soviet-inspired Khalq, or "Masses" faction of the People's Democratic Party of Afghanistan (PDPA), which traced its roots back to the late 1960s. Taraki, with the assistance of his deputy, Hafizullah Amin, soon marginalized and then exiled Babrak Karmal, the leader of a rival party faction, and began a brutal campaign against the "enemies of the revolution." [57] Taraki and Amin's attempt to impose Marxist-Leninist policies upon the population was supported by the Soviet Union, which initially sent a small number of military and political advisers to Afghanistan.

In Herat, in northwestern Afghanistan, in April 1979, the "Saur (April) Revolution" was threatened when Afghan Army soldiers and officers abandoned their positions and joined a rebellion against the new government's efforts to impose secular laws, which threatened to undermine centuries of tradition in one of the most religious, remote, and premodern societies in the world. These rebels imposed a terror of their own, leading to the violent death in Herat of numerous Afghan Communist Party officials and their Soviet military and political advisers. Taraki, from the capital, Kabul, pleaded with the Kremlin for more help. Soviet troops, he suggested, could come in disguise to Afghanistan; no one would be the wiser. The Soviets recommended mobilizing "the workers," forcing Taraki to attempt to explain just how underdeveloped and rural Afghanistan was (**Document 8.7**). The Soviet Politburo decided against open intervention at the time but created an Afghanistan Commission, headed by KGB chief Yuri Andropov. The commission would direct the Soviet Union's policy on Afghanistan through the remainder of the year.

A struggle for power between Taraki and Amin forced the Soviets into direct action. Amin was considered suspect in the Kremlin; he spoke English but not Russian, and he was even rumored to be in league with the CIA. General Secretary Brezhnev suggested to Taraki that he remove his rival from the government. Before Taraki could do so, however, he was killed by order of Amin. This assassination, Soviet foreign minister Andrei Gromyko recalled, was "a slap in the face to which he [Brezhnev] had to respond."[58] Fearing that Amin, possibly with secret U.S. backing, might turn to the West—as had Egypt's Anwar al-Sadat just two years previously, in signing the Camp David Accords—Andropov's committee recommended the use of force. It would, Andropov said, be a relatively easy military operation to bring Afghanistan under Soviet control. On December 25, 1979, the Soviet Union invaded Afghanistan. Within two days, Amin had been killed, and Karmal had been brought back by the Soviets in apparent triumph. The Afghanistan Commission reported on New Year's Eve that "it is possible to be sure" that Karmal will "stabilize completely the situation in the country."[59]

President Carter was shocked by the Soviets' behavior in Afghanistan. He withdrew SALT II from consideration by the Senate and spoke openly of his disappointment and surprise. This was much more serious than even the hostage situation, he lectured his chief of staff, Hamilton Jordan: "Capturing those Americans was an inhumane act committed by a bunch of radicals and condoned by a crazy old man. But this is deliberate aggression that calls into question détente and the way we have been doing business with the Soviets for the past decade."[60] In a television interview, the president said that the invasion had shaken his previous opinion of the Soviets (**Document 8.8**). This was music to the ears of the many critics of the president's foreign policy.

In a speech to the nation on January 4, 1980, one day after withdrawing SALT II from Senate consideration, Carter announced how else he intended to respond to this grave action by the Soviets. He would, he said, take under consideration a boycott of the upcoming Olympic Games, which were to be held in Moscow. More substantively and decisively, he announced an embargo of U.S. grain sales to the Soviet Union. In his final State of the Union address on January 23, 1980, Carter repeated his statement regarding the Olympics and announced a series of additional actions. These included ordering that American men ages eighteen to twenty-six register for a possible resumption of Selective Service; increasing the pace of his previously announced defense buildup—moving to a 5 percent per year target; and providing substantial military and economic aid for Afghanistan's neighbor, Pakistan. The president also hinted at a deepening of the ties between the United States and China. Finally, the president articulated what became known as the Carter Doctrine: "An attempt by any outside force to gain control of the Persian Gulf region will be regarded as an assault on the vital interests of the United States of America, and such an assault will be repelled by any means necessary, including military force" (**Document 8.9**). The administration had come full circle. Jimmy Carter had entered office dedicated to the proposition that the world was far too complex for Cold War doctrines. Now Carter had a doctrine of his own.

The Soviets thought they saw through the president's maneuver. The members of the Afghanistan Commission advised the Central Committee:

> The USA, its allies, and the PRC have set themselves the goal of using to the maximum extent the events in Afghanistan to intensify the atmosphere of anti-Sovietism and to justify long-term foreign policy acts . . . directed at changing the balance of power in their favor. . . .
>
> Henceforth, in relations with the USA, [it should be Soviet policy] to maintain a firm line in opposition to the Carter Administration's provocative steps. (**Document 8.10**)

When the dissident Andrei Sakharov denounced the Soviet invasion, officials did not hesitate to arrest and relocate him, although they could surely have predicted the reaction of the U.S. president (**Document 8.11**). Remarkably, the KGB told the Politburo that most Western media outlets *supported* the Soviet government's decision to deal forcefully with the troublemaking Sakharov (**Document 8.12**).

The president was determined to make the Soviet intervention as costly to them as possible.[61] Unfortunately for Carter, the public was not impressed. By midsummer, with the duration of the hostage crisis well into triple digits—"America Held Hostage, Day 201, Day 202, Day 203 . . ."—and no apparent change in the situation in Afghanistan, President Carter's approval ratings reached a remarkable low of 28 percent.

In his campaign for reelection in 1980, the president emphasized his determination to face squarely the threat of Soviet strategic advance. It was not enough. Dedicated doves despaired at the "new" Carter, while more hawkish commentators, opponents, and rivals suggested that Carter's early weakness in the presidency had created the situation that the president was now, belatedly, trying to address. The reaction to some of Carter's specific policies demonstrated this dynamic. Students questioned the need for Selective Service registration in a meeting with the president at the White House (**Document 8.13**), while the military establishment challenged the president's conversion to preparedness.

The president wanted real defense increases—a 5.4 percent increase, above inflation, for the coming year—but the service chiefs and many members of Congress were not satisfied. The chairman of the JCS, Gen. David C. Jones, testified before the House Budget Committee that the nation needed "substantial" increases above and beyond what the president's budget proposed.[62] The president lobbied the chairman of the Senate Armed Services Committee, Mississippi Democrat John Stennis, to help him hold the line. Carter urged Stennis to say no to stepped-up production schedules for the F-18, the refurbishing of retired battleships, the construction of additional submarines, and the resurrection of the B-1 bomber and the navy's previously cancelled new aircraft carrier. After members of the House and Senate worked out a compromise bill, which included billions more in defense spending than the president desired, he came out in opposition. Sen. Ernest "Fritz" Hollings, South Carolina Democrat and chairman of the Senate Budget Committee, attacked the president's veto, calling it "outrageous" and "deplorable."[63]

Rather than surrender to the president, the military fought back in House hearings before the Armed Services Committee. All the chiefs testified in favor of greater defense spending. The highlight of those hearings was the testimony of Army Chief of Staff Gen. Edward "Shy" Meyer, who testified on May 29, 1980, that America's national security was "protected" by a "hollow Army" (**Document 8.14**). Carter thereupon reversed himself and endorsed substantial increases, including funding for particular items that he had singled out for rejection earlier, such as the navy's new nuclear aircraft carrier.

CONCLUSION: PRESIDENTIAL INEPTITUDE AND COLD WAR MENACE

By the time Carter left office, the Americans and Soviets regularly exchanged threats and complaints. The president insisted to a Yugoslav reporter on June 12, 1980, that détente was still relevant and the policy of the United States, but the record belied that statement. President Carter signed an agreement on August 22, 1980, for military basing rights in Somalia, and he pledged at a press conference in September that the United States would use nuclear weapons against the Soviet Union to defend the itself and its allies. He also continued to speak out against human rights violations behind the iron curtain. The Soviets condemned the president for carrying out warfare against the people of Afghanistan (that is, opposing the Soviet war to take control of the country), for forging an anti-Soviet triangle with the People's Republic of China and Japan, and for a host of other alleged bellicose actions.

When Presidential Directive 59, regarding the selection of targets in the Soviet Union in the event of a nuclear war, was leaked to the press on August 6, the Soviets claimed it was evidence of a misguided American desire to abandon détente and to embrace a potentially destabilizing new doctrine of winnable nuclear war. The new directive actually *was* an effort to break away from the doctrine of mutual assured destruction (MAD), but it was designed largely by Brzezinski and Secretary of Defense Harold Brown in response to the emerging consensus among arms control strategists and Kremlin watchers that the Soviets had themselves moved beyond that doctrine and now possessed the will as well as the weaponry and targeting to engage in limited nuclear wars. The United States, Brzezinski and Brown reasoned, could continue credibly to deter the Soviets only if it could respond in kind to a Soviet attack. The directive, by permitting the president greater flexibility in targeting—for instance, by giving the president the flexibility to target military installations rather than urban populations—was designed to achieve this result.[64] After one last crisis—a postelection war scare over Poland, where the Soviets were attempting to quell protests against government policies—and one last laugh at the president's expense—when Carter suggested in a debate with his Republican challenger, Ronald Reagan, that he sought advice on the nuclear arms race from his teenage daughter—Jimmy Carter's eventful presidency came to a close (**Document 8.15**).

Carter's presidency was one in which movement in foreign policy was characterized by sudden twists and turns. It is possible after the fact to identify consistent themes, such as the promotion of human rights and the desire to reverse a decline in U.S. military power associated with the debacle in Vietnam. Some commentators have gone so far as to praise Jimmy Carter as the president who first dared attempt "to wean Russians away from Communism." [65] There is certainly a measure of truth to this assessment, but it misleads by its suggestion that the Carter presidency was anything but chaotic and confused in its conduct of a Cold War foreign policy. The Carter administration illustrates, perhaps more than any other, the intersection of presidential ineptitude and Cold War menace.

NOTES

1. Steven M. Gillon, "Jimmy Carter," in *The American Presidency,* ed. Alan Brinkley and Davis Dyer (Boston: Houghton Mifflin, 2004), 456.
2. The "Jimmy Who?" label was so widely used during the campaign that the Jimmy Carter Library and Museum entitled a 25th campaign anniversary exhibition, "From 'Jimmy Who?' to 'Mr. President.'" Jimmy Carter Library and Museum, press release, August 27, 2001, www.jimmycarterlibrary.org/pastexhibits/jim_who.phtml.
3. Quoted in Fred Greenstein, *The Presidential Difference: Leadership Style from FDR to Clinton* (New York: Free Press, 2000), 142.
4. William Quandt, "Discussant's Remarks," in *Jimmy Carter: Foreign Policy and Post-Presidential Years,* ed. Herbert D. Rosenbaum and Alexej Ugrinsky (Westport, Conn: Greenwood Press, 1994), 62. Quandt was a foreign policy adviser to the president.
5. Leslie Gelb, director of the State Department's Bureau of Politico-Military Affairs from 1977 to 1979, quoted in Richard A. Melanson, *American Foreign Policy after Vietnam: The Search for Consensus from Nixon to Clinton,* 3d ed. (Armonk, N.Y.: M. E. Sharpe, 2000), 99.
6. Jerel A. Rosati, "The Rise and Fall of America's First Post-Cold War Foreign Policy," in Rosenbaum and Ugrinsky, *Jimmy Carter,* 36, 39.
7. A presidential aide had changed the wording in this speech, from a prior draft's "seventeen years ago." The president kept the rewrite. Robert A. Strong, *Working in the World: Jimmy Carter and the Making of American Foreign Policy* (Baton Rouge: Louisiana State University Press, 2000), 225.
8. Jimmy Carter, "Address at Commencement Exercises at the University of Notre Dame," May 22, 1977, in *Public Papers of the Presidents of the United States: Jimmy Carter, 1977–1981,* from the American Presidency Project, University of California, Santa Barbara, www.presidency.ucsb.edu.
9. Ibid.
10. Oswald Johnston, "Sakharov Pleads for Carter to Aid Soviet Dissidents," *Los Angeles Times,* January 29, 1977.
11. "Tass Assails 'Slander' in U.S.," *Washington Post,* January 30, 1977.
12. Raymond L. Garthoff, *Détente and Confrontation: American-Soviet Relations from Nixon to Reagan,* rev. ed. (Washington, D.C.: Brookings Institution Press, 1994), 633.
13. Burton I. Kaufman, *The Presidency of James Earl Carter, Jr.* (Lawrence: University Press of Kansas, 1993), 39.
14. Jimmy Carter, *Keeping Faith: Memoirs of a President* (New York: Bantam, 1982), 149.
15. Ibid., 65.
16. Ibid., 145.
17. Young made the remarks in an interview with a French journalist. He referred to his own experience and that of other civil rights activists who had been jailed for organizing or participating in protests. Cyrus Vance was said to have had an "unprintable" response. The president called Young to rebuke him. See Richard L. Homan, "Administration Criticizes Remark by Young," *Washington Post,* July 13, 1978. For a recent, positive, reference to Young's remarks, see Joe Allen and Paul D'Amato, "The Persecution of Leonard Peltier," *Socialist Worker Online,* February 10, 2006, www.socialistworker.org/2006-1/575/575_08_Peltier.shtml.
18. Walter Parchomenko, *Soviet Images of Dissidents and Nonconformists* (New York: Praeger, 1986), 133.
19. Yuri Andropov to the Central Committee of the Communist Party, December 29, 1975, Document 108 in *The KGB File of Andrei Sakharov,* ed. Joshua Rubenstein and Alexander Gribanov (New Haven, Conn.: Yale University Press, 2005), 211.
20. Parchomenko, *Soviet Images of Dissidents,* 208–209.

21. Dale Herspring, *The Pentagon and the Presidency: Civil-Military Relations from FDR to George W. Bush* (Lawrence: University Press of Kansas, 2005), 243.

22. Paul C. Warnke, "Apes on a Treadmill," *Foreign Policy,* no. 18 (Spring 1975): 12–29.

23. Betty Glad, "Discussant's Remarks," in Rosenbaum and Ugrinsky, *Jimmy Carter,* 387.

24. The president still hoped for something more, and he spoke of a 50 percent reduction in nuclear forces in a speech before the United Nations. See Jimmy Carter, "United Nations Address before the General Assembly," October 4, 1977, in *Public Papers of the Presidents of the United States: Jimmy Carter, 1977–1981,* from the American Presidency Project, University of California, Santa Barbara, www.presidency.ucsb.edu.

25. Garthoff, *Détente and Confrontation,* 654.

26. Zbigniew Brzezinski, *Power and Principle: Memoirs of the National Security Advisor, 1977–1981* (New York: Farrar, Strauss, Giroux, 1983), 188–189.

27. Garthoff, *Détente and Confrontation,* 666.

28. See Strong, *Working in the World,* chapter 4.

29. Erwin C. Hargrove, *Jimmy Carter as President: Leadership and the Politics of the Public Good* (Baton Rouge: Louisiana State University Press, 1988), 117–118.

30. Garthoff, *Détente and Confrontation,* 662.

31. Kaufman, *Presidency of James Earl Carter,* 130.

32. Carter, *Keeping Faith,* 234.

33. "Text of Carter's and Brezhnev's Remarks at Signing of the Treaty," *New York Times,* June 19, 1979.

34. The Soviets failed to keep these promises. See Federation of American Scientists, "TU-22M Backfire (Tupolev)," in *Russia/ Soviet Nuclear Forces Guide,* www.fas.org/nuke/guide/russia/bomber/tu-22m.htm.

35. Kaufman, *Presidency of James Earl Carter,* 151.

36. Jimmy Carter, "Panama Canal Treaties Address to the Nation," February 1, 1978, in *Public Papers of the Presidents of the United States: Jimmy Carter, 1977–1981,* from the American Presidency Project, University of California, Santa Barbara, www.presidency.edu.

37. Kenneth Morris, *Jimmy Carter, American Moralist* (Athens: University of Georgia Press, 1996), 267.

38. The president spoke of the B-1 in the context of a "gross waste of money in the Pentagon." See Herspring, *Pentagon and the Presidency,* 244.

39. Gary Jacobsen, *Congress and the Cold War* (New York: Cambridge University Press, 2006), 230–232.

40. Ibid., 245.

41. Ibid., 250.

42. Strong, *Working in the World,* 217.

43. Stephen G. Rabe, review of *The Soviet Brigade in Cuba: A Study in Political Diplomacy,* by David D. Newsom, *Slavic Review* 47, no. 3 (1988): 548–549.

44. Jimmy Carter, "Peace and National Security Address to the Nation on Soviet Combat Troops in Cuba and the Strategic Arms Limitation Treaty," October 1, 1979, in *Public Papers of the Presidents of the United States: Jimmy Carter, 1977–1981,* from the American Presidency Project, University of California, Santa Barbara, www.presidency.ucsb.edu.

45. Strong, *Working in the World,* 225.

46. The Senate Armed Services Committee had no formal jurisdiction over the treaty, but voted on it anyway. Their vote was 10-0 against, with 7 abstentions, on December 20, 1979. Jacobsen, *Congress and the Cold War,* 246.

47. Sherri L. Wasserman, *The Neutron Bomb Controversy: A Study in Alliance Politics* (New York: Praeger, 1983), 40.

48. Brooks Jackson, "Bunny Goes Bugs, Rabbit Attacks President," *Washington Post,* August 30, 1979.

49. "A Tale of Carter and the Killer Rabbit," *New York Times,* August 30, 1979.

50. Cyrus Vance, *Hard Choices: Critical Years in American Foreign Policy* (New York: Simon and Schuster, 1983), 371.

51. Stephen Skowronek, *The Politics Presidents Make: Leadership from John Adams to George Bush* (Cambridge, Mass.: Harvard University Press, Belknap Press, 1993), 401.

52. Ibid.

53. Ted Koppel and Kyle Gibson, *Nightline: History in the Making and the Making of Television* (New York: Random House, 1996), 10–11.

54. Skowronek, *Politics Presidents Make,* 402.

55. Carter, *Keeping Faith,* 4.

56. Steve Galster, "Afghanistan: The Making of U.S. Policy, 1973–1990," in *The September 11 Sourcebooks,* vol. 2, *Afghanistan: Lessons from the Last War,* ed. John Prados and Svetlana Savranskaya (electronic briefing book 57, National Security Archive, George Washington University, Washington, D.C., October 9, 2001), www.gwu.edu/~nsarchiv/NSAEBB/NSAEBB57/essay.html.

57. Taraki's own words, as quoted in Christopher M. Andrew and Vasili Mitrokhin, *The World Was Going Our Way: The KGB and the Battle for the Third World* (New York: Basic Books, 2005), 389.

58. Ibid., 397.

59. Ibid., 404.

60. Hamilton Jordan, *Crisis: The Last Year of the Carter Presidency* (New York: Putnam, 1982), 99.

61. Carter, *Keeping Faith,* 476.

62. Herspring, *Pentagon and the Presidency,* 251. This was on March 1, 1980.

63. Ibid., 252.

64. Kaufman, *Presidency of James Earl Carter,* 192.

65. Douglas Brinkley, *The Unfinished Presidency: Jimmy Carter's Journey Beyond the White House* (New York: Viking, 1998), 21.

Document 8.1
President Jimmy Carter Offers His Support to Andrei Sakharov, Telegram, February 5, 1977

During the 1976 presidential campaign, the well-known Soviet dissident Andrei Sakharov wrote to both Jimmy Carter and Gerald Ford, urging them to speak out about human rights in his nation in light of the 1975 Helsinki Accords. Sakharov wrote again to Carter at the time of his inauguration. President Carter replied via a telegram that was hand delivered to Sakharov at the U.S. embassy in Moscow. Yuri Andropov, the head of the KGB (the Soviet intelligence agency and secret police), relayed the telegram to his comrades in the Central Committee of the Soviet Communist Party several days later.

Dear Professor Sakharov:

I received your letter of January 21, and I want to express my appreciation to you for bringing your thoughts to my personal attention.

Human rights are a central concern of my administration. In my inaugural address I stated: "Because we are free, we can never be indifferent to the fate of freedom elsewhere." You may rest assured that the American people and our government will continue our firm commitment to promote respect for human rights not only in our country, but also abroad.

We shall use our good offices to seek the release of prisoners of conscience, and we will continue our efforts to shape a world responsive to human aspirations in which nations of different cultures and histories can live side by side in peace and justice.

I am always glad to hear from you, and I wish you well.

Sincerely,

J. CARTER

Source: Yuri Andropov to the Central Committee, February 9, 1977, Andrei Sakharov Archive, MS Russ 79, Houghton Library, Harvard University.

Document 8.2
President Jimmy Carter Advocates a Foreign Policy to Promote Human Rights, Commencement Address at the University of Notre Dame, May 22, 1977

President Carter forcefully articulated his views on the importance of human rights to U.S. foreign policy in a commencement address during the spring of his first year in office. The strategy of the containment of an expansionist Soviet Union, Carter said, represented an old and tired way of thinking about the world and its problems. That policy's "intellectual and moral poverty" were revealed in the Vietnam War. A "new world" demanded a new strategy, one that would make Americans "proud to be Americans" again.

. . . For too many years, we've been willing to adopt the flawed and erroneous principles and tactics of our adversaries, sometimes abandoning our own values for theirs. We've fought fire with fire, never thinking that fire is better quenched with water. This approach failed, with Vietnam the best example of its intellectual and moral poverty. But through failure we have now found our way back to our own principles and values, and we have regained our lost confidence.

By the measure of history, our Nation's 200 years are very brief, and our rise to world eminence is briefer still. It dates from 1945, when Europe and the old international order lay in ruins. Before then, America was largely on the periphery of world affairs. But since then, we have inescapably been at the center of world affairs.

Our policy during this period was guided by two principles: a belief that Soviet expansion was almost inevitable but that it must be contained, and the corresponding belief in the importance of an almost exclusive alliance among non-Communist nations on both sides of the Atlantic. That system could not last forever unchanged. Historical trends have weakened its foundation. The unifying threat of conflict with the Soviet Union has become less intensive, even though the competition has become more extensive.

The Vietnamese war produced a profound moral crisis, sapping worldwide faith in our own policy and our system of life, a crisis of confidence made even more grave by the covert pessimism of some of our leaders. . . .

The world is still divided by ideological disputes, dominated by regional conflicts, and threatened by danger that we will not resolve the differences of race and wealth without violence or without drawing into combat the major military powers. We can no longer separate the traditional issues of war and peace from the new global questions of justice, equity, and human rights.

It is a new world, but America should not fear it. It is a new world, and we should help to shape it. It is a new world that calls for a new American foreign policy—a policy based on constant decency in its values and on optimism in our historical vision.

We can no longer have a policy solely for the industrial nations as the foundation of global stability, but we must respond to the new reality of a politically awakening world.

We can no longer expect that the other 150 nations will follow the dictates of the powerful, but we must continue—confidently—our efforts to inspire, to persuade, and to lead.

Our policy must reflect our belief that the world can hope for more than simple survival and our belief that dignity and freedom are fundamental spiritual requirements. Our policy must shape an international system that will last longer than secret deals.

We cannot make this kind of policy by manipulation. Our policy must be open; it must be candid; it must be one of constructive global involvement, resting on five cardinal principles.

I've tried to make these premises clear to the American people since last January. Let me review what we have been doing and discuss what we intend to do.

. . . [W]e have reaffirmed America's commitment to human rights as a fundamental tenet of our foreign policy. In ancestry, religion, color, place of origin, and cultural background, we Americans are as diverse a nation as the world has even seen. No common mystique of blood or soil unites us. What draws us together, perhaps more than anything else, is a belief in human freedom. We want the world to know that our Nation stands for more than financial prosperity.

This does not mean that we can conduct our foreign policy by rigid moral maxims. We live in a world that is imperfect and which will always be imperfect—a world that is complex and confused and which will always be complex and confused. . . .

Throughout the world today, in free nations and in totalitarian countries as well, there is a preoccupation with the subject of human freedom, human rights. And I believe it is incumbent on us in this country to keep that discussion, that debate, that contention alive. No other country is as well-qualified as we to set an example. We have our own shortcomings and faults, and we should strive constantly and with courage to make sure that we are legitimately proud of what we have. . . .

Let me conclude by summarizing: Our policy is based on an historical vision of America's role. Our policy is derived from a larger view of global change. Our policy is rooted in our moral values, which never change. Our policy is reinforced by our material wealth and by our military power. Our policy is designed to serve mankind. And it is a policy that I hope will make you proud to be Americans.

Source: Jimmy Carter, "Address at Commencement Exercises at the University of Notre Dame," May 22, 1977, in *Public Papers of the Presidents of the United States: Jimmy Carter, 1977–1981,* from the American Presidency Project, University of California, Santa Barbara, www.presidency.ucsb.edu.

Document 8.3
President Jimmy Carter Creates Confusion over His Foreign Policy, Commencement Address at the United States Naval Academy, June 7, 1978

In response to press accounts that called his foreign policy incoherent, the president set out to clarify his purposes in foreign policy. The result was this speech, which only resulted in greater confusion. "Two Different Speeches" was the headline that the influential Washington Post *ran the next day to describe the president's effort. On the one hand, the president spoke optimistically of détente and human rights, and he dismissed the idea that either side could ever truly gain superiority over the other. On the other, he issued a stern warning to the Soviets: continue to intervene in the affairs of poor nations, as in Africa, and continue to repress your citizens at home, and the United States will confront you with its superior might.*

. . . Today I want to discuss one of the most important aspects of that international context—the relationship between the world's two greatest powers, the United States of America and the Soviet Union.

We must realize that for a very long time our relationship with the Soviet Union will be competitive. That competition is to be constructive if we are successful. Instead it could be dangerous and politically disastrous. Then our relationship must be cooperative as well.

We must avoid excessive swings in the public mood in our country—from euphoria when things are going well, to despair when they are not; from an exaggerated sense of compatibility with the Soviet Union, to open expressions of hostility.

Detente between our two countries is central to world peace. It's important for the world, for the American public, and for you as future leaders of the Navy to understand the complex and sensitive nature. . . .

To be stable, to be supported by the American people, and to be a basis for widening the scope of cooperation, then détente must be broadly defined and truly reciprocal. Both nations must exercise restraint in troubled areas and in troubled times. Both must honor meticulously those agreements which have already been reached to widen cooperation, naturally and mutually limit nuclear arms production, permit the free movement of people and the expression of ideas, and to protect human rights.

Neither of us should entertain the notion that military supremacy can be attained, or that transient military advantage can be politically exploited. . . .

We desire to dominate no one. We will continue to widen our cooperation with the positive new forces in the world.

We want to increase our collaboration with the Soviet Union, but also with the emerging nations, with the nations of Eastern Europe, and with the People's Republic of China. We are particularly dedicated to genuine self-determination and majority rule in those areas of the world where these goals have not yet been attained.

Our long-term objective must be to convince the Soviet Union of the advantages of cooperation and of the costs of disruptive behavior. . . .

I'm glad to report to you today that the prospects for a SALT II agreement are good.

Beyond this major effort, improved trade and technological and cultural exchange are among the immediate benefits of cooperation between our two countries. However, these efforts to cooperate do not erase the significant differences between us.

What are these differences?

To the Soviet Union, détente seems to mean a continuing aggressive struggle for political advantage and increased influence in a variety of ways. The Soviet Union apparently sees military power and military assistance as the best means of expanding their influence abroad. Obviously, areas of instability in the world provide a tempting target for this effort, and all too often they seem ready to exploit any such opportunity.

As became apparent in Korea, in Angola, and also, as you know, in Ethiopia more recently, the Soviets prefer to use proxy forces to achieve their purposes. . . .

The abuse of basic human rights in their own country, in violation of the agreement which was reached at Helsinki, has earned them the condemnation of people everywhere who love freedom. By their actions, they've demonstrated that the Soviet system cannot tolerate freely expressed ideas or notions of loyal opposition and the free movement of peoples.

The Soviet Union attempts to export a totalitarian and repressive form of government, resulting in a closed society. Some of these characteristics and goals create problems for the Soviet Union.

Outside a tightly controlled bloc, the Soviet Union has difficult political relations with other nations. Their cultural bonds with others are few and frayed. Their form of government is becoming increasingly unattractive to other nations, so that even Marxist-Leninist groups no longer look on the Soviet Union as a model to be imitated. . . .

In contrast to the Soviet Union, we are surrounded by friendly neighbors and wide seas. Our societal structure is stable and cohesive, and our foreign policy enjoys bipartisan public support, which gives it continuity.

We are also strong because of what we stand for as a nation: the realistic chance for every person to build a better life; protection by both law and custom from arbitrary exercise of government power; the right of every individual to speak out, to participate fully in government, and to share political power. Our philosophy is based on personal freedom, the most powerful of all ideas, and our democratic way of life warrants the admiration and emulation by other people throughout the world.

Our work for human rights makes us part of an international tide, growing in force. We are strengthened by being part of it.

Our growing economic strength is also a major political factor, potential influence for the benefit of others. Our gross national product exceeds that of all nine nations combined in the European Economic Community and is twice as great as that of the Soviet Union. Additionally, we are now learning how to use our resources more wisely, creating a new harmony between our people and our environment.

Our analysis of American military strength also furnishes a basis for confidence. We know that neither the United States nor the Soviet Union can launch a nuclear assault on the other without suffering a devastating counterattack which could destroy the aggressor nation. Although the Soviet Union has more missile launchers, greater throw-weight, and more continental air defense capabilities, the United States has more warheads, generally greater accuracy, more heavy bombers, a more balanced nuclear force, better missile submarines, and superior antisubmarine warfare capability. . . .

The Soviet Union can choose either confrontation or cooperation. The United States is adequately prepared to meet either choice. . . .

Source: Jimmy Carter, "United States Naval Academy Address at the Commencement Exercises," June 7, 1978, in *Public Papers of the Presidents of the United States: Jimmy Carter 1977–1981,* from the American Presidency Project, University of California, Santa Barbara, www.presidency.ucsb.edu.

Document 8.4
President Jimmy Carter's New Year's Greetings to the People's Republic of China, January 1, 1979

On December 15, 1978, the United States and the People's Republic of China released a joint communiqué establishing normal diplomatic relations. This move, by which the United States recognized the government of the PRC as the sole legal government of all China, paradoxically caused great frustration in both the Soviet Union and among conservative American defenders of Taiwan. On January 1, the president sent New Year's greetings to the PRC. Later that month, the president hosted Chinese premier Deng Xiaoping in Washington, D.C.

Today, after a generation of isolation from each other, the United States of America and the People's Republic of China establish full diplomatic relations between our governments. The cause of world peace will be served by this historic act of reconciliation.

The estrangement of our peoples has sometimes produced misunderstanding, confrontation and enmity. That era is behind us. We can now establish normal patterns of commerce, and scholarly and cultural exchange. Through common effort, we can deepen the new ties of friendship between our peoples, and we can jointly contribute to the prosperity and stability of Asia and the Pacific region.

Precisely because our two countries have different traditions, cultures, and political and economic systems, we have much to gain from each other. The United States prizes the great variety of opinions and origins among its own citizens. Similarly, the United States desires a world of diversity in which each nation is free to make a distinctive contribution to express the manifold aspirations, cultures, traditions, and beliefs of mankind.

The American people value the enormous contributions the Chinese people have made to the achievements of humanity. And we welcome the growing involvement of the People's Republic of China in world affairs. We consider China as a key force for global peace.

We wish to cooperate closely with the creative Chinese people on the problems that confront all people.

Your Excellency, in our country, the first day of the New Year is a time of rededication and resolve. In that spirit, we pledge during the coming years:

- to continue as an enlightened Asian and Pacific power, determined to help maintain peace and stability in the region;
- to enrich the lives of our peoples, both spiritually and materially, through expanded trade, tourism, and student and cultural exchanges, and cooperation in the sciences, all on a basis of equality and mutual benefit; and
- to extend our hands across the Pacific to you in friendship and peace.

Source: Jimmy Carter, "Premier Hua Guofeng of the People's Republic of China New Year's Message from the President," January 1, 1979, in *Public Papers of the Presidents of the United States: Jimmy Carter 1977–1981,* from the American Presidency Project, University of California, Santa Barbara, www.presidency.ucsb.edu.

Document 8.5
Second Strategic Arms Limitation Talks Agreement (SALT II), June 18, 1979

Negotiations in the second round of Strategic Arms Limitation Talks (SALT) began in November 1972. The two sides were close to agreement on the basic provisions of the treaty to replace SALT I when President Carter took office. Political difficulties between the two nations prevented formal agreement until June 18, 1979, when Carter and General Secretary Leonid Brezhnev signed SALT II in Vienna. In the new treaty, each superpower agreed to cap its arsenal of strategic nuclear delivery vehicles—launchers for intercontinental ballistic missiles (ICBMs), submarine-launched ballistic missiles (SLBMs), air-to-surface ballistic missiles (ASBMs), and heavy bombers—at 2,400 total, to be reduced to 2,250 by 1982. Each side also agreed to limit itself to 1,320 ballistic missiles with multiple independently targeted reentry vehicles (MIRVs), and heavy bombers with long-range cruise missiles. The treaty's text further banned deployment of some untested technologies, such as seabed ballistic missile launchers, and otherwise sought to set boundaries around the arms race. Although the treaty was never ratified by the Senate, Presidents Carter and Reagan both affirmed its importance and conformed to its limits.

The United States of America and the Union of Soviet Socialist Republics, hereinafter referred to as the Parties,

Conscious that nuclear war would have devastating consequences for all mankind,

Proceeding from the Basic Principles of Relations Between the United States of America and the Union of Soviet Socialist Republics of May 29, 1972,

Attaching particular significance to the limitation of strategic arms and determined to continue their efforts begun with the Treaty on the Limitation of Anti-Ballistic Missile Systems and the Interim Agreement on Certain Measures with Respect to the Limitation of Strategic Offensive Arms, of May 26, 1972,

Convinced that the additional measures limiting strategic offensive arms provided for in this Treaty will contribute to the improvement of relations between the Parties, help to reduce the risk of outbreak of nuclear war and strengthen international peace and security,

Mindful of their obligations under Article VI of the Treaty on the Non-Proliferation of Nuclear Weapons,

Guided by the principle of equality and equal security,

Recognizing that the strengthening of strategic stability meets the interests of the Parties and the interests of international security,

Reaffirming their desire to take measures for the further limitation and for the further reduction of strategic arms, having in mind the goal of achieving general and complete disarmament,

Declaring their intention to undertake in the near future negotiations further to limit and further to reduce strategic offensive arms,

Have agreed as follows: . . .

ARTICLE III

1. Upon entry into force of this Treaty, each Party undertakes to limit ICBM launchers, SLBM launchers, heavy bombers, and ASBMs to an aggregate number not to exceed 2,400.
2. Each Party undertakes to limit, from January 1, 1981, strategic offensive arms referred to in paragraph 1 of this Article to an aggregate number not to exceed 2,250, and to initiate reductions of those arms which as of that date would be in excess of this aggregate number.
3. Within the aggregate numbers provided for in paragraphs 1 and 2 of this Article and subject to the provisions of this Treaty, each Party has the right to determine the composition of these aggregates. . . .

ARTICLE IV

1. Each Party undertakes not to start construction of additional fixed ICBM launchers.
2. Each Party undertakes not to relocate fixed ICBM launchers.
3. Each Party undertakes not to convert launchers of light ICBMs, or of ICBMs of older types deployed prior to 1964, into launchers of heavy ICBMs of types deployed after that time.
4. Each Party undertakes in the process of modernization and replacement of ICBM silo launchers not to increase the original internal volume of an ICBM silo launcher by more than thirty-two percent. Within this limit each Party has the right to determine whether such an increase will be made through an increase in the original diameter or in the original depth of an ICBM silo launcher, or in both of these dimensions. . . .

5. Each Party undertakes:
   (a) not to supply ICBM launcher deployment areas with intercontinental ballistic missiles in excess of a number consistent with normal deployment, maintenance, training, and replacement requirements;
   (b) not to provide storage facilities for or to store ICBMs in excess of normal deployment requirements at launch sites of ICBM launchers;
   (c) not to develop, test, or deploy systems for rapid reload of ICBM launchers. . . .
7. Each Party undertakes not to develop, test, or deploy ICBMs which have a launch-weight greater or a throw-weight greater than that of the heaviest, in terms of either launch-weight or throw-weight, respectively, of the heavy ICBMs deployed by either Party as of the date of signature of this Treaty. . . .
10. Each Party undertakes not to flight-test or deploy ICBMs of a type flight-tested as of May 1, 1979 with a number of reentry vehicles greater than the maximum number of reentry vehicles with which an ICBM of that type has been flight-tested as of that date. . . .
14. Each Party undertakes not to deploy at any one time on heavy bombers equipped for cruise missiles capable of a range in excess of 600 kilometers a number of such cruise missiles which exceeds the product of 28 and the number of such heavy bombers. . . .

ARTICLE V

1. Within the aggregate numbers provided for in paragraphs 1 and 2 of Article III, each Party undertakes to limit launchers of ICBMs and SLBMs equipped with MIRVs, ASBMs equipped with MIRVs, and heavy bombers equipped for cruise missiles capable of a range in excess of 600 kilometers to an aggregate number not to exceed 1,320.
2. Within the aggregate number provided for in paragraph 1 of this Article, each Party undertakes to limit launchers of ICBMs and SLBMs equipped with MIRVs, and ASBMs equipped with MIRVs to an aggregate number not to exceed 1,200.
3. Within the aggregate number provided for in paragraph 2 of this Article, each Party undertakes to limit launchers of ICBMs equipped with MIRVs to an aggregate number not to exceed 820. . . .

ARTICLE IX

1. Each Party undertakes not to develop, test, or deploy:
   (a) ballistic missiles capable of a range in excess of 600 kilometers for installation on waterborne vehicles other than submarines, or launchers of such missiles;
   (b) fixed ballistic or cruise missile launchers for emplacement on the ocean floor, on the seabed, or on the beds of internal waters and inland waters, or in the subsoil thereof, or mobile launchers of such missiles, which move only in contact with the ocean floor, the seabed, or the beds of internal waters and inland waters, or missiles for such launchers;
   (c) systems for placing into Earth orbit nuclear weapons or any other kind of weapons of mass destruction, including fractional orbital missiles;

(d) mobile launchers of heavy ICBMs;

(e) SLBMs which have a launch-weight greater or a throw-weight greater than that of the heaviest, in terms of either launch-weight or throw-weight, respectively, of the light ICBMs deployed by either Party as of the date of signature of this Treaty, or launchers of such SLBMs; or

(f) ASBMs which have a launch-weight greater or a throw-weight greater than that of the heaviest, in terms of either launch-weight or throw-weight, respectively, of the light ICBMs deployed by either Party as of the date of signature of this Treaty.

ARTICLE XI

1. Strategic offensive arms which would be in excess of the aggregate numbers provided for in this Treaty as well as strategic offensive arms prohibited by this Treaty shall be dismantled or destroyed under procedures to be agreed upon in the Standing Consultative Commission. . . .

ARTICLE XIX

1. This Treaty shall be subject to ratification in accordance with the constitutional procedures of each Party. This Treaty shall enter into force on the day of the exchange of instruments of ratification and shall remain in force through December 31, 1985, unless replaced earlier by an agreement further limiting strategic offensive arms. . . .

Source: "Treaty Between the United States of America and the Union of Soviet Socialist Republics on the Limitation of Strategic Offensive Arms," June 18, 1979, from the Federation of American Scientists, http://fas.org/nuke/control/salt2/index.html.

Document 8.6
NATO Agrees to Deploy Cruise Missiles in Its "Dual-Track" Decision, Special Meeting of Foreign and Defense Ministers, Brussels, Belgium, December 12, 1979

In 1977 the Soviet Union deployed a new intermediate range nuclear missile targeted at Western Europe. Each SS-20 was a mobile weapon that carried three warheads. NATO's response was to replace Western Europe's short-range Pershing I-A missiles with intermediate-range MIRV missiles, Pershing IIs, and Tomahawk cruise missiles; however, the change would not take place until 1983. The lag was intended to give negotiators a chance to make the deployment unnecessary and to provide political cover for nervous West European governments.

1. At a special meeting of Foreign and Defence Ministers in Brussels on 12 December 1979.

2. Ministers recalled the May 1978 Summit where governments expressed the political resolve to meet the challenges to their security posed by the continuing momentum of the Warsaw Pact military build-up.

3. The Warsaw Pact has over the years developed a large and growing capability in nuclear systems that directly threaten Western Europe and have a strategic significance for the Alliance in Europe. This situation has been especially aggravated over the last few years by Soviet decisions to implement programmes modernising and expanding their long-range nuclear capability substantially. In particular, they have deployed the SS-20 missile, which offers significant improvements over previous systems in providing greater accuracy, more mobility, and greater range, as well as having multiple warheads, and the Backfire bomber, which has a much better performance than other Soviet aircraft deployed hitherto in a theatre role.

During this period, while the Soviet Union has been reinforcing its superiority in Long-Range Theatre Nuclear Forces (LRTNF) both quantitatively and qualitatively, Western LRTNF capabilities have remained static. Indeed these forces are increasing in age and vulnerability and do not include land-based, long-range theatre nuclear missile systems.

4. At the same time, the Soviets have also undertaken a modernisation and expansion of their shorter-range TNF and greatly improved the overall quality of their conventional forces.

These developments took place against the background of increasing Soviet inter-continental capabilities and achievement of parity in inter-continental capability with the United States.

5. These trends have prompted serious concern within the Alliance, because, if they were to continue, Soviet superiority in theatre nuclear systems could undermine the stability achieved in inter-continental systems and cast doubt on the credibility of the Alliance's deterrent strategy by highlighting the gap in the spectrum of NATO's available nuclear response to aggression.

6. Ministers noted that these recent developments require concrete actions on the part of the Alliance if NATO's strategy of flexible response is to remain credible. After intensive consideration, including the merits of alternative approaches, and after taking note of the positions of certain members, Ministers concluded that the overall interest of the Alliance would best be served by pursuing two parallel and complementary approaches of TNF modernisation and arms control.

7. Accordingly Ministers have decided to modernise NATO's LRTNF by the deployment in Europe of US ground-launched systems comprising 108 Pershing II launchers, which would replace existing US Pershing I-A, and 464 Ground-Launched Cruise Missiles (GLCM), all with single warheads. All the nations currently participating in the integrated defence structure will participate in the programme: the missiles will be stationed in selected countries and certain support costs will be met through NATO's existing common funding arrangements.

The programme will not increase NATO's reliance upon nuclear weapons. In this connection, Ministers agreed that as an integral part of TNF modernisation, 1,000 US nuclear warheads will be withdrawn from Europe as soon as feasible. Further, Ministers decided that the 572 LRTNF warheads should be accommodated within that reduced level, which necessarily implies a numerical shift of emphasis away from warheads for delivery systems of other types and shorter ranges In addition they noted with satisfaction that the Nuclear Planning Group is undertaking an examination of the precise nature, scope and basis of the adjustments resulting from the LRTNF deployment and their possible implications for the balance of roles and systems in NATO's nuclear armoury as a whole. This examination will form the basis of a substantive report to NPG Ministers in the Autumn of 1980.

8. Ministers attach great importance to the role of arms control in contributing to a more stable military relationship between East and West and in advancing the process of détente. This is reflected in a broad set of initiatives being examined within the Alliance to further the course of arms control and détente in the 1980s. Ministers regard arms control as an integral part of the Alliance's efforts to assure the undiminished security of its member States and to make the strategic situation between East and West more stable, more predictable, and more manageable at lower levels of armaments on both sides. In this regard they welcome the contribution which the SALT II Treaty makes towards achieving these objectives. . . .

11. The Ministers have decided to pursue these two parallel and complementary approaches in order to avert an arms race in Europe caused by the Soviet TNF build-up, yet preserve the viability of NATO's strategy of deterrence and defence and thus maintain the security of its member States. . . .

Source: North Atlantic Treaty Organization, "Special Meeting of Foreign and Defence Ministers (The 'Double Track' Decision on Theatre Nuclear Forces)," December 12, 1979, www.nato.int/docu/basictxt/b791212a.htm.

Document 8.7
Soviet Premier Alexei Kosygin and Afghan Prime Minister Nur Mohammed Taraki Discuss Islamic Rebellion and Soviet Intervention in Afghanistan, March 17 or 18, 1979

Soviet premier Alexei Kosygin spoke on the telephone in early 1979 with Afghan prime minister Nur Mohammed Taraki about the Islamic rebellion against which Taraki's government was struggling. The Soviet leader's line of questioning reveals a serious ignorance of conditions in one of the world's most remote and least developed nations.

Kosygin: Ask Comrade Taraki, perhaps he will outline the situation in Afghanistan.

Taraki: The situation is bad and getting worse.

Kosygin: Do you have support among the workers, city dwellers, the petty bourgeoisie, and the white collar workers in Herat? Is there still anyone on your side?

Taraki: There is no active support on the part of the population. It is almost wholly under the influence of Shiite slogans—follow not the heathens, but follow us. The propaganda is underpinned by this.

Kosygin: Are there many workers there?

Taraki: Very few—between 1,000 and 2,000 people in all. . . .

Kosygin: Hundreds of Afghan officers were trained in the Soviet Union. Where are they all now?

Taraki: Most of them are Moslem reactionaries. We are unable to rely on them, we have no confidence in them.

Kosygin: Can't you recruit a further 50,000 soldiers if we quickly airlift arms to you? How many people can you recruit?

Taraki: The core can only be formed by older secondary school pupils, students, and a few workers. The working class in Afghanistan is very small, but it is a long affair to train them. But we will take any measures, if necessary.

Kosygin: We have decided to quickly deliver military equipment and property to you and to repair helicopters and aircraft. All this is for free. We have also decided to deliver to you 100,000 tons of grain and to raise gas prices from $21 per cubic meter to $37.

Taraki: That is very good, but let us talk of Herat. Why can't the Soviet Union send Uzbeks, Tajiks, and Turkmens in civilian clothing? No one will recognize them. They could drive tanks, because we have all these nationalities in Afghanistan. Let them don Afghan costume and wear Afghan badges and no one will recognize them. It is very easy work, in our view. . . .

Kosygin: You are, of course, oversimplifying the issue. It is a complex political and international issue, but irrespective of this, we will hold consultations again and get back to you.

Source: "Transcript of Telephone Conversation Between Soviet Premier Alexei Kosygin and Afghan Prime Minister Nur Mohammed Taraki, 17 or 18 March 1979," *Cold War International History Project Bulletin,* no. 8–9 (Winter 1996–1997): 145–146, www.cwihp.org.

Document 8.8
President Jimmy Carter Reacts to the Soviet Invasion of Afghanistan, ABC News Interview, December 31, 1979

In an interview with Frank Reynolds of ABC News, President Carter spoke candidly of his surprise and horror at the Soviet invasion of Afghanistan. Carter perhaps meant to underline the seriousness of the event, but his confessional remarks also provided ammunition to his critics, who had long assailed the president for his alleged naïvety.

President Carter: He [Brezhnev] responded in what I consider to be an inadequate way. He claimed that he had been invited by the Afghan Government to come in and protect Afghanistan from some outside third nation threat. This was obviously false because the person that he claimed invited him, President Amin, was murdered or assassinated after the Soviets pulled their coup. . . .

Mr. Reynolds: Well, he's lying, isn't he, Mr. President?

President Carter: He is not telling the facts accurately, that's correct.

Mr. Reynolds: Have you changed your perception of the Russians in the time that you've been here? . . .

President Carter: My opinion of the Russians has changed most [sic] dramatically in the last week than even the previous two and a half years before that. It's only now dawning on the world the magnitude of the action that the Soviets undertook in invading Afghanistan. . . . [W]hat we will do about it I cannot yet say.

But to repeat myself, this action of the Soviets has made a more dramatic change in my opinion of what the Soviets' ultimate goals are than anything they've done in the previous time I've been in office.

Source: Edward H. Judge and John W. Langdon, *The Cold War: A History through Documents* (Upper Saddle River, N.J.: Prentice-Hall, 1999), 200.

Document 8.9
President Jimmy Carter's Final State of the Union Address, January 23, 1980

In the aftermath of the twin shocks of 1979, the hostage-taking in Iran and the Soviet invasion of Afghanistan, President Carter focused his State of the Union address on foreign affairs and called for what he considered a substantial enhancement of U.S. military strength. His frustration with the Soviets was evident in his unusual decision to send to Congress a different, much more comprehensive, 33,000 word State of the Union "message" two days before he delivered his 3,500 word "address." The president who had come into office focused intently on domestic and economic issues now did not want concerns over inflation or the energy crisis to detract from his area of principal concern: the Cold War.

. . . At this time in Iran, 50 Americans are still held captive, innocent victims of terrorism and anarchy. Also at this moment, massive Soviet troops are attempting to subjugate the fiercely independent and deeply religious people of Afghanistan. These two acts—one of international terrorism and one of military aggression—present a serious challenge to the United States of America and indeed to all the nations of the world. Together, we will meet these threats to peace. . . .

I'm determined that the United States will remain the strongest of all nations, but our power will never be used to initiate a threat to the security of any nation or to the rights of any human being. We seek to be and to remain secure—a nation at peace in a stable world. But to be secure we must face the world as it is.

Three basic developments have helped to shape our challenges: the steady growth and increased projection of Soviet military power beyond its own borders; the overwhelming dependence of the Western democracies on oil supplies from the Middle East; and the press of social and religious and economic and political change in the many nations of the developing world, exemplified by the revolution in Iran.

Each of these factors is important in its own right. Each interacts with the others. All must be faced together, squarely and courageously. We will face these challenges, and we will meet them with the best that is in us. And we will not fail.

In response to the abhorrent act in Iran, our Nation has never been aroused and unified so greatly in peacetime. Our position is clear. The United States will not yield to blackmail. . . .

But now we face a broader and more fundamental challenge in this region because of the recent military action of the Soviet Union.

Now, as during the last 3½ decades, the relationship between our country, the United States of America, and the Soviet Union is the most critical factor in determining whether the world will live at peace or be engulfed in global conflict.

Since the end of the Second World War, America has led other nations in meeting the challenge of mounting Soviet power. This has not been a simple or a static relationship. Between us there has been cooperation, there has been competition, and at times there has been confrontation. . . .

Preventing nuclear war is the foremost responsibility of the two superpowers. That's why we've negotiated the strategic arms limitation treaties—SALT I and SALT II. Especially now, in a time of great tension, observing the mutual constraints imposed by the terms of these treaties will be in the best interest of both countries and will help to preserve world peace. I will consult very closely with the Congress on this matter as we strive to control nuclear weapons. That effort to control nuclear weapons will not be abandoned.

We superpowers also have the responsibility to exercise restraint in the use of our great military force. The integrity and the independence of weaker nations must not be threatened. They must know that in our presence they are secure.

But now the Soviet Union has taken a radical and an aggressive new step. It's using its great military power against a relatively defenseless nation. The implications of the Soviet invasion of Afghanistan could pose the most serious threat to the peace since the Second World War.

The vast majority of nations on Earth have condemned this latest Soviet attempt to extend its colonial domination of others and have demanded the immediate withdrawal of Soviet troops. The Moslem world is especially and justifiably outraged by this aggression against an Islamic people. No action of a world power has ever been so quickly and so overwhelmingly condemned. But verbal condemnation is not enough. The Soviet Union must pay a concrete price for their aggression.

While this invasion continues, we and the other nations of the world cannot conduct business as usual with the Soviet Union. That's why the United States has imposed stiff economic penalties on the Soviet Union. I will not issue any permits for Soviet ships to fish in the coastal waters of the United States. I've cut Soviet access to high-technology equipment and to agricultural products. I've limited other commerce with the Soviet Union, and I've asked our allies and friends to join with us in restraining their own trade with the Soviets and not to replace our own embargoed items. And I have notified the Olympic Committee that with Soviet invading forces in Afghanistan, neither the American people nor I will support sending an Olympic team to Moscow. . . .

The region which is now threatened by Soviet troops in Afghanistan is of great strategic importance: It contains more than two-thirds of the world's exportable oil. The Soviet effort to dominate Afghanistan has brought Soviet military forces to within 300 miles of the Indian Ocean and close to the Straits of Hormuz, a waterway through which most of the world's oil must flow. The Soviet Union is now attempting to consolidate a strategic position, therefore, that poses a grave threat to the free movement of Middle East oil. . . .

Let our position be absolutely clear: An attempt by any outside force to gain control of the Persian Gulf region will be regarded as an assault on the vital interests of the United States of America, and such an assault will be repelled by any means necessary, including military force.

During the past 3 years, you have joined with me to improve our own security and the prospects for peace, not only in the vital oil-producing area of the Persian Gulf region but around the world. We've increased annually our real commitment for defense, and we will sustain this increase of effort throughout the Five Year Defense Program. It's imperative that Congress approve this strong defense budget for 1981, encompassing a 5-percent real growth in authorizations, without any reduction.

We are also improving our capability to deploy U.S. military forces rapidly to distant areas. We've helped to strengthen NATO and our other alliances, and recently we and other NATO members have decided to develop and to deploy modernized, intermediate-range nuclear forces to meet an unwarranted and increased threat from the nuclear weapons of the Soviet Union. . . .

We've also expanded our own sphere of friendship. Our deep commitment to human rights and to meeting human needs has improved our relationship with much of the Third World. Our decision to normalize relations with the People's Republic of China will help to preserve peace and stability in Asia and in the Western Pacific. . . .

The men and women of America's Armed Forces are on duty tonight in many parts of the world. I'm proud of the job they are doing, and I know you share that pride. I believe that our volunteer forces are adequate for current defense needs, and I hope that it will not become necessary to impose a draft. However, we must be prepared for that possibility. For this reason, I have determined that the Selective Service System must now be revitalized. I will send legislation and budget proposals to the Congress next month so that we can begin registration and then meet future mobilization needs rapidly if they arise. . . .

Our material resources, great as they are, are limited. Our problems are too complex for simple slogans or for quick solutions. We cannot solve them without effort and sacrifice. Walter Lippmann once reminded us, "You took the good things for granted. Now you must earn them again. For every right that you cherish, you have a duty which you must fulfill. For every good which you wish to preserve, you will have to sacrifice your comfort and your ease. There is nothing for nothing any longer." . . .

Source: Jimmy Carter, "The State of the Union Address Delivered Before a Joint Session of the Congress," January 23, 1980, in *Public Papers of the Presidents of the United States: Jimmy Carter 1977–1981,* from the American Presidency Project, University of California, Santa Barbara www .presidency.ucsb.edu.

Document 8.10
Soviet Perspective on the Situation in Afghanistan, Report to the Central Committee of the Communist Party of the Soviet Union, January 27, 1980

This report by KGB chief Yuri Andropov, Soviet foreign minister Andrei Gromyko, and the other members of the Afghanistan Commission, a special ad hoc committee that controlled decision making on Afghanistan for the Soviet government, reveals what some Soviet leaders thought of their role in Afghanistan. According to Andropov, the "stabilization" of Afghanistan was important to counteract provocative moves against the Soviet Union undertaken by President Jimmy Carter. It is entirely possible that Andropov, who was an intelligent and wily hardliner, and the other commission members were playing to the fears of their less sophisticated comrades in making this argument.

. . . The provision by the USSR of many-sided, including military, assistance to Afghanistan and the coming to power of the government of Babrak Karmal created the necessary conditions for the stabilization of the situation in the DRA [Democratic Republic of Afghanistan]and put an end to certain tendencies in the development of the situation in the Middle East which are dangerous for us.

Along with this the development of events bears witness to the fact that the USA, its allies, and the PRC [People's Republic of China] have set themselves the goal of using to the maximum extent the events in Afghanistan to intensify the atmosphere of anti-Sovietism and to justify long-term foreign policy acts which are hostile to the Soviet Union and directed at changing the balance of power in their favor. Providing increased assistance to the Afghan counter-revolution, the West and the PRC are counting on the fact that they will succeed in inspiring an extended conflict in Afghanistan, as the result of which, they believe, the Soviet Union will get tied up in that country. . . .

In the future as well, the necessity of providing for the broad foreign policy interests and the security of the USSR will demand the preservation of the offensive measures which we undertake in relation to the Afghan events. In working out and conducting them, we would suggest that it is expedient to be guided by the following.

—Henceforth, in relations with the USA, to maintain a firm line in opposition to the Carter Administration's provocative steps. . . .

—To intensify our influence on the positions of various NATO allies of the USA, particularly on France and the FRG [Federal Republic of Germany, or West Germany], to the greatest possible extent using in our interest the differences which have been revealed between them and the USA in the approach to the choice of measures in response to the actions of the Soviet Union in Afghanistan.

—Keeping in mind that the events in Afghanistan are being used by the USA and the PRC as a convenient pretext for a further rapprochement on an anti-Soviet basis, to plan long-term measures to complicate relations between Washington and Beijing. . . .

—Bring into life measures directed at the preservation of the anti-imperialist, primarily anti-American, elements in the foreign policy of Iran, insofar as the continuation of the crisis in Iran-American relations limits the potential possibilities of the Khomeini regime to inspire anti-government uprisings on Moslem grounds in Afghanistan. . . .

—While conducting foreign policy and propagandistic measures, to use even more widely the thesis that the Soviet Union's provision of military assistance to Afghanistan cannot be viewed in isolation from the USA's provocative efforts, which have already been undertaken over the course of a long time, to achieve unilateral military advantages in regions which are strategically important to the USSR.

In relation to the difficult domestic political and economic situation in the DRA, along with the intensification of anti-Soviet moods which are taking place among part of the Afghan population as the result of the criminal activity of H. Amin and his circle, a certain period of time evidently will be required for the normalization of the situation in Afghanistan itself. . . .

Source: "CPSU CC Politburo Decision, 28 January 1980, with Report by Gromyko-Andropov-Ustinov-Ponomarev, 27 January 1980," *Cold War International History Project Bulletin*, no. 8–9 (Winter 1996–1997): 163–165, www.cwihp.org.

Document 8.11
President Jimmy Carter Condemns the Banishment of Andrei Sakharov, White House Statement, January 23, 1980

Dissident Andrei Sakharov's public protest against the Soviet war in Afghanistan was too much for the KGB to stand. At the urging of KGB chief Yuri Andropov, Sakharov was stripped of the awards and medals that the Soviet government had bestowed upon him for his scientific discoveries, and he was forcibly relocated to the remote city of Gorky. The White House released the following statement in response.

The decision by Soviet authorities to deprive Nobel laureate Andrei Sakharov of his honors and to send him into exile arouses worldwide indignation. This denial of basic freedoms is a direct violation of the Helsinki Accords and a blow to the aspirations of all mankind to establish respect for human rights. The American people join with free men and women everywhere in condemning this act.

We must, at the same time, ask why the Soviet Union has chosen this moment to persecute this great man. What has he done in the past few months that is in any way different from what he was doing for the past 20 years? Why the need to silence him now? Is it because of the invasion and occupation of Afghanistan?

Just as we have welcomed Solzhenitsyn, Brodsky, Rostropovich, and thousands of others who have fled Soviet oppression, so we would welcome Dr. Sakharov. It is part of our proud and sacred heritage.

The arrest of Dr. Sakharov is a scar on their system that the Soviet leaders cannot erase by hurling abuse at him and seeking to mask the truth. His voice may be silenced in exile, but the truths he has spoken serve as a monument to his courage and an inspiration to man's enduring quest for dignity and freedom.

Source: Jimmy Carter, "Nobel Laureate Andrei Sakharov White House Statement," January 23, 1980, in *Public Papers of the Presidents of the United States: Jimmy Carter 1977–1981,* from the American Presidency Project, University of California, Santa Barbara, www.presidency.ucsb.edu.

Document 8.12
KGB Chief Yuri Andropov Analyzes the Western Response to Andrei Sakharov's Punishment, Report to the Central Committee of the Communist Party, January 24, 1980

The KGB provided the Central Committee of the Communist Party with false reassurances about reaction in the West to Sakharov's banishment. The Western press widely condemned the Soviet action but observed that in the old days of Stalin, a troublemaker like Sakharov would have been dealt with even more harshly. Time *magazine, in the story misquoted in the document below, in fact stated, "The Soviets did show a certain restraint by merely banishing Sakharov, instead of putting him on trial." The KGB report's claim—that* Time*'s correspondent thought being sent to Gorky was not so bad—was a misrepresentation of an unfortunately snide remark by a U.S. State Department official: "Said one State Department official: 'Being exiled to Gorky is a little like being sent to Detroit; it ain't great but it ain't so bad.'" (See "The Silencing of Sakharov,"* Time, *February 4, 1980, www.time.com/time/magazine/article/0,9171,954512,00.html.)*

. . . For instance, a correspondent of the English newspaper "Times" stated: "The Soviet authorities chose a perfectly good time for putting things in order in their country because the USA froze détente. It is high time to do this."

The BBC correspondent in Moscow said: "What has happened to Sakharov evidently shows that the Soviet upper crust has taken a decision not to waste more time on the Americans, renounce them as a thankless job, not to pay attention to the Western criticism, and to emphasize quite plainly the main problem, that is the security of the Soviet Union."

A correspondent of the American agency "United Press International" while regarding Sakharov as a prominent figure among Soviet "dissidents" wrote that "having removed Sakharov from the scene, the Soviets deprived the whole dissident organization in the USSR of the opportunity to communicate with the Western public."

"The decision of the Soviet authorities about Sakharov," observed a correspondent of the American magazine "Times", "is rather mild, it could be harsher as well. He is the one to blame for what has happened because he perorated too much. And the fact that he will live in Gorky is not such an awful thing." . . .

Source: Yuri Andropov to the Central Committee, January 24, 1980, Andrei Sakharov Archive, MS Russ 79, Houghton Library, Harvard University.

Document 8.13
President Jimmy Carter Defends His Decision to Resume Selective Service Registration, Meeting with Student Leaders, February 15, 1980

In a White House meeting with elected leaders of student bodies from across the United States, President Carter replied to pointed questions about his decision to resume Selective Service registration in order to speed mobilization in the event of a return to the draft.

The President: First of all, let me welcome you to the White House and to an opportunity for us to let you know what is going on in our own administration and for you to give us advice on what our administration ought to do in the future. I understand you've had good meetings with my staff members and others. This is very helpful to us and, I hope, to you.

I'd like to say just a few words from the perspective of the Oval Office, as President, undoubtedly repeating some of the points that you have heard during the earlier part of the day. Then I'd like to answer a few questions. And if you all have the time, I would like to stand outside the door and have an individual photograph made with each one of you before you leave.

Also, Dr. Brzezinski has informed me that seven or eight of you had expressed a desire to volunteer for the Army. [Laughter] I have an Army recruiting officer out there with me. [Laughter] The ones who don't come through the line—I know you've changed your mind. [Laughter] . . .

Q.: President Carter, my name is Jerry Kerwin. I'm the student body president at UCLA.

And just the other day you made a comment about students overreacting to the registration plan. A lot of students have been looking at other alternatives—like Congressman McCloskey has a plan in Congress right now which would bring up national service, a plan for that. [Inaudible]—just brought up other ways to strengthen the military, and there's other things also. I'd like to know if in your staff discussions what are the kinds of things you looked at before deciding to come out with the proposed registration?

The President: Yes, we looked at those considerations, and they're still viable. Let me repeat, which I'm sure you have heard often today: We have no plans for the initiation of the draft. We do not need it now. There is no need for our country to be mobilized with the involuntary recruitment of anyone. We are now getting along very well with our voluntary military forces.

We are also getting along very well with the voluntary service of young and old people in the Peace Corps, other ACTION programs. There is a constitutional question involved in the involuntary recruitment of people for nonmilitary service; there is a constitutional provision against involuntary servitude. And it would not be constitutionally permissible, according to some lawyers, if we conscripted people for the purpose of rejuvenating communities or solving our energy problem or service in mental health centers or working in hospitals or that sort of thing. So, absent a time of crisis when our Nation was mobilized to defend itself militarily, it would not be feasible, in my opinion, to have the broader based public service as a result of conscription.

I think that many of you would consider, though, a formal public service, perhaps early in your professional career, in some of the forms that I've just described. I don't think many of you are likely to go into the military. I wish you would. I was in there for 11 years and enjoyed it and got a lot out of it and ultimately did okay in politics. [Laughter] But there are many other very strong programs.

I don't know if you all met with Sam Brown today or not. Did Sam talk to you? Well Sam, as you know, is in charge of our ACTION program, under which comes the Peace Corps and other volunteer service programs. You might want to consider those. But I think voluntarily it would be great; conscription for that purpose would be doubtful of legality or need.

Q.: My name is Russ Lamp, Wayne State University. We heard the National Security Adviser, Dr. Brzezinski, and the Director of Selective Service make presentations on the world situation, registration, and draft, and so forth. And hearing your position, our school has taken a position in opposition to registration and the draft, and we still hold that.

It hasn't been clearly established what the military need is, and I believe the word "preparedness," a rather vague word, has been given as the rationale. We want to say, and I feel I am obligated from my constituency to communicate to you, as you've requested to hear from us, that we're opposed to it, we're concerned about the use of the military and continued prospects for intervention in the Third World—[inaudible]—military force—that is being considered—our policies in—[inaudible]. We're concerned about this, and we're concerned about whether the draft is a way of responding to a war with the Soviet Union, when the prospects of a nuclear war would loom very large. Since those military questions are very serious and haven't been addressed yet, we're concerned and do not agree that registration is appropriate at this time.

The President: I understand. I presume that there was not a question. [Laughter] Right?

Q.: No, sir. Thank you.

Source: "Meeting with Student Leaders, Remarks and a Question-and-Answer Session," February 15, 1980, in *Public Papers of the Presidents of the United States: Jimmy Carter, 1977–1981,* from the American Presidency Project, University of California, Santa Barbara, www.presidency.ucsb.edu.

Document 8.14
Army Chief of Staff Gen. Edward Meyer Declares that the United States Has a "Hollow Army," Congressional Hearing, May 29, 1980

The military buildup that was completed under President Ronald Reagan began under Jimmy Carter. President Carter, however, fought with his Joint Chiefs of Staff over the magnitude and speed of the necessary changes. In congressional hearings late in Carter's term, the chiefs spoke out more forcefully against an executive budget than they had since the Eisenhower years. In testimony given before the House Committee on Armed Services' Investigations Subcommittee, Army Chief of Staff Gen. Edward "Shy" Meyer proclaimed that the nation was utterly unprepared for war, had a "hollow Army," and needed bigger and faster improvements than those called for by the president's plan.

General Meyer: We have a tremendous shortfall in our ability to modernize the Army as quickly as I believe we must in order to respond to the threat. . . .

I do not believe that the current budget responds to the Army's needs in meeting the challenge of the eighties. . . .

Right now, as I have said before, we have a hollow Army. Our forward deployed forces are at full strength in Europe, in Panama, and in Korea. Our tactical forces in the United States are some 17,000 under strength. Therefore, anywhere you go in the United States, except for the 82d Airborne Division, which is also filled up, you will find companies and platoons which have been zeroed out.

Gillespie V. "Sonny" Montgomery (D-MS): In other words, we're about two infantry divisions short because, as I understand it, of a shortfall in young men who would fill the combat slots.

General Meyer: The current shortfall is in the combat arms. Although from a pure numbers point of view, if you believe pure numbers, enlistments for the combat arms are up this year because that is where we focused our recruiting effort. Right now, we have filled the infantry requirements.

Mr. Montgomery: Only 38 percent of the young men you recruit today have a high school education or diploma. The other 62 percent are not high school graduates. Is that correct?

General Meyer: That is correct if you mean those we have actually brought on board. It is not correct if you add in those we have recruited under the delayed entry program. Right now, about 50 percent of our recruitments are high school graduates.

Mr. Montgomery: What worries me is if we have to move these units. . . . In effect, they're going to have to go as they are. I'm worried that you're going to take young men and put them in these combat units and they're not going to be trained. They're going overseas, and they're going to get killed.

Where are you going to get the trained personnel to go into these units if you don't have any way to fill them? Of course, I'm going back to the Individual Ready Reserve. We're going to have to get some trained personnel in the Individual Ready Reserve. Where do we get these people? We don't even have an Individual Ready Reserve per se.

General Meyer: You have two choices as far as I am concerned. You are going to have to ultimately return to a draft, along the lines that General Barrow pointed out, or you are going to have to go to an adequately resourced approach to the All-Volunteer Force. Today we have neither, and the country has to come to grips with that very serious problem.

Source: U.S. Congress, House Committee on Armed Services, *National Defense Funding Levels for Fiscal Year 1981: Hearing before the Investigations Subcommittee of the Committee on Armed Services,* 96th Cong., 2d sess., May 29, 1980, H.A.S.C. No. 96-41 (Washington, D.C.: U.S. Government Printing Office, 1961), 9, 11, 18.

Document 8.15
President Jimmy Carter and Governor Ronald Reagan's Presidential Debate, October 28, 1980

In their one debate, President Carter and the man who would succeed him traded accusations and barbs about a number of topics, including arms control. The president's reference to having consulted his daughter, Amy, about the weighty issues of the day entered the folklore surrounding presidential debates.

. . .

Mr. Stone: Governor Reagan—arms control: The President said it was the single most important issue. Both of you have expressed the desire to end the nuclear arms race with Russia, but by methods that are vastly different. You suggest that we scrap the SALT II treaty already negotiated, and intensify the build-up of American power to induce the Soviets to sign a new treaty—one more favorable to us. President Carter, on the other hand, says he will again try to convince a reluctant Congress to ratify the present treaty on the grounds it's the best we can hope to get. Now, both of you cannot be right. Will you tell us why you think you are?

Mr. Reagan: Yes. I think I'm right because I believe that we must have a consistent foreign policy, a strong America, and a strong economy. And then, as we build up our national security, to restore our margin of safety, we at the same time try to restrain the Soviet build-up, which has been going forward at a rapid pace, and for quite some time. The SALT II treaty was the result of negotiations that Mr. Carter's team entered into after he had asked the Soviet Union for a discussion of actual reduction of nuclear strategic weapons. And his emissary, I think, came home in 12 hours having heard a very definite *nyet.* But taking that one no from the Soviet Union, we then went back into negotiations on their terms, because Mr. Carter had canceled the B-1 bomber, delayed the MX, delayed the Trident submarine, delayed the cruise missile, shut down the Missile Man—the three—the Minuteman missile production line, and whatever other things that might have been done. The Soviet Union sat at the table knowing that we had gone forward with unilateral concessions without any reciprocation from them whatsoever. . . .

Mr. Smith: Governor, I have to interrupt you at that point. The time is up for that. But the same question now to President Carter.

Mr. Stone: Yes. President Carter, both of you have expressed the desire to end the nuclear arms race with Russia, but through vastly different methods. The Governor suggests we scrap the SALT II treaty which you negotiated in Vienna or signed in Vienna, intensify the build-up of American power to induce the Soviets to sign a new treaty, one more favorable to us. You, on the other hand, say you will again try to convince a reluctant Congress to ratify the present treaty on the grounds it is the best we can hope to get from the Russians. You cannot both be right. Will you tell us why you think you are?

Mr. Carter: Yes, I'd be glad to. Inflation, unemployment, the cities are all very important issues, but they pale into insignificance in the life and duties of a President when compared with the control of nuclear weapons. Every President who has served in the Oval Office since Harry Truman has been dedicated to the proposition of controlling nuclear weapons. To negotiate with the Soviet Union a balanced, controlled, observable [agreement], and then reducing levels of atomic weaponry, there is a disturbing pattern in the attitude of Governor Reagan. He has never supported any of those arms control agreements—the limited test ban, SALT I, nor the Antiballistic Missile Treaty, nor the Vladivostok Treaty negotiated with the Soviet Union by President Ford—and now he wants to throw into the wastebasket a treaty to control nuclear weapons on a balanced and equal basis between ourselves and the Soviet Union, negotiated over a seven-year period, by myself and my two Republican predecessors. . . .

Mr. Smith: Governor Reagan, you have an opportunity to rebut that.

Mr. Reagan: Yes, I'd like to respond very much. First of all, the Soviet Union [—] if I have been critical of some of the previous agreements, it's because we've been out-negotiated for quite a long time. . . . I am not talking of scrapping. I am talking of taking the treaty back, and going back into negotiations. And I would say to the Soviet Union, we will sit and negotiate with you as long as it takes, to have not only legitimate arms limitation, but to have a reduction of these nuclear weapons to the point that neither one of us represents a threat to the other. That is hardly throwing away a treaty and being opposed to arms limitation.

Mr. Smith: President Carter?

Mr. Carter: Yes. Governor Reagan is making some very misleading and disturbing statements. . . . If President Brezhnev said, we will scrap this treaty, negotiated under three American Presidents over a seven-year period of time, we insist upon nuclear superiority as a basis for future negotiations, and we believe that the launching of a nuclear arms race is a good basis for future negotiations, it's obvious that I, as President, and all Americans, would reject such a proposition. This would mean the resumption of a very dangerous nuclear arms race. It would be very disturbing to American people. It would change the basic tone and commitment that our nation has experienced ever since the Second World War, with all Presidents, Democratic and Republican. And it would also be very disturbing to our allies, all of whom support this nuclear arms treaty. In addition to that, the adversarial relationship between ourselves and the Soviet Union would undoubtedly deteriorate very rapidly. This attitude is extremely dangerous and belligerent in its tone, although it's said with a quiet voice.

Mr. Smith: Governor Reagan?

Mr. Reagan: I know the President's supposed to be replying to me, but sometimes, I have a hard time in connecting what he's saying, with what I have said or what my positions are. I sometimes think he's like the witch doctor that gets mad when a good doctor comes along with a cure that'll work. . . .

Mr. Smith: President Carter, you have the last word on this question.

Mr. Carter: I think, to close out this discussion, it would be better to put into perspective what we're talking about. I had a discussion with my daughter, Amy, the other day, before I came here, to ask her what the most important issue was. She said she thought nuclear weaponry—and the control of nuclear arms. This is a formidable force. Some of these weapons have 10 megatons of explosion. If you put 50 tons of TNT in each one of railroad cars, you would have a carload of TNT—a trainload of TNT stretching across this nation. That's one major war explosion in a warhead. We have thousands, equivalent of megaton, or million tons, of TNT warheads. The control of these weapons is the single major responsibility of a President, and to cast out this commitment of all Presidents, because of some slight technicalities that can be corrected, is a very dangerous approach.

Source: Commission on Presidential Debates, "The Carter-Reagan Presidential Debate," Debate Transcript, October 28, 1980, www.debates.org/pages/trans80b.html.

CHAPTER NINE

Ronald Reagan

Reviving the Cold War and the Presidency

R onald Reagan was elected president because he was not Jimmy Carter. By election day, November 5, 1980, a majority of voters had had enough of the Carter presidency. That summer, only 28 percent of American adults polled by the Gallup Organization approved of the way Carter was doing his job, one of the lowest presidential job approval ratings ever recorded.[1] Although the state of the economy was the public's overriding complaint, President Carter's leadership in foreign affairs was likewise a cause for concern. In 1979 the Soviets had invaded Afghanistan and Iranian radicals had taken hostage

President Ronald Reagan gives a speech on Strategic Arms Reduction Talks (START) at the National Press Club in Washington, D.C., on November 18, 1981. Source: Ronald Reagan Presidential Library.

the American workforce of the U.S. embassy in Tehran. President Carter had been surprised in both cases and seemed helpless to force the Soviets out and to bring the hostages home. The combination of economic suffering and international humiliation was enough to spur anxiety for the nation's future among commentators and ordinary Americans alike.

Ronald Reagan's supporters could not have scripted a better story for his assumption of the presidency. Reagan was a gifted political actor. He had, in fact, been a Hollywood actor before making the move to politics, and he had a talent for conveying to an audience, on screen or in person, his good-natured, deeply felt faith in the American spirit. Whereas Jimmy Carter had first contributed to a crisis of confidence and then scolded the American people for their low morale, Ronald Reagan continuously celebrated "We the People."[2]

Ronald Reagan had been preaching this secular sermon for decades. In the early 1940s, he was involved in liberal politics, but by the end of the decade, he had become persuaded of the threat posed to the United States by Communists, including those believed to be attempting to infiltrate and subvert the Screen Actors Guild, of which he had been elected president in 1947. As his movie career faded, Reagan found new life in 1952 as a celebrity spokesman for General Electric (G.E.). For eight years, he hosted the G.E. Theater, a Sunday night movie, and made increasingly political speeches during his appearances at G.E. plants around the country. Reagan's turn to politics alienated him from his corporate sponsors, who preferred that he focus on noncontroversial themes, but endeared him to conservative Republicans.

During Barry Goldwater's 1964 campaign for the presidency, Reagan was called upon to give a nationally televised speech at the end of October, just days before the polls. The speech, entitled "A Time for Choosing," helped the Goldwater campaign set new records for fundraising. In the address, which came to be known in conservative circles simply as "The Speech," Reagan articulated a Manichean view of the Cold War:

> You and I are told increasingly that we have to choose between a left or right, but I would like to suggest that there is no such thing as a left or right. There is only an up or down—up to a man's age-old dream, the ultimate in individual freedom consistent with law and order—or down to the ant heap of totalitarianism, and regardless of their sincerity, their humanitarian motives, those who would trade our freedom for security have embarked on this downward course. . . .
>
> You and I have a rendezvous with destiny. We will preserve for our children this, the last best hope of man on Earth, or we will sentence them to take the last step into a thousand years of darkness.[3]

Two years later, in 1966, Reagan was elected governor of California. In 1968, Reagan's backers in California began trying to elect their man president. When he at last became president, after serving two terms as governor of California, Reagan not surprisingly embarked on what his ardent conservative supporters, many of whom had been following his career for more than fifteen years, dubbed the "Reagan Revolution."[4] Reagan, like other conservatives, reacted harshly against the perceived failures of modern liberalism. Government had grown too big and too expensive, he declared, sapping the initiative of the entrepreneur and demoralizing the worker.[5] The predictable result was the economic mess that beset the nation in the late 1970s, when "stagflation" brought about double-digit inflation at the same time as unemployment rates rose. In foreign affairs, Reagan reacted against not only Carter's presidency but also the policies of Richard Nixon and Gerald Ford, Carter's Republican predecessors. They, guided by their controversial secretary of state, Henry Kissinger, had pursued détente with the Soviet Union. Détente, Reagan had protested in 1976 during his campaign against sitting president Ford for the Republican nomination, was a sellout to the Soviets. "Détente," Reagan liked to quip, was "what a farmer had with his turkey until Thanksgiving Day."[6]

Détente had weakened the nation's security, conservatives argued. To make the country safe, they asserted, a restoration was in order. Only by restoring the nation to its founding principles, including respect for traditional values and peace through strength, could the damage wrought by liberalism be repaired.

President Reagan's agenda promised a restoration of the American presidency as well. Ever since the impassioned politics of the late 1960s—since Lyndon Johnson's presidency—a succession of chief executives had suffered at the hands of investigative journalists, citizen activists, public-interest lawyers, rapidly multiplying interest groups, and a resurgent Congress. As a result, no president who held office from 1964 to 1980 had managed to serve two full terms, and all four of them left office with their leadership impugned. Johnson had declined to run for reelection in 1968; Richard Nixon had been forced from office in his second term; Gerald Ford, the only president elected to neither the presidency nor the vice presidency, was defeated in 1976; and Jimmy Carter was the first elected president to attempt reelection and fail since Herbert Hoover's disastrous campaign of 1932. Experts on the presidency began to wonder whether the fault lay not in the presidents but in the office itself. Perhaps the demands made of modern presidents were simply so great as to make failure unavoidable. Presidents, it had begun to seem, were captives in a gilded cage. They might, in some destructive sense, hold "the most powerful office in the world," but—short of starting World War III—what could they actually accomplish?

By the end of Reagan's second term, experts no longer spoke of an impossible presidency. Although critics and supporters evaluated Reagan's presidency differently, no one could deny that the presidency was again at the center of American politics, and that Reagan's leadership had had consequences, including a prominent revival of American patriotic expression, which contributed to an ideological offensive in the renewed Cold War. In the 1980s the Cold War and the presidency both made a comeback.

PSYOPs, REBELS, DISSIDENTS, AND ALLIES: THE BUILDING BLOCKS OF A NEW COLD WAR ASSERTIVENESS

The Reagan administration was unusually disciplined, especially in its first term. During that time, a highly effective team of senior officials within the White House established priorities and controlled, to the greatest extent possible, the public perception of the president and the expenditure of his political capital. Because President Reagan's highest priority upon taking office was rebuilding the nation's economy, the president's considerable ambitions to reinvigorate the Cold War were at first often pursued indirectly, even covertly.

PSYOPs and Rebellion

President Reagan wanted to keep the Soviets guessing about American intentions. To accomplish this, he authorized a highly secret campaign of psychological operations (PSYOPs) against the Soviets. At the heart of every PSYOP is deception, the intentional dissemination of false information. In this instance, the president employed battleships, submarines, fighter jets, nuclear-powered submarines, and strategic bombers. All of these were ordered into operation near Soviet borders in mid-February 1981, in ways guaranteed to provoke and worry the Soviets. " 'Sometimes we would send bombers over the North Pole and their radars would click on,' recall[ed] Gen. [John T.] Chain, [a] former Strategic Air Command commander. 'Other times fighter-bombers would probe their Asian or European periphery.' " To make the operation all the more unsettling, they would follow no pattern. In some weeks, several such "false alarms" would be sent. Then the flights would suddenly be halted, only to restart a few weeks later.[7]

The U.S. Navy also contributed to this operation to unsettle the Soviets. Entire aircraft carrier battle groups were ordered into waters where they had never strayed before, close to Soviet borders. Using a variety of deceptive practices, they managed on many occasions to maneuver into their final, provocative positions without first being detected by the Soviets. During one such maneuver, involving a transit of the Greenland-Iceland-United Kingdom Gap, navy fighters conducted "an unprecedented simulated attack on Soviet long-range reconnaissance planes as they refueled in-flight."[8] In May 1981 the Soviet Politburo (the top executive council of the Central Committee of the Communist Party of the Soviet Union) approved a request by General Secretary Leonid Brezhnev and KGB chief Yuri Andropov to initiate a large-scale intelligence-gathering operation. The United States was making preparations for an attack, Andropov asserted.

Reagan gave the Soviets further reason for concern in Central America. There is some irony to this, because the president's unwillingness in 1981 to rally the public behind any sort of overt military action was regarded as timidity by some cold warriors at home, including Reagan's first secretary of state, Gen. Alexander Haig. Haig bridled at the White House's tight control of the administration's agenda and Reagan's decision to focus the public's attention first on domestic economic issues rather than foreign problems. He was so heedless of the president's priorities that at a National Security Council (NSC) meeting just three months into the Reagan presidency, he recommended that the United States launch a military offensive against Fidel Castro's Cuba.

Cuban forces had been serving as proxies for the Soviet Union in Africa for years. More recently, Cuban arms, imported from the Soviet Union and Eastern Europe, had begun to be smuggled in large quantities to Central America to prop up the new Communist government of Nicaragua, headed by president Daniel Ortega and the Sandinista regime, and to spur a Communist insurgency in El Salvador. "Just give me the word," Haig is reported to have told the president, forgetting decorum as well as the fact that the secretary of state is not in the military chain of command, "and I'll make that [expletive] island a parking lot."[9]

President Reagan was not about to bomb Cuba, but neither was he going to invite Ortega to the White House, as President Carter had. Reagan cut off aid to the Sandinista government and ordered U.S. naval exercises off the coast of neighboring Honduras, to remind the Nicaraguan government of the United States' ability to project its military power to Central America. In March 1981, after rejecting Secretary Haig's provocative advice, the president authorized the Central Intelligence Agency (CIA) to interdict arms flows through Nicaragua to other Central American countries. In August 1981 officials of the U.S. government helped create a small 500-man paramilitary organization of Nicaraguans in exile, known as the "Contras," to carry out this mission. By the end of the year, the president had authorized the CIA, under the direction of committed cold warrior and CIA director William Casey, to "support and conduct" operations against Nicaragua (**Document 9.1**). The Contras, who were reminiscent of the Cuban exiles trained by the CIA during the Eisenhower and Kennedy administrations, would remain neither small nor covert for long.

The U.S. public was never successfully mobilized behind the administration's fight against Communist expansion in Central America. In 1982 only 19 percent of adults in the United States favored the use of U.S. forces in a hypothetical scenario to prevent the government of El Salvador from being defeated by "leftist rebels." Four years later, the figure had only risen to 25 percent.[10] Many people could not even keep straight which side the United States was on in the Nicaraguan civil war, which was not necessarily a bad thing for the White House. The beauty of the Contra operation was that it was relatively cost-free to the U.S. public, and therefore to the president.

The support of indigenous rebel fighters had been favored by previous presidents as a means to fight the Cold War. The 1970s expansion of Soviet influence into new parts of the world, however, presented the United States with unparalleled opportunities to strike against Soviet interests. In the 1980s the Reagan administration embraced several such opportunities and codified the practice as the Reagan Doctrine. Under the direction of Director of Central Intelligence Casey, an NSC planning group elaborated upon the doctrine in the document the president endorsed as National Security Decision Directive 75 (NSDD 75) in January 1983. According to NSDD 75, it was U.S. policy to "contain and over time reverse Soviet expansionism" by targeting Soviet client states. The United States would use covert and overt means in such countries "to encourage democratic movements and forces," that is, rebel fighters.[11]

The Contra project was an early proving ground of the Reagan Doctrine. There were other countries that were also potentially appropriate for the application of this policy; these included Afghanistan; Cambodia; and several in Africa, namely Angola, Ethiopia, and Mozambique. Congressional reluctance to back rebels in Ethiopia and Mozambique prevented the administration from sending any aid to the forces fighting in those countries against Soviet-directed governments. Very limited aid was provided in Cambodia, by a Congress still leery of intervention in Southeast Asia. The United States provided more support for Angolan forces but did so inconsistently. Afghanistan was the only country in addition to Nicaragua in which the Reagan Doctrine was conspicuously and consistently applied.

Under Reagan, with significant help from certain Republicans in Congress who made Afghanistan a personal cause, money, arms, and intelligence flowed to the rebels who were fighting a holy war against the infidel Soviets who had invaded their country. Regarding Afghanistan, Casey exulted:

> Here's the beauty of the Afghanistan operation. Usually it looks like the big bad Americans are beating up on the natives. Afghanistan is just the reverse. . . . We don't make it our war. The *mujahedin* [Afghan resistance fighters] have all the motivation they need. All we have to do is give them help, only more of it.[12]

The military rulers of Pakistan, located between India and Afghanistan, allowed American aid to be funneled through their country and eventually gave the rebel fighters sanctuary and the civilian populations of entire Afghan villages and towns refuge along the border. The price of Pakistan's assistance was high, as it included the United States' developing "a blind spot concerning Pakistan's nuclear weapons development capability."[13] Early in Reagan's second term, a turning point was reached in the Afghanistan mission, when the White House decided to support the rebels with "all available means," including portable shoulder-fired anti-aircraft weapons with automated targeting. These Stinger missiles proved remarkably effective in the hands of the Afghan rebels. Even after the

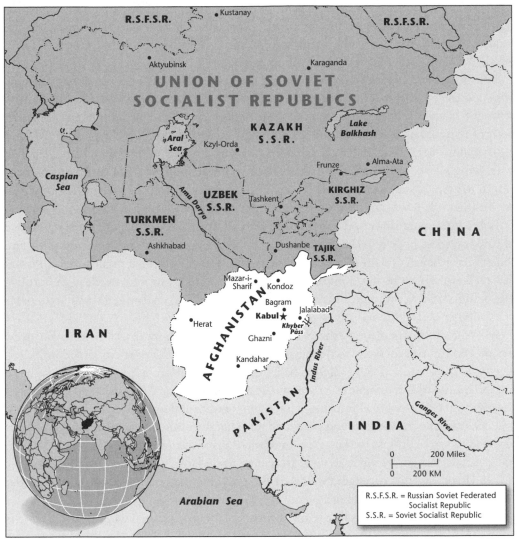

Afghanistan and Neighboring Soviet Republics, 1979

Soviet Union began to extricate its armed services from this quagmire—tentatively in 1986 and in earnest in 1988—the CIA kept open the flow of arms to those willing to use them against Soviet troops.

Supporting Dissent in Eastern Europe

The Carter administration had pursued a controversial policy of openly promoting human rights around the world. Republicans, including Reagan, had ridiculed Carter's seemingly naïve demand for human rights under authoritarian governments allied with the United States. They made a distinction, however, between the pursuit of human rights in such countries and in totalitarian states such as the Soviet Union.[14] In the latter case, a human-rights foreign policy was not only appropriate but imperative. Events in Poland gave the Reagan administration the opportunity to promote both human rights and its broader Cold War aim of rolling back Soviet dominance.

Polish dissidents appealed to the West for support in 1981, as a decade-long economic crisis led to a government crackdown on reformers. During the 1970s, the Polish government made a series of concessions to rioting students and striking laborers, which bought temporary social peace but did nothing to improve the Polish economy. To fund industrial modernization, the government borrowed heavily from Western banks. The borrowing proved sufficient to burden the state with debt but was not sufficient to arrest a decline in living standards. While the economic situation worsened, the Polish political environment grew unstable with the emergence of two new political actors.

Poles derived enormous pride in the election of Cardinal Karol Wojtyla, the archbishop of Krakow, to be pope in 1978. The dissonance between national pride in a new pope and the official atheism of Communist doctrine strengthened Polish nationalists, who wished to break away from Soviet domination. Pope John Paul II, moreover, though hardly a "Reaganite" in his pronouncements on international affairs, challenged totalitarian practices and hypocrisy.

In 1980 another new force emerged in Polish politics. The trade union Solidarity grew out of a committee formed to coordinate strike activities at the port city of Gdansk. Solidarity, and its leader, Lech Walesa, challenged the Polish government for the right to organize industrial trade unions, as well as the release of political prisoners, an end to censorship, and other political reforms. The union's political demands grew out of its own practice of democracy. All its top positions were filled through open elections, a process that was in stark contrast to the practices of the Polish Communist government. To gain social peace, the government acceded to many of Solidarity's demands. With this highly visible victory against the state, Solidarity became, in a matter of months, a rival to the Communist Party for control of Poland.

In 1981, Ronald Reagan's first year in office, Poland experienced wildcat strikes (unannounced work stoppages), a veiled threat of military intervention from the Warsaw Pact nations, an emotional appeal to dissidents for calm by the Catholic primate of Poland, and the elevation of the nation's defense minister, Gen. Wojciech Jaruzelski, first to the premiership of the government and then to the position of first secretary of the Polish Communist Party. After Solidarity demanded a national referendum on the future of the Communist Party in Poland, Jaruzelski declared martial law on December 12, 1981, suspended Solidarity, and arrested Walesa and thousands of other dissidents. The Polish ambassador to the United States and his family defected to America.

President Reagan gave the United States' response to these actions in a Christmas message on December 23 (**Document 9.2**). He announced economic sanctions intended to punish the Polish government, including the termination of Export-Import Bank credit insurance, which had provided financial incentives for U.S. firms to export goods and services to Poland. The following week, the president announced further sanctions, this time directed against the Soviet Union. Most U.S. observers of events in Poland by this time had concluded that there remained little Polish sovereignty. The surest way to influence Warsaw's ruling elite was, therefore, to influence Soviet leaders in the Kremlin. Reagan's new sanctions included the postponement of talks on a new long-term grain agreement and the suspension of the issuance or renewal of U.S. export licenses for electronic equipment, computers, and other high-tech products.

Working within the Alliance: NATO and the Euromissiles

The United States had little success in leading its major European allies to join in sanctions in response to events in Poland. Even Prime Minister Margaret Thatcher, Reagan's firmest ally in the Cold War, "resented this American policy, which fell outside the 'norm' of consensus on NATO foreign policy."[15] Germany was greatly opposed to sanctions, as it went against the grain of the policy of Ostpolitik, which aimed to change Eastern Europe through increased economic and cultural exchanges. In a communiqué issued in January 1982, the foreign ministers of the member states of the North Atlantic Treaty Organization (NATO) condemned the Polish military government for imposing martial law and the Soviet Union for intervening in the affairs of another state. As for sanctions against the Soviets, though, the ministers merely agreed that each NATO member country would have to examine its own relations with the Soviet Union and come to its own decision (**Document 9.3**).

This outcome was disappointing to the United States because Germany and especially France were heavily involved in a major pipeline project with the Soviets, which U.S. conservatives viewed as a threat. The Trans-Siberian Pipeline, when completed, would considerably enhance the Soviet Union's capability to earn much-needed hard currency by directly transporting to the West a portion of the nation's vast petrochemical reserves. As President Reagan recounted bitterly in his memoirs, "The reaction of some of our allies suggested that money spoke louder to them than principle."[16]

The Reagan administration had greater success, however, when it mattered the most—in the pursuit of the "dual-track" deployment of intermediate-range nuclear missiles to Europe. Under this approach, a continuation of Carter-era policy, the Americans pursued a deal with the Soviets that would make the deployment of such missiles by the West unnecessary, while simultaneously preparing the missiles to be delivered on schedule, in November 1983. The Soviets, naturally, worked assiduously on their own dual track, by which they attempted to block the deployment of U.S. missiles—essentially by cheering on and, to the extent possible, manipulating the peace movement in Western Europe—while declining to take seriously Western demands for the removal of the Soviet intermediate-range missiles that already threatened Western Europe. Meanwhile, the Soviets reinforced their considerable Soviet and Warsaw Pact advantage in a possible European war (**Document 9.4**). Ultimately, the Euromissile deployment took place as planned, giving Reagan (and Carter, by extension) a gratifying diplomatic victory. After a year's hiatus, during which the Soviets declined to negotiate in protest of the West's alleged belligerency, negotiations resumed, this time in earnest.

CONFRONTATION

The Reagan administration's purpose in asserting U.S. interests against the Soviet Union and associated states was not to confront the enemy for confrontation's sake. Nor was the defeat or demise of the Soviet Union considered at the time to be a plausible goal. Rather, the point was to regain the initiative in what was presumed to be a struggle without end. By taking the initiative, the United States might demonstrate its resolve and compel the Soviets to negotiate in good faith. The ultimate objective, according to an administration strategy document written in the spring of 1982, was "a fundamentally different East-West relationship by the end of this decade" (**Document 9.5**). To put it another way, the Reagan administration wanted détente but believed that the only way to get a relaxation of tensions worthy of the name "détente" was to frighten the Soviets into submission.

Public confrontation with the Soviet Union on the battlefield of ideas was an integral part of the plan. Such confrontation served two purposes. It reclaimed for the United States the moral high ground abandoned in détente. It also provided the emotional foundation for the only sort of sacrifice that most Americans were ever asked to make in the renewed Cold War: to support with their tax dollars, their votes, and their scientifically sampled opinions a substantial arms buildup so that the United States might negotiate with the Soviets from a position of strength.

Because there was ground to make up in the arms race, and the Soviets had extended their influence over much of the globe, the confrontation was bound to take time, years if not decades. Therefore, in the rhetorically charged atmosphere of ideological combat—as well as at the peripheries of the Soviet and American spheres of influence, where actual armed conflict took place through intermediaries—things were going to have to get worse before they could get better.

President Reagan launched a remarkable ideological assault on the enemy in June 1982 in a speech before the British Parliament, in which he prophesied that communism, because of its own inherent frailties, would be placed on the "ashheap of history" (**Document 9.6**). The words were harsh, but the concept was a throwback to the Cold War's origins. Like George Kennan, the author of the original containment doctrine (see **Document 1.6**), Reagan viewed communism as an aberrant and ultimately doomed form of government. Under the right circumstances, which the United States and its allies had an obligation to bring about, communism's internal contradictions would come to the fore, revealing its weakness and absurdity.

Ideological confrontation was just part of the Reagan plan. The comprehensive strategy, as detailed in a January 1983 NSC document intended for the administration's foreign policy elite, also called for a sustained military buildup, nonmilitary efforts to undermine Soviet domination of Eastern Europe, the provision of aid to rebels in the third world, and even support for the Communist People's Republic of China to increase Soviet vulnerability in the East (**Document 9.7**). Politically, the strategy involved hanging tough against critics who were perceived as likely to decry the departure from presumably friendly relations.

As the ideological offensive continued into 1983, the key players were high-level Reagan appointees, including Jeane Kirkpatrick, U.S. ambassador to the United Nations; Michael Novak, Reagan's pick to represent the United States on the UN Commission on Human Rights; and Charles Wick, an old friend Reagan appointed to head the United States Information Agency. The State Department, meanwhile, under the leadership of Haig and then George Shultz, published a series of damning reports detailing Soviet perfidy, including the use of chemical weapons in Afghanistan, the abuse of human rights, the promotion of terrorism, and the systematic and flagrant violation of arms control treaties with the United States.

The most memorable ideological assaults, however, were those made by the president himself. Reagan boldly proclaimed that the Soviet Union was "the focus of evil in the world" and called the rival superpower an "evil empire" in a March 1983 speech at the annual convention of the National Association of Evangelicals (NAE; **Document 9.8**). Evangelical Christians were becoming an increasingly important constituency for the Republican Party. As voters, they were most interested in social issues, and the majority of Reagan's speech to the NAE on this occasion addressed themes such as abortion and school prayer. To Reagan, it made perfect sense to seek religiously based support in the Cold War as well, for he saw the war in profoundly moralistic and spiritual terms. He had been denouncing "Godless Communism" for decades.[17] After he survived a nearly successful assassination attempt on March 30, 1981, moreover, some authors speculated that the president believed he had been spared so that he could continue God's work in the Cold War.[18] Such commentators have made a great deal of Reagan's diary entry the day he returned to work at the White House: "Whatever happens now, I owe my life to God and will try to serve Him in any way I can."[19] Others said more simply that the president was unabashed in his belief in America's goodness and eager to recruit new converts to the support of his foreign policy. Critics called him paranoid and deluded. The debate over the character of Reagan's beliefs became especially bitter in the wake of his surprise announcement of a new Cold War program: the Strategic Defense Initiative, or "Star Wars."

"Star Wars" and an Arms Buildup

Ronald Reagan proved surprisingly pragmatic on some points as president. He compromised, for example, on the need for tax increases not long after leading Congress to enact a historic income tax cut in 1981. On certain matters, however, he gave no ground over the course of his presidency. The Strategic Defense Initiative (SDI) was one of those issues about which the president displayed an "awesome stubbornness."[20]

Confrontation with the "evil empire" through rhetoric and an arms buildup, in the strategic view promulgated by the Reagan administration, was intended to lead to a solidly grounded reduction in hostilities and a "new relationship." Not all of the administration officials debating foreign and military policy were fully committed to this goal, but Reagan was sincere. He went so far as to envision the possibility of ridding the world of nuclear weapons altogether, thereby placing at least an upper limit to the destructiveness of armed conflict. If the United States' scientists and engineers could provide the nation with protection against strategic nuclear missiles, he reasoned in a March 1983 address, the country would be safe from the fear of nuclear war. By sharing the anti-missile technology with its adversaries, the United States could make freedom from such fear a universal human right (**Document 9.9**).

The impetus for SDI, which critics labeled "Star Wars," came from a loose-knit group of cold warriors in Congress and the defense community. In 1979 Sen. Malcolm Wallop, R-Wyo., lobbied his fellow senators and others to support of a laser-based space weapon system to defend against nuclear missile attacks. He was supported in his efforts by Lt. Gen. Daniel O. Graham, the former director of the Defense Intelligence Agency, and Edward Teller, a legendary nuclear scientist who favored conservative defense policies. In May 1981 these three helped to found High Frontier, a private organization committed to advancing missile defense.

High Frontier's ideas appealed to an influential group within the Reagan White House and on Capitol Hill: the critics of the 1972 Anti-Ballistic Missile (ABM) Treaty (see **Document 6.17**). To Richard Allen, Reagan's first national security adviser, and others, including William Schneider, chief of the national security division within the Office and Management and Budget, anything that would break apart the ABM Treaty regime was a step in the right direction. The treaty, Allen and Schneider believed, represented the defeatist policies of the past and was a psychological as well as a technical barrier to restarting the arms race, which they thought essential for the United States' security.

Attempts to launch the effort for a new anti-missile defense system faced substantial opposition, however, even from within the administration. The mere pursuit of SDI had the potential to destabilize the very balance of terror that it was meant to supersede. If the Americans were to come remotely close to achieving a defense against strategic weapons, the Soviets might well reason that it would be preferable to use theirs while they still had value. Pragmatists within the administration, such as Secretary of State George Shultz and White House chief of staff James Baker, urged caution in the face of such a potentially destabilizing outcome. In addition, SDI might simply be impossible. There was no guarantee of success, and the scientific, engineering, and financial challenges were staggering.

Regardless, President Reagan was deeply committed to the program. He believed that SDI would threaten the Soviets in an area where they were particularly vulnerable: high technology. High technology had two major attributes that gave the advantage to the United States. First, it was expensive. SDI was potentially so expensive that critics warned it might bankrupt the U.S. government. The president did not back down. "Defense," Reagan repeatedly insisted, "is not a budget issue. You spend what you need." [21] In the aftermath of the Cold War, a myth developed that SDI's enormous potential cost was actually an ingenious plot to bankrupt the Soviet government. However, according to Jack Matlock Jr., who served as U.S. ambassador to the Soviet Union during the late Reagan administration, "none of the key players were operating from the assumption that we were going to do the Soviet Union in" by pushing them into bankruptcy through the pursuit of missile defense. [22] Still, over time, the spending demanded by the program would be difficult for the Soviets to match.[23] But SDI was more than expensive; it was at or beyond the cutting edge of science and technology.

There was a new attitude among U.S. defense planners in the 1980s about technology and science in the arms race. In the 1950s U.S. experts were sometimes openly envious of the Soviet Union's alleged advantage in technological competition. After all, the Soviet government could simply *command* heavy industry to build more missiles, rather than more luxury cars, and scientists to research military, not consumer, technologies. By the 1980s, however, the advantages of a capitalist market in balancing the need for both consumer goods and national security were widely apparent. The shift in military technology and the arms race, moreover, from heavy industrial manufacturing to increasing reliance on information technology and computing undercut whatever advantage the Soviets might once have enjoyed. Computers, which had become essential to the arms race, were difficult for a totalitarian government to embrace. President Reagan saw in this a great opportunity.

A final reason why the president favored SDI was that he viewed the long-standing balance of terror, rationalized in the doctrine of mutual assured destruction, as exactly what its acronym implied: MAD. Reagan shared with many other Americans of his and his children's generations a visceral fear of nuclear weapons and nuclear war. In the words of Lt. Gen. Edward L. Rowney, Reagan's chief arms control negotiator, "Reagan really want [ed] to abolish nuclear weapons."[24]

SDI thus became the cornerstone of an across-the-board military buildup aimed at retaking the initiative in the Cold War. In the pro-defense atmosphere of the 1980 campaign season, Jimmy Carter had proclaimed that if elected to a second term, he would spend $1.27 trillion on defense, from fiscal year 1982 to fiscal year 1986. Reagan had promised to spend more. In the emergency budgeting process that Reagan oversaw in the first month of his presidency, during which the outgoing Carter administration's budgets were reworked to conform to the promise of the Reagan Revolution, projected defense spending over this same time frame was increased by 10 percent per year. The members of the Joint Chiefs of Staff (JCS) thought it was "Christmas in February."[25]

The Reagan arms buildup was so substantial and fast-paced that it was criticized even by its beneficiaries. The real Reagan strategy, said a senior academic specialist on defense, was not MAD, it was "M-O-R-E."[26] The assumption behind the rapid buildup, however, was that the armed forces, their supporters in Congress, and the nation's major defense contractors had a good grasp of what was needed. They had been asking for what they needed for years; now it was time to give it to them. As a consequence, although the Reagan buildup did not overlook the need for greater pay for military personnel and an expansion of their numbers, the percentage of the defense budget spent on weapons acquisition increased substantially, from 26 percent in 1981 to 38 percent in 1987. There was waste involved, but in the Pentagon as well as at the White House, there was a feeling that this was a historic opportunity that must not be missed. "More was available than Defense could spend wisely," admitted Adm. William Crowe Jr., who became chairman of the JCS in October 1985. But he readily acknowledged that it had been the sensible thing to "spend it anyway even if not wisely, knowing that in five years we won't have it."[27]

The Reagan military buildup also expanded the U.S. arsenal across the spectrum of possible conflict. New strategic weapons—the B-1 bomber and the MX missile—were at last taken beyond the prototype phase, produced in quantity, and deployed. The U.S. Navy undertook to enlarge its battle fleet to 600 ships, a number endorsed in the Republican Party Platform of 1980,[28] and this goal became a rallying cry for two successive navy secretaries under Reagan, John F. Lehman and James Webb. The strengthening of conventional fighting forces, the last step in the buildup, was the manifestation of a new doctrine of horizontal escalation. Utilizing this concept, the United States might respond to a provocation in one area of the globe with an assault upon Soviet interests elsewhere, such as North Korea, Cuba, or even Vietnam.

Reagan's endorsement of the MX missile was a particularly symbolic act. The MX was a proposed heavy intercontinental ballistic missile (ICBM) intended to counter the Soviet deployment in the mid-1970s of the SS-18, the most powerful ICBM ever. The Soviet SS-18 arsenal could theoretically, according to 1987 Defense Department projections, "destroy 65–80% of the U.S. ICBM force, using two warheads against each. Even after such an attack, there would still be more than 1,000 SS-18 warheads available for further strikes against U.S. targets."[29] In the event of a nuclear exchange, the MX arsenal would presumably not share the same fate as the rest of the American ICBM force because it would be based in such a way as to lessen its vulnerability. That, at least, had been the promise, but also the source of much controversy during the Carter Administration. The debate raged over whether the MX missiles should be based on a rail system, to keep them mobile, or in silos.

The Reagan administration opted at first for the simplest of solutions to the MX basing controversy: the new missiles would be housed in existing, but "hardened," silos. As a further protective measure, the missiles would be concentrated rather than dispersed. This counterintuitive measure would arguably increase the survivability of the missiles, if the blast from the first incoming ICBM detonated the second Soviet missile, which in turn detonated the third, and so on, leading to a series of explosions at ever-greater heights above the target. Only a fraction of the missile field would, if this bit of theorizing was correct, be destroyed. Congress rejected this quick-fix approach to the basing problem that had dogged MX development for years and required further studies.

The administration followed Congress's mandate by turning the problem of MX basing over to a presidential commission headed by Brent Scowcroft, President Ford's former national security adviser and a retired general. After analyzing all options, the commission agreed with the administration's initial idea to utilize existing silos. The ostensibly nonpolitical commission had wisely made the influential Democratic chairman of the House Armed Services Committee, Leslie "Les" Aspin of Wisconsin, a virtual coauthor of its report. With his support, a sufficient number of Democrats voted with the Republicans to provide funding for fifty MX missiles—one half the number initially requested by the administration, but still a considerable enhancement of the American nuclear deterrent.

The Reagan buildup also led to the 1985 deployment of the U.S. Air Force's B-1 bomber. The B-1, put into production as the B-1B, is a "stealthy" aircraft designed to avoid radar detection. It can carry a payload of air-launched cruise missiles, short-range attack missiles, and plain-old gravity bombs. Officially designated the Advanced Manned Strategic Aircraft (AMSA), the craft was unofficially known as "America's Most Studied Aircraft," and it was a considerable political achievement for President Reagan to push it, finally, into production.[30] Also entering the U.S. arsenal during the Reagan years were the U.S. Army's first new tank since 1959, the M1A1 or "Abrams," a 57-ton behemoth capable of 66 miles per hour, and the two tactical nuclear weapons systems deployed by NATO in 1983, the Pershing II and Tomahawk ground-launched cruise missiles.

A Year of Maximum Danger: The War Scares of 1983

The world took notice of Reagan's confrontational approach in the Cold War. In Western Europe and the United States, a peace movement materialized that took for its aim to freeze the nuclear arms race. The movement's adherents demanded an immediate moratorium on the development or deployment of additional nuclear weapons, unilaterally on the part of the United States if need be. President Reagan's supporters sometimes derided American and European peace activists as part of the "peace at any price" constituency, unwittingly (or perhaps not) doing the bidding of the Soviets. The president himself, however, shared the dream of a world without nuclear weapons, and he continuously asserted that the ultimate goal of building up U.S. military strength was to permit the superpowers to draw down, equally, to reduced levels. But despite the administration's sustained effort to remind the U.S. public of the stakes involved and the necessity of developing new weapons, polls in 1982 and 1983 showed that 70 percent of the nation's adult population believed that both the United States and the Soviet Union should immediately halt "the testing, production, and deployment of nuclear weapons." [31]

In June 1982 the Democratic chairman of the House Committee on Foreign Affairs, Clement Zablocki of Wisconsin, proposed an immediate freeze. His resolution was countered by one sponsored by two Republicans and one Democrat that called for an eventual freeze at "equal and substantially reduced levels." [32] After a lengthy debate over both resolutions that extended into the evening of August 5, 1982, the president won a "major symbolic victory," in the words of the *New York Times,* with a two-vote margin of victory in favor of the White-House backed resolution.[33]

The 1982 midterm elections brought a net increase of twenty-six seats in the House for the Democratic Party, which interpreted its victory as a mandate to oppose Reagan's foreign policy, among other things. Even before the new Congress came into session, the invigorated Democratic majority passed the first Boland Amendment prohibiting covert support for the Contras, and—as discussed earlier—forced the administration to study MX basing options yet again. After the new Congress was seated in January 1983, the House Foreign Affairs Committee voted overwhelmingly, 27-9, to recommend the Zablocki Resolution to the full House for reconsideration. On the floor, the resolution was damaged by its author's "humiliating" performance in debate. Zablocki was unprepared to defend his own resolution, and "appeared bewildered and unable to answer pointed questions about how a nuclear freeze would work." [34] Even so, his resolution passed this time, after over forty hours of debate, by a vote of 278 to 149 (**Document 9.10**). The resolution forced no change in the U.S., much less the Soviet, arsenal or weapons programs and thus was "more symbolic than real," in the words of the *New York Times*.[35] But symbolism, especially in the Reagan years, was a force to be reckoned with.

Soviet officials were even more alarmed about the potential for nuclear war in 1983 than were all but Reagan's most harsh domestic critics. Of course, the Soviets had been subjected to the president's PSYOPs campaign, which had been designed precisely to unnerve them. Two years into the Reagan presidency, the Soviet debate over the president's intentions—did he or did he not intend to launch a surprise nuclear attack on the Soviet Union?—had sparked a fear of war among the Soviet general population, not just the elite. The Soviet leadership inflamed the public's fear. General Secretary Yuri Andropov reacted to President Reagan's announcement of the Strategic Defense Initiative in March 1983 with harsh rhetoric of his own. He accused Reagan of "deliberately lying" about Soviet military power to justify SDI. He asserted to the Soviet press that Reagan's pursuit of the missile defense system "is not just irresponsible, it is insane." The president was "putting the entire world in jeopardy."[36]

In November 1983 an annual NATO command exercise, ABLE ARCHER 83, was undertaken. The 1983 operation featured two innovations that triggered a Soviet panic. First, initial plans (later modified) called for the participation of high-level U.S. officials, even the president. Second, "ABLE ARCHER 83 included a practice drill that took NATO forces through a full-scale simulated release of nuclear weapons."[37] Based on these changes to the yearly routine, when the exercise began, the KGB concluded that it was the U.S. president's intention to use the exercise as a cover for the start of a nuclear war. KGB headquarters sent urgent messages to its officers throughout Europe seeking confirmation.

The CIA learned of the Soviet misinterpretation of the training operation through a double agent. President Reagan, upon reading a report about the episode, commented to National Security Adviser Robert "Bud" McFarlane, "I don't see how they could believe that—but it's something to think about." In a later meeting that same day, the president "spoke about the biblical prophecy of Armageddon, a final world-ending battle between good and evil, a topic that fascinated the President. McFarlane thought it was not accidental that Armageddon was on Reagan's mind."[38]

In December 1983, Reagan reached out to General Secretary Andropov, and initiated a new approach to the Soviet Union. He personally wrote to the Soviet leader, affirming his interest in arms reduction and seeking to assure Andropov that the United States' intentions were purely pacific. In January 1984, President Reagan gave a major address on U.S.-Soviet relations (**Document 9.11**). It was time, said the president, to seek out avenues for cooperation, while not overlooking the considerable gulf between the two sides. In addition to human rights and regional issues, the president pointed to bilateral relations and arms control as areas in which he believed relations could and should be improved. When Andropov died on February 9, 1984, Reagan immediately wrote to his successor, Konstantin Chernenko, to assure him personally that the United States "do not seek to challenge the security of the Soviet Union."[39]

Results from this new orientation were slow to come, in part because of continued instability in the leadership of the Kremlin. Chernenko's reign lasted just thirteen months before he too died in office. Only when his successor, the much younger Mikhail Gorbachev, consolidated power, was there sufficient stability on the Soviet side to justify optimism regarding the prospects for difficult, possibly protracted, negotiations on issues such as arms control. Before then, in any event, the Reagan administration faced serious challenges closer to home. The president's response to these new troubles revealed that—however much the war scare of 1983 may have unsettled him, and however much he hoped to improve bilateral relations with the Soviets—the Cold War was still on.

THE USE OF FORCE

The Reagan administration, as determined as it was to build up the military, was decidedly reluctant to deploy U.S. armed forces in combat. In part, this reflected priorities. The White House focused on the threat from the Soviet Union, where the imperative response was to maintain a credible deterrence: as long as the United States maintained sufficient force, it would never have to fight its principal adversary directly. Also, like the Ford and Carter administrations, the Reagan administration was constrained by the legacy of the Vietnam War. The Reagan Doctrine provided one way out of the resultant dilemma, as the United States could sometimes rely on fighters of other countries. But what about situations in which there was no alternative to the use of U.S. troops?

In 1982 President Reagan ordered U.S. forces into Lebanon. This was not a Cold War mission, but rather an effort to promote security after the Israeli Defense Forces had pushed the Palestine Liberation Organization (PLO) out of Lebanon. As the Lebanese political situation deteriorated, armed militias battled one another against a backdrop of terrorist assaults. With U.S. forces in harm's way, Reagan's cabinet and senior military officials debated among themselves the criteria for the use of U.S. forces in hostilities.

Defense Secretary Casper Weinberger and the members of the JCS did not see any value or a clear military objective for the United States in the Lebanese operation. Secretary of State Shultz argued that the mission was an essential counterpart to diplomatic efforts underway to restore Lebanese sovereignty. Weinberger and the service chiefs, he believed, were still not over Vietnam. Before the debate was over in Washington, it was settled in Lebanon. On October 23, 1983, a truck carrying 5,000 pounds of explosives slammed into the U.S. Marine barracks at the Beirut Airport, killing 241 marines. National Security Adviser McFarlane, on Weinberger's side in the internal conflict, ignored the president's order to devise a retaliatory strike.[40] The marines were withdrawn from Lebanon in February 1984.

Just two days after the bombing in Beirut, however, marines, sailors, airmen, and soldiers were deployed into combat in Grenada, an island in the Caribbean, against Latin American leftists. Grenada had been a British colony until 1974. In a bloodless coup, Maurice Bishop, the leader of the leftist New Jewel Movement, took power in 1979. With financial backing from East Germany and the Soviet Union, as well as from Canada and the European Community, he stabilized control. The press was heavily censored, political opposition outlawed and potential rivals imprisoned. When church leaders spoke out about such abuses, Bishop threatened them with the same fate as befell his secular critics. Meanwhile, Cuban construction workers were brought in to build an airport at Port Salinas, supposedly to accommodate the tourist trade.

President Reagan responded to Bishop's actions by adding Grenada to a list of nations to which the United States opposed lending from international financial institutions. The president also scoffed publicly at the rationale for the Cuban-built air base, and he warned that events in Grenada were part of the overall plan of the Soviet Union to undermine U.S. security and "limit our capacity to act in more distant places, such as Europe, the Persian Gulf, the Indian Ocean, the Sea of Japan."[41] In a dramatic speech that recalled the theatrics of Adlai Stevenson at the UN during the Cuban Missile Crisis, Reagan gave a televised address, on March 23, 1983, in which he displayed aerial reconnaissance photographs of Grenada and Nicaragua, making the case that both countries were being used by the Soviets, operating through the Cubans, to funnel arms into El Salvador, Honduras, and Costa Rica.

Bishop, fearing a U.S. invasion, freed political prisoners and took other steps to reform his image. Ironically, this made an invasion more likely, because in response to Bishop's veer to the center, a more dangerous man, Bernard Coard, took power from and executed Bishop on October 19, 1983. Six days later, after an urgent appeal from the Organization of Eastern Caribbean States for assistance, the United States launched its first significant military operation since the Vietnam War.

With the participation of about 300 troops from Jamaica, some 7,000 U.S. forces invaded the island on October 25, 1983, engaged in combat with the approximately 700 Cubans there, overwhelmed the armed supporters and functionaries of the Grenadian People's Revolutionary Government, and took possession of the capital, the airport, and everything else that might be considered a strategic asset. Eighteen Americans, forty-five Grenadians, and twenty-four Cubans were killed in the fighting.

The operation had been championed by Secretary of State Shultz and resisted by the Pentagon. At the UN, Ambassador Kirkpatrick gave an impassioned speech in support of the action, arguing that Grenada had surrendered its sovereignty by allowing itself to be permanently overtaken by outsiders. The fighting was over in just a few days, but news reports highlighted massive confusion among the U.S. forces, and many Democratic members of Congress hesitated before rallying to the president's side. Although the White House had justified the invasion as a battle in the Cold War, and supporters yearned to lay to rest the ghost of Vietnam by show of a successful use of force, the administration stilled its critics by focusing on the fate of Americans resident in Grenada, especially a group of students at a Grenada medical school. When the medical students were returned to the United States on October 26, they thanked the armed forces for their rescue. One of the first students off the plane that carried them back home kissed the ground. Few voices criticized the mission after this dramatic show of gratitude. The Grenada operation was, then, a victory, but its meaning was far from clear. Even Gerald Ford and Jimmy Carter, after all, had sent American service members on potentially dangerous *rescue* missions.

The most significant legacies of Grenada were a reform of the JCS that would arguably make the use of force more effective in the future and, paradoxically, a restrictive doctrine on the use of force in the first place. The first, the Goldwater-Nichols Act, was the most significant change in the organization of the military command structure since the 1947 National Security Act.

The Grenada invasion was marred by numerous instances of interservice rivalry, pettiness, and communication fiascoes. In one notorious example, a soldier needing to communicate with a ship just off shore had to use his personal calling card at a pay phone to call his superiors on base in the United States, to implore their assistance in getting a message to the ship for support fire. In another instance, Army Maj. Gen. Norman Scwharzkopf had to threaten to court martial a marine colonel before the colonel would agree to fly Army Rangers ashore in marine helicopters. The Rangers were ready to go, while the colonel's marines needed another twenty-four hours before they would be in position to launch, but the colonel at first insisted, "We don't fly Army soldiers in Marine helicopters."[42] In the Grenada operation, such incidents were farcical but not consequential. As the acerbic former secretary of state Alexander Haig commented, the "Providence Police Force" could have carried out the mission.[43] In a more serious encounter, farce could become tragedy. As a result, a boost was given to an ongoing effort to strengthen the position of the chairman of the Joint Chiefs of Staff (CJCS) and otherwise to create the conditions under which true "jointness" could prevail among the armed services.

The Goldwater-Nichols Act was signed into law October 1, 1986, after several years of hearings and maneuvering on Capitol Hill and within defense policy circles. The act's major provisions designated the CJCS as *the* principal military adviser to the secretary of defense and the president and took the remaining members of the JCS out of the chain of command. The president could decide to place the CJCS in the chain of command, between the secretary of defense and the combatant commanders. The uniformed heads of the services, the chiefs, would command nothing more than a desk. To further strengthen the CJCS, the entire JCS staff (more than 1,000 officers) was assigned to work for the CJCS, not the JCS collectively. In addition, "purple" (multiservice) commands were made requisite for advancement to flag and general officer rank in all the armed services. As the military was not again sent into combat in the Cold War, the significance of these changes at the time was more potential than actual. Still, Goldwater-Nichols had the effect of promoting military reform and efficiency, and the act provided a platform for the CJCS to emerge as a front-line policymaker in the critical last years of the Cold War.

The other important legacy of Grenada—the articulation of a new doctrine on the use of force—similarly has had its greatest influence in the post–Cold War era. Secretary of Defense Weinberger had opposed what he saw as the cavalier use of the armed forces in Grenada and Lebanon. The Weinberger Doctrine, influenced by his senior military assistant, Maj. Gen. Colin Powell, put forth a number of tests "to help avoid being drawn inexorably into an endless morass, where it is not vital to our national interest to fight"[44] (**Document 9.12**). The doctrine held that the United States should commit forces to combat only:

- in the defense of vital interests
- with the clear intention to win
- with a clearly defined military objective

- with sufficient force to achieve the objective
- with the support of the American people and Congress
- as a last resort, when other means have failed

As a correspondent for the *New York Times* observed, these tests "seemed to echo criteria that military officers have propounded since the end of the war in Vietnam."[45] At the time Weinberger made his remarks in November 1984, he was lobbying within the government against what he considered another ill-advised military adventure, this one into Central America.

REELECTION AND A SECOND-TERM SCANDAL

Ronald Reagan won a decisive victory in his 1984 reelection campaign, with 59 percent of the popular vote and an electoral college landslide. Polls taken before the elections had indicated that Reagan's Democratic opponent, Walter Mondale, held views that were closer to those of the average voter on a range of issues, foreign as well as domestic. Mondale, and most Americans, opposed giving military aid to the Contras, wanted to cut the military budget to close the budget deficit, and even agreed, by a 56–40 percent margin (with 4 percent undecided), that "under the Reagan administration the elderly, the poor, and the handicapped have been especially hard hit, while the rich and big business have been much better off."[46] But on election day, issues were not as decisive as economic recovery and charisma.

Reagan had asked voters in 1980 whether they thought they were better off after four years of President Carter's leadership than they had been before. Most did not think that they were. In 1984 a majority of voters felt they were better off than they had been under Carter, and they were willing to give the president the credit. Reagan also benefited from his charismatic, unifying leadership, which enabled him to win the affection, trust, and the votes of millions who were closer to Mondale on the issues, including many working-class voters who typically thought of themselves as Democrats. These so-called Reagan Democrats looked beyond the issues in their support of what Reagan represented to them: faith in America's goodness, optimism about its future, and strength in national defense.[47]

Of course, presidents are not bound to respect political scientists' and pollsters' interpretation of events. Reagan was buoyed by his reelection and took it as a mandate to continue the initiatives of his first term. If not for two dramatic events in the Cold War, the second term of Reagan's presidency might simply have represented a continuation of the policies of his first term. The first event nearly derailed Reagan's presidency, but the other provided the president with an opportunity to negotiate a historic reduction in nuclear arms, which set the Cold War on a path to its demise.

The Reagan administration's Contra operation in Nicaragua had been restricted by the first Boland Amendment, passed in December 1982. Named for its chief sponsor, Rep. Edward Boland, D-Mass., the bill had authorized the CIA to aid the Contras in interdicting arms shipments to other countries, but it had prevented the U.S. government from aiding in the attempted overthrow of the Nicaraguan government. Even before the second, more restrictive, Boland Amendment was passed in October 1984—severely restricting the funds that the U.S. government might make available to the Contras for any purpose—the administration had turned to foreign and private sources of funding to keep the Contras in the field.

The Contra operation had been in trouble repeatedly since its inception because of unsteady congressional support. The administration's effort to overcome its troubles with Congress led to the creation of an off-the-books enterprise, run out of the National Security Council, to raise and disburse funds from nonappropriated sources. The protagonists in this drama—including Vice Adm. John Poindexter, who was Reagan's national security adviser from late 1985 to late 1986—insisted that Boland II did not apply to the NSC, because it specifically referred to "the Central Intelligence Agency, the Department of Defense, or any agency or entity involved in intelligence activities" as those government entities banned from assisting the Contras.[48] With the critical assistance of the NSC enterprise, the Contras survived.

In 1985, someone (NSC staff member Lt. Col. Oliver North is generally credited) had the idea to secure additional funds for the Contra enterprise from the profits made in another under-the-radar NSC endeavor—the sale of arms to Iran in order to win Iran's influence to bring about the release of some American hostages held by Muslim extremists in Lebanon. When the arms sales were discovered by the press in November 1986, and then the diversion of funds was revealed several weeks later by the attorney general, the Iran-Contra affair became the sort of news scandal that the nation had not witnessed since Watergate.

In riveting congressional hearings that were aired live on television, Watergate-style, Lt. Col. North, testifying in his marine uniform, spoke of his efforts with pride and defiance. His "dewy-eyed patriotism" and "Red-haunted alarm" were mocked in the *New York Times,* but his personal impact was impossible to ignore.[49] The White House boasted of a shift in public opinion in favor of the Contras, which they attributed to North's presence before the cameras. Turner Home Entertainment rushed to release a videotape of North's testimony to video rental stores based on what the company termed the "unbelievable" response to North's testimony. His message itself was newsworthy, explained the company's general manager, but "how he said it . . . made it a video spectacular."[50] Admiral Poindexter, for his part, gave what was probably the most significant testimony of the hearings, testifying that he had neither received nor sought the explicit approval of the president for the illegal diversion of funds.

Reagan's staffers may have saved him from impeachment, but his presidency was still in serious trouble as a result of this scandal and his stubborn insistence for months that he had done nothing wrong. While it was essential that the president maintain his innocence regarding the illegal diversion of funds to Central America, it was just as important to maintain his credibility by acknowledging the plain truth—that he had indeed traded arms for hostages and otherwise violated U.S. policy by entering into deal making with the sponsors of terrorism. The president came clean in an awkward but effective speech, delivered after much deliberation on March 4, 1987 (**Document 9.13**).

REAGAN, GORBACHEV, AND THE END OF THE COLD WAR?

During his first year in office, President Reagan had put forward an agenda for arms control talks in a letter to General Secretary Brezhnev. He had proposed a "zero-zero" option with regard to intermediate-range nuclear forces in Europe. If the Soviets withdrew their weapons, the United States would cancel its planned deployment of comparable weapons in Europe. Regarding strategic weapons, the president had suggested his version of a nuclear freeze: the superpowers would reduce their arsenals to equal and verifiable levels. Conventional force numbers might also be lowered.

These proposals led nowhere in Reagan's first term, which the president may have expected based on his belief that it was imperative to build up American military strength to induce the Soviets to negotiate seriously. Strategic Arms Reduction Talks (START) did begin in 1982 but were suspended, along with talks on intermediate-range forces, after U.S. missiles were delivered, on schedule, to Europe in November 1983. In the aftermath, the conservative, pro-deployment governments of Germany and Holland were maintained in office by their electorates. As it became clear that neither the United States nor its NATO allies could be pressured to rescind the deployment, the Soviets dispatched Foreign Minister Andrei Gromyko to Washington, D.C., to initiate a new effort at arms talks. When talks resumed in March 1985, they were divided into separate but linked negotiations over intermediate forces, strategic offensive forces, and ballistic-missile defense.

In the same month as arms talks resumed, Mikhail Gorbachev came to power in the Soviet Union. General Secretary Gorbachev was as committed to the Soviet Union and to the success of communism as had been his predecessors. Unlike them, however, he was willing to experiment to achieve his aims. Perestroika, his campaign to restructure the ailing Soviet command economy, was designed "to release scarce capital assets from the military-industrial complex without a palpable loss of military security vis-à-vis the West." [51] The launching of perestroika was preceded by a policy of openness, or glasnost, intended to mobilize support for the restructuring and to weaken the entrenched government bureaucracy, which could be expected to fight against change. Gorbachev also demonstrated openness to summitry and arms reductions.

Reagan and Gorbachev forged a personal working relationship when they met at Geneva, Switzerland, in November 1985, although they made no substantive progress toward agreement. According to the U.S. record of one of the leaders' conversations, Gorbachev

appealed to the President to recognize the true signal he was conveying to him as President and to the United States Administration as a whole. The Soviet Union did indeed wish to establish a new relationship with the United States and deliver our two nations from the increasing fear of nuclear weapons. [52]

The president confided to a friend afterward that Gorbachev "is practical and knows his economy is a basket case." [53]

After the meeting at Geneva, U.S. and Soviet negotiators continued to struggle toward an agreeable formula for arms reductions. The president's insistence that SDI not be treated as a bargaining chip—that restrictions on SDI not be agreed to in exchange for reductions in strategic weapons—continued to be a critical impediment to a comprehensive agreement. To Reagan, SDI was a moral imperative and should not threaten any nation with truly peaceful intentions. At a small, informal summit in Reykjavik, Iceland, in October 1986, Reagan and Gorbachev came close to agreeing to a deal that would have eliminated *all* U.S. and Soviet ballistic nuclear weapons within ten years and would have removed all Soviet and U.S. intermediate nuclear weapons from Europe.[54] However, Gorbachev, who saw SDI as a threat, required Reagan to agree to limit the program's research and testing to the laboratory. Secretary of State George Shultz told the *New York Times* that the Americans were willing to negotiate a reduction in the proposed space-based system, but "the Soviet Union's objective was effectively to kill off the SDI program," and that was something to which Reagan would not agree.[55]

Criticism of the deal-that-almost-was came from both conservatives and liberals. Conservatives were aghast that the president had almost consented to give away the entire U.S. ICBM arsenal, without even consulting senior military officers. The meeting in Iceland was supposed to be an informal, limited affair. Gorbachev, conservatives speculated, had intended to ambush Reagan with tempting proposals for which he had not had time to prepare a thoughtful reply. "Gorbachev's goal is still military superiority," warned the conservative columnist George Will; Reagan must not let himself be deluded into believing outrageous lies about Soviet disaffection with the Cold War or "the supposedly 'strapped' Soviet economy."[56] Liberals were dismayed that Reagan would forego the opportunity to realize his alleged dream of a world free from the threat of nuclear Armageddon because of what they saw as his irrational attachment to a technologically dubious and possibly financially ruinous space shield. When the Iran-Contra scandal broke in November 1986, shortly after Reykjavik, the initiative to move arms talks forward was left to the Soviets.

Gorbachev soon took that initiative. He was not, as it turns out, scheming to catch Reagan off guard. He was simply desperate. The Soviet economy was indeed "a basket case," and the Soviet government was in trouble. The Soviets also had problems in Afghanistan, where the U.S.-backed rebels were winning the war. In Eastern Europe, meanwhile, economic setbacks and social unrest had grown to alarming proportions. During a June 1987 visit to West Berlin, Reagan seized the opportunity to comment upon the Communists' difficulties in controlling an increasingly restive East European empire. During his speech before the Brandenburg Gate separating West Berlin from East, he uttered a famous challenge to Gorbachev: "Mr. Gorbachev, tear down this wall!" (**Document 9.14**)

Against a backdrop of mutual challenges, including the arrest by both sides of alleged spies and the exchange of insults over such past events as the Soviet response to the Hungarian uprising in 1956, Gorbachev in February 1987 broke an impasse at the Intermediate Nuclear Force (INF) talks at Geneva by agreeing to separate those discussions from ongoing negotiations over strategic weapons and space. By the end of the year, the two sides reached agreement and signed the INF Treaty (**Document 9.15**). Under this treaty, both sides would dismantle *and* destroy their intermediate nuclear weapons systems. Intrusive verification procedures were detailed in the treaty so that each side could be certain that the other kept its word. As the president liked to say about dealing with the Soviets, it was necessary to "trust, but verify."[57] Reagan joked that he had used this adage so often that Gorbachev had become tired of hearing these words, which were an English translation of a Russian saying. So, the president said, "I'm now using an American one to let him know where I stand: Trust everybody, but cut the cards."[58]

On his visit to Washington, D.C., where the treaty was signed on December 8, 1987, Gorbachev was treated as a celebrity. He returned the favor by acting like an American politician, stopping his motorcade at one point to work the crowd that had lined up to watch the Soviet premier pass. "Gorby" was a hit, as was the treaty that he and Reagan signed.

In the summer of Reagan's last year as president he and Gorbachev met in Moscow for a final summit. In Russia President Reagan spoke of freedom and the free market to an audience of students at Moscow State University, and he praised Gorbachev to reporters for his contribution to improved U.S.-Soviet relations. But despite the friendly visits both men made to the rival superpower's capital, Reagan and Gorbachev, and their respective governments, continued to trade challenges and barbs and to fight against one another through proxies in such places as Afghanistan and Central America. Reagan repeatedly raised the issues of human rights and the Brezhnev Doctrine, by which the former Soviet leader had asserted for the Soviet Union the right to intervene in Eastern Europe to "protect" socialism.[59]

In December 1988, after Vice President George Bush had been elected to succeed Reagan as president, Gorbachev made a dramatic speech before the UN General Assembly. He declared unilateral reductions in the conventional arms that threatened Western Europe and implicitly renounced the Brezhnev Doctrine. The general secretary proclaimed:

> Freedom of choice is a universal principle to which there should be no exceptions. We have not come to the conclusion of the immutability of this principle simply through good motives. We have been led to it through impartial analysis of the objective processes of our time. The increasing varieties of social development in different countries are becoming an ever more perceptible feature of these processes. This relates to both the capitalist and socialist systems. (**Document 9.16**)

In another remarkable statement of principle, which could be read as a concession to decades of Western criticism of the Soviet Union as a lawless dictatorship, Gorbachev went on to state that the Soviet Union, as part of a "truly revolutionary upsurge," had "gone substantially and deeply into the business of constructing a socialist state based on the rule of law."

Was this the beginning of the end of the "evil empire"? Some observers thought so and noted that while Gorbachev spoke hopefully in New York, his nation's affairs were in a shambles. Two thousand persons a day were being registered in places of temporary refuge in the southern part of the Soviet Union, as they fled from ethnic conflict among armed groups anxious to control their own provinces; the Baltic states were discussing secession and their citizens had turned out in large numbers to protest against Soviet control; and in Eastern Europe, particularly in Czechoslovakia and Hungary, "incipient rebellion [was] endemic."[60] In Afghanistan, meanwhile, the rebels were winning, and nobody in the West took seriously the Kremlin's tough talk about using Backfire bombers and SCUD missiles to halt the supply of arms from Pakistan. It would be up to George Bush to ponder the meaning of such events and of Gorbachev's articulation of new principles and to make an authoritative American reply.

CONCLUSION

Ronald Reagan believed in the Cold War and the fight against communism. On his way to the White House and once in office, he preached that it was both foolish and dangerous to think that the struggle was in any significant sense over, just because treaties had slowed the arms race and U.S. presidents had begun to treat the Soviets with respect. Such an assumption was foolish because it confused the shadow of conflict—the rhetoric of presidents and the protocol of international summitry—with the substance—the irreducible and unbridgeable gap between totalitarianism and freedom. It was dangerous because it took only one superpower to fight the war. If the United States were to continue down the path of détente and appeasement, Reagan and his fellow conservatives argued, it would be fine with the Soviets, who would continue to use force to expand their influence around the globe while proclaiming their pacifism and complimenting the United States for its maturity in recognizing Soviet intentions as purely peaceful. At the end of the day, Reagan believed, the United States and the West would be presented with a choice: surrender or die.

Because he believed in the Cold War, Ronald Reagan believed that the United States had no choice but to *fight* the war. He took advantage of both the president's unilateral powers and his bully pulpit of persuasion to prosecute his foreign policy agenda. In doing so, he gave new force to the presidency, an institution that had lost much of its power during the 1970s. Because Reagan was adept at using these powers, he was able to launch a broad offensive against the Soviet Union and sustain the fight through eight years. Reagan relied upon persuasion and deal making as he led the Democratic-controlled Congress to join his crusade against "evil" by supporting his significant and expensive rearmament campaign; without their votes, his plan would have been just talk. He demonstrated the president's unilateral power by backing indigenous rebels fighting against Communist governments in Central America and on the periphery of the Soviet Union. Although the Cold War did not end during his presidency, Reagan's policies helped push the Soviet Union toward collapse.

Among the unilateral powers of the presidency employed to great effect by Reagan, the power of decision was critical. Reagan preferred to delegate many decisions and was surprisingly conciliatory on some issues presumably close to his heart, such as tax cuts, but he was doggedly decisive about some things, including support for the rebels in Central America and Afghanistan and SDI. His refusal to compromise on his support for these policies forced others to acknowledge the president's priorities.

Reagan also utilized another significant unilateral power of the presidency—the power to hold the nation's attention. This was important in two ways. First, Reagan was a master of symbolic rhetoric and he "performed" the role of head of state better than any other Cold War president save, perhaps, Dwight Eisenhower and John F. Kennedy. This helped Reagan gain rapport with the American public, which secured his reelection in a highly personalized campaign, and permitted him to withstand the hard times that befell him in the second term, especially in the wake of the Iran-Contra scandal. Second, Reagan's ability to hold the people's attention was important because it provided the foundation for a sleight-of-hand approach to governing not seen since Eisenhower. President Reagan, and the senior White House staff who worked for him, well understood what some of his admirers forgot: the president is not the presidency. In the Reagan years, covert operations and bureaucratic subterfuge were as important as the president's speeches, so much so that in Iran-Contra, their collision almost toppled Reagan's presidency.

By the end of the his presidency, Reagan's first-term ideological offensive and arms buildup had given way to (or prepared the way for, depending on one's point of view) serial summitry and historic arms reductions. By the end of Reagan's time in office, it was apparent that a new era had begun in the relationship of the superpowers.

NOTES

1. Fred Greenstein, *The Presidential Difference: Leadership Style from FDR to Clinton* (New York: The Free Press, Martin Kessler Books, 2000), 235.
2. "We the people" is of course drawn from the preamble to the U.S. Constitution. Reagan spoke of "We the People, this breed called Americans" in both of his inaugural addresses. See Ronald Reagan, "Inaugural Address," January 20, 1981, and "Inaugural Address," January 21, 1985, in *Public Papers of the Presidents of the United States: Ronald Reagan, 1981–1989,* from the American Presidency Project, University of California, Santa Barbara, www.presidency.ucsb.edu.
3. Ronald Reagan, "A Time for Choosing," October 27, 1964, from the Ronald Reagan Presidential Foundation, www.reaganfoundation.org/reagan/speeches/rendezvous.asp.
4. President Reagan's ambition, and the ambition of those around him, was indicated by the free use his subordinates and admirers made of the language of "revolution." See, for example, the following memoirs by administration figures: Martin Anderson, *Revolution* (San Diego: Harcourt, Brace, Jovanovich, 1988); Peggy Noonan, *What I Saw at the Revolution: A Political Life in the Reagan Era* (New York: Random House, 1990); David Stockman, *The Triumph of Politics: Why the Reagan Revolution Failed* (New York: Harper and Row, 1986).
5. In Reagan's first inaugural address, he famously declared that "government is not the solution to our problem; government is the problem." See Ronald Reagan, "Inaugural Address," January 20, 1981, in *Public Papers of the Presidents of the United States: Ronald Reagan, 1981–1989,* from the American Presidency Project, University of California, Santa Barbara, www.presidency.ucsb.edu.
6. Ronald Reagan, *Reagan, In His Own Hand,* ed. Kiron K. Skinner et al. (New York: Free Press, 2001), 12.
7. Peter Schweizer, *Victory: The Reagan Administration's Secret Strategy that Hastened the Collapse of the Soviet Union* (New York: The Atlantic Monthly Press, 1994), 8.
8. Benjamin B. Fischer, "A Cold War Conundrum" (unclassified monograph, Central Intelligence Agency, Center for the Study of Intelligence, Washington, D.C., 1997), https://www.cia.gov/csi/monograph/coldwar/source.htm#ft22.
9. Chester J. Pach Jr., "Sticking to His Guns, Reagan and National Security," in *Reagan Presidency: Pragmatic Conservatism and Its Legacies,* ed. W. Elliot Brownlee and Hugh Davis Graham (Lawrence: University Press of Kansas, 2003), 98.
10. Eugene R. Wittkopf, *Faces of Internationalism: Public Opinion and American Foreign Policy* (Durham, N.C.: Duke University Press, 1990), 247–248.
11. James M. Scott, *Deciding to Intervene: The Reagan Doctrine and American Foreign Policy* (Durham, N.C.: Duke University Press, 1996), 16.
12. Steve Coll, *Ghost Wars: The Secret History of CIA, Afghanistan, and Bin Laden, from the Soviet Invasion to September 11, 2001* (New York: Penguin, 2004), 97.
13. Condoleezza Rice, "U.S.-Soviet Relations," in *Looking Back on the Reagan Presidency,* ed. Larry Berman (Baltimore, Md.: Johns Hopkins University Press, 1990), 76.
14. Jeane Kirkpatrick, "Dictatorships and Double Standards," *Commentary* 68 (November 1979): 34–45.

15. Anna M. Cienciala, review of *The United States, Western Europe and the Polish Crisis: International Relations in the Second World War,* by Helene Sjursen, *American Historical Review* 109, no. 4 (October 2004), available online (subscription required) from the History Cooperative, www.historycooperative.org.

16. Ronald Reagan, *An American Life* (New York: Simon and Schuster, 1990), 307.

17. In Reagan's classic speech, "A Time for Choosing," he explicitly compared the United States' fight against the Soviet Union to Jesus's martyrdom on the cross. See Reagan, "A Time for Choosing."

18. Paul Kengor, *God and Ronald Reagan: A Spiritual Life* (New York: Regan Books, 2004) and *Crusader: Ronald Reagan and the Fall of Communism* (New York: Regan Books, 2006).

19. Edmund Morris, "At the Edge of Death," Newsweek, October 4, 1999, 35, and *Dutch: A Memoir of Ronald Reagan* (New York: Random House, 1999), 434–435. *Washington Post* investigative reporter Carl Bernstein suggested that both Reagan and Pope John Paul II believed they had been spared from death in 1981 assassination attempts to confront the evil of Soviet communism. See Bernstein, "The Holy Alliance," *Time,* February 24, 1992, 28, 30.

20. I. M. Destler, "Reagan and the World: An 'Awesome Stubbornness,'" in *The Reagan Legacy: Promise and Performance,* ed. Charles O. Jones (Chatham, N.J.: Chatham House, 1988).

21. Pach, "Sticking to His Guns," 90. This was a mantra that infuriated Reagan's first director of the Office of Management and Budget, David Stockman. See Stockman's *The Triumph of Politics: How the Reagan Revolution Failed* (New York: Harper and Row, 1986).

22. Ambassador Jack Matlock Jr., as quoted by Beth A. Fischer, "Reagan and the Soviets: Winning the Cold War?" in Brownlee and Graham, *Reagan Presidency,* 122.

23. The ever-practical George Shultz cautioned Reagan, though, that "it would be a mistake to assume that the Soviet capacity for competition with us will diminish at any time during *your presidency*"(emphasis added). Ibid., from a January 1983 memorandum from Shultz to the president.

24. Samuel F. Wells Jr., "Reagan, Euromissiles, and Europe," in Brownlee and Graham, *Reagan Presidency,* 141.

25. Dale Herspring, *The Pentagon and the Presidency: Civil-Military Relations from FDR to Clinton* (Lawrence: University Press of Kansas, 2005), 277.

26. Ibid., 273.

27. Ibid., 277.

28. The 1980 Republican Party Platform, from the American Presidency Project, University of California, Santa Barbara, www.presidency.ucsb.edu.

29. U.S. Department of Defense, *Soviet Military Power: 1987* (Washington, D.C.: U.S. Government Printing Office, 1987), 29.

30. David Miller, *The Cold War: A Military History* (New York: St. Martin's Press, 1998), 126–127.

31. Pach, "Sticking to His Guns," 103.

32. Robert David Johnson, *Congress and the Cold War* (New York: Cambridge University Press, 2006), 266.

33. Ibid.

34. Ibid., 269, quoting the *Washington Post.*

35. Ibid., 270.

36. Benjamin B. Fischer, *Cold War Conundrum.*

37. Ibid.

38. Ibid., quoting Don Oberdorfer, *The Turn: From the Cold War to a New Era* (New York: Poseidon, 1991), 67.

39. Beth A. Fischer, "Reagan and the Soviets," 18.

40. Herspring, *Pentagon and the Presidency,* 284.

41. In a speech of March 10, 1983, quoted in Richard A. Melanson, *American Foreign Policy since the Vietnam War: The Search for Consensus from Nixon to Clinton* (Armonk, N.Y.: M.E. Sharpe, 1990), 161.

42. Herspring, *The Pentagon and the Presidency,* 289.

43. Ibid., 169.

44. Casper W. Weinberger, "The Uses of Military Power, Remarks at the National Press Club, November 28, 1984," Department of Defense News Release No. 609-84, from *Air Force Magazine: Journal of the Air Force Association* 87, no.1 (January 2004), 42; full text online at www.afa.org/magazine/Jan2004/0104keeperfull.html.

45. Richard Halloran, "U.S. Will Not Drift into a Latin War, Weinberger Says," *New York Times,* November 29, 1984.

46. Seymour Martin Lipset, "The Elections, the Economy, and Public Opinion: 1984," *PS* 18, no.1 (Winter 1985): 29.

47. Jeff Manza and Clem Brooks, *Social Cleavages and Political Change: Voter Alignments and U.S. Party Coalitions* (New York: Oxford University Press, 1999), 49.

48. United States Congress, House Select Committee to Investigate Covert Arms Transactions with Iran, *Report of the Congressional Committees Investigating the Iran-Contra Affair: With the Minority Views,* ed. Joel Brinkley and Stephen Engelberg (New York: Times Books, 1998), 51.

49. Tom Wicker, "In the Nation: Don't Count on Ollie," *New York Times,* July 22, 1987.

50. Lisa Belkin, "North's Testimony Set for Release on Cassette," *New York Times,* July 23, 1987.

51. Joseph Smith and Simon Davis, *The A to Z of the Cold War* (Lanham, Md.: Scarecrow Press, 2005), 155.

52. Wells, "Reagan, Euromissiles, and Europe," 143.

53. Ibid.

54. Bernard Weintraub, "Summit Aftermath: Outlook for Bargaining on Arms; How Grim Ending in Iceland Followed Hard-Won Gains," *New York Times,* October 14, 1986. The president confused things when he reportedly told members of Congress that he had almost agreed at Iceland to the abolition of *all* nuclear weapons, a move which would, arguably, leave Western Europe virtually defenseless against the Warsaw Pact's massive advantage in conventional forces. The White House spokesperson at first suggested that the president had "misspoken," but later declared that his surely accurate statements might have been "misunderstood." See Bernard Gwertzman, "Shultz Details Reagan's Arms Bid at Iceland to Clarify U.S. Position," *New York Times,* October 18, 1986.

55. Weintraub, "Summit Aftermath." In the immediate aftermath of the summit, General Secretary Gorbachev had said "only a madman" would believe as the Americans apparently did that development of a space-based missile defense system should be permitted to proceed outside the laboratory. See Philip Taubman, "The Iceland Summit: 'A Difficult Dialogue'; Gorbachev Angrily Accuses Reagan of Scuttling an Accord at Reykjavik," *New York Times,* October 13, 1986.

56. George F. Will, "Gorbachev's Goal Is Still Military Superiority," *The Toronto Star,* December 8, 1988.

57. "I actually learned a couple of words in Russian in order to talk about this with the General Secretary," said Reagan. "Dovorey no provorey . . . Trust, but verify." See his "Remarks to Administration Supporters at a White House Briefing on Arms Control, Central America, and the Supreme Court," November 23, 1987, *Public Papers of the Presidents of the United States: Ronald Reagan, 1981–1989,* from the American Presidency Project, University of California, Santa Barbara, www.presidency.ucsb.edu.

58. Ronald Reagan, "Remarks at a Fundraising Luncheon for Senator Pete Wilson in Irvine, California," August 23, 1988, in *Public Papers of the Presidents of the United States: Ronald Reagan, 1981–1989,* from the American Presidency Project, University of California, Santa Barbara, www.presidency.ucsb.edu.

59. See, for example, Ronald Reagan, "Radio Address to the Nation on the Soviet-United States Summit Meeting in Moscow," May 28, 1988, in *Public Papers of the Presidents of the United States: Ronald Reagan, 1981–1989,* from the American Presidency Project, University of California, Santa Barbara, www.presidency.ucsb.edu.

60. Joseph C. Harsch, "Is This the Beginning of the End of the Soviet Empire?" *The New York Times,* December 9, 1988.

Document 9.1
President Ronald Reagan Approves Covert Action against the Communist Government of Nicaragua, December 1, 1981

In the summer of 1979 the repressive Nicaraguan government was overthrown by the Sandinista National Liberation Front (FSLN), Cuban-backed revolutionaries led by Daniel Ortega. President Jimmy Carter's emphasis on human rights had led him to distance the United States from the previous regime in Nicaragua, which had long enjoyed American support, despite its poor human rights record. President Reagan was determined to reverse what he saw as the most egregious example of Communist expansion close to American borders since Fidel Castro's rise to power in Cuba. In this presidential "finding," the Central Intelligence Agency was called upon to lead the effort. The Xs in the document indicate where words were blacked out during declassification.

NSC/ICS 33340

Finding Pursuant to Section 662 of
The Foreign Assistance Act of 1961,
As Amended, Concerning Operations
Undertaken by the Central Intelligence
Agency in Foreign Countries, Other Than
Those Intended Solely for the Purpose
of Intelligence Collection

I hereby find that the following operation in a foreign country (including all support necessary to such operation) is important to the national security of the United States, and direct the Director of Central Intelligence, or his designee, to report this Finding to the intelligence committees of the Congress pursuant to Section 501 of the National Security Act of 1947, as amended, and to provide such briefings as necessary.

SCOPE	PURPOSE
Central America	Support and conduct XXXXXXXXX paramilitary operations against XXX XXXXXXXXXXXXXXX Nicaragua XXXXXXXXXXXXXXXXXXXXX XXXXXXXXXXXXXXXXXXXXX XXXXXX

RONALD REAGAN

The White House
Washington, D.C.
December 1, 1981

Source: Ronald Reagan, "Document 2: Ronald Reagan's Secret Presidential Finding on Covert Operations which Officially Authorized the CIA's Contra War against Nicaragua," December 1, 1981, in *Nicaragua: The Making of U.S. Policy 1978–1990,* June 1991, from the National Security Archive, George Washington University, www.gwu.edu/~nsarchiv/nsa/publications/nicaragua/nidoc2.html.

Document 9.2
A Cold War Christmas, President Ronald Reagan's Address on the Imposition of Martial Law in Poland, December 23, 1981.

In the East European satellite Poland, the Solidarity trade union emerged in 1980 as a major voice demanding workers' rights and other freedoms. The Polish state, led by the Polish United Workers' Party national secretary and prime minister Gen. Wojciech Jaruzelski, imposed martial law in December 1981 in an attempt to arrest the "downward" spiral of events and, he said, to forestall Soviet invasion. President Reagan, in response, imposed economic sanctions against Poland and condemned the Soviet Union for its intervention. As the president announced his response, he underlined the spiritual dimension of the Cold War battle in this Cold War Christmas address.

. . . As I speak to you tonight, the fate of a proud and ancient nation hangs in the balance. For a thousand years, Christmas has been celebrated in Poland, a land of deep religious faith, but this Christmas brings little joy to the courageous Polish people. They have been betrayed by their own government.

The men who rule them and their totalitarian allies fear the very freedom that the Polish people cherish. They have answered the stirrings of liberty with brute force, killings, mass arrests, and the setting up of concentration camps. Lech Walesa and other Solidarity leaders are imprisoned, their fate unknown. Factories, mines, universities, and homes have been assaulted.

The Polish Government has trampled underfoot solemn commitments to the UN Charter and the Helsinki accords. It has even broken the Gdansk agreement of August 1980, by which the Polish Government recognized the basic right of its people to form free trade unions and to strike. . . .

It's ironic that we offered, and Poland expressed interest in accepting, our help after World War II. The Soviet Union intervened then and refused to allow such help to Poland. But if the forces of tyranny in Poland, and those who incite them from without, do not relent, they should prepare themselves for serious consequences. Already, throughout the Free World, citizens have publicly demonstrated their support for the Polish people. Our government, and those of our allies, have expressed moral revulsion at the police state tactics of Poland's oppressors. The Church has also spoken out, in spite of threats and intimidation. But our reaction cannot stop there.

I want emphatically to state tonight that if the outrages in Poland do not cease, we cannot and will not conduct "business as usual" with the perpetrators and those who aid and abet them. Make no mistake, their crime will cost them dearly in their future dealings with

America and free peoples everywhere. I do not make this statement lightly or without serious reflection. . . .

The United States is taking immediate action to suspend major elements of our economic relationships with the Polish Government. We have halted the renewal of the Export-Import Bank's line of export credit insurance to the Polish Government. We will suspend Polish civil aviation privileges in the United States. We are suspending the right of Poland's fishing fleet to operate in American waters. And we're proposing to our allies the further restriction of high technology exports to Poland.

These actions are not directed against the Polish people. They are a warning to the Government of Poland that free men cannot and will not stand idly by in the face of brutal repression. To underscore this point, I've written a letter to General Jaruzelski, head of the Polish Government. In it, I outlined the steps we're taking and warned of the serious consequences if the Polish Government continues to use violence against its populace. I've urged him to free those in arbitrary detention, to lift martial law, and to restore the internationally recognized rights of the Polish people to free speech and association.

The Soviet Union, through its threats and pressures, deserves a major share of blame for the developments in Poland. So, I have also sent a letter to President Brezhnev urging him to permit the restoration of basic human rights in Poland provided for in the Helsinki Final Act. In it, I informed him that if this repression continues, the United States will have no choice but to take further concrete political and economic measures affecting our relationship.

When 19th century Polish patriots rose against foreign oppressors, their rallying cry was, "For our freedom and yours." Well, that motto still rings true in our time. There is a spirit of solidarity abroad in the world tonight that no physical force can crush. It crosses national boundaries and enters into the hearts of men and women everywhere. In factories, farms, and schools, in cities and towns around the globe, we the people of the Free World stand as one with our Polish brothers and sisters. Their cause is ours, and our prayers and hopes go out to them this Christmas.

Yesterday, I met in this very room with Romuald Spasowski, the distinguished former Polish Ambassador who has sought asylum in our country in protest of the suppression of his native land. He told me that one of the ways the Polish people have demonstrated their solidarity in the face of martial law is by placing lighted candles in their windows to show that the light of liberty still glows in their hearts.

Ambassador Spasowski requested that on Christmas Eve a lighted candle will burn in the White House window as a small but certain beacon of our solidarity with the Polish people. I urge all of you to do the same tomorrow night, on Christmas Eve, as a personal statement of your commitment to the steps we're taking to support the brave people of Poland in their time of troubles.

Once, earlier in this century, an evil influence threatened that the lights were going out all over the world. Let the light of millions of candles in American homes give notice that the light of freedom is not going to be extinguished. We are blessed with a freedom and abundance denied to so many. Let those candles remind us that these blessings bring with them a solid obligation, an obligation to the God who guides us, an obligation to the heritage of liberty and dignity handed down to us by our forefathers and an obligation to the children of the world, whose future will be shaped by the way we live our lives today.

Christmas means so much because of one special child. But Christmas also reminds us that all children are special, that they are gifts from God, gifts beyond price that mean more than any presents money can buy. In their love and laughter, in our hopes for their future lies the true meaning of Christmas.

So, in a spirit of gratitude for what we've been able to achieve together over the past year and looking forward to all that we hope to achieve together in the years ahead, Nancy and I want to wish you all the best of holiday seasons. As Charles Dickens, whom I quoted a few moments ago, said so well in "A Christmas Carol," "God bless us, every one."

Good night.

Source: Ronald Reagan, "Address to the Nation about Christmas and the Situation in Poland," December 23, 1981, in *Public Papers of the Presidents of the United States: Ronald Reagan, 1981–1989,* from the American Presidency Project, University of California, Santa Barbara, www.presidency.ucsb.edu.

Document 9.3
NATO Allies Condemn the Soviet-Directed Crackdown in Poland, Ministerial Communiqué, January 11, 1982

In a ministerial communiqué, the members of the North Atlantic Treaty Organization (NATO) emphasized common ground. While they joined together to condemn the Polish government for the imposition of martial law and the Soviet Union for its intervention in the internal affairs of Poland, they could not agree on how to translate their words into action. The ministers could only say that each NATO country would have to examine its relations with the Soviet Union and come it its own decisions.

1. The Allied governments condemn the imposition of martial law in Poland and denounce the massive violation of human rights and the suppression of fundamental civil liberties in contravention of the United Nations Charter, the Universal Declaration on Human Rights and the Final Act of Helsinki.

2. The process of renewal and reform which began in Poland in August 1980 was watched with sympathy and hope by all who believe in freedom and self determination; it resulted from a genuine effort by the overwhelming majority of the Polish people to achieve a more open society in accordance with the principles of the Final Act of Helsinki.

3. The imposition of martial law, the use of force against Polish workers, with the thousands of internments, the harsh prison sentences and the deaths that followed, have deprived the Polish people of their rights and freedoms, in particular in the field of trade unions. These acts threaten to destroy the basis for reconciliation and compromise which are necessary to progress and stability in Poland. They are in clear violation of Polish commitments under the Helsinki Final Act, particularly the principle relating to respect for human rights and fundamental freedoms. Developments in Poland demon-

strate once again the rigidity of the Warsaw Pact regimes with respect to those changes necessary to meet the legitimate aspirations of their peoples (1). This endangers public confidence in co-operation between East and West and seriously affects international relations.

4. The Allies deplore the sustained campaign mounted by the Soviet Union against efforts by the Polish people for national renewal and reform, and its active support for the subsequent systematic suppression of those efforts in Poland. . . . The Soviet Union has no right to determine the political and social development of Poland.

5. The Allies call upon the Polish leadership to live up to its declared intention to re-establish civil liberties and the process of reform. They urge the Polish authorities to end the state of martial law, to release those arrested, and to restore immediately a dialogue with the Church and Solidarity. . . .

6. The Allies call upon the Soviet Union to respect Poland's fundamental right to solve its own problems free from foreign interference and to respect the clear desire of the overwhelming majority of the Polish people for national renewal and reform. Soviet pressure, direct or indirect, aimed at frustrating that desire, must cease. The Allies also warn that if an outside armed intervention were to take place it would have the most profound consequences for international relations.

7. In their communiqué of 11th December, 1981, NATO Ministers reaffirmed their commitment to work for a climate of confidence and mutual restraint in East-West relations; what has since happened in Poland has great significance for the development of security and co-operation in Europe. The persistence of repression in Poland is eroding the political foundation for progress on the full agenda of issues which divide East and West.

8. The Allies remain committed to the policies of effective deterrence and the pursuit of arms control and in particular have welcomed the initiatives contained in President Reagan's 18th November speech. The Soviet Union will bear full responsibility if its actions with regard to Poland and its failure to live up to existing international obligations damage the arms control process. . . .

14. In the current situation in Poland, economic relations with Poland and the Soviet Union are bound to be affected. Soviet actions towards Poland make it necessary for the Allies to examine the course of future economic and commercial relations with the Soviet Union. Recognising that each of the Allies will act in accordance with its own situation and laws, they will examine measures which could involve arrangements regarding imports from the Soviet Union, maritime agreements, air services agreements, the size of Soviet commercial representation and the conditions surrounding export credits (1).

(1) The Greek delegation has reserved its position on these paragraphs

Source: NATO, "Declaration on Events in Poland," January 11, 1982, Ministerial Communiqué, www.nato.int/docu/comm/49-95/c820111a.htm.

Document 9.4
NATO and Warsaw Pact Force Comparisons, 1982–1983

The Communist countries of the Warsaw Pact had long enjoyed numerical superiority in conventional forces, relative to those of the North Atlantic Treaty Organization's European members. As long as the United States credibly threatened to respond to a Warsaw Pact invasion with nuclear war, the conventional force imbalance was a cause for worry but not alarm in the West. But would the Americans really risk their own destruction in a nuclear war, to save Europe? This question, which haunted U.S.-European relations throughout the Cold War, became urgent when the Soviets deployed the SS-20, beginning in 1976. The SS-20 was a sophisticated intermediate-range nuclear missile that posed no danger to the United States but could destroy European cities.

NATO and Warsaw Pact Force Comparisons, 1982–1983

	NATO	Warsaw Pact
Conventional Forces		
Aircraft in Europe	2,975	7,240
Main battle tanks	13,000	42,500
Anti-tank guided weapon launchers	8,100	24,300
Artillery/mortars	10,750	31,500
Armored personnel carriers and Infantry fighting vehicles	30,000	78,800
Attack helicopters	400	700
Total military personnel	2.6 million	4.0 million
Nuclear Forces		
Strategic missiles and bombers	2,022[1]	2,704[2]
Of which		
ICBMs	1,052	1,398
SLBMs	560	950
Bombers	410	356
Longer-range INF missiles systems	0	600
Of which		
SS-4s		275
SS-5s		25
SS-20s		300

Note: ICBMs, intercontinental ballistic missiles; INF, intermediate-range nuclear forces; SLBMs, submarine-launched ballistic missiles.

[1] NATO strategic weapons include US strategic missiles, B-52s, FB-11s, FB-111, and 64 British Polaris SLBMs.

[2] Warsaw Pact strategic weapons include Soviet strategic missiles and intercontinental bombers, including the Backfire.

Source: Terry McNeill, *The Kremlin and the Peace Offensive* (London: British Atlantic Publications, 1983), 15.

Document 9.5
The Reagan Administration's National Security Strategy, National Security Decision Directive 32, May 20, 1982

To President Reagan, national security strategy was, first and foremost, Cold War strategy. To advance the cause of freedom against the forces of evil, which is how the president articulated the purpose of his strategy, the United States would upgrade and expand its conventional forces, reach out increasingly to its allies, and prepare to fight a "protracted nuclear conflict." By thus demonstrating its resolve, the United States might achieve, according to this document, a "fundamentally different East-West relationship by the end of this decade."

U.S. NATIONAL SECURITY STRATEGY

. . .

The national security policy of the United States shall be guided by the following global objectives:

- To deter military attack by the USSR and its allies against the U.S., its allies, and other important countries across the spectrum of conflict; and to defeat such attack should deterrence fail.
- To strengthen the influence of the U.S. throughout the world by strengthening existing alliances, by improving relations with other nations, by forming and supporting coalitions of states friendly to U.S. interests, and by a full range of diplomatic, political, economic, and information efforts.
- To contain and reverse the expansion of Soviet control and military presence throughout the world, and to increase the costs of Soviet support and use of proxy, terrorist, and subversive forces.
- To neutralize the efforts of the USSR to increase its influence through its use of diplomacy, arms transfers, economic pressure, political action, propaganda and disinformation.
- To foster, if possible in concert with our allies, restraint in Soviet military spending, discourage Soviet adventurism, and weaken the Soviet alliance system by forcing the USSR to bear the brunt of its economic shortcomings, and to encourage long-term liberalizing and nationalist tendencies within the Soviet Union and allied countries.
- To limit Soviet military capabilities by strengthening the U.S. military, by pursuing equitable and verifiable arms control agreements, and by preventing the flow of militarily significant technologies and resources to the Soviet Union.
- To ensure the U.S. access to foreign markets, and to ensure the U.S. and its allies and friends access to foreign energy and mineral resources.
- To ensure U.S. access to space and the oceans.
- To discourage further proliferation of nuclear weapons.
- To encourage and strongly support aid, trade, and investment programs . . . in the Third World.
- To promote a well-functioning international economic system. . . .

Threats to U.S. National Security

The key military threats to U.S. security during the 1980s will continue to be posed by the Soviet Union and its allies and clients. . . .

Unstable governments, weak political institutions, inefficient economies, and the persistence of traditional conflicts create opportunities for Soviet expansion in many parts of the developing world. The growing scarcity of resources, such as oil, increasing terrorism, the dangers of nuclear proliferation, uncertainties in Soviet political succession, reticence on the part of a number of Western countries, and the growing assertiveness of Soviet foreign policy all contribute to the unstable international environment. For these reasons, the decade of the eighties will likely pose the greatest challenge to our survival and well-being since World War II and our response could result in a fundamentally different East-West relationship by the end of this decade.

The Role of Allies and Others

Given the loss of U.S. strategic superiority and the overwhelming growth of Soviet conventional forces capabilities, together with the increased political and economic strength of the industrial democracies and the heightened importance of Third World resources, the United States must increasingly draw upon the resources and cooperation of allies and others to protect our interests and those of our friends. There is no other alternative. . . .

Nuclear Forces

. . . The United States will enhance its strategic nuclear deterrent by developing a capability to sustain protracted nuclear conflict. . . .

General Purpose Forces

. . . In order to close the gap between strategy and capabilities, the U.S. must undertake a sustained and balanced force development program. First priority is to improve the operational capabilities of forward or early deploying forces and their associated lift. Second priority is to be accorded to U.S.-based late deploying forces and then third priority to expanding the force structure. . . .

Source: National Security Council, "U.S. National Security Strategy" (NSC-NSDD-32), from the Federation of American Scientists, www.fas.org/irp/offdocs/nsdd/nsdd-032.htm.

Document 9.6
President Ronald Reagan Proclaims that Communism Will Be Placed on the "Ashheap of History," Address to Parliament, June 8, 1982

Public confrontation with the Soviet Union on the battlefield of ideas was a key component of the Reagan administration's approach to the Soviet Union. More than any president since John F. Kennedy, President Reagan spoke confidently, and provocatively, of the certain triumph of freedom and democracy over totalitarianism, as illustrated by this address to the British Parliament during his first term.

. . . We have not inherited an easy world. If developments like the Industrial Revolution, which began here in England, and the gifts of science and technology have made life much easier for us, they have also made it more dangerous. There are threats now to our freedom, indeed to our very existence, that other generations could never even have imagined.

There is first the threat of global war. No President, no Congress, no Prime Minister, no Parliament can spend a day entirely free of this threat. And I don't have to tell you that in today's world the existence of nuclear weapons could mean, if not the extinction of mankind, then surely the end of civilization as we know it. That's why negotiations on intermediate-range nuclear forces now underway in Europe and the START talks—Strategic Arms Reduction Talks—which will begin later this month, are not just critical to American or Western policy; they are critical to mankind. Our commitment to early success in these negotiations is firm and unshakable, and our purpose is clear: reducing the risk of war by reducing the means of waging war on both sides.

At the same time there is a threat posed to human freedom by the enormous power of the modern state. History teaches the dangers of government that overreaches—political control taking precedence over free economic growth, secret police, mindless bureaucracy, all combining to stifle individual excellence and personal freedom.

Now, I'm aware that among us here and throughout Europe there is legitimate disagreement over the extent to which the public sector should play a role in a nation's economy and life. But on one point all of us are united—our abhorrence of dictatorship in all its forms, but most particularly totalitarianism and the terrible inhumanities it has caused in our time—the great purge, Auschwitz and Dachau, the Gulag, and Cambodia.

Historians looking back at our time will note the consistent restraint and peaceful intentions of the West. They will note that it was the democracies who refused to use the threat of their nuclear monopoly in the forties and early fifties for territorial or imperial gain. Had that nuclear monopoly been in the hands of the Communist world, the map of Europe—indeed, the world—would look very different today. And certainly they will note it was not the democracies that invaded Afghanistan or suppressed Polish Solidarity or used chemical and toxin warfare in Afghanistan and Southeast Asia.

If history teaches anything it teaches self-delusion in the face of unpleasant facts is folly. We see around us today the marks of our terrible dilemma—predictions of doomsday, anti-nuclear demonstrations, an arms race in which the West must, for its own protection, be an unwilling participant. At the same time we see totalitarian forces in the world who seek subversion and conflict around the globe to further their barbarous assault on the human spirit. What, then, is our course? Must civilization perish in a hail of fiery atoms? Must freedom wither in a quiet, deadening accommodation with totalitarian evil?

Sir Winston Churchill refused to accept the inevitability of war or even that it was imminent. He said, "I do not believe that Soviet Russia desires war. What they desire is the fruits of war and the indefinite expansion of their power and doctrines. But what we have to consider here today while time remains is the permanent prevention of war and the establishment of conditions of freedom and democracy as rapidly as possible in all countries."

Well, this is precisely our mission today: to preserve freedom as well as peace. It may not be easy to see; but I believe we live now at a turning point.

In an ironic sense Karl Marx was right. We are witnessing today a great revolutionary crisis, a crisis where the demands of the economic order are conflicting directly with those of the political order. But the crisis is happening not in the free, non-Marxist West, but in the home of Marxist-Leninism, the Soviet Union. It is the Soviet Union that runs against the tide of history by denying human freedom and human dignity to its citizens. It also is in deep economic difficulty. The rate of growth in the national product has been steadily declining since the Fifties and is less than half of what it was then.

The dimensions of this failure are astounding: A country which employs one fifth of its population in agriculture is unable to feed its own people. Were it not for the private sector, the tiny private sector tolerated in Soviet agriculture, the country might be on the brink of famine. These private plots occupy a bare 3 percent of the arable land but account for nearly one-quarter of Soviet farm output and nearly one-third of meat products and vegetables. Overcentralized, with little or no incentives, year after year the Soviet system pours its best resource into the making of instruments of destruction. The constant shrinkage of economic growth combined with the growth of military production is putting a heavy strain on the Soviet people. What we see here is a political structure that no longer corresponds to its economic base, a society where productive forces are hampered by political ones.

The decay of the Soviet experiment should come as no surprise to us. Wherever the comparisons have been made between free and closed societies—West Germany and East Germany, Austria and Czechoslovakia, Malaysia and Vietnam—it is the democratic countries what are prosperous and responsive to the needs of their people. And one of the simple but overwhelming facts of our time is this: Of all the millions of refugees we've seen in the modern world, their flight is always away from, not toward the Communist world. Today on the NATO line, our military forces face east to prevent a possible invasion. On the other side of the line, the Soviet forces also face east to prevent their people from leaving.

The hard evidence of totalitarian rule has caused in mankind an uprising of the intellect and will. Whether it is the growth of the new schools of economics in America or England or the appearance of the so-called new philosophers in France, there is one unifying thread running through the intellectual work of these groups—rejection of the arbitrary power of the state, the refusal to subordinate the rights of the individual to the superstate, the realization that collectivism stifles all the best human impulses. . . .

In the Communist world as well, man's instinctive desire for freedom and self-determination surfaces again and again. To be sure, there are grim reminders of how brutally the police state attempts to snuff out this quest for self-rule—1953 in East Germany, 1956 in Hungary, 1968 in Czechoslovakia, 1981 in Poland. But the struggle continues in Poland. And we know that there are even those who strive and suffer for freedom within the confines of the Soviet Union itself. How we conduct ourselves here in the Western democracies will determine whether this trend continues.

No, democracy is not a fragile flower. Still it needs cultivating. If the rest of this century is to witness the gradual growth of freedom and democratic ideals, we must take actions to assist the campaign for democracy.

Some argue that we should encourage democratic change in right-wing dictatorships, but not in Communist regimes. Well, to accept this preposterous notion—as some well-meaning people have—is to invite the argument that once countries achieve a nuclear capability, they should be allowed an undisturbed reign of terror over their own citizens. We reject this course.

As for the Soviet view, Chairman Brezhnev repeatedly has stressed that the competition of ideas and systems must continue and that this is entirely consistent with relaxation of tensions and peace.

Well, we ask only that these systems begin by living up to their own constitutions, abiding by their own laws, and complying with the international obligations they have undertaken. We ask only for a process, a direction, a basic code of decency, not for an instant transformation.

We cannot ignore the fact that even without our encouragement there has been and will continue to be repeated explosions against repression and dictatorships. The Soviet Union itself is not immune to this reality. Any system is inherently unstable that has no peaceful means to legitimize its leaders. In such cases, the very repressiveness of the state ultimately drives people to resist it, if necessary, by force.

While we must be cautious about forcing the pace of change, we must not hesitate to declare our ultimate objectives and to take concrete actions to move toward them. We must be staunch in our conviction that freedom is not the sole prerogative of a lucky few, but the inalienable and universal right of all human beings. . . .

Now, I don't wish to sound overly optimistic, yet the Soviet Union is not immune from the reality of what is going on in the world. It has happened in the past—a small ruling elite either mistakenly attempts to ease domestic unrest through greater repression and foreign adventure, or it chooses a wiser course. It begins to allow its people a voice in their own destiny. Even if this latter process is not realized soon, I believe the renewed strength of the democratic movement, complemented by a global campaign for freedom, will strengthen the prospects for arms control and a world at peace.

I have discussed on other occasions . . . the elements of Western policies toward the Soviet Union to safeguard our interests and protect the peace. What I am describing now is a plan and a hope for the long term—the march of freedom and democracy which will leave Marxism-Leninism on the ashheap of history as it has left other tyrannies which stifle the freedom and muzzle the self-expression of the people. . . .

I've often wondered about the shyness of some of us in the West about standing for these ideals that have done so much to ease the plight of man and the hardships of our imperfect world. This reluctance to use those vast resources at our command reminds me of the elderly lady whose home was bombed in the Blitz. As the rescuers moved about, they found a bottle of brandy she'd stored behind the staircase, which was all that was left standing. And since she was barely conscious, one of the workers pulled the cork to give her a taste of it. She came around immediately and said, "Here now—there now, put it back. That's for emergencies." [Laughter]

Well, the emergency is upon us. Let us be shy no longer. Let us go to our strength. Let us offer hope. Let us tell the world that a new age is not only possible but probable.

During the dark days of the Second World War, when this island was incandescent with courage, Winston Churchill exclaimed about Britain's adversaries, "What kind of a people do they think we are?" Well, Britain's adversaries found out what extraordinary people the British are. But all the democracies paid a terrible price for allowing the dictators to underestimate us. We dare not make that mistake again. So, let us ask ourselves, "What kind of people do we think we are?" And let us answer, "Free people, worthy of freedom and determined not only to remain so but to help others gain their freedom as well." . . .

Source: Ronald Reagan, "Address to Members of the British Parliament," June 8, 1982, in *Public Papers of the Presidents of the United States: Ronald Reagan, 1981–1989,* from the American Presidency Project, University of California, Santa Barbara, www.presidency.ucsb.edu.

Document 9.7
The Reagan Administration's Long-Range Plan for Confronting the Soviet Union, National Security Decision Directive 75, January 17, 1983

President Reagan's plan for fighting the Cold War involved a sustained military buildup to change the Soviets' calculation of the perceived costs and benefits of military aggression. In addition, the United States would attempt to undermine Soviet domination of Eastern Europe and to work cooperatively with Communist China, so as to increase the Soviet Union's vulnerability along its Asian border. Reagan administration planners hoped that these policies would eventually lead to an improvement in superpower relations, but they understood that, in political terms, superpower tensions were going to have to get worse before they could get better.

U.S. RELATIONS WITH THE USSR

U.S. policy toward the Soviet Union will consist of three elements: external resistance to Soviet imperialism; internal pressure on the USSR to weaken the sources of Soviet imperialism; and negotiations to eliminate, on the basis of strict reciprocity, outstanding disagreements. Specifically, U.S. tasks are:

1. To contain and over time reverse Soviet expansionism by competing effectively on a sustained basis with the Soviet Union in all international arenas—particularly in the overall military balance and in geographical regions of priority concern to the United States. This will remain the primary focus of U.S. policy toward the USSR.

2. To promote, within the narrow limits available to us, the process of change in the Soviet Union toward a more pluralistic political and economic system in which the power of the privileged ruling elite is gradually reduced. . . .

3. To engage the Soviet Union in negotiations to attempt to reach agreements which protect and enhance U.S. interests and which are consistent with the principle of strict reciprocity and mutual interest. . . .

In order to implement this threefold strategy, the U.S. must convey clearly to Moscow that unacceptable behavior will incur costs that would outweigh any gains. At the same time, the U.S. must make clear to the Soviets that genuine restraint in their behavior would create the possibility of an East-West relationship that might bring important benefits for the Soviet Union. . . .

Shaping the Soviet Environment: Arenas of Engagement

. . .

A. Functional

1. *Military Strategy:* The U.S. must modernize its military forces—both nuclear and conventional—so that Soviet leaders perceive that the U.S. is determined never to accept a second place or a deteriorating military posture. Soviet calculations of possible war outcomes under any contingency must always result in outcomes so unfavorable to the USSR that there would be no incentive for Soviet leaders to initiate an attack. . . .

3. *Political Action:* U.S. policy must have an ideological thrust which clearly affirms the superiority of U.S. and Western values of individual dignity and freedom, a free press, free trade unions, free enterprise, and political democracy over the repressive features of Soviet Communism. . . .

B. Geopolitical

. . .

3. *The Soviet Empire* . . . U.S. policies should seek whenever possible to encourage Soviet allies to distance themselves from Moscow in foreign policy and to move toward democratization domestically.

  (a) *Eastern Europe:* The primary U.S. objective in Eastern Europe is to loosen Moscow's hold on the region while promoting the cause of human rights in individual East European countries. . . .

  (b) *Afghanistan:* The U.S. objective is to keep maximum pressure on Moscow for withdrawal and to ensure that the Soviets' political, military, and other costs remain high while the occupation continues. . . .

4. *China:* China continues to support U.S. efforts to strengthen the world's defenses against Soviet expansionism. The U.S. should over time seek to achieve enhanced strategic cooperation and policy coordination with China, and to reduce the possibility of a Sino-Soviet rapprochement. . . .

Priorities in the U.S. Approach: Maximizing Restraining Leverage over Soviet Behavior

The interrelated tasks of containing and reversing Soviet expansion and promoting evolutionary change within the Soviet Union itself cannot be accomplished quickly. The coming 5–10 years will be a period of considerable uncertainty in which the Soviets may test U.S. resolve by continuing the kind of aggressive international behavior which the U.S. finds unacceptable. . . .

. . . The heart of U.S. military strategy is to deter attack by the USSR and its allies against the U.S., its Allies, or other important countries, and to defeat such an attack should deterrence fail. . . . This military strategy will be combined with a political strategy attaching high priority to the following objectives:

—*Sustaining steady, long-term growth in U.S. defense spending and capabilities—both nuclear and conventional.* This is the most important way of conveying to the Soviets U.S. resolve and political staying-power.

—*Creating a long-term Western consensus for dealing with the Soviet Union.* . . .

Articulating the U.S. Approach: Sustaining Public and Congressional Support

The policy outlined above is one for the long haul. It is unlikely to yield a rapid breakthrough in bilateral relations with the Soviet Union. In the absence of dramatic near-term victories in the U.S. effort to moderate Soviet behavior, pressure is likely to mount for change in U.S. policy. There will be appeals from important segments of domestic opinion for a more "normal" U.S.-Soviet relationship, particularly in a period of political transition in Moscow.

It is therefore essential that the American people understand and support U.S. policy. This will require that official U.S. statements and actions avoid generating unrealizable expectations for near-term progress in U.S.-Soviet relations. At the same time, the U.S. must demonstrate credibly that its policy is not a blueprint for an open-ended, sterile confrontation with Moscow, but a serious search for a stable and constructive long-term basis for U.S.-Soviet relations.

RONALD REAGAN

Source: National Security Council, "U.S. Relations with the USSR" (NSC-NSDD-75), from the Federation of American Scientists, www.fas.org/irp/offdocs/nsdd/nsdd-075.htm.

Document 9.8
"An Evil Empire," President Ronald Reagan's Address to the National Association of Evangelicals, March 8, 1983

In his address at the annual convention of the National Association of Evangelicals in Orlando, Florida, President Reagan depicted the Soviet Union as "the focus of evil in the modern world" and referred to the rival superpower as "an evil empire." The speech touched on a number of moral and religious themes, but it had an overtly political rationale. The president was calling upon the "Religious Right" to embrace his foreign policy agenda as he had embraced its agenda on social policy.

. . . There is sin and evil in the world, and we're enjoined by Scripture and the Lord Jesus to oppose it with all our might. Our nation, too, has a legacy of evil with which it must deal. The glory of this land has been its capacity for transcending the moral evils of our past. For example, the long struggle of minority citizens for equal rights, once a source of disunity and civil war, is now a point of pride for all Americans. We must never go back. There is no room for racism, anti-Semitism, or other forms of ethnic and racial hatred in this country. . . .

But whatever sad episodes exist in our past, any objective observer must hold a positive view of American history, a history that has been the story of hopes fulfilled and dreams made into reality. Especially in this century, America has kept alight the torch of freedom, but not just for ourselves but for millions of others around the world.

And this brings me to my final point today. During my first press conference as President, in answer to a direct question, I pointed out that, as good Marxist-Leninists, the Soviet leaders have openly and publicly declared that the only morality they recognize is that which will further their cause, which is world revolution. I think I should point out I was only quoting Lenin, their guiding spirit, who said in 1920 that they repudiate all morality that proceeds from supernatural ideas—that's their name for religion—or ideas that are outside class conceptions. Morality is entirely subordinate to the interests of class war. And everything is moral that is necessary for the annihilation of the old, exploiting social order and for uniting the proletariat.

Well, I think the refusal of many influential people to accept this elementary fact of Soviet doctrine illustrates an historical reluctance to see totalitarian powers for what they are. We saw this phenomenon in the 1930's. We see it too often today.

This doesn't mean we should isolate ourselves and refuse to seek an understanding with them. I intend to do everything I can to persuade them of our peaceful intent, to remind them that it was the West that refused to use its nuclear monopoly in the forties and fifties for territorial gain and which now proposes a 50-percent cut in strategic ballistic missiles and the elimination of an entire class of land-based, intermediate-range nuclear missiles.

At the same time, however, they must be made to understand we will never compromise our principles and standards. We will never give away our freedom. We will never abandon our belief in God. And we will never stop searching for a genuine peace. But we can assure none of these things America stands for through the so-called nuclear freeze solutions proposed by some.

The truth is that a freeze now would be a very dangerous fraud, for that is merely the illusion of peace. The reality is that we must find peace through strength. . . .

Yes, let us pray for the salvation of all of those who live in that totalitarian darkness—pray they will discover the joy of knowing God. But until they do, let us be aware that while they preach the supremacy of the state, declare its omnipotence over individual man, and predict its eventual domination of all peoples on the Earth, they are the focus of evil in the modern world. . . .

So, I urge you to speak out against those who would place the United States in a position of military and moral inferiority. You know, I've always believed that old Screwtape [a devil in C. S. Lewis's *Screwtape Letters*] reserved his best efforts for those of you in the church. So, in your discussions of the nuclear freeze proposals, I urge you to beware the temptation of pride—the temptation of blithely declaring yourselves above it all and label both sides equally at fault, to ignore the facts of history and the aggressive impulses of an evil empire, to simply call the arms race a giant misunderstanding and thereby remove yourself from the struggle between right and wrong and good and evil.

I ask you to resist the attempts of those who would have you withhold your support for our efforts, this administration's efforts, to keep America strong and free, while we negotiate real and verifiable reductions in the world's nuclear arsenals and one day, with God's help, their total elimination.

While America's military strength is important, let me add here that I've always maintained that the struggle now going on for the world will never be decided by bombs or rockets, by armies or military might. The real crisis we face today is a spiritual one; at root, it is a test of moral will and faith. . . .

I believe we shall rise to the challenge. I believe that communism is another sad, bizarre chapter in human history whose last pages even now are being written. I believe this because the source of our strength in the quest for human freedom is not material, but spiritual. And because it knows no limitation, it must terrify and ultimately triumph over those who would enslave their fellow man. For in the words of Isaiah: "He giveth power to the faint; and to them that have no might He increaseth strength. . . . But they that wait upon the Lord shall renew their strength; they shall mount up with wings as eagles; they shall run, and not be weary. . . ."

Yes, change your world. One of our Founding Fathers, Thomas Paine, said, "We have it within our power to begin the world over again." We can do it, doing together what no one church could do by itself.

God bless you, and thank you very much.

Source: Ronald Reagan, "Remarks at the Annual Convention of the National Association of Evangelicals in Orlando, Florida," March 8, 1983, in *Public Papers of the Presidents of the United States: Ronald Reagan, 1981–1989,* from the American Presidency Project, University of California, Santa Barbara, www.presidency.ucsb.edu.

Document 9.9
President Ronald Reagan Announces the Strategic Defense Initiative, March 23, 1983

President Ronald Reagan was captivated by the idea that nuclear weapons might be made technologically obsolete. If the nation's scientific and engineering community could somehow perfect a defense against strategic nuclear missiles, then the horrifying, if thus far successful, doctrine of mutual assured destruction (MAD) could be laid to rest, along with the world's stockpiles of nuclear missiles. The president's critics labeled the proposal "Star Wars," to suggest that the program was based more in science fiction than science fact.

. . . [T]hus far tonight I've shared with you my thoughts on the problems of national security we must face together. My predecessors in the Oval Office have appeared before you on other occasions to describe the threat posed by Soviet power and have proposed steps to address that threat. But since the advent of nuclear weapons, those steps have been increasingly directed toward deterrence of aggression through the promise of retaliation.

This approach to stability through offensive threat has worked. We and our allies have succeeded in preventing nuclear war for more than three decades. In recent months, however, my advisers, including in particular the Joint Chiefs of Staff, have underscored the necessity to break out of a future that relies solely on offensive retaliation for our security.

Over the course of these discussions, I've become more and more deeply convinced that the human spirit must be capable of rising above dealing with other nations and human beings by threatening their existence. Feeling this way, I believe we must thoroughly examine every opportunity for reducing tensions and for introducing greater stability into the strategic calculus on both sides.

One of the most important contributions we can make is, of course, to lower the level of all arms, and particularly nuclear arms. . . .

If the Soviet Union will join with us in our effort to achieve major arms reduction, we will have succeeded in stabilizing the nuclear balance. Nevertheless, it will still be necessary to rely on the specter of retaliation, on mutual threat. And that's a sad commentary on the human condition. Wouldn't it be better to save lives than to avenge them? Are we not capable of demonstrating our peaceful intentions by applying all our abilities and our ingenuity to achieving a truly lasting stability? I think we are. Indeed, we must.

After careful consultation with my advisers, including the Joint Chiefs of Staff, I believe there is a way. Let me share with you a vision of the future which offers hope. It is that we embark on a program to counter the awesome Soviet missile threat with measures that are defensive. Let us turn to the very strengths in technology that spawned our great industrial base and that have given us the quality of life we enjoy today.

What if free people could live secure in the knowledge that their security did not rest upon the threat of instant U.S. retaliation to deter a Soviet attack, that we could intercept and destroy strategic ballistic missiles before they reached our own soil or that of our allies?

I know this is a formidable, technical task, one that may not be accomplished before the end of this century. Yet, current technology has attained a level of sophistication where it's reasonable for us to begin this effort. It will take years, probably decades of effort on many fronts. There will be failures and setbacks, just as there will be successes and breakthroughs. And as we proceed, we must remain constant in preserving the nuclear deterrent and maintaining a solid capability for flexible response. But isn't it worth every investment necessary to free the world from the threat of nuclear war? We know it is.

In the meantime, we will continue to pursue real reductions in nuclear arms, negotiating from a position of strength that can be ensured only by modernizing our strategic forces. At the same time, we must take steps to reduce the risk of a conventional military conflict escalating to nuclear war by improving our nonnuclear capabilities.

America does possess—now—the technologies to attain very significant improvements in the effectiveness of our conventional, nonnuclear forces. Proceeding boldly with these new technologies, we can significantly reduce any incentive that the Soviet Union may have to threaten attack against the United States or its allies.

As we pursue our goal of defensive technologies, we recognize that our allies rely upon our strategic offensive power to deter attacks against them. Their vital interests and ours are inextricably linked. Their safety and ours are one. And no change in technology can or will alter that reality. We must and shall continue to honor our commitments.

I clearly recognize that defensive systems have limitations and raise certain problems and ambiguities. If paired with offensive systems, they can be viewed as fostering an aggressive policy, and no one wants that. But with these considerations firmly in mind, I call upon the scientific community in our country, those who gave us nuclear weapons, to turn their great talents now to the cause of mankind and world peace, to give us the means of rendering these nuclear weapons impotent and obsolete.

Tonight, consistent with our obligations of the ABM treaty and recognizing the need for closer consultation with our allies, I'm taking an important first step. I am directing a comprehensive and intensive effort to define a long-term research and development program to begin to achieve our ultimate goal of eliminating the threat posed by strategic nuclear missiles. This could pave the way for arms control measures to eliminate the weapons themselves. We seek neither military superiority nor political advantage. Our only purpose—one all people share—is to search for ways to reduce the danger of nuclear war.

My fellow Americans, tonight we're launching an effort which holds the promise of changing the course of human history. There will be risks, and results take time. But I believe we can do it. As we cross this threshold, I ask for your prayers and your support.

Thank you, good night, and God bless you.

Source: Ronald Reagan, "Address to the Nation on Defense and National Security," March 23, 1983, in *Public Papers of the Presidents of the United States: Ronald Reagan, 1981–1989,* from the American Presidency Project, University of California, Santa Barbara, www.presidency.ucsb.edu.

Document 9.10
Nuclear Freeze Resolution, Joint Resolution 13, May 4, 1983

President Ronald Reagan's military buildup and his sometimes bellicose rhetoric about the Soviet Union ironically helped to mobilize support for a nuclear freeze—a moratorium on the development or deployment of additional nuclear weapons. The freeze was endorsed in numerous states before a resolution won a majority vote in Congress. In reply, the president continued to insist that freezing weapons at their current level would lock into place a Soviet advantage. He argued that the United States first had to respond to the latest Soviet provocations, including the Soviet arms buildup of the previous decade. Only then would it be possible to freeze weapons—and to look forward to their reduction and eventual elimination.

JOINT RESOLUTION

Calling for a mutual and verifiable freeze on and reductions in nuclear weapons.

Whereas the greatest challenge facing the Earth is to prevent the occurrence of nuclear war by accident or design;

Whereas the increasing stockpiles of nuclear weapons and nuclear delivery systems by both the United States and the Soviet Union have not strengthened international peace and security but in fact enhance the prospect for mutual destructions;

Whereas adequate verification of compliance has always been an indispensable part of any international arms control agreement; and

Whereas a mutual and verifiable freeze followed by reductions in nuclear weapons and nuclear delivery systems would greatly reduce the risk of nuclear war:

Now, therefore, be it

Resolved by the Senate and House of Representatives of the United States of America in Congress assembled, That the strategic arms reduction talks (START) between the United States and the Soviet Union should have the following objectives:

(1) Pursuing a complete halt to the nuclear arms race.

(2) Deciding when and how to achieve a mutual verifiable freeze on testing, production, and further deployment of nuclear warheads, missiles, and other delivery systems.

(3) Giving special attention to destabilizing weapons whose deployment would make such a freeze more difficult to achieve.

(4) Proceeding from this mutual and verifiable freeze, pursuing substantial, equitable, and verifiable reductions through mutual ceilings, annual percentages, or any other equally effective and verifiable means of strengthening strategic stability.

(5) Preserving present limitations and controls on current nuclear weapons and nuclear delivery systems.

(6) Incorporating ongoing negotiations in Geneva on land-based intermediate-range nuclear missiles into the START negotiations.

In those negotiations, the United States shall make every effort to reach a common position with our North Atlantic Treaty Organization allies on any element of an agreement which would be inconsistent with existing United States commitments to those allies.

Source: H.J. Res. 13, 98th Cong., 1st sess., January 3, 1983, in U.S. Congress, House Committee on Foreign Affairs, *Calling for a Mutual and Verifiable Freeze on and Reductions in Nuclear Weapons: Hearings and Markup before the Committee on Foreign Affairs, House of Representatives,* 98th Cong., 1st sess., on H.J. Res. 13, February 17, March 2 and 8, 1983 (Washington, D.C.: U.S. Government Printing Office, 1983), Appendix I, 243–245.

Document 9.11
President Ronald Reagan's Address on Changing the Tone of U.S.-Soviet Relations, January 16, 1984

After a year of harsh rhetoric and widespread fear that the Cold War was spiraling toward a nuclear Armageddon, President Reagan announced his intention to change the tone of U.S.-Soviet Union relations. Without being blind to the deep differences that divide them, he said, the superpowers should seek areas in which cooperation might prevail, including the resolution of regional conflicts and arms control leading to arms reduction. Some commentators saw a new Reagan in this speech, on the defensive in response to the domestic and international peace movement; others said it was the same Reagan, now speaking from a position of national strength, following a three-year military buildup.

. . . I believe that 1984 finds the United States in the strongest position in years to establish a constructive and realistic working relationship with the Soviet Union. We've come a long way since the decade of the seventies, years when the United States seemed filled with self-doubt and neglected its defenses, while the Soviet Union increased its military might and sought to expand its influence by armed forces and threat. . . .

Three years ago, we embraced a mandate from the American people to change course, and we have. With the support of the American people and the Congress we halted America's decline. Our economy is now in the midst of the best recovery since the sixties. Our defenses are being rebuilt, our alliances are solid, and our commitment to defend our values has never been more clear.

America's recovery may have taken Soviet leaders by surprise. They may have counted on us to keep weakening ourselves. They've been saying for years that our demise was inevitable. They said it so often they probably started believing it. Well, if so, I think they can see now they were wrong.

This may be the reason that we've been hearing such strident rhetoric from the Kremlin recently. These harsh words have led some to speak of heightened uncertainty and an increased danger of conflict. This is understandable but profoundly mistaken.

Look beyond the words, and one fact stands out: America's deterrence is more credible, and it is making the world a safer place—safer because now there is less danger that the Soviet leadership will underestimate our strength or question our resolve.

Yes, we are safer now, but to say that our restored deterrence has made the world safer is not to say that it's safe enough. We're witnessing tragic conflicts in many parts of the world. Nuclear arsenals are far too high, and our working relationship with the Soviet Union is not what it must be. These are conditions which must be addressed and improved. . . .

I propose that our governments make a major effort to see if we can make progress in three broad problem areas. First, we need to find ways to reduce, and eventually to eliminate, the threat and use of force in solving international disputes. . . .

Our second task should be to find ways to reduce the vast stockpiles of armaments in the world. It's tragic to see the world's developing nations spending more than $150 billion a year on armed forces—some 20 percent of their national budgets. We must find ways to reverse the vicious cycle of threat and response which drives arms races everywhere it occurs. . . .

Our third task is to establish a better working relationship with each other, one marked by greater cooperation and understanding. Cooperation and understanding are built on deeds, not words. Complying with agreements helps; violating them hurts. Respecting the rights of individual citizens bolsters the relationship; denying these rights harms it. Expanding contacts across borders and permitting a free exchange or interchange of information and ideas increase confidence; sealing off one's people from the rest of the world reduces it. Peaceful trade helps, while organized theft of industrial secrets certainly hurts.

Cooperation and understanding are especially important to arms control. In recent years we've had serious concerns about Soviet compliance with agreements and treaties. Compliance is important because we seek truly effective arms control. However, there's been mounting evidence that provisions of agreements have been violated and that advantage has been taken of ambiguities in our agreements. . . .

In our discussions with the Soviet Union, we will work to remove the obstacles which threaten to undermine existing agreements and a broader arms control process. Examples I've cited illustrate why our relationship with the Soviet Union is not what it should be. We have a long way to go, but we're determined to try and try again. We may have to start in small ways, but start we must.

In working on these tasks, our approach is based on three guiding principles—realism, strength, and dialog. Realism means we must start with a clear-eyed understanding of the world we live in. We must recognize that we are in a long-term competition with a government that does not share our notions of individual liberties at home and peaceful change abroad. We must be frank in acknowledging our differences and unafraid to promote our values.

Strength is essential to negotiate successfully and protect our interests. If we're weak, we can do neither. Strength is more than military power. Economic strength is crucial, and America's economy is leading the world into recovery. Equally important is our strength of spirit and unity among our people at home and with our allies abroad. We're stronger in all these areas than we were 3 years ago. Our strength is necessary to deter war and to facilitate negotiated solutions. Soviet leaders know it makes sense to compromise only if they can get something in return. Well, America can now offer something in return.

Strength and dialog go hand in hand, and we're determined to deal with our differences peacefully through negotiations. We're prepared to discuss the problems that divide us and to work for practical, fair solutions on the basis of mutual compromise. We will never retreat from negotiations.

I have openly expressed my view of the Soviet system. I don't know why this should come as a surprise to Soviet leaders who've never shied from expressing their view of our system. But this doesn't mean that we can't deal with each other. We don't refuse to talk when the Soviets call us imperialist aggressors and worse, or because they cling to the fantasy of a Communist triumph over democracy. The fact that neither of us likes the other system is no reason to refuse to talk. Living in this nuclear age makes it imperative that we do talk. Our commitment to dialog is firm and unshakeable, but we insist that our negotiations deal with real problems, not atmospherics.

In our approach to negotiations, reducing the risk of war, and especially nuclear war, is priority number one. A nuclear conflict could well be mankind's last. And that is why I proposed over 2 years ago the zero option for intermediate-range missiles. Our aim was and continues to be to eliminate an entire class of nuclear arms. Indeed, I support a zero option for all nuclear arms. As I've said before, my dream is to see the day when nuclear weapons will be banished from the face of the Earth. . . .

Our challenge is peaceful. It will bring out the best in us. It also calls for the best in the Soviet Union. We do not threaten the Soviet Union. Freedom poses no threat. It is the language of progress. We proved this 35 years ago when we had a monopoly on nuclear weapons and could have tried to dominate the world, but we didn't. Instead, we used our power to write a new chapter in the history of mankind. We helped rebuild war-ravaged economies in Europe and the Far East, including those of nations who had been our enemies. Indeed, those former enemies are now among our staunchest friends.

We can't predict how the Soviet leaders will respond to our challenge. But the people of our two countries share with all mankind the dream of eliminating the risk of nuclear war. It's not an impossible dream, because eliminating these risks are so clearly a vital interest for all of us. Our two countries have never fought each other. There's no reason why we ever should. Indeed, we fought common enemies in World War II. Today our common enemies are poverty, disease, and above all, war.

More than 20 years ago, President Kennedy defined an approach that is as valid today as when he announced it. "So let us not be blind to our differences," he said, "but let us also direct attention to our common interests and to the means by which those differences can be resolved."

Well, those differences are differences in governmental structure and philosophy. The common interests have to do with the things of everyday life for people everywhere. Just suppose with me for a moment that an Ivan and an Anya could find themselves, oh, say, in a waiting room, or sharing a shelter from the rain or a storm with a Jim and Sally, and there was no language barrier to keep them from getting acquainted. Would they then debate the differences between their respective governments? Or would they find themselves comparing notes about their children and what each other did for a living?

Before they parted company, they would probably have touched on ambitions and hobbies and what they wanted for their children and problems of making ends meet. And as they went their separate ways, maybe Anya would be saying to Ivan, "Wasn't she nice? She also teaches music." Or Jim would be telling Sally what Ivan did or didn't like about his boss. They might even have decided they were all going to get together for dinner some evening soon. Above all, they would have proven that people don't make wars.

People want to raise their children in a world without fear and without war. They want to have some of the good things over and above bare subsistence that make life worth living. They want to work at some craft, trade, or profession that gives them satisfaction and a sense of worth. Their common interests cross all borders.

If the Soviet Government wants peace, then there will be peace. Together we can strengthen peace, reduce the level of arms, and know in doing so that we have helped fulfill the hopes and dreams of those we represent and, indeed, of people everywhere. Let us begin now.

Source: Ronald Reagan, "Address to the Nation and Other Countries on U.S.-Soviet Relations," January 16, 1984, in *Public Papers of the Presidents of the United States: Ronald Reagan, 1981–1989,* from the American Presidency Project, University of California, Santa Barbara, www.presidency.ucsb.edu.

Document 9.12
The Weinberger Doctrine, Secretary of Defense Casper Weinberger's Address on Restricting the Use of Force, November 28, 1984

Secretary of Defense Casper Weinberger viewed the use of armed forces for military operations other than war (MOOTWA, in mil-speak) and low-intensity conflicts as a distraction from preparation for war and perhaps an invitation to a Vietnam-like quagmire. Therefore, in a speech at the National Press Club in Washington, D.C., he set forth criteria for the use of force. The Weinberger Doctrine was influenced by the secretary's senior military assistant, Maj. Gen. Colin Powell, who later articulated an overlapping doctrine of overwhelming force as the chairman of the Joint Chiefs of Staff during the Persian Gulf War. Whether termed the "Weinberger Doctrine," the "Weinberger-Powell Doctrine," or the "Powell Doctrine," the idea that the United States should use military force only under certain conditions, set by the military establishment itself, exerted a powerful influence over military planning and debates about military deployments into the post–Cold War era.

. . . We should only engage our troops if we must do so as a matter of our own vital national interest. We cannot assume for other sovereign nations the responsibility to defend their territory without their strong invitation when our freedom is not threatened.

On the other hand, there have been recent cases where the United States has seen the need to join forces with other nations to try to preserve the peace by helping with negotiations, and by separating warring parties, and thus enabling those warring nations to withdraw from hostilities safely. In the Middle East, which has been torn by conflict for millennia, we have sent our troops in recent years both to the Sinai and to Lebanon, for just such a peacekeeping mission. But we did not configure or equip those forces for combat—they were armed only for their self-defense. Their mission required them to be and to be recognized as peacekeepers. We knew that if conditions deteriorated so they were in danger, or if because of the actions of the warring nations, their peacekeeping mission could not be realized, then it would be necessary either to add sufficiently to the number and arms of our troops, in short to equip them for combat, or to withdraw them. And so in Lebanon, when we faced just such a choice, because the warring nations did not enter into withdrawal or peace agreements, the President properly withdrew forces equipped only for peacekeeping.

In those cases where our national interests require us to commit combat force we must never let there be doubt of our resolution. When it is necessary for our troops to be committed to combat, we must commit them, in sufficient numbers, and we must support them, as effectively and resolutely as our strength permits. When we commit our troops to combat we must do so with the sole object of winning.

Once it is clear our troops are required, because our vital interests are at stake, then we must have the firm national resolve to commit every ounce of strength necessary to win the fight to achieve our objectives. In Grenada we did just that.

Just as clearly, there are other situations where United States combat forces should not be used. I believe the postwar period has taught us several lessons, and from them I have developed six major tests to be applied when we are weighing the use of US combat forces abroad. Let me now share them with you:

(1) First, the United States should not commit forces to combat overseas unless the particular engagement or occasion is deemed vital to our national interest or that of our allies. That emphatically does not mean that we should declare beforehand, as we did with Korea in 1950, that a particular area is outside our strategic perimeter.

(2) Second, if we decide it is necessary to put combat troops into a given situation, we should do so wholeheartedly, and with the clear intention of winning. If we are unwilling to commit the forces or resources necessary to achieve our objectives, we should not commit them at all. Of course if the particular situation requires only limited force to win our objectives, then we should not hesitate to commit forces sized accordingly. When Hitler broke treaties and remilitarized the Rhineland, small combat forces then could perhaps have prevented the holocaust of World War II.

(3) Third, if we do decide to commit forces to combat overseas, we should have clearly defined political and military objectives. And we should know precisely how our forces can accomplish those clearly defined objectives. And we should have and send the forces needed to do just that. As Clausewitz wrote, "no one starts a war—or rather, no one in his senses ought to do so—without first being clear in his mind what he intends to achieve by that war, and how he intends to conduct it."

War may be different today than in Clausewitz's time, but the need for well-defined objectives and a consistent strategy is still essential. If we determine that a combat mission has become necessary for our vital national interests, then we must send forces capable to do the job and not assign a combat mission to a force configured for peacekeeping.

(4) Fourth, the relationship between our objectives and the forces we have committed—their size, composition and disposition—must be continually reassessed and adjusted if necessary. Conditions and objectives invariably change during the course of a conflict. When they do change, then so must our combat requirements. We must con-

tinuously keep as a beacon light before us the basic questions: "Is this conflict in our national interest?" "Does our national interest require us to fight, to use force of arms?" If the answers are "yes," then we must win. If the answers are "no," then we should not be in combat.

(5) Fifth, before the US commits combat forces abroad, there must be some reasonable assurance we will have the support of the American people and their elected representatives in Congress. This support cannot be achieved unless we are candid in making clear the threats we face; the support cannot be sustained without continuing and close consultation. We cannot fight a battle with the Congress at home while asking our troops to win a war overseas or, as in the case of Vietnam, in effect asking our troops not to win, but just to be there.

(6) Finally, the commitment of US forces to combat should be a last resort.

I believe that these tests can be helpful in deciding whether or not we should commit our troops to combat in the months and years ahead. The point we must all keep uppermost in our minds is that if we ever decide to commit forces to combat, we must support those forces to the fullest extent of our national will for as long as it takes to win. So we must have in mind objectives that are clearly defined and understood and supported by the widest possible number of our citizens. And those objectives must be vital to our survival as a free nation and to the fulfillment of our responsibilities as a world power. We must also be farsighted enough to sense when immediate and strong reactions to apparently small events can prevent lion-like responses that may be required later. We must never forget those isolationists in Europe who shrugged that "Danzig is not worth a war," and "why should we fight to keep the Rhineland demilitarized?"

These tests I have just mentioned have been phrased negatively for a purpose they are intended to sound a note of caution—caution that we must observe prior to committing forces to combat overseas. When we ask our military forces to risk their very lives in such situations, a note of caution is not only prudent, it is morally required.

In many situations we may apply these tests and conclude that a combatant role is not appropriate. Yet no one should interpret what I am saying here today as an abdication of America's responsibilities either to its own citizens or to its allies. Nor should these remarks be misread as a signal that this country, or this Administration, is unwilling to commit forces to combat overseas.

We have demonstrated in the past that, when our vital interests or those of our allies are threatened, we are ready to use force, and use it decisively, to protect those interests. Let no one entertain any illusions—if our vital interests are involved, we are prepared to fight. And we are resolved that if we must fight, we must win.

So, while these tests are drawn from lessons we have learned from the past, they also can and should be applied to the future. For example, the problems confronting us in Central America today are difficult. The possibility of more extensive Soviet and Soviet-proxy penetration into this hemisphere in months ahead is something we should recognize. If this happens we will clearly need more economic and military assistance and training to help those who want democracy.

The President will not allow our military forces to creep or be drawn gradually into a combat role in Central America or any other place in the world. And indeed our policy is designed to prevent the need for direct American involvement. This means we will need sustained Congressional support to back and give confidence to our friends in the region.

I believe that the tests I have enunciated here today can, if applied carefully, avoid the danger of this gradualist incremental approach, which almost always means the use of insufficient force. These tests can help us to avoid being drawn inexorably into an endless morass, where it is not vital to our national interest to fight. . . .

Source: Casper W. Weinberger, "The Uses of Military Power," November 28, 1984, Department of Defense News Release no. 609-84, in "The Keeper File: Weinberger's Six Tests," *Air Force Magazine* 87, no. 1 (January 2004), www.afa.org/magazine/jan2004/military_power.pdf.

Document 9.13
President Ronald Reagan Acknowledges Fault in the Iran-Contra Affair, March 4, 1987

In the Iran-Contra affair, President Reagan authorized the sale of arms to Iran, as part of an arms-for-hostages deal. The president at first denied that he had done so, but he was forced by the release of relevant documents to acknowledge his role, even though his "heart and [his] best intentions" still attested to his innocence. Reagan thus took limited responsibility for the first, ill-advised half of the Iran-Contra affair, and he vowed to implement the recommendations of a bipartisan commission—the "Tower Board," named for its chairman, Sen. John Tower, R-Texas—that had recently reported on the administration's mismanagement of national security. The president never acknowledged any responsibility for the second, illegal half of the Iran-Contra affair, the diversion of profits from the arms sales to the anti-Communist "Contra" paramilitary in Central America.

My fellow Americans:

I've spoken to you from this historic office on many occasions and about many things. The power of the Presidency is often thought to reside within this Oval Office. Yet it doesn't rest here; it rests in you, the American people, and in your trust. Your trust is what gives a President his powers of leadership and his personal strength, and it's what I want to talk to you about this evening.

For the past 3 months, I've been silent on the revelations about Iran. And you must have been thinking: "Well, why doesn't he tell us what's happening? Why doesn't he just speak to us as he has in the past when we've faced troubles or tragedies?" Others of you, I guess, were thinking: "What's he doing hiding out in the White House?" Well, the reason I haven't spoken to you before now is this: You deserve the truth. And as frustrating as the waiting has been, I felt it was improper to come to you with sketchy reports, or possibly even erroneous statements, which would then have to be corrected, creating even more doubt and confusion. There's been enough of that. I've paid a price for my silence in terms of your trust and confidence. But I've had to wait, as you have, for the complete story. . . .

I've studied the Board's report. Its findings are honest, convincing, and highly critical; and I accept them. And tonight I want to share with you my thoughts on these findings and report to you on the actions I'm taking to implement the Board's recommendations. First, let me say I take full responsibility for my own actions and for those of my administration. As angry as I may be about activities undertaken without my knowledge, I am still accountable for those activities. As disappointed as I may be in some who served me, I'm still the one who must answer to the American people for this behavior. And as personally distasteful as I find secret bank accounts and diverted funds—well, as the Navy would say, this happened on my watch.

Let's start with the part that is the most controversial. A few months ago I told the American people I did not trade arms for hostages. My heart and my best intentions still tell me that's true, but the facts and the evidence tell me it is not. As the Tower Board reported, what began as a strategic opening to Iran deteriorated, in its implementation, into trading arms for hostages. This runs counter to my own beliefs, to administration policy, and to the original strategy we had in mind. There are reasons why it happened, but no excuses. It was a mistake. I undertook the original Iran initiative in order to develop relations with those who might assume leadership in a post-Khomeini government.

It's clear from the Board's report, however, that I let my personal concern for the hostages spill over into the geopolitical strategy of reaching out to Iran. I asked so many questions about the hostages' welfare that I didn't ask enough about the specifics of the total Iran plan. Let me say to the hostage families: We have not given up. We never will. And I promise you we'll use every legitimate means to free your loved ones from captivity. But I must also caution that those Americans who freely remain in such dangerous areas must know that they're responsible for their own safety.

Now, another major aspect of the Board's findings regards the transfer of funds to the Nicaraguan contras. The Tower Board wasn't able to find out what happened to this money, so the facts here will be left to the continuing investigations of the court appointed Independent Counsel and the two congressional investigating committees. I'm confident the truth will come out about this matter, as well. As I told the Tower Board, I didn't know about any diversion of funds to the contras. But as President, I cannot escape responsibility. . . .

Now, what should happen when you make a mistake is this: You take your knocks, you learn your lessons, and then you move on. That's the healthiest way to deal with a problem. This in no way diminishes the importance of the other continuing investigations, but the business of our country and our people must proceed. I've gotten this message from Republicans and Democrats in Congress, from allies around the world, and—if we're reading the signals right—even from the Soviets. And of course, I've heard the message from you, the American people. You know, by the time you reach my age, you've made plenty of mistakes. And if you've lived your life properly—so, you learn. You put things in perspective. You pull your energies together. You change. You go forward.

My fellow Americans, I have a great deal that I want to accomplish with you and for you over the next 2 years. And the Lord willing, that's exactly what I intend to do.

Good night, and God bless you.

Source: Ronald Reagan, "Address to the Nation on the Iran Arms and Contra Aid Controversy," March 4, 1987, in *Public Papers of the Presidents of the United States: Ronald Reagan, 1981–1989,* from the American Presidency Project, University of California at Santa Barbara, www.presidency.ucsb.edu.

Document 9.14:
"Mr. Gorbachev: Tear Down This Wall!" President Ronald Reagan Makes a Prescient Rhetorical Demand in Berlin, June 12, 1987

Not even Ronald Reagan, one of the most optimistic leaders of the Cold War, could have imagined that the reviled Berlin Wall would soon be demolished, when he stood before the Brandenburg Gate and challenged Soviet leader Mikhail Gorbachev to "tear down this wall!"

. . . Twenty-four years ago, President John F. Kennedy visited Berlin, speaking to the people of this city and the world at the city hall. Well, since then two other presidents have come, each in his turn, to Berlin. And today I, myself, make my second visit to your city.

We come to Berlin, we American Presidents, because it's our duty to speak, in this place, of freedom. But I must confess, we're drawn here by other things as well: by the feeling of history in this city, more than 500 years older than our own nation; by the beauty of the Grunewald and the Tiergarten; most of all, by your courage and determination. Perhaps the composer, Paul Lincke, understood something about American Presidents. You see, like so many Presidents before me, I come here today because wherever I go, whatever I do: "Ich hab noch einen koffer in Berlin." [I still have a suitcase in Berlin.]

Our gathering today is being broadcast throughout Western Europe and North America. I understand that it is being seen and heard as well in the East. To those listening throughout Eastern Europe, I extend my warmest greetings and the good will of the American people. To those listening in East Berlin, a special word: Although I cannot be with you, I address my remarks to you just as surely as to those standing here before me. For I join you, as I join your fellow countrymen in the West, in this firm, this unalterable belief: Es gibt nur ein Berlin. [There is only one Berlin.]

Behind me stands a wall that encircles the free sectors of this city, part of a vast system of barriers that divides the entire continent of Europe. From the Baltic, south, those barriers cut across Germany in a gash of barbed wire, concrete, dog runs, and guardtowers. Farther south, there may be no visible, no obvious wall. But there remain armed guards and checkpoints all the same—still a restriction on the right to travel, still an instrument to impose upon ordinary men and women the will of a totalitarian state. Yet it is here in Berlin where the wall emerges most clearly; here, cutting across your city, where the news photo and the television screen have imprinted this brutal division of a continent upon the mind of the world. Standing before the Brandenburg Gate, every man is a German, separated from his fellow men. Every man is a Berliner, forced to look upon a scar.

President von Weizsacker has said: "The German question is open as long as the Brandenburg Gate is closed." Today I say: As long as this gate is closed, as long as this scar of a wall is permitted to stand, it is not the German question alone that remains open, but the question of freedom for all mankind. Yet I do not come here to lament. For I find in Berlin a message of hope, even in the shadow of this wall, a message of triumph. . . .

In the 1950's, Khrushchev predicted: "We will bury you." But in the West today, we see a free world that has achieved a level of prosperity and well-being unprecedented in all human history. In the Communist world, we see failure, technological backwardness, declining standards of health, even want of the most basic kind-too little food. Even today, the Soviet Union still cannot feed itself. After these four decades, then, there stands before the entire world one great and inescapable conclusion: Freedom leads to prosperity. Freedom replaces the ancient hatreds among the nations with comity and peace. Freedom is the victor.

And now the Soviets themselves may, in a limited way, be coming to understand the importance of freedom. We hear much from Moscow about a new policy of reform and openness. Some political prisoners have been released. Certain foreign news broadcasts are no longer being jammed. Some economic enterprises have been permitted to operate with greater freedom from state control. Are these the beginnings of profound changes in the Soviet state? Or are they token gestures, intended to raise false hopes in the West, or to strengthen the Soviet system without changing it? We welcome change and openness; for we believe that freedom and security go together, that the advance of human liberty can only strengthen the cause of world peace.

There is one sign the Soviets can make that would be unmistakable, that would advance dramatically the cause of freedom and peace. General Secretary Gorbachev, if you seek peace, if you seek prosperity for the Soviet Union and Eastern Europe, if you seek liberalization: Come here to this gate! Mr. Gorbachev, open this gate! Mr. Gorbachev, tear down this wall! . . .

Source: Ronald Reagan, "Remarks on East-West Relations at the Brandenburg Gate in West Berlin," June 12, 1987, in *Public Papers of the Presidents of the United States: Ronald Reagan, 1981–1989,* from the American Presidency Project, University of California at Santa Barbara, www.presidency.ucsb.edu.

Document 9.15
Intermediate Nuclear Forces Treaty, December 8, 1987

In the first arms reduction (as opposed to arms limitation) treaty of the Cold War, the Soviets and Americans agreed to remove intermediate-range and shorter-range nuclear missiles from Europe. The treaty, signed at a Washington, D.C., summit, contained stringent verification procedures. Its completion capped many years of often dramatic negotiation, beginning after the Soviet Union's deployment of the powerful intermediate-range SS-20 in 1976. The agreement did not include limits on tactical nuclear devices, those with a range less than approximately 300 miles.

TREATY BETWEEN THE UNITED STATES OF AMERICA AND THE UNION OF SOVIET SOCIALIST REPUBLICS ON THE ELIMINATION OF THEIR INTERMEDIATE-RANGE AND SHORTER-RANGE MISSILES
Signed at Washington December 8, 1987
Ratification advised by U.S. Senate May 27, 1988
Instruments of ratification exchanged June 1, 1988
Entered into force June 1, 1988

. . .

ARTICLE I

In accordance with the provisions of this Treaty which includes the Memorandum of Understanding and Protocols which form an integral part thereof, each Party shall eliminate its intermediate-range and shorter-range missiles, not have such systems thereafter, and carry out the other obligations set forth in this Treaty. . . .

ARTICLE IV

1. Each Party shall eliminate all its intermediate-range missiles and launchers of such missiles, and all support structures and support equipment of the categories listed in the Memorandum of Understanding associated with such missiles and launchers, so that no later than three years after entry into force of this Treaty and thereafter no such missiles, launchers, support structures or support equipment shall be possessed by either Party. . . .

ARTICLE V

1. Each Party shall eliminate all its shorter-range missiles and launchers of such missiles, and all support equipment of the categories listed in the Memorandum of Understanding associated with such missiles and launchers, so that no later than 18 months after entry into force of this Treaty and thereafter no such missiles, launchers or support equipment shall be possessed by either Party. . . .

ARTICLE XI

1. For the purpose of ensuring verification of compliance with the provisions of this Treaty, each Party shall have the right to conduct on-site inspections. The Parties shall imple-

ment on-site inspections in accordance with this Article, the Protocol on Inspection and the Protocol on Elimination.

2. Each Party shall have the right to conduct inspections provided for by this Article both within the territory of the other Party and within the territories of basing countries. . . .

5. Each Party shall have the right to conduct inspections pursuant to this paragraph for 13 years after entry into force of this Treaty. Each Party shall have the right to conduct 20 such inspections per calendar year during the first three years after entry into force of this Treaty, 15 such inspections per calendar year during the subsequent five years, and ten such inspections per calendar year during the last five years. Neither Party shall use more than half of its total number of these inspections per calendar year within the territory of any one basing country. . . .

ARTICLE XII

1. For the purpose of ensuring verification of compliance with the provisions of this Treaty, each Party shall use national technical means of verification at its disposal in a manner consistent with generally recognized principles of international law. . . .

Source: "Treaty between the United States of America and the Union of Soviet Socialist Republics on the Elimination of their Intermediate-Range and Shorter-Range Missiles," December 8, 1987, from the Federation of American Scientists, www.fas.org/nuke/control/inf/text/inf.htm.

Document 9.16
Soviet General Secretary Mikhail Gorbachev Implicitly Renounces the Use of Force to Retain the Soviets' Hold on Eastern Europe, December 7, 1988

In a speech before the UN General Assembly, General Secretary Gorbachev stunned the West by announcing unilateral steps to de-escalate the Cold War in Europe. Of even greater consequence was the Soviet leader's implicit renunciation of the Brezhnev Doctrine. From now on, Gorbachev suggested, Eastern Europe would be free to find its own way, even if that meant finding its way toward an accommodation with the West. The countries of Eastern Europe did so, far faster and more completely than the Soviet leader had imagined.

Two great revolutions, the French revolution of 1789 and the Russian revolution of 1917, have exerted a powerful influence on the actual nature of the historical process and radically changed the course of world events. Both of them, each in its own way, have given a gigantic impetus to man's progress. They are also the ones that have formed in many respects the way of thinking which is still prevailing in the public consciousness.

That is a very great spiritual wealth, but there emerges before us today a different world, for which it is necessary to seek different roads toward the future, to seek—relying, of course, on accumulated experience—but also seeing the radical differences between that which was yesterday and that which is taking place today.

The newness of the tasks, and at the same time their difficulty, are not limited to this. Today we have entered an era when progress will be based on the interests of all mankind.

Consciousness of this requires that world policy, too, should be determined by the priority of the values of all mankind. . . .

The compelling necessity of the principle of freedom of choice is also clear to us. The failure to recognize this, to recognize it, is fraught with very dire consequences, consequences for world peace. Denying that right to the peoples, no matter what the pretext, no matter what the words are used to conceal it, means infringing upon even the unstable balance that is, has been possible to achieve.

Freedom of choice is a universal principle to which there should be no exceptions. We have not come to the conclusion of the immutability of this principle simply through good motives. We have been led to it through impartial analysis of the objective processes of our time. The increasing varieties of social development in different countries are becoming in ever more perceptible feature of these processes. This relates to both the capitalist and socialist systems. The variety of sociopolitical structures which has grown over the last decades from national liberation movements also demonstrates this. This objective fact presupposes respect for other people's vies and stands, tolerance, a preparedness to see phenomena that are different as not necessarily bad or hostile, and an ability to learn to live side by side while remaining different and not agreeing with one another on every issue.

The de-ideologization of interstate relations has become a demand of the new stage. We are not giving up our convictions, philosophy, or traditions. Neither are we calling on anyone else to give up theirs. Yet we are not going to shut ourselves up within the range of our values. That would lead to spiritual impoverishment, for it would mean renouncing so powerful a source of development as sharing all the original things created independently by each nation. . . .

Our country is undergoing a truly revolutionary upsurge. The process of restructuring is gaining pace; we started by elaborating the theoretical concepts of restructuring; we had to assess the nature and scope of the problems, to interpret the lessons of the past, and to express this in the form of political conclusions and programs. This was done. The theoretical work, the re-interpretation of what had happened, the final elaboration, enrichment, and correction of political stances have not ended. They continue. However, it was fundamentally important to start from an overall concept, which is already now being confirmed by the experience of past years, which has turned out to be generally correct and to which there is no alternative.

In order to involve society in implementing the plans for restructuring it had to be made more truly democratic. Under the badge of democratization, restructuring has now encompassed politics, the economy, spiritual life, and ideology. . . .

. . . We have gone substantially and deeply into the business of constructing a socialist state based on the rule of law. A whole series of new laws has been prepared or is at a completion stage. Many of them come into force as early as 1989, and we trust that they will correspond to the highest standards from the point of view of ensuring the rights of the individual. Soviet democracy is to acquire a firm, normative base. This means such acts as the Law on Freedom of Conscience, on glasnost, on public associations and organizations, and on much else. There are now no people in places of imprisonment in the country who have been sentenced for their political or religious convictions. . . .

Now about the most important topic, without which no problem of the coming century can be resolved: disarmament. . . .

Today I can inform you of the following: The Soviet Union has made a decision on reducing its armed forces. In the next two years, their numerical strength will be reduced by 500,000 persons, and the volume of conventional arms will also be cut considerably. These reductions will be made on a unilateral basis, unconnected with negotiations on the mandate for the Vienna meeting. By agreement with our allies in the Warsaw Pact, we have made the decision to withdraw six tank divisions from the GDR, Czechoslovakia, and Hungary, and to disband them by 1991. Assault landing formations and units, and a number of others, including assault river-crossing forces, with their armaments and combat equipment, will also be withdrawn from the groups of Soviet forces situated in those countries. The Soviet forces situated in those countries will be cut by 50,000 persons, and their arms by 5,000 tanks. All remaining Soviet divisions on the territory of our allies will be reorganized. They will be given a different structure from today's which will become unambiguously defensive, after the removal of a large number of their tanks. . . .

Source: Mikhail Gorbachev, "Address to the 43rd United Nations General Assembly Session," December 7, 1988, from CNN, *Cold War*, www.cnn.com/SPECIALS/cold.war/episodes/23/documents/gorbachev/.

CHAPTER TEN

George Bush

Caution in the Face of Victory

G eorge Bush was the last president of the Cold War. In his four years as chief executive, the Cold War came to an almost mysterious end as the adversary—the "evil empire," as Ronald Reagan had called it—imploded.[1] As the Cold War unraveled in the East, President Bush sought leverage over events from Washington, D.C., through leadership of the Western Cold War alliance. His difficulty steering events seemed to make a mockery at times of the premise of the Cold War presidency, that the U.S. president was the most powerful democratically elected official on earth.

Secretary of State James Baker and President George Bush at the Conference on Security and Cooperation in Europe, Paris France, on November 19, 1990. Source: George Bush Presidential Library.

During the Cold War, presidents were inescapably entangled in national security and military affairs. No president, no matter his personal inclination and practical experience, could place a lower priority on national security than on domestic affairs without inviting trouble. Those who dared to make the attempt or seemed weak, principally Presidents Lyndon Johnson, Gerald Ford, and Jimmy Carter, paid a heavy price. Johnson abandoned the presidency after trying to hide the costs of America's military commitment to Vietnam, so that he would not have to sacrifice for his foreign policy his cherished domestic goal of building a Great Society. Gerald Ford's bid to win election to the position to which he had been appointed was undermined in the Republican primaries by a challenger—Ronald Reagan—who decried the incumbent's alleged naïveté in the face of the Communist threat. Ford was beaten by Carter, who met a similar fate. Carter lost the presidency to an opponent—Ronald Reagan, again—who effectively castigated him for failing to maintain American strength in a hostile global environment. In the Cold War, the president had to be an effective commander in chief and a strong symbolic head of state. For presidents who excelled at these roles, there were big payoffs in prestige and approval.

One might go so far as to say that, during the Cold War, the people of the United States and their presidents entered into a revised social contract. In exchange for taking onto their shoulders the sobering responsibility of maintaining the nation's safety against a deadly foe with a stockpile of nuclear weapons to match that of the United States, the American people, and their representatives in Congress, agreed to permit the president expanded powers, as well as the discretion to use such powers as he saw fit. There were, of course, boundaries to be observed. When President Johnson tried the patience and assumed the gullibility of the public in pursuit of victory in Vietnam, there was a backlash against presidential power. And when President Richard Nixon, seeking peace, expanded the war in Vietnam (and on the home front), he too was brought to heel. The power and prestige of the presidency underwent a considerable rehabilitation, however, under Ronald Reagan, and it was as the heir to Reagan that George Bush came into office in 1989. It became Bush's fate, then, to hold an office of renewed strength at a time when the very foundation of its modern meaning was undergoing daily challenge.

ORDER, PRUDENCE, AND A RED, WHITE, AND BLUE CAMPAIGN

George Bush's handling of American foreign policy in the twilight of the Cold War reflected his beliefs, his personality, and his path to the presidency. His fondness for order and remarkable skill at "personal diplomacy" were evident even in his childhood, when he was nicknamed "Have Half" because he was always eager to share.[2] The scion of Prescott Bush, a partner at a leading Wall Street investment bank who served in the Eisenhower years as a Republican senator from Connecticut, George Bush made his fortune as a partner in an independent oil exploration firm. By the mid-1960s, he was ready to make the move into politics, and he won election in 1966 to the House of Representatives as a Republican representing one of the more wealthy enclaves of Houston, Texas.

Bush went from the House to the White House through a succession of appointive positions, including U.S. ambassador to the United Nations, chairman of the Republican National Committee, U.S. envoy to Communist China (before the United States had a formal ambassador to the People's Republic), and director of the Central Intelligence Agency. His résumé and his skill at building relationships put him in a position where he could call on thousands of personal acquaintances to back his bid for the presidency in 1980. He lost the contest for the Republican nomination that year, but he did well enough to be invited to join the ticket with Ronald Reagan.

In the elections of 1988, after eight years of loyal service as vice president, Bush won a historic but incomplete victory as president. The good news for Bush was that he was the first sitting vice president to succeed to the presidency since Martin Van Buren in 1836. The bad news was that Democrats gained seats in both chambers of Congress, increasing their majorities to ten in the Senate and eighty-five in the House. Bush could clearly not claim a partisan mandate as president. Nor could he claim a personal one, for voters seemed to be thinking more of how much they appreciated *Reagan* not how much they liked Bush as they cast their ballots. "Underlying all specific considerations," observed political scientist Gerald M. Pomper in one postelection analysis, "was the electorate's attitude toward the outgoing President. Whatever the issue, those who approved 'of the way

Ronald Reagan has handled his job as President since 1981' voted for Bush, and those who disapproved voted for Dukakis."[3]

Although President Reagan and his supporters had declared the Cold War all but over in the final months of his presidency, neither Bush nor his Democratic opponent in 1988, Massachusetts governor Michael Dukakis, could afford to agree. Bush naturally sought to hold together the electoral coalition that Reagan had pieced together. Moreover, foreign policy was his area of core expertise and interest. Governor Dukakis, for his part, could ill afford to invite criticism for being naïve or gullible about the Communist threat. Ever since the Democratic Party had shifted to the left during the late 1960s, Republicans had scored victories by accusing Democrats of just these traits. The consequence was a red, white, and blue campaign, in which pride in country, and skepticism about the durability of changes underway in the Soviet Union, loomed large.

In one of the more memorable moments of Cold War presidential politicking, candidate Bush attacked his opponent for allegedly having a "problem" with the Pledge of Allegiance. "I believe that schoolchildren should have the right to say the pledge," said the vice president. "I don't know what his problem is with the pledge."[4] As governor, Dukakis had vetoed a bill, on constitutional grounds, requiring teachers to lead the recitation of the Pledge of Allegiance in the commonwealth's public schools. Running for president, Dukakis did not seem to understand that millions of Americans across the nation thought of patriotism as a nonnegotiable value—the sort that permitted no compromise, not even with the Constitution. Rather than place himself squarely behind the Pledge when questioned about his veto, he lectured reporters on the finer points of constitutional law. In this, the "last campaign of the Cold War," the law was not the issue.[5] The issue, as defined by the Bush camp, was each candidate's love of country and fitness to defend it against all enemies. When Dukakis attempted to burnish his image as a potential commander in chief by taking a ride in a tank, he managed to look simultaneously desperate and silly, and his tank ride was lampooned by cartoonists and comedians.

After the polls closed and the political mud slinging ended, the more refined and dignified Bush reappeared. Candidate Bush's skepticism about the changes under way in the Soviet system remained, however, for George Bush was less than romantic about popular democracy. Therefore, when Bush entered the presidency, he had a number of reasons to look askance at the idea of making any big changes in foreign policy. He faced an expanding Democratic majority in the House and Senate; he had won his office by promising to be resolute, not dynamic; and he was, by upbringing as well as disposition, inclined to caution. Even at the moment of his triumph, when he delivered his inaugural address, the president's ambition was not grand, but elegantly understated:

> Some see leadership as high drama and the sound of trumpets calling, and sometimes it is that. But I see history as a book with many pages, and each day we fill a page with acts of hopefulness and meaning. The new breeze blows, a page turns, the story unfolds. And so, today a chapter begins.[6]

It was not Bush's job, as he saw it, to sound a trumpet, and he was too well bred to blow his own horn. As he took office, he was prepared to manage, not end, the Cold War. How, then, did the Cold War end?

A POLICY OF CAUTION

The general secretary of the Soviet Union, Mikhail Gorbachev, and his comrades in the Politburo (the inner circle of the Soviet Communist Party) correctly perceived Bush's inclination to go slow in the Cold War. At a December 1988 meeting of the Politburo, Gorbachev appraised the president-elect "on the basis of contacts and some information," while conceding that his evaluation was "still premature":

> First, it is hard to expect that this administration will aggravate relations with the USSR or will get involved in some risky international adventure that can undermine these relations. On the other hand, Comrades, I believe with full certainty that the administration is not ready for a new serious turn in relations with the USSR which would correspond to the steps that our side has undertaken. At least such is the picture today. So they say: we stay prudent, we will not hurry. (**Document 10.1**)

What, then, could "make Bush act"? Gorbachev asked his comrades. Only the threat of a "loss of prestige," he reasoned. Therefore, the Soviet Union must take the initiative so as to present Bush with the choice of either acquiescing to Soviet leadership of the "entire world" or cooperating with the Soviets in a mutual effort to remake the superpower relationship.

President Bush and his foreign policy team naturally had their own ideas about the choices before them, and they refused to be hurried into setting forth their policy for dealing with the Soviet Union. The president acknowledged positive steps made by Moscow—steps that presumably had in fact been designed to make Bush act—but evinced no compulsion to respond with bold steps of his own. Thus, on February 15, 1989, after Soviet military forces at last withdrew from Afghanistan, the president neither claimed victory for the United States, lest such boasting incline the Soviets to reconsider their move, nor accepted the change in Soviet policy as sufficient to merit praise, much less a change in the basic relationship between the United States and the Communist superpower. Rather, President Bush demanded that the Soviets stop *all* interference in the internal affairs of Afghanistan, not just end their military domination of the country.

Similarly, although Bush did praise Gorbachev for his helpful attitude in working with the United States to resolve certain other issues around the globe, such as the civil war in Angola, Secretary of State James Baker regularly criticized the Soviets in 1989 for their continued support for the governments of Nicaragua and Cuba. Secretary Baker also called repeatedly for Gorbachev to make a clear and explicit renunciation of the Brezhnev Doctrine—the statement of Soviet policy articulated by former general secretary Leonid Brezhnev, by which the Soviets claimed the right to intervene in Eastern Europe to defend communism against all enemies, including the Eastern Europeans themselves, should they seek to change their Soviet-backed governments.

By May 1989 President Bush had settled upon a general approach to the Soviet Union. The theme was prudence, as emphasized in the president's May 12 commencement speech at Texas A&M University, in which he observed that it would be foolish to base U.S. policy on Soviet words or even Soviet good intentions. The United States must respond instead to the Soviet Union's enormous and threatening military might and actions that continued to threaten the peace and stability of the world. In Europe, the Soviets had unilaterally reduced their forces, but the Warsaw Pact, Bush observed, still possessed hundreds of thousands more troops than the North Atlantic Treaty Organization (NATO) and still divided the East from the West with barbed wire and concrete. Finally, with regard to the third world, Bush invited General Secretary Gorbachev to

> work with the West in positive, practical—not merely rhetorical—steps toward diplomatic solution to . . . regional disputes around the world. I welcome the Soviet withdrawal from Afghanistan, and the Angola agreement. But there is much more to be done around the world. We're ready. Let's roll up our sleeves and get to work.[7]

In two more commencement speeches, at Boston University and the United States Coast Guard Academy, and then in a major address in West Germany at the end of the month, the president elaborated on the importance of a step-by-step, cautious approach to changes under way in the world and stated plainly the steps he expected the Soviets to take to demonstrate their good faith. In addition to adhering to the human rights demands of the 1975 Helsinki Final Act (see **Document 7.1**), to which the Soviets had formally subscribed, the president called on Gorbachev to dismantle the Berlin Wall and to make concessions in negotiations that would soon resume on conventional as well as nuclear arms.

Over the next several months, the Soviets took steps of their own choosing in order to undermine, as they saw it, the American stubbornness to let go of the Cold War. In September Soviet foreign minister Eduard Shevardnadze, in negotiations with Bush and Baker, agreed to dismantle the Soviet radar site at Krasnoyarsk, which the Americans had long claimed was in violation of the 1972 Anti-Ballistic Missile (ABM) Treaty (see **Document 6.17**), and to drop the Soviets' previous insistence that a new nuclear arms agreement be linked to concessions by the United States on its missile defense system, the Strategic Defense Initiative (SDI), or "Star Wars." Later in the year, the Soviets discontinued military aid to Nicaragua, as the United States had discontinued military aid to the anti-Marxist Contras. (In April 1989 Bush had agreed with Congress on a compromise bill that would clothe, shelter, and feed, but not further arm, the U.S.-backed rebels until national elections scheduled for February 1990. When the elections took place, the Marxist Sandinista regime lost the presidency.)

The Bush administration set forth its fullest statement on foreign policy with regard to the Soviet Union in September 1989 through National Security Directive 23, which was signed by the president and addressed to the administration's most senior officials (**Document 10.2**). NSD 23 held that "the Soviet military threat has not diminished" but rather increased. "The character of the changes taking place in the Soviet Union," the report continued, "leads to the possibility that a new era may be upon us"—but only the possibility. Moreover, "the transformation of the Soviet Union from a source of instability to a productive force in the family of nations is a long-term goal that can only be pursued from a position of American strength, and with patience and creativity." It would take "decades," according to NSD 23, for the changes occurring in the Soviet Union to assume their final shape.

The president, of course, was wrong, but then so was virtually everyone else who gave serious thought at the time to the future of the Soviet Union. Even while the Bush administration carefully formulated its policy, a series of momentous events unfolded. In the

Baltic region, nationalist sentiment had been organized into non-Communist political organizations, which agitated openly for a restoration of national rights. Even the Baltic Communist parties joined in the movement toward autonomy, and in February 1989 Estonia began to fly its prewar national flag over all government buildings, to the enormous consternation of Soviet officials. In May representatives of the three Baltic states—Estonia, Lithuania, and Latvia—adopted resolutions calling on the Soviet Union to recognize their right to make their own choices regarding their economy. In Russia itself, meanwhile, political elites emerged, foremost among them Boris Yeltsin, who openly criticized the Communist Party as a reactionary organization and who seemed more interested in the future of Russia than of the Soviet state. President Bush reacted cautiously; he feared giving encouragement to nationalists who might provoke the Soviets to violence. When Yeltsin, recently elected to represent Moscow in the Congress of Deputies and by then the undisputed leader of the aggressive reformers in Moscow, visited the White House in 1989, he was brought in via a side entrance and given an audience not with Bush, but with the president's national security adviser, Brent Scowcroft, and the National Security Council's top Russian expert, Condoleezza Rice.

Even when, in the same momentous year, Communist China witnessed mass demonstrations against totalitarian rule, the president and his senior foreign policy team took caution, not hope, from events. After Communist Party Chairman Mao Zedong's death in 1976, limited but potent reforms had been undertaken in China, granting minimal property rights to farmers and opening defined sectors of the economy to foreign investment. An experiment with limited democratic rights, which involved a loosening of state censorship, encouraged a movement on college campuses and among educated urbanites in favor of a further expansion of liberties. The movement took inspiration in part from Gorbachev's reforms in the Soviet Union. A recent rapprochement between the two leading Communist nations, moreover, had increased the receptivity of the Chinese people to viewing events in the Soviet Union favorably. Gorbachev was even scheduled to visit Beijing in May 1989, for the first visit to China by a Soviet head of state since the Sino-Soviet split of the 1950s.

On May 13, 1989, just a day before Gorbachev's arrival and after several weeks of mass protests that had led to no observable change in the government's willingness to expand its reforms, several thousand students gathered in Tiananmen Square, a vast public plaza in Beijing, and announced a hunger strike to demand that the government open a dialogue with the students' leaders. For weeks, the West was captivated by televised images of Chinese youth protesting for freedom. Finally, on June 4, the government took action. Troops of the People's Liberation Army, brought into the city for the occasion from rural provinces—where soldiers were thought likely to have less sympathy with urban youth and their romantic ideals—forcibly scattered the demonstrators, arrested the leaders, and killed those who dared to resist.

Amid cries of outrage from Capitol Hill and demands that the president condemn and punish the People's Republic of China, President Bush responded with understated rhetoric, mild dispensations, and a secret high-level mission by the national security adviser to China. When the Democratic-controlled Congress passed a law automatically extending the visas of Chinese students in America by four years, the president used his veto. After the House voted overwhelmingly, 390 to 25, to override the president's veto, Bush and Secretary of State Baker intensely lobbied Republican senators for their support. "Things are at a very sensitive stage over there [in China]," Baker said after a lunch with Republican senators. An override would undermine the administration in delicate negotiations.[8] The president's veto was sustained, just barely; the Senate's vote of 62 to 37 to override fell 4 votes short of the required two-thirds majority. The president made the most of his narrow victory, telling reporters, "When they heard the full argument, I think they decided, 'Well, we should support the President on this one.'"[9]

To Bush, the moral of Tiananmen was to beware the backlash of a Communist state when challenged beyond its endurance. Because President Bush saw Gorbachev as the best hope for moderation and stability in the Soviet Union, he thus worried about Gorbachev's ability to maintain his power against both popular pressure to increase the pace of change and elite pressure from hard-liners and military leaders to slow it down. To support Gorbachev and the moderate path that he seemed to represent, Bush agreed in October to an informal summit, to take place December 2 and 3, for which the Soviets had been lobbying the White House. Before the two leaders could meet at Malta, however, the world changed, effectively bringing the Cold War to an abrupt end.

"AWKWARD AND UNCOMFORTABLE": THE FALL OF THE BERLIN WALL

In September 1989 East Germans, residents of the "crown jewel" of Eastern Europe, as their nation was widely known in the East, began to vote with their feet for freedom. This became possible when Hungary opened its borders with Austria on September 10, 1989, as a step toward abandoning its own ties to the Soviet Union. In response to the Hungarian border opening, tens of thousands of people in East Germany (the German Democratic Republic, GDR) simultaneously decided to "go on vacation" to Hungary—which had always been a simple matter, since both countries were behind the Iron Curtain— from which they could then enter Austria, and from Austria, travel freely to West Germany (the Federal Republic of Germany, FRG). By FRG law, they could then claim automatic citizenship. Thousands of other East Germans sought asylum at Western embassies in Czechoslovakia, Poland, and in East Germany itself. The East German government responded by seeking to close its borders with its suddenly unreliable East European neighbors, which provoked massive demonstrations.

Earlier in the Cold War, the Soviets might well have reacted, as they did in Hungary in 1956 and Czechoslovakia in 1968, by crushing the dissenters by force. Gorbachev, however, was disenchanted with the precedents set by the leaders of his youth. In his memoirs, Gorbachev described his profound distress at the Soviet invasion of Czechoslovakia. The Prague Spring "stood on the threshold of important developments," according to Gorbachev. When the Soviets crushed the rebellion, they drove "a stake" into the heart of "all later searches to transform the system."[10] In addition, Gorbachev was absorbed with his own domestic problems.

The Soviet economy had been in a slow decline for years. The arms race had taken a toll, as had the expensive war in Afghanistan. Even more important, the Soviets had come to grief through the accumulated inefficiencies of a command economy, in which prices were set by the state, resources were allocated by bureaucrats, and individual initiative was punished rather than rewarded. The Soviets also suffered greatly from their inability to match Western technological innovation. By the time Gorbachev came to power, growth rates were barely above zero.

A different sort of Soviet leader might have pushed grimly forward without attempting reform, but Gorbachev had staked his reputation within and without the Soviet Union on his ability to reform the ailing Soviet economy by implementing "New Thinking," which became the foundation for his signature policies of perestroika (restructuring) and glasnost (openness).[11] Taking on the burdens of Eastern European states, themselves coping with the accumulated miseries of Soviet-style command economies and the oil price shocks of the era, would make Gorbachev's job more difficult. In the old days, when Soviet leaders judged their success primarily in terms of their raw power—whether they were in charge of the empire or not—the economic costs of keeping the countries of Eastern Europe dependent on the Soviet Union would not have been such a great concern. Gorbachev's decision to prioritize the Soviet national economy encouraged him to watch passively as Eastern Europe crumbled.

On a visit to East Germany on October 7, 1989, Gorbachev pointedly stated that policy for the GDR was made "not in Moscow, but in Berlin."[12] After GDR president Erich Honecker resigned on October 18, Gorbachev reiterated his position that the Soviet Union had "no right to interfere" in the affairs of East Germany. The new president, Egor Krenz, would have to resolve his country's troubles on his own.

Elsewhere in Eastern Europe, popular demonstrations contributed to a spate of complementary changes in leaders and even forms of government in 1989. Poland continued its progress toward open government; during the summer, the first free Polish elections since before World War II took place. In Hungary in October, the parliament adopted a new constitution that relinquished the Communist Party's monopoly on power. Radio stations broadcast the speeches of the hero of Hungary's attempted revolution against Soviet control, the late Imre Nagy, who was executed in 1958, and 250,000 people assembled in the capital for a lengthy ceremony in which his body was reinterred. (He had originally been buried in an unmarked grave.) In Yugoslavia the government was forced by popular pressures to endorse free elections, independent labor unions, and individual rights.

The spread of pluralism in the Soviet satellites and the apparent willingness of the Soviet Union, as led by General Secretary Gorbachev, to tolerate this enormous transformation posed a problem for President Bush, focused as he was on Soviet capabilities, which continued to threaten the Western alliance. If the United States' allies were to become so enamored of Gorbachev that they agreed to the Soviet position on arms control, the Soviets might temporarily lose a measure of control over Eastern Europe (Bush always worried that the Soviets might reverse course and crack down at any moment) but gain a permanent military advantage.

As a consequence, the president worked hard in 1989 to maintain positive relations with the FRG and consensus within the NATO military alliance. It was not an easy task. Gorbachev wanted to place priority in arms talks on reducing short-range nuclear forces, which were important to the West's defense strategy. President Bush was adamant that conventional force reductions come first, because it was in that realm that the East still possessed superiority in Europe. Despite the hard realism of Gorbachev's position, whereby he clearly sought an advantage for his side, not a pacifist abandonment of war, many Europeans were tempted to see the problem in arms talks in the same way that Gorbachev did. Many Europeans were, in fact, frankly skeptical of American intentions, while they had come to perceive Soviet intentions through the lens of Gorbachev's status as a world celebrity. From this point of view, Gorbachev was the "good guy" now and Bush the militarist keeping the Cold War alive. Bush fought back in his own way, by working the telephone and meeting as frequently as possible with other heads of state. At least in part because of the president's skillful diplomacy with his NATO partners, in particular with Chancellor Helmut Kohl of the FRG, the alliance held firm.

President Bush reviewed the changes taking place in Eastern Europe with Kohl in a conversation on October 23, 1989 (**Document 10.3**). In their talk, the U.S. and German heads of state agreed that East Europeans were pushing forward these changes on their own, with considerable courage, and that, as Kohl remarked, "none of us can give a prognosis" of how the situation would develop. In East Germany, they agreed, a great deal depended on Krenz, the new president.

General Secretary Gorbachev, as it happens, also agreed. On November 1, he sought to reassure Krenz of Krenz's own ability to meet the challenge before him (**Document 10.4**). Gorbachev could offer Krenz nothing beyond advice and hope, as both men worked to save, not end, Communist rule in the East. Krenz should not fear that his country might be dissolved by being incorporated into the West, Gorbachev reasoned, because no one was "looking forward to German unification." "History itself," he declared, "decided that there should be two German states." Krenz merely needed to keep ties between his nation and the FRG "under control."

While dispensing his advice to Krenz, Gorbachev seemed to seek sympathy as he reviewed for his new colleague the economic troubles of the East. In both Hungary and Poland, he pointedly observed, utter economic dependence on the West made it impossible for the Soviets to rescue those nation's failing economies, for "we cannot take Poland on our balance [sheet]." The situation in East Germany was much the same.

Within weeks, further demonstrations led to mass mobilizations of East Germans, who on November 9 pressed to cross into West Berlin. When guards at the various checkpoints decided on their own not to use force to halt them—apparently having no current orders from the government as to how to respond to mass civil disobedience of this sort—thousands of East Germans crossed joyously into West Berlin. East and West Germans, amid celebrations carried around the world by live television, assaulted the wall with hammers, crowbars, and whatever else they had on hand. "This," reflected Gorbachev's senior foreign policy aide, A. S. Chernyaev, "is the end of Yalta" (**Document 10.5**).

At the White House, the president held an impromptu press conference in the Oval Office. It was "awkward and uncomfortable," the president recalled in his foreign policy memoirs:

> Of course I was thankful about the events in Berlin, but as I answered questions my mind kept racing over a possible Soviet crackdown, turning all the happiness to tragedy. My answers were cautious. I tried to explain that we were handling the event in a way that would not goad the Soviets. Lesley [Stahl, a White House correspondent for CBS News] poised over me, remarked that "this is a sort of great victory for our side in the big East-West battle, but you don't seem elated."
>
> "I'm not an emotional kind of guy," I said.
>
> "Well, how elated are you?" she demanded.
>
> "I'm very pleased," I replied evenly.[13]

Stahl's line of questioning was, thought the president, "pure foolishness," repeated by Democratic leaders on Capitol Hill, one of whom urged the president to go to Berlin to "dance" on the wall.[14]

It was against this backdrop, and the November 11 resignation of Bulgaria's president for life as a result of mass protests, that Bush and Gorbachev met for talks on December 2–3 aboard a Soviet ship, the *Maxim Gorky*, off of Malta, in the Mediterranean Sea. At Malta, Bush and Gorbachev began to "look ahead to a new relationship between East and West, a new Europe, and in some respects a new world." Gorbachev informed the president that the Soviets "don't consider you an enemy any more" and Bush spoke of his desire for a "cooperative" relationship with the Soviet Union.[15] At the end of the talks, the two leaders held a joint press conference, at which the general secretary reported, "We stated, both of us, that the world leaves one epoch of cold war and enters another epoch" (**Document 10.6**).

Before the end of the year, the separation of Eastern Europe from the Soviet Union was nearly complete. In Czechoslovakia the Communist president was forced into early retirement. In December Alexander Dubcek, the reformist Communist leader who was deposed when the Soviets crushed the Sprague Spring of 1968, was elected chairman of the Czech parliament, and a leading dissident, Vaclav Havel, was elected president. Also in December, the brutally repressive dictator of Romania, Nicolae Ceausescu, was executed along with his wife after a military coup overthrew his regime.

Given these changes in the governments of Eastern Europe, it was not long before the institutions that had tied the region to the Soviet Union became obsolete and failed. In January 1990, at the annual meeting of the Council for Mutual Economic Assistance (COMECON), a number of the newly reconfigured Eastern European states called for the dissolution of "that fundamental economic organization of the Soviet empire."[16] Within a year, COMECON had ceased to exist. The Warsaw Pact, the military alliance of the Soviet Union and Eastern Europe, also collapsed in the aftermath of the revolutions in Eastern Europe. Ignoring Gorbachev's call to recast the alliance as a nonmilitary organization, the pact's Eastern European members disbanded the organization in the summer of 1991 and demanded the withdraw of Soviet troops from their now sovereign nations.

GERMAN REUNIFICATION AND A BRIEF SOVIET-AMERICAN CONDOMINIUM OF POWERS

Over 1990 and 1991, the two years following the fall of the Berlin Wall, the forces pushing the Eastern European countries away from the Soviet Union and on independent paths toward pluralism spread to the Soviet Union itself. There were two issues of great concern for the president during this time: German reunification and Baltic independence. In both cases, President Bush continued to approach events with great caution, anxious not to provoke a Soviet military crackdown or an unraveling of stability and order within the Soviet Union. Although, in hindsight, many observers identify the fall of the Berlin Wall as the certain end of the Cold War, Bush and his national security adviser were not so certain. They still thought it possible, in Scowcroft's words, that the end result of all the changes sweeping the former Soviet bloc might be a "Brezhnev system [of Communist dictatorship in eternal conflict with the West] with a humanitarian paint job."[17]

German reunification came to pass, despite the opposition of both the Soviets and the British as well as the ambivalence of the Americans. Margaret Thatcher, the conservative British prime minister, expressed the historic aversion of her country to the domination of the continent of Europe by any single nation. Chancellor Kohl attempted to make light of such concerns in conversation with Bush by remarking, "Frankly, sixty-two million prosperous Germans are difficult to tolerate—add seventeen million more [the population of East Germany] and they [other European states] have big problems."[18] The Bush administration did share at least a measure of Thatcher's concern. Its more conservative members, in particular Scowcroft, were frankly wary of German reunification. Ultimately, however, it was the Germans who would decide the issue.

After the collapse of the wall, the West German government sought to stabilize the GDR to prevent an uncontrolled depopulation of the East. (More than 130,000 East Germans emigrated to the FRG in November 1989 alone.)[19] Principally, this meant the FRG began to provide a great deal of "foreign" aid to the GDR, on condition that the GDR commit to radical, promarket reforms. In the GDR, meanwhile, popular pressure for political reform undermined the authority of the Communist government, which had hoped to maintain power by appeasing citizens with free elections, political transparency, and calls to end to the Soviet military presence in their country. Crowds of East Germans, unimpressed with the new face of East German communism, forced their way into government buildings to seize Communist Party records, lest they be destroyed by bureaucrats hoping to hide the misdeeds of the past. Even Soviet military installations were assaulted by demonstrators. In the first free elections in GDR history, on March 19, 1990, a coalition of pro-unification candidates linked to the party of Chancellor Kohl in the West won an overwhelming victory. German reunification, barring military intervention, was now a foregone conclusion.

The Bush administration accepted the Germans' decision for unity and established a forum for the negotiation of reunification, to which the Soviets would be a part. In the "two plus four" process, the two Germanys took the lead, while the four Allies of World War II—the United States, the Soviet Union, Britain, and France, which still held occupation rights under agreements signed at the end of the war—were secondary partners in the talks. In February 1990 Gorbachev dropped his opposition to reunification and accepted the two plus four process. To sweeten the deal, Secretary of State Baker assured Gorbachev that in a NATO incorporating a reunified Germany, NATO's foreign military forces would not be moved eastward from their present positions.

Gorbachev was still not in complete agreement with the West on German reunification when he traveled to the United States at the end of May 1990 for a summit with Bush. At that summit, however, the president successfully exploited the Soviet leader's desperation for Western economic assistance to win the final, critical concession. Conditions were so bad in the Soviet Union that summer that a massive food shortage was feared. In Washington, Gorbachev "virtually begged" the president to sign a trade deal in order to help feed the Soviet people.[20] In exchange, Gorbachev at last surrendered his opposition to a reunified Germany's membership in NATO. Later that summer, the two Germanys signed a unification treaty and the four occupying powers agreed to recognize complete German sovereignty. The two superpowers further declared the soon-to-be-former East Germany off limits for nuclear weapons and Soviet troops. The Treaty on the Final Settlement with Respect to Germany was signed in Moscow September 12.

President Bush was also able at the May 1990 summit to gain Soviet concessions on the arms balance. The Soviets were simply in no position to negotiate. Gorbachev's reforms, although heralded in the West as a great success for having eased tensions in the Cold War, had weakened the general secretary at home and worsened the economic troubles that had inspired the reforms in the first place.

As a complement to perestroika, the attempted reconstruction of the Soviet economy, Gorbachev had implemented a policy of glasnost, or openness, for Soviet citizens. The idea had been to focus popular anger at perestroika's old guard opponents, the faceless but privileged apparatchiks (Communist officials) whose regulations and red tape were strangling the economy. But the process had gotten out of hand as the Soviet people began to decide what it was they wished to criticize about the old Stalinist system under which they lived. Soviet workers complained bitterly about stagnant wages. Inexperienced in handling such situations, the government responded to wage demands by printing currency to pay the workers. Banking on inflation, enterprising Soviet citizens with cash reserves or connections then began to buy out the merchandise at government stores, to resell it on the mushrooming black market. Convinced that government planners were making matters worse, Gorbachev and his reformers slashed the budgets and staffs of state ministries "involved in the economy in order to prevent them from further tampering with it. Without the state and the party to hold it together and guide it, the economy went into free-fall."[21]

Angered by the unintended consequences of glasnost, hard-line members of the Communist Party stubbornly refused to embrace perestroika. In response, Gorbachev unwittingly deepened the hole he was digging for himself with a refinement of glasnost: demokratizatsiya, or democratization. Under the rubric of spreading "democracy," Gorbachev permitted the formation of factions within the Communist Party and even experimented with multicandidate, though not multiparty, elections. Again, the results were unexpected. Exercising their new freedom of association, Soviet citizens established informal groups that became the basis for political parties that challenged not only the hardliners, but Gorbachev himself. Civil society, which had been tightly controlled in the old Soviet system, flourished with even the most minimal encouragement from the state.

Everything Gorbachev tried, it seemed, only further undermined his ability to control events. Still, he continued to try. Like President Hoover when he was faced with the Great Depression, Gorbachev thought that perhaps if he could only cut government expenses sufficiently, then things might improve.

Cutting expenses in the Soviet Union really meant one thing—reducing the tremendous burden of defense expenditures. Making concessions to the West would help cut these expenses. Making concessions might also, Gorbachev hoped, stimulate loans and grants from Western sources. When he went to Washington in the summer of 1990, Gorbachev wanted, in fact, some very concrete help from Bush, including membership in the International Monetary Fund and the right to join meetings of the G-7, the seven leading industrialized countries.

The president pursued a balancing act before and after this summit, leading the allies to offer the Soviets a portion of what they wanted, such as observer status at the next G-7 meeting (at which Gorbachev presented his ideas for a Western bailout of the Soviet economy) in exchange for ever greater concessions on outstanding security concerns, including the reduction of conventional forces in Europe. The last point was particularly momentous, for the superpowers had negotiated with one another without result from 1973 to 1989 in the Mutual and Balanced Forces Reduction Talks. (After Bush took office, the name of those talks was changed to Conventional Forces in Europe.) On November 19, 1990, the two sides agreed to a treaty signed by all twenty-two members of NATO and the Warsaw Pact, substantially reducing conventional forces (including combat troops, as well as tanks, artillery systems, armored combat vehicles, and fighter aircraft) in Europe. To make the treaty possible, Gorbachev had reversed himself by accepting the Americans' demand that the United States be permitted to retain a significant number of troops in Europe.

By late summer 1990, the nature of the relationship between the superpowers had definitely changed. Although Bush and his top advisers, with good reason as it would turn out, still feared that Gorbachev might not last in the top job in the Soviet Union, Bush was more than happy to accept "Gorby's" friendship when Iraq invaded and occupied Kuwait in August 1990. The response to the Iraqi invasion of neighboring Kuwait (the long-lost nineteenth province of Iraq, according to Iraqi dictator Saddam Hussein) became the defining moment of George Bush's presidency.

Declaring immediately that Iraq's aggression "would not stand," President Bush defined the situation in the sort of stark moralistic terms that no longer applied to U.S. relations with the Soviet Union. In doing so, the president harkened back to World War II, in which the United States had allied with the Soviets to overcome a greater evil, that of Adolph Hitler's Nazi regime. General Secretary Gorbachev's cooperative attitude, and desire to win further U.S. and Western support to prop up the Soviet economy (and, thereby, extend his own stay in office), led him to play his part in this drama well. Gorbachev joined Bush in denouncing Iraq's actions and supported United Nations resolutions demanding the restoration of Kuwaiti sovereignty.

The high point for Soviet-Western cooperation was reached in November 1990, when the Soviet Union and the nations of Eastern and Western Europe (plus Canada) signed the Charter of Paris for a New Europe during the Conference on Security and Cooperation in Europe (CSCE).[22] The charter was an amplification of the 1975 Helsinki Accords, which had done so much to inspire dissidents in the Soviet Union and Eastern Europe. On November 21 in Paris, at the close of the charter conference, President Bush read some prepared remarks. "We're going to have a statement on what transpired here in the CSCE talks," the president began, haltingly. He continued:

> And really, the first sentence, although written in the past tense, says it all: that in signing the Charter of Paris this morning, we have closed a chapter of history. I'm about to sign this, and we are closing a chapter in history. The cold war is over, and now we move on to working with the various countries in the CSCE and others for a peaceful and stable Europe.[23]

After commending those who worked on the Conventional Forces in Europe Treaty, concluded simultaneously with the charter, the president made a few comments drawing a parallel between Eastern Europe and Kuwait (both were victims of aggression and force) and then invited questions. In the press conference at which the president of the United States declared the end of the Cold War, not a single reporter asked him to expand upon his remarks. They presumably considered the end of the Cold War yesterday's news and were interested only in today's: the looming war with Iraq.

BALTIC INDEPENDENCE AND THE END OF THE SOVIET UNION

The end of the Cold War was not truly complete without the end of the Soviet Union. The latter came to pass as suddenly as the former. The trigger was the drive for Baltic independence.

Both the Soviet Union and the Bush administration were less than enthusiastic about independence for the Baltic states. Estonia, Latvia, and Lithuania were part of the Soviet Union, and if the Soviets accepted the right of secession for these republics, it was reasonable to fear that the precedent thus established would lead to the ruin of the empire. Even though Bush repeatedly "warned Gorbachev to find a peaceful solution," he "declined to do more for fear of provoking the violent disintegration of the Soviet Union."[24] The bipolar global balance of power had been the foundation of the Cold War's conflicts and proxy wars, but it was also a source of stability. The bipolar world was "the devil we knew," which to George Bush was preferable to the chaos that might engulf the world should the other pole suddenly disappear. As events unfolded, however, it quickly became apparent that it really did not matter what the superpowers' leaders might prefer.

Nationalist aspirations had never been entirely extinguished in the Soviet states. Most previous Soviet leaders, beginning with Joseph Stalin, had risen through the ranks of the Soviet system by helping to suppress nationalism brutally in such vital parts of the empire as the Ukraine. Gorbachev was less attuned to and less comfortable with this part of his job than those who had gone before him. Still, early in his tenure, he responded with force to the occasional ethnic riot in the provinces, as in December 1986 when residents of Kazakhstan protested the replacement of the first secretary of the Kazakh Communist Party with an ethnic Russian. While in office, Gorbachev continued to call upon force to quell disturbances that challenged the central government's authority. In 1989 more than twenty Georgians were killed in the provincial capital, Tbilisi, when Soviet troops crushed a demonstration organized by a pro-independence faction or popular front—one of those informal institutions that Gorbachev had permitted under glasnost, in the expectation that they would encourage and enable critics to voice their disappointment at Gorbachev's opponents, not with him or with his hopes for a reinvigorated Soviet Union.

Gorbachev was ill prepared, though, for what happened the next year. In spring 1990, following more than a year of preparation, the Baltic states moved decisively toward independence. Lithuania, Latvia, and Estonia all passed resolutions condemning Soviet occupation as illegal and indicating their intention to change their relationship with Moscow. Lithuania was the first to defy Moscow openly by declaring its complete independence on March 11. The Latvian government's highest body, the Supreme Soviet—under intense pressure from the population, which had mobilized behind a dues-paying organization, the Latvian Popular Front—followed with a May declaration of its intent to become independent following a period of transition.

Soviet authorities responded at first with economic sanctions and political pressure. Finally, on January 11, 1991, after the Lithuanian government refused to rescind its proclamation of independence, Soviet tanks rolled through the streets of the capital, Vilnius. Troops seized the parliament building and fired on civilian protestors while fighter jets flew menacingly overhead. Soviet soldiers withdrew within days from most government offices, but they continued to occupy the capital's television station for the next eight months. On the night of January 20, Soviet troops struck the Latvian capital, Riga. Only Estonia was spared outright assault.

President Bush, once again urged by Democratic opponents in Congress to respond forcefully, saw no benefit to threatening tougher action than the United States was truly prepared to take. As the president well understood, it was inconceivable that the United States or NATO would use force in defense of secessionist movements in the Soviet Union. Even to grant encouragement to such movements carried substantial risks of unintended escalation of conflict between the superpowers. The president had to be content with rhetorical denunciations of the violence. Blasting the U.S. president for alleged appeasement, the Baltic states sought help from other sources, including Boris Yeltsin, who pledged his and Russia's support against Gorbachev and the Soviet Union.

If the drive for independence had been limited to the Baltic region, the Soviet Union might have survived. Unfortunately for Gorbachev, however, events in the Baltic states were followed by secessionist declarations in the more vital provinces of Georgia, Ukraine, and Russia. In Tbilisi, Georgia, anti-Soviet demonstrators had been dispersed with force on April 9, 1989; twenty were killed. On the second anniversary of that event, Georgia declared independence. In Ukraine, sovereignty was declared July 1990, although full independence was not proclaimed until over a year later. In the heart of the Soviet Union,

Russia, the independence movement had a champion who rivaled Gorbachev in his charismatic appeal to the people.

Boris Yeltsin's power grew as he won leadership of newly legalized institutions, such as the Russian Congress of People's Deputies. In May 1990 he was elected chairman of the Russian Supreme Soviet, a subgroup of the Congress. By this election, he became the de facto president of Russia. His standing was given further democratic legitimacy in a republic-wide election for president in June 1991. In the same month, Russia issued its own declaration of sovereignty.

In the midst of this turmoil, Bush and Gorbachev met in Moscow for a final time. At the conclusion of their talks, the two leaders signed a new arms control agreement, the Strategic Arms Reduction Treaty (START I; **Document 10.7**). The historic treaty, which mandated significant reductions in nuclear arms by both sides, was soon overshadowed in the news by an attempted overthrow of the crumbling Soviet government.

In August 1991 eight antireformist leaders of the Soviet government, including Vladimir Kriuchov, the chief of the KGB; Dmitrii Iazov, the minister of defense; and Lasilii Starodubtsev, the head of the Peasants' Union, initiated a coup. They attempted to prevent further erosion of the Soviet system by placing Gorbachev under house arrest in his summer home and ordering the Soviet military to take possession of all the key government buildings in Moscow. Yeltsin, at first from within the Russian parliament building and then on the streets of the capital, rallied large public protests against the attempted coup and won the loyalty of many persons within the military and security agencies.

After the failure of the August coup, the Soviet Union quickly collapsed. Yeltsin's loyalists took possession of the Soviet Union's central government offices and decreed the end of union-wide institutions, including the Communist Party of the Soviet Union. By the end of the year, the Baltic states and all the other Soviet republics had declared or affirmed their independence. On December 25, 1991, the leaders of the newly formed Commonwealth of Independent States—the Soviet successor nations—dissolved the Union of Soviet Socialist Republics. President Bush addressed the United States on the occasion of the collapse of the Soviet Union and expressed his appreciation for former general secretary Gorbachev (**Document 10.8**).

CONCLUSION

George Bush tried hard as president to go slow and be careful. Events did not permit him to go slow, but he was careful. Perhaps it was as a consequence of his caution that the Soviet Union achieved an almost bloodless crash landing. Perhaps it really did not matter what position the U.S. president took during the death throes of the nation's fifty-year adversary. As the president might have said, however, it is best in such a situation to be prudent and to act as if the position of the United States was indeed potentially critical. Eight presidents before him, from Harry Truman through Ronald Reagan, had borne the responsibility of defending the United States against what was thought to be an enduring and enormous threat from the Soviet Union. That threat came not just from the attitude of the Soviet head of state, which might change overnight with a change in personnel, but also from the existence of all the institutions and resources of a rival superpower, including a vast arsenal of weapons, both nuclear and conventional. The period from 1989 to 1991 was surely no time to throw caution to the wind in confronting that reality.

The reserved President Bush permitted himself few moments of celebration. At last, in the heady atmosphere of early 1992, following the collapse of both the Cold War and the Soviet Union and the defeat of Saddam Hussein, President Bush reflected on the end of the Cold War and took a bow. (**Document 10.9**). It was, he said in his State of the Union address on January 28, a victory, not just an event: "The Cold War didn't end. It was won." Those who won it included generations of American servicemen and women as well as generations of American taxpayers, who for half a century "shouldered the burden and paid taxes that were higher than they would have been to support a defense that was bigger than it would have been if imperial communism had never existed." At long last, "the long, drawn-out dread is over."

Was the Cold War social contract between the people and their president thereby over as well? At the very least it was in trouble. President Bush discovered this to his chagrin in his campaign for reelection. In 1991, the year before the election, the president had led an impressively diverse coalition of nations to push Saddam Hussein's army out of Kuwait and had won the world's support for this action through the United Nations. The victory, indeed the *effort,* was the start of something truly big, according to Bush. "This is an historic moment," said the president in announcing the start of military action against Iraq:

> We have in this past year made great progress in ending the long era of conflict and cold war. We have before us the opportunity to forge for ourselves and for future generations a new world order—a world where the rule of law, not the law of the jungle, governs the conduct of nations. When we are successful—and we will be—we have a real chance at this new world order, an order in which a credible United Nations can use its peacekeeping role to fulfill the promise and vision of the U.N.'s founders.[25]

A "New World Order" was to be created on the ashes of the Cold War's world order. In this new age, as envisioned by Bush, nations that threatened the common good would face the common wrath of an organized society of states. Force and belligerence would become a thing of the past, as would perhaps war itself, once the community of states had demonstrated its will to police bad states by acting against one of the worst of all, Iraq under Hussein.[26]

The U.S. public rallied around the president in enormous numbers immediately after the stunningly successful military operation to force Iraq's army out of Kuwait. President Bush, for a moment, even enjoyed unprecedented public approval for his handling of the presidency. The people's enthusiasm did not translate, however, into a winning majority of votes in November 1992. In that election, the public rejected the experienced and steady leadership of the president that they had so recently celebrated, and instead entrusted the presidency to Bill Clinton, a Democratic former governor of Arkansas who not only had never served in the armed forces, but also had manipulated the system to avoid such service during the Vietnam War. It seemed, in the end, that it was not a New World Order after all, but a New (and diminished) Presidential Order that George Bush had brought into being.

NOTES

1. President Ronald Reagan famously termed the Soviet Union an "evil empire" (see Document 9.8).
2. Peter Schweizer and Rochelle Schweizer, *The Bushes: Portrait of a Dynasty* (New York: Double-day, 2004), 54.
3. Gerald M. Pomper, "The Presidential Election," in Gerald M. Pomper et al., *The Election of 1988: Reports and Interpretations,* ed. (Chatham, N.J.: Chatham House Publishers, 1989), 144.
4. Marjorie Randon Hershey, "The Campaign and the Media," in Gerald M. Pomper et al., *The Election of 1988* (Chatham, N.J.: Chatham House Publishers, 1989), 85.
5. Sidney Blumenthal, *Pledging Allegiance: The Last Campaign of the Cold War* (New York: Harper Collins, 1990).
6. George Bush, "Inaugural Address," January 20, 1989, in *Public Papers of the Presidents of the United States: George Bush, 1989–1993,* from the American Presidency Project, University of California, Santa Barbara, www.presidency.ucsb.edu.
7. George Bush, "Remarks at the Texas A&M University Commencement Ceremony in College Station," May 12, 1989, in *Public Papers of the Presidents of the United States: George Bush, 1989–1993,* from the American Presidency Project, University of California, Santa Barbara, www.presidency.ucsb.edu.
8. Thomas L. Friedman, "White House Asks an Irate Congress for China Support," *New York Times,* January 24, 1990, ProQuest Historical Newspapers.
9. As quoted in Helen Dewar, "Senate Narrowly Votes to Sustain Veto of Chinese Students Bill," *Washington Post,* January 26, 1990.
10. Jeremi Suri, "Explaining the End of the Cold War: A New Historical Consensus," *Journal of Cold War Studies* 4, no.4 (2002), 77.
11. Ibid., 77–79.
12. Richard A. Melanson, *American Foreign Policy since the Vietnam War: The Search for Consensus from Nixon to Clinton* (Armonk, N.Y.: M. E. Sharpe, 2000), 197.
13. George Bush and Brent Scowcroft, *A World Transformed* (New York: Knopf, 1988), 149.
14. Ibid.
15. Raymond L Garthoff, *The Great Transition: Soviet-American Relations and the End of the Cold War* (Washington, D.C.: Brookings Institution, 1994), 406.
16. The Library of Congress, "Russia, New Thinking: Foreign Policy under Gorbachev," http://countrystudies.us/russia/17.htm.
17. Bush and Scowcroft, *World Transformed,* 155.
18. Ibid., 199.
19. Ibid., 194.
20. John Robert Greene, *The Presidency of George Bush* (Lawrence: University Press of Kansas, 2000), 107.
21. The Library of Congress, "Russia, New Thinking: Foreign Policy under Gorbachev," http://countrystudies.us/russia/17.htm.
22. The CSCE did not become a "full blown organization" until 1995, by which time it was renamed OSCE, the Organization for Security and Cooperation in Europe. See OCSE, "CSCE/OSCE Timeline," www.osce.org/item/15659.html.
23. George Bush, "Remarks and a Question-and-Answer Session with Reporters in Paris, France," November 21, 1990, in *Public Papers of the Presidents of the United States: George Bush, 1989–1993,* from the American Presidency Project, University of California, Santa Barbara, www.presidency.ucsb.edu.
24. As quoted by Melanson, *American Foreign Policy,* 207.
25. George Bush, "Address to the Nation Announcing Allied Military Action in the Persian Gulf," January 16, 1991, in *Public Papers of the Presidents of the United States: George Bush, 1989–1993,* from the American Presidency Project, University of California, Santa Barbara, www.presidency.ucsb.edu.
26. Ibid.

Document 10.1
Soviet Leaders Discuss the World Situation and President-elect George Bush, December 27–28, 1988

In a meeting of the top leadership of the Soviet Union, the Politburo of the Central Committee of the Communist Party of the Soviet Union (CC CPSU), General Secretary Mikhail Gorbachev and his "comrades" reviewed Western reaction to Gorbachev's recent speech to the United Nations, where he revealed unilateral arms reductions and discussed the urgent need to promote peace between Communist and Western nations. If the United States did not want the Soviet Union to "lead the entire world," it would be up to the new president, George Bush, to respond positively to Soviet initiatives. Bush was an exceedingly cautious man, the Soviets observed, but could be made to act.

Top Secret
Single Copy
(Draft record)
process
Meeting of the Politburo of the CC CPSU
27–28 December 1988

Chaired: Cde. M.S. Gorbachev
Present: Cdes. V.I. Vorotnikov, L.N. Ziakov, E.K. Ligachev, V.A. Medvedev, V.P. Nikonov, N.I. Ryzhkov, N.N. Sliunkov, V.M. Chebrikov, E.A. Shevardnadze, A.N. Yakovlev, A.P. Biriukova, A.V. Vlasov, A.I. Lukiuanov, Yu. D. Masliukov, G.P. Rzumosvskii, Yu.F. Soloviev, N.V. Talyzin, D.T. Yazov.

 1. About practical implementation and practical support of the results of the visit of Cde. M. S. Gorbachev to the U.N.

Gorbachev: . . . We can state that our initiatives pulled the rug [out] from under the feet of those who have been prattling, and not without success, that new political thinking is just about words. The Soviet Union, they [political leaders and commentators in the United States, Britain, and elsewhere in the West] said, should still provide evidence. There was plenty of talk, many nice words, but not a single tank is withdrawn, not a single cannon. Therefore the unilateral reduction left a huge impression, and, one should admit, created an entirely different background for perceptions of our policies and the Soviet Union as a whole.

 . . . Such impressive positive shifts created among the conservative part of the US political elite, and not only in the US, concern, anxiety, and even fear. [British prime minister Margaret] Thatcher also shares some of it. This breeds considerations of another kind, the essence of which is—to lower expectations, to sow doubts, even suspicions. Behind it is the plot to stop the process of erosion [and], disintegration of the foundations of the "Cold War." That is the crux of the matter. We are proposing and willing to build a new world, to destroy the old basis. Those who oppose it are in the minority, but these circles are very influential.

In the classified information which we receive they speak directly: we cannot allow the Soviet Union to seize the initiative and lead the entire world. . . .

What kind of policy will the US conduct with regard to us? There are several very interesting and serious versions. . . .

Here is one: changes in the policy of the USSR are caused by the profound crisis of communism and socialism. . . . In other words we are dismantling socialism with our *perestroika* and renouncing communist goals. This version is used to devalue our peace initiatives. These are just forced steps, so they say, they do not have another option. Well, there is some grain of realism in this, but only to a degree. We had something different in mind when we formulated our policy. . . .

On the basis of this version comes the conclusion that the United States should do nothing on its part to consolidate positive shifts in international relations. The Soviet Union as well as other socialist countries, so they say have no way out. . . . This is serious, comrades. The "Washington Times" writes about it. And the "Heritage Foundation" prepared recommendations for the Bush administration along these lines.

And here is the viewpoint of liberal circles: The USSR is not renouncing socialism, instead it is rescuing it, as President [Franklin D.] Roosevelt once rescued American capitalism through the New Deal. . . .

If this [conservative] version prevails, it will have a serious political effect. Incidentally, some elements of this concept are present in the thinking of [President-elect George] Bush. As if they are passing from Reagan to Bush. They are present in Western Europe: they say that under Reagan the United States has built up its military potential, activated their support to freedom fighters in various regions, and thereby convinced the Soviet Union that expansionist policy has no future. Some Europeans also want to consider the source of change of Soviet policy as American power.

This seems to be the most influential current. In essence it is close to the official viewpoint. Its danger is obvious, since, if it takes root and becomes the foundation of the policy of the future administration, it will contribute to the arms race and to military interference by the US in other countries. . . .

Of course, it is still premature to draw serious conclusions about the policy of the future administration, but something can be said on the basis of contacts and some information. First, it is hard to expect that this administration will aggravate relations with the USSR or will get involved in some risky international adventure that can undermine these relations. On the other hand, Comrades, I believe with full certainty that the administration is not ready for a new serious turn in relations with the USSR which would correspond to the steps our side has undertaken. At least such is the picture today. So they say: we stay prudent, we will not hurry.

Still, at the last moment, when I managed to break away from Reagan I spoke to Bush about this indecisiveness. He snapped back: you must understand my position. I can not, according to American tradition, step up front until a formal transfer of power has taken place. This I understand, no question about it. We will have understanding. And he assured me—there will be continuity. He believes we should build on what has been achieved, and he will make his own contribution. . . .

We should take into account that Bush is a very cautious politician. They say his idiosyncratic feature is the "natural caution" of Bush. It is inside him. We should see it. And what can make Bush act? Only [a threat] of the loss of prestige for the administration. So we need circumstances which we have now created by our initiatives to promote this process.

The mood of the present administration mostly reflects centrist sentiments in the political circles of the US and Bush himself says: I am in the center. Most of those who today turn out to be in Bush's team are people who in America are called traditionalists. These people were brought up in the years of the Cold War and still do not have any foreign policy alternative to the traditional post-war course of the United States with all its zigzags to the Right, to the Left, even with its risky adventures. . . .

Yakovlev: Yesterday I met with [U.S. ambassador Jack] Matlock. He told me that Bush is more professional, better informed, but at the same time is more cautious. He tried to convince me that he always took part in the preparation of specific decisions, was interested in details, knew many, that is: he cast the new president in the best possible light.

What else should we keep in mind in terms of putting pressure on the Americans? They are very afraid of our European and Pacific policies. They would not like to [have to] jump on [an already] departing train, a runaway train no less. They are used to being in the driver's seat. They are upset by our active foreign policy in other regions. . . .

Most importantly, Mikhail Sergeevich [Gorbachev], you spoke many times about it, is the disappearance of the enemy image. If we continue to advance in this direction and carry out this business, we will ultimately pull the carpet from under the feet of the military-industrial complex [of the United States]. Of course, the Americans will be forced to change their approaches radically. . . .

Ligachev: . . . Foreign policy is a very large complex of issues. And most important among them, cardinal, is disarmament. . . . We need disarmament most of all. We carried this burden, with relation to the military budget, with the result that in the economic area we could hardly solve anything important. . . .

But this does not mean that we should weaken the defense preparedness of the country. We have enough ways, approaches, and means to reduce the excessively large military expenditures and to use rationally, pragmatically the means for strengthening the defense readiness of the country. We should tell this to the party, to the party activists. Today, when the world has already begun to disarm, slowly but surely, in the final analysis, the power of the state will be determined not by military might, but by a strong economy and by political cohesion of society. . . .

Gorbachev: . . . Vitaly Ivanovich [Vorotnikov] said that people ask within the country: how did it come about that we "strip down" independently? And Yegor Kuzmich [Ligachev] approached this theme from another angle: the Party should know. We will keep it a secret, speaking frankly. And we will keep this secrecy for one reason: if we admit now that we cannot build a longer-term economic and social policy without [unilateral cuts], then we will be forced to explain—why. Today we cannot tell even the Party about it; first of all we should bring about some order. If we say today how much we are removing for defense from the national revenue, this may reduce to naught [the effect] of the speech at the United Nations. Since such a [disastrous] situation does not exist in any other country. Perhaps only in poor countries, where half of their budget goes to military spending.

Shevardnadze: For instance, in Angola.

Gorbachev:. . . First, in our plans we build in military expenses twice as large as the growth of national income, then our national income turns out to be going down the tubes, but we stick to our military plans. So you should [be able to] figure out what is going on here. For that reason we should be patient for a little bit longer. . . . By the time of the 13th Five-Year Plan [for 1991–1995], . . . we will have something to say. . . .

Source: "Minutes of the Meeting of the Politburo of the Central Committee of the Communist Party of the Soviet Union, 27–28 December 1988 (Excerpts)," trans. Vladislav Zubok, from "On the Eve: A Glimpse Inside the Politburo at the End of 1988," *Cold War International History Project Bulletin*, no. 12–13 (Fall–Winter 2001): 24–29, www.cwihp.org.

Document 10.2
U.S. Relations with the Soviet Union, National Security Directive 23, September 22, 1989

In a major review of Cold War strategy, the Bush administration appraised events in the Soviet Union. It was possible, but not certain, declared the president, that "a new era may be upon us." The United States would remain vigilant in the face of the continuing Soviet threat and test the Soviets' willingness to live up to their new rhetoric of openness and respect for human rights.

. . .

For forty years the United States has committed its power and will to containing the military and ideological threat of Soviet communism. Containment was never an end in itself; it was a strategy born of the conditions of the postwar world. The United States recognized that, while Soviet military power was not the only threat to international stability, it was the most immediate and grave one. The U.S. challenge was to prevent the spread of Soviet communism while rebuilding the economic, political and social strength of the world's long-standing and new democracies. Those who crafted the strategy of containment also believed that the Soviet Union, denied the course of external expansion, would ultimately have to face and react to the internal contradictions of its own inefficient, repressive and inhumane system.

This strategy provided an enduring pillar for the growth of Western democracy and free enterprise. While the most important goal of containment has been met—the development of free and prosperous societies in Western Europe and in other parts of the world—the Soviet military threat has not diminished. Rather, in the last two decades, the Soviet Union has increased its military power across the spectrum of capabilities, drawing on that power to exacerbate local conflicts and to conduct a global foreign policy opposed to Western interests.

The Soviet Union has stood apart from the international order and often worked to undermine it.

The character of the changes taking place in the Soviet Union leads to the possibility that a new era may now be upon us. We may be able to move beyond containment to a U.S. policy that actively promotes the integration of the Soviet Union into the existing international system. The U.S.S.R. has indicated an interest in rapprochement with the international order and criticized major tenets of its own postwar political-military policy.

These are words that we can only applaud. But a new relationship with the international system can not simply be declared by Moscow. Nor can it be granted by others. It must be earned. . . .

The transformation of the Soviet Union from a source of instability to a productive force within the family of nations is a long-term goal that can only be pursued from a position of American strength and with patience and creativity. Our policy is not designed to help a particular leader or set of leaders in the Soviet Union. We seek, instead, fundamental alterations in Soviet military force structure, institutions, and practices which can only be reversed at great cost, economically and politically, to the Soviet Union. If we succeed, the ground for cooperation will widen, while that for conflict narrows. The U.S.-Soviet relationship may still be fundamentally competitive, but it will be less militarized and safer.

. . . Moscow will find the United States a willing partner in building a better relationship. The foundation of that relationship will grow firmer if Soviet reforms lead to conditions that will support a new cooperative relationship between Moscow and the West. Those conditions include:

> Deployment of a Soviet force posture that is smaller and less threatening. . . .
>
> Renunciation of the principle that class conflict is a source of international tension and establishment of a record of conduct consistent with that pledge.
>
> Adherence to the obligation that it undertook at the end of World War II to permit self-determination for the countries of East-Central Europe. Moscow must authoritatively renounce the "Brezhnev Doctrine". . . .
>
> Demilitarization of Soviet foreign policy in other regions of the world and serious participation in efforts to ameliorate conflict, including bringing pressure to bear on Soviet clients who do not recognize the legitimate security interests of their neighbors.
>
> Participation in cooperative efforts to stop the proliferation of ballistic missile technology as well as nuclear, chemical and biological weapons.
>
> Willingness to cooperate with the United States to address pressing global problems, including the international trade in drugs and narcotics, terrorism, and dangers to the environment.
>
> Institutionalization of democratic internal laws and human rights practices, political pluralism, and a more market-oriented economic structure, which will establish a firm Soviet democratic basis for a more productive and cooperative relationship with the free nations of the world.

STRATEGIC-MILITARY OBJECTIVES

The United States must maintain modern military forces that strengthen deterrence and enhance the security of our allies and friends. The United States will seek to protect and sustain its military-technological advantages. The purpose of our forces is not to put pressure on a weak Soviet economy or to seek military superiority. Rather, U.S. policy recognizes the need to provide a hedge against uncertain long-term developments in the Soviet Union and to impress upon the Soviet leadership the wisdom of pursuing a responsible course. Moscow must be convinced that nothing can be gained by turning back to a more militaristic policy. Most importantly, American forces are a reliable and credible guarantee of our safety and of our commitment to the security of our allies in the face of Soviet forces that, even if restructured, will be large and modern.

At the same time, the United States will seek verifiable arms control agreements with the Soviet Union and its allies. . . .

POLITICAL-DIPLOMATIC OBJECTIVES

Regional Issues

U.S. policy will encourage fundamental political and economic reform, including freely contested elections, in East-Central Europe, so that states in that region may once again be productive members of a prosperous, peaceful, and democratic Europe, whole and free from fear of Soviet intervention. . . .

We will engage the Soviet Union on a variety of regional issues not only to seek their resolution, but also in order to test the reality of new Soviet thinking and whether Soviet behavior matches rhetoric in key areas around the world. . . .

Democratization

The United States is encouraged by emerging trends in the internal political processes in the Soviet Union. . . . We welcome the positive changes that have taken place and we will continue to encourage greater recognition of human rights, market incentives, and free elections. To the extent that Soviet practices are modified and institutions are built based on popular will, we may find that the nature of the threat itself has changed, though any such transformation could take decades. . . .

GEORGE BUSH

Source: National Security Council, "National Security Decision Directive 23," September 22, 1989, from the George Bush Presidential Library, http://bushlibrary.tamu.edu/research/directives.html.

Document 10.3
President George Bush and German Chancellor Helmut Kohl Discuss Events in Eastern Europe, October 23, 1989

President Bush worked closely with Chancellor Kohl of the Federal Republic of Germany (FRG) to coordinate their responses to fast-moving events in the East. In an October 1989 telephone conversation, they discussed Hungary, Poland, and East Germany (the German Democratic Republic, or GDR). With regard to the last, they agreed that German reunification, should it happen, would mean the integration of the GDR into the West, not the neutralization of West Germany.

. . .

Chancellor Kohl: I wanted to tell you briefly how I see events in Hungary, Poland, and the GDR. In Hungary, things are going the best. The people are incredibly courageous, and very determined. The present government is taking an enormous risk: the changes have their origin with the reform movement in the Communist Party, but it is not at all certain that the reformers will be able to get credit in the course of the election. It is quite possible that the Party will come in only second, and there might be a coalition. We have supported the Hungarians quite vigorously. In December, I will go over for two days to give further support, also optically.

The President: Where will you go?

Chancellor Kohl: I will go to Budapest. . . . They can make it, though the next two years will be decisive. On November 9 I will go to Poland for four days. Our negotiations have been essentially concluded. I will do all I can to support the new government, especially in the economic area. With the EC [European Community], I intend to give assistance in human resources. This seems to be the problem, if I may put it bluntly: there is a lot of good will and many good ideas, but the Poles do not know how to put them into practice. They have to introduce currency reforms, a new banking system, and other steps to open up a new market-oriented economy. I will be doing what I can, and I will also take into account and work on what you have suggested, so that Western activities can be homogeneous. . . . I also want to enter into a new phase with the Poles, 50 years after the outbreak of war.

In the GDR, changes are quite dramatic. None of us can give a prognosis. It is not clear whether the new man will have the determination and the strength to carry out reform. Gorbachev told me that he had encouraged reform during his visit, but I am not sure how courageous he [new Party and state leader Egon Krenz] is. There is an enormous unrest among the population. Things will become incalculable if there are no reforms. My interest is not to see so many flee the GDR, because the consequences there would be catastrophic. Our estimates are that by Christmas we will have reached a total of 150,000 refugees, with an average age of under 30.

My last point concerns the climate among the media in New York, the coast, London, the Hague, Rome, and Paris that, crudely speaking, holds that Germans are now committed to Ostpolitik and discussion about reunification and that they are less interested in the EC and the West. This is absolute nonsense! I will again and again explain and declare my position. . . . I will say publicly . . . that without a strong NATO, without the necessary development of the EC, none of these developments in the Warsaw Pact would have occurred. I am firmly convinced of that, and that will be my message. It would also be good for you, as soon as you can, to deliver a public message that progress in disarmament and changes in the east are possible only if we stand together.

The President: I couldn't agree more. I have seen some of those stories, but I know your position and think I know the heartbeat of Germany. The strength of NATO has made possible these changes in Eastern Europe. We are seeing a spate of stories about German reunification resulting in a neutralist Germany and a threat to Western security. We do not believe that. We are trying to react very cautiously and carefully to change in the GDR. We have great respect for the way the FRG under your leadership has been handling this situation. You have done a great job.

I understand that Horst [Teltschik, the Chancellor's security advisor] is coming soon. We are very anxious to talk with him on this subject and also about Poland and Hungary. We are getting criticism in the Congress from liberal Democrats that we ought to be doing more to foster change, but I am not going to go so fast as to be reckless. . . .

Information in brackets appears in original document and is attributed to an NSC notetaker.
Source: "Memorandum of Telephone Conversation: Telephone Call from Chancellor Helmut Kohl of the Federal Republic of Germany, October 23, 1989, 9:02-9:26 a.m. EDT," from the George Bush Presidential Library, http://bushlibrary.tamu.edu/research/pdfs/telcon6-23-89.pdf.

Document 10.4
Soviet Premier Mikhail Gorbachev Advises East German President Egon Krenz on Managing the Crisis in East Germany, November 1, 1989

The Soviet and East German leaders were desperate to head off reunification of the two Germanys. In this conversation, they took comfort in their perception that leaders in the West were likewise alarmed about the possibility of East Germany's failure. They also discussed the conciliatory measures taken by the East German state, measures designed to keep the German Democratic Republic (GDR) from falling apart. Soviet Premier Gorbachev expresses his view that Eastern Europe's travails could be traced to economic dependence on the West.

. . .

Gorbachev: Yesterday Alexander N. Yakovlev received [former US National Security Adviser] Zbigniew Brzezinski, who, as you know, has a head with "global brains." And he said: If today the events turned out in such a way that unification of Germany became a reality, it would mean a collapse of many things. I think so far we have held the correct line: stood firmly in favor of the coexistence of two German states, and as a result, came to a wide international recognition of the GDR, achieved the Moscow Treaty, gave a boost to the Helsinki Process. Therefore we should confidently follow this same course.

You must know: all serious political figures—[British Prime Minister Margaret] Thatcher, [French President François] Mitterrand, [Italian Prime Minister Giulio]

Andreotti, [Polish President Wojciech] Jaruzelski, and even the Americans—though their position has recently exhibited some nuances—are not looking forward to German unification. Moreover, in today's situation it would probably have an explosive character. The majority of Western leaders do not want to see the dissolution of NATO and of the Warsaw Treaty Organization. Serious politicians understand that they are factors of a necessary equilibrium. However, Mitterrand feels like he has to mention his sympathy for the idea of the German unification. The Americans are also speaking about such sympathies for the Germans' pull toward the unification. But I think that they do it as a favor to Bonn, and also because to some extent, they are anxious about too much rapprochement between the FRG and the USSR. Therefore, I repeat, the best course of action now is to continue the same line in the German affairs which we have successfully developed so far. By the way, [former FRG Chancellor and Social Democratic Party leader] Willy Brandt shares this opinion as well. He believes that the GDR is a great victory of socialism, even though he has his own understanding of socialism. A liquidation of the republic, in his opinion, would have been a bust for the Social Democrats. Therefore, I think, we all should start from the following formula: history itself decided that there should be two German states. But of course, you cannot get away from the FRG. The need for human contacts presumes normal relations with the FRG. You should not disrupt your ties with the FRG, although, certainly, they should be kept under control.

I am convinced that we should coordinate our relations with the FRG better, although [Erich] Honecker [Krenz's predecessor in the GDR] tried to evade this necessity. We know about your relations with the FRG, and you know about our relations with it. Why should we try to hide anything from each other! It would make sense to talk about the possibilities of trilateral cooperation between the USSR, the GDR, and the FRG, especially in the economic sphere. . . .

The situation in Hungary and Poland today is such that they have nowhere else to go, as they say, because they have drowned in financial dependence on the West. Today some people criticize us: they say, what is the Soviet Union doing—allowing Poland and Hungary to "sail" to the West[?] But we cannot take Poland on our balance. [Former Polish leader Edward] Gierek accumulated $48 billion dollars of debt. Poland has already paid off $49 billion, and it still owes almost $49 billion. As far as Hungary is concerned, the International Monetary Fund has dictated its harsh ultimatum already under the late Hungarian leader János Kádár.

Krenz: This is not our way.

Gorbachev: You need to take this into account in your relationship with the FRG.

[. . .] *Gorbachev:* We need to think through all of this, and to find formulas that would allow people to realize their human needs. Otherwise we will be forced to accept all kinds of ultimatums. Maybe we can direct our International Departments and Foreign Ministries to think about possible initiatives together. Clearly, your constructive steps should be accompanied with demands for certain obligations from the other side. Chancellor Helmut Kohl keeps in touch with me and with you. We need to influence him. Once under the pressure of the opposition, he found himself on the horse of nationalism. The right wing starts to present their demands for the unification of Germany to the Soviet Union, and appeals to the US. The logic is simple—all the peoples are united, why do we Germans not have this right?

Krenz: We have already taken a number of steps. First of all, we gave orders to the border troops not to use weapons at the border, except in the cases of direct attacks on the soldiers. Secondly, we adopted a draft of Law on Foreign Travel at the Politburo. We will present it for a public discussion, and we plan to pass it in the Volkskammer even before Christmas.

Source: "Soviet Record of Conversation between M. S. Gorbachev and the General Secretary of the Central Committee of the Socialist Unity Party of Germany Egon Krenz," Notes of A. S. Chernyaev, Archive of the Gorbachev Foundation, f. 2, op. 2, trans. Svetlana Savranskaya (National Security Archive), from the Cold War International History Project, Woodrow Wilson International Center for Scholars, www.cwihp.org.

Document 10.5
Senior Communist Party Member Anatoly Chernyaev Reflects on the Fall of the Berlin Wall, November 10, 1989

Mikhail Gorbachev's senior foreign policy aide, Anatoly Chernyaev, confided to his diary his personal interpretation of the meaning of the fall of the Berlin Wall.

The Berlin Wall has collapsed. This entire era in the history of the Socialist system is over. Following the [Polish United Socialist Party] PUWP and the [Hungarian Socialist Workers' Party] HSWP Honecker has left. Today we received messages about the "retirement" of [Chinese Communist Party leader] Deng Xiaopeng and [Bulgarian leader Todor] Zhivkov. Only our "best friends" [Cuban leader Fidel] Castro, [Romanian leader Nicolae] Ceausescu, [and North Korean leader] Kim Il Sung are still around—people who hate our guts.

But the main thing is the GDR, the Berlin Wall. For it has to do not only with "socialism" but with the shift in the world balance of forces. This is the end of Yalta. . . of the Stalinist legacy and the "defeat of Hitlerite Germany."

That is what Gorbachev has done. And he has indeed turned out to be a great leader. He has sensed the pace of history and helped history to find a natural channel.

Source: "Excerpts from Anatoly Chernyaev's Diary," Notes of A. S. Chernyaev, Archive of the Gorbachev Foundation, f. 2, op. 2, trans. Vladislav Zubok (National Security Archive), from the Cold War International History Project, Woodrow Wilson International Center for Scholars, www.cwihp.org.

Document 10.6
President George Bush and Soviet Premier Mikhail Gorbachev Discuss Their Informal Summit, December 3, 1989

Just weeks after the fall of the Berlin Wall, President Bush and Soviet Premier Gorbachev met aboard the Soviet passenger liner Maxim Gorky, *off the coast of Malta, in the Mediterranean Sea. In a session with reporters following the summit, Bush expressed his support for Gorbachev's agenda of domestic reform, and both leaders spoke, in their own ways—Bush with reference to his trademark prudence, and Gorbachev with reference to historical dialectics—about the remarkable changes under way in Eastern Europe.*

The President: . . . For 40 years, the Western alliance has stood together in the cause of free-dom. And now, with reform underway in the Soviet Union, we stand at the threshold of a brand-new era of U.S.-Soviet relations. And it is within our grasp to contribute, each in our own way, to overcoming the division of Europe and ending the military con-frontation there. We've got to do more to ameliorate the violence and suffering that afflicts so many regions in the world and to remove common threats to our future: the deterioration of the environment, the spread of nuclear and chemical weapons, ballistic missile technology, the narcotics trade. And our discussions here will give greater impe-tus to make real progress in these areas.

There's also a great potential to develop common opportunities. For example, the Soviet Union now seeks greater engagement with the international market economy, a step that certainly I'm prepared to encourage in every way I can.

As I leave Malta for Brussels and a meeting with our NATO allies, I am optimistic that as the West works patiently together and increasingly cooperates with the Soviet Union, we can realize a lasting peace and transform the East-West relationship to one of endur-ing cooperation. And that is a future that's worthy of our peoples. And that's the future that I want to help in creating. And that's the future that Chairman Gorbachev and I began right here in Malta.

Thank you, sir, for your hospitality.

The Chairman: Ladies and gentlemen, comrades, there are many symbolic things about this meeting, and one of them—it has never been in the history that the leaders of our two coun-tries hold a joint press conference. This is also an important symbol. I share the view voiced by President Bush that we are satisfied, in general, with the results of the meeting. . . .

Well, we have made our contact, a good contact. The atmosphere was friendly, straightforward, open; and this enabled us to make good work. In our position, the most dangerous thing is to exaggerate. And it is always that we should preserve elements of cautiousness, and I use the favorite word by President Bush. [Laughter] Our world and our relations are at a crucial juncture. We should be highly responsible to face up to the challenges of today's world. And the leaders of our two countries cannot act as a fire brigade, although fire brigades are very useful. We have to keep it in mind also. This ele-ment was also present. . . .

Q.: Chairman Gorbachev, President Bush called on you to end the cold war once and for all. Do you think that has been done now?

The Chairman: In the first place, I assured the President of the United States that the Soviet Union would never start hot war against the United States of America, and we would like our relations to develop in such a way that they would open greater possibilities for cooperation. Naturally, the President and I had a wide discussion—rather, we sought the answer to the question where we stand now. We stated, both of us, that the world leaves one epoch of cold war and enters another epoch. This is just the beginning. We're just at the very beginning of our long road to a long-lasting peaceful period.

Thus, we were unanimous in concluding about the special responsibility of such countries as the United States and the Soviet Union. Naturally, we had a rather long discussion, but this is not for the press conference; that is, we shouldn't explain that discussion regarding the fact that the new era calls for a new approach. And thus, many things that were characteristic of the cold war should be abandoned, both the—[inaudible]—in force, the arms race, mistrust, psychological and ideological struggle, and all that. All that should be things of the past. . . .

Q.: My question is to President Bush. You, as President of the United States, participate for the first time at the summit meeting, but you were the Vice President of the previous administration that took part in forming foreign policies. So, what is your assessment of the course that our two countries have passed since Geneva to Malta?

The President: That's what we call a "slow ball" in the trade. [Laughter] It's an easy question because I really think they are improving dramatically. There is enormous support in our country for what Chairman Gorbachev is doing inside the Soviet Union. There is enormous respect and support for the way he has advocated peaceful change in Europe. And so, this meeting accomplished everything that I had hoped it would. It was a no-agenda meeting, and yet it was a meeting where we discussed, as the Chairman said, many, many subjects. So, I think if a meeting can improve relations, I think this one has. . . .

Q.: I'm from the group of Czechoslovak journalists. President Gorbachev, did you assure President Bush that the changes in Eastern Europe are irreversible and that the Soviet Union has forsaken the right to intervene there militarily? And President Bush, similarly, as a result of this meeting, are you now more trusting that the Soviets have indeed renounced the Brezhnev doctrine?

The Chairman: I wouldn't like you to consider me here or to regard me as a full-fledged representative of all European countries. This wouldn't be true. We are a part of Eastern Europe, of Europe. We interact with our allies in all areas, and our ties are deep. However, every nation is an independent entity in world politics, and every people has the right to choose its own destiny, the destiny of its own state. And I can only explain my own attitude.

I believe that those changes, both in the Soviet Union and in the countries of Eastern Europe, have been prepared by the course of the historic evolution itself. No one can avoid this evolutionary process; and those problems should be resolved on a new basis, taking into account the experience and the potential of those countries, opening up possibilities for utilizing anything positive that has been accumulated by mankind. And I believe that we should welcome the thrust of those processes because they are related to the desire of the people to make those societies more democratic, more humane, and to face the world. Therefore, I'm encouraged by the thrust of those processes, and I believe that this is highly assisted by other countries.

I also see deep, profound changes in other countries, including Western European countries, and this is also very important because this is a reciprocal movement so that the people will become more close around the continent, and preserving at the same time the identity of one's own people. This is very important for us to understand.

Q.: I ask a question on the part of the Czechoslovak journalists. We are discussing the future of Europe?

The President: May I just respond briefly? There is no question that there is dramatic change. Nobody can question it. And as President Gorbachev talks about democratic change and peaceful—that certainly lays to rest previous doctrines that may have had a different approach. And so, he knows that not just the President but all the people in the United States would like to see this peaceful, democratic evolution continue. And so, I think that's the best way to answer the question because the change is so dramatic and so obvious to people. . . .

Q.: Whether the German question was discussed and your attitude toward the Kohl [Chancellor of the Federal Republic of Germany] plan.

The President: The United States, as part of NATO, has had a longstanding position. Helsinki spells out a concept of permanent borders. I made clear to President Gorbachev that we, for our part, do not want to do anything that is unrealistic and causes any country to end up going backwards or end up having its own people in military conflict, one with the other. And so, I think we have tried to act with the word that President Gorbachev has used to—and that is, with caution—not to go demonstrating on top of the Berlin Wall to show how happy we are about the change. We are happy about the change.

I've heard many leaders speak about the German question. And I don't think it is a role of the United States to dictate the rapidity of change in any country. It's a matter for the people to determine themselves. So, that's our position, and the last word goes to the Chairman on this.

The Chairman: Yes, and the President wrote a note to me in English. I don't read English, but I answered in Russian—he doesn't read Russian—but we agreed on it anyway. [Laughter]

I'll be brief. In the past few days, I already answered a few times on the question. I can only confirm what I said before. But as we have discussed with the President this question, I can say that we approach this subject on the basis of the Helsinki process, which summed up the results of the Second World War and consolidated the results of the war. And those are realities. And the reality is such that we have today's Europe with two German states, the Federal Republic of Germany and the German Democratic Republic, which are both members of the United Nations and sovereign states.

This was the decision of history. And I always revert to this subject, or thesis, which saves me. Indeed, in order to remain realists, we should say that history itself decides the processes and fates on the European continent and also the fates of those two states. I think this is a common understanding shared by anyone. And any artificial acceleration of the process would only exacerbate and make it more difficult to change in many European countries those changes that are now taking place now in Europe. Thus, we wouldn't serve that process by an artificial acceleration or prompting of the processes that are going on in those two countries.

I think we can thank the media for their cooperation. We are not yet aware of what they will write about us.

The President: Right to thank them afterward you mean? [Laughter] After they've written?

The Chairman: We should thank them in advance, and therefore, they will do better in the future. . . .

Source: George Bush, "Remarks of the President and Soviet Chairman Gorbachev and a Question-and-Answer Session with Reporters in Malta," December 3, 1989, in *Public Papers of the Presidents of the United States: George Bush, 1989–1993,* from the American Presidency Project, University of California, Santa Barbara, www.presidency.ucsb.edu.

Document 10.7
Strategic Arms Reduction Treaty (START I), July 31, 1991

After seven years of negotiation, the Soviet Union and the United States agreed in 1991 to a comprehensive and complex treaty reducing the most feared type of Cold War weaponry: offensive strategic nuclear missiles, intercontinental ballistic missiles (ICBMs), submarine-launched ballistic missiles (SLBMs), and heavy bombers. The treaty was signed just five months before the collapse of the Soviet Union, causing a delay of several years before it finally entered into force on December 5, 1994, after all the nuclear successor states to the Soviet Union—Russia, Belarus, Kazakhstan, and Ukraine—ratified the treaty. The last three eliminated their nuclear weapons completely, transferring their weapons to Russia. In START I, both sides agreed to gradually reduce the number of deployed warheads and weapons delivery systems. On December 5, 2001, Russia and the United States reached the target of a "mere" 6,000 deployed nuclear warheads. Before that landmark was reached, the United States had completed the called-for destruction of all 600 of its Minuteman II and III silos, iconic structures of the Cold War.

ARTICLE I

Each Party shall reduce and limit its strategic offensive arms in accordance with the provisions of this Treaty, and shall carry out the other obligations set forth in this Treaty and its Annexes, Protocols, and Memorandum of Understanding.

ARTICLE II

1. Each Party shall reduce and limit its ICBMs and ICBM launchers, SLBMs and SLBM launchers, heavy bombers, ICBM warheads, SLBM warheads, and heavy bomber armaments, so that seven years after entry into force of this Treaty and thereafter, the aggregate numbers, as counted in accordance with Article III of this Treaty, do not exceed:

    (a) 1600, for deployed ICBMs and their associated launchers, deployed SLBMs and their associated launchers, and deployed heavy bombers, including 154 for deployed heavy ICBMs and their associated launchers;

    (b) 6000, for warheads attributed to deployed ICBMs, deployed SLBMs, and deployed heavy bombers

        (i)   4900, for warheads attributed to deployed ICBMs and deployed SLBMs;

        (ii) 1100, for warheads attributed to deployed ICBMs on mobile launchers of ICBMs;

        (iii) 1540, for warheads attributed to deployed heavy ICBMs. . . .

ARTICLE III

. . .

4. For the purposes of counting warheads:

    (a) The number of warheads attributed to an ICBM or SLBM of each existing type shall be the number specified in the Memorandum of Understanding on the Establishment of the Data Base Relating to this Treaty, hereinafter referred to as the Memorandum of Understanding.

    (b) The number of warheads that will be attributed to an ICBM or SLBM of a new type shall be the maximum number of reentry vehicles with which an ICBM or SLBM of that type has been flight-tested. The number of warheads that will be attributed to an ICBM or SLBM of a new type with a front section of an existing design with multiple reentry vehicles, or to an ICBM or SLBM of a new type with one reentry vehicle, shall be no less than the nearest integer that is smaller than the result of dividing 40 percent of the accountable throw-weight of the ICBM or SLBM by the weight of the lightest reentry vehicle flight-tested on an ICBM of SLBM of a new type. In the case of an ICBM or SLBM of a new type with a of warheads that will be attributed to an ICBM of SLBM of a new type with a front section of a fundamentally new design, the question of the applicability of the 40-percent rule to such an ICBM or SLBM shall be subject to agreement within the framework of the Joint Compliance and Inspection Commission. Until agreement has been reached regarding the rule that will apply to such an ICBM or SLBM, the number of warheads that will be attributed to such an ICBM or SLBM shall be the maximum number of reentry vehicles with which an ICBM or SLBM of that type has been flight-tested. The number of new types of ICBMs or SLBMs with a front section of a fundamentally new design shall not exceed two for each Party as long as this Treaty remains in force. . . .

ARTICLE V

. . .

2. Each Party undertakes not to:
   (a) produce, flight-test, or deploy heavy ICBMs of a new type, or increase the launch weight or throw-weight of heavy ICBMs of an existing type;
   (b) produce, flight-test, or deploy heavy SLBMs;
   (c) produce test, or deploy mobile launchers of heavy ICBMs;
   (d) produce, test, or deploy additional silo launchers of ICBMs of heavy ICBMs, except for silo launchers of heavy ICBMs that replace silo launchers of heavy ICBMs that have been eliminated in accordance with Section II of the Conversion or Elimination Protocol, provided that the limits provided for in Article II of this Treaty are not exceeded;
   (e) convert launchers that are not launchers of heavy ICBMs into launchers of heavy ICBMs;
   (f) produce, test, or deploy launchers of heavy SLBMs;
   (g) reduce the number of warheads attributed to a heavy ICBM of an existing type.

3. Each Party undertakes not to deploy ICBMs other than in silo launchers of ICBMs, on road-mobile launchers of ICBMs, or on rail-mobile launchers of ICBMs. Each Party undertakes not to produce, test, or deploy ICBM launchers other than silo launchers of ICBMs, road-mobile launchers of ICBMs, or rail-mobile launchers of ICBMs. . . .

15. Each Party undertakes not to use ICBMs or SLBMs for delivering objects into the upper atmosphere or space for purposes inconsistent with existing international obligations undertaken by the Parties.

16. Each Party undertakes not to produce, test, or deploy systems for rapid reload and not to conduct rapid reload.

17. Each Party undertakes not to install SLBM launchers on submarines that were not originally constructed as ballistic missile submarines. . . .

28. Each Party undertakes not to base strategic offensive arms subject to the limitations of this Treaty outside its national territory. . . .

Source: U.S. State Department, "Treaty between the United States of America and the Union of Soviet Socialist Republics on the Reduction and Limitation of Strategic Offensive Arms," July 31, 1991, www.state.gov/t/ac/trt/18535.htm.

Document 10.8
President George Bush's Address on the Dissolution of the Soviet Union, December 25, 1991

When the Soviet Union ceased to be on Christmas Day 1991, President Bush at last announced victory for the West in the Cold War. Because many U.S. voters had already put the Cold War behind them, and because Bush would stand for reelection in less than a year, the president ended his remarks by assuring his audience of his commitment to fight for yet another victory, this time against transitory hard economic times at home. "I am committed," said the president "to attacking our economic problems at home with the same determination we brought to winning the cold war." Even after Bush won another foreign victory in the Persian Gulf War, a majority of Americans were unimpressed. They sent the last president of the Cold War home after just one term.

During these last few months, you and I have witnessed one of the greatest dramas of the 20th century, the historic and revolutionary transformation of a totalitarian dictatorship, the Soviet Union, and the liberation of its peoples. As we celebrate Christmas, this day of peace and hope, I thought we should take a few minutes to reflect on what these events mean for us as Americans.

For over 40 years, the United States led the West in the struggle against communism and the threat it posed to our most precious values. This struggle shaped the lives of all Americans. It forced all nations to live under the specter of nuclear destruction.

That confrontation is now over. The nuclear threat, while far from gone, is receding. Eastern Europe is free. The Soviet Union itself is no more. This is a victory for democracy and freedom. It's a victory for the moral force of our values. Every American can take pride in this victory, from the millions of men and women who have served our country in uniform, to millions of Americans who supported their country and a strong defense under nine Presidents.

New, independent nations have emerged out of the wreckage of the Soviet empire. Last weekend, these former Republics formed a Commonwealth of Independent States. This act marks the end of the old Soviet Union, signified today by Mikhail Gorbachev's decision to resign as President.

I'd like to express, on behalf of the American people, my gratitude to Mikhail Gorbachev for years of sustained commitment to world peace, and for his intellect, vision, and courage. I spoke with Mikhail Gorbachev this morning. We reviewed the many accomplishments of the past few years and spoke of hope for the future.

Mikhail Gorbachev's revolutionary policies transformed the Soviet Union. His policies permitted the peoples of Russia and the other Republics to cast aside decades of oppression and establish the foundations of freedom. His legacy guarantees him an honored place in history and provides a solid basis for the United States to work in equally constructive ways with his successors.

The United States applauds and supports the historic choice for freedom by the new States of the Commonwealth. We congratulate them on the peaceful and democratic path they have chosen, and for their careful attention to nuclear control and safety during this transition. Despite a potential for instability and chaos, these events clearly serve our national interest.

We stand tonight before a new world of hope and possibilities for our children, a world we could not have contemplated a few years ago. The challenge for us now is to engage these new States in sustaining the peace and building a more prosperous future.

And so today, based on commitments and assurances given to us by some of these States, concerning nuclear safety, democracy, and free markets, I am announcing some important steps designed to begin this process.

First, the United States recognizes and welcomes the emergence of a free, independent, and democratic Russia, led by its courageous President, Boris Yeltsin. Our Embassy in Moscow will remain there as our Embassy to Russia. We will support Russia's assumption of the U.S.S.R.'s seat as a permanent Member of the United Nations Security Council. I look forward to working closely with President Yeltsin in support of his efforts to bring democratic and market reform to Russia.

Second, the United States also recognizes the independence of Ukraine, Armenia, Kazakhstan, Belarus, and Kyrgyzstan, all States that have made specific commitments to us. We will move quickly to establish diplomatic relations with these States and build new ties to them. We will sponsor membership in the United Nations for those not already members.

Third, the United States also recognizes today as independent States the remaining six former Soviet Republics: Moldova, Turkmenistan, Azerbaijan, Tadjikistan, Georgia, and Uzbekistan. We will establish diplomatic relations with them when we are satisfied that they have made commitments to responsible security policies and democratic principles, as have the other States we recognize today.

These dramatic events come at a time when Americans are also facing challenges here at home. I know that for many of you these are difficult times. And I want all Americans to know that I am committed to attacking our economic problems at home with the same determination we brought to winning the cold war.

I am confident we will meet this challenge as we have so many times before. But we cannot if we retreat into isolationism. We will only succeed in this interconnected world by continuing to lead the fight for free people and free and fair trade. A free and prosperous global economy is essential for America's prosperity. That means jobs and economic growth right here at home.

This is a day of great hope for all Americans. Our enemies have become our partners, committed to building democratic and civil societies. They ask for our support, and we will give it to them. We will do it because as Americans we can do no less.

For our children, we must offer them the guarantee of a peaceful and prosperous future, a future grounded in a world built on strong democratic principles, free from the specter of global conflict.

May God bless the people of the new nations in the Commonwealth of Independent States. And on this special day of peace on Earth, good will toward men, may God continue to bless the United States of America. Good night.

Source: George Bush, "Address to the Nation on the Commonwealth of Independent States," December 25, 1991, in *Public Papers of the Presidents of the United States: George Bush, 1989–1993,* from the American Presidency Project, University of California, Santa Barbara, www.presidency.ucsb.edu.

Document 10.9

"By the Grace of God, America Won the Cold War," President George Bush's State of the Union Address, January 28, 1992

In his final State of the Union message, President Bush reflected on the end of the Cold War: its meaning for the United States, for the world, and for the future. Then the president got down to the ever-present business of politics: addressing the anxiety of the moment by putting forth a nine-point plan for economic recovery.

. . . We gather tonight at a dramatic and deeply promising time in our history and in the history of man on Earth. For in the past 12 months, the world has known changes of almost Biblical proportions. And even now, months after the failed coup that doomed a failed system, I'm not sure we've absorbed the full impact, the full import of what happened. But communism died this year.

Even as President, with the most fascinating possible vantage point, there were times when I was so busy managing progress and helping to lead change that I didn't always show the joy that was in my heart. But the biggest thing that has happened in the world in my life, in our lives, is this: By the grace of God, America won the cold war.

I mean to speak this evening of the changes that can take place in our country, now that we can stop making the sacrifices we had to make when we had an avowed enemy that was a superpower. Now we can look homeward even more and move to set right what needs to be set right.

I will speak of those things. But let me tell you something I've been thinking these past few months. It's a kind of roll call of honor. For the cold war didn't end; it was won. And I think of those who won it, in places like Korea and Vietnam. And some of them didn't come back. Back then they were heroes, but this year they were victors.

The long roll call, all the G.I. Joes and Janes, all the ones who fought faithfully for freedom, who hit the ground and sucked the dust and knew their share of horror. This may seem frivolous, and I don't mean it so, but it's moving to me how the world saw them. The world saw not only their special valor but their special style: their rambunctious, optimistic bravery, their do-or-die unity unhampered by class or race or region. What a group we've put forth, for generations now, from the ones who wrote "Kilroy was here" on the walls of the German stalags to those who left signs in the Iraqi desert that said, "I saw Elvis." What a group of kids we've sent out into the world.

And there's another to be singled out, though it may seem inelegant, and I mean a mass of people called the American taxpayer. No one ever thinks to thank the people who pay a country's bill or an alliance's bill. But for half a century now, the American people have shouldered the burden and paid taxes that were higher than they would have been to support a defense that was bigger than it would have been if imperial communism had never existed. But it did; doesn't anymore. And here's a fact I wouldn't mind the world acknowledging: The American taxpayer bore the brunt of the burden and deserves a hunk of the glory.

So now, for the first time in 35 years, our strategic bombers stand down. No longer are they on 'round-the-clock alert. Tomorrow our children will go to school and study history and how plants grow. And they won't have, as my children did, air raid drills in which they crawl under their desks and cover their heads in case of nuclear war. My grandchildren don't have to do that and won't have the bad dreams children had once, in decades past. There are still threats. But the long, drawn-out dread is over. . . .

Source: George Bush, "Address before a Joint Session of Congress on the State of the Union," January 28, 1992, in *Public Papers of the Presidents of the United States: George Bush, 1989–1993,* from the American Presidency Project, University of California, Santa Barbara, www.presidency.ucsb.edu.

CHAPTER ELEVEN

Aftermath

Legacies of a Fifty-Year War

For fifty years, the Cold War defined the lower limits of presidential power. During the war, no president was free to ignore national security or the imperative for executive leadership. A president who harkened back to an old-fashioned conception of presidential deference to the legislative branch—what was once called the Whig theory of the presidency—would have been not only an anachronism but also a danger. With the threat of global war a constant worry, deliberation and debate had to give way to decision and dispatch in the conduct of foreign affairs. Alexander Hamilton, the architect of the Constitution's executive branch, would not have been pleased by the Cold War—who would have been?—but he would have been pleased by the presidency's capacity to manage and, ultimately, contain such a vast undertaking. "Energy in the executive," he wrote, "is a leading character in the definition of good government. It is essential to the protection of the community against foreign attacks." Indeed, he added, "[e]very man the least conversant in Roman history knows how often that republic was obliged to take refuge in the absolute power of a single man, under the formidable title of dictator." [1]

Nine years after the fall of the Berlin Wall in 1989, cars drive through the Brandenburg Gate, one of the famous East Berlin–West Berlin border crossings. Source: AP Images/Sven Kaestner.

For the same fifty years, the Cold War also defined the upper limits of presidential power. No president ever held the title "dictator," but several were accused of longing for the role. In truth, the machinery of government devised by the constitutional framers proved sufficiently robust and flexible to permit a considerable expansion of presidential power without a complete debasement of the countervailing powers of the legislative and judicial branches. Throughout the Cold War, presidential power increased through an accumulation of precedents as particular presidents responded to particular crises. On occasion, a president reached too far and had his pretensions to powers checked.

Among the more notable occasions for the exercise of presidential power during the Cold War were:

- President Harry Truman's issuance of an executive order ending segregation in the armed forces
- Truman's decision to take the nation to war in Korea with the sanction of the United Nations *rather than* the U.S. Congress
- Presidents Dwight Eisenhower's and John F. Kennedy's administrations' plots to assassinate Cuban Communist dictator Fidel Castro
- Eisenhower's and Kennedy's operation, conceived in the earlier administration and implemented in the latter, for a surreptitious hand in the overthrow of Castro's Cuban regime
- Kennedy's decision to blockade Soviet delivery of nuclear missiles to Cuba, setting the stage for a possible nuclear showdown
- President Lyndon Johnson's decision to send U.S. armed forces to the Dominican Republic, to prevent a takeover of the government by presumed Marxists
- Johnson's decision to Americanize the Vietnam War and to commit U.S. ground troops to battle, with a minimum of congressional debate or public excitement
- President Richard Nixon's expansion of the American war in Vietnam into Cambodia, unleashing a furious protest against the government
- Nixon's executive decision to violate the law in order, as he saw it, to defend the United States against its domestic enemies, who happened also to be his partisan opponents
- President Gerald Ford's pardon of Nixon to heal the wounds of Vietnam and, he hoped, gain the attention of the public for all the things *he* wanted to accomplish in the White House
- President Jimmy Carter's unconditional pardon of Vietnam War draft evaders, and his decision to embark on a failed rescue mission to free Americans held hostage in Iran
- President Ronald Reagan's extensive (and, in a single notable instance, illegal) use of covert means to harass Soviet-backed governments, from Afghanistan to Nicaragua
- Reagan's refusal to place his Strategic Defense Initiative (SDI), or "Star Wars," missile defense program on the bargaining table in negotiations with the Soviet Union

In some of the cases above—for example, President Ford's pardon of Nixon and President Reagan's refusal to bargain with SDI—the president exercised a power explicitly granted under the Constitution. In other cases—for example, the decisions of Presidents Truman, Kennedy, and Johnson to threaten or order the nation into hot war—the president took upon himself the prerogative power long claimed by strong executives, to defend the community against its enemies in an emergency. Such power may or may not be granted between the lines of the U.S. Constitution, but in the Cold War it was accepted that the president's "war powers" included the power to respond with force to attacks halfway around the world, as in Korea and Vietnam, and to control every facet of the potential use of nuclear weapons, as in the Cuban Missile Crisis. Finally, in some cases—such as the illegal operations conducted to further the goals of Presidents Nixon and Reagan—

presidents or those who worked for them tried to claim powers that they simply did not have, not even in fighting the Cold War. These attempts were rebuffed. The Cold War gave presidents license to lead, but not to dictate to the rest of the government.

The Cold War president, one might conclude, occupied an office with expansive although hardly unlimited powers. Typically, the president handled this responsibility with a clear sense of responsibility to the people of the United States and accountability to the electorate and to the judgment of history. This is a long leash upon which to place a chief executive, but the times were clearly exceptional. In the aftermath of the Cold War, the limits of presidential power have been contested.

President George Bush was the first to suffer the indifference to foreign affairs of a post–Cold War electorate. Although he had led the nation and an international coalition to what he hoped would be a defining victory in battle—the first (and, he hoped, the last) battle to establish a veritable New World Order—just the year before he stood for reelection, the voting public was seemingly unimpressed in 1992. Instead of returning to office the victor of Operation Desert Storm and the man who led the nation as its arch foe in the Cold War collapsed, the electorate turned to a very different sort of man: Bill Clinton.

A POST–COLD WAR PRESIDENT

President Bill Clinton was the first nonveteran to hold the office of president since the Cold War began. Of course, that was in part the consequence of a generational shift. While military service was a rite of passage for able-bodied men of George Bush and Ronald Reagan's generation, it was increasingly a matter of choice or luck for baby boomers like Clinton. Eventually, therefore, someone without a service record would be elected president. But the chances were good that, as long as the Cold War was still on, that someone would not have been Bill Clinton. The former Arkansas governor simply had too much baggage associated with his nonveteran status to make him a plausible candidate in the Cold War era. He had maneuvered himself out of harm's way in the closing years of the Vietnam War draft by feigning interest in the Arkansas National Guard. His knowledge of the military was minimal, and he was looked upon with barely concealed contempt by the overwhelming majority of the military officers whom he would command as president.[2] Moreover, his passion in politics and government was domestic policy, not foreign. All of this would surely have mattered to the electorate during the Cold War.

Coming into office, then, Bill Clinton had peculiar weaknesses as a commander in chief and minimal interest in post–Cold War foreign policy. But thanks to the expansion of the presidency during the Cold War, Clinton had resources for leadership at which peacetime presidents of old would have marveled. This was fortunate for Clinton, because as the first post–Cold War president, he could not simply ignore or defer the pressing challenges he faced in military policy and foreign affairs.

The Military

As commander in chief, Bill Clinton struggled with the Joint Chiefs of Staff (JCS), which had grown used to deciding for themselves matters related to personnel and enlistment, training, and even the sort of combat operations that were suitable for the U.S. armed forces. Presidents Reagan and Bush had usually agreed with the military chiefs on these issues, so the JCS and the commanders in chief had gotten along well during the late stages of the Cold War, in part because there was a war on. Civilian leaders often (though by no means always) defer in times of war to the judgment of military professionals. By Clinton's inauguration, however, the war was over. In addition, Clinton had promised during his campaign to make some changes in military personnel policy and to be more liberal in the use of the armed forces to address global humanitarian crises. As a result, the Clinton presidency was a period of intense conflict between the White House and the JCS, on issues ranging from permitting gays to serve in the military and allowing women in combat roles to using the armed forces for humanitarian deployments and missions other than war.

The president backed down on the topic of gays and compromised on that of women, but he used his power to declare the nation's strategic direction, regardless of whether the military liked it.[3] In the Clinton administration, therefore, the national security strategy of the United States entered into a post–Cold War phase, where the military would be used routinely for global humanitarian missions and peacekeeping operations (**Document 11.1**). Because, however, a great many influential people both within the military and in Congress simply did not believe that the end of the Cold War meant the end of the threat of major war, and because of simple policy inertia, change in the nation's security *policies* far outpaced change in the nation's military *capabilities*.

Through the 1990s, the military went through four major reviews of its force structure, organization, size, deployment, training, and doctrine. Despite being constantly studied, the military was not seriously reconfigured, although it was gradually downsized. By the end of the 1990s, the military services and the civilian command structure of the Pentagon were still very much as they had been in 1989, only about one-third smaller. Gen. Colin Powell, as chairman of the JCS under Presidents George Bush and Bill Clinton, had preemptively suggested the first round of cuts. Powell knew that the Democratic majority in Congress was eager to begin disbursing the "Peace Dividend" to its constituents. To diminish the possibility that congressional committees would trim the military with a butcher's knife, he ordered the service chiefs to assault it with their scalpels even before everyone on Bush's cabinet had acknowledged that the Cold War was indeed over. Powell's vision of a "Base Force"—a bare minimum force needed to confront the capabilities, if not the ambitions, of other military forces around the globe—was too expensive for Congress and for Clinton.[4] But the precedent had been set: the post–Cold War military would be a scaled-down version of the Cold War military. The issue of a Cold War–style force for a post–Cold War world was still being debated in the first year of George W. Bush's presidency.

Challenges to the Power of the Presidency

President Clinton also struggled to maintain the prestige and power of the office that had been defined for so long by war. In this, he was perhaps more successful than it first appears. In the midterm elections of 1994, just two years into his presidency, Bill Clinton faced the indignity of a massive partisan defeat. The Republicans became the majority party in the House and Senate for the first time since Dwight Eisenhower was a newly elected president. Moreover, the new Speaker of the House, Rep. Newt Gingrich of Georgia, challenged the president for leadership in a way little seen in the past. He claimed, first of all, a national mandate on the basis of his party's victory in the midterm elections. Under his tutelage, the Republicans elected in that year had run on a written platform, a "Contract with America." This gave Gingrich, promptly selected by his party as Speaker, a claim to national leadership unique in congressional history. For the following four years, Gingrich battled Clinton for the right to set the national government's agenda and shape its predominant policy. As a result, "the decline of the presidency and the rise of Congress" became the new "conventional wisdom" in Washington, D.C.[5] But alarm about the shrinking presidency proved unwarranted.

Gingrich attempted to consolidate his power by imitating the very war-inflated presidency that he claimed to challenge. Like "Bill," "Newt" thus became a household name, and he aspired to his own cult of personality. Like any modern president, he attempted to rally the public through televised speeches and sound bites written to capture the Americans' short attention spans. Like a president, he sought a platform on the world stage, where he might stand symbolically and represent the nation. In this contest, Gingrich was seriously outmatched by Clinton, who, as president, had sharpened his political skills in a true national election and had a much easier task commanding the nation's attention. When the nation needed a symbolic head, it gravitated naturally to its president. When Gingrich and Clinton squared off over the federal government's budget in the winter of 1995–1996, the public sided with the president and blamed Congress for forcing repeated government shutdowns. After the April 1995 bombing of the Alfred P. Murrah Federal Building in Oklahoma City, it was President Clinton who effortlessly assumed the role of head of state and comforted a grieving nation.

Then there was the matter of the president's command authority. Ever since Harry Truman's presidency, it has been widely accepted—even by members of Congress—that a president does not have to ask Congress or anyone else for permission to accomplish a military goal. In the early twentieth century, before the permanent mobilization of the armed forces, the commander in chief was typically at the mercy of Congress unless the nation was involved in a hot war. Even then, a clever and ambitious president could still get around Congress, on occasion. President Theodore Roosevelt brilliantly exploited this fact. After Congress denied him the funds to send the U.S. Navy on a cruise around the world, something he wanted in order to impress nations such as Japan with the United States' growing power, Roosevelt used his command authority to send them halfway—and dared Congress not to bring them back. (He well knew that Congress would cave into pressure to return home the nation's sailors, who otherwise would bake in the sun halfway around the world.) But since the Korean War, presidents had not needed to be so creative.

Thus, when President Clinton decided (in part for domestic political reasons) to use force in response to a crisis in Haiti, like any Cold War president faced with a similarly small operation, he simply acted, without even the nicety of a congressional resolution to authorize the potential use of force. In 1990 Haiti's elected president, Jean-Bertrand Aristide, was removed from power in a military coup. Since then, the United States had been working to return him to office. As the situation in Haiti worsened, with periodic bloodshed between rival factions and economic collapse, the Congressional Black Caucus in the U.S. House of Representatives and Florida politicians who feared a massive influx of Haitian refugees joined together to lobby Clinton to take action. In September 1994, after securing a United Nations Security Council mandate, Clinton ordered a U.S. invasion force into position. The invasion was averted only at the last minute when former general Colin Powell, joined by former president Jimmy Carter, brokered a deal in which Haiti's military dictators surrendered power but remained in the country. As a result, U.S. forces waded ashore on September 19, facing television cameras rather than small-arms fire.

In 1995 and 1999, President Clinton employed lethal force in a different part of the world. After the Cold War, Yugoslavia broke apart violently, as a decade-long war erupted between rival states within the former Communist republic. During the Bush presidency, the president had resisted calls for the introduction of U.S. military forces into the Balkans. President Clinton, during his election campaign, had occasionally taken time from his economic message to call for "heat" in Bosnia and Herzegovina—presumably U.S. air strikes— but he had largely stayed away from the issue. Once in office, though, the European Union's inability to handle the crisis, plus televised coverage of the Bosnian Serb Army's bombardment of the United Nation's "safe havens," pressed the president to action.

In Operation Deliberate Force, a U.S.-led NATO air campaign was carried out between August 30 and September 20, 1995. With the critical assistance of ground forces from Bosnia and Herzegovina, one of the breakaway republics of the former Yugoslavia, the operation created the conditions necessary for a peace agreement, which was signed at Wright-Patterson Air Force Base in Dayton, Ohio. The Dayton Accords resolved the crisis in Bosnia and Herzegovina, but in the ethnic Albanian province of Kosovo, conflict escalated between the armed forces of the Federal Republic of Yugoslavia and paramilitary rebels fighting for Kosovo's independence, the Kosovo Liberation Army (KLA). As the final step in a campaign to bring Kosovo to heel, Slobodan Milosevic, the president of the Federal Republic of Yugoslavia, ordered a full-scale military offensive against the ethnically distinct Albanian majority in Kosovo. President Clinton, with NATO backing, employed massive air power in Operation Allied Force. In early June 1999, after eleven weeks, the operation succeeded.

President Clinton, like Cold War presidents before him, informed Congress prior to each of these operations, as he did on more than sixty other occasions when he ordered the use of "armed forces abroad in situations of military conflict or potential conflict or for other than normal peacetime purposes" during his eight years in office. But he never asked Congress for its permission.[6] Answering criticism about his failure to consult Congress prior to the Haiti operation, the president cited the precedent of the Cold War, as if there were no distinction to be observed between Cold War and post–Cold War chief executives: "I would welcome the support of the Congress, and I hope that I will have that. Like my predecessors of both parties, I have not agreed that I was constitutionally mandated to get it."[7] Similarly, he treated the sanction of the United Nations, which he secured for Operation Uphold Democracy, as preferable but not mandatory. The Balkans bombing of 1999 proceeded in defiance of Russian and Chinese protests and, therefore, without the approval of the Security Council. (Russia occupies the seat held by the former Soviet Union.) It appears as if international responsibilities and global military options are still very much incumbent upon the president.

Even the impeachment of President Clinton did not seriously detract from his powers. Certainly the prestige of the presidency, if not its power, was damaged in January 1998, when Clinton's disastrous dalliance with a White House intern, Monica Lewinsky, became public. That month, Clinton was deposed in a lawsuit brought against him by Paula Jones, who was suing him for alleged sexual harassment while he was governor of Arkansas and she an employee of the state. During his deposition in the case, while answering questions about whether he had had sex with other women who were in his employ, Clinton allegedly perjured himself by stating that he had not had "sexual relations" with Lewinsky. Clinton was also accused of obstructing justice by allegedly encouraging Lewinsky to lie in her affidavit in the Jones case.[8] The resulting impeachment by the House of Representatives and trial by the Senate did not, however, damage the president's place in government.

In fact, Clinton and the Democratic Party were ultimately the beneficiaries of a backlash against the Republican Party. The attempt to unseat the president on this account was simply too much for many Americans, and the president's job approval ratings improved while the public's perception of Congress soured. Democrats did surprisingly well in the 1998 midterm elections, conducted in the midst of the impeachment scandal; House Republicans, who had taken the lead in the impeachment proceedings, suffered. As a consequence of this and other setbacks, Gingrich abruptly resigned his position as Speaker on November 6, 1998, and indicated that he would not take his seat when the House reconvened in January.

It is possible that, over the long term, Clinton's contempt for judicial process in the Jones suit and the subsequent investigation into his sworn testimony in that case may be seen as a low point for the post–Cold War presidency. His actions may be compared in time with those of Nixon or Reagan, who were also alleged to have placed themselves above the law. What is clear, however, is that this was a presidential scandal of a different sort, as Clinton could not claim that his misconduct was intended to defend the nation against its enemies. If only because of the domestic, even personal, nature of the underlying facts at issue, the Clinton impeachment stands as an intriguing symbol of the post–Cold War, indeed, post-modern, political era.

The United States' Role in the World

Finally, President Clinton struggled with the problem of defining the United States' international role in a world that was no longer bipolar. To begin with, there was the matter of accounting for all of the former Soviet Union's nuclear weapons. Fortunately for Clinton, his predecessor had already made substantial progress on this front before leaving office.

The Strategic Arms Reduction Treaty (START I) was signed by President Bush just months before the Soviet state collapsed (see **Document 10.7**). In a remarkably smooth transition, however, the treaty was ratified by the nuclear successor states to the Soviet

Union—Russia, Belarus, Kazakhstan, and Ukraine—within a year. The last three, during the 1990s, eliminated their nuclear weapons completely, transferring them to Russia. The U.S. State Department, along with other federal agencies, worked assiduously in the 1990s and beyond, moreover, to ensure the integrity of the Russian nuclear arsenal against possible threat or attack. In a series of diplomatic moves, the United States and Russia slowly but methodically decreased the threat that each might potentially pose to the other, retargeting their missiles and further decreasing their stockpiles in accordance with a successor treaty, START II.

Under START I, each side agreed to reduce their warheads to 6,000 apiece. In START II, signed by Bush and Russian president Boris Yeltsin on January 3, 1993, just weeks before Clinton took office, each side agreed to reduce nuclear stockpiles by about two-thirds more and to ban all MIRVed ICBMs (strategic intercontinental ballistic missiles with multiple warheads). Additional complex limits and sublimits were agreed to, all of which dramatically reduced the nuclear threat faced by both powers. Following difficult diplomatic talks between the Clinton administration and the other Eastern nuclear successor states, the treaty was at last ratified by the U.S. Senate in 1996. It was formally ratified in 2000 by the Russian government after considerable further negotiation (over such issues as how much of the costs of compliance the U.S. government would pay).

On the issue of how the United States should relate to the wider world after the Cold War, there were several possible answers. All of them had their proponents in the 1990s.

Clinton's post–Cold War vision was of a decidedly committed United States, generously giving of its leadership and, when useful, its military might. Thus, when ethnic and nationalist tensions, coupled with the dizzying opportunity for political power, brought the former Yugoslavia to civil war, Clinton was pleased to step into the power vacuum left by the collapse of the Soviet empire. Working through international organizations, most prominently NATO, Clinton deployed military forces and used diplomacy and economic aid to encourage the factions to end the fighting. When faced with the challenge of the People's Republic of China—still defiantly Communist but embracing, by ever-greater degrees, the economic principles of the West—Clinton eschewed calls to punish the country for its social and political repressions. Instead, he attempted to shape its domestic and international policies through positive engagement in bilateral and multilateral negotiations and exchanges.

Clinton's vision had its adherents, but it also had its detractors. Some critics blamed Clinton for attempting to do too much on the international scene. The United States should draw back, they argued, and take care of its internal problems before worrying so much about the quality of life in the former Yugoslavia or the People's Republic of China. Although there were occasional voices raised in support of a new isolationism, perhaps one of the biggest changes in American life brought about by the Cold War was the consensus among the nation's elite, both Republicans and Democrats, in favor of the United States being committed around the world. U.S. leadership in foreign affairs was a foregone conclusion to most senators, senior members of the House, newspaper publishers and editors, and writers and academics who studied foreign affairs.[9]

A more important criticism of the Clinton camp came from mainstream Republicans who wanted to maintain the United States' leadership in world affairs, while being more cautious and selective about deploying the nation's armed forces. Let the military have a rest, they said, from the non-war deployments of the 1990s. Let the armed services focus instead on preparing for the next "real" war, however hard it might be at the moment to imagine when, or against whom, that war might be fought.

Finally, there were critics of the Clinton administration who argued throughout the 1990s that the president was doing not too much but too little to maintain U.S. leadership. These critics, many of whom were the same hard-liners who had buttressed President Reagan in his first term, argued that the United States was letting a historic opportunity slip by. If the United States committed to *more* military spending and active engagement around the world, it could ensure that there would never be a future peer adversary against which the nation would have to arm itself and with whom it would have to once again divide the world. The end of a bipolar world, they said, offered the opportunity to create a *unipolar* one. The United States was and should remain the sole superpower.[10]

THE END OF ANOTHER ERA?

What was the proper role of the U.S. armed forces after the end of the Cold War? Should the troops be used for peacekeeping and humanitarian missions, since it was unlikely that they would asked to fight a war anytime soon? How much power did the United States really require in its fighting forces? Was it prudent or just wasteful to keep maintaining and replacing fleets of nuclear bombers and aircraft carriers as well as battle tanks designed to meet the Warsaw Pact on the plains of Europe? What was the proper role of the United States in international affairs? Should it take the lead on all issues? Was it not time for the nations of Eastern and Western Europe to begin to play a more responsible role for events in their parts of the world? What did the United States owe the nations over which it had fought proxy wars in the Cold War? What did those nations owe to the United States? Did NATO still have a military role in Europe or in the world beyond? What should the relationship be between NATO and Russia?

The end of the Cold War brought all of these questions, and many more, to the forefront of debate among defense professionals, presidential contenders, members of Congress, and ordinary Americans. All were still being debated on September 11, 2001, when the United States was attacked by al-Qaida. It was clearly hyperbole that led President George W. Bush, like so many others, to say that "everything changed" on that day. Some things stayed the same. In a time of crisis, the nation still turns to the president and defers to the president's judgment to define the threat and devise a response. Because, however, of the way in which the president chose to respond to that attack—through a dramatic reliance upon military power to wage a punitive war in Afghanistan and a preemptive war in Iraq—it is clear that the United States has now entered a new phase, the post-post–Cold War era. As the nation returned to war, the Cold War was rhetorically laid to rest all over again, when Bush and Russian president Vladimir Putin issued a "Joint Statement on a New Relationship between the United States and Russia" (**Document 11.2**). At the same time, Cold War arguments about the extent of presidential power relative to that of Congress became central to political discussion once again. Because of the nature of the "war on terror" and its prosecution, a new debate began about the limits of presidential power in taking action against suspected terrorists.

Although it is the Cold War that nourished the strong executive powers that President George W. Bush has employed in the war on terror, the president's rhetoric has invoked not that struggle but rather the "good war," World War II. Nazi Germany, not the Stalinist Soviet Union, remains the symbolic embodiment of evil in U.S. political culture. The Cold War, perhaps because it simply faded away, seems poised to fade away likewise in the popular imagination. It should not be permitted to do so, however, for the Cold War's lasting effects on our national institutions, not least among them the presidency, are too great to be ignored.

NOTES

1. Alexander Hamilton, *Federalist Paper* no. 70, in Alexander Hamilton, James Madison, John Jay, *The Federalist Papers,* ed. Clinton Rossiter (New York: New American Library, 1961), 423.

2. Thomas S. Langston, *Uneasy Balance: Civil-Military Relations in Peacetime America since 1783* (Baltimore, Md.: Johns Hopkins University Press, 2003), 1–2, 110. See also Peter D. Feaver and Richard K. Kohn, eds., *Soldiers and Civilians: The Civil-Military Gap and American National Security* (Cambridge, Mass.: MIT Press, 2001), especially chapters 1 and 5 (Ole R. Holsti, "Of Chasms and Convergences: Attitudes and Beliefs of Civilians and Military Elites at the Start of a New Millennium," 15–100; Russell F. Weigley, "The American Civil-Military Cultural Gap: A Historical Perspective, Colonial Times to the Present," 215–246).

3. President Clinton attempted in his first weeks in office to lift the ban on service by homosexuals in the armed forces. He was forced by opposition from the JCS and members of Congress to embrace a "don't ask, don't tell" policy that actually led to an increase in the number of gay service personnel driven from military duty. The president similarly settled for less than he wanted with regard to lifting restrictions on gender integration in the military. See Laura L. Miller and John Allen Williams, "Do Military Policies on Gender and Sexuality Undermine Combat Effectiveness?" in Feaver and Kohn, *Soldiers and Civilians,* 361–402.

4. Lorna Jaffe, *The Development of the Base Force, 1989–1992* (Washington, D.C.: Joint Chiefs of Staff, Office of the Chairman, Joint History Office, 1993); Sharon K. Weiner, "The Politics of Resource Allocation in the Post Cold-War Pentagon," *Security Studies* 5, no. 4 (Summer 1996): 125–142.

5. Michael Lind, "The Out-of-Control Presidency," *The New Republic* (August 14, 1995): 18.

6. Richard F. Grimmett, *Instances of Use of United States Armed Forces Abroad, 1798–2004,* Congressional Research Service report RL30172, available online from the Naval Historical Center, www.au.af.mil/au/awc/awcgate/crs/rl30172.htm.

7. William J. Clinton, "The President's News Conference," August 3, 1994, in *Public Papers of the Presidents of the United States: William J. Clinton, 1993–2001,* from the American Presidency Project, University of California, Santa Barbara, www.presidency.ucsb.edu.

8. See Richard A. Posner, *An Affair of State: The Investigation, Impeachment, and Trial of President Clinton* (Cambridge, Mass.: Harvard University Press, 1999).

9. See Eric A. Nordlinger, *Isolationism Reconfigured: American Foreign Policy for a New Century* (Princeton, N.J.: Princeton University Press, 1996); Joshua Muravcik, *The Imperative of American Leadership: A Challenge to Neo-Isolationism* (Washington, D.C.: AEI Press, 1996).

10. See Robert Kagan and William Kristol, *Present Dangers: Crisis and Opportunity in American Foreign and Defense Policy* (San Francisco: Encounter Books, 2000); Stefan Halper and Jonathan Clarke, *America Alone: The Neo-Conservatives and the Global Order* (Cambridge, England: Cambridge University Press, 2004).

Document 11.1
The National Security Strategy of Engagement and Enlargement, February 1995

President Bill Clinton proclaimed a new national security strategy for the post–Cold War era. His strategy began with the premise that national security is not based on weapons and soldiers alone. Economic and environmental security are equally important components of the nation's defense, especially in a world where the United States stands alone in its military power. Therefore, to promote the United States' security, the federal government would commit itself to economic revitalization at home, as well as to maintaining a strong military. Because democracies pose less of a threat to peace than dictatorships, moreover, the United States would endeavor to spread democracy around the globe. With regard to the military, President Clinton's new strategy declared that the armed forces would and should be used for missions other than war. These were fighting words to a military establishment forged during the Cold War.

PREFACE

Protecting our nation's security—our people, our territory and our way of life—is my Administration's foremost mission and constitutional duty. The end of the Cold War fundamentally changed America's security imperatives. The central security challenge of the past half-century—the threat of communist expansion—is gone. The dangers we face today are more diverse. Ethnic conflict is spreading and rogue states pose a serious danger to regional stability in many corners of the globe. The proliferation of weapons of mass destruction represents a major challenge to our security. Large scale environmental degradation, exacerbated by rapid population growth, threatens to undermine political stability in many countries and regions.

At the same time, we have unparalleled opportunities to make our nation safer and more prosperous. Our military might is unparalleled. We now have a truly global economy linked by an instantaneous communication network, which offers growing opportunity for American jobs and American investment. The community of democratic nations is growing, enhancing the prospects for political stability, peaceful conflict resolution and greater dignity and hope for the people of the world. The international community is beginning to act together to address pressing global environmental needs.

Never has American leadership been more essential—to navigate the shoals of the world's new dangers and to capitalize on its opportunities. American assets are unique: our military strength, our dynamic economy, our powerful ideals and, above all, our people. We can and must make the difference through our engagement; our involvement must be carefully tailored to serve our interests and priorities.

This report . . . elaborates a national security strategy tailored for this new era. Focusing on new threats and new opportunities, its central goals are:

- To sustain our security with military forces that are ready to fight.
- To bolster America's economic revitalization.
- To promote democracy abroad. . . .

Deciding When and How to Employ U.S. Forces

. . . There are three basic categories of national interests which can merit the use of our armed forces. The first involves America's vital interests, i.e., interests which are of broad, overriding importance to the survival, security and vitality of our national entity—the defense of U.S. territory, citizens, allies and economic well-being. We will do whatever it takes to defend these interests, including—when necessary—the unilateral and decisive use of military power. . . .

The second category involves cases in which important, but not vital, U.S. interests are threatened. That is, the interests at stake do not affect our national survival, but they do affect importantly our national well-being and the character of the world in which we live. In such cases, military forces should only be used if they advance U.S. interests, they are likely to be able to accomplish their objectives, the costs and risks of their employment are commensurate with the interests at stake, and other means have been tried and have failed to achieve our objectives. Such use of force should also be limited, reflecting the relative saliency of the interests we have at stake. Haiti is the most recent example in this category.

The third category involves primarily humanitarian interests. Here, our decisions focus on the resources we can bring to bear by using unique capabilities of our military rather than on the combat power of military force. Generally, the military is not the best tool to address humanitarian concerns. But under certain conditions, the use of our armed forces may be appropriate: when a humanitarian catastrophe dwarfs the ability of civilian relief agencies to respond; when the need for relief is urgent and only the military has the ability to jump-start the longer-term response to the disaster; when the response requires resources unique to the military; and the risk to American troops is minimal. . . .

Source: National Security Council, *A National Security Strategy of Engagement and Enlargement,* February 1995, from the Defense Technical Information Center, www.dtic.mil/doctrine/jel/research_pubs/nss.pdf.

Document 11.2
Joint Statement by President George W. Bush and President Vladimir V. Putin on a New Relationship between the United States and Russia, November 13, 2001

Shortly after the attacks of September 11, 2001, President George W. Bush and his Russian counterpart, President Vladimir Putin, promised to cooperate with one another in the war on terror. At a Washington, D.C., summit, the two leaders signed a number of agreements, pledging cooperation on bioterrorism, on the Middle East, and on the effort to stop the international flow of illegal drugs, and published this broad statement on the nature of the Russian-American relationship.

Our countries are embarked on a new relationship for the 21st century, founded on a commitment to the values of democracy, the free market, and the rule of law. The United States and Russia have overcome the legacy of the Cold War. Neither country regards the other as an enemy or threat. Aware of our responsibility to contribute to international security, we are determined to work together, and with other nations and international organizations, including the United Nations, to promote security, economic well-being, and a peaceful, prosperous, free world.

We affirm our determination to meet the threats to peace in the 21st century. Among these threats are terrorism, the new horror of which was vividly demonstrated by the evil crimes of September 11, proliferation of weapons of mass destruction, militant nationalism, ethnic and religious intolerance, and regional instability. These threats endanger the security of both countries and the world at large. Dealing with these challenges calls for the creation of a new strategic framework to ensure the mutual security of the United States and Russia, and the world community.

We have agreed that the current levels of our nuclear forces do not reflect the strategic realities of today. Therefore, we have confirmed our respective commitments to implement substantial reductions in strategic offensive weapons. On strategic defenses and the ABM Treaty, we have agreed, in light of the changing global security environment, to continue consultations within the broad framework of the new strategic relationship. On nonproliferation matters, we reaffirm our mutual commitment to the Biological and Chemical Weapons Conventions, and endorse efforts to strengthen the Nuclear Nonproliferation Treaty. Both sides agree that urgent attention must continue to be given to improving the physical protection and accounting of nuclear materials of all possessor states, and preventing illicit nuclear trafficking.

We support the building of a European-Atlantic community whole, free, and at peace, excluding no one, and respecting the independence, sovereignty and territorial integrity of all nations. To this end, the United States and Russia will work, together with NATO and other NATO members, to improve, strengthen, and enhance the relationship between NATO and Russia, with a view to developing new, effective mechanisms for consultation, cooperation, joint decision, and coordinated/joint action. . . .

We recognize a market economy, the freedom of economic choice and an open democratic society as the most effective means to provide for the welfare of our citizens. The United States and Russia will cooperate, including through the support of direct contacts between the business communities of our countries, to advance U.S.-Russian economic, trade, and investment relations. The achievement of these goals requires the removal of legislative and administrative barriers, a transparent, predictable investment climate, the rule of law, and market-based economic reforms. To this end, it is important to reduce bureaucratic constraints on the economy and to combat economic crime and corruption.

Reaffirming our commitment to advance common values, the United States and Russia will continue to work together to protect and advance human rights, tolerance, religious freedom, free speech and independent media, economic opportunity, and the rule of law. In keeping with these commitments, we welcome the initiative of Russian and American media executives, journalists, and independent organizations to convene a Russian-American Media Entrepreneurship Dialogue. We will promote intense people-to-people exchanges as an important factor for enhancing mutual understanding between the American and Russian peoples. We pledge ourselves to the principles and values that represent the best traditions of both our nations, and to cooperation in order to realize them now and in the future.

Source: "Joint Statement by President George W. Bush and President Vladimir V. Putin on a New Relationship between the United States and Russia," November 13, 2001, in *Public Papers of the Presidents of the United States: George W. Bush, 2001–*, from the American Presidency Project, University of California, Santa Barbara, www.presidency.ucsb.edu.

Selected Bibliography

This bibliography includes online and print resources on the Cold War. In the print section, general reference works and specialized studies of the Cold War, the military, the presidency, and Congress are provided first. These are followed by resources on each of the nine presidents profiled in this book as well as the origins and aftermath of the Cold War. Works considered especially noteworthy are preceded by an asterisk (*).

ONLINE RESOURCES

Assassination Archives and Research Center Public Digital Library. www.aarclibrary.org/publib.htm.

Avalon Project at Yale Law School: Documents in Law, History, and Diplomacy. www.yale.edu/lawweb/avalon.

* CNN. *Cold War.* www.cnn.com/SPECIALS/cold.war/.

Cold War History Research Center. Budapest, Hungary. www.coldwar.hu.

Cold War International History Project and George Washington University Cold War Group. Cold War Files. www.coldwarfiles.org.

Cold War Museum. www.coldwar.org.

Commission on Presidential Debates. www.debates.org/pages/debtrans.html.

Davis Center for Russian and Eurasian Studies. Cold War Studies at Harvard University. www.fas.harvard.edu/~hpcws/index2.htm.

* Federation of American Scientists. Arms Control Agreements. www.fas.org/nuke/control.

* ———. Intelligence Resource Program. www.fas.org/irp/offdocs/index.html.

Ferraro, Vincent. Mount Holyoke College. Documents Relating to American Foreign Policy: The Cold War. www.mtholyoke.edu/acad/intrel/coldwar.htm.

* George Washington University. National Security Archive. www.nsarchive.org. Includes numerous microfiche collections and electronic briefing books.

Library of Congress. Country Studies. http://lcweb2.loc.gov/frd/cs/cshome.html.

Moïse, Edwin E. Clemson University. Vietnam War Bibliography. www.clemson.edu/caah/history/facultypages/EdMoise/bibliography.html.

* National Archives. Presidential Libraries. www.archives.gov/presidential-libraries.

Parallel History Project on NATO and the Warsaw Pact. www.isn.ethz.ch/php.

Texas Tech University. Vietnam Project. www.vietnam.ttu.edu.

University of Michigan Library. Federal Government Resources: Historic Documents. www.lib.umich.edu/govdocs/fedhis.html#coldwar.

University of Oregon. East and Southeast Asia: An Annotated Directory of Internet Resources. http://newton.uor.edu/Departments&Programs/AsianstudiesDept/index.html.

* U.S. Department of State. Foreign Relations of the United States. www.state.gov/r/pa/ho/frus/c1716.htm

* Woodrow Wilson International Center for Scholars. Cold War International History Project. www.cwihp.org. Includes a bulletin, working papers, e-dossiers, and a virtual archive.

* Woolley, John, and Gerhard Peters. American Presidency Project. www.presidency.ucsb.edu. Includes searchable edition of the *Public Papers of the Presidents of the United States.*

BOOKS

Reference Works

* Arms, Thomas S. *Encyclopedia of the Cold War.* New York: Facts on File, 1994.

Brune, Lester H. *Chronology of the Cold War: 1917–1992.* New York: Routledge, 2005.

Chambers, John Whiteclay, II, ed. *The Oxford Companion to American Military History*. New York: Oxford University Press, 1999.

Edwards, George C., III. *Presidential Approval: A Sourcebook*. Baltimore, Md.: Johns Hopkins University Press, 1990.

Genovese, Michael A., ed. *Encyclopedia of the American Presidency*. New York: Facts on File, 2004.

* Hill, Kenneth L. *Cold War Chronology: Soviet-American Relations, 1945–1991*. Washington, D.C.: CQ Press, 1993.

Nelson, Michael, ed. *The Presidency A to Z*. 3d ed. Washington, D.C.: CQ Press, 2003.

Schwartz, Richard Alan. *The Cold War Reference Guide: A General History and Annotated Chronology, with Selected Biographies*. Jefferson, N.C.: McFarland and Company, 1997.

Smith, Joseph, and Simon Davis. *The A to Z of the Cold War*. Lanham, Md.: Scarecrow Press, 2005.

Surveys of the Cold War

Andrew, Christopher M., and Vasili Mirokhin. *The World Was Going Our Way: The KGB and the Battle for the Third World*. New York: Basic Books, 2005.

Brands, H. W. *The Devil We Knew: Americans and the Cold War*. New York: Oxford University Press, 1993.

* Crockatt, Richard. *The Fifty Years War: The United States and the Soviet Union in World Politics, 1941–1991*. New York: Routledge, 1994.

* Gaddis, John Lewis. *Strategies of Containment: A Critical Appraisal of Postwar American National Security Policy*. New York: Oxford University Press, 1982.

* ———. *We Now Know: Rethinking Cold War History*. New York: Oxford University Press, 1997.

Judge, Edward H., and John W. Langdon, comps. and eds. *The Cold War: A History through Documents*. Upper Saddle River, N.J.: Prentice Hall, 1998.

LaFeber, Walter. *America, Russia, and the Cold War, 1945–2002*. Updated 9th ed. New York: McGraw Hill, 2004.

Lind, Michael. *The American Way of Strategy: U.S. Foreign Policy and the American Way of Life*. New York: Oxford University Press, 2006.

* Walker, Martin. *Cold War, A History*. New York: Henry Holt, 1993.

Specialized Studies of the Cold War

Chen, Jian. *Mao's China and the Cold War*. Chapel Hill: University of North Carolina Press, 2000.

* Friedberg, Aaron. *In the Shadow of the Garrison State: America's Anti-Statism and Its Cold War Grand Strategy*. Princeton, N.J.: Princeton University Press, 2000.

* Garthoff, Raymond L. *Détente and Confrontation: American-Soviet Relations from Nixon to Reagan*. Rev. ed. Washington, D.C.: Brookings Institution Press, 1994.

Ippolito, Dennis S. *Uncertain Legacies: Federal Budget Policy from Roosevelt through Reagan*. Charlottesville: University Press of Virginia, 1990.

Ouimet, Matthew J. *The Rise and Fall of the Brezhnev Doctrine in Soviet Foreign Policy*. Chapel Hill: University of North Carolina Press, 2003.

Prados, John. *Presidents' Secret Wars: CIA and Pentagon Covert Operations from World War II through the Persian Gulf*. Rev. and updated ed. Chicago: Ivan R. Dee, 1996.

Riley, Russell L. *The President and the Politics of Racial Inequality: Nation Keeping from 1831 to 1965*. New York: Columbia University Press, 1999.

* Wittkopf, Eugene R. *Faces of Internationalism: Public Opinion and American Foreign Policy*. Durham, N.C.: Duke University Press, 1990.

Zhai, Qiang. *China and the Vietnam Wars, 1950–1975*. Chapel Hill: University of North Carolina Press, 2000.

Zubok, Vladislav, and Constantine Speshakov. *Inside the Kremlin's Cold War: From Stalin to Khrushchev*. Cambridge, Mass.: Harvard University Press, 1996.

Surveys and Specialized Studies of the Military

Cohen, Eliot A. *Citizens and Soldiers: The Dilemmas of Military Service*. Ithaca, N.Y.: Cornell University Press, 1985.

Flynn, George Q. *The Draft, 1940–1973*. Lawrence: University Press of Kansas, 1993.

Hammond, Paul. *Organizing for Defense: The American Military Establishment in the Twentieth Century*. Princeton, N.J.: Princeton University Press, 1961.

* Herspring, Dale R. *The Pentagon and the Presidency: Civil-Military Relations from FDR to George W. Bush.* Lawrence: University Press of Kansas, 2005.

Huntington, Samuel P. *The Soldier and the State: The Theory and Practice of Civil-Military Relations.* Cambridge, Mass.: Harvard University Press, Belknap Press, 1959.

Janowitz, Morris. *The Professional Soldier: A Social and Professional Portrait.* Glencoe, Ill.: Free Press, 1960.

Matloff, Maurice, ed. *American Military History.* Vol. 2, *1902–1996.* Conshohocken, Pa.: Combined Books, 1996.

Miller, David. *The Cold War: A Military History.* New York: St. Martin's, 1998.

* Millet, Allan R., and Peter Maslowski. *For the Common Defense: A Military History of the United States of America.* New York: Free Press, 1984.

Millis, Walter. *Arms and Men: A Study in American Military History.* New York: Putnam, 1956.

Weigley, Russell F. *The American Way of War: A History of United States Military Strategy and Policy.* Bloomington: Indiana University Press, 1977.

Surveys and Specialized Studies of the Presidency

Bose, Meena. *Shaping and Signaling Presidential Policy: The National Security Decision Making of Eisenhower and Kennedy.* College Station: Texas A&M University Press, 1998.

Brinkley, Alan, and Davis Dyer, eds. *The American Presidency.* Boston: Houghton Mifflin, 2004.

Burke, John P., and Fred I. Greenstein. *How Presidents Test Reality: Decisions on Vietnam, 1954 and 1965.* With Larry Berman and Richard Immerman. New York: Russell Sage Foundation, 1989.

Corwin, Edward S. *The President, Office and Powers, 1787–1957.* 4th rev. ed. New York: New York University Press, 1957.

Greenstein, Fred I. *The Presidential Difference, Leadership Style from FDR to Clinton.* New York: Martin Kessler Books, 2000.

Hamby, Alonzo L. *Liberalism and Its Challengers: FDR to Reagan.* New York: Oxford University Press, 1985.

Koh, Harold Hongju. *The National Security Constitution: Sharing Power after the Iran-Contra Affair.* New Haven, Conn.: Yale University Press, 1990.

* Lowi, Theodore. *The Personal President: Power Invested, Promise Unfulfilled.* Ithaca, N.Y.: Cornell University Press, 1985.

* Mueller, John. *War, Presidents and Public Opinion.* New York: Wiley, 1973.

* Neustadt, Richard E. *Presidential Power: The Politics of Leadership.* New York: Wiley, 1960.

* Pious, Richard M. *The American Presidency.* New York: Basic Books, 1979.

* Schlesinger, Arthur M., Jr. *The Imperial Presidency.* Boston: Houghton Mifflin, 1973.

Skowronek, Stephen. *The Politics Presidents Make: Leadership from John Adams to Bill Clinton.* Cambridge, Mass.: Harvard University Press, Belknap Press, 1997.

Studies of Congress

Ely, John Hart. *War and Responsibility: Constitutional Lessons of Vietnam and Its Aftermath.* Princeton, N.J.: Princeton University Press, 1993.

Fisher, Louis. *Congressional Abdication on War and Spending.* College Station: Texas A&M University Press, 2000.

Hinkley, Barbara. *Less Than Meets the Eye: Foreign Policy Making and the Myth of the Assertive Congress.* Chicago: University of Chicago Press, 1994.

* Johnson, Robert David. *Congress and the Cold War.* New York: Cambridge University Press, 2006.

Sundquist, James L. *Decline and Resurgence of Congress.* Washington, D.C.: Brookings Institution Press, 1982.

Foreign Heads of State

Brezhnev, Leonid. *Memoirs.* Oxford, England: Pergamon Press, 1982.

* Chang, Jung and Jon Halliday. *Mao: The Unknown Story.* New York: Knopf, 2005.

Duiker, William J. *Ho Chi Minh: A Life.* New York: Hyperion, 2000.

Gorbachev, Mikhail. *Memoirs.* New York: Doubleday, 1996.

* Khrushchev, Nikita Sergeevich. *Khrushchev Remembers.* Translated and edited by Strobe Talbot. New York: Bantam Books, 1971.

Marshall, Barbara. *Willy Brandt: A Political Biography.* London: Palgrave Macmillan, 1997.

Thatcher, Margaret. *The Downing Street Years.* New York: Harper Collins, 1993.

CHAPTER ONE: ORIGINS

Acheson, Dean. *Present at the Creation: My Years at the State Department.* New York: Norton, 1969.

Alperovitz, Gar. *Atomic Diplomacy: Hiroshima and Potsdam, the Use of the Atomic Bomb and the American Confrontation with Soviet Power.* New York: Elisabeth Sifton Books, 1985.

Gaddis, John Lewis. *The United States and the Origins of the Cold War, 1941–1947.* New York: Columbia University Press, 1972.

* Isaacson, Walter, and Evan Thomas. *The Wise Men: Six Friends and the World They Made.* New York: Touchstone, 1986.

Kennan, George. *Memoirs.* Boston: Little, Brown, 1967.

* Klehr, Harvey, John Earl Haynes, and Kyrill M. Anderson. *The Soviet World of American Communism.* New Haven: Yale University Press, 1998.

Leffler, Melvyn P. *The Specter of Communism: The United States and the Origins of the Cold War, 1917–1953.* New York: Hill and Wang, 1994.

Reynolds, David. *The Origins of the Cold War in Europe: International Perspectives.* New Haven: Yale University Press, 1994.

Woods, Randall Bennett. *Dawning of the Cold War: The United States' Quest for Order.* Athens: University of Georgia Press, 1991.

Yergin, Daniel. *The Shattered Peace: The Origins of the Cold War and the National Security State.* Boston: Houghton Mifflin, 1977.

CHAPTER TWO: HARRY TRUMAN

Dalfiume, Richard M. *Desegregation of the U.S. Armed Forces; Fighting on Two Fronts, 1939–1953.* Columbia: University of Missouri Press, 1969.

* Donovan, Robert J. *Conflict and Crisis: The Presidency of Harry S. Truman, 1945–1948.* New York: Norton, 1997.

* ———. *Tumultuous Years: The Presidency of Harry S. Truman, 1949–1954.* New York: Norton, 1982.

Jones, Joseph Marion. *The Fifteen Weeks, February 21–June 5, 1947.* New York: Viking, 1955.

Leffler, Melvyn P. *A Preponderance of Power: National Security, the Truman Administration, and the Cold War.* Palo Alto, Calif.: Stanford University Press, 1992.

Lowitt, Richard. *The Truman-MacArthur Controversy.* Chicago: Rand McNally, 1967.

McCoy, Donald R. *Presidency of Harry S. Truman.* Lawrence: University Press of Kansas, 1984.

McCullough, David. *Truman.* New York: Simon and Schuster, 1992.

Millett, Allan. *The War for Korea, 1945–1950: A House Burning.* Lawrence: University Press of Kansas, 2005.

Spanier, John W. *The Truman-MacArthur Controversy and the Korean War.* New York: Norton, 1965.

Truman, Harry S. *Defending the West: The Truman-Churchill Correspondence, 1945–1960.* Edited by G. W. Sand. Westport, Conn.: Praeger, 2004.

———. *Memoirs.* Vol. 1, *Year of Decision.* Garden City, N.Y.: Doubleday, 1955.

———. *Memoirs.* Vol. 2, *Years of Trial and Hope.* Garden City, N.Y.: Doubleday, 1956.

CHAPTER THREE: DWIGHT EISENHOWER

Ambrose, Stephen E. *Eisenhower.* Vol. 2, *The President.* New York: Simon and Schuster, 1984.

Billings-Yun, Melanie. *Decision against War: Eisenhower and Dien Bien Phu.* New York: Columbia University Press, 1988.

* Bowie, Robert R., and Richard H. Immerman. *Waging Peace: How Eisenhower Shaped an Enduring Cold War Strategy.* New York: Oxford University Press, 1998.

Chambers, Whittaker. *Witness.* New York: Random House, 1952.

Divine, Robert A. *Eisenhower and the Cold War.* New York: Oxford University Press, 1981.

* ———. *The Sputnik Challenge.* New York: Oxford University Press, 1993.

Eisenhower, Dwight D. *The Eisenhower Diaries.* Edited by Robert H. Ferrell. New York: Norton, 1981.

———. *The White House Years.* Vol. 1, *Mandate for Change, 1953–1956.* Garden City, N.Y.: Doubleday, 1963.

———. *The White House Years.* Vol. 2, *Waging Peace, 1956–1961.* Garden City, N.Y.: Doubleday, 1965.

Fried, Richard. *Nightmare in Red: The McCarthy Era in Perspective.* New York: Oxford University Press, 1990.

Greenstein, Fred. *The Hidden-Hand Presidency: Eisenhower as Leader.* New York: Basic Books, 1982.

Hiss, Alger. *In the Court of Public Opinion.* New York: Knopf, 1957.

Immerman, Richard H. *The CIA in Guatemala: The Foreign Policy of Intervention.* Austin: University of Texas Press, 1982.

Kahn, Herman. *On Thermonuclear War: Thinking about the Unthinkable.* Princeton, N.J.: Princeton University Press, 1960.

Laswell, Harold. *National Security and Individual Freedom.* New York: McGraw-Hill, 1950.

Melanson, Richard A., and David Mayers, eds. *Reevaluating Eisenhower: American Foreign Policy in the 1950s.* Urbana: University of Illinois Press, 1987.

* Pach, Christopher J., and Elmo Richardson. *The Presidency of Dwight D. Eisenhower.* Rev. ed. Lawrence: University Press of Kansas, 1991.

CHAPTER FOUR: JOHN F. KENNEDY

Ball, Desmond. *Politics and Force Levels: The Strategic Missile Program of the Kennedy Administration.* Berkeley: University of California Press, 1980.

* Beschloss, Michael. *The Crisis Years: Kennedy and Khrushchev, 1960–1963.* New York: Harper Collins, 1991.

Blight, James, and David Welch. *On the Brink: Americans and Soviets Examine the Cuban Missile Crisis.* New York: Hill and Wang, 1989.

Borstelman, Thomas. *The Cold War and the Color Line: American Race Relations in the Global Arena.* Cambridge, Mass.: Harvard University Press, 2001.

Frankel, Max. *High Noon in the Cold War: Kennedy, Khrushchev, and the Cuban Missile Crisis.* New York: Ballantine Books, 2004.

Fursenko, Aleksandr, and Timothy J. Naftali. *One Hell of a Gamble: Khrushchev, Castro, and Kennedy, 1958–1964.* New York: Norton, 1998.

Giglio, James N. *Presidency of John F. Kennedy.* Lawrence: University Press of Kansas, 2006.

* Giglio, James N., and Stephen G. Rabe. *Debating the Kennedy Presidency.* Lanham, Md.: Rowman & Littlefield, 2003.

Halberstam, David. *The Best and the Brightest.* New York: Random House, 1972.

* Higgins, Trumbull. *The Perfect Failure: Kennedy, Eisenhower, and the CIA at the Bay of Pigs.* New York: Norton, 1987.

Mahoney, Richard D. *JFK: Ordeal in Africa.* New York: Oxford University Press, 1983.

May, Ernest, and Philip D. Zelikow. *The Kennedy Tapes: Inside the White House during the Cuban Missile Crisis.* Cambridge, Mass.: Harvard University Press, 1997.

Miroff, Bruce. *Pragmatic Illusions: The Presidential Politics of John F. Kennedy.* New York: McKay, 1976.

Parmet, Herbert S. *JFK: The Presidency of John F. Kennedy.* New York: Dial Press, 1983.

Paterson, Thomas G., ed. *Kennedy's Quest for Victory: American Foreign Policy, 1961–1963.* New York: Oxford University Press, 1989.

Preble, Christopher A. *John F. Kennedy and the Missile Gap.* DeKalb: Northern Illinois University Press, 2004.

Rabe, Stephen G. *The Most Dangerous Area in the World: John F. Kennedy Confronts Communist Revolution in Latin America.* Chapel Hill: University of North Carolina Press, 1999.

Reeves, Thomas C. *A Question of Character: A Life of John F. Kennedy.* New York: Macmillan, 1991.

Schlesinger, Arthur M., Jr. *A Thousand Days: John F. Kennedy in the White House.* Boston: Houghton Mifflin, 1965.

* Stern, Sheldon M. *Averting 'The Final Failure': John F. Kennedy and the Secret Cuban Missile Crisis Meetings.* Palo Alto, Calif.: Stanford University Press, 2003.

CHAPTER FIVE: LYNDON JOHNSON

Berman, Larry. *Planning for a Tragedy: The Americanization of the War in Vietnam.* New York: Norton, 1982.

Bernstein, Irving. *Guns or Butter: The Presidency of Lyndon Johnson.* New York: Oxford University Press, 1990.

* Beschloss, Michael R., ed. *Reaching for Glory: Lyndon Johnson's Secret White House Tapes, 1964–1965.* New York: Simon and Schuster, 2001.

* ———, ed. *Taking Charge: The Johnson White House Tapes, 1963–1964.* New York: Simon and Schuster, 1997.

Bornet, Vaughn Davis. *The Presidency of Lyndon B. Johnson.* Lawrence: University Press of Kansas, 1983.

Dallek, Robert. *Flawed Giant: Lyndon Johnson and His Times, 1961–1973.* New York: Oxford University Press, 1998.

Dugger, Ronnie. *The Politician: The Life and Times of Lyndon Johnson.* New York: Norton, 1982.

Goodwin, Doris Kearns. *Lyndon Johnson and the American Dream.* New York: St. Martin's, 1991.

Johnson, Lyndon Baines. *The Vantage Point: Perspectives on the Presidency, 1963–1969.* New York: Holt, Rinehart, and Winston, 1971.

Langston, Thomas S. *Lyndon Baines Johnson.* Washington, D.C.: CQ Press, 2002.

* Lind, Michael. *Vietnam: The Necessary War, a Reinterpretation of America's Most Disastrous Military Conflict.* New York: Free Press, 1999.

Maclear, Michael. *The Ten Thousand Day War: Vietnam, 1945–1975.* New York: St. Martin's, 1981.

McMaster, H. R. *Dereliction of Duty: Lyndon Johnson, Robert McNamara, the Joint Chiefs of Staff, and the Lies That Led to Vietnam.* New York: Harper Perennial, 1997.

McNamara, Robert S. *In Retrospect: The Tragedy and Lessons of Vietnam.* With Brian VanDeMark. New York: Times Books, 1995.

Sheehan, Neil, Nedrick Smith, E. W. Kenworthy, and Fox Butterfield. *The Pentagon Papers as Published by the* New York Times. New York: Bantam Books, 1971.

CHAPTERS SIX AND SEVEN: RICHARD NIXON AND GERALD FORD

Ambrose, Stephen E. *Nixon, Ruin and Recovery: 1973–1990.* New York: Simon and Schuster, 1991.

———. *Nixon, The Triumph of a Politician: 1962–1972.* New York: Simon and Schuster, 1989.

Asselin, Pierre. *A Bitter Peace: Washington, Hanoi, and the Making of the Paris Agreement.* Chapel Hill: University of North Carolina Press, 2002.

Berman, Larry. *No Peace, No Honor: Nixon, Kissinger, and Betrayal in Vietnam.* New York: Free Press, 2001.

Cannon, James. *Time and Chance: Gerald Ford's Appointment with History.* New York: Harper Collins, 1994.

Erlichman, John. *Witness to Power: The Nixon Years.* New York: Simon and Schuster, 1982.

Firestone, Bernard J., and Alexej Ugrinsky. *Gerald R. Ford and the Politics of Post-Watergate America.* Westport, Conn.: Greenwood Press, 1993.

Ford, Gerald R. *A Time to Heal: The Autobiography of Gerald R. Ford.* New York: Harper and Row, 1979.

Greene, John Robert. *The Presidency of Gerald Ford.* Lawrence: University Press of Kansas, 1995.

* Haldeman, H. R. *The Haldeman Diaries: Inside the Nixon White House.* New York: Putnam, 1994.

Herring, George C. *America's Longest War: The United States and Vietnam, 1950–1975.* New York: John Wiley and Sons, 1979.

Hoff, Joan. *Nixon Reconsidered.* New York: Basic Books, 1994.

* Kimball, Jeffrey. *The Vietnam War File: Uncovering the Secret History of Nixon-Era Strategy.* Lawrence: University Press of Kansas, 2003.

Kissinger, Henry. *White House Years.* Boston: Little, Brown, 1979.

Nixon, Richard. *RN: The Memoirs of Richard Nixon.* New York: Grosset & Dunlap, 1978.

Small, Melvin. *At the Water's Edge: American Politics and the Vietnam War.* New York: Ivan R. Dee, 2005.

* ———. *The Presidency of Richard Nixon.* Lawrence: University Press of Kansas, 2003.

Summers, Harry G. *On Strategy.* San Rafael, Calif.: Presidio Press, 1986.

Westmoreland, William C. *A Soldier Reports.* Garden City, N.Y.: Doubleday, 1976.

CHAPTER EIGHT: JIMMY CARTER

Brzezinski, Zbigniew. *Power and Principle: Memoirs of the National Security Advisor, 1977–1981.* New York: Farrar, Strauss, and Giroux, 1983.

Carter, Jimmy. *Keeping Faith: Memoirs of a President.* New York: Bantam, 1982.

Hargrove, Erwin C. *Jimmy Carter as President: Leadership and the Politics of the Public Good.* Baton Rouge: Louisiana State University Press, 1988.

Jordan, Hamilton. *Crisis: The Last Year of the Carter Presidency.* New York: Putnam, 1982.

Kaufman, Burton I. *The Presidency of James Earl Carter Jr.* Lawrence: University Press of Kansas, 1993.

Moens, Alexander. *Foreign Policy under Carter: Testing Multiple Advocacy Decision Making.* Boulder, Colo.: Westview Press, 1990.

Morris, Kenneth. *Jimmy Carter, American Moralist.* Athens: University of Georgia Press, 1996.

Rosenbaum, Herbert D., and Alexej Ugrinsky, eds. *Jimmy Carter: Foreign Policy and Post-Presidential Years.* Westport, Conn.: Greenwood Press, 1994.

* Smith, Gaddis. *Morality, Reason, and Power: American Diplomacy in the Carter Years.* New York: Hill and Wang, 1986.

Strong, Robert A. *Working in the World: Jimmy Carter and the Making of American Foreign Policy.* Baton Rouge: Louisiana State University Press, 2000.

Vance, Cyrus. *Hard Choices: Critical Years in American Foreign Policy.* New York: Simon and Schuster, 1983.

CHAPTER NINE: RONALD REAGAN

Anderson, Martin. *Revolution.* New York: Harcourt Brace Jovanovich, 1988.

Berman, Larry, ed. *Looking Back on the Reagan Presidency.* Baltimore, Md.: Johns Hopkins University Press, 1990.

Brownlee, W. Elliot, and Hugh Davis Graham, eds. *The Reagan Presidency: Pragmatic Conservatism and Its Legacies.* Lawrence: University Press of Kansas, 2003.

Cannon, Lou. *President Reagan: The Role of a Lifetime.* New York: Simon and Schuster, 1991.

* ———. *Reagan.* New York: Putnam's, 1982.

Coll, Steve. *Ghost Wars: The Secret History of CIA, Afghanistan, and Bin Laden, from the Soviet Invasion to September 11, 2001.* New York: Penguin, 2004.

Draper, Theodore. *A Very Thin Line: The Iran-Contra Affair.* New York: Hill and Wang, 1991.

Erikson, Paul D. *Reagan Speaks: The Making of an American Myth.* New York: New York University Press, 1985.

* Evangelista, Matthew. *Unarmed Forces: The Transnational Movement to End the Cold War.* Ithaca, N.Y.: Cornell University Press, 1999.

* Fitzgerald, Frances. *Way Out There in the Blue: Reagan, Star Wars, and the End of the Cold War.* New York: Simon and Schuster, 2000.

Morris, Edmund. *Dutch: A Memoir.* New York: Random House, 1999.

Reagan, Ronald. *An American Life.* New York: Simon and Schuster, 1990.

* ———. *Reagan, in His Own Hand.* Edited by Kiron K. Skinner, Annelise Anderson, and Martin Anderson. New York: Free Press, 2001.

Regan, Donald T. *For the Record: From Wall Street to Washington.* San Diego, Calif.: Harcourt Brace Jovanovich, 1988.

Scott, James M. *Deciding to Intervene: The Reagan Doctrine and American Foreign Policy.* Durham, N.C.: Duke University Press, 1996.

Shultz, George P. *Turmoil and Triumph: My Years as Secretary of State.* New York: Scribner's, 1993.

Stockman, David. *The Triumph of Politics: How the Reagan Revolution Failed.* New York: Harper and Row, 1986.

Wirls, Daniel. *Buildup: The Politics of Defense in the Reagan Era.* Ithaca, N.Y.: Cornell University Press, 1992.

CHAPTER TEN: GEORGE BUSH

Baker, James A., III. *The Politics of Diplomacy: Revolution, War, and Peace, 1989–1993.* New York: Putnam's, 1995.

Blumenthal, Sidney. *Pledging Allegiance: The Last Campaign of the Cold War.* New York: Harper Collins, 1990.

Bush, George, and Brent Scowcroft. *A World Transformed.* New York: Knopf, 1988.

Campbell, Colin, and Bert A. Rockman, eds. *The Bush Presidency, First Appraisals.* Chatham, N.J.: Chatham House Publishers, 1991.

de Nevers, Renée. *Comrades No More: The Seeds of Political Change in Eastern Europe.* Cambridge: MIT Press, 2003.

Greene, John Robert. *The Presidency of George Bush.* Lawrence: University Press of Kansas, 2000.

Matlock, Jack F., Jr. *Autopsy of an Empire: The American Ambassador's Account of the Collapse of the Soviet Union*. New York: Random House, 1995.

* Oberdorfer, Don. *From the Cold War to a New Era*. Baltimore, Md.: Johns Hopkins University Press, 1998.

Parmet, Herbert S. *George Bush: The Life of a Lone Star Yankee*. New York: Scribner and Sons, 1997.

* Pons, Silvio. *Reinterpreting the End of the Cold War*. London: Frank Cass, 2004.

Wohlforth, William C., ed. *Witnesses to the End of the Cold War*. Baltimore, Md.: Johns Hopkins University Press, 1996.

CHAPTER ELEVEN: AFTERMATH

* Bacevich, Andrew. *American Empire*. Cambridge, Mass.: Harvard University Press, 2002.

Betts, Richard K., ed. *Conflict after the Cold War: Argument on Causes of War and Peace*. New York: Macmillan, 1994.

Ferguson, Niall. *Colossus: The Rise and Fall of the American Empire*. New York: Penguin, 2005.

Fukuyama, Francis. *The End of History and the Last Man*. New York: Free Press, 1992.

Kagan, Donald, and Frederick W. Kagan. *While America Sleeps: Self-Delusion, Military Weakness, and the Threat to Peace Today*. New York: St. Martin's, 2000.

Langston, Thomas. *Uneasy Balance: Civil-Military Relations in Peacetime America since 1783*. Baltimore, Md.: Johns Hopkins University Press, 2003.

Lebow, Richard Ned, and Janice Gross Stein. *We All Lost the Cold War*. Princeton: Princeton University Press, 1994.

Mueller, John. *Retreat from Doomsday: The Obsolescence of Major War*. New York: Basic Books, 1989.

Schwartz, Stephen I. *Atomic Audit: The Costs and Consequences of U.S. Nuclear Weapons since 1940*. Washington, D.C.: Brookings Institution Press, 1998.

Appendix A
Notable Figures of the Cold War

Abrams, Creighton, Jr.
General Abrams (September 15, 1914–September 4, 1974), a distinguished World War II veteran, commanded troops in postwar Europe, Korea, and the United States before being appointed army vice chief of staff (1964–1967). Abrams served as deputy commander and then commander of the U.S. Military Assistance Command in Vietnam (1968–1972). During a time of domestic resistance to the war, Abrams administered President Nixon's Vietnamization program by gradually withdrawing American troops and training South Vietnamese officers. Abrams returned to the United States to serve as army chief of staff (1972–1974) and executed a significant reorganization of the U.S. Army. He died seven months before the fall of Saigon.

Acheson, Dean
Acheson (April 11, 1893–October 12, 1971) was a primary author of postwar American foreign policy as undersecretary (1945–1949) and secretary of state (1949–1953). Acheson espoused containment through the appropriation of funds to the non-Communist bloc to rebuild and rearm America's allies; accordingly, he assisted in the formulation and implementation of the Marshall Plan, the Truman Doctrine, and the North Atlantic Treaty Organization (NATO) military alliance. Acheson also supported increased defense spending for nuclear technology, conventional forces, and overseas operations. He played an instrumental role in supporting President Truman's decision to respond with force to North Korea's invasion of South Korea, by securing UN Security Council approval for military action. Acheson informally advised Presidents Kennedy and Johnson on foreign policy issues. Acheson, a staunch cold warrior, made a deep impression on President Johnson when he expressed skepticism about the efficacy of America's involvement in Vietnam.

Andropov, Yuri
Andropov (June 15, 1914–February 9, 1984) was chairman of the KGB, the Soviet state security agency (1967–1982), general secretary of the Communist Party of the Soviet Union (CPSU) (1982–1984), and president of the USSR (1983–1984). Andropov organized German guerrillas during World War II and served as ambassador to Hungary (1953–1957) during its 1956 revolution. After serving as secretary to the CPSU central committee (1962–1967), Andropov was later admitted as a full member of the party's elite Politburo (1973). Andropov gained considerable power during his reign as KGB chief. Because of his age and severe health problems during his tenure as general secretary and president, Andropov's attempts to reform the Soviet economy and negotiate arms control with the United States were largely ineffective.

Baker, James, III
After coordinating the 1988 campaign of President Bush, Baker (b. April 28, 1930) became secretary of state in 1989 and served until returning to the White House to run the president's reelection campaign from the position of chief of staff in late 1992. Baker was President Reagan's chief of staff (1981–1985) and secretary of the Treasury (1985–1988). A consummate Republican insider known for avoiding ideological disputes, Baker won respect during his long service to both presidents. As secretary of state, he pursued the Bush administration's policy to encourage Eastern Europe defection from the Soviet camp. He was instrumental in guiding the diplomatic process by which East and West Germany were reunited after the fall of the Berlin Wall.

Ball, George
Ball (December 21, 1909–May 26, 1994), an attorney, diplomat, and financier, served as undersecretary of state for the Kennedy and Johnson administrations (1961–1966). Ball advised several wartime diplomatic and military organizations and supervised economic affairs in Kennedy's State Department, where he promoted European economic integration and development. An advocate of caution in the use of force, Ball

lobbied for the successful naval quarantine of Cuba during the missile crisis, as an alternative to an outright invasion, and questioned the Americanization of the war in Vietnam. After resigning in 1966, he returned to government briefly as a UN ambassador (1968) and, later, foreign policy adviser to President Carter.

Baruch, Bernard

Baruch (August 19, 1870–June 20, 1965), a prosperous investor and generous donor to the Democratic Party, used his vantage point as a high-level presidential appointee to regulate the American economy for war production during the world wars. In 1946 President Truman appointed Baruch chief U.S. representative to the UN Atomic Energy Commission. Baruch helped author and then presented to the United Nations the "Baruch Plan" to transfer jurisdiction over atomic weapons to that body.

Bradley, Omar

General Bradley (February 12, 1893–April 8, 1981), a revered World War II commander, was President Truman's head of the Veterans Administration (1945–1948) and army chief of staff (1948–1949) before being appointed the first chairman of the Joint Chiefs of Staff (1949–1953). As a member of the Joint Chiefs, Bradley worked to limit defense spending and invest in development of the hydrogen bomb. An advocate of containment, Bradley supported restricting the Korean War to the Korean peninsula and backed Truman's decision to dismiss General Douglas MacArthur, who urged the president to expand the conflict. After his term as JCS chairman, Bradley retired from active military duties.

Brezhnev, Leonid

Brezhnev (December 19, 1906–November 10, 1982) succeeded Nikita Khrushchev as General Secretary of the Soviet Communist Party (1964–1982). A Red Army political commissar during World War II, Brezhnev rose in the party hierarchy and was elected to the Central Committee (1952) and Presidium (1957), serving as chairman of the Presidium (1960–1964) and secretary of the Central Committee (1963–1964), before joining the coalition that ousted Khrushchev from power.

As general secretary, Brezhnev maintained a strong, centralized, repressive government. He expanded the defense industry at the expense of other economic sectors, which resulted in an economic decline and shortages of consumer goods. Following his predecessors, he supported Communist regimes and revolutionaries, particularly in the Middle East and Africa, and he proclaimed the Brezhnev doctrine, a pledge to intervene with force to defend communism in client states such as Czechoslovakia (1968). In 1975 Brezhnev signed the Helsinki Final Act, by which he gained Western recognition of the Soviet absorption of Eastern Europe in exchange for a Soviet promise to respect national self-determination and human rights. During the 1970s Brezhnev met with Presidents Nixon (1972), Ford (1974), and Carter (1979); cooperated with the United States on trade and disarmament; and signed the first and second Strategic Arms Limitation Talks treaties (SALT I and II).

Brown, Harold

Brown (b. September 19, 1927), a nuclear physicist, served as secretary of defense (1977–1981) in the Carter administration. After holding civilian Defense Department positions in the Kennedy and Johnson administrations as a research director and secretary of the Air Force (1965–1969), Brown taught at the California Institute of Technology until returning to government service in 1977. As secretary of defense, Brown developed new weapons programs and backed the revamping of American nuclear strategy. As a SALT II negotiator, Brown successfully opposed deep cuts in American cruise missiles, but he failed to secure congressional approval of the treaty. An advocate of improved American-Chinese relations, the defense secretary visited China in 1980.

Brzezinski, Zbigniew

Brzezinski (b. March 28, 1928), a Polish-American political scientist, served as President Carter's national security adviser (1977–1981). A prolific academic with strong anti-Communist views, Brzezinski directed the Trilateral Commission (1973–1976), an organization promoting American, Japanese, and European cooperation. As national security advisor, Brzezinski sought to enhance the United States' strategic position in relation to the Soviet Union by improving relations with China and selectively enhancing U.S. military forces. Brzezinski was instrumental in negotiating the SALT II and the Israel–Egypt Peace (Camp David) Accords in 1979. During the Iranian hostage crisis, Brzezinski supported the abortive helicopter mission to rescue the American captives.

Bundy, McGeorge

As national security adviser, Bundy (March 30, 1919–September 16, 1996) played a major role in the coordination of foreign policy during the Kennedy and Johnson administrations (1961–1966). An accomplished academic (he became dean of Harvard College at thirty-four years of age), World War II veteran, and foreign policy expert, Bundy mediated the national security policies of rival agencies and actors, most notably as a manager of EXCOMM (executive committee) during the Cuban Missile Crisis in the Kennedy presidency. In the early 1960s he encouraged escalating U.S. military intervention in Vietnam but became disillusioned with the war and eventually advocated the withdrawal of American troops.

Byrnes, James F.

During World War II, President Roosevelt chose Byrnes (May 2, 1882* –April 9, 1972) as his informal second-in-command on the home front. A Democratic U.S. representative (1911–1925) and senator (1931–1941) from South Carolina, and, briefly, a Supreme Court justice (1941–1942), Byrnes directed Roosevelt's Office of Economic Stabilization and Office of War Mobilization. As Truman's secretary of state in 1945, Byrnes advocated the deployment of atomic weapons in Japan, was instrumental in the establishment of the UN Atomic Energy Commission, and took the lead in negotiating several postwar international agreements. Criticized for wanting to appease Josef Stalin in postwar negotiations, Byrnes eventually adopted a more confrontational approach toward the Soviet Union, most notably over the division of Germany. Byrnes's personal relationship with Truman was poor, and he resigned in January 1947. Remaining active in politics, he served as governor of South Carolina (1951–1955).

(*As a young man, Byrnes falsified his age to procure a competitive position as a court stenographer; accordingly, the year of his birth is often mistakenly cited as 1879. See David Robertson, *Sly and Able: A Political Biography of James F. Byrnes* [New York: W.W. Norton, 1994] 23–24.)

Casey, William

After directing Reagan's 1980 presidential campaign, Casey (March 13, 1913–May 6, 1987) was appointed director of the Central Intelligence Agency (CIA) in 1981. During World War II, Casey directed American reconnaissance activities in Europe for the Office of Strategic Services (OSS). In 1971 President Nixon appointed Casey chair of the Securities and Exchange Commission (SEC). As CIA director, Casey combated communism with zeal unmatched since the early Cold War. His support for Islamic rebels fighting the Soviets in Afghanistan helped to roll back Soviet expansion in Asia. Under Casey's direction, the CIA also backed the anti-Communist Contra rebels fighting the Sandinista government of Nicaragua. Casey was scheduled to testify before Congress regarding his alleged involvement in the Iran–Contra Affair, which involved giving more support to the Contras than the law allowed, when he was diagnosed with a malignant brain tumor requiring his immediate hospitalization.

Castro (Ruz), Fidel

Castro (Ruz) (b. August 13, 1926), prime minister (1959–1967) and president (1967–) of Cuba, led the 26th of July Movement that toppled Fulgencio Batista's U.S.-backed regime in 1959. Following Castro's revolution, Cuba's unique position as a Marxist outpost in the Western hemisphere made it a leading Cold War battleground. As U.S.-Cuban relations deteriorated, Castro aligned with the Soviet Union, provoking the bungled Bay of Pigs invasion and the 1962 missile crisis. A leader of several international Marxist organizations, particularly among developing nations, Castro supported Communist insurgencies with weapons and troops in Latin America and Africa. While the Soviet Union's collapse severely strained Cuba economically and isolated Cuba politically, Castro's power remained uncontested until July 2006 when, citing failing health, Castro temporarily ceded presidential power to his brother.

Chernenko, Konstantin

Chernenko (September 24, 1911–March 10, 1985) was general secretary of the Soviet Union from February 1984 until his death in March 1985. Having joined the Communist Party in 1931, he met and became close friends with Leonid Brezhnev while serving in the Moldovan Soviet Republic. As Brezhnev advanced, so did Chernenko, who became a full member of the Central Committee in 1971 and Politburo in 1978. After Brezhnev's death in 1982, Yuri Andropov became general secretary following a short power struggle with Chernenko. Andropov died shortly after taking office, leaving Chernenko to become general secretary. During his brief tenure, the Soviets boycotted the 1984 Olympics in Los Angeles and further agitated relations with the United States by negotiating a trade pact with China.

Church, Frank

Church (July 25, 1924–April 7, 1984), a Democratic U.S. senator from Idaho (1957–1981), led the movement to contain executive power during the 1970s and influenced foreign policy as chairman of the Senate Foreign Relations Committee (1979–1981). After studying law and fighting in World War II, Church was elected to the Senate at the age of thirty-two. One of the earliest critics of the Vietnam War, Church cosponsored the Cooper-Church and Case-Church Amendments, which curtailed U.S. operations in Southeast Asia. As chairman of the "Church Committee" (1975–1976), the senator publicly scrutinized abuses in the Federal Bureau of Investigation (FBI) and CIA, which resulted in greater oversight of intelligence activities.

Clay, Lucius

General Clay (April 23, 1897–April 16, 1978) played a crucial role in the postwar reconstruction of West Germany. A U.S. Army logistician and engineer, Clay was named commander in chief of the American forces in Europe and military governor of occupied Germany in 1947. Following the Soviet blockade of West Berlin in 1948, Clay organized a monumental airlift to supply the city with resources. As military governor, Clay laid the foundations for the West German government and economy. In 1949 Clay retired from military service to pursue a successful career in business, though he maintained close ties to many politicians, including President Eisenhower. In 1961 President Kennedy appointed Clay special representative to Berlin to symbolize U.S. commitment to the region.

Clifford, Clark

Clifford (December 25, 1906–October 11, 1998) was an influential consultant for several Democratic administrations during the Cold War. As an adviser to President Truman, Clifford drafted the influential Clifford-Elsey report, which demonstrated to Truman that almost all members of his administration—who were consulted for the study—supported a tougher stance toward the Soviet Union. Clifford played an important part in the formulation of the Truman Doctrine, Marshall Plan, and the National Security Act of 1947 and its amendments of 1949. From 1950, Clifford pursued a career in corporate law, although he continued to advise Democratic administrations. After the resignation of Robert McNamara, Clifford joined President Johnson's cabinet as secretary of defense in 1968.

Colby, William

Colby (January 4, 1920–April 27, 1996), director of the CIA (1973–1975), was responsible for airing much of the agency's dirty laundry during the congressional investigations of the 1970s. A member of the Office of Strategic Services (OSS) during World War II, Colby joined the CIA after the war and directed the CIA's Far East operations, particularly in Vietnam, during the 1960s. He returned to the United States in 1971 to serve as executive director and director of the CIA. President Ford dismissed Colby after he released damaging information on CIA activities that was published in the *New York Times*.

Colson, Charles "Chuck"

Colson (b. October 16, 1931), an attorney and President Nixon's special counsel (1969–1973), was one of the Nixon's most loyal aides. As a member of the clandestine "Plumbers" outfit, Colson was implicated in the cover-up of the Plumbers' burglary of Nixon critic Daniel Ellsberg's psychiatrist's office. In 1973 Colson resigned under a cloud of suspicion and returned to the private sector. He pled guilty to obstruction of justice in 1974 and served seven months in prison.

Crowe, William, Jr.

Admiral Crowe (b. January 2, 1925) was chairman of the Joint Chiefs of Staff (CJCS) in the Reagan administration from 1985 until he retired from the U.S. Navy in 1989. He served as an assistant to the naval aide for President Eisenhower from 1954 to 1955. He was appointed commander of NATO's southern flank in 1980 and commander in chief of the United States Pacific Command in 1983. As CJCS, Crowe supported the Reagan military buildup as well as the Goldwater-Nichols Act, a major reform in military command organization, designed to curb interservice rivalry.

Dobrynin, Anatoly

The diplomatic career of Dobrynin (b. November 16, 1919), Soviet ambassador to the United States (1962–1986), spanned the entire length of the Cold War. After entering the Soviet foreign ministry in 1946, Dobrynin served as assistant deputy minister of foreign affairs (1949–1952, 1955–1957), counsel to the Washington embassy (1952–1955), undersecretary of the United Nations (1957–1960), and head of the foreign ministry's American affairs division (1960–1961). In October 1962, just months after being appointed American ambassador, Dobrynin played a pivotal role in the Cuban Missile Crisis through his secret negotiations with Attorney General Robert Kennedy. In later years, the ambassador pursued détente with the United States and collaborated on disarmament initiatives. Dobrynin returned to the Soviet Union in 1986 to lead the Communist Party Central Committee's international relations department.

Dulles, Allen

Dulles (April 7, 1893–January 29, 1969), diplomat and World War II intelligence officer, helped the administration of President Truman draft the National Security Act of 1947, which created the Central Intelligence Agency (CIA). From 1950 to 1953, he served in the new agency as deputy director and from 1953 to 1961 as director. With the support of his brother, Eisenhower's secretary of state John Foster Dulles, Dulles pioneered the use of covert operations to accomplish U.S. objectives in the third world, successfully staging coups in Iran in 1953 and Guatemala in 1954. Dulles chafed at congressional oversight and contributed to a climate of mutual distrust between Congress and the CIA. He was forced into retirement by President Kennedy for his part in the 1961 Bay of Pigs fiasco.

Dulles, John Foster

Dulles's (February 25, 1888–May 24, 1959) distinguished diplomatic career spanned more than five decades. Following World War I Dulles unsuccessfully opposed harsh German reparations at Versailles, and after World War II he negotiated the 1951 Peace Treaty with Japan. He represented the United States in the United Nations during Truman's administration before being appointed secretary of state by President Eisenhower in 1953.

During his tenure in the Eisenhower administration, Dulles established himself as a fervent anti-Communist and, although he held sophisticated views on foreign policy, he is best remembered for the incendiary, moralistic rhetoric in which he publicized his views. In 1956 Dulles withdrew financing for the Aswan Dam following Egyptian president Gamal Abdel Nasser's purchase of Soviet bloc weapons, which instigated the Suez Crisis. A strong supporter of West Germany, Dulles traveled to Germany in January 1959, despite suffering from terminal cancer, to pledge U.S. support personally to Chancellor Konrad Adenauer.

Ehrlichman, John

Ehrlichman (March 20, 1925–February 14, 1999), counsel, then domestic affairs adviser, to President Nixon, was a powerful member of the inner circle within the highly centralized Nixon White House. Beginning in 1960, Ehrlichman, along with H. R. Haldeman, his longtime friend and Nixon supporter, advised and managed Nixon's political campaigns. In the Nixon administration, Ehrlichman directed the "Plumbers" unit, established to plug leaks and discredit Nixon's many "enemies," and concealed the White House's role in the Watergate break-in. After President Nixon demanded Ehrlichman's resignation in April 1973, Ehrlichman was convicted for his role in the Watergate conspiracy and served eighteen months in federal prison.

Ellsberg, Daniel

A defense analyst specializing in Vietnam policy during the Kennedy, Johnson, and Nixon administrations, Ellsberg (b. April 7, 1931) provoked a Nixon administration crisis by leaking the classified Pentagon Papers, a lengthy analytical history of the American war in Vietnam. Ellsberg, disenchanted by the war following a two-year stint in Vietnam, smuggled the study out of the Pentagon and offered it to the press. The *New York Times* first published excerpts of the papers in June 1971, instigating the landmark Supreme Court case *New York Times Co. v. the United States*. In 1973 the government's case against Ellsberg for theft of government property and other alleged crimes was dismissed because of misconduct on the part of the White House.

Forrestal, James

In 1947, after working with Congress and President Truman to unify and restructure the American military, Navy secretary Forrestal (February 15, 1892–May 22, 1949) became the first U.S. secretary of defense. Forrestal, a vocal anti-Communist and advocate of containment, was instrumental in advancing the case for strengthening and expanding the armed forces during the early Cold War. Forrestal defended the need to mobilize conventional forces as well as train personnel in guerrilla warfare, intelligence, and covert operations. President Truman's differences of opinion with Forrestal led the president to replace him with Louis Johnson in 1949.

Fulbright, J. William

Fulbright (April 9, 1905–February 9, 1995), a Democratic U.S. representative (1942–1944) and U.S. senator (1944–1974) from Arkansas, chaired the Senate Foreign Relations Committee from 1959–1974. As a freshman member of Congress, Fulbright passed the resolution that laid the foundation for the United Nations, an institution he supported throughout his career. A committed anti-Communist, Fulbright supported such initiatives as the Truman Doctrine, the Marshall Plan, the NATO military alliance, and intervention in Korea. Although he was initially supportive of President Johnson's policies in Vietnam, Fulbright later questioned the war's value and necessity and held a series of hearings in the mid- and late 1960s that fueled domestic opposition to the war.

Gorbachev, Mikhail
Following the death of Konstantin Chernenko in 1985, Gorbachev (b. March 2, 1931) became general secretary of the Soviet Union. Gorbachev joined the Communist Party in 1952 and became a full member of the Central Committee in 1971. In 1980 he became the youngest full member of the Politburo and rose under the tutelage of Yuri Andropov. He initiated the reforms of glasnost (openness) and perestroika (reconstruction) in hopes of helping the ailing Soviet economy and weakening the Communist bureaucracy's debilitating hold on Soviet institutions. His policies led instead to economic shortages, nationalist uprisings, and the eventual collapse of the Soviet Union. In 1991, following a failed coup attempt in August and the declaration of independence by numerous Soviet republics, Gorbachev resigned as the general secretary and disbanded the Central Committee. Despite these failures, he earned celebrity status in the West for his embrace of new ideas and the gratitude of the world for refusing to resort to military means to rescue the Soviet Union.

Gromyko, Andrei
Gromyko's (July 18, 1909–July 2, 1989) diplomatic career spanned nearly five decades. In 1939 Gromyko, an economist, entered the Soviet foreign ministry and was appointed ambassador to the United States four years later. Gromyko attended many pivotal wartime negotiations, including conferences in Tehran (1943), San Francisco (1945), Yalta (1945), and Potsdam (1945). After representing the Soviet Union at the United Nations (1946–1948), he worked his way up the ranks at the foreign ministry and became foreign minister in 1957, a post he held until 1985. As foreign minister, he oversaw the Soviet response to countless Cold War crises and negotiated with U.S. presidents and secretaries of state during periods of tension as well as détente. Within the Soviet government, he advocated intervention in Czechoslovakia (1968), Afghanistan (1979), and Poland (1981). In 1985 Gromyko, a member of the Central Committee of the Communist Party since 1973, was given the ceremonial role of head of state, a position in which he served until being forced into retirement by General Secretary Mikhail Gorbachev because of his hard-line views.

Guevara, Ernesto "Che"
Guevara (June 14, 1928–October 8, 1967), an Argentinean-born doctor, writer, and icon among revolutionaries, wandered Latin America as a young adult, allying himself with a variety of Marxist groups. In 1956 he joined Fidel Castro's 26th of July Movement. After several years of guerilla warfare, Guevara rose to power along with Castro in 1959. He became Castro's chief economic adviser. In 1965 he left Cuba in an effort to export its revolution to other countries in Latin America and Africa. He was captured and killed by U.S.-trained Bolivian special forces in 1967.

Haig, Alexander, Jr.
Haig (b. December 2, 1924), a former four-star U.S. Army general, was President Reagan's secretary of state (1981–1982). During the Nixon administration, he served as Henry Kissinger's military aide (1969), deputy assistant to the president for national security affairs (1970–1972), and, briefly, army vice chief of staff (1972) before becoming chief of staff (1973–1974). As chief of staff he helped Nixon confront the reality of the choice he faced—resignation or impeachment—and helped manage a smooth transition to the Ford administration. As Supreme Allied Commander in Europe (1974–1979), Haig pursued strong ties between NATO allies before resigning in protest against President Carter's foreign policies. Haig's impatience and assertiveness as Reagan's secretary of state led to power struggles with other cabinet officials and the White House. He resigned in 1982.

Haldeman, H. R.
Haldeman (October 27, 1926–November 12, 1993), was President Nixon's chief of staff (1969–1973). In 1956 Haldeman, then an advertising executive, began campaigning for Nixon. He managed and advised several Nixon campaigns throughout the 1960s and in 1968 was rewarded by the president-elect with a White House position. As chief of staff and a member of Nixon's inner circle, Haldeman was implicated in the Watergate cover-up, and the president pressured him to resign in 1973. In 1975 a federal jury convicted

Haldeman of conspiracy, obstruction of justice, and perjury, for which he served eighteen months in federal prison.

Harriman, Averell

Harriman (November 15, 1891–July 26, 1986), a wealthy industrialist, was an adviser to Democratic administrations from the 1940s through the 1960s. After being appointed President Roosevelt's special representative to the United Kingdom, Harriman went on to serve as U.S. ambassador to the Soviet Union from 1943–1946 and then, briefly, to the United Kingdom. From 1946–1948, as Truman's secretary of commerce, Harriman lobbied Congress on behalf of the Marshall Plan, a program he helped implement as a member of the Economic Cooperation Administration from 1948–1950 and director of the Mutual Security Administration from 1951–1953. Harriman served as governor of New York from 1955–1959. He helped negotiate the 1963 Limited Nuclear Test Ban Treaty for President Kennedy and the Vietnam Paris Peace Talks under President Johnson.

Ho Chi Minh

Ho (May 19, 1890–September 3, 1969), prime minister (1946–1955) and president (1955–1969) of North Vietnam, spearheaded the movements for Vietnamese independence and unification under Communist rule. While living abroad for three decades, Ho was a founding member of the French Communist Party, studied party ideology and revolutionary tactics in the Soviet Union, and helped to organize Communist activities throughout Asia. Upon returning to Vietnam, he led the Vietminh's successful struggles against the Japanese during World War II and the U.S.-backed French colonialists during the First Indochina War (1946–1954). In 1945 he established the Democratic Republic of Vietnam (DRV) and was elected its president in 1946.

Though Ho professed to have nothing but the greatest admiration for American revolutionary history, he pursued a Maoist campaign in the North Vietnamese countryside in the 1950s that resulted in the death or imprisonment of thousands of Vietnamese guilty only of being in the wrong class. In the 1960s his government mobilized and funded a Communist insurgency in the South and then accepted the challenge of open warfare against the United States, which intervened to protect South Vietnam.

Honecker, Erich

Honecker (August 25, 1912–May 29, 1994) was the chief executive of the German Democratic Republic (GDR, or Communist East Germany) from 1971 to 1989. Honecker joined the Communist Party of Germany (KPD) in 1929. After a brief academic stint in Russia, Honecker returned to Germany in 1931, was arrested by the Nazis in 1935 for Communist activity, and spent the remainder of their reign in captivity. After World War II, Honecker helped form the Socialist Unity Party of Germany (SED) and led them to victory in the 1946 elections. Honecker became a full member of the Central Committee in 1958 and coordinated the construction of the Berlin Wall in 1961. In 1971 Honecker garnered Soviet support and became leader of Germany and the SED. Honecker propped up the GDR through economic cooperation and loans from the Federal Republic of Germany (FRG, or West Germany). Honecker took a dim view of Soviet General Secretary Mikhail Gorbachev's reforms, but massive demonstrations and an exodus of East Germans fleeing into the FRG through the recently opened Hungarian border led to Honecker's forced resignation in 1989.

Hoover, J. Edgar

Hoover (January 1, 1895–May 2, 1972) substantially expanded and modernized the Federal Bureau of Investigation (FBI) during his five-decade reign as its assistant director (1921–1924) and director (1924–1972). Under Hoover's leadership, the FBI pursued foreign radicals, high-profile gangsters, Nazis, spies, Communists, subversives, and—eventually—ordinary citizens who ran afoul of Hoover's bosses, the presidents of the United States. After his death, Hoover's controversial methods of hounding suspected Communists and dissidents, including peaceful civil rights leaders such as Martin Luther King Jr., were exposed in an investigation by Sen. Frank Church.

Humphrey, George

Humphrey (March 8, 1890–January 20, 1970), a prominent industrialist, lawyer, and governmental consultant, was President Eisenhower's secretary of the Treasury from 1953–1957. A close friend of the president and one of his most trusted advisers, Humphrey shared his perspective that balancing the budget, reducing the national debt, and combating inflation were top priorities, even if doing those things meant spending less for defense than the military establishment thought wise. As the administration's chief economic adviser, Humphrey implemented policies that cut expenditures held over from the Truman administration and generated a budget surplus of $1.6 billion.

Hussein, Saddam

Hussein (b. April 28, 1937) led Iraq as president and dictator from 1979 until 2003. He joined the pan-Arab Baath Party in 1957, and after attempting to assassinate Prime Minister Abdul Karim Qassim, he was forced to live in exile in Egypt. Hussein returned to Iraq in 1963 following a U.S.-supported Baath coup, but he was jailed as the government fell apart. Hussein helped to lead a 1968 coup that restored Baath power and became vice president. Fearing loss of power in a potential treaty with Syria, Hussein forced President Ahmed Hassan al-Bakr to resign in 1979 and rose to the presidency. He consolidated power through intimidation and execution of rivals and in the Iraq-Iran War (1980–1988), he used mustard gas in violation of international norms of war. To pay off war debts, Hussein invaded and attempted to take over Kuwait in 1990 but was driven out in 1991 by the United States and United Kingdom, with the unanimous support of the UN Security Council. President Bush heralded the war as a sign of the "New World Order" that he hoped would replace the Cold War. After the U.S.-led invasion of Iraq in 2003, Hussein went into hiding and was captured in December 2003.

Jackson, Henry "Scoop"

Jackson (May 31, 1912–September 1, 1983) was a Democratic U.S. representative (1941–1953) and senator (1953–1983) from Washington State with hawkish foreign policy views. Jackson advocated interventionism abroad, particularly in Vietnam and Israel, and resisted détente with the Soviet Union. Domestically, Jackson's views were much more liberal, as he championed the labor and civil rights movements and supported increased funding for environmental and social welfare initiatives. Jackson successfully led an effort in Congress to link U.S. trade with the Soviet Union to Soviet concessions on the treatment of dissidents and "refuseniks," Soviet Jews who were refused emigration to Israel. An unsuccessful candidate for his party's presidential nomination in 1972 and 1976, his greatest legacy was as a mentor to a number of hawkish foreign policy experts who left the Democratic Party in the late 1970s and became "neoconservative" supporters of Republican presidents.

Johnson, Louis

Johnson (January 10, 1891–April 24, 1966), a World War I veteran and former assistant secretary of war (1937–1940), became President Truman's secretary of defense in 1949, but his brief tenure was largely unsuccessful. First, Johnson's decision shortly after taking office to halt construction of the naval aircraft carrier U.S.S. *United States* exacerbated interservice rivalries and provoked the "revolt of the admirals," in which U.S. Navy commanders publicly criticized the secretary's policies. The outbreak of the Korean War also exposed Johnson to criticism for his insistence on trimming defense budgets. Truman called for Johnson's resignation and appointed Gen. George Marshall as his replacement.

Jones, David

General Jones (b. July 9, 1921), air force chief of staff (1974–1978) and chairman of the Joint Chiefs of Staff (CJCS; 1978–1982), played a major role in boosting the air force's preparedness during the 1970s and early 1980s. A bomber during the Korean War, Jones worked his way up the air force command, serving as a naval commander in Vietnam (1969–1971) and as vice commander in chief and commander in chief of the American Air Force in Europe (1971–1974). As air force chief of staff, Jones was criticized for not securing the production of a B-1 bomber; however, he argued for defense spending increases and encouraged the development of the MX missile system. While serving as CJCS, Jones, anxious over increased Soviet militarization, expressed apprehension about SALT II, although he ultimately supported the treaty. He gave critical help to military reformers by expressing his support for the Goldwater-Nichols Act shortly before leaving office.

Kennan, George

Kennan (February 16, 1904–March 17, 2005), a Soviet expert in the State Department, gave intellectual substance to America's early Cold War policy. In 1946 Kennan, from his position in the U.S. embassy in Moscow, wrote the "Long Telegram" in which he expressed apprehension about Soviet ambitions and argued for a policy of military and nonmilitary "containment" of the Soviet Union. In 1947 Kennan authored the famous "X" article in *Foreign Affairs,* in which he popularized his argument for acknowledging the irreducible antagonism between Soviet and U.S. interests in the world. After serving as the first director of the Policy Planning Staff within the State Department (1947–1949), Kennan was appointed ambassador to the Soviet Union (1952) and Yugoslavia (1961–1963).

Kennedy, Robert

Kennedy (November 20, 1925–June 6, 1968) established himself as a congressional legal counsel before managing his brother's presidential campaign. In 1961 President Kennedy appointed him attorney general, a position from which the younger Kennedy pursued highly publicized investigations against organized crime and racial segregation. During the Cuban Missile Crisis, Kennedy played a pivotal role as the president's secret intermediary with the Soviet ambassador to the United States, Anatoly Dobrynin. After President Kennedy's assassination in 1963, Kennedy served briefly as attorney general for President Johnson, with whom he shared a mutual loathing. In 1964 he was elected U.S. senator from New York. Kennedy became an outspoken critic of the Johnson administration and was assassinated in Los Angeles in 1968 while campaigning for the presidency.

Khrushchev, Nikita

Khrushchev (April 17, 1893–September 11, 1971) headed the Soviet Communist Party (1953–1964) and served as premier of the Soviet Union (1958–1964). After studying Marxism and fighting in the Russian Civil War, Khrushchev entered Soviet politics. His loyalty to Josef Stalin allowed him to rise quickly in the party and become one of Stalin's top advisers. After Stalin's death in 1953, Khrushchev became first secretary of the Communist Party. Khrushchev solidified his command in 1957 following power struggles with the Presidium, and in March 1958 he assumed the position of premier.

As demonstrated in the famous 1959 "Kitchen Debate" with Vice President Nixon, Khrushchev stressed the importance of economic and technological growth. Like President Eisenhower, Khrushchev deemphasized the role of conventional arms in favor of nuclear technology. Through such technological successes as the launching of Sputnik and Soviet ICBMs in the late 1950s, he aroused fear of a "missile gap" in the United States. An advocate of "peaceful coexistence" with the West, the premier became the first Soviet leader to visit the United States in his September 1959 meeting with Eisenhower at Camp David, Maryland. Khrushchev also reduced Soviet troop levels in 1960 and signed the Nuclear Test Ban Treaty with President Kennedy in 1963. Nevertheless, the premier squared off with the United States during some of the tensest junctures of the Cold War, including the building of the Berlin Wall and the 1962 Cuban Missile Crisis. Soviet capitulation to the West during the missile crisis jeopardized his power at home.

On October 13, 1964, a group of high-ranking members of the Soviet Communist Party, led by Leonid Brezhnev and Anastas Mikoyan, removed Khrushchev from power while he was on vacation. After this bloodless coup, Brezhnev succeeded Khrushchev as first secretary and Mikoyan succeeded him as head of state.

Kirkpatrick, Jeane

Kirkpatrick (b. November 19, 1926) became the first woman to serve as U.S. ambassador to the United Nations (1981–1985). She was still a Democrat during her service for President Reagan but was a vocal critic of her party's shift away from confrontation of international rivals. Although she was a Marxist in her early career, she was an ardent anti-Communist who came to the attention of Reagan through her argument for unapologetic U.S. support for anti-Communist dictatorships. As UN ambassador, she was a strong critic of Communist regimes and defender of American interests as defined by the Reagan administration.

Kissinger, Henry

Kissinger (b. May 27, 1923), national security adviser (1969–1975) and secretary of state (1973–1977) during the Nixon and Ford administrations, was one of the most influential figures in postwar U.S. foreign policy. A Jewish refuge of Nazi Germany, Kissinger served in the U.S. Army during World War II and in occupied Germany after the war. After earning his PhD, Kissinger joined the faculty of Harvard University and later served as a foreign policy adviser to the Eisenhower, Kennedy, and Johnson administrations.

As national security adviser and secretary of state, Kissinger served as Nixon and Ford's chief foreign policymaker. Concerned with the decline of U.S. power, Kissinger conceptualized the United States' role in the international arena in terms of balance of power and *realpolitik* theory whereby a nation's actions and nonactions were calculated objectively in terms of power and national interest. Through this lens, Kissinger developed Vietnamization and the Nixon Doctrine, which limited U.S. military interventionism abroad. Meanwhile, he supported the pursuit of U.S. interests by orchestrating controversial covert operations in the third world and supporting brutal yet U.S.-friendly dictatorships.

Kissinger's greatest victories include the warming of relations with China, the negotiation of trade and disarmament agreements with both China and the Soviet Union, and the formal recognition of Europe's postwar boundaries. Involved in Vietnam policy since the Johnson administration, Kissinger won a Nobel Peace Prize for negotiating the Paris Peace Accords in 1973, which he attempted to return when Saigon fell to the Communist North Vietnamese.

Kohl, Helmut

Kohl (b. April 3, 1930) served as chancellor of West Germany (1982–1990) and chancellor of Germany (1990–1998). Kohl became a controversial figure in West German politics during the Reagan presidency through his support of the deployment by NATO of intermediate-range nuclear missiles. In 1990 Kohl and his party, the Christian Democratic Union, won electoral support at home and diplomatic support abroad for rapid German reunification after East Germany broke free of the Soviet Union and began to hold free elections. Kohl worked closely with President Bush in pursuing a peaceful but decisive end to the Cold War in Germany.

Kosygin, Alexei

Kosygin (February 21, 1904–December 18, 1980) joined the Communist Party after fighting in the Russian Civil War. A technocrat, Kosygin survived Stalin's purges and rose in the party hierarchy, becoming a full member of the Politburo (1948–1953) and the Presidium (1960–1980). Kosygin served in several high-level positions in the economic ministry under Stalin and Khrushchev, and he succeeded Khrushchev as premier in 1964. Formally, he, along with Leonid Brezhnev and Anastas Mikoyan (and, later, Nikolay Pogorny), was but one member of a troika that wielded executive power. In reality, Brezhnev soon emerged as the ultimate leader.

Mao Zedong

Mao (December 26, 1893–September 9, 1976), chairman of the Chinese Communist Party for more than three decades, was the leading architect of the People's Republic of China (PRC). Mao helped establish the Chinese Community Party (CCP) in 1921 and developed and popularized Maoism, which blended communism, Chinese nationalism, and a cult of personality. In the Chinese Civil War, Mao led the Communists to victory over Chiang Kai-shek's nationalist forces and proclaimed the establishment of the PRC in 1949. The chairman reorganized the Chinese economy, redistributed land, and brutally repressed opponents and potential opponents. After a failed economic revitalization program known as the Great Leap Forward, in which millions died from starvation as a result of the government's agricultural policies, Mao briefly stepped down as head of state only to remerge in 1966 after launching the Great Proletarian Cultural Revolution, a violent purge of the government and the CCP.

On the international stage, Mao actively supported Communist revolutions in the third world and advocated the use of the guerrilla tactics adopted by the CCP in the Chinese Civil War. He committed the People's Liberation Army to fight in Korea against the UN army and provided aid to Ho Chi Minh's forces in Vietnam. Third world support for Mao's China helped earn its recognition in the United Nations in 1971.

Competition for influence in the third world, coupled with differences with Josef Stalin and Nikita Khrushchev on Communist ideology and bilateral relations, provoked tensions between the Soviet Union and the PRC. Although Mao accused Khrushchev of being soft on the West, particularly in Berlin and Cuba, Mao cultivated ties with the United States later in his career, most likely as a result of the Sino-Soviet split. In 1971 the PRC hosted the U.S. table tennis team, the first Americans permitted to visit since 1949. The next year, during President Nixon's successful visit with the chairman, the PRC and the United States agreed to greater economic, cultural, and technological cooperation.

Marshall, George

General Marshall (December 31, 1880–October 16, 1959) was first celebrated as army chief of staff during World War II; during his tenure Marshall increased the size of the U.S. Army eightfold from 1932–1941 and organized the Allies' successful military strategy. Marshall served as President Truman's special representative in China before being appointed to his cabinet. As secretary of state (1947–1949), Marshall played a key role in the formulation of the Truman Doctrine and other significant Cold War foreign policies. In a 1947 speech at Harvard University, Marshall outlined the "Marshall Plan," through which the United States dispensed more than $12 billion to rebuild war-torn Western Europe. As secretary of defense (1950–1951) during the Korean War, Marshall supported Truman's controversial decision to relieve General Douglas MacArthur.

McCarthy, Joseph

McCarthy (November 14, 1908–May 2, 1957), the anti-Communist Wisconsin senator, served as the state's youngest circuit court judge and fought in the U.S. Marines in World War II before being elected to the U.S. Senate in 1946. In 1950, McCarthy delivered a speech in Wheeling, West Virginia, in which he accused the Truman administration's State Department of harboring hundreds of Communists. The ensuing search for subversives, dubbed "McCarthyism," made the senator a hero to millions but alienated him from many of his party's elites, including President Eisenhower, who thought McCarthy reckless and vain. In 1953, McCarthy became chair of the Senate Government Operations Committee and its Permanent Subcommittee on Investigations, which held several hearings on communism and un-American activities in the federal government. Hearings in 1954 on subversion in the U.S. Army exposed McCarthy's bombast and cruelty before a televised audience and led to his censure by the Senate.

McNamara, Robert

Secretary of defense for the Kennedy and Johnson administrations, McNamara (b. June 9, 1916), a former Ford Motor Company executive, used his managerial acumen and knowledge of systems analysis to restructure the Pentagon and reduce waste in defense spending. Skeptical of Eisenhower's policy of massive retaliation, McNamara embraced "flexible response" instead and worked with Congress to increase troop levels and special operations capabilities. Believing that formidable offensive forces served as a deterrent to a nuclear first strike, McNamara also led a build up of U.S. conventional weaponry and accelerated the Pentagon's research and development work.

McNamara's career as secretary of defense is marked with substantial successes and failures. During the Kennedy administration he supported both the Bay of Pigs invasion and the naval quarantine of Cuba. Although McNamara advocated escalation of U.S. involvement in Vietnam and was responsible for the much-maligned emphasis that the military placed during the war on quantifiable metrics such as body counts, the secretary of defense became disillusioned with the war later in his career. Isolated from Johnson and the Joint Chiefs of Staff over the future of Vietnam policy, McNamara resigned in 1967.

Molotov, Vyacheslav

A top advisor to Josef Stalin, Molotov (March 9, 1890–November 8, 1986) became active in Marxist politics as teenager. He ascended quickly in the party and was named secretary of the Central Committee of the Communist Party of the Soviet Union in 1921. As Soviet foreign minister (1939–1949, 1953–1956), Molotov steered Soviet foreign policy during World War II and the early Cold War. Although Hitler's breech of the Soviet-German Nonaggression Pact led him to align the Soviet Union with the United States and Britain, he took a confrontational stance with the West following the war. Molotov's influence waned after Stalin's death; he organized an unsuccessful revolt against Nikita Khrushchev in 1957 and was ultimately dismissed from the Communist Party in 1962.

Nasser, Gamal Abdel

Nasser (January 15, 1918–September 28, 1970), the charismatic prime minister (1954–1955) and president (1956–1970) of Egypt, supported the coups that overthrew King Farouk's monarchy in 1952 and established an authoritarian, socialist republic. Although he was a founder of the Non-Aligned Movement, an organization of third-world nations that eschewed Soviet and American hegemony, Nasser's socialist leanings tied him to the Soviet Union. In 1956 his nationalization of the Suez Canal provoked the French, British, and Israelis to launch an orchestrated assault, which was condemned by President Eisenhower. Following border skirmishes, Israel launched an attack on Egypt in 1967; the Six-Day War resulted in the humiliating defeat of Egypt, Jordan, Iraq, and Syria.

Ngo Dinh Diem

Diem (January 3, 1901–November 2, 1963) was the first president (1955–1963) of the Republic of Vietnam. In the 1930s, Diem resigned as an official in Bao Dai's imperial government, citing French encroachment on Vietnamese affairs. After being captured by the Vietminh (the South Vietnamese Communist insurgency) and refusing a position in Ho Chi Minh's Communist government, Diem spent the early 1950s in exile in the United States. Upon his return, Diem was named premier of South Vietnam, which had been divided from North Vietnam following the struggle for Indochina after World War II. In 1955 Diem refused to hold a referendum concerning Vietnam's reunification, declared independence for the Republic of Vietnam, and became its president. Although the United States supported Diem, his corrupt and abusive regime was a source of constant worry in Washington, D.C. On November 2, 1963, he was assassinated in a coup that had been approved by President Kennedy.

Nguyen Van Thieu
Thieu (April 5, 1923–September 29, 2001), a South Vietnamese army commander and later president of the Republic of Vietnam (1967–1975), joined several coup d'états during the 1960s, including the bloody ousting of South Vietnamese president Ngo Dinh Diem, and held leadership positions in a series of unstable revolutionary governments. In 1967 Thieu was elected president of South Vietnam; during his administration he oversaw Vietnamization and signed the Paris Peace Accords. He resigned shortly before the fall of Saigon, after blasting the U.S. government for failing to live up to its promises to protect South Vietnam from North Vietnamese attack after the peace accords had been signed. He lived the rest of his life in exile.

Novikov, Nikolai
Novikov (b. February 7, 1903–?), an influential Soviet diplomat, worked in academia before joining the People's Commissariat for Foreign Affairs in 1938. He held various positions in the Soviet foreign service before being assigned to the U.S. embassy in 1944. Over the next two years, Novikov acted as Soviet ambassador Andrei Gromyko's second-in-command while Gromyko traveled to participate in postwar negotiations. Novikov was appointed ambassador to the United States in 1946 and he represented the Soviet Union at the 1946 UN General Assembly and the Paris Peace Conference the same year. Novikov is most remembered for authoring a telegram in September 1946 warning of American imperialist ambitions.

Ortega, Daniel
Ortega (b. November 11, 1945) was president of Nicaragua between 1985 and 1990. He joined the Sandinista National Liberation Front (FSLN) in 1963 and became its leader. FSLN overthrew dictator Anastasio Somoza in 1979, leaving the FSLN to rule through the Junta for National Reconstruction, of which Ortega was a member. Soon after Somoza's overthrow, Ortega and the Sandinistas assumed control of the junta and the country. In 1984 Ortega's leadership received the imprimatur of a national election, although the Reagan administration, which considered Ortega a dictator in league with international communism, condemned the elections as unfair. The Reagan administration worked to unseat Ortega and to cut off the flow of arms both into the country—from Cuba and the Soviet Union—and out to Marxist guerilas in Central America. Under pressure from the United States and the Contra rebels that the United States funded and trained, Ortega and FSLN agreed to hold open elections in 1990. To his great surprise, Ortega lost the presidency to Violeta Chamorro and the anti-Sandinista National Opposition Union (UNO).

Powell, Colin
General Powell (b. April 5, 1937) was national security adviser (1987–1989) under President Reagan before becoming chairman of the Joint Chiefs of Staff (1989–1993) under Presidents Bush and Clinton. He was secretary of state for President George W. Bush (2001–2004). Powell served in the U.S. Army in Korea and Vietnam and rose to the rank of general in 1989. He was instrumental in the revitalization of the army following its defeat in Vietnam. In the late Cold War and early post–Cold War period, Powell was known for his doctrine, which proclaimed that U.S. military force should only be used under restrictive conditions, including the clear support of the public and Congress. The Persian Gulf War of 1990–1991 exemplified the style of warfare endorsed by Powell.

Radford, Arthur
A naval officer and aviator, Admiral Radford (February 27, 1896–August 17, 1973) served in World War I, and during World War II, he climbed the ranks as a commander in the Pacific theater. In 1953 Radford became the first naval officer to chair the Joint Chiefs of Staff. As chairman, the admiral earned a hawkish reputation by advocating intervention in Indochina and the use of atomic weapons, as necessary, to defend against Communist advances, particularly in East Asia. Although Radford strongly supported President Eisenhower's New Look strategy, he later battled the administration over cuts in defense spending.

Randolph, Philip
Randolph (April 15, 1889–May 16, 1979) was a prominent labor and civil rights leader. Through his radical magazine *Messenger,* first published in 1917, and its successor, *African American Labor,* Randolph, a

socialist, advocated interracial labor unity. During the 1920s Randolph organized and led the Brotherhood of Sleeping Car Porters, one of the most successful black unions; he later served as vice president of the AFL-CIO for more than a decade. A pacifist who advocated nonviolent protest, Randolph is credited with pressuring the government to adopt President Truman's Executive Order 9981, which desegregated the armed forces.

Regan, Donald
Regan (December 21, 1918–June 10, 2003) served under President Reagan as secretary of the Treasury from 1981 to 1985, and then as chief of staff from 1985 to 1987. During his tenure, he was an ardent supporter of supply-side economics, promoting tax cuts as a means of economic stimulation. Regan was often the public spokesperson for Reaganomics. He was pressured to resign amidst the Iran-Contra affair, in which members of the White House staff ran an illegal funding operation benefiting the Contra rebels in Nicaragua.

Rice, Condoleezza
Rice (b. November 14, 1954) is secretary of state (2005–present) under President George W. Bush, having replaced Colin Powell after his resignation. Rice served as George W. Bush's national security adviser (2001–2005) during his first term. Rice was a political science professor at Stanford University (1981–2000) and served as provost there from 1993 to 1999. She also served as senior director of Soviet and East European Affairs in the National Security Council and as special assistant to the president for national security affairs for President George H. W. Bush between 1989 and 1991—the period of the dissolution of the Soviet Union and the reunification of East and West Germany.

Ridgway, Matthew
One of the most celebrated U.S. military commanders of his generation, General Ridgway (March 3, 1895–July 26, 1993) commanded paratroopers of the Eighty-second Airborne Division in Sicily during Operation Husky and in Normandy on D-Day and, later, led the XVIII Corps in the Battle of the Bulge. Before joining Eisenhower's Joint Chiefs of Staff in 1953, Ridgway led the Eighth Army to victories in Korea and served as supreme commander of the NATO military alliance. Ridgway objected strongly to Eisenhower's "New Look" strategy. He supported the use of conventional forces to deter nuclear threats and was denied reappointment to the Joint Chiefs in 1955.

Rockefeller, Nelson
Rockefeller (July 8, 1908–January 26, 1979), President Ford's vice president (1974–1977), was a three-time presidential candidate. An internationalist and philanthropist, Rockefeller advised the Roosevelt, Truman, Eisenhower, Johnson, and Nixon administrations on foreign policy issues and led several organizations committed to Latin American economic development. As governor of New York (1958–1973), Rockefeller consolidated and expanded the state government. After the resignation of President Nixon, the new president, Ford, chose "Rocky" to be his vice president. Rockefeller's liberal views and aggressive personal style created a rift between him and such Ford administration officials as Chief of Staff Dick Cheney and Defense Secretary Donald Rumsfeld.

Rostow, Walt
Rostow (October 7, 1916–February 13, 2003), an economic historian and adviser to the Eisenhower, Kennedy, and Johnson administrations, played a key role in escalating the Vietnam War. Rostow was an intelligence officer during World War II and then worked on European recovery as an economist for the State Department. As special assistant to the national security adviser (1961–1963), chair of the State Department policy planning council (1961–1966), and national security adviser (1966–1969), Rostow influenced military policy in Vietnam, where he believed intensification of bombing campaigns was the key to victory.

Rusk, Dean
Secretary of state under the Kennedy and Johnson administrations, Rusk (February 9, 1909–December 20, 1994) considerably, albeit quietly, influenced U.S. Cold War foreign policy. After serving in the U.S. Army during World War II, Rusk joined the State Department in 1947. Through his work in the State Department, Rusk, an internationalist, solicited greater U.S. support for the United Nations and garnered prominence within the department bureaucracy. As assistant secretary for Far Eastern affairs from 1950–1952, Rusk played a key role in developing policy toward China and Korea. President Kennedy, seeking a moderate who would not compete with him for leadership of the government's foreign policy, appointed Rusk as secretary of state in 1961. Rusk held a relatively weak position within the Kennedy presidency but

became more influential in the Johnson administration through his unwavering support for President Johnson's policies in Vietnam.

Sakharov, Andrei

Sakharov (May 21, 1921–December 14, 1989), a leading Soviet nuclear physicist, human rights activist, and Nobel laureate (1975), became a popular figure in the West during the Cold War. A member of the team of researchers that developed the Soviet hydrogen bomb (1948–1953), Sakharov's belief that nuclear technology should be reserved for peaceful means barred him from state-sponsored weapons research. Increasingly critical of Soviet military policies and civil liberties abuses, Sakharov founded the Moscow Committee for Human Rights in 1970 and authored numerous political essays circulated in the Western press. In 1980, after denouncing the Soviet invasion of Afghanistan, Sakharov was arrested and sent to live in internal exile under tight KGB surveillance. President Carter, who met with Sakharov in 1977, publicly deplored the exile, which was ended by Mikhail Gorbachev six years later.

Schlesinger, James

A hawkish economist and consultant, Schlesinger (b. February 15, 1929) served in the Nixon, Ford, and Carter administrations as assistant director of the Office of Management and Budget (1970–1971), chair of the Atomic Energy Commission (1971–1973), director of the Central Intelligence Agency (1973), secretary of defense (1973–1975), and secretary of energy (1977–1979). As secretary of defense, Schlesinger resisted arms control, lobbied for increased military spending, and advocated bringing into U.S. strategy the concept of a winnable, limited nuclear war. Such policies alienated him from the Ford administration and led to his dismissal in 1975. He later served as President Carter's first energy secretary.

Scowcroft, Brent

Scowcroft (b. March 9, 1925) was national security adviser to President Ford (1975–1977) and President Bush (1989–1993). Scowcroft served in the U.S. military for twenty-nine years, graduating from West Point and earning the rank of lieutenant general in the U.S. Air Force. Scowcroft was skeptical of the durability of changes in the Soviet regime under Mikhail Gorbachev and urged caution upon an already cautious Bush. Although he had his own views, Scowcroft was an honest broker as national security adviser, ensuring that Ford and Bush heard the views of all their key foreign policy advisers. He and Bush coauthored a memoir of foreign policymaking in the administration shortly after they left office.

Shevardnadze, Eduard

Shevardnadze (b. January 25, 1928) was president of Georgia from 1995 to 2003, before resigning amidst criticism and popular discontent. Shevardnadze joined the Communist Party of the Soviet Union in 1948 and was promoted to the Georgian Supreme Soviet in 1959. In 1972 Shevardnadze became the first secretary of the Georgian Communist Party. He joined the Soviet Central Committee in 1976 and became Soviet minister of foreign affairs in 1985. Shevardnadze was instrumental in refusing Soviet support to the Communist leaders of Eastern bloc countries at the end of the Cold War. Old guard Stalinists in Moscow began to view him as a traitor for not attempting to retain the Soviet republics, and Shevardnadze resigned in 1990 amid a growing rift with Gorbachev, who himself was under intense pressure from the same critics. In Georgia, Shevardnadze orchestrated a violent coup in 1992, deposing the democratically elected Zviad Gamsakhurdia, and ascended to the presidency. In 2003 protesters took to the streets and demanded Shevardnadze's resignation. Shevardnadze resigned in what is now called the "Rose Revolution."

Shultz, George

President Reagan appointed Shultz (b. December 13, 1920) secretary of state in 1982 and he served the remainder of Reagan's tenure, until 1989. Shultz had previously served as President Nixon's secretary of labor from 1969 to 1970 and secretary of the Treasury from 1972 to 1974. He helped reform U.S. currency policy during this period and pulled the dollar from the gold standard. Shultz contributed significantly to all the major foreign policy accomplishments and treaties of Reagan's presidency. He often advocated caution in diplomacy and restraint in the face of such temptations as the Iran-Contra deal. He was more willing, than other members of Reagan's cabinet, however, to advise consideration of the use of force in Lebanon and even in Nicaragua.

Stettinius, Edward, Jr.

Stettinius (October 22, 1900–October 31, 1949), an American businessman and diplomat, was a founder of the United Nations. In 1939 Stettinius left a successful business career to join the Roosevelt administration; he led several wartime organizations, most notably the Lend-Lease Administration (1942–1943). After being appointed undersecretary (1943–1944) and then secretary of state (1944–1945), Stettinius advised President Truman at Yalta and led the U.S. delegation at the 1945 San Francisco Conference, where he helped forge a consensus, especially with the Soviets, regarding the formation of the United Nations. In 1945 he stepped down as secretary of state to become a U.S. representative to the UN, but he resigned a year later because of disagreements with Truman's foreign policies.

Stevenson, Adlai

Stevenson (February 5, 1900–July 14, 1965) was a lawyer and New Dealer. With the support of the outgoing Democratic President Truman, Stevenson, then the governor of Illinois, won the Democratic nomination for president in 1952, before being soundly defeated by Republican Dwight Eisenhower. Stevenson repeated the experiment four years later, with similar results. Although unsuccessful as a presidential candidate, Stevenson won praise for his intelligence and rectitude. He strongly supported John F. Kennedy in the 1960 election and was appointed his ambassador to the United Nations. During the Cuban Missile Crisis, he famously got the better of his Soviet counterpart, displaying for all the world to see the photographic evidence of missile sites in Cuba and demanding a Soviet acknowledgment.

Stimson, Henry

In 1940 President Roosevelt appointed Stimson (September 21, 1867–October 20, 1950) secretary of war, the year before U.S. entry into World War II. Stimson was an accomplished internationalist and had served in high positions in every Republican administration since that of Theodore Roosevelt. In Franklin Roosevelt's cabinet, Stimson pressed for war preparedness and encouraged intervention in World War II even before the attack on Pearl Harbor. Stimson also managed the Manhattan Project and advised Presidents Roosevelt and Truman, who kept him on in his administration, on atomic energy policy and nuclear strategy. In this capacity, Stimson influenced Truman's decision to use atomic weapons against Japan in 1945. Despite his skepticism of Soviet ambitions, Stimson urged Truman to seek mutual cooperation with the Soviet Union on nuclear arms control.

Taylor, Maxwell

A hero of World War II, General Taylor (August 26, 1901–April 19, 1987) became an influential figure during the Cold War. During 1953–1995, he brilliantly commanded the Eighth Army in the Korean War before accepting a position as commander of U.S. and UN operations in the Far East. As army chief of staff (1955–1959), Taylor advocated strong conventional armies rather than nuclear deterrence and, consequently, often came into conflict with the Eisenhower administration. Following a brief retirement, Taylor was solicited by President Kennedy to investigate the Bay of Pigs debacle in 1961 and earned recognition within the administration for his frank assessment. A few weeks after being named chairman of Kennedy's Joint Chiefs of Staff in October 1962, Taylor aided the president as the only uniformed member of EXCOMM (executive committee) during the Cuban Missile Crisis. As chairman of the Joint Chiefs, ambassador to South Vietnam (1964–1965), and special adviser to the Johnson administration, the general played a major role in escalating the Vietnam War.

Thatcher, Margaret

Thatcher (b. October 13, 1925) was prime minister of the United Kingdom from 1979 to 1990. After more than a decade's service to her Conservative Party in the House of Parliament, she became secretary of state for education and science under Prime Minister Edward Heath following the 1970 elections. After the Conservatives lost the 1974 elections, Thatcher defeated Heath and William Whitelaw to become the Conservative Party leader. During her more than a decade as prime minister, Thatcher supported Reagan's deterrence policies against the Soviet Union. Domestically, Thatcher promoted tax cuts and government deregulation and, in non–Cold War foreign affairs, led the nation to victory in its war with Argentina over the Falkland Islands and oversaw negotiations over Northern Ireland. In relation to European integration, Thatcher was a staunch oppositionist.

Vance, Cyrus

Vance (March 27, 1917–January 12, 2002) was President Carter's first secretary of state (1977–1980). An attorney and naval officer, Vance served in the Kennedy and Johnson administrations as counsel to the Pentagon (1961–1962), secretary of the army (1962–1964), deputy secretary of defense (1964–1967), and delegate to the Paris Peace Talks (1968–1969). As secretary of state, Vance negotiated the Panama Canal Treaty (1977), SALT II (1979), and the Camp David Accords (1978–1979), and he worked to establish official diplomatic relations with the People's Republic of China (1979). Vance and National Security Adviser Zbigniew Brzezinski contested for influence within the Carter cabinet. Their rivalry, which was personal as well as ideological, diminished the president's reputation for managerial competence and policy consistency. Vance resigned in 1980 following Carter's attempted helicopter rescue of the American hostages in Iran, an operation which he had opposed. Under President Clinton, he served as a UN negotiator in the Balkans (1991–1993).

Wallace, Henry

Wallace (October 7, 1888–November 18, 1965), a liberal internationalist, was a leading critic of such post-war policies as the Truman Doctrine and the Marshall Plan. In the 1940 election, President Roosevelt chose Wallace, his skillful, progressive secretary of agriculture (1933–1941), as his running mate. During World War II, Wallace led Roosevelt's Board of Economic Warfare (1941–1943) and lobbied for the establishment of a strong international organization. Replaced by Harry Truman in the 1944 election, Wallace served briefly as secretary of commerce. After Roosevelt's death, Wallace's idealistic beliefs increasingly isolated him from the Truman administration; in 1946 the President dismissed him after criticizing the administration's policies toward the Soviet Union. Wallace was unsuccessful in his campaign for president in 1948.

Warnke, Paul

Warnke (January 31, 1920–October 31, 2001), an arms control advocate, directed President Carter's U.S. Arms Control and Disarmament Agency (ACDA; 1977–1978). During the Johnson administration, as the general counsel to the Pentagon (1966) and assistant secretary of defense for international security affairs (1967–1969), Warnke pushed for a negotiated settlement in Vietnam and restraint in arms production. In 1975 Warnke published an article ("Apes on a Treadmill") in *Foreign Affairs* that derided the arms race as nonsensical and advocated cuts in weapons development. As director of the ACDA, Warnke negotiated SALT II; he resigned over perceived concessions granted to the Soviets during the talks.

Weinberger, Casper

Weinberger (August 18, 1917–March 28, 2006) was appointed secretary of defense by President Reagan in 1981 and held the position until 1987. Weinberger served in the California State Assembly from 1952 to 1958 and later became chair of the California Republican Party in 1962. As secretary of defense, he sided with President Reagan in increasing the defense budget and expanding the U.S. military. He strongly advocated the Strategic Defense Initiative, also known as the "Star Wars" missile shield, as well as increasing and modernizing nuclear weapons. Weinberger approved the transfer of weapons to Iran involved in the Iran-Contra affair and was later indicted on felony charges for his actions. He resigned from his post in 1987. President Bush pardoned Weinberger in 1992 for his participation in Iran-Contra.

Westmoreland, William

General Westmoreland (March 26, 1914–July 18, 2005) fought in World War II and Korea before he was deployed to Vietnam in 1963, where he assumed the role of commander of the U.S. Military Assistance Command (1964–1968). In that post, Westmoreland oversaw a twenty-five-fold expansion of American forces in the region. Some historians blame Westmoreland's strategy of attrition for the failure in Vietnam. Following the Tet Offensive, he was replaced by Gen. Creighton Williams Abrams Jr., and he returned to the United States to serve as army chief of staff (1968–1972).

Wheeler, Earle

General Wheeler (January 13, 1908–December 18, 1975) served as army chief of staff (1962–1964) and chairman of the Joint Chiefs of Staff (1964–1970) after holding a variety of domestic and foreign assignments. Wheeler is credited with improving and enlarging the armed forces while successfully pursuing nuclear arms reductions. However, he is faulted by some for failing to challenge President Johnson's limited war strategy. During the Nixon administration, Wheeler carried out controversial clandestine bombing campaigns against Cambodia (1969–1970).

Yeltsin, Boris

Yeltsin (b. February 1, 1931) became the first president of Russia in 1991 and served until 1999. Yeltsin joined the Communist Party in 1961, rising to the Politburo in 1985, before being demoted due to confrontations with Mikhail Gorbachev in 1987. During his time in the party leadership, Yeltsin was an avid reformer and a moderate Russian nationalist. As the elected president of the Russian Republic, Yeltsin won international respect when he helped to overturn the August 1991 coup against Soviet leader Mikhail Gorbachev. After this, Yeltsin played a key role in the formation of the Commonwealth of Independent States, the creation of which marked the dissolution of the Soviet Union.

Young, Andrew, Jr.

Young (b. March 12, 1932), a civil rights activist and ordained Protestant minister, was the first African American to serve as U.S. ambassador to the United Nations. Young worked closely with Martin Luther King Jr. to end segregation, serving as executive director of the Southern Christian Leadership Conference (1964–1970). In 1977 President Carter, a former Georgia governor, appointed Young as UN ambassador, a position Young used to promote human rights and economic development in the third world. He was forced to resign in 1979 after he violated administration policy by meeting with the Palestinian Liberation Organization (PLO).

Zhou Enlai

The first premier (1949–1976) and foreign minister (1949–1958) of the People's Republic of China (PRC), Zhou (March 5, 1898–January 8, 1976) was a leading architect of Chinese foreign policy. During the Chinese civil war he negotiated with the nationalists on behalf of the Communist Party of China and backed Mao's rise to power. As premier of the newly established PRC, Zhou criticized imperialism and encouraged Communist movements in the third world. While Chinese relations with the Soviet Union deteriorated, Zhou eased tensions with the United States in the 1970s and won UN membership for the PRC in 1971.

Appendix B
Key Events in the Cold War

This chronology was compiled by CQ Press editors with the assistance of Kenneth Hill's *Cold War Chronology: Soviet-American Relations 1945–1991* (Washington, D.C.: Congressional Quarterly, 1993). Documents from Chapters 1 through 11 appear as key events here for readers' reference.

1944

August 29 Shape of Peace to Come (see Document 1.1). President Roosevelt speaks to the press about the newly established United Nations (UN).

1945

February 11 Churchill and Stalin on Yalta (see Document 1.2). At the Yalta Conference, the "Big Three"— Josef Stalin, Winston Churchill, and Franklin Roosevelt—reach agreement on the division of Germany into zones of occupation and the veto power of permanent members of the planned UN Security Council. In a secret side agreement, the Soviets agree to enter the war against Japan in exchange for territorial concessions.

April 12 Roosevelt's Death. President Roosevelt's death leaves his vice president, Harry Truman, to take over the office.

June 26 United Nations Charter (see Document 1.3). Per the agreement reached at Yalta, the Allies organize a conference of forty-six nations in San Francisco that culminates in the signing of the UN Charter.

July 17–August 2 Potsdam Conference (see Document 1.4). Stalin, President Truman, and Churchill (who is replaced by Clement Atlee, who arrives after becoming the new prime minister) meet to consider terms of German occupation and the division of Europe.

September 11 Council of Foreign Ministers. The first meeting of the Council of Foreign Ministers, representing China, France, the Soviet Union, the United Kingdom, and the United States, convenes in London to consider territorial questions and other issues resulting from World War II.

October 23 Truman on the Military. President Truman urges Congress to adopt a program of universal military training, arguing that America's strength would be used to help enforce the authority of the UN.

December 14 Atomic Energy Committee. Members of the Senate Atomic Energy Committee meet with President Truman about proposals that Secretary of State James Byrnes might make to the Soviets while attending the Big Three foreign ministers meeting in Moscow.

1946

January 14 Truman on Foreign Policy. In his State of the Union address, President Truman pledges to support the principles of the UN charter.

February 9 Stalin on Communism (see Document 1.5). In Josef Stalin's speech to "voters" in Moscow, the Soviets' preeminent leader attributes Soviet success in the war to the Communist Party's economic and social policies prior to war.

February 22 "Long Telegram" (see Document 1.6). George Kennan warns that the United States must mobilize all its resources to confront the challenge of Soviet-led communism. His ideas provide an intellectual foundation upon which the Cold War strategy of "containment" will be constructed.

March 5 Iron Curtain (see Document 1.7). Speaking in Missouri, Winston Churchill declares that an "iron curtain" has descended across Europe and notes Soviet domination of Eastern Europe and the transformation of East Germany into a pro-Communist state. He calls for a greater degree of cooperation between the United States and Britain.

March 14 Stalin on Churchill (see Document 1.8). In *Pravda,* Stalin takes strong exception to Churchill's "Iron Curtain" speech.

June 14 Baruch Plan. The United States, at the first meeting of the UN Atomic Energy Commission, presents a plan for the control, supervision, and peaceful use of atomic energy.

July 1 Atomic Bomb Survey (see Document 1.10). The report assesses the effectiveness of the bombs dropped by the United States on the Japanese cities of Hiroshima and Nagasaki.

September 27 Novikov Telegram (see Document 1.9). The Soviet ambassador to the United States, Nikolai Novikov, analyzes events in terms ironically similar to those employed in Kennan's famous "Long Telegram."

1947

February 21 Britain and Aid to Greece and Turkey. The British ambassador to the United States delivers an urgent message to the U.S. Department of State that Britain will cease aid to Greece and Turkey.

March 12 Truman Doctrine (see Document 2.1). President Truman announces his Cold War doctrine—providing economic and military assistance to nations threatened by communism—at a joint session of Congress. He requests $400 million to aid Greece and Turkey.

March 21 Executive Order 9835 (see Document 2.2). President Truman commands that loyalty investigations be conducted on all persons applying for federal government positions and that the heads of government agencies and departments establish procedures to dismiss disloyal employees.

June 5 Marshall Plan (see Document 2.3). Secretary of State George Marshall calls for the United States to provide temporary but massive economic aid to Europe for four years.

July "Containment." "Mr. X" (a pseudonym for George Kennan) offers his famous analysis of "The Sources of Soviet Conduct" for readers of *Foreign Affairs*. The article helps to legitimize President Truman's efforts to contain the Soviet Union.

September "Cold War." The columnist Walter Lippmann popularizes the phrase "Cold War," but the term had been used by others, including writer George Orwell, before.

September 25 Soviet Response to Marshall Plan (see Document 2.4). At the UN, Deputy Foreign Minister Andrei Vishinsky declares that the Marshall Plan is nothing more than economic imperialism and nothing less than a violation of the fundamental principles that the United States has agreed to uphold by joining the UN.

October 5 Cominform Manifesto (see Document 2.5). The Communist Information Bureau (Cominform), which disseminates propaganda and encourages Communist solidarity, issues a manifesto urging Communist parties everywhere to oppose U.S. policies and to undermine support for the Marshall Plan.

1948

January 7 Truman on Foreign Policy. President Truman, in his State of the Union address, emphasizes the growing interdependence of nations and stresses that any nation losing its independence and democracy would affect the United States. To keep the country militarily strong, he again asks Congress to approve a universal military training bill and urges lawmakers to authorize funds for the European Recovery Program.

February 25 Czechoslovakia Coup. In a coup, backed by Josef Stalin, the Communists remove their rivals from political power in Czechoslovakia.

April 3 Marshall Plan. President Truman signs into law the European Economic Recovery Program (the Marshall Plan).

June 11 Vandenberg Resolution (see Document 2.8). Congress authorizes the Truman administration to join negotiations for membership in the emerging anti-Soviet Atlantic alliance, signifying a consensus on U.S. support for collective security.

June 12 Truman on Foreign Policy. President Truman, in an address in California, criticizes the Soviet Union for its rejection of the Marshall Plan, excessive use of the veto in the UN Security Council, indirect aggression in Eastern Europe, and interference in the affairs of nations. The president outlines a plan for peace that includes controlling atomic energy, various economic assistance programs, and support for the UN.

June 24 Berlin Blockade. The Soviets impose a complete land and water blockade of Berlin.

June 24 Berlin Airlift (see Document 2.6). The United States begins flying food and supplies into Berlin in response to the Soviet blockade. The airlift will become the main method for supplying the people of Berlin until the Soviets lift the blockade in May 1949.

July 26 Desegregation of the Armed Forces (see Document 2.7). Truman issues Executive Order 9981 to desegregate the military and to improve U.S. civil rights to battle Soviet propaganda.

1949

January 20 Truman on Collective Security (see Document 2.10). In his inaugural address, President Truman outlines a four-point program to win the Cold War that focuses on the UN, the Marshall Plan, the North Atlantic Treaty Organization (NATO), and exporting scientific and technological advances to underdeveloped countries.

April 4 NATO Alliance (see Document 2.9). President Truman signs the treaty creating the NATO military alliance.

May 9 End of Berlin Blockade. The Soviets announce the end of the Berlin blockade, almost a year after its imposition.

September 21 West Germany Established. The Federal Republic of German is officially established.

September 23 President on Soviet Atomic Bomb (see Document 2.11). President Truman announces to the American people that the Soviets have tested an atomic bomb.

October 1 People's Republic of China (see Document 2.12). Mao Zedong's Communist forces succeed and the People's Republic of China is established, with its national capital at Beijing.

October 8 German Democratic Republic. The German Democratic Republic (East Germany) is formally established, although the Soviet Union continues to exercise control over the government.

1950

January 26 U.S. Aid to South Korea. The United States and South Korea sign a mutual defense assistance agreement.

January 31 Hydrogen Bomb. President Truman announces that the Atomic Energy Commission will continue work on the development of a hydrogen bomb.

February 9 McCarthy Speech (see Document 2.13). In a speech in West Virginia, Sen. Joseph McCarthy of Wisconsin announces that there are Communists in the Truman administration

February 14 Soviet-Chinese Treaty. The Soviet Union and People's Republic of China sign a Treaty of Friendship, Alliance, and Mutual Aid.

April 7 National Security Council Report (see Document 2.14). National Security Council (NSC) Report 68 describes the Soviet Union as an expansionist power and calls for massive and sustained U.S. rearmament to fight the Cold War.

June 25 Truman on Korea (see Document 2.15). After North Korea invades South Korea, President Truman seeks support from the UN Security Council, which passes a resolution condemning the invasion.

June 27 Assistance to South Korea (see Document 2.16). President Truman announces his decision to send military assistance to help South Korea. Truman adds that the United States will align itself with the French effort in Vietnam, Laos, and Cambodia—or "Indochina."

July 19 Truman Address on the War (see Document 2.17). President Truman addresses the nation on the war and explains in stark terms the consequences of defeat. He asks Congress to approve a supplemental emergency appropriation of $10 billion.

November 30 Truman on Atomic Bomb. President Truman causes a controversy when, in response to a question at a news conference, he says that the United States is considering using the atomic bomb in Korea.

1951

April 5 General MacArthur on Conduct of War (see Document 2.19). In a public letter to a U.S. representative, Gen. Douglas MacArthur denounces President Truman's conduct of the war and his refusal to attack China after it entered the Korean War.

April 11 Truman on MacArthur Firing (see Documents 2.20 and 2.21). President Truman fires MacArthur and makes a televised speech justifying his removal. The same day Truman also defends his conduct of the war.

1952

June 5 Court Ruling on War Powers (see Document 2.22). The Supreme Court decides that President Truman's war powers have limits and overrules the president's assertion of prerogative powers to resolve a labor-management dispute in the nation's steel mills.

November 1 Hydrogen Bomb. The United States tests its first device for a hydrogen bomb.

1953

January 15 Truman on Communism. President Truman, in his farewell address, says that the values of democracy will prevail over communism.

March 4 Stalin's Death. Josef Stalin dies and is succeeded by Georgi Malenkov.

April 16 Eisenhower on Atomic Energy (see Document 3.2). In his "Chance for Peace" speech, President Eisenhower appeals to the new Soviet leadership for the international control of atomic energy.

July 2 Eisenhower on Capitalism (see Document 3.1). President Eisenhower reflects in his diary on the challenges facing the United States and contrasts his views with those of Vladimir Lenin.

July 27 Korean Armistice. The Korean War ends as China and North Korea are more willing to end the fighting after Stalin's death and the new Soviet leaders seek to improve relations with the United States.

August 20 Soviet Hydrogen Bomb. The Soviet Union announces it has exploded a hydrogen bomb.

September 8 Eisenhower to Dulles (see Document 3.4). In a memorandum to Secretary of State John Foster Dulles, President Eisenhower considers the possibility of a nuclear first strike.

September 13 First Secretary Khrushchev. Nikita Khrushchev becomes first secretary of the Communist Party, making him the most powerful leader in the Soviet Union.

October 30 National Security Report (see Document 3.3). NSC-162/2 presents a review of U.S. security policy and becomes the official underpinning of "massive retaliation."

December 8 Eisenhower "Atoms for Peace" Speech (see Document 3.12). The president speaks to the UN openly about the capabilities of the American nuclear arsenal and the nuclear arms race. He ends the speech with a plea to the Soviets to join the United States in diverting nuclear technology to peaceful purposes.

December 10 Eisenhower Reflection on "Atoms for Peace." (see Document 3.13) In his diary, the president describes the multiple purposes served by his dramatic speech before the UN.

1954

January 12 "Massive Retaliation" (see Document 3.5). Secretary of State John Foster Dulles's speech in New York City emphasizes "massive retaliatory power," in contrast to the crisis-driven policies that prevailed under President Truman.

February 1/10 Soviet Peace Proposals. During the Berlin Conference, Soviet Foreign Minister Vyacheslav Molotov proposes a peace treaty for Germany, a collective security treaty for Europe, and a neutral German treaty where foreign forces withdraw from the state. Western nations reject all Soviet proposals.

April 7 "Falling Dominoes" (see Document 3.6). President Eisenhower, in a press conference, employs the metaphor "falling dominoes" to describe the stakes involved in the Cold War contest for Indochina.

September 8 Southeast Asia Collective Defense Treaty (see Document 3.7). Australia, France, New Zealand, Pakistan, the Philippines, Thailand, the United Kingdom, and the United States agree to come to the aid of one another in the event of a military strike against any one of the signatories or against Vietnam.

1955

January 29 Formosa Resolution (see Document 3.8). Congress passes a resolution proclaiming American determination to defend Formosa in the first Taiwan Straits crisis.

January 31 Ridgway Criticism of Military Cuts (see Document 3.9). In an unusual display of military dissent, Army Chief of Staff Gen. Matthew Ridgway criticizes President Eisenhower's proposal to reduce the nation's conventional armed forces.

February 2 President on General Ridgway (see Document 3.10) President Eisenhower replies to General Ridgway's criticism of proposed cuts to army strength.

(no date) Bricker Amendment. U.S. senator John Bricker proposes an amendment to the Constitution requiring presidents to consult Congress before reaching agreements with foreign governments.

July 21 Open-Sky Proposal. At the Big Four summit meeting, President Eisenhower suggests that the United States and the Soviet Union should exchange blueprints of their military establishments and that both nations should be allowed to conduct reconnaissance flights over each other's territory.

December 25 Eisenhower Christmas Message. President Eisenhower sends a Christmas message to the Soviet satellite countries through Radio Free Europe. The president says he supports these countries' efforts to regain their freedom.

1956

January 5 Eisenhower State of the Union Address. President Eisenhower, in his State of the Union address, comments on Soviet tactics of "division, enticement, and duplicity" rather than violence to create disunity among Western nations.

April 18 Cominform Dissolved. The Soviet Union announces the dissolution of the Cominform, established in 1947.

April 21 Eisenhower on Foreign Policy. President Eisenhower, in an address to the American Society of Newspaper Editors, states that a new, more peaceful era is developing as more nations support freedom.

September 1 Soviet Nuclear Tests. TASS, the Soviet news agency, announces that the Soviet Union has carried out nuclear tests because the United States refused to agree to a nuclear test ban treaty.

November 4 Hungary Invasion. Soviet Union invades Hungary to end rebellion against Communist government.

November 5 New Government in Hungary. The Soviet Union installs a new government in Hungary under the leadership of Janos Kadar.

1957

January 5 Eisenhower Doctrine (see Document 3.14). President Eisenhower pledges U.S. resistance to Communist aggression in the Middle East and requests military and economic aid to countries in the region endangered by communism.

August 27 Soviet ICBM. Soviets launch the first intercontinental ballistic missile (ICBM).

October 4 Sputnik. The Soviet Union launches *Sputnik,* the first earth satellite.

December 17 U.S. ICBM. The United States launches an ICBM.

1958

January 9 Eisenhower State of the Union Address. President Eisenhower says that the United States has adequate deterrent capability to prevent war but emphasizes the necessity of waging a "total peace" to cope with the "total cold war" conducted by the Soviet Union.

March 27 New Soviet Leader. Nikita Khrushchev replaces Nikolai Bulganin as premier and retains his position as first secretary of the Communist Party, officially making him the undisputed leader of the Soviet Union.

July 22 Eisenhower Letter to Khrushchev. President Eisenhower defends U.S. actions in the Middle East, including deployment of troops to Lebanon to protect its independence.

August 13 Eisenhower at the UN. President Eisenhower presents a six-point peace plan to bring stability to the Middle East.

1959

July 24 "Kitchen Debate" (see Document 3.15). At opening of the U.S. National Exhibit in Moscow, Vice President Richard Nixon and Soviet premier Nikita Khrushchev hold an impromptu debate on the virtues of capitalism and socialism in a model of a modern American kitchen.

September 27 Camp David Talks. President Eisenhower and Khrushchev issue a joint statement at the conclusion of their talks on disarmament, Berlin, Germany, and trade.

1960

May 1 U-2 Flight. President Eisenhower approves one more spy plane flyover of the Soviet Union before Paris meetings with Nikita Khrushchev. The plane is shot down over the Soviet Union and the pilot, Francis Gary Powers, is captured.

May 3 U-2 Cover Story (see Document 3.16). A NASA spokesperson issues a preestablished cover story, which indicates that a weather plane has been lost on a routine flight over Turkey.

May 7 Change in U-2 Story (see Document 3.17). The United States admits that the U-2 plane shot down on May 1 was on a spy mission.

May 11 Eisenhower on U-2 Incident (see Document 3.18). President Eisenhower accepts responsibility for the U-2 flight and affirms his belief that the spy flight had been necessary.

May 17 Covert Action against Cuba. President Eisenhower approves a covert action program against the new Cuban government of Fidel Castro. The plan calls for the training of Cuban exiles intent on overthrowing Castro.

October 18 Kennedy on "Missile Gap." Sen. John F. Kennedy from Massachusetts urges action to stop what he calls a retreat of freedom around the world under President Eisenhower.

1961

January 17 Eisenhower's Farewell (see Document 3.19). The president warns that if the United States departs from pursuing peace through moderated expenditures and the avoidance of war, it risks falling into the embrace of the "military-industrial complex."

January 20 Kennedy Inaugural Address (see Document 4.1). President Kennedy summons a new generation to the task of "defending freedom in its hour of maximum danger" and evokes a spirit of common sacrifice for the common good. He also issues a warning that the United States would "pay any price, bear any burden . . . to assure the survival and the success of liberty."

March 13 Alliance for Progress. In Latin America, Peace Corps volunteers are integrated into a program known as the Alliance for Progress, which combines three principal elements: monetary aid, land and tax reform, and democratization.

April 17 Bay of Pigs. Cuban exiles, with support from the Central Intelligence Agency (CIA), launch an attack to overthrow Fidel Castro's government. The mission fails when they are met by 25,000 Cuban soldiers with armored vehicles and tanks.

April 20 Kennedy's Response to the Bay of Pigs (see Document 4.2). President Kennedy speaks about the recent defeat of the "small band of freedom fighters" in Cuba and warns that the United States will not always be so reluctant to join in.

April 21 Bay of Pigs Press Conference (see Document 4.3). President Kennedy acknowledges responsibility for the botched operation in Cuba.

April 25 Bay of Pigs Off-the-Record (see Document 4.4). At the State Department, President Kennedy admits off-the-record that the invasion was planned in Washington and suggests to his audience that it had enjoyed the enthusiastic endorsement of the nation's military and spy chiefs.

May 25 Kennedy on Foreign and Domestic Policy (see Document 4.5). In a special message to the Congress, President Kennedy emphasizes the need for civil defense (that is, fallout shelters) and pledges to land a man on the moon before the end of the decade.

August 13 Berlin Wall. The Communists begin to erect a wall to prevent East Germans from fleeing into West Berlin.

September 5 Nuclear Testing. President Kennedy announces that the United States will resume underground nuclear testing because the Soviet Union is testing again.

October 21 Nuclear Power of the United States. The Kennedy administration informs the public that the United States has several times the nuclear power of the Soviets.

1962

February 21 Khrushchev to Kennedy. Premier Nikita Khrushchev congratulates President Kennedy on astronaut John Glenn's successful orbit around the earth. Kennedy welcomes the Soviet suggestion that the two nations should cooperate in the exploration of space.

June 6 President on the Military (see Document 4.6). President Kennedy, at the United States Military Academy at West Point, New York, addresses the need to rethink the role of the military in order to win the Cold War.

October 15 Evidence of Nuclear Missiles in Cuba. Analysts at the National Photographic Interpretation Center discover unmistakable evidence of nuclear-missile launching sites under construction in Cuba.

October 18 An Exchange of Warnings (see Document 4.7). President Kennedy meets with Soviet foreign minister Andrei Gromyko and conceals his knowledge of Soviet missiles in Cuba while hinting at a compromise. Both sides acknowledge "grave" consequences should their conflict over Cuba escalate.

October 19 "Situation Completely Satisfactory" (see Document 4.8). After meeting with President Kennedy, the Soviet foreign minister delivers a positive report to the Kremlin.

October 22 Quarantine (see Document 4.9). President Kennedy informs the public about Soviet missiles in Cuba and announces a "quarantine" on ships carrying military equipment to Cuba. Kennedy avoids using the more common term "blockade" because a blockade has been recognized for several centuries in international law as an act of war.

October 23 Dobrynin Analysis of Kennedy's Actions (see Document 4.10). Soviet ambassador to the United States Anatoly Dobrynin's telegram to Moscow describes the mood in Washington and analyzes the Kennedy administration's actions.

October 26 Khrushchev Offer (see Document 4.11). In a letter to President Kennedy, Khrushchev offers to remove missiles from Cuba if the United States promises not to invade the country.

October 27 Second Letter from Khrushchev (see Document 4.12). Before the United States can respond to the Soviets' first offer, Khrushchev adds another demand: the removal of U.S. missiles from Turkey.

October 27 Kennedy Back Channel (see Document 4.13). The president sends his brother, Attorney General Robert Kennedy, to make private promises to Ambassador Dobrynin to end the missile crisis. President Kennedy agrees publicly not to invade Cuba in exchange for the removal of the Soviet missiles. Privately, he accedes to the removal of its missiles from Turkey.

October 27–28 Formal Exchange of Letters (see Document 4.14). The leaders of the two superpowers exchange formal letters ending the crisis in Cuba.

1963

June 10 Speech at American University (see Document 4.15). In a commencement address, President Kennedy speaks of world peace and of his hopes for a relaxation of tensions between the United States and the Soviet Union.

June 20 Superpower "Hot Line." The United States and the Soviet Union establish the famous "hot line" linking the American presidents and the Soviet premiers.

June 26 "Ich bin ein Berliner" (see Document 4.16). In a celebrated trip to West Berlin, President Kennedy affirms U.S. commitment to West Berlin and declares himself a citizen of Berlin.

August 5 Partial Test Ban Treaty (see Document 4.17). Britain, the Soviet Union, and the United States sign a partial nuclear test ban treaty prohibiting testing in the atmosphere, outer space, and under water.

November 22 Kennedy Assassinated. President Kennedy is assassinated in Dallas; he is succeeded by Vice President Lyndon Johnson.

November 22 Possible Soviet Plot (see Document 5.1). President Johnson speculates that the Soviets might have killed President Kennedy.

1964

August 7 Gulf of Tonkin Resolution (see Document 5.3). President Johnson finally rallies Congress behind the Vietnam War when he receives congressional approval to use "all necessary measures" to retaliate against suspected North Vietnamese attacks on U.S. ships.

October 5 Mao's View on Vietnam and Gulf of Tonkin Resolution (see Document 5.4). Chinese leader Mao Zedong is unimpressed with the U.S. response in Vietnam and urges greater action and patience by North Vietnam.

October 14 Khrushchev Removed. Soviet Premier Nikita Khrushchev is removed from power in a bloodless coup; he is replaced by Aleksei Kosygin as premier and Leonid Brezhnev as first secretary of the Communist Party.

November 29 United States: "Why We Fight" (see Document 5.5). Defense planner John McNaughton analyzes U.S. war aims and claims the situation in Vietnam is "bad and deteriorating."

1965

March Public Opinion on the Vietnam War (see Document 5.10). Polls show that support for the war is highest among Americans under thirty years of age.

March 30 and April 2 Chinese Foreign Minister's Analysis of Vietnam (see Document 5.6). In talks with the leaders of Algeria and Pakistan, Chinese foreign minister Zhou Enlai affirms the Chinese government's commitment to send ground troops into the fight, just as it did in Korea, should the United States attack North Vietnam.

April 7 "Peace without Conquest" (See Document 5.7). In an address at Johns Hopkins University, President Johnson offers to fund a massive development program in Vietnam if the Communists will relent.

July 27 Americanizing the War (see Document 5.8). President Johnson attempts to walk a tightrope in Vietnam: Americanize the war but do not provoke the Soviets and Chinese.

1966

January 31 Resumption of Bombing. President Johnson orders the renewed bombing of North Vietnam. For thirty-seven days the United States did not bomb North Vietnam, but still the Hanoi government gave no indication it was willing to seek a negotiated settlement.

September 5 "Bridges of Friendship." President Johnson, in a speech in Ohio, says the United States is attempting to build "bridges of friendship" to the nations of Eastern Europe. The Soviet Union views Johnson's policies as an attempt to interfere in the internal affairs of Eastern Europe.

1967

May 23 Grim Outlook for Summer (see Document 5.11). The Federal Bureau of Investigation (FBI) reports that the prospects are high for racial and antiwar turbulence and violence during the summer.

October 25 Mansfield Resolution (see Document 5.12). The Senate passes a resolution calling on President Johnson to send the issue of the Vietnam War to the UN.

1968

February 1 Possible Use of Nuclear Weapons (see Document 5.13). A memorandum from Gen. Earle Wheeler, chairman of the Joint Chiefs of Staff, raises the possibility of tactical nuclear strikes in Vietnam.

February 2 "Fracture Jaw" Telegram (see Document 5.14). Adm. Alexander Sharp informs Wheeler that planning (with the project name "Fracture Jaw") is already under way for possible use of nuclear weapons in Vietnam.

February 2 Nuclear Issue (see Document 5.15). National Security Adviser Walt Rostow warns President Johnson that the military might raise the "nuclear issue" and advises him on how to avoid considering the issue.

February 3 Rostow Apology (see Document 5.16). Rostow accepts responsibility for accidentally setting in motion nuclear contingency planning.

February 16 Johnson Denial of Nuclear Planning (see Document 5.17). In a press conference, President Johnson denies rumors that he or anyone in his government has discussed the possible use of nuclear weapons in Vietnam.

March Hawks and Doves (see Documents 5.9 and 5.10). A Gallup Poll indicates for the first time that "doves" (opponents of the war) outnumber "hawks" (supporters of the war).

March 4 Request for More Troops (see Document 5.18). In the wake of the massive Tet Offensive launched by the Communists, President Johnson's team considers Gen. William Westmoreland's request for 200,000 more troops but ultimately deploys only 22,000.

March 26 "Wise Men" Briefing (see Document 5.19). President Johnson shows anger at the Vietnam War and domestic politics when he meets with his generals and secretary of state to plan a briefing for senior foreign policy veterans.

March 31 Unilateral Bombing Halt and Johnson Withdrawal from Campaign (see Document 5.20.) At the end of a televised speech announcing the de-escalation of the Vietnam War, President Johnson announces his withdrawal from the presidential contest.

May 3 Vietnam Talks. President Johnson announces that representatives of the United States and North Vietnam will meet in Paris to begin preliminary negotiations on ending the Vietnam War. The talks begin on May 13.

July 1 Nuclear Non-Proliferation Treaty (see Document 5.2). After a three-year negotiation process conducted by the UN, the United States, the Soviet Union, the United Kingdom, and fifty non-nuclear-weapon nations sign a treaty in which nuclear-weapon states pledge not to transfer weapons technology to non-nuclear-weapon states but acknowledge the right of such states to make peaceful use of nuclear power.

August 21 Intervention in Czechoslovakia. Soviet and Warsaw Treaty Organization (or Warsaw Pact) countries invade Czechoslovakia.

November 6 Nixon Victory. With President Johnson out of the race, Republican Richard Nixon defeats Democrat Hubert Humphrey in the presidential election.

1969

January 27 Nixon on Linkage. President Nixon implicitly links arms control agreements with the resolution of political issues. The question of "linkage" becomes an important issue in U.S.-Soviet relations until the end of 1991, when the Soviet Union ceases to exist.

August 2 Nixon Visits Romania. President Nixon visits Romania; he is the first American president to do so. The Romanian government demonstrates its independence from the Soviet Union by welcoming Nixon warmly.

July 25 Nixon Doctrine. At a press conference in Guam, the president announces a new self-help containment doctrine under which the United States would help a nation fight for its freedom against Communist forces but would no longer make the sort of open-ended promises that had been made to the government of South Vietnam. Applying this policy to Vietnam, President Nixon calls for "Vietnamization" of the war.

September 18 Nixon at the UN. President Nixon says he hopes relations between the United States and the Soviet Union will improve despite their differences. He wants the two countries to negotiate on a broad range of issues and to engage the People's Republic of China in a diplomatic exchange. The president calls on the Soviet Union to set a date for the beginning of strategic arms control negotiations and on the United Nations to help bring the Vietnam War to an end.

November 3 Nixon and the "Silent Majority" (see Document 6.1). President Nixon criticizes protestors and makes his case for the war in Vietnam. Nixon attempts to mobilize the great majority of Americans who neither fought against nor fought in the war in Vietnam. He rallies them to support the "Nixon Doctrine."

November 12 My Lai Massacre. The massacre at My Lai—the killing of hundreds of unarmed Vietnamese civilians, mostly women and children, by U.S. soldiers on March 16, 1968—is reported publicly.

November 17 SALT Talks. Phase one of the Strategic Arms Limitation Talks (SALT) talks begins in Helsinki, Finland. These talks eventually lead to the signing of the SALT I treaty in May 1972.

1970

February 6 Johnson on Tonkin Resolution. Former president Lyndon Johnson says he viewed the Tonkin Gulf Resolution as the equivalent to a declaration of war. He also insists that Congress similarly viewed it as authorizing war.

March 18 Nol in Power. After almost a year of Operation Menu, the codename for the U.S. bombing of neutral Cambodia during the Vietnam War, Cambodia's prime minister Gen. Lon Nol deposes President Norodom Sihanouk while the latter is on a diplomatic mission to Moscow and Beijing.

March 21 Nixon and the Soviets. President Nixon, in a statement at a news conference, says the United States had received reports that the Soviet Union was delivering SA-3 missiles to the United Arab Republic. Nixon says he will reevaluate U.S. policies if the Soviets bring about a change in the balance of power in the Middle East.

April 30 Nixon and Cambodia (see Document 6.2). President Nixon, in a radio and television address to the nation, announces that U.S. military units were sent into Cambodia to stop the Communist military forces from using portions of that country as a sanctuary to launch attacks against South Vietnam.

May 4 Kent State. Four students are killed by National Guardsman at Kent State University in Ohio during protests against the invasion of Cambodia.

June 29 Cooper-Church Amendment (see Document 6.4). Idaho Democratic senator Frank Church and liberal Kentucky Republican senator John Sherman Cooper cosponsor an amendment to restrain the president's discretion in the conduct of the war in Vietnam. After considerable debate, including a seven-week filibuster, a modified version of the amendment is approved by both houses of Congress in December 1970 and becomes law in January 1971.

October 7 Nixon Peace Initiative. President Nixon, in an address to the nation, presents a new initiative for peace in Indochina. He calls for a cease-fire throughout Indochina to be put into place and supervised by international observers.

1971

January 11 Violence against the Soviets. President Nixon sends a message to American Jewish leaders deploring the bombing of a Soviet-occupied building in Washington, D.C., allegedly by a Zionist group. These groups were engaged in frequent demonstrations against the Soviet Union to protest the trial in Leningrad of eleven people, nine of whom were Jews, for attempting to hijack an airplane to flee the Soviet Union.

January 21 Soviet Propaganda (see Document 6.14). Soviet documents show that ideological warfare between the superpowers continues even during détente.

February 25 Nixon and China. President Nixon, in his second "Annual State of the World" report to Congress, says the United States would not exploit Sino-Soviet differences. The president wants better relations with the People's Republic of China, but he is not optimistic relations will soon improve.

March 11 "Get the Hell Out" (see Document 6.5). In an Oval Office conversation with his national security adviser, Henry Kissinger, President Nixon declares his impatience with the war in Vietnam. Nixon and Kissinger share no apparent illusions about the prospects for peace, with or without a suitable agreement to end the U.S. presence in the war.

March 19 Nixon and Kissinger on Vietnam and Elections (see Document 6.6). In a taped phone conversation, President Nixon and Kissinger put the need for withdrawal into the context of the upcoming 1972 election.

April 4 Groundwork for Rapprochement (see Document 6.9). Communist Chinese leader Mao Zedong's decision to initiate rapprochement with the United States through "Ping-Pong diplomacy" is nearly derailed when his assistant questions whether he has reversed his earlier decision to turn down the U.S. request to visit China while under the influence of sleeping pills.

April 10 "Ping-Pong Diplomacy" (see Document 6.10). The hand of Mao in the Chinese invitation to American table tennis players is evident to the *New York Times,* which celebrates the emergence of a new form of dialogue between nations: "Ping-Pong diplomacy."

April 14 Policy toward China (see Document 6.7). President Nixon and Kissinger discuss the costs and benefits of normalizing relations with the People's Republic of China. The president and Kissinger discuss the possibility of the mutual opening of China and the United States to one another. The implications for Taiwan, they agree, are sad, but normalizing relations will provide a welcome diversion from the war in Vietnam and provide leverage against the Soviet Union.

May 20 Nixon on Arms Control. President Nixon announces that the United States and the Soviet Union will concentrate on reaching an agreement to limit the deployment of antiballistic missile (ABM) systems and offensive nuclear weapons. While the Soviet Union wants to proceed with an initial agreement limiting only defensive weapons, the United States insists that both defensive and offensive weapons be covered.

June 10 Trade with China. The White House announces that controls on trade with the People's Republic of China are being further reduced. This is one of several steps taken to demonstrate the American desire to improve relations with Beijing.

June 30. Pentagon Papers Court Decision (see Document 6.3). A defense analyst with a troubled conscience leaks to the press the contents of a 7,000-page secret history of the War in Vietnam, from 1945 to 1971. The Nixon White House attempts to stop the publication of the document, but the Supreme Court holds that the First Amendment guarantee of free expression prohibits after-the-fact censorship.

July U.S. Aims in Vietnam (see Document 6.8). During his visit to brief the Chinese foreign minister on U.S. intentions in Vietnam, Kissinger makes clear his and the president's private policy in Vietnam: peace for the United States with the withdrawal of U.S. troops and continued war between the North and South Vietnam.

July 15 Nixon to China. President Nixon announces he has received and accepted an invitation to visit the People's Republic of China. The invitation is a result of a secret trip to China made by Kissinger from July 9 to 11.

September Clandestine White House Operation. In an attempt to punish Defense Department official Daniel Ellsberg for leaking a top-secret Pentagon study of the Vietnam War to the *New York Times,* President Nixon orders the Special Investigations Unit to find damaging information about him. The operatives break into Ellsberg's psychiatrist's office.

September 3 Quadripartite Agreement (see Document 6.15). The United States, Soviet Union, Britain, and France establish the rights of civilians to travel freely in and out of West Berlin.

September 25 Nixon on Arms. President Nixon asserts that the superpowers have rough parity in their nuclear arsenals; therefore, neither country could gain any advantage by launching a first strike.

September 30 Nuclear War Treaty. The United States and the Soviet Union sign a Nuclear Accidents Measures agreement that is designed to prevent the accidental outbreak of nuclear war.

1972

January 3 U.S. Diplomacy in China (see Document 6.11). Gen. Alexander Haig exchanges views with the foreign minister to the People's Republic of China in Beijing. Henry Kissinger's deputy promises to pass along to the Chinese U.S. intelligence about the Soviet threat to China.

January 4 Chinese Diplomacy (see Document 6.12). Chinese premier Zhou Enlai meets with Chairman Mao Zedong to review Haig's comments and to consider an appropriate reply. Mao likens the U.S. diplomatic moves to "a cat feeling sorry for a mouse."

January 20 Nixon State of the Union. President Nixon says he will visit the People's Republic of China and the Soviet Union to explore the possibility of negotiating differences and thereby lowering international tensions.

February 21–28 Nixon in China. President Nixon arrives in China for a summit meeting with Chinese leaders. He meets with Mao and attends a banquet given by Zhou.

February 27 Shanghai Communiqué (see Document 6.13). President Nixon's momentous trip to China is capped with the issuance of a joint communiqué, describing not only their agreements but also their disagreements regarding Japan, Korea, Indochina, and Taiwan.

May 22 Moscow Summit. President Nixon arrives in Moscow to begin a summit meeting with Soviet chairman Leonid Brezhnev.

May 26 SALT I (see Document 6.16). This "interim agreement," reached at the conclusion of the first round of Strategic Arms Limitation Talks in Moscow, seeks to limit the arms race by imposing numerical as well as qualitative limits on ballistic missile launchers of all types. The treaty is acknowledged by both sides to be a holding action, with the Soviet Union continuing to enjoy an advantage in the total number ICBMs.

May 26 Anti-Ballistic Missile Treaty (see Document 6.17). Under the ABM Treaty, the superpowers agree to leave unchallenged each nation's ability to strike at the other with its nuclear arsenal, thus preserving the "balance of terror." The treaty permits each side only two local-area ABM deployments. (A protocol to the treaty, agreed to in 1976, reduces the agreed-to deployment areas to one apiece.)

May 29 Basic Principles Agreement. President Nixon and General Secretary Brezhnev sign an agreement with twelve principles intended to serve as a political framework for relations between the two superpowers. Among other things, they agree to avoid military confrontations and to respect each other's legitimate security interests.

June 1 Nixon to Joint Session of Congress. After signing the SALT I and ABM agreements, President Nixon gives a triumphal speech to a joint session of Congress. This is, he says, the "beginning of the end of the era which began in 1945."

June 17 Watergate. A clandestine unit operating out of the Committee to Re-Elect the President breaks into the Democratic National Committee in the Watergate complex in Washington, D.C.

June 23 "Smoking Gun" Tape. President Nixon uses claim of national security to mislead the FBI's investigation into the Watergate break-in.

October 4 Jackson Amendment. (see Document 6.18). Sen. Henry "Scoop" Jackson champions the rights of Soviet Jews to emigrate to Israel and attempts to force President Nixon to link Soviet policy on Jewish emigration to the relaxation of trade barriers between the United States and the Soviet Union, a key item in Nixon's agenda for détente.

October 18 U.S.-Soviet Trade. The United States and the Soviet Union sign a three-year trade agreement that grants the Soviet Union most-favored-nation (MFN) status, subject to U.S. Senate approval. The agreement is one aspect of President Nixon's plan to create a web of interlocking relations between the United States and the Soviet Union.

December 15–30 "Christmas Bombing." After Kissinger formally breaks off talks in Paris with North and South Vietnam, President Nixon unleashes "Linebacker II." The "Christmas Bombing" campaign, as the press christens the operation, is even more intense than the bombing of the North before the election.

1973

January 23 Peace in Vietnam (see Document 6.19). In a televised address to the nation, President Nixon announces "peace with honor" in Vietnam.

January 27 Paris Peace Accords. The agreement officially ends direct U.S. involvement in the Vietnam conflict.

February Senate Watergate Investigation. The Senate empanels a select committee to investigate the Watergate burglary and associated allegations of corruption in the Nixon campaign.

June 21 Nixon to Moscow. President Nixon, at a state dinner for the Soviet leaders, announces that he has accepted an invitation to visit the Soviet Union in 1974. The president says that he supports regularly scheduled summit meetings.

June 22 Prevention of Nuclear War. President Nixon and General Secretary Leonid Brezhnev sign an Agreement on the Prevention of Nuclear War. It is, in effect, a declaration of intentions by the United States and the Soviet Union to avoid creating situations conducive to conflict between the superpowers.

June 24 Brezhnev Address to the United States. General Secretary Brezhnev, in a televised address to the American people, discusses the improvement in Soviet-American relations and the importance of détente.

August 22 Kissinger as Secretary of State. President Nixon announces that Henry Kissinger will be nominated as secretary of state to replace William Rogers.

September 11 Coup in Chile. The military in Chile carry out a coup and seize control of the government. President Salvador Allende, a Marxist supported by Cuba and the Soviet Union, is allegedly killed opposing the coup, but others maintain he committed suicide. Supporters of Allende accuse the Central Intelligence Agency of being responsible for the coup and Allende's death.

September 28 Nixon-Gromyko Talks. Soviet foreign minister Andrei Gromyko meets with President Nixon in Washington, D.C. Among other things, the two leaders discuss the SALT II negotiations. President Nixon pledges to carry out his promise to have the Soviet Union granted MFN status.

October 6 Yom Kippur War. In a coordinated, surprise assault on Israel, Syria and Egypt initiate the conflict in the Golan Heights and the Sinai, respectively. The conflict lasts sixteen days.

October 25 Military Alert. President Nixon, in part to dissuade the Soviet Union from militarily intervening in the Middle East, issues a worldwide military alert of U.S. forces. The Soviets do not intervene.

October 26 Impeachment Crisis (see Document 6.21). In a television interview, the president speaks about the recently concluded Arab-Israeli War and answers questions regarding his possible impeachment.

November 7 War Powers Resolution (see Document 6.20). The apogee of congressional resistance to the "imperial presidency" is the passage over President Nixon's veto of an act intended to prohibit the president from taking the nation to war without adequate consultation with Congress.

1974

June 25 Nixon to Moscow. President Nixon, before leaving for Moscow, says he wants to achieve three objectives in his meetings with General Secretary Leonid Brezhnev: strengthen U.S.-Soviet relations, develop further areas of superpower cooperation, and make progress completing the SALT negotiations.

July 2 Nixon on Russian Television. President Nixon, in a radio and television address to the Russian people, says that despite U.S.-Soviet differences, the two nations are learning to cooperate on behalf of world peace.

July 3 ABM Treaty. The United States and the Soviet Union sign an agreement limiting each nation to one ABM site, rather than the two sites agreed to in 1972.

July 3 Threshold Test Ban Treaty. The United States and the Soviet Union sign a Threshold Test Ban Treaty (TTB) prohibiting underground nuclear explosions in excess of 150 kilotons.

July 3 Soviet-American Communiqué. President Nixon and General Secretary Brezhnev issue a communiqué at the close of their summit meeting. The leaders say that they are satisfied with the improved relations between the superpowers since 1972, they plan to continue to improve relations, and they hope recent improvements would prove "irreversible." The summit produces modest results, in part because it takes place during the Watergate scandal.

August 8 Nixon Resigns. President Nixon, in an address to the American people, announces his resignation effective at noon the following day. Nixon is succeeded by Vice President Gerald Ford.

1975

March 12 Stearman Memorandum (see Document 7.2). A memorandum, written by an NSC staffer to Secretary of State Henry Kissinger, warns of a coming North Vietnamese offensive but fails to anticipate the imminent collapse of South Vietnam.

April 12 Withdrawal from Cambodia. The United States airlifts its embassy staff from Phnom Penh, Cambodia, as the "dominoes" begin to fall.

April 21 Ford on Vietnam (see Document 7.3). President Ford answers questions in a prime-time interview on CBS, as the fall of Saigon draws near.

April 23 Ford and South Vietnam (see Document 7.4). President Ford declares in a speech delivered at Tulane University that the war is "finished as far as America is concerned."

April 29 Evacuation from Saigon (see Document 7.5). President Ford issues a statement on the U.S. withdrawal from Vietnam.

August 1 Helsinki Accord (see Document 7.1). President Ford and General Secretary Leonid Brezhnev (along with leaders of thirty-three other nations) acknowledge the legitimacy of Europe's postwar boundaries and agree to defend human rights in domestic affairs.

September 18 SALT II. President Ford and Secretary of State Kissinger meet with Soviet foreign minister Andrei Gromyko at the White House to discuss arms control issues. In a statement following the meeting, Kissinger says about 85 percent of the SALT II treaty has been completed.

November 11 Church Committee Report. (see Documents 7.6 and 7.7). A Senate committee interim report is released containing dramatic evidence of the CIA's attempts to use political assassination during the Cold War.

1976

January 19 Ford State of the Union Address. In his State of the Union address, President Ford asks for aid to forces fighting the Communists in Angola, a policy opposed by many members of Congress.

February 10 No Aid to Angola. President Ford signs a Defense Department appropriation bill that prohibits U.S. aid to Angolan rebels fighting the Soviet-backed regime.

February 18 Executive Order 11905 (see Document 7.9). In response to politically damaging reports published by the Church Committee, President Ford signs an executive order that forbids participation of U.S. government employees in political assassination.

April Mayaguez Incident (see Document 7.10). President Ford answers questions about decisions he made following the seizure of an American merchant ship by Cambodian forces the previous spring.

April 26 Church Committee Report. (see Document 7.8). A Senate committee report discloses that domestic intelligence operations conducted by the CIA and FBI during the Cold War have often violated the constitutional rights of Americans.

October 6 Presidential Debate (see Document 7.12). During his second debate with former Georgia Democratic governor Jimmy Carter, President Ford rhetorically "liberates" Romania and Poland from Soviet hegemony.

November 2 1976 Presidential Election. Challenger Carter defeats incumbent Ford in a very close election.

December 1 Team "B" Report. (see Document 7.11). The report of Team "B," an assessment of the CIA's analysis of the Soviet threat that was leaked to the press in October, is published. The classified report argues that the CIA has consistently underestimated the Soviet threat and disparages détente policy and ongoing SALT negotiations.

1977

January 12 Ford State of the Union Address. President Ford, in his State of the Union address, emphasizes the need to remain militarily strong to meet the Soviet challenge. He supports the development of the Trident submarine, the B-1 bomber, and survivable ICBMs.

January 21 Draft Evader Pardon. President Carter issues a presidential pardon to approximately 100,000 Vietnam War draft evaders. He also condemns the war as immoral and unnecessary.

January 26 Troop Withdrawal from South Korea. Carrying out a campaign promise, President Carter orders the withdrawal of U.S. Army combat forces from South Korea (although defensive forces remain) despite heavy protest by both military and civilian defense leaders.

February 5 Carter and Sakharov (see Document 8.1). President Carter sends a telegram to Soviet nuclear physicist and dissident Andrei Sakharov, assuring him that the United States will continue to support human rights at home and abroad, as well as the release of prisoners of conscience. Soviet authorities react strongly, terming it "sabotage" from the West.

March 17 President Carter at the UN. In a speech to the UN, the president announces that he intends to prioritize human rights in U.S. foreign policy.

May 9 Nixon on Presidential Power (see Document 6.22). In a televised interview with David Frost, former president Nixon asserts that the actions that forced his resignation were justified by the "war at home" over the war abroad.

May 22 Carter at Notre Dame (see Document 8.2). In a commencement address, President Carter explains his foreign policy. He reaffirms the U.S. commitment to human rights and says the United States is "now free of that inordinate fear of communism" that characterized American policy in the past.

June 30 President Carter Announces Opposition to the B-1 Bomber. The president announces his opposition to a major U.S. defense initiative, and he proposes to zero-out funding. Congress agrees to accept elimination of development funding.

October 4 Carter at the UN. President Carter says the superpowers are close to completing the SALT II treaty. He expresses support for a 50 percent reduction in nuclear weapons and a comprehensive test ban treaty.

December 15 Carter on Human Rights. President Carter says he thinks that the 1948 Universal Declaration of Human Rights permits nations to criticize human rights abuses in other nations. He says the criticism does not mean these nations are enemies.

1978

January 12 Carter and the Soviet Union. President Carter says unlike the Soviet Union, the United States will not send arms to any of the nations involved in the conflict in the Horn of Africa. He says the United States will do whatever it can to help resolve the conflict between Somalia and Ethiopia, and he calls on the Soviet Union and Cuba to stop sending arms and personnel to the region.

January 19 Carter State of the Union Address. President Carter reaffirms his commitment to human rights, claiming that America has regained a moral basis for its foreign policy. He expects the SALT II treaty to be completed in 1978, and he expresses the wish to negotiate a comprehensive nuclear test ban treaty with the Soviet Union.

March 2 Carter on Soviet Policy in Africa. President Carter says Soviet activities in the Horn of Africa will not be linked to negotiations for a SALT II treaty. The president says he has been assured by Foreign Minister Andrei Gromyko that Ethiopian troops, supplied by the Soviet Union, will not cross the border to fight in Somalia.

May 5 Carter Critical of the Soviets. President Carter accuses the Soviet Union of interfering in the internal affairs of the African nations. He is particularly critical of Soviet willingness to ship arms to African nations involved in internal or external conflicts.

May 30 Carter to NATO. President Carter, in a speech to the heads of state attending the North Atlantic Council meeting in Washington, says the Soviet Union and its Warsaw Pact allies are continuing to expand their military might beyond their legitimate security requirements. He says the United States will use whatever force is necessary, including nuclear weapons, to defend the NATO nations.

June 7 Carter on Relations with the Soviets (see Document 8.3). President Carter, in a commencement address to the United States Naval Academy, discusses U.S.-Soviet relations and the need for a policy of détente. He says the Soviets defined détente in a manner that exacerbates relations between the superpowers.

November 19 Brezhnev Warning. General Secretary Leonid Brezhnev, in response to a question from a *Pravda* reporter, warns the United States not to intervene in Iran. The Soviet leader says that any military intervention would impinge on the security interests of the Soviet Union.

December 15 U.S.-China Recognition. In what is considered a surprise statement, President Carter announces that the United States and the People's Republic of China have agreed to establish diplomatic relations effective January 1, 1979.

1979

January 1 U.S. Relations with China (see Document 8.4). President Carter celebrates the landmark U.S. decision to institute normal diplomatic relations with the People's Republic of China.

January 17 Carter on Triangular Diplomacy. President Carter says he does not plan to use improved relations with the People's Republic of China against the Soviet Union. He adds that if U.S.-Soviet relations improve, he will not use that against China.

January 23 Carter State of the Union Address. President Carter, in his State of the Union address, opines that the U.S. military might help to strengthen world peace. He says he supports modernizing NATO's military forces and reaffirms the U.S. commitment to the SALT process, which he does not think will weaken the nation's nuclear capabilities. The president also says he would like General Secretary Leonid Brezhnev to visit the United States.

February 1 Joint Communiqué. Deng Xiaoping and President Carter issue a joint communiqué at the close of their summit meeting in Washington, D.C. The two sides sign a number of agreements pertaining to science, technology, and culture. Carter accepts an invitation to visit the People's Republic of China.

March 17 or 18 Soviet-Afghan Relations (see Document 8.7). Soviet Premier Alexei Kosygin speaks on the telephone with the Afghan prime minister, Nur Mohammed Taraki, about the Islamic rebellion against which Taraki's government is struggling. The Soviet premier's line of questioning reveals a serious ignorance of conditions in one of the world's most remote, undeveloped nations.

April 25 Carter and SALT. President Carter, in a speech to the American Newspaper Publishers Association, says the Senate's rejection of the SALT II treaty could increase U.S.-Soviet tensions and might cause the Soviet Union to adopt a more aggressive foreign policy.

May 9 SALT Treaty Completed. Secretary of State Cyrus Vance and Secretary of Defense Harold Brown announce that the United States and the Soviet Union have completed the SALT II treaty. The agreement is to last for ten years once it is ratified by the U.S. Senate.

June 18 SALT II Treaty (see Document 8.5). President Carter and General Secretary Brezhnev sign a treaty addressing all strategic launch platforms for nuclear weapons, including bombers, which were not included in SALT I. The ceilings set ensure that both sides could have no more than 2,400 ICBMs, submarine-launched ballistic missiles (SLBMs), and strategic bombers.

July 19 Nicaragua. The government of Anastasio Somoza in Nicaragua is overthrown by the Sandinistas, who organize a government similar to the one in Cuba. Nicaragua's Marxist policies become a major source of tension in Soviet-American relations.

September 7 Soviet Troops in Cuba. President Carter, in remarks to reporters, confirms the presence of a Soviet combat unit in Cuba and terms its presence unacceptable. The president says the Soviet troops might have been in Cuba "for quite a few years." These troops had been there since 1962—a fact not mentioned in the official statement. The information stalls U.S. Senate debate on the SALT II Treaty.

September 7 Harder Line with the Soviets. President Carter approves a basing plan for the controversial MX missile.

October 1 Carter on Troops in Cuba. President Carter, in an address to the nation, declares that the presence of Soviet troops in Cuba is not going to lead to a war or to a major superpower confrontation. He says the United States would assist any nation threatened by Soviet or Cuban troops.

November 4 U.S. Hostages Seizure. With the deposed Iranian Shah's medical condition deteriorating, President Carter allows him entry into the United States for medical treatment. Iranian radicals, vying for power within the not-yet-stable environment of postrevolution Iran, seize the opportunity and take hostage sixty-three Americans at the U.S. Embassy in Tehran. The event and ensuing crisis draw the president's attention away from the Soviets and, by some estimates, gives strength to the Soviet decision to invade Afghanistan that December.

December 12 NATO Foreign Ministers' Agreement to Deploy U.S. Cruise Missiles (see Document 8.6). The United States gains agreement among it European allies regarding deployment of new nuclear missiles.

December 12 Carter on Foreign Policy. President Carter says that in real terms Soviet defense spending has been increasing for twenty years while U.S. spending declined from 1968 to 1976. The president says the United States is now embarking on a program to meet the Soviet military challenge.

December 25 Soviet Invasion of Afghanistan. The Soviet Union begins its invasion of Afghanistan. The State Department calls on the international community to condemn the Soviet aggression.

December 28 Carter and Afghanistan. President Carter issues a statement condemning the Soviet Union for its "gross interference" in Afghanistan's internal affairs. He labels the Soviet intervention a "blatant violation" of international standards.

December 31 Carter on ABC News (see Document 8.8). In an interview with ABC News, President Carter speaks candidly of his surprise and horror at the Soviet move into Afghanistan, providing ammunition to his critics, who had long assailed the president for his alleged naïvety.

1980

January 3 SALT II. The White House announces that President Carter has asked Senate leaders to delay discussions on the ratification of the SALT II treaty because of the Soviet invasion of Afghanistan.

January 4 U.S. Response to Soviet Invasion of Afghanistan. The Soviet invasion of Afghanistan creates a crisis in U.S.-Soviet relations.

January 8 Carter and Afghanistan. President Carter, in comments to members of Congress, says the Soviet invasion of Afghanistan is the greatest threat to peace since World War II.

January 20 Carter and the Olympics. President Carter, in a letter to Robert Kane, president of the U.S. Olympic Committee, suggests that if Soviet troops remain in Afghanistan, the Olympics scheduled to take place in Moscow should be moved to another site or be cancelled.

January 23 Carter and Sakharov (see Document 8.11). The White House issues a statement denouncing the decision of the Soviet government on January 22 to send Soviet nuclear physicist and dissident Andrei Sakharov and his wife into internal exile.

January 23 Carter Doctrine (see Document 8.9). President Carter, in his State of the Union address, enunciates the Carter Doctrine. He says the United States will regard any effort by an outside power to gain control of the Persian Gulf region "as an assault on the vital interests of the United States, and such an assault will be repelled by any means necessary, including military force."

January 24 KGB on Sakharov (see Document 8.12). Yuri Andropov, chief of the KGB (the Soviet state security agency), analyzes the Western response to Sakharov's punishment in a report to the Central Committee of the Communist Party.

January 27 Soviet Afghanistan Commission Report to Communist Party (see Document 8.10). KGB chief Andropov, Soviet foreign minister Andrei Gromyko, and the other members of a special ad hoc committee release a report containing an optimistic outlook on combating the guerilla insurgency the Soviets face in Afghanistan.

February 13 Carter on Foreign Policy. President Carter says the Soviet invasion of Afghanistan creates a dangerous situation because the country is located in an area vital to the transportation of oil. The president is confident that the United States' military capabilities are sufficient to deal with any Soviet military threat.

February 15 Carter on Selective Service (see Document 8.13). President Carter defends his decision to resume Selective Service registration in a question-and-answer session with student leaders.

February 19 Carter on Foreign Policy. President Carter, in an address to the American Legion, reviews the steps he has taken to improve U.S. military might. He calls for an increase in defense spending, accelerated development of cruise missiles, the building of the MX missile and the Trident submarine, and the strengthening of NATO.

February 26 Carter on Foreign Policy. President Carter says the United States is prepared to help Turkey, Iran, and Pakistan if they are attacked by the Soviet Union.

March 5 Carter and Schmidt. President Carter and Chancellor Helmut Schmidt of the Federal Republic of Germany, at the conclusion of their meeting in Washington, D.C., issue a joint statement condemning the Soviet Union for invading Afghanistan. They agree that participation in the summer Olympics in Moscow will be unacceptable while Soviet forces are in Afghanistan.

April 13 Carter and Afghanistan. President Carter, in response to a question at a news conference, says he decided to react to the Soviet invasion of Afghanistan in economic and political terms because those actions, as well as those of other nations, will eventually result in a Soviet withdrawal from Afghanistan.

May 29 U.S. Army on Carter's Plan (see Document 8.14). At a congressional hearing, Army Chief of Staff Gen. Edward Meyer declares the United States has a "hollow army" and is unprepared for war. The general calls for bigger and faster improvements than are laid out in President Carter's plan.

August 5 Presidential Directive 59. The *New York Times* reports that President Carter has signed Presidential Directive 59, which lists targets to be hit in the Soviet Union in case of a nuclear war and, in effect, gives the president more targeting options than he had in the past.

October 28 Carter-Reagan Debate (see Document 8.15). President Carter and former Republican California governor Ronald Reagan offer contrasting perspectives on U.S. policy for the Cold War.

1981

January 16 Carter State of the Union Address. President Carter says that the Soviet Union now realizes it will pay a price for its aggression in Afghanistan.

March 31 Reagan Assassination Attempt. President Reagan and three others are wounded by John Hinckley Jr. outside a Washington, D.C., hotel.

December 1 CIA Training for Counter-Communist Rebels in Central America (see Document 9.1). The president approves covert action to overthrow a Communist government in Central America.

December 17 Reagan on Poland. President Reagan says that the denial of human rights in Poland and the government's reliance on coercive power would not take place without Soviet support.

December 23 Poland (see Document 9.2). President Reagan announces sanctions on Poland because of the government's decision to impose martial law. The president blames the Soviets for the imposition of martial law in Poland and orders sanctions imposed on the Soviet Union a week later.

1982

January 11 NATO and Poland (see Document 9.3). NATO members condemn Soviet action in Poland but decline to join the embargo against Soviet pipeline construction.

January 26 Reagan State of the Union Address. President Reagan defends the sanctions imposed by the United States on Poland and the Soviet Union.

(no date) NATO and Warsaw Pact Force Comparisons, 1982–1983 (see Document 9.4). The Communist countries of the Warsaw Pact have long enjoyed numerical superiority in conventional forces, relative to those of the NATO's European members.

March 16 Missile Deployment. The White House rejects the Soviet-proposed moratorium on medium-range missiles west of the Ural Mountains. The moratorium would permit the Soviet Union to continue deploying SS-20 missiles east of the Ural Mountains, and the NATO nations would be threatened by the SS-20s already deployed west of the mountains.

March 31 Arms Control. President Reagan says the United States would be ready to negotiate with the Soviet Union for strategic arms reductions during the summer. The president, however, rejects the idea of a nuclear freeze. He supports force reductions to equal levels.

April 17 Nuclear Weapons. President Reagan says the United States has to increase its military capabilities to balance the Soviet Union.

May 13 Nuclear First Use. President Reagan rejects the idea of a "no first strike" pledge. He also would like to reduce the large land-based strategic missiles in the Soviet arsenal because they are the most destabilizing weapons.

May 20 National Security Strategy (see Document 9.5). The United States seeks to expand its conventional forces, reach out increasingly to its allies, and prepare to fight a "protracted nuclear conflict."

June 8 Reagan at Westminster (see Document 9.6). Communism will be placed on "the ash heap of history," proclaims President Reagan in his address to the British Parliament, pointing out that no Communist regime in Eastern Europe since coming to power thirty years ago has permitted free elections. He asks Western nations to promote democratic ideals and to build democratic infrastructures. He advocates a "crusade for freedom" and says the Russian people are not immune to the demands for greater freedom.

June 17 Reagan and Disarmament. President Reagan, in an address to the UN General Assembly, accuses the Soviet Union of a massive military buildup during the decade of détente, manipulating the peace movement in the West, and preventing the development of a peace movement within the Soviet Union. He advocates a stage reduction in strategic weapons and a common ceiling of 900,000 troops for the NATO and the Warsaw Pact nations.

July 1 Reagan on Arms Control. President Reagan says the Soviet Union agreed to the intermediate-range nuclear forces (INF) negations in November 1981 only because the United States intends to deploy Pershing II and cruise missiles to match the Soviets' SS-20s.

October 8 Solidarity Outlawed. The Polish government outlaws Solidarity, the Polish labor union led by Lech Walesa. President Reagan denounces the decision and says he will seek to revoke Poland's MFN status.

November 10 Death of Brezhnev. General Secretary Leonid Brezhnev dies; he is succeeded by Yuri Andropov.

December 8 Boland Amendment. Congress restricts U.S. support for anti-Communist rebels in Central America.

1983

January 17 Strategy for the Cold War (see Document 9.7). The Reagan administration develops a blueprint for battling the Soviet Union.

January 25 Reagan State of the Union Address. President Reagan says the United States has strengthened its military capabilities and is using diplomatic initiatives to resolve outstanding problems. He hopes the new Soviet leadership will demonstrate its willingness for solutions to common problems. However, General Secretary Yuri Andropov is as critical of Reagan's policies as was his predecessor, Leonid Brezhnev.

February 18 Reagan on Foreign Policy. President Reagan says that one of his foreign policy goals is to publicize unsavory aspects of Soviet policy; he mentions the use of forced labor for the building of the Soviet gas pipeline, the use of chemical warfare in Kampuchea, and repressive Soviet policies in Poland.

February 22 Reagan on Foreign Policy. President Reagan says a major Soviet foreign policy objective is to drive a wedge between the United States and its European allies by using the Soviet nuclear arsenal to spread insecurity in NATO.

March 8 "Evil Empire" Speech (see Document 9.8). President Reagan refers to the Soviet Union as the "evil empire" and describes Soviet communism as the "focus of evil" in the world.

March 23 Strategic Defense Initiative (see Document 9.9). President Reagan decides to try to develop a system of defense to counter the Soviet missile threat. This program, officially known as the Strategic Defense Initiative (SDI) and unofficially as "Star Wars," becomes a major source of tension between the superpowers.

May 4 Nuclear Freeze Resolution in Congress (see Document 9.10). The peace movement reaches the U.S. House of Representatives, which passes a resolution in favor of a nuclear freeze.

May 5 Reagan and the Nuclear Freeze. President Reagan, in response to the House's resolution, expresses his opposition to a nuclear freeze. He favors reducing arms rather than maintaining them at the existing high levels.

May 17 Soviets and SALT. President Reagan says the Soviets may have tested a new ICBM and, if so, they are in violation of SALT II.

June 8 Reagan and START. President Reagan, on the day the Strategic Arms Reduction Treaty (START) talks resume in Geneva, says the U.S. goal is to reduce ICBMs by one-third. The president wants a more stable strategic balance at reduced force levels.

September 1 Korean Airliner Downed. The Soviet Union shoots down a Korean passenger plane in Soviet airspace, killing 269 people. Two days later, President Reagan says the Soviet Union owes the world an explanation and an apology.

September 26 Reagan at the UN. President Reagan, in his address to the UN General Assembly, says the Soviets increasingly resort to violence for political gains. He criticizes the Soviet Union for shooting down the Korean airliner, for violating the 1975 Helsinki Final Act, and for using chemical weapons in Afghanistan.

October 3 Reagan and Democracy. President Reagan says a willingness to speak out against the evils of communism helps make U.S. foreign policy more effective. He adds that a democratic revolution is under way around the world.

October 25 Grenada. A U.S. military force invades Grenada with forces from members of the Organization of Eastern Caribbean States (OECS). President Reagan says the intervention is necessary to protect the Americans in Grenada and to restore democracy.

November 2–11 ABLE ARCHER 83. The NATO allies conduct a full-scale simulated release of nuclear weapons. Such activity and KGB intelligence errors lead the Soviet Union to believe that the allies are preparing for an attack. Tensions finally ease when the drill ends ten days later.

November 22–23 INF Deployment. The West German parliament approves Pershing II missile deployments on November 22. The first U.S. INF missiles arrive in Europe the next day, and the Soviet delegation walks out of the INF negotiations in Geneva. The United States offers to resume the talks when the Soviets are willing to return.

1984

January 16 Reagan and Arms Control (see Document 9.11). President Reagan says the harsh rhetoric coming out of the Soviet Union is the result of United States recently strengthening its military posture.

January 23 Soviet Treaty Violations. President Reagan sends Congress a list of Soviet violations of arms control treaties. The message is in keeping with the fiscal year 1984 Arms Control and Disarmament Act passed by Congress requiring the president to issue such a report.

February 6 Reagan on Foreign Policy. President Reagan declares that a willingness to draw distinctions between freedom and communism "is the moral center of our foreign policy."

February 10 Death of Andropov. General Secretary Yuri Andropov dies; he is succeeded by Konstantin Chernenko.

March 27 Reagan and Arms Control. President Reagan points out that since the signing of SALT I in 1972, the Soviets have added 7,950 strategic nuclear warheads to their arsenal.

April 6 Reagan on Foreign Policy. President Reagan says the Soviet Union would have little incentive to negotiate with the United States if the 1979 dual-track decision is abandoned, the production of the MX missile cancelled, and a nuclear freeze implemented.

April 26 China Summit. President Reagan arrives in People's Republic of China for a six-day visit.

April 28 Reagan on China Visit. President Reagan says he repeatedly told the Chinese leaders that differences between the United States and China are less important than their common interests. He says China is opposing Soviet aggression, thus contributing to peace.

May 9 Reagan and Central America. President Reagan speaks about efforts to bring freedom and economic well-being to the nations of Central America despite the policies of Cuba, Nicaragua, and the Soviet Union to promote and support communism.

August 3 Sanctions on Poland. The White House announces that some sanctions imposed on Poland in 1981 are being lifted because the Polish government released and granted amnesty to political prisoners in an effort to bring order and stability.

September 24 Reagan at the UN. President Reagan, in an address to the UN General Assembly, says the United States has regained its military strength and is now ready for negotiations with the Soviet Union.

September 28 Reagan and Gromyko. President Reagan meets with Soviet foreign minister Andrei Gromyko in Washington. The two leaders discuss a broad range of issues, including resuming suspended arms control talks. After the meeting, Gromyko says he does not see any change in U.S. foreign policies.

October 10 Soviet Treaty Violations. President Reagan sends Congress a report entitled "A Quarter Century of Soviet Compliance Practices under Arms Control Commitments: 1958–1983." The report, in effect a record of Soviet treaty violations and alleged violations, is prepared by the General Advisory Committee on Arms Control and Disarmament, a White House advisory panel.

November 28 Restrictive Doctrine on the Use of Force (see Document 9.12). Secretary of Defense Casper Weinberger sets the rules for use of force to limit military involvement and prevent situations like Vietnam.

1985

March 11 Death of Chernenko. General Secretary Konstantin Chernenko dies; he is succeeded by Mikhail Gorbachev.

April 15 Reagan and Nicaragua. President Reagan calls on Congress to approve aid for the Contras fighting the Sandinista government in Nicaragua. He accuses the Nicaraguan government of atrocities that he says were the "natural expression" of a Communist regime.

July 8 Reagan on Terrorism. President Reagan identifies Cuba, Iran, Libya, Nicaragua, and North Korea as countries supporting and sponsoring international terrorism. He says the United States would not tolerate attacks "from outlaw states run by the strangest collection of misfits, loony tunes, and squalid criminals since the advent of the Third Reich." He notes the close ties of all the states sponsoring terrorism to the Soviet Union.

October 24 Reagan at the UN. President Reagan, in an address to the UN General Assembly, calls on the Soviet Union to help resolve regional conflicts. The president links improved U.S.-Soviet relations to the resolution of regional conflicts.

November 18 Gorbachev and Reagan. President Reagan meets with Gorbachev in Geneva, Switzerland.

November 21 U.S.-Soviet Statement. The United States and the Soviet Union issue a joint statement emphasizing that "a nuclear war cannot be won and must never be fought."

November 21 Reagan on the Summit. President Reagan addresses a joint session of Congress on the results of his summit meeting with Gorbachev. Gorbachev agrees to visit the United States in 1986, and Reagan accepts an invitation to visit the Soviet Union in 1987.

November 23 Reagan on SDI. President Reagan says a major Soviet goal at the Geneva summit is to get the United States to abandon SDI. The president says he made it clear to Gorbachev that the United States would continue SDI research.

December 23 Soviet Treaty Violations. President Reagan, as required by law, sends Congress a memorandum on "Soviet Noncompliance with Arms Control Agreements." The president says the evidence supports the conclusion that "there is a pattern of Soviet noncompliance."

1986

February 4 Reagan State of the Union Address. President Reagan expresses support for the insurgents fighting Communist regimes in Afghanistan, Angola, Cambodia, and Nicaragua. He also expresses the hope that relations with the Soviet Union would improve as a result of General Secretary Mikhail Gorbachev's forthcoming visit to the United States.

March 14 Reagan and Regional Conflicts. President Reagan, in a message to Congress, says Soviet involvement in regional conflicts in the 1970s "produced victims on a scale unknown since the genocides of Hitler and Stalin."

March 29 Reagan on Arms Control. The White House announces the arms control proposals made by Gorbachev that same day. President Reagan repeats proposals he had made in the past regarding verification measures for the Threshold Test Ban treaty and the Peaceful Nuclear Explosion treaty, and he rejects Gorbachev's proposal for another nuclear test ban moratorium.

April 14 U.S. Attack on Libya. President Reagan says that U.S. warplanes attacked Libya a few hours earlier in retaliation for its alleged attack against U.S. military personnel in Berlin on April 5.

April 15 Soviets Cancel Meeting. The Soviet Union condemns the bombing of Libya, accusing the United States of engaging in "aircraft-carrier diplomacy." As a sign of their displeasure, the Soviets cancel the scheduled May 14 meeting between Soviet foreign minister Eduard Shevardnadze and U.S. secretary of state George Shultz.

April 28 Nuclear Accident. The Soviet government announces that a nuclear accident has occurred at a power plant in Chernobyl, located in the Ukraine.

May 14 Reaction to Chernobyl. President Reagan issues a statement on the Chernobyl accident, denying the Soviet allegation that the United States and allied nations are exploiting the accident by spreading inaccurate information. The president criticizes the Soviet Union for its failure to make more information available to the media.

July 25 Gorbachev and Reagan. President Reagan, in a letter to Gorbachev, suggests that the United States and the Soviet Union should share the benefits of SDI research and should negotiate an agreement eliminating all offensive ballistic missiles. The president also suggests that the superpowers agree to abide by the terms of the ABM treaty for seven-and-a-half more years. Gorbachev favors extending the ABM treaty for fifteen years and ties the proposal to reductions of long-range missiles.

August 5 Arms Control. President Reagan sends Congress a list of arms control treaty violations committed by the Soviet Union. The president reiterates his policy, announced on May 27, of no longer abiding by SALT II.

October 13 Reagan on Reykjavik. President Reagan evaluates his meeting with Gorbachev at Reykjavik. The president emphasizes differences between the United States and the Soviet Union that result from Reagan's commitment to SDI.

October 19–22 Diplomats Ousted. The Soviet Union expels fifteen American diplomats in retaliation for the American ouster of eighty Soviet diplomats and also calls back the remaining 260 Russians working at the U.S. embassy.

November 28 SALT II Exceeded. The United States exceeds the limits imposed by SALT II by deploying a B-52 bomber capable of carrying cruise missiles.

1987

February 19 Sanctions Lifted against Poland. The U.S. government lifts sanctions against Poland that have been in place since 1982.

March 4 Reagan and the Iran-Contra Affair (see Document 9.13). President Reagan accepts limited responsibility for the Iran-Contra affair and vows to implement the recommendations of the investigative commission.

April 6 Reagan and the Soviet Union. President Reagan insists that the Soviet Union comply with the provisions of the 1975 Helsinki Final Act. He says if the Soviet Union liberalized its society, the Soviet economy would improve, and the Soviet people could then enjoy a better life.

June 12 Reagan in Berlin (see Document 9.14). President Reagan calls on General Secretary Mikhail Gorbachev to tear down the Berlin Wall.

September 15 Nuclear Risk Reduction Centers. President Reagan announces that the United States and the Soviet Union signed a treaty to establish nuclear risk reduction centers in Washington and Moscow. The purpose of the centers is to avoid conflicts that might result from accidents, misinterpretations, or miscalculations.

September 16 Reagan on Foreign Policy. President Reagan rejects the idea of a moral equivalency between the United States and the Soviet Union. He asserts there could be no moral equivalency between democratic and totalitarian regimes.

December 8 Gorbachev to Washington. President Reagan welcomes Gorbachev to Washington, D.C. Reagan hopes the meeting with Gorbachev will result in improved relations and a greater degree of cooperation in resolving issues such as arms control, human rights, and regional conflicts. Gorbachev hopes the INF treaty will lead to other agreements between the superpowers and to diminishing tensions.

December 8 INF Treaty (see Document 9.15). The United States and the Soviet Union sign the INF treaty eliminating intermediate-range missiles.

December 10 Reagan on the Summit. President Reagan labels the meeting a "clear summit" and he says the INF treaty is the most important step since World War II to halt the arms race.

1988

April 14 Afghanistan Agreement. The United States and the Soviet Union sign an agreement refraining from interfering in the internal affairs of Afghanistan and Pakistan.

May 29 Reagan and Gorbachev. President Reagan meets with General Secretary Mikhail Gorbachev in Moscow.

May 30 Reagan Meets Religious Leaders. President Reagan, in a talk to religious leaders at the Danilov Monastery in Moscow, says he hopes that soon all the Soviet people will enjoy freedom of religion. In a separate meeting with a number of dissidents at the Spaso House in Moscow, Reagan expresses support for their efforts to promote human rights and assures them of the support of the American people.

May 31 Reagan at Moscow State University. President Reagan speaks about the value of freedom and its links to other aspects of life. He says that he and Gorbachev want to have student exchange programs involving thousands of students a year, but the president would also like to see individuals have the right to travel free from government restrictions.

June 1 U.S.-Soviet Joint Statement. The United States and the Soviet Union, at the conclusion of the Moscow summit meeting, issue a joint statement reviewing progress that was made and the problems that remained on the four major agenda items of arms control, human rights, regional problems, and bilateral issues.

June 1 Reagan and the Soviet Union. President Reagan says that U.S.-Soviet relations are quite different now compared with 1981. He attributes the change to the leadership of Gorbachev and the trust that has developed.

August 27 Reagan on Foreign Policy. President Reagan, in a radio address, reviews policy events. He welcomes the cease-fire in the Iran-Iraq War, the withdrawal of half the Soviet forces from Afghanistan, and the announcement of Vietnam to withdraw its forces from Cambodia.

September 26 Reagan at the UN. President Reagan, in an address to the UN General Assembly, speaks about changes taking place in Communist nations and the growing commitment of nations to peace and freedom. He welcomes the improvement in U.S.-Soviet relations and says that if reforms in the Soviet Union continue, there would be further improvement.

November 8 Bush Elected. Vice President George Bush, the Republican candidate for president, defeats his Democratic opponent, Massachusetts governor Michael Dukakis.

December 3 Reagan on Foreign Policy. President Reagan reviews U.S.-Soviet relations since he took office. He is generally optimistic about the superpower relationship, but he is looking forward to the Berlin Wall being torn down and the works of Alexandr Solzhenitsyn being published in the Soviet Union.

December 7 Bush and Reagan Meet Gorbachev. Gorbachev meets with President Reagan and President-elect Bush. The meeting demonstrates continuity in U.S.-Soviet relations.

December 7 Reagan on Foreign Policy. President Reagan comments on his meeting earlier in the day with Gorbachev. The two leaders agree that there has been substantial improvement in U.S.-Soviet relations since the first summit meeting in Geneva in 1985.

December 7 Gorbachev and Eastern Europe (see Document 9.16). Gorbachev, in a speech before the UN General Assembly, unilaterally renounces the Brezhnev Doctrine, allowing Eastern Europe to tread its own political path.

December 22 Angola and Cuba. President Reagan welcomes the signing of the agreement between Angola and Cuba calling for the withdrawal of Cuban troops to be completed by July 1, 1991.

December 27–28 Soviet Politburo View on Bush (see Document 10.1). The Politburo concludes that the policy of President-elect Bush will be slow and cautious, unless there is a threat to American prestige. The Soviet Union will act first and present Bush with the choice of either acquiescing to or joining the Soviet Union in remaking the superpower relationship.

1989

February 15 Bush and Afghanistan. President Bush, on the day after the withdrawal of all Soviet troops from Afghanistan, calls on the Soviet Union to stop interfering in Afghanistan's internal affairs

February 15 Bush and China. President Bush, at a reception on the first day of a two-day visit to China, says he welcomes improved relations between China and the Soviet Union, and he suggests that their rapprochement could lead to a resolution of the Cambodia problem and greater stability on the Korean peninsula.

May 13 Baltic States Independence Movements. Representatives of Estonia, Lithuania, and Latvia meet in Tallin to elect the Baltic People's Deputies and to coordinate their efforts for economic independence from the Soviet Union.

May 31 Bush Speech in Germany. In a major speech in the Federal Republic of Germany, Bush welcomes General Secretary Mikhail Gorbachev's foreign policy initiatives but insists that more has to be done. Specifically, he proposes strengthening the Helsinki process to promote human rights in Eastern Europe and the Soviet Union; tearing down the Berlin Wall; cooperating to address environmental dangers; and moving toward demilitarization of Europe.

June 4 Tiananmen Square Massacre. The Chinese People's Liberation Army, under orders from the government, enters Tiananmen Square in Beijing to suppress the students, intellectuals, and labor activists who, protesting for greater freedom, have occupied the square since May 13, 1989. Although images from the violence, which killed as many as 3,000 civilians, prompt an outcry from Congress and the American public, Bush responds with limited public condemnation of the People's Republic of China but dispatches his national security adviser on a top-secret mission to China.

June 4 Elections in Poland. Poland holds its first free elections since the Communists came to power. The candidates supported by Solidarity, the Polish trade union, win a decisive victory.

September 10 Hungary and Austria. Hungary opens its borders with Austria, allowing tens of thousands of East Germans to enter West Germany via Hungary and Austria. East Germany seeks to close its borders but encounters widespread protest. Gorbachev, concerned with internal affairs, declares that the Soviet government has no say in the policies of the German Democratic Republic.

September 22 Bush National Security Directive 23 (Document 10.2). President Bush signs National Security Directive 23, which addresses the changes taking place in the Soviet Union yet recognizes that the threat from the Soviet Union is still undiminished. The document predicts final transformation of the Soviet Union will take place only after decades, and the United States must not let down its guard in testing the Soviet Union's willingness to open up to more changes.

October 18 Honecker Resigns. Erick Honecker, the Communist leader of the German Democratic Republic for eighteen years and an opponent of Gorbachev's reforms, is forced to resign. He is replaced by Egon Krenz.

October 23 Bush and Kohl (see Document 10.3). President Bush and German Chancellor Helmut Kohl discuss the political changes in Hungary, Poland, and East Germany. Although the situation in East Germany would depend on the actions of its new leader, Egon Krenz, President Bush and Kohl agree that reunification of East and West Germany should mean that the German Democratic Republic will integrate into the West.

November 1 Gorbachev and Krenz (see Document 10.4). Gorbachev meets with East German leader Krenz to discuss the challenge of preventing reunification of West and East Germany, with Gorbachev assuring Krenz of the improbability of this event.

November 9 Fall of the Berlin Wall (see Document 10.5). The German Democratic Republic opens the Berlin Wall and allows thousands of East Germans to travel freely to West Germany. President Bush, at a question-and-answer session with reporters, welcomes the decision of the East German government.

November 11 Zhivkov Resignation. Todor Zhivkov, the leader of Bulgaria since 1954, resigns as a result of mass protests against Communist rule. Gorbachev sends a congratulatory message to Petar Mladenov, Zhivkov's successor.

December 2–3 Malta Summit (see Document 10.6). President Bush and Gorbachev meet for a superpower summit on the *Maxim Gorky* off the coast of Malta and hold a joint press conference. The leaders respond to questions related to the apparent end of Cold War.

December 4 Bush on Foreign Policy. President Bush, in an address to the NATO ministers representing the member nations in Brussels, says the division of Europe is coming to an end, thus bringing about the outcome the United States has sought since 1945. He says the NATO nations should take the lead in promoting freedom and reforms throughout Europe.

December 10 Husak Resignation. President Gustav Husak of Czechoslovakia resigns after being forced to accept a cabinet with a non-Communist majority.

December 27 Demise of Romanian Leader. *Pravda* reports that Romanian president Nicolae Ceausescu and his wife were executed after having been found guilty of "crimes against the Romanian people and Romania."

December 29 New Czech Leader. President Bush sends a message of congratulations to Vaclav Havel, author and human rights activist, on his election as president of Czechoslovakia.

1990

January 31 Bush State of the Union Address. President Bush praises the improved relations with the Soviet Union and progress toward democratization. He proposes deep reductions in conventional force levels in Europe by both sides.

February 7 Bush on Containment. President Bush, in a speech in California, says it took nearly fifty years to vindicate the strategy of containing the Soviet Union. He says the United States is taking steps to ensure a lasting peace now that the Cold War is coming to an end and the Soviet system is undergoing change.

February 12 Bush and Troop Reductions. President Bush rejects a Soviet proposal for lowering conventional military forces in Europe to equal levels. The president insists on having 30,000 more U.S. troops than the Soviet forces in Europe because they contribute to political stability. On February 13

General Secretary Mikhail Gorbachev reverses his position without explanation and accepts the American counterproposal for conventional troop reductions in Europe.

February 13 German Reunification. The ministers of Britain, France, the United States, the Soviet Union, the German Democratic Republic, and the Federal Republic of Germany adopt a framework for German unification at a meeting in Ottawa, Canada. They agree to a two-plus-four process whereby the two German states would negotiate with each other and the Big Four would also negotiate.

March 11 Lithuanian Independence. The Lithuanian parliament declares Lithuania to be independent and sovereign. The desire of the Lithuanians to free themselves from Soviet control becomes a contentious issue in U.S.-Soviet relations.

March 19 Kohl in Germany. In the first free elections in East German history, a coalition of pro-unification candidates linked to the West German party of Chancellor Helmut Kohl wins an overwhelming victory.

March 20 National Security Strategy. President Bush sends Congress the annual National Security Strategy Report. The report expresses support for integrating the Soviet Union into the international political system. Bush also favors the unification of Germany and its incorporation into NATO.

June 1 U.S.-Soviet Agreements. President Bush and Gorbachev sign a number of arms control agreements pertaining to chemical weapons, nuclear testing, and the peaceful uses of atomic energy during a summit meeting in Washington, D.C. They also issue a joint statement expressing their satisfaction with the progress being made in completing a START treaty.

June 3 Gorbachev and Bush. President Bush and Gorbachev, at a news conference, express satisfaction with the results of the summit meeting, although they disagree about whether Germany should become a member of NATO.

June 15 Nuclear Weapons. The White House issues a statement opposing the Soviet desire to begin negotiations on short-range nuclear weapons in Europe before completing an agreement on conventional forces in Europe.

July 6 Bush and NATO. President Bush, at a news conference following the NATO summit in London, comments on changes for NATO that represent a "historic turning point." He invites the Soviet Union and the nations of Eastern Europe to "establish regular diplomatic liaison with the alliance."

August 2 Iraq Attack on Kuwait. The UN Security Council passes a resolution, with the support of the United States and the Soviet Union, condemning Iraq for its invasion of Kuwait earlier that day.

September 9 Bush and Gorbachev. President Bush and Gorbachev meet in Helsinki to discuss the Persian Gulf crisis. They call on all nations "to adhere to sanctions mandated by the United Nations" and on Iraq to unconditionally withdraw its forces from Kuwait.

September 12 Agreement on Germany. France, Britain, the United States, the Soviet Union, and East and West Germany sign an agreement ending Allied occupation rights. Germany is united and its sovereignty fully restored.

October 1 Bush at the UN. President Bush praises the Soviet Union for supporting the UN activities in the Persian Gulf. The support, says Bush, indicates a new and different relationship between the superpowers whereby they cooperate to solve international problems.

December 29 Jackson-Vanik Amendment. President Bush issues an Executive Order waiving the Jackson-Vanik Amendment, approved in 1974, thus permitting the Soviet Union to receive credit guarantees to purchase agricultural products.

1991

January 21 Bush and the Baltics. President Bush appeals to the Soviet Union "to resist using force" in the Baltic republics. The same day the NATO ministers meeting in Brussels, Belgium, consider imposing sanctions on the Soviet Union if the violence in the Baltics does not cease.

May 8 Bush and the Baltics. President Bush meets with the leaders of Lithuania, Latvia, and Estonia and expresses the hope that the three Baltic republics can resolve their problems with the Soviet Union.

June 12 Yeltsin in Russia. Boris Yeltsin wins 57 percent of the popular vote in the democratic presidential elections for the Russian republic, defeating Soviet leader Mikhail Gorbachev's preferred candidate, Nikolai Ryzhkov.

July 31 Strategic Arms Reduction Treaty (see Document 10.7). The end of the Cold War yields major arms restrictions through the Strategic Arms Reduction Treaty (START). The Soviet Union and the United States agree to a complex and gradual reduction of warheads and weapons deployment systems. After the collapse of the Soviet Union, all four nuclear successor states—Russia, Belarus, Kazakhstan, and Ukraine—ratify the treaty.

August 1 Bush in the Ukraine. President Bush, in an address to the Supreme Soviet of the Ukrainian Soviet Socialist Republic, says the United States will not choose between supporting Gorbachev or leaders in various Soviet republics desiring independence: the United States supports freedom, democracy, and economic reforms.

August 19 Soviet Coup. Gorbachev, while vacationing in the Crimea, is ousted as general secretary in a coup by opponents of his reforms.

August 21 Bush and Gorbachev. President Bush, in remarks to reporters at a news conference, discusses his phone conversation with Gorbachev in which the Soviet leader said that events are under control and that he will return to Moscow. The coup has failed.

September 2 Relations with the Baltics. President Bush announces that the United States "is now prepared immediately to establish diplomatic relations" with the Baltic States.

September 27 Unilateral Arms Cuts. President Bush moves beyond START, acknowledging rapidity of events in USSR. President Bush says the United States will eliminate all tactical nuclear weapons in Europe and Asia. He also announces an end to the twenty-four-hour alert for American bombers, and he calls on the Soviet Union to negotiate additional arms control measures.

October 29 Bush and Gorbachev. President Bush meets with Gorbachev in Spain to discuss the Middle East peace process. The two leaders pledge to do whatever they can to help resolve problems in the Middle East.

November 20 Aid to the Soviet Union. President Bush announces that the United States will make available an additional $1.5 million in food assistance for the Soviet Union and the various republics. The president previously made available $585 million to the Soviet Union in October.

December 25 Gorbachev Resigns. Gorbachev resigns as president of the Union of Soviet Socialist Republics (USSR). The leaders of the newly formed Commonwealth of Independent States—the Soviet successor nations—dissolve the USSR.

December 25 End of the Soviet Union (see Document 10.8). In a Christmas Day address to the American people, President Bush declares a "victory for democracy and freedom" after the formal dissolution of the Soviet Union. Bush praises Gorbachev "for his intellect, vision, and courage."

1992

January 28 Bush's Victory Speech (see Document 10.9). President Bush reflects on the end of the Cold War and its implications for the nation and the world in his final State of the Union address.

1993

January 3 START II Treaty. Further dramatic arms cuts are achieved.

1995

February Engagement and Enlargement (see Document 11.1). President Clinton declares a new national security strategy for the post–Cold War era: pursuit of economic development and environmental security in the domestic front, and humanitarian missions and peacekeeping operations abroad.

1999

March Clinton and Kosovo. President Clinton orders an extensive air bombardment of Serbian forces on the offensive in the province of Kosovo.

2001

November 13 George W. Bush and Putin (see Document 11.2). President George W. Bush and Russian president Vladimir Putin issue a joint statement that promises cooperation between the two countries in the newly redefined war on terror.

Image and Text Credits

CQ Press and the author would like to acknowledge the valuable assistance and vast resources provided by the libraries and archives of Presidents Truman, Eisenhower, Kennedy, Johnson, Nixon, Ford, Carter, Reagan, and Bush.

CHAPTER 1: ORIGINS OF THE COLD WAR

Images
p. 1: Courtesy of the Library of Congress. **p. 3:** Copyright 2007, CQ Press.

Documents
1.1, 1.2: Reprinted courtesy of John Woolley and Gerhard Peters, The American Presidency Project, University of California, Santa Barbara, www.presidency.ucsb.edu. **1.3:** Copyright © United Nations. **1.4:** Reprinted courtesy of William C. Fray, The Avalon Project at Yale Law School, www.yale.edu/lawweb/avalon/avalon.htm. **1.6:** Reprinted courtesy of the National Security Archive, www.nsarchive.org. **1.7:** Reproduced with permission of Curtis Brown Ltd, London on behalf of The Estate of Winston Churchill. Copyright Winston S. Churchill.

CHAPTER 2: HARRY TRUMAN

Images
p. 47: Courtesy of the Harry S. Truman Presidential Museum and Library. **p. 52:** Courtesy of the Department of History, United States Military Academy.

Documents
2.1, 2.10, 2.11, 2.16, 2.17, 2.20, 2.21, 2.22: Reprinted courtesy of John Woolley and Gerhard Peters, The American Presidency Project, University of California, Santa Barbara, www.presidency.ucsb.edu. **2.3:** Reprinted from the *Department of State Bulletin.* **2.4, 2:15:** Copyright © United Nations. **2.5:** Edward H. Judge and John W. Langdon, *The Cold War: A History through Documents,* 1st edition, © 1999. Reprinted by permission of Pearson Education, Inc., Upper Saddle River, N.J. **2.6:** Reprinted courtesy of Texas A&M University Press. **2.7:** Reprinted from the *Federal Register.* **2.8:** Reprinted courtesy of William C. Fray, The Avalon Project at Yale Law School, www.yale.edu/lawweb/avalon/avalon.htm. **2.9:** Reprinted courtesy of the North Atlantic Treaty Organization. **2.12:** From *The Writings of Mao Zedong, 1949–1976. Vol I: September 1949–December 1955,* ed. Michael Y. M. Kau and John K. Leung (Armonk, N.Y: M. E. Sharpe, 1986), pp. 10–11. Translation © 1986 by M. E. Sharpe, Inc. Reprinted with permission. **2.14:** Reprinted courtesy of the Federation of American Scientists. **2.18:** Reprinted from the Cold War International History Project (CWIHP), www.cwihp.org, by permission from the Woodrow Wilson International Center for Scholars.

CHAPTER 3: DWIGHT EISENHOWER

Images
p. 98: Courtesy of the United Nations, Department of Public Information. **p. 102:** Copyright 2007, CQ Press. **p. 116** Copyright 1955, U.S. News & World Report, L.P. Reprinted with permission.

Documents
3.1, 3.13: Reprinted courtesy of the Dwight D. Eisenhower Library, DDE Diary Series, Dwight D. Eisenhower's Papers as President. **3.2, 3.6, 3.10, 3.12, 3.14, 3.18, 3.19:** Reprinted courtesy of John Woolley and Gerhard Peters, The American Presidency Project, University of California, Santa Barbara, www.presidency.ucsb.edu. **3.3, 3.8:** Reproduced from *Foreign Relations of the United States* with the permission of the Department of State, Office of the Historian. **3.4:** © 1996 The Johns Hopkins University

CHAPTER 4: JOHN F. KENNEDY

Images

Documents

CHAPTER 5: LYNDON JOHNSON

Images

Documents

CHAPTER 6: RICHARD NIXON

Images

Documents

CHAPTER 7: GERALD FORD

Image
p. 328: Courtesy of the Gerald R. Ford Presidential Library and Museum.

Documents
7.1: Reprinted courtesy of the Organization for Security and Co-operation in Europe. **7.3, 7.4, 7.5, 7.10:** Reprinted courtesy of John Woolley and Gerhard Peters, The American Presidency Project, University of California, Santa Barbara, www.presidency.ucsb.edu. **7.6, 7.8:** Reprinted courtesy of the Assassination Archives and Research Center. **7.9:** Reprinted courtesy of the Federation of American Scientists.

CHAPTER 8: JIMMY CARTER

Images
p. 371: Courtesy of the Jimmy Carter Presidential Library. **p. 378:** Copyright 1978, CQ Press.

Documents
8.1, 8.12: By permisson of the Houghton Library, Harvard University. **8.2, 8.3, 8.4, 8.9, 8.11, 8.13:** Reprinted courtesy of John Woolley and Gerhard Peters, The American Presidency Project, University of California, Santa Barbara, www.presidency.ucsb.edu. **8.5:** Reprinted courtesy of the Federation of American Scientists. **8.6:** Reprinted courtesy of the North Atlantic Treaty Organization. **8.7, 8.10:** Reprinted from the Cold War International History Project (CWIHP), www.cwihp.org, by permission from the Woodrow Wilson International Center for Scholars. **8.8:** Edward H. Judge and John W. Langdon, *The Cold War: A History through Documents,* 1st edition, © 1999. Reprinted by permission of Pearson Education, Inc., Upper Saddle River, N.J.

CHAPTER 9: RONALD REAGAN

Images
p. 418: Courtesy of the Ronald Reagan Presidential Library. **p. 423:** Copyright 2007, CQ Press.

Documents
9.1: This material is published with permission of ProQuest Information and Learning Company and the National Security Archive. Further reproduction is prohibited without permission. **9.2, 9.6, 9.8, 9.9, 9.11, 9.13, 9.14:** Reprinted courtesy of John Woolley and Gerhard Peters, The American Presidency Project, University of California, Santa Barbara, www.presidency.ucsb.edu. **9.3:** Reprinted courtesy of the North Atlantic Treaty Organization. **9.5, 9.7, 9.15:** Reprinted courtesy of the Federation of American Scientists. **9.12:** Reprinted courtesy of *Air Force Magazine.* **9.16:** Copyright © United Nations.

CHAPTER 10: GEORGE BUSH

Image
p. 478: Courtesy of the George Bush Presidential Library.

Documents
10.1, 10.4, 10.5: Reprinted from the Cold War International History Project (CWIHP), www.cwihp .org, by permission from the Woodrow Wilson International Center for Scholars. **10.6, 10.8, 10.9:** Reprinted courtesy of John Woolley and Gerhard Peters, The American Presidency Project, University of California, Santa Barbara, www.presidency.ucsb.edu.

CHAPTER 11: AFTERMATH

Image
p. 516: AP Images/Sven Kaestner.

Documents
11.2: Reprinted courtesy of John Woolley and Gerhard Peters, The American Presidency Project, University of California, Santa Barbara, www.presidency.ucsb.edu.

Index

Document reprints are indicated by page numbers in italics.